POLITIES

STUDIES IN INTERNATIONAL RELATIONS

Charles W. Kegley, Jr., and Donald J. Puchala

General Editors

POLITIES

Authority, Identities, and Change

Yale H. Ferguson
and
Richard W. Mansbach

University of South Carolina Press

Published in Columbia, South Carolina, by the
University of South Carolina Press

Manufactured in the United States of America

00 99 98 97 96   5 4 3 2 1

Library of Congress Cataloging-in-Publication Data

Ferguson, Yale H.
    Polities: authority, identities, and change / Yale H. Ferguson
and Richard W. Mansbach.
        p.   cm. — (Studies in international relations)
        ISBN 1-57003-128-2 (cloth)
        ISBN 1-57003-077-4 (paper)
        1. State, The—History.   2. National state—History.
    3. International relations—History.   I. Mansbach, Richard W.,
    1943– . II. Title. III. Series: Studies in international
    relations (Columbia, S.C.)
    JC11.F45   1996
    321'.14—dc20   95-50229

To our daughters,

Rachael Alexandra Mansbach
and
Caitlin Christiana Ferguson

CONTENTS

ILLUSTRATIONS

PREFACE

The publication of *Polities* marks two decades of fruitful collaboration between the authors, during which time we have grown increasingly skeptical about the dominant theories and methodologies in our field and the prospect that they might shed light on the crucial issues of our time. During the first years of our collaboration, we became convinced that the model of the world inherited from the mainstream European tradition of power politics, with its emphasis on structural determinants and states-as-actors, was irredeemably flawed and curiously out of touch with the real world. In addition, it seemed to us that the subfield of international relations was inexplicably isolated from the remainder of political science, history, and the other social sciences.

Thereafter, our belief in the positivist underpinnings of the subfield gradually eroded until we were persuaded that its exacting epistemological claims were partly responsible for fragmentation and compartmentalization in the subfield and were deterring scholars from speculating in a manner conducive to the flourishing of what critics called "grand theory." The irony was that in the absence of competitors, realism and its variants continued to dominate the marketplace of ideas in international relations, even to the point that its premises were (tacitly) embraced by the very "scientists" who sought to displace it.

It seemed to us not only that realism continued to dominate the scholarly agenda but also that it shaped, reflected, and even legitimated the image of the world of practitioners. Notwithstanding the rhetoric of strict empiricists, their values and the values of their cultural milieu were inextricably woven into the fabric of their scholarship. What had changed was that self-conscious empiricists were less conscious of their values and less forthcoming about them than their classical predecessors—Thucydides, Hobbes, Bodin, and others of this ilk. In a very real sense, our knowledge of international relations actually deteriorated between the 1960s and the 1990s, as students accepted

xiii

realist and neorealist norms, while rigorously limiting research to testable propositions or shaping it to use accessible data. At the same time, they increasingly accepted the world of their imagination as unchanging and ignored the historical roots of the present and future.

Frustrated by the growing gap between international-relations theory and discourse and the world it purports to explain, we sought to break decisively with the past, while avoiding the despair and relativism that characterize those approaches variously labeled postpositivism, postmodernism, deconstructionism, and so forth. The result was the Polities project, from which this book has emanated.

Of the many persons to whom we owe thanks, Don Puchala and Nicholas Onuf merit special praise. Others who offered helpful suggestions on portions of the manuscript were Gavin Boyd, R. J. Barry Jones, Peter Krüger, Richard Little, and Mark Zacher. The present work reflects their comments and criticism, though errors of fact or logic remain the sole responsibility of the authors. Professor Ferguson also wishes to express his deep gratitude for support during periods as a visiting fellow at the University of Cambridge, to the Centre of International Studies (especially its former director, Richard T. B. Langhorne, now at Wilton Park) and to Clare Hall. He owes additional thanks to the Rutgers University Graduate School-Newark and the Austrian-American Fulbright Commission for grant assistance, and to Anselm Skuhra and the Senatsinstitut für Politikwissenschaft at the University of Salzburg.

Last, but certainly not least, our collaboration has been sustained by the love of our spouses and children.

POLITIES

Part I

THEORY

1

INTRODUCTION
New Paths to Theory

The aim of theory is to make sense of what happens in the world. Inevitably, theories tell us what to look at and, by inference, what can be safely ignored. "Theories," as Pierre Allan (1992, 240) expresses it, "remain an indispensable tool for organizing our pictures of the world and guiding us in our practical and ethical decisions." Theory simplifies reality, allowing us to focus on selected phenomena that help us to explain and predict what is important to scholars and policymakers. Unfortunately, contemporary theories of global politics fall far short of these goals, even as a rapidly changing world makes it all the more urgent for us to have good theory. The disjunction between theory and practice appears as an abyss in the failure to predict or adequately to explain, even in retrospect, the end of the Cold War. "Not only did almost nobody in politics or academia predict these changes," declare two observers (Grunberg and Risse-Kappen 1992, 105), "most forecasts pointed in the opposite direction of what actually happened." Failures at least provide us with healthy incentives to revise our theories about the world.

International-relations theorists, especially those in the power-politics tradition, seem to have particular difficulty in accounting for radical change that entails massive shifts in loyalties from one set of authorities to others. They did not understand the French Revolution or the explosion of nationalism that was its companion, nor could they make sense of the Russian revolutions of 1917 or 1991. The demise of the Soviet Union surprised power theorists because their theories were focused on states and their relations rather than empires and also were unable to comprehend the revival of old identities that began in Eastern Europe and fed back to the USSR itself. Power theorists have been equally at a loss to address the post–Cold War political disintegration occurring in much of the developing world from ethnic, religious, and class conflict. In sum, academics and practitioners are ill-prepared to make sense of events that do not fit statist theory—and few events that fill today's print media and television screens do! It is no exaggeration to suggest that ordinary citizens who follow the daily news may have a better picture of the way the world actually works than the vast majority of blinkered IR theorists.

Nevertheless, when we abandon what theories we have because they cannot account for what appear to be important anomalies, we must do so with care. "If we discarded existing theories," warns Allan, "what alternative(s) would we have? One cannot beat something with nothing—even something not very satisfactory" (1992, 240). Our response in this book is to insist upon theory that focuses on change in global politics and a wider range of polities than the Westphalian state (hereafter, Westphalian polity). (See chapter 2 for a full definition of "polity" and an explanation of the "Westphalian" type.) We argue that the subject of study should be politics as a whole, rather than international relations as traditionally understood, and that politics primarily involves relationships between, among, and within different polity types.

The impetus for this book lies partly in the authors' disillusionment with the proliferation of tiny theoretical islands in the field whose members speak only to one another, the growing rebellion against "positivism" and the claims of "science," and the prospect of new disciplinary wars among scholars over epistemological issues (Ferguson and Mansbach 1988). Similar wars in the past—between "realists" and "idealists" and "traditionalists" and "scientists"—led to the ruin of departments; the imposition of virtual loyalty tests upon graduate students and nontenured faculty; conflicts for control of journals, professional organizations, and access to grant funding; and, of course, to clashes among strong personalities.[1]

The time has obviously come for an approach to theory-building that will at once be more constructive and more imaginative (Ferguson and Mansbach 1991). Inductivist empiricism continues to impede theoretical progress, especially in the United States where it remains perhaps the dominant approach. It perforce focuses attention on

---

1. To date, there has been less acrimony in the current debate. As Peter J. Katzenstein (1989, 302) observes: "The discussion is being conducted in muted tones. Claims of the superiority of one's preferred paradigm are not made, and the opposition is not hooted."

questions—some important, many trivial—that are susceptible to measurement and, to get on with the task of measurement, has tended to proceed uncritically upon some very dubious theoretical premises. For example, as John A. Vasquez (1993) points out, much of the quantitative work on war has been of limited utility because it rests upon arguable realist assumptions. Inductivist empiricism has directed attention away from (prior) problems posed by murky concepts and has also often been conducted from a woefully ahistorical and Eurocentric perspective. No wonder that positivism has proved such an easy target for postmodernists! Yet many postmodernists in our field appear content to criticize the best efforts of others rather than offer any usable substitute for bad theory. It is not enough to suggest that everything is subjective, for anyone knows that some spectacles seem to bring more of the world in focus than others. Are there no better lenses available, or shall we persist in celebrating blindness?

At the outset, then, let us explain in some detail what we perceive to be the impediments to building fruitful theory in global politics.

RETHINKING THE TOOLS OF OUR TRADE

The discipline's failure to fulfil the extravagant promise of the "scientific revolution" (see Knorr and Rosenau 1969) and the absence of a cumulative body of knowledge about global politics—especially after repeated predictions of breakthroughs just around the corner—have shaken the confidence of scholars and produced a "Third Debate."[2] Some have so lost faith in the dominant strict empiricism of recent decades and its positivist premises that they pronounce the death of objectivity and its accompanying truth claims and accept the relativism of deconstructionism (Lapid 1989b, 235–54, and 1989a, 77–88). We subscribe to some of the reservations and conclusions of these self-styled "dissidents" (Ashley and Walker 1990, 259–68), for example, that "the orthodoxies of our social and political worlds are created in the process of writing" (Shapiro 1989, 18). We share a "general sense of dissatisfaction" that "must become especially acute when the historically specific understandings of space and time that inform the primary categories and traditions of international relations theory are challenged by speculations about the accelerative tendencies of contemporary political life" (Walker 1993, 6).

---

2. See Lapid 1989a and 1989b.

We do not accept, as some of our dissident colleagues appear to, that we must throw the baby out with the bath water, and we, unlike them, remain confident that it is possible to penetrate the "external reality" behind the "texts" that purport to describe reality. Although theoretical statements have an explicit or implicit political agenda and, in this sense, have the attributes of ideology (defined by Mann 1993, 227, as "a meaning system embodying ultimate values, norms, and ritual and aesthetic practices"), they usually correspond to some aspects of reality. Our task is to interpret both that slice of reality that theories shed light upon and the remainder of that reality about which they remain silent. Even if our theories do not provide eternal truths and invariable laws, they can be judged according to what Donald J. Puchala calls "pragmatic truth," by which he means "interpretations of the record" that can contribute to "present-day problem-solving" (1995, 15).

The sense of frustration over the failure of scholars to provide the tools for prediction and explanation is more acute because we are experiencing heightened uncertainty at a time of dramatic and rapid global change. Much international-relations theory, as we have noted, has been curiously irrelevant to the political earthquakes of recent years. Indeed, part of the Third Debate is about what is an appropriate scholarly attitude to uncertainty. Should it be one of "celebration" or "despair," or should we, as Yosef Lapid (1989c) argues, stake out a middle ground by pursuing a less absolute standard of truth through "science," recognizing that there are no "guarantees" of payoffs?

It is hardly surprising that we have been disappointed by the crude, often ahistorical—even antihistorical—empiricism that has dominated research in international relations. Charles Tilly correctly observes that social scientists "have sought to escape the tyranny of the past through the employment of techniques developed in fields oriented to the present" (1975, 3). Empiricism must be tempered to reflect a field that is closer to the humanities than to the natural sciences, and methodology should be sensitive to the contextual nature of research and the explicit or implicit aspirations of those undertaking it. Social-science concepts are inescapably value-laden; social-science theories inevitably are a mix of fact and wish, reflecting the society in which they arise and power relations in the profession and that society more generally (Ferguson and Mansbach 1988, 32–48). "Facts" have little meaning outside of context, and context has a critical historical dimension. One is reminded of Francis Bacon's biblical paraphrase: "What is truth? suggested Pilate; and would not stay for an answer."

All of the foregoing points up the wisdom of Raymond Martin's (1989) cautious suggestion that "modest empirical subjectivism" might be a reasonable substitute for the sort of certainty demanded by rigorous empiricists. James N. Rosenau (1990, 27–28) similarly maintains that: "To be short on evidence is not to be inattentive to the need for evidence." He approaches the heart of the issue when he adds that "the processes of knowledge building are variable, . . . they can only be as rigorous as prior understandings of the subject allow, and . . . the methods one uses must . . . be compatible with these substantive limits."

As Rosenau recognizes, not everything of theoretical significance can be directly observed or precisely measured. Whether this situation is because our tools are poorly honed (as optimists claim) or because the concepts are inherently unobservable and/or unmeasurable (as pessimists argue), the fact remains that phenomena that defy precise measurement should not *for that reason* be ignored. Methodology must not be permitted to drive theory. "The tasks of the normal scientist," Rosenau (1986, 853) contends, "can be undertaken only after her revolutionary counterpart has paved the way."

What few scholars as yet have come to accept is the possibility of an empiricism that not only is sensitive to changing political and social norms but also can make the process of evolving norms itself an object of investigation. It is not enough to accept the importance of norms in world politics; we must also identify the manner in which they change (Kreml and Kegley 1990, 155–75). And, as norms change, theory follows that legitimizes and reinforces those norms, and tends to dictate what scholars and practitioners will observe or ignore.

Just as the normative content of concepts makes it difficult to achieve consensus about their meaning, so the normative commitment of scholars makes the scientific ideal of falsification largely impossible to attain. Social scientists are not really interested in "knowledge for its own sake." They are up to their ears in "reality," and they hope their scholarship will have an impact on society. Robert Jervis (1989, 397) readily admits that "events in the real world" strongly influence the topics about which he writes. Oran R. Young (1989, 69) likewise describes how his "formative experiences involved events occurring in the realm of applied politics," and the late Karl W. Deutsch (1989, 15) declared that his first encounters with public affairs were "with real political events." Because social scientists deliberately seek to change reality, perhaps they should neither expect nor necessarily wish for actual confirmation of their truth claims.

A spirit of empiricism that deemphasizes induction and measurement would presumably be sensitive to what Raymond F. Hopkins (1987) felicitously calls "the subjective dimension of international politics." Some scholars have repeatedly acknowledged the importance of this aspect of external reality. What Harold and Margaret Sprout (1965) three decades ago called "the psychological dimension" of foreign affairs has been an important focus for those interested in the psychobiographical attributes of leaders and the perceptual bases of decision making (see George and George 1964; Jervis 1976; Janis and Mann 1977). Nevertheless, preoccupation with parsimony and replicable data have prevented the field from taking seriously the Sprouts' insight that what we *think about* the world around us is at least partially responsible for creating (or destroying) that world.

The subjective dimension has been central to that strand of scholarship that began with international law and more recently has taken the form of "regime theory." Subjectivity is implicit in the most widely accepted definition of regimes—"principles, norms, rules, and decision-making procedures around which actor expectations converge" (Krasner 1982b, 185). Robert O. Keohane (1984, 17) identifies another key subjective element—"the value of information produced and distributed by international regimes." In the same vein, Friedrich V. Kratochwil and John Gerard Ruggie (1986, 764) rightly insist that "the ontology of regimes rests upon a strong element of intersubjectivity," and they capture one of the essential qualities of regimes in declaring that regimes are known primarily "by their principled and shared understandings of desirable and acceptable forms of social behavior."

These are refreshing acknowledgements of the centrality of the subjective dimension of political life and specifically of how perceptions and "ideas" (Onuf 1989, and Kratochwil 1989)—loyalties, identities, expectations, and goals—shape structures. However, our field is still largely dominated by those who focus on tangible and easily measurable capabilities and neglect the critical role of attitudes in explaining and predicting behavior. Strict empiricists have avoided analyzing such subjective phenomena as affect, expectations, loyalties, and identities (Goldstein 1993, 9–13), not because they are unimportant or in principle impossible to infer empirically, but for other reasons. One reason for this yawning gap in many models is that it is difficult, time-consuming, and costly to obtain data about key attitudes for large numbers of people, not least in developing societies. More important, perhaps, is that inclusion of subjective factors threatens the parsimony of theories.

Scholars yearn for elegant models that explain everything. Regrettably, the world refuses to oblige by being—or revealing itself to be—as simple as they wish. A preference for parsimony may result in models that are near-ridiculous caricatures of reality. There is wisdom in Imre Lakatos's (1978, 35; 1970) suggestion that we evaluate theory not only on the basis of parsimony but also on the grounds of the comprehensiveness of the explanation it advances and, most important, its likely contribution to theoretical progress. Parsimony is valuable but not as an end in itself. However aesthetic parsimony may be, it should be abandoned if it fails to capture the reality we hope to explain and thereby does not contribute to theoretical progress.

A final impediment to freeing ourselves from the past is that, after a generation of critical analysis, realism/neorealism[3] with its emphasis on structure and especially distributions of capabilities and perceptions of relative gains (see Waltz 1979, 1993, and Grieco 1988, 1993), retains a powerful grip on our field. The widely accepted realist assumption that distributions of attitudes are somehow derivative from capabilities needs to be revised. Since capabilities define the realm of the possible and attitudes the realm of the probable, it is likely that the two are reciprocally related. The distribution of capabilities affects the way people view the world, but those perceptions in turn provide incentives for efforts to redistribute capabilities.

Even in the absence of shifts in the distribution of capabilities in a system, the policies of actors are usually altered when the ideas and expectations of elites and/or masses change. And, when capabilities are altered, policy disasters may ensue if attitudes remain unchanged. Several of our historical cases reflect changing attitudes brought about

---

3. There is disagreement over the difference between realism and neorealism. One view (Keohane 1986, 158–203) is that neorealism is primarily a revolt against the "reductionist" aspects of realism. Keohane associates "neorealism" in this sense with Waltz's *Theory of International Politics*. By contrast, Jeffrey A. Hart (1991, 17, fn. 14) reserves the term "neorealism" "for those scholars who argue that strategic/military power must have an economic underpinning." He maintains that neorealism, as he defines it, has led to some opening of the state "black box." Still others might suggest that even Keohane's self-styled "institutionalism" is neorealist insofar as it rests upon assumptions about the centrality of power and "state interests."

by the conquest of a mature culture by "barbarians" who are absorbed into the dominant culture and provide it with new capabilities. Babylon was conquered by Assyria, yet it was the Assyrians who assumed the trappings of the Babylonians; the Greek cities were conquered first by Macedon and then by Rome, yet Hellenistic culture thrived and spread; the Mongols conquered China and were sinicized by those whom they defeated in battle.

THE REALIST/NEOREALIST LEGACY AND THE STATE

One reason for the failure of international-relations "scientists" to deliver the goods, as noted earlier, is that many remained saddled with the baggage of realism and its rigid assumptions. Vasquez (1983, 21) argues: "From the behavioralist perspective, what was in contention was not the . . . fundamental assumptions of the realist paradigm but how the realists had conceived of science, particularly scientific methodology."[4] An alliance of realist/neorealist theory and scientific methodology tried to build a field around the concept of the (ill-defined) Westphalian state/polity, ignoring other political collectivities.[5] "All too many studies," Rosenau observes, "posit the state as a symbol without content, as an actor whose nature, motives, and conduct are so self-evident as to obviate any need for precise conceptualizing" (1990, 117).

The state has so many different, competing, and loaded meanings that it is largely useless for theory-building (Ferguson and Mansbach 1989). Is it a Hegelian symbol of collectivist identity, the highest realization of self? Is it a "nation," connoting ethnic and/or cultural identity? A legal system? A "country," with both territorial and perhaps ethnic/cultural overtones? In perhaps its most useful conception, the state is a territory with legal boundaries, with a "government" somewhere inside. The government of a state is a set of authorities and a symbol of identity that competes with other authorities and identities for human loyalties. To the extent that governments can link themselves to other symbols of identity, they enhance their

---

4. For Vasquez, the debate between the scientists and the traditionalists "was over method and not substance."

5. The authors originally addressed this problem in Mansbach, Ferguson, and Lampert 1976.

legitimacy and security. Some (for example, Shi'ite Iran and Catholic Ireland) seek to harness religious identities, while others (for example, Muslim Egypt and Turkey) resist at their peril becoming closely identified with a particular religion. Other governments buttress themselves by blurring the line between state and a particular ethnicity. As events in the former Yugoslavia or Nazi Germany suggest, the linking of state and ethnicity may produce communal solidarity but at the risk of dangerous extremism.

Governments typically have *some* military forces (of varying reliability) and some tax revenues (whether at home or in Swiss bank accounts) at their disposal; there may be *some* concentration of resources at the "center," whether willingly given or not. The symbols of statehood have both normative and legal implications. Politicians and bureaucrats *claim* a monopoly of the legitimate exercise of violence and other "sovereign" powers within state boundaries. They *attempt* to establish an effective legal order that, among other things, assures stable property relations (Thomson and Krasner 1989, 214–16). They act in the name of the state in trying to *persuade* various audiences that their policies embody "the national interest." They usually enjoy *some* control over the movement of goods and persons across state boundaries.

From the vantage of the global system, sovereignty *by definition*, "signifies," as Ruggie (1983, 276) points out, "a form of legitimation that pertains to a system of relations" among "possessive individualists." In the broad sweep of human history, state sovereignty is a relatively recent idea, arising in a specific historical context as a solution to a crisis of legitimacy that followed "the rediscovery from Roman law of the concept of absolute private property and the simultaneous emergence of mutually exclusive territorial state formations." Writes Ruggie: "How can one justify absolute individuation when one's frame of reference is inclusive natural rights? And if one justifies such individuation, what basis is left for political community? The works we regard today as the modern classics in political theory and international legal thought were produced in direct response to this legitimation crisis" (1983, 276).

Sovereignty was a viable, even a vital, source of legitimacy for European princes who had repudiated the universalist pretensions of Holy Roman Emperor and Roman Pope. Princes sought to assure social cohesion in their domains while confronting the challenges of natural law and individual rights. Indeed, sovereignty was bestowed by them upon one another and was not some independent attribute. In cases of disputed territory, sovereign states accepted the principle of fixed and exclusive territorial frontiers, by contrast to imperial and transnational political forms (Spruyt 1994, 34–36). Even then, however, the Weberian idea that the state enjoyed a coercive monopoly was purely aspirational. As Janice E. Thomson (1994, 3) demonstrates: "States did not monopolize violence even within their territorial borders. Urban militias, private armies, fiscal agents, armies of regional lords, and rival claimants to royal power, police forces, and state armies all claimed the right to exercise violence." In short, the modern doctrine of sovereignty was an ideological invention that legitimated the efforts of feudal princes to throw off the legal and ideational shackles imposed by those higher in the feudal hierarchy and to control other challengers.

We no longer live in eighteenth-century Europe, and the realist/ neorealist conception of a tidy world of Westphalian polities presents about as accurate a vision of today's reality as a Hollywood stage set does of the American West or as a Potemkin village did of Tsarist Russia. "Sovereignty," as Nicholas G. Onuf (1989, 142) argues, "is not a condition. . . . Instead it is an ideal that is never reached, in a world where each step toward the ideal takes effort and costs resources, possibly in increasing increments, to prevent ever smaller amounts of unwanted behavior."[6] The sources of legitimacy have evolved, and we must begin to correct what Rosenau (1990, 117) identifies as scholars' failure to focus attention "on the conditions whereby authority is created, legitimacy sustained, and compliance achieved."

Old habits die hard, however, and many theorists continue to deny that there has been any reduction in "the significance of sovereign statehood as the fundamental way in which the world is politically organized," insisting that the "vast majority of people still owe their allegiance to the independent countries to which they belong—which for most people is the primary loyalty" (Jackson and James 1993, 6). Some neorealist, institutional, and agent/structure theorists concede that the effects of sovereignty are limited but nonetheless retain sovereign states at the center of their analyses.[7] Declares Keohane (1988, 385): "Sover-

---

6. For discussions of sovereignty as a variable, see Krasner 1993; Kratoch-wil n.d.; and Onuf 1989.

7. The editors of a recent volume of empirical efforts to test realism admit that the state-centric proposition "is largely unchallenged in this volume"

eignty is . . . a relatively precise legal concept: a question of law, not of fact, of authority, not sheer power. . . . It does not imply that the sovereign entity possesses de facto independence, although as a political matter, the fact that an entity is sovereign can be expected to have implications for its power and autonomy."[8] These "implications" are not trivial but are not so important that we should allow ourselves to be diverted from questions of how much autonomy "sovereign states" actually enjoy and how this compares to the effective control exercised by a variety of "nonsovereign" political actors.[9]

There is no escaping three essential points: First, the state is only one of many collective symbols with which people identify and to which they may be loyal.[10] Individuals are subject to crosscutting pressures arising from diverse identities and loyalties. Loyalties to self and extensions of self—family, clan, caste, village, tribe, city, nation, homeland, church, political party, class, and so on—undermine the political capacity of officials and compete with loyalty to the Westphalian polity. As Ernst B. Haas (1986, 742) asks: "Can the simultaneous pressure of domestic turmoil and international interdependence lead to political constructs that are quite different from what we know and that therefore imply a different kind of world order? . . . Just as in a previous age [people] sought a new identity in nationalism once the old identities ceased being useful rationalizers, the newly disoriented must search for an alternative nationalism." There are other ways to

---

(Wayman and Diehl 1994, 251). Had the proposition been challenged, many of the other propositions examined in the book could not have been tested.

8. Keohane (1988, 385, fn. 6) distances himself from Waltz's claim that sovereignty means that a state "decides for itself how it will cope with its internal and external problems."

9. Perhaps, as Kratochwil (n.d.) suggests, we should return to the original notion of sovereignty as *dominium*. His view is that early-modern kings and their subjects never conceived of sovereignty as implying full autonomy and control, merely certain powers—that is, a limited and nonexclusive domain of authority—that belonged to the king.

10. Combining the symbols of "nation" and "state" after the French Revolution made both more attractive to large numbers of people. Yet, however "nation" is to be defined (except *as* "state"), it is clear that most "nations" today are not "states" and most "states" are not "nations." "Nation-state," though a widely used term, can be seriously misleading. Cf. Hobsbawn 1992; Smith 1991; and Ferguson 1994.

identify political and psychological boundaries on maps in addition to the frontiers of states.

Second, given adequate information, the sources of all supposed "state" behavior can be traced to "nonstate" sources. Scholars of international relations and international law may choose to define their subjects so narrowly as to focus exclusively on the interplay of "state" policy positions in world affairs, but they will be hard-pressed to explain where policies come from and to account for changes in them. No state is a unitary actor, and there is no such thing as an objectively-conceived "national (state) interest." Governments are composed of numerous individuals and groups, responding in turn to other persons and groups, and all are profoundly influenced by broad rules and systemic trends.

Third, sovereignty as a normative/legal concept has only modest practical consequences. There are always more interesting and important things to apprehend about any state than its sovereign condition. As Rosenau (1990, 3–20) argues, most governments are confronted by growing challenges to their autonomy and control arising from micro and macro factors like the technological revolution; a better informed, less passive citizenry; and transaction flows "managed" by transnational firms and banks.[11] Even if there were consensus about where sovereignty resides, no government enjoys the degree of control over inhabitants or over its own fate that the concept implies. Democratic theorists who held that only "the people" are sovereign may have been close to the mark; this apparent contradiction in terms at least entailed a recognition that shifts in ideology may force authorities to become more responsive to popular demands. Partisans of diverse causes are available to authorities that compete with governments for citizens' loyalties and resources. Mobilization of the masses, whether by governments or their opponents, is an increasingly important factor in world politics,[12] or what Rosenau (1990, 6) calls "postinternational politics."

---

11. These factors are as not as "unprecedented" as Rosenau claims. Although the technology of contemporary societies is new, "ideological/knowledge" shifts have been at the heart of historical watersheds from the "fall" of Rome to Japan's Meiji Reformation. Such shifts and their sources are among the matters we consider in later chapters.

12. Mass politics and the participation of nonprofessionals in foreign affairs are anathema to realists.

Some governments face a breakdown in law and order because there is no normative consensus among those whom they seek to govern. The Weberian ideal of the state's having a monopoly of the legitimate use of force is remote to governments that are routinely challenged by restive military establishments, street demonstrations, tribal passions, rural guerrillas, urban terrorists, ethnic riots, or drug cartels. In all instances, surely, the existence of the violence itself is as significant as its "illegitimate" or "outlaw" nature.

If governments are beset from "below," they are also constrained from "above." Neorealists envision an anarchic universe, with an absence of central authority that is mitigated only by the widely accepted rights and duties of states enshrined in international law, the presence of issue-specific regimes, and the exchange of certain considerations among states. In fact, structural interdependence limits governments at every turn. In some cases, pressures on governments from "below" provide additional incentives for cooperation; in others, such pressures make cooperation more difficult. All in all, Alexander E. Wendt's (1992) observation that "anarchy is what states make of it" is not entirely correct, in part because states are not unitary actors, but also because they are far from free agents. Considerations such as these are at the center of the current debate between neorealists and neoliberals.[13]

The degree of anarchy varies by issue; some are more Hobbesian than others. Ironically, the potential for a Hobbesian "state of nature" may grow under the "atomized" conditions, described above, in failed states such as Somalia and Sierra Leone, even as the state-centric world recedes. Nevertheless, widespread coordination of behavior *among governments* exists and persists, not because "idealists" or "utopians" were right in believing that there is a broad harmony of interests but because players regard the alternatives as undesirable and avoidable. Policy goals clash and must be reconciled, yet countless transactions and consultative mechanisms testify to the humdrum regularity of much day-to-day life in global politics.

The unwillingness of many scholars to see global politics as more than an anarchic universe of Westphalian polities is partly a consequence of the desire for parsimony we noted earlier. State-centric assumptions enable scholars to treat the objects of their enquiry as

---

13. See especially Baldwin 1993; Kegley 1995; and Ruggie 1993a.

though each occupies a unique space and enjoys control over a discernible population and set of resources. These assumptions greatly simplify the tasks of data creation, gathering, and analysis. Comparison, too, is facilitated when one assumes that actors are essentially homologous. In sum, realist/neorealist theory is theory about state behavior, and the Western tradition (which is largely realist) encourages us, as Martin Wight (1968, 21) put it, "to think of international relations as the untidy fringe of domestic politics."[14]

Yet there is no logical, historical, or empirical justification for universalizing the Westphalian polity, which is only one of many forms of political organization. A reality of overlapping authorities, organizing citizens in different ways and attracting their resources for limited purposes, is messier than the myth of a system of states, but it is closer to what actually prevails in the world. The difficulty is not simply that the state is "a conceptual variable" (Nettl 1968, 559–92) or that the idea of an "impenetrable" state providing inhabitants with a protective "hard shell" (Herz 1959, 96–108) is an ideal type. More important, scholars fixated on the state are ignoring the most interesting question in world politics: How do individuals come together (or are brought together) to behave collectively?[15]

The elevated status of the ahistorical unitary state reflects inadequate attention to the dynamic side of world politics—the sources and consequences of change[16]—and a normative bent in favor of "stability." As Peter J. Katzenstein (1989, 291, 292) concludes: "The core paradigm of international relations theory, neorealism, emphasizes not change but continuity. . . . Neorealism . . . provides a parsimonious explanation of *stability*. Yet much of what we need to understand is *change*" (emphasis in original). Without agreeing that "structure" and "history" are antithetical, we accept R. B. J. Walker's (1987, 70) verdict: "Some of the more powerful forms of realist analysis in international political theory draw upon traditions that are

---

14. Wight (1968, 18) argues that international politics came to be regarded as "a tradition of speculation about the society of states, or the family of nations, or the international community."

15. This question was central to political theorists like Hobbes, Hegel, and Rousseau. For an effort to theorize about the processes of actor formation and dissolution, see Mansbach and Vasquez (1981, 143–85).

16. This point is not new. See, for example, Huntington 1971, 283–322.

less concerned with change and history than with stasis and structure."[17]

BEYOND THE NATION-STATE[18]

While realist/neorealist assumptions have persisted, there has been steady but gradual movement away from the dominant model of black-boxed states.[19] Many students of foreign policy have come to acknowledge that conceptions of national interest—however widely shared and parroted—are inherently subjective and parochial. They also recognize that expressions of phenomena like ideology, ruling-elite beliefs, and foreign-policy consensus are usually internally contradictory and are, in any event, too amorphous to explain policy. Actual decision making requires participants to debate which policies will serve general goals and then often to make hard choices among conflicting goals.

Theories of decision making and bureaucratic politics, some dating back four decades, were a step forward. Bureaucratic analysis proposed that "what a government does in any particular instance can be understood largely as a result of bargaining among players positioned hierarchically in the government," (Allison and Halperin 1972, 43). Hopkins (1976, 406) grasped the wider implications in urging us also to think of international organization "as including those officials who

---

17. Walker tends to identify "realism/neorealism" with "structure"; although his criticisms of realists like Waltz are appropriate, they are not applicable to all who are concerned with structure. While remaining sensitive to change, it is also important to identify *relatively* constant structural attributes. "Relatively constant" attributes correspond to what Rosenau (1990, 78–82) calls "parameters," which he distinguishes from "variables."

18. Subheading from Haas 1964.

19. Despite neorealist emphasis on state-centricity and insistence on system-level theory, political science departments routinely offer courses in international politics and foreign policy. The former usually stress system-level, and the latter, subsystem-level description and explanation. In this way, most departments, at least implicitly, "hedge" their teaching and research bets. For us, a more important question is whether the two arenas should be regarded as sufficiently distinct to be separated. We believe not. The same might be said for the traditional distinction between international and comparative politics.

are part of the organizational networks that perform international functions, whether they are formally in international or domestic bureaucracies, within governments or in the private sector." This directed our attention toward transnational coalitions of bureaucrats in alliance with subnational groups, which, in turn, might be in conflict with authorities in their own country.

Recent efforts to rescue the idea of the unitary state-as-actor at least have begun to differentiate state from society. By admitting that the interests of state decision makers "are separate and distinct from the interests of any particular societal group" and that, in pursuing interests, "decision-makers may be frustrated not only by other states but also by their inability to overcome resistance from within their own society," Stephen D. Krasner (1978, 10; also Katzenstein 1978) comes close to identifying the state with its government. As such, he allows for competition between "official" and "unofficial" authorities. "The objectives sought by the state," he argues (1978, 5–6), "cannot be reduced to some summation of private desires." The wall between the domestic and international arenas still stands, but it is unclear what function it serves any longer.

Efforts to salvage the national interest inevitably maintain some semblance of the Rational Actor Model, described by Graham T. Allison (1971, 10) as an "attempt to explain events by recounting the aims and calculations of nations or governments." Despite evidence to the contrary, some scholars still posit collective actors as "rational" under all circumstances. Even if we accept only "bounded" rationality, where precisely are such bounds? (See Ferguson and Manbach 1988, chapter 6.) In fact, "empirically no individual manages fully to offset all the components of habit, . . . behavior originates in response to internal conditioning as well as external stimuli, and . . . thus the rational actor who only calculates interests or recognizes preferences is an ideal type" (Rosenau 1986, 862). Rational-choice and game theorists push this ideal type so far that it becomes little more than a logician's mathematical exercise.[20] The fact remains, as Robert D.

---

20. Like game theorists, rational choicers may succeed in illuminating the logic of some strategic options, but that is about the only direct application to world politics. Both schools of theory draw their inspiration from economists, whose models based on supposedly rational behavior are daily confounded by real-world consumers and investors—not to mention politicians.

Putnam (1988, 432) reminds us, that "on nearly all important issues 'central decision-makers' disagree about what the national interest and the international context demand."

Rosenau's (1969, 2) original conception of national-international "linkages" was an explicit attempt to open up the black box and look at the relationship between behavior within and without states. "Almost every day," he declared, "incidents are reported that defy the principles of sovereignty. Politics everywhere . . . are related to politics everywhere else."[21] He spotlighted the obstacles posed by state-centric premises, arguing that "national-international linkages have never been subjected to systematic, sustained, and comparative inquiry" because the "traditional subdivisions of political science" lead analysts to "treat linkages as parameters rather than as data." A major conundrum, however, was whether the impact of "domestic" factors on "international" outcomes was greater than the impact of systemic/structural factors on the internal arena. Peter Gourevitch, for example, argued: "Instead of being a cause of international politics, domestic structure may be a consequence of it. . . . Put more simply, political development is shaped by war and trade" (1978, 882, 883). Paradoxically, structural realists, including more conventional power theorists like Kenneth N. Waltz, continued to insist on the primacy of state actors.

From "linkages," it was a small step to transnationalism. The key insight was that a "good deal of intersocietal intercourse, with significant political importance takes place without governmental control," and, as a consequence, nonstate entities may be "actors in the international arena and competitors of the nation-state" (Nye and Keohane 1971, x). Recognition of issues involving collective goods and linked fates further eroded the metaphorical walls around states. Important in this regard was the development by Keohane and Joseph S. Nye, Jr., (1987, 731; also 1989, 23–37) of the concept of "complex interdependence," defined as "an ideal type of international system, deliberately constructed to contrast with a 'realist' ideal type" and as "a situation among a number of countries in which multiple channels of contact [that states do not monopolize] connect societies."

---

21. Rosenau's still earlier efforts (1966, 71–92; and 1967, 11–50) to provide a framework for the comparative study of foreign policy and theorize about "issue areas" were steps toward developing the "linkage" concept.

Even as structural neorealists put their spin on linkage theory, so some regime theorists subsequently diverted transnationalism in a more conventional realist direction. When all is said and done, about the only difference between what Keohane (1988) classifies as "rationalistic" and "reflective" approaches to regimes is whether states (still undifferentiated entities) calculate the "national interest" in a rational cost/benefit fashion or whether regimes emerge almost absentmindedly as decision makers "learn" over time in specific contexts. Keohane acknowledges that domestic politics has been a "blind spot" for regime theorists, and Stephan Haggard and Beth A. Simmons (1987, 513, 515–16) see the source of this "blind spot" as "the lure of parsimonious systemic theory":

> Growing interdependence means the erasure of boundaries separating international and domestic politics. "Domestic" political issues spill over into international politics and "foreign policy" has domestic roots and consequences. Governments, when making choices about regime creation and compliance, try to preserve the benefits of cooperation while minimizing the costs that may fall on politically important groups. This insight appears to have been lost in much recent writing about regimes.

Regime theory thus seemed to lose sight of the shared fates of actors on both sides of the great divide of state boundaries.

Rosenau's recent work has moved even farther away from state-centricity. He declared (1984, 263) that "the worldwide crisis of authority can be viewed as having so thoroughly undermined the prevailing distribution of global power as to alter the significance of the State as a causal agent in the course of events." Eventually, he neared a decisive break with the state:

> With the globe becoming smaller and more interdependent, with causal flows cascading among and within collectivities in crazy-quilt patterns new to world politics, and with Western perspectives no longer predominant, we can break free by conceiving of humanity, not as a collection of countries or relations among states, but as congeries of authority relationships, some of which are coterminous with countries and states and others of which are either located within or extend beyond state boundaries. Mapped in this way, the globe more nearly approximates present-

day experience than does the conventional portrayal of some 160 territorial units. (1990, 37)[22]

If we accept this argument, then we must heed Waltz's (1990, 37) advice that "systems populated by units of different sorts in some way perform differently" and draw conclusions with which he would not sympathize.

THE NEED FOR A HISTORICAL AND MULTICULTURAL PERSPECTIVE

The realist/neorealist tradition, with roots in theorists like Thucydides, Hobbes, and Machiavelli, grew out of the European experience.[23] The tradition's static bias is partly a consequence of "parochial and ethnocentric" (Gilpin 1981, 5) theorizing about political life as though the Westphalian polity and the European state system that matured in the eighteenth and nineteenth centuries could be generalized across time and place (see Walker 1989, 163–83).[24] The absence of historical perspective and the Eurocentric propensity in global politics are closely related.

The Westphalian state was a product of historical forces that reached their climax in a particular time and place. As Thomson (1994, 4, also 10–11) observes, "the transition from heteronomy to sovereignty" was a European phenomenon that took place following the medieval period when rulers sought to delegitimate nonstate violence. The resulting system of competitive states, historian William H. McNeill (1982, 114) argues, was largely responsible for the growth and expansion of the technology and organization that in due course permitted the European conquest of much of the world. Europe's "peculiarly fragmented political geography" in which Westphalian

---

22. This imagery recalls Burton (1972, 42).

23. Of course, examples of "power politics" theory can be found in many cultures, and one might cite Kautilya, and Lord Shang and the Chinese Legalist tradition to illustrate how widespread aspects of realism have been. Although no civilization has been dominated so systematically by realism as the West since the fifteenth century, realist theory would be enriched if it took fuller account of its non-European variants.

24. Whether or not the Eurocentric bias reflects an assumption that things European are inherently superior is beyond the scope of this analysis.

polities were cheek to jowl produced intense rivalry among them and fostered unbridled entrepreneurship. Tilly (1975, 29) maintains that conditions were historically "ripe" for the emergence of territorial states in Europe: "If lineages controlling land, labor and loyalty had sprawled across the European map, it would have been harder to break up the population into discrete territories, co-opt powerful members of local elites without extending privileges to their clienteles or reinforcing the lineages as such, differentiate government from kinship, and so on." Nor was there anything inevitable about the way the map of Europe unfolded. In Tilly's (1975, 7) words, "as seen from 1600 or so, the development of the state was very contingent; many aspiring states crumpled and fell along the way."

The flowering of the centralized territorial state in Europe with "the bureaucratization of military administration" gave Europeans additional advantages. McNeill (1982, 117) explains the relationship between the Westphalian state/polity and the external expansion of European power:

> A well-drilled army, responding to a clear chain of command that reached down to every corporal and squad from a monarch claiming to rule by divine right, constituted a more obedient and efficient instrument of policy than had ever been seen on earth before. Such armies could and did establish a superior level of public peace within all the principal European states. This allowed agriculture, commerce, and industry to flourish, and, in turn, enhanced the taxable wealth that kept the armed forces in being. A self-sustaining feedback loop thus arose that raised Europe's power and wealth above levels other civilizations had attained. Relatively easy expansion at the expense of less well organized and disciplined armed establishments became assured, with the result that that Europe's world-girdling imperial career extended rapidly to new areas of the globe.

The European conquest overwhelmed other forms of political organization and produced the antihistorical idea that the Westphalian polity is a universal form. As European empires spread across the globe, their organizing principle and its ideological baggage reappeared in what was usually highly distorted local caricature. We still live with the bloody vestiges of the triumph of the statist idea in persistent civil strife in Africa, the Middle East, and Asia. Such strife reflects the reemergence of nested loyalties that were dormant, and resistance from different sources of authority, to colonial entities that the Europeans imposed. The new states never had much in common with their European progenitors, and loyalty patterns continue to have less to do with national frontiers and flags than with precolonial political forms.

A comparison of contemporary states reveals that definitions of the state like that of Theda Skocpol (1979, 29)—"a set of administrative, policing, and military organizations headed, and more or less well coordinated by, an executive authority"—are seldom realized in practice. In the words of Walter Carlsnaes (1992, 267), "comparative analysis must perforce be circumscribed by the *a priori* recognition that although state actors may possess many *analogous* characteristics, they are nevertheless *always* constituted by *different* real-world structures" (emphasis in original).

Although concentrations of coercive capability have existed for all of recorded history, the bases and extent of such coercion, the manner of its organization, and its relationship to individuals have varied so much that to regard every manifestation as a "state" hopelessly muddies the waters. It implies that highly centralized Pharonic Egypt, the complex tribal groups of pre-Columbian America, the spiritual union of the early Islamic empire, the monarchies of eighteenth-century Europe, and the feeble states in today's Africa have more in common than is even remotely the case.

More important, *at any given moment,* there exist numerous actual and potential political forms that attract and sometimes compete for human loyalties. Just as governments today compete with tribal entities, kinship groups, and even interstate and transnational organizations, so imperial forms in ancient Sumer or China contended with rival suitors for the affections of inhabitants. In every historical context, human beings are subject to crosscutting pressures arising from multiple identities. Loyalties to self and many extensions of self limit the capacity of any political form to command resources, including the support of members.[25]

Labeling all political entities "states" also masks genuine change. Revolutions may transform states like "France" and "Russia" and dramatically alter the loyalties of inhabitants. Language that leaves

---

25. See, for example, the collection edited by Thorburn and Tura 1989 on "Pluralism, Regionalism, Nationalism"; also Walker and Mendlovitz 1993; and Haas 1986, 707–44.

an impression of continuity is misleading. "France" and "Russia" remained as states in a legal sense but with significant shifts in perceived "national interests," sources of decision making, and patterns of behavior. The propensity to regard the Westphalian polities as timeless has an ideological side as well, reinforcing the institution it purports to describe and explain. In Wight's (1968, 21) words: "The principle that every individual requires the protection of a state . . . is a juristic expression of the belief in the sovereign state as the consummation of political experience and activity which has marked political thought since the Renaissance."[26] These observations return us to the need to focus on change itself, which is possible only through historical consciousness.

Historical consciousness is also necessary to escape the false dichotomy between "domestic" and "international" politics, a necessary step toward breaking down the false maps in our minds (Ferguson and Mansbach 1995).[27] A wall between "interstate" and "intrastate" politics is enshrined in the "classical tradition." K. J. Holsti remarks (1985, 9, 10): "Nation states are the essential actors, not only because they share the legal attribute of sovereignty and because many norms and practices are designed to protect their independence, but because they are the actors that *engage in war and are essential in organizing the norms and institutions which provide more or less stability, security, order, and/or peace for the system.* . . . International theory properly focuses on the consequences of a world made up of sovereign states" (emphasis in original).[28] Separating the two arenas distorts analysis at the outset and precludes thinking about politics as a

---

26. With a similar disregard for logic and experience, Hegel declared that history had come to an abrupt end with the flowering of the Frederickian state in Prussia.

27. The implications of changing views of space and time are elaborated by Ruggie (1993b).

28. It is, of course, tautological to identify one type of actor as "essential" because it is defined as such (e.g., sovereignty) or because it has the capacity to wage war. By implication, either interstate "war" is the *only* form of large-scale violence (which is false) or only "sovereign" states have the capacity to engage in large-scale violence (also false). Finally, the normative assumption that war is the only phenomenon worth studying (and, for that reason, states are the only actors worth observing) is by no means self-evident.

seamless whole. By developing the field with a focus on behavior between or among states and calling it "international," scholars transformed a variable (actor) into a constant (state) and cut themselves off from much of political life.

Despite considerable progress away from fixation on the unified state, scholars have not yet gone far enough to integrate insights from the several subfields in political science, not to mention other disciplines, into a single framework of politics. The wall between inside and outside the Westphalian state/polity—though increasingly permeable, even sievelike—still stands. Putnam reflects a discipline-wide uncertainty about how to deal with the problem: "Domestic politics and international relations are often somehow entangled, but our theories have not yet sorted out the puzzling tangle" (1988, 427).

The question is how to tear down the wall. Rosenau (1990, 97), for instance, recognizes the obsolescence of state-centricity, yet still finds it necessary to posit "*two* interactive worlds with overlapping memberships" (emphasis in original).[29] Why does he retain this separation? Virtually every issue in global politics involves both worlds. As long as the barrier between inside and outside exists, it obscures the degree to which there is a single arena. That arena encompasses numerous layered, overlapping, and interacting authorities, which represent the shifting perceived interests and loyalties of individuals. As a result, the idea that politics can be expressed as "between" and "across" needs to be supplemented by "above" and "below," without any implication of hierarchy among polities and certainly not for all issues. Authorities are engaged in countless issues, some of which are related and some not. Competition for loyalties—politics in its purest form—is visible in the pulling and hauling that takes place between and among the various arenas. As we have noted, the very language of international relations, evolved from the metaphor of the Westphalian polity, disguises what is taking place. Competition for the loyalties of elites and publics is simultaneously conducted among authorities situated inside and outside sovereign borders, and "insiders" and "outsiders" seek allies with each other.

The concept of national interest hides this pulling and hauling and produces the impression that a "state" serenely presides over the political process. In fact, political preferences often reflect values that

---

29. One of these worlds is state-centric, and the other is not.

grow out of loyalties to something other than a state. National-interest claims are attempts to legitimize those preferences and disguise "alien" loyalties. Rhetoric notwithstanding, one supports higher or lower tariffs because one's labor union desires to protect jobs; one's corporation sees opportunities or fears competition in world markets; or one's family likes Japanese cars and electronic equipment.

Such non-national interests constitute more than affiliations or personal quirks. They reflect commitments to authoritative others. In some cases, authoritative others may be located in clear and coherently hierarchical organizations, such as corporations, churches, labor unions, or even government bureaucracies. In others, authorities are more difficult to locate in a precise way because of the diffuse manner in which an interest is organized—gender, class, race, ethnicity—but role models and spokespersons can usually be identified.

The only way to overcome time-bound tunnel vision and the statist ideologies that reinforce it is to study the past. In Michael Mann's (1986b, 32) words: "World history develops. Through historical comparison we can see that the most significant problems of our time are novel. That is why they are difficult to solve: They are interstitial to institutions that deal effectively with the more traditional problems for which they were set up."[30] As we look back, we learn that familiar theories and approaches—for example, realism—appear over and over because they legitimize and underwrite particular political forms, policies, or modes of behavior.

The imperative to study history goes beyond the limited historiocity that is fashionable in some regime-theory and postmodernist circles. To be sure, there are risks in using history. Scholars who venture beyond the customary confines of their discipline invite criticisms both from colleagues in their own discipline and others in the discipline to be explored. Traditional historians are suspicious of social-science "theories" in general and offer a litany of warnings about macrohistory: There is too much information and not enough "evidence"; historical complexity precludes establishing "causation"; one can be an expert only on a limited period of history; significant exceptions contradict every generalization; no one outside of a specific historical time can reconstruct the perceptions of those who strutted

---

30. For a discussion of the static bias of international- relations theory, see Gilpin (1981, 6–8).

across the stage;[31] and so on. Fortunately, historians like McNeill, Fernand Braudel, and Barbara Tuchman have dramatically and successfully broken out of the narrow mold. Others we can only wish well in their archival research and proceed to mine their work for larger insights they may not be disposed to develop. All scholarly investigation, even theirs, rests on theoretical assumptions that might as well be articulated and improved[32]—and we must have much greater historical perspective to do that effectively in our field. We return to our assumptions about the use of history in chapter 2.

LEVELS OF ANALYSIS: NECESSITY OR IMPEDIMENT TO THEORY?

When J. David Singer (1961, 78) set out to describe "the levels-of-analysis problem" in international relations more than three decades ago, he tried to "examine the theoretical implications and consequences of two of the more widely employed levels of analysis: the international system and the national sub-systems." That "problem"—in reality a logical pitfall involving the relationship between complex wholes and the parts of which they consist[33]—strict empiricists and realists employ to discourage defections from state-centric premises. Singer's (1961, 77) original (and correct) formulation of the issue, as whether an observer chooses "to focus upon the parts or upon the whole, upon the components or upon the system," was translated into a stark choice between conducting research at the level of the "state" or the level of the "system of states."[34]

A corollary of this limited menu was the implied claim that, if an

---

31. The counter to this assertion is that those who lived in a certain era were too close to events to appreciate their wider significance, and the same may apply to experts who limit themselves to the study of that period.

32. Hall and Kratochwil (1993) observe that "history is not simply a tale of how it actually happened but a construct in which data and sources are not theory-independent." Nonetheless, as we explain in chapter 2, such an admission does not mean that *any* interpretation of history is equally plausible.

33. The issue is summarized in the "ecological" and "individualistic" fallacies.

34. Waltz (1959), who has a strong preference for system-level analysis, offered scholars a choice among focusing on systems of states, states, or individuals.

entity were enclosed in the boundaries of a Westphalian state/polity, it would be regarded as part of that state. If *some* of the units of analysis were states (or, more accurately the governments of states), then *all* of them had to be states—a claim that assumes all "other" entities are loyal and provide resources to the state in which they are situated. In some instances, these assumptions are correct, but in others they plainly are not. Although nested within state borders, an entity (including a part of the government) may successfully deny access to its resources, defy the "official" policies, alter the nature and direction of those policies, and actively compete for the loyalties and resources of individuals and groups. Under those conditions, the entity may function with substantial autonomy, and those who support it may even regard the state as an illegitimate agent.

The problem posed by the "levels-of-analysis problem" is contextual and issue-specific. As our gaze moves from issue to issue, the cast of actors—the dramatis personae, so to speak—changes, as do relations among the players. This view challenges the premise that the cast is constant, with a few powerful states in starring roles. In fact, the cast of actors in global politics constantly changes, with numerous nonexclusive and mobilized groups—next to, overlapping, above, and below—interacting at, between, and among various levels. When Waltz (1979, 102) argues that "among states, the state of nature is a state of war," he is also (wrongly) implying that the cast of actors, the structure in which they interact, and, consequently, resulting patterns of behavior remain constant. Since the cast of actors is a key structural attribute, moving from one issue to another—by definition—means changing structure. Some contexts resemble a "state of nature," while others feature norms and institutions that not only preclude violence but also foster community or, in Hedley Bull's (1977, 4, 5) words, "an arrangement [that] promotes certain goals or values" and "sustains elementary, primary or universal goals of social life."

Some of the agent-structure literature, drawing upon structuration theory (cf. Cohen 1989, Giddens 1984, and Bashkar 1979), recognizes the constraints posed by these assumptions.[35] Wendt (1987, 368; also Carlsnaes 1992, 245–70) decries the overemphasis on state agents at the expense of structure and the reverse emphasis—especially evident in the work of Waltz and Immanuel Wallerstein—on structure at the

---

35. For an excellent analysis of structuration, see Onuf (1989, 52–65).

expense of state agents. What is needed, Wendt argues, is a focus on "the historical specificity and contingency of the structuring of social structures." Once we accept the causal impact of "unobservable generative structures," it will clear the way for appreciating that agent and structure enjoy a dynamic relationship. We will then presumably be able to answer the sort of question that Haggard and Simmons (1987, 492) ask about regimes: "Do regimes have independent influence on state behavior and, if so, how?"

It is agent-structure interaction that determines the nature of society (rules of the game, institutions, and so on). Although their language seems to imply the primacy of Westphalian polities, Wendt and Raymond Duvall (1989, 66; also Wendt 1990) observe that they are not trying to make a "substantive argument about the relative importance of states in the modern international system" but are instead contending that "the powers, interests, and indeed identities of *all* actors in the international system . . . have social conditions of existence that are embodied in the structural or 'socially integrative' dimension of institutions at various levels of structuration in the international system." This approach does not escape the "levels-of-analysis problem," but it intends to move freely among levels.[36] Although the actor-structure debate has retained the baggage of statist terminology and too uncritically accepts the "generative structures" version of realism/neorealism, it reminds us that the diverse nature of collectivities makes it virtually impossible to cut up reality in the manner in which scholars like Waltz and Singer wish. Since some actors occupy the same space, are located entirely within one another or stretch across other actors, what functions as "structures" in some contexts will become "agents" in other contexts.

Another effort to confront levels of analysis while providing a framework for linking "state" and "system" is Putnam's (1988, 434) imaginative conceptualization of a "two-level game." He writes: "At the national level, domestic groups pursue their interests by pressuring the government to adopt favorable policies, and politicians seek power by constructing coalitions among those groups. At the international level, national governments seek to maximize their own ability to

---

36. The agent-structure literature is compatible with the effort of Sprout and Sprout (1969, 41–56) to define an "ecological triad" that encompasses actor, environment, and the relationship between actor and environment.

satisfy domestic pressures, while minimizing the adverse consequences of foreign developments. Neither of the two games can be
ignored by central decision-makers so long as their countries remain
interdependent, yet sovereign." Putnam's approach overcomes some
of regime theory's failure to take cognizance of intrastate politics
and appreciates the porous nature of state borders. However, while
recognizing a need to move freely between levels, the framework ends
up enshrining only two levels, with "government" as the gatekeeper
between outside and inside, and relegates nongovernmental authorities—wherever they might be situated—to the roles of lobbyist and
special pleader.

CONCLUSION

Weaving together observations about the importance of attitudes
and their distribution, and the agent-structure debate, it is clear that
there are as many "agents" and "structures" as there are issues, and
in principle each may reflect a unique set of levels of analysis. In
making sense of agent-structure relationships, we must consider phenomena from both micro and macro perspectives,[37] the latter conceived not as a single "level" but as a panoply of overarching actors
and relationships in which individuals are enmeshed. Rosenau (1986,
866–67) once again:

> By their very nature, the macro structures and processes of any
> social system are rooted in and sustained by the habits that
> prevail at the micro level—in the routinized ways individuals
> strive for goals, remember the past, cope with challenges, resist
> demands, make decisions, follow leaders, lead followers, or
> otherwise conduct their lives—and that therefore the macro
> phenomena are subject to alteration if their micro components
> undergo major transformation. To be sure, the more firmly macro
> structures are in place, the more they reinforce the habitual
> patterns of the micro actors who are embraced by them. This is
> why global structures and processes do not readily change. . . .
> Notwithstanding this central tendency, however, macro-micro

---

37. If there exists a genuine levels-of-analysis problem, it entails the
careless mixing of "micro" and "macro" properties.

interactions cannot be taken for granted because the impetus to fundamental, parametric change can originate at the micro level. Macro-micro links are as much two-way flows as they are unidirectional.

Following Rosenau, we focus attention on the manner in which individuals have directed and redirected their loyalties (micro components) and have strengthened or weakened polities (macro structures) that were competing for their loyalties. This is an effort to shed light on what Lapid and Kratochwil (1994, 5) describe as "the neglected role played by identity-driven dynamics in global affairs."[38] In the next chapter, we present a framework for analyzing these processes and explain the core concepts on which that framework is built. Thereafter, we apply the framework to an analysis of six historical cases. In the last chapter, we draw some conclusions from the cases and return to argue the case for reform of international theory.

---

38. Lapid and Kratochwil build on Boulding's (1978, 333) concept of three interactive systems.

2

THE SUBJECT IS POLITICS

Our concern in this book is the myriad and overlapping ways in which individuals and groups have organized themselves in world politics or, more accurately, the world *of* politics. A "state system"— the framework employed in traditional Western approaches to international relations—is, as we observed in the introduction, only one possible context with specific historical and geographic attributes (Rosenau 1990, 97–98, and Spruyt 1994, 11–33). Indeed, the notion of a system of bounded territorial entities is an incomplete and misleading model of world politics and, even in eighteenth-and nineteenth-century Europe, was probably not a very good representation of reality.[1] One cannot assume that other contexts—past or future—will be the same, for as Edward Vose Gulick (1955, 5–6) notes, "the historian can readily point to other times and places . . . where a state system has not existed."

When we escape Eurocentric and ahistorical biases, it becomes apparent that political life has typically resembled Mann's (1986b, 1, 16–17, and 1986a) description of societies as "multiple overlapping and intersecting sociospatial networks of power." Although Mann overemphasizes the supposed "autonomous power of the state" at the expense of attitudes and especially identities, he does recognize that there is a good deal more to the story than Westphalian polities: "Human beings do not create unitary societies but a diversity of intersecting networks of social interaction."

---

1. Global politics has almost always had what Rosenau calls multi-centric and state-centric features. The problem is that few scholars paid attention to the multi-centric side of things. The world has changed in the dramatic ways that Rosenau describes, but those changes have not produced multi-centric features so much as they have accelerated and accentuated them.

For some important purposes, the national state represents a real interaction network with a degree of cleavage at its boundaries. . . . Complexities proliferate the more we probe. Military alliances, churches, common language, and so forth, all add powerful sociospatially different networks of interaction. . . . The contemporary world is not exceptional. Overlapping interaction networks are the historical norm. . . . Social relationships have rarely aggregated into unitary societies—although states sometimes had unitary pretensions. . . . The forms of overlap and intersection have varied considerably, but they have been always there.

The "networks" to which Mann refers are often more than mere social categories. They can give rise to identities and symbols around which people organize themselves for political purposes, seeking greater value satisfaction. Sometimes those identities/symbols coexist peaceably, but other times, as in the collision between the Tudor "state" and the "church" in sixteenth-century England, they clash violently.[2]

THE POLITY CONCEPT

Far from falling exclusively into the neat territorial-state pigeonholes described by generations of international-relations scholars and practitioners,[3] global politics has always been a seamless web, encompassing numerous layered, overlapping, and interacting political au-

---

2. Rosenau (1990, 104, 93) asks: "Why now, late in the twentieth century, has turbulence overcome world politics, weakening national states to the point where they must share the political stage with private subgroups, transnational organizations, and their own bureaucratic agencies?" He thus regards the disappearance of "the relative tidiness provided by customary jurisdictions and stable polities" and the existence of geographic borders that "surround partial or mixed populations" as "anomalies." Although these are important characteristics of contemporary political life, they are not anomalies. They have, to some extent, always characterized global politics, but our theoretical blinders prevented us from noticing them. This is a case in which the world— changing today at an apparently faster pace— has nonetheless changed less than the lens through which it is being viewed.

3. For a description of the classical conception of international relations, see Holsti 1985, 7–10.

thorities. The political universe is at once more complex and shifting, as well as integrated, than the traditional picture of an interstate system reveals. We urgently need unified theory of—or, at least, a unified approach to understanding—politics. But to achieve that goal, we must stop thinking of global politics exclusively as the preserve of Westphalian states/polities and begin to conceptualize it in terms of the relationships and evolution of many polities of different types, which often occupy at least some of the same space.

A polity (or political authority) has a distinct identity; a capacity to mobilize persons and their resources for political purposes, that is, for value satisfaction; and a degree of institutionalization and hierarchy (leaders and constituents). It should be stressed that a polity in our conception is distinguishable from any unitary notion of society (about which Mann rightly cautions) and even from social networks. Social networks, interactions, or transactions—for example, a market—that produce value satisfaction may lack sufficient identity, institutionalization, and hierarchy to be a polity. Social categories that may be useful analytically, like "unwed mothers," may likewise lack identity, institutionalization, and hierarchy—and a capacity for mobilization as well. However, because they do meet our criteria, most organized social groups, from families to transnational firms, are polities. Let us examine more closely each of the criteria that define a polity.

First, a polity must have an identity that is distinct, though many polities seek to bolster their influence by associating with other identities as well. For example, the National Association for the Advancement of Colored People (NAACP) in the United States cultivated its own somewhat more conservative and "responsible" identity within the black community, but it nonetheless presumed to speak for black Americans in general, albeit not exclusively. The Palestine Liberation Organization (PLO) has its own identity as the self-proclaimed voice of the Palestinian people, though its identity is undermined by factionalism within the organization, the defection of radical groups like Hamas, and an absence of consensus about goals and means among Palestinians as a whole. Those who are members of a polity must *perceive* that they share some trait(s) or quality(ies)—minimally, association with the group itself—that distinguishes them from others outside the polity. Thus, any identity or sense of "we-ness" presupposes the existence of one or more alternate identities or "other-ness(es)."

Second, a polity must have the capacity to mobilize individuals and/or groups for political ends, that is, for value satisfaction. Leaders must be able to call upon the support and resources of those for whose identity(ies) they are surrogates. Those persons who are associated with a polity will regard it as having *authority—although not necessarily exclusive authority—over a specified domain.* A polity's *domain* includes the *persons* who identify with it and their *resources,* the *space* those persons occupy,[4] and the *issue(s)* over which the polity exercises influence.[5]

Authority is the ability to exercise influence or control across space over persons, resources, and issue outcomes; in other words, it is the capacity to govern. The capacity to govern is rarely exclusive, as pluralists and Marxists have long recognized, and it certainly is not limited to what are usually termed governments. In Rosenau's and Ernst-Otto Czempiel's (1992) phrase, we need to pay greater attention to "governance without government."

Authority is obviously more secure when those who are subject to it regard it as right and proper, but *neither legitimacy nor enshrinement in formal law are prerequisites for authority to be effective.*[6] Latin American specialists, for example, traditionally made the distinction between the nominal and real constitutions of some of the countries they studied, by way of accounting for the de facto "authoritarian rule" of successive dictators or military regimes when the formal constitution was democratic.[7] Virtually all polities have some means of disciplining or coercing persons within their domain. That said, in fact, individuals rarely accept authority just to avoid punishment; rather, they expect benefit(s) in exchange, including the psychological satisfaction of group identity and ideology. The cruelest and most

---

4. Space is a more appropriate term than territory, especially when considering phenomena like financial markets or electronic networks ("cyberspace"). However, it is important to recognize that all polities, not just the Westphalian variety, have a territorial reach of sorts.

5. This definition of domain combines the attributes of what Lasswell and Kaplan (1950, 73–74) mean by "scope" and "domain." See also Deutsch 1978, 32–44.

6. In this regard, we differ with Lasswell's and Kaplan's (1950, 133) definition of authority as "expected and legitimate possession of power."

7. Entrenched military regimes in Brazil, Chile, and elsewhere eventually began to write their own constitutions.

corrupt dictatorship would not last long if it did not deliver the goods at least to key elites.

Although individuals have numerous traits in common, many of which remain unperceived, it is a *belief* in linked fates that produces *loyalties*. Loyalties, in turn, provide the only firm foundation for the exercise of authority. Each set of loyalties is a social network, with territorial and functional dimensions, in which participants *perceive* one another as sharing some trait(s) or quality(ies) that place them in a common situation of actual or potential advantage or disadvantage (Mansbach and Vasquez 1981, 143–85). A polity may be grounded in ethnicity, economic status, territorial contiguity, language, gender,[8] or any of the other myriad ways that people believe link their aspirations to others who share that identity and, presumably, related interests and goals. Authority, then, is *an exchange phenomenon* in which loyalties and other resources are provided in return for value satisfaction (or relief from value deprivation). Just as observant Catholics regard the word of their Church as critical in helping them sort out religious and moral questions, so members of the National Organization of Women or Amnesty International look to their group for guidance and concerted action on issues relevant to their concerns.

If a polity succeeds in providing satisfaction, it may prevent new loyalties from forming, as Peter Sahlins (1989, 291) illustrates by explaining why Catalan nationalism was weaker in France than Spain: "The French Catalans were bound to the French state by its ability to satisfy their needs. The French state had created the ties of loyalty and identity instrumentally, by fulfilling the material needs of its citizens. For the people of the borderland, the greater advantage lay in being French than in defining their national identity as Catalans, which would only be meaningful in opposition to the Spanish state." Conversely, failure to provide satisfaction may provoke shifts in loyalties. When values cease being allocated in an acceptable fashion, even durable loyalties erode and fade, and the stage is set for their redistribution and a shift in authority patterns. This process usually occurs incrementally (though not always, as in times of war or other catastrophe) because human loyalties, anchored by custom, tradition, and a host of psychological mechanisms, are resistant to change. Hence there is usually a time-lag between events that alter the distribu-

---

8. See especially Sylvester 1994, Agger 1994, and Tickner 1992.

tion of values and the subsequent shift in authority patterns. Those whose behavior initially eats away at loyalties, like the French aristocracy under Louis XIV and eighteenth-century colonial authorities in North America, may not be present to see the consequences of their acts.

Finally, a polity must have an identifiable hierarchy with roles that provide institutional continuity. Polities consist of structures and rules that facilitate the achievement of common ends. There must be individuals who speak or act on behalf of persons identifying with the polity, who provide leadership and inspiration, and can call upon followers for resources and support. The polity need not have a literal "center," nor must members live in vicinity or even contiguously; but sufficient leadership and role differentiation must exist for institutional memory, historical continuity, and resource mobilization. At one extreme are polities like the Catholic Church with a clear hierarchy and (in modern times) a single center. Yet, even Judaism at the height of the Diaspora, though lacking a physical center or a clearly defined hierarchy, may be regarded as a polity. Rabbis acted as figures of authority; scripture provided differentiation from other communities; and Jews from around the world treated one another as though all belonged to a single community.

However varied polities may be in their institutions and sociocultural environments, all allocate values authoritatively. There is no simple threshold that a group passes to become a polity. Among other things, polities differ in degree of hierarchy, centralization of authority, institutionalization, mobilization capacity, homogeneity, and size. These differences are not trivial and affect both the staying power of polities and their ability to compete successfully with one another when necessary.

Today, as in the past, a rich variety of polity types interact across global and regional issues. There is, moreover, great variety *within* each type—family, tribe, city, and so on. Each is merely an ideal construct, or model, which manifests itself in a range of forms in real-world polities during a particular time and also over time.[9] As George Liska (1990, 18) observes: "To posit the particular organizational

---

9. Westphalian polities are by no means exempted from this observation. See Krasner 1993, for instance, for a discussion of the evolution of the idea of sovereignty as a defining element in statehood.

characteristics of, say, antique empires in general or the Assyrian Empire in particular as defining the entity called 'empire' for all time leads through a preliminary finding—to the effect that more recent power and interest aggregations such as the British and the American were no empires at all—to the seemingly incontrovertible conclusion of radical or qualitative change having taken place over time."

Each historical era produces its own particular distribution and ranking of polities as well as some idiosyncratic permutations and combinations of earlier forms. The break with the past is, very occasionally, dramatic enough—e.g., the development of the Catholic Church late in the Roman era—to suggest the emergence of a genuinely new polity type. Considering this discussion, then, it should not be surprising that there is not only considerable duplication in the lists of polity types for each of our historical cases but also that no two lists are exactly the same. For similar reasons, we have not attempted to construct any definitive list of polity types, although many of the same types appear again and again. Using our criteria for the existence of a polity, then, let each individual analyst construct his or her own list of relevant polities for the time frame and/or issue(s) under investigation.

Polities of one type routinely shade into another or evolve from one into another type, but the moment of transformation is rarely precise. Sometimes evolution is so slow as to be almost imperceptible, and sometimes the process of "coming from" or "moving toward" another type of polity is very rapid. In addition, the continuous interaction among polities of different types produces important reciprocal influences. Rome, for example, was first a city polity, then—with the conquest of its Etruscan rival and expansion beyond the plain of Latium—became a large regional polity, and eventually, even before the Augustan era, assumed the trappings of empire (Scullard 1959, 2–5). After the collapse of the empire, many of its provincial boundaries were transformed into the frontiers of European protostates. Clive Parry (1968, 11) declares: "As the barbarians abandoned their nomadic ways . . . what began as a principle of personality became a principle of territoriality. Laws and systems of law became local. And the lines of division between them came to correspond roughly with the Roman provincial frontiers."

Political evolution has never been unilinear (Spruyt 1994, 20–21). Imperial and city polities, for example, have in the past devolved into chiefdoms, as happened in Italy under the Lombards and in post-Mycenaean Greece, respectively (see chapters 13–14 and 5–6). Parts of contemporary Africa are witnessing a devolution of failed postcolonial states into tribes and clans, and the dissolution of the Soviet Union brought an end to the last of the nineteenth-century multinational empires.

Given the rise and fall of practically everything in history, one should be circumspect in crediting the supposed growth of "the autonomous power of the state" over the last few centuries that so impresses scholars like Mann (1986a). Every process of political integration (fusion) carries the seeds of its own destruction (fission). First, the growth of any central authority tends to generate a substantial bureaucracy, and individual units thereof often pursue their own perceived interests. "Government" itself becomes harder to manage. Second, the creation of a central authority and possible extension of the territory under its control typically produces profound economic and social changes. Old identities and loyalties are absorbed, and new ones arise. The polity's constituency becomes all the more difficult to govern. At a minimum, this trend translates into a proliferation of factions and competing demands upon the center. At worst, discordant identities and loyalties may produce powerful centrifugal forces that ultimately result in the original polity's destruction. Rosenau refers to the simultaneous presence of these two processes as "fragmegration" (1994, 256). Third, the rise of any new polity can have a transforming impact on others outside its domain, either through a "demonstration effect" or because outsiders are energized by fear or predatory instincts. The polity's external universe may become more unpredictable and dangerous.

The first two considerations explain why Rousseau and Confucius had a preference for small polities. Size—population and space—has consequences. Expansion entails the digestion of new identities and old loyalties and produces a more heterogeneous population. Distance attentuates coercive and administrative capacity. The experience of expansive empires confirms Kenneth E. Boulding's (1962, 230, 231) idea of a "loss-of-strength gradient" or "the further the weaker" by which "strength declines as it moves away from its home base." Not only does distance impose physical barriers to the use of coercion by a center, it may require the appointment of local surrogates—"governors," "proconsuls," or "viceroys." Separated from the center, they may become foci for local loyalties and even rival polities. Whether the commanders of Roman legions on the frontier, governors of the Islamic caliphate in Spain and North Africa, or local princes in medieval Europe, such individuals potentially threaten the center.

A small polity is likely to be more homogeneous than a large one and have fewer conflicting identities. Smallness permits more intensive contacts among citizens and makes possible a web of reinforcing bonds among individuals and groups. However, the multiple fissures in polities like classical Athens and Renaissance Florence remind us not to carry this line of reasoning too far. Indeed, Spruyt (1994, 173) distinguishes city-states from sovereign states by their lack of "a clear sovereign." A small polity is at least easier to administer, and coercion is more effective if its target is physically close. On the deficit side, a small polity has fewer persons to mobilize for war and normally less material resources than larger polities.

AUTHORITY PATTERNS AND COMPETITION FOR LOYALTIES

The we/they cleavages that are characteristic of politics result to a significant extent from competition among polities. Such cleavages reflect psychological distance among peoples organized around diverse symbols. The Westphalian polity is only one such symbol, and its marriage to "nation" and the invention of "popular sovreignty" in the eighteenth and nineteenth centuries made it unusually powerful. That symbol and the type of polity it represented were reinforced by the durable and elastic ideology of "nationalism."[10] In Spruyt's words: "The emergence of sovereign, territorial rule was . . . not merely a fight between the forces favoring fragmentation versus centralization; it was a contest about the very nature of authority and kingship" (1994, 68).

In mobilizing adherents for political ends, polities function as authoritative allocators; and global politics, in turn, involves a variety of interacting authorities and the attendant loyalties that nourish and sustain them. The manner in which loyalties are distributed and the cooperation and/or competition among authorities for them are dynamic aspects of world politics. What Rosenau calls the "micro parameter"—"those predispositions and practices by which people

---

10. Realists and neorealists largely ignore the "national" side of the nation-state (Lapid and Kratochwil 1994). However, the upsurge in nationality-based conflict since the end of the Cold War has produced renewed interest in nationalism (for example, the new journal *Nations and Nationalism* from Cambridge University Press; Krüger 1993; Pfaff 1993; Hopf 1993, 207; Tamir 1993, ix; Snyder 1993, 179; Buzan 1993, 338).

relate to higher authority" (1990, 89)[11]—is at the heart of the matter and determines which authority patterns arise, survive, and succeed. Familiar types like tribe, state, and empire are ways of denoting different patterns of authority that have evolved to mobilize identities.

The concept of polities as political authorities grows out of Easton's (1965) durable definition of politics as the authoritative allocation of values by a political system. It incorporates, too, Harry Eckstein's and Ted Robert Gurr's (1975) conception of politics as "asymmetric relationships."[12] One must, however, exercise caution with Easton's concept of political system lest it imply a Platonic degree of discreteness, autonomy, power, and exclusivity that few real-world polities ever achieve. In addition, as Eckstein and Gurr point out, Easton excludes from the realm of the political nongovernmental social asymmetries. That exclusion is overly restrictive.

We also do not follow Easton in reserving "authoritative" for the (supposedly) legally binding actions of governments. Value allocation is authoritative if it is effective. Government actions, whatever their legal status, may be ineffective. It would be illogical, for instance, to describe as authoritative the commands of the Lebanese government between 1975 and 1990 or even the Eighteenth Amendment to the United States Constitution that outlawed the sale and consumption of alcoholic beverages. Governments in the developing world are often not effective allocators in any sense. Such putative authorities behave as special pleaders or lobbyists outside their own territory and enjoy limited control over persons and things inside or outside their legal borders. Law, then, is only one possible source of whatever legitimacy enhances the capacity of polities to govern effectively (as an "authority" or "authoritatively").

The authoritative allocation of values has *never* been confined to governments, even when conceived as nonunitary coteries of bureaucracies, supplemented by overarching international regimes. Early entities that archaeologists classify as "states" evinced many charac-

---

11. Rosenau also identifies what he calls "structural" and "relational" parameters that are characteristics of collectivities and the system in which they are found.

12. We do not accept Eckstein's and Gurr's conclusion that there are sufficient differences between "domestic" and "international" politics to justify treating them as separate fields of study.

teristics customarily associated with Westphalian polities—territory, executives, legislatures, judges, bureaucracies, taxes, armed forces, interest groups, social classes. They also had problems of succession, peer-polity and often center-periphery relations, alliances, wars, and trade. Prehistoric hunter-gatherers and nomadic herders even had a process for allocating values by a shaman or other elders who enjoyed authority. Hunter-gatherer society was "exceptionally complex; . . . highly varied, with a single 'mode of production' being as capable of supporting differing political 'superstructures' as are agrarian and industrial productive systems" (Hall 1987, 12). Far from being simple creatures who eked out survival as best they could, prehistoric hunters and gatherers "were seen as economic savants making perfectly judged decisions. . . . They were resource managers guided by the principle of least effort, the efficient conservation of calories in the pursuit of optimal behaviour" (Gamble 1987, 30).[13]

Today a wide variety of authorities exercise influence or effective control, as well as enjoy legitimacy, within particular domains—the persons, resources, space, and range of issues over which the authority of a polity extends. Legal and organizational boundaries condition and constrain behavior, but none encompass governmental/intergovernmental authorities with complete control of the allocation-of-values process. Bureaucracies may have extensive (rarely exclusive) control over selected processes. In some cases, they presume to allocate values authoritatively only for those residing in the territory of a single nation-state. In others, they allocate on a far greater scale, as did the British Admiralty and Foreign Office in the nineteenth century and the U.S. State Department and the Red Army during the Cold War.[14]

Ultimately, the individual is the bedrock unit of analysis. As Douglass C. North expresses it: "Institutions are a creation of human beings. They evolve and are altered by human beings; hence our theory must begin with the individual" (1990, 5). The effectiveness of

---

13. Analyses of nomadic societies, like the Comanches in North America prior to the European conquest, reinforce the conclusion that such societies had significant political institutions and hiearchy, which made them efficient allocators.

14. Sovereignty may be used as a defense against the extraterritorial pretensions of others, but it provides no explanation of or justification for such pretensions.

governance rests on the loyalties of those for whom authorities claim to act and on the willingness of the governed to contribute resources to the collectivities of which they are part. As we have stressed, few authorities can govern effectively for any length of time by means of coercion alone. Large-scale desertion rates from the armed forces, rising crime rates, declining labor productivity, growing numbers of refugees, and spiraling tax evasion typify declining legitimacy and a constriction of loyalties.

Individuals typically have numerous identities and loyalties, partly because it is impossible for any polity to satisfy all of an individual's core values. There are broad loyalties to family, tribe, class, religion, caste, race, ethnicity, gender, or nation that may elicit obedience from individuals in diverse locations over a broad range of issues. By contrast, narrow authorities like the Greek amphictiony supervising the shrine of Delphi operate only in highly specialized areas of political life. Individuals view different authorities as germane to particular issues and, therefore, as the ones to be obeyed as regards those issues. Perceptions of factors like relationship to the issue, function, past success, aspirations for the future, and control over rewards and penalties determine which authority individuals will turn to in a particular context.

Consequently, individuals are enmeshed in a complex web of relationships, inextricably intertwined with a large number of politically active entities. Sometimes identities and loyalties coexist easily, and sometimes issues force choices among them. Such issues may produce dissonance, as in medieval Europe where, Ruggie (1983, 274) observes, politics "reflected 'a patchwork of overlapping and incomplete rights of government,' which were 'inextricably superimposed and tangled,' and in which 'different juridical instances were geographically interwoven and stratified, and plural allegiances, asymmetrical suzerainties and anomalous enclaves abounded.' ''[15] The Holy Roman Empire was managed by barons who also were Catholic bishops. From the point of view of the German emperors, those barons provided security from potential dynastic competitiors because they were celibate. During good times when pope and emperor got along, the barons enjoyed two sources of funds (the church collection and

---

15. Ruggie is citing Perry Anderson *Lineages of the Absolutist State* (London: New Left Books, 1974), 37–38.

imperial taxes), but when a reformist pope took office, they had to make invidious choices between competing authorities.

The allocation of values by social networks and the authorities that govern them routinely cross the territorial boundaries of other polities. Like the Westphalian polity, all networks of authority have their own conceptions of space. Families and kinship groups have homes and localities, sedentary tribes their lands, nomadic tribes their home range, religions their faithful, ethnic and language groups their "nation," transnational corporations their production centers and markets, and so on. In sum, world politics is characterized by sometimes isolated but commonly crisscrossing webs of loyalties.

The pulling and hauling of competition among authorities alters a polity's territory and other aspects of its domain. Conquest, proselytism, diplomacy, changing economic and social ties, and additional mechanisms of global intercourse may lead to an expansion or retrenchment of the number of persons and/or space over which polities exercise authority. Change will also take place in the number and/or range of issues in which polities engage and in the weight of their authority over specific issues. Figure 1, adapted from Philippe Schmitter's analysis of variation in regional integration, illustrates possible variation in range and weight of authority.

Polities require ideological justification, whether crude or elaborate, that legitimizes them and anchors and interprets the loyalties of adherents. Nearly all draw on the norms of their era, but those that are most successful enhance their identity by evolving their own distinctive ideology—"divine right of kings," "civilizing mission," "Mandate of Heaven," "papal infallibility," or "dictatorship of the proletariat." If what E. J. Hobsbawm calls "the sentiments and symbols of 'imagined community' " (1992, 91) can be anchored, then ideology is serving its purpose. A polity is more durable to the extent it co-opts or incorporates competing ideologies and identities into its ideological framework. For example, polities supported by a dominant religion may incorporate into their pantheon of gods those carried on the horses of others. Or, in the face of conquest, a polity may absorb outsiders by co-opting them into other aspects of a dominant culture. In any event, old identities, loyalties, and ideas remain to "haunt" a new polity and ultimately may prove to be a key factor in its collapse. Since they are only slowly, if ever, eliminated in any final way, the stability and durability of a polity depend on its capacity to integrate them.

Variation in Regional Integration

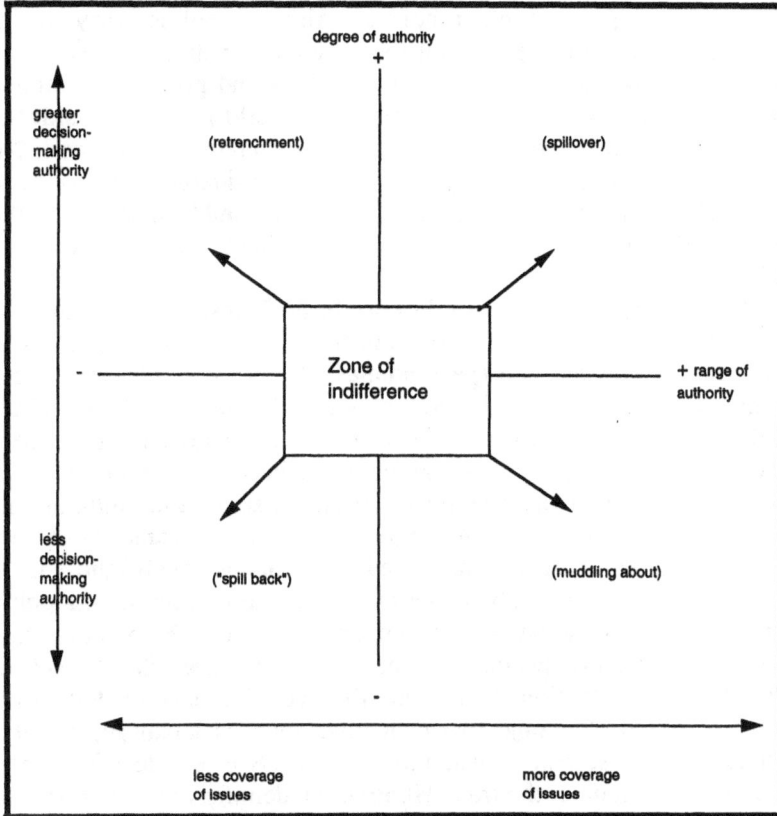

Adapted from Philip C. Schmitter, "A Revised Theory of Regional Integration," *International Organization*, 24:4 (Autumn 1970), p. 845.

Loyalties, as any pluralist knows,[16] can be shared among numerous authorities, and the manner in which they are divided and redivided is central to politics. As we shall see in the chapters that follow, competition for loyalties among authorities of very different stripes has been an engine of political change since the dawn of history. Elections, wars, ideology, and even advertising—though apparently disparate enterprises—may all be seen, at root, as contests for human

---

16. This reference should not be construed as an acceptance or advocacy of pluralist ideology in a state context. See, for example, Dahl 1967, 22–24.

loyalties among competing authorities. Although polities vary significantly in the ratio of persuasion to coercion that they employ, all of them manipulate symbols to attract loyalties and procure resources. Onuf (1989, 243-44) wisely observes that "world politics are still the terrain upon which belief systems are most intensely contested. No differently from priests, today's propagandists, ideologues, teachers, and publicists attempt to spell out the meaning and significance of the human situation in ways that inevitably affect the distribution of influence and rewards."

Competition for loyalties takes two basic forms. The first and most frequently studied is the competition between and among polities of the same or similar type (peer polities). Thus, the Cold War was a competition between the United States and its allies and the members of the Soviet bloc. Although there have been exceptions to the propensity to look at world politics as contests between like polities (for example, studies of the relationship between states and multinational corporations[17]), the long-term competition for loyalties among different *types* of polities—arguably the more important—is largely ignored.

Failure to theorize about the changing relationship among polity types at least partly explains the commotion caused by Samuel Huntington's (1993, 24) speculation that individuals have other "levels of identity" than "nation-state" and that conflict may explode over loyalties based "on objective elements, such as language, history, religion, customs, institutions, and . . . subjective self-identification of people."[18] Of course, the traits Huntington identifies may reinforce, as well as divide, polities and may be the bases of new polity types.

ANALYTIC ISSUES

One purpose of the historical materials that follow is to identify both the processes of decay and shifts in loyalties and the factors that seem to trigger and feed these processes. We can, in principle, conduct

---

17. See, for example, Barnet and Muller 1974, Tolchin and Tolchin 1988, Vernon 1971 and 1977.

18. Huntington's claim that these identities constitute "civilizations" is arbitary and probably misleading. Rather, each identity—religion, ethnicity, and so forth—forms a distinct pattern of authority with its own scope and domain.

an analysis of changes in authorities and competition among them at either a micro or macro level. Micro analysis requires observing individuals and groups whose loyalties competing authorities seek to attract. Individuals in each temporal and spatial context identify with selected authorities, and their multiple loyalties are tested with regard to specific issues. If authorities adopt divergent issue positions on specific issues, individuals have to make hard choices among the positions and, therefore, rank their own loyalties. A succession of such conflicts, or a single one if it is central enough to the lives of those involved, may force a fundamental reevaluation and reordering of loyalties.

Micro analysis can explain why individuals made the choices they did under the pressure of cognitive dissonance. In medieval Europe, how did the bishop-barons choose (when they had to) between and among pope and emperor, extended family, and local secular and/or religious authorities; and why did they make the choices they did? In early twentieth-century China, what bonds tied military officers to the Manchus, the Kuomintang, the communists, local warlords, or other would-be authorities; and how did such bonds influence political outcomes? In post-Columbian Mexico and Peru, what persuaded some indigenous nobles to collaborate with European *conquistadores* and what persuaded others to resist? Broadly speaking, such questions probe the changing cognitions, perceptions, and skills of individuals. They inquire into individual hopes and fears and try to determine which symbols were most persuasive and why. They ask, too, about what constituted successful manipulation of symbols, and which efforts failed. These are questions of growing relevance for our own times, because of the proliferation of ethnic contests and the major political shifts underway in Europe, the former USSR, and elsewhere. Although they are difficult questions to answer, especially in historical contexts where information is limited, they tap the wellsprings of politics.

A macro perspective looks at the big picture, especially the manner in which micro factors converge to produce emergent properties, which then encourage or constrain individual and/or group behavior. The power-politics tradition has confined itself largely to macro analysis, insisting that micro-factor reductionism should not be permitted to dilute the parsimony that can only be achieved at the macro level. "Low-level explanations," argues Waltz (1979, 67), "are repeatedly defeated, for the similarity and repetition of international outcomes persist despite wide variations in the attributes and in the interactions of the agents that supposedly cause them."

At the macro level, the study of international relations is normally concerned with the distribution of resources and attitudes among the principal polities across space—a *horizontal dimension.*[19] In this dimension, interaction is conceived in the familiar sense of "between" or "among" actors occupying spaces that exclude one another. This conception of space is compatible with theory that limits international politics to Westphalian polities and analyzes the patterns of behavior that are presumed to flow from their relationships. Yet such theory ignores head-on horizontal clashes between nonpeer polities like the UN versus Somali warlord bands, Rome versus tribal barbarians, or Spain versus the Aztec empire. Horizontal analysis also tends to dismiss layering or overlap among polities as "domestic" or "internal" politics, thereby overlooking multiple loyalties.

In fact, many of the most interesting and consequential aspects of political life flow from the fact that polities share space and can claim the loyalties of all or some of the same constituents. *The phenomenon in which some polities are encapsulated by others and embedded within them, we refer to as nesting.* Within a given space, one or another polity type may stand at the apex of an authority hierarchy, in the sense of enjoying first call on the affections of adherents with multiple loyalties, having access to more resources, or affecting more issues than others; but such a hierarchy cannot be assumed. Even where a hierarchy does exist, the polity or polities at the top will still have to interact, sometimes compete, and may be influenced by other polities below.

A frequent result of nesting is a process in which a dominant polity is modified and assumes some of the characteristics of the polity it has not entirely digested—and the nested polity is also affected. Nesting is sometimes the outcome of horizontal contests. As we shall see in chapters 9–10, when Spanish and Aztecs collided, many of the institutions of the latter slid under and into those of their conquerors like a

---

19. Typical of the horizontal focus of most international relations are the seven variables identified by Zinnes (1980, 10–12) to map and compare international systems. Rosenau (1990, 79, fn. 16) maintains that "most analysts would agree" these factors "are central to the operation of any international system."

tectonic plate. Neither conqueror nor conquered were ever the same again, and certainly this was the case with governance in Mexico. But nesting need not orginate in horizontal contests, for, indeed, it is a normal condition whenever there is any degree of social complexity.

Interactions among polities that occupy some or all of the same space constitute a *vertical dimension* of political life.[20] The vertical dimension involves relationships that arise from the overlapping and layering of polities,[21] and from their fission and fusion. Unlike the horizontal dimension, the vertical dimension routinely involves a variety of polity types.[22] Although they occupy the same space, polity types may coexist amicably either because each has its own issue domain or because crosscutting among issues allows them to bargain and achieve trade-offs. Some authorities like ethnic communities, churches, and regional governments are physically within Westphalian polities.

State-centric theory presumes the superiority (autonomy, power, and perhaps even contribution to the moral order) of state polities over both those polities they physically enclose and those international organizations and regimes that encompass the state. It is interesting to observe in this connection that Westphalian polities were born and grew powerful as parts of larger secular and religious entities; their leaders were relatively low in the medieval hierarchy. As was the case in that epoch, some of the most salient aspects of contemporary world politics involve not relations among peer polities but rather the efforts of Westphalian polities to resist and repress claims of autonomy from "below" and retain their own autonomy in the face of newly empowered regional and global institutions.

The distinction between the horizontal and vertical dimensions of

---

20. By emphasizing relations between ruling and subject classes, Marxist analysis centered on a critical vertical dimension.

21. Layering is the appropriate description when a clear hierarchy exists within the given space. By contrast, overlapping better describes a situation in which hierarchy is low, and interaction and competition is typical of relations among various polities occupying some or all of the same space.

22. The number of actors in a system—a system's polarity—is often a concern of international-relations scholars. By introducing a vertical dimension, it becomes difficult to determine polarity for a particular social space, since this will vary by issue and context.

political life, while serving an important analytic purpose, does not imply the kind of impermeable separation or compartmentalization that characterizes the traditional statist distinction between inter- and intranational politics. In reality, the two dimensions freely intermingle and have reciprocal effects on each other.[23] Analytically, they are reunited by the concept of issue—a single arena that replaces the two arenas called "domestic" and "international." Some polities are energized by only one or a few issues, whereas others cooperate and/ or compete across a wide range of issues. When polities are involved in only a few issues, the prospects for trade-offs are obviously fewer than if they are involved in many. If the same sets of authorities are present in several issues, those issues will be linked, so that outcomes in any of them will have an impact on the others.

In addition, although we will continue to use the terms "inside" and "outside"[24] to denote the location or source of phenomena, this distinction, unlike statist theory, neither implies the existence of qualitatively different political processes nor the shielding of one arena from the other. Instead, owing to the presence of numerous, sometimes overlapping, and nested polities, the idea of inside/outside varies as one's attention shifts from polity to polity. There are as many "boundaries" between the units and their environment as there are polities (Kratochwil 1986).

The importance of linkages between the horizontal and vertical dimensions is illustrated by the relationship between the seventeenth- and eighteenth-century Franco-British (horizontal) rivalry, French support for Catholic pretensions in England and American resistance to British colonial rule (vertical), and the inspiration provided by the English bourgeoisie to both the American and French middle classes in their revolutions (vertical) against British colonial authorities and the French monarchy respectively. Ironically, Napoleon Bonaparte, the product of (vertical) revolution in France, was responsible for the (horizontal) expansion of France at the expense of other Westphalian polities and fostered popular (vertical) movements against conservative monarchies in countries like Italy and Spain.

In this century, the combination of World War I (horizontal) and

---

23. This is what Robert Putnam (1988) seeks to express with the concept of "two-level games."

24. This language is borrowed from R. B. J. Walker (1993).

class warfare in Germany and Russia (vertical)—which led to the triumph of Bolshevism in the Soviet Union, the emergence of the Weimar Republic, and the later triumph of the Nazis in Germany—illustrates the consequences of the intersection of the two dimensions. The assumption of power by Lenin and Hitler and their followers in their respective countries was linked to the onset of World War II. The conflict between Trotsky and Stalin was partly a conflict over the relative significance of the horizontal and vertical dimensions in global politics, and changing Soviet policies toward the forces of international communism entailed uncertainty about how to forge policy that could take account of the two dimensions.

Linkages between the two dimensions exist at both the global and local levels. Thus, there was an interactive relationship between clan and class politics in classical Athens and Athenian relations with other Greek city polities, especially Sparta, and with imperial policy more generally. "Empire and mass democracy rose together," argues Liska (1990, 80), "when shifting from hoplite infantry to sea-borne triremes required enfranchising more manpower; and, outdoing the Themistoclean precedent, the material exigencies of the new property-less citizens inspired increasingly demagogic politicians (the Cleons, Cleophons, and Alcibiades) to complete under pressures of war the decay begun with the mid-course Periclean welfare state" (see chapters 5–6).

Similarly, family feuds and class politics in the cities of twelfth- and thirteenth-century Italy were closely linked to the combat between the German emperor and the Papacy for system-wide supremacy. Each city had its Guelph (anti-imperial) and Ghibelline (proimperial) partisans. Ultimately, local princes were able to manipulate imperial-papal hostility to achieve greater independence, and this helped pave the way for the emergence of Westphalian polities in Europe (see chapters 13 and 14).

POLITIES AND CHANGE

The evolution of political forms is not predestined to move in one direction, and no single type of polity implies "progress." The absorption of older entities by newer and larger ones does *not* mean that the former are irrelevant but may merely signify a shift in the political arena and a new set of rules for waging conflict. The fact that classical Athens and Renaissance Florence were swallowed up by larger territorial entities implies neither the irrelevance nor the obsolescence of the city polity. Indeed, Singapore is among the most modern and viable of contemporary political entities. Today, global politics is witnessing the reemergence of entities that were once thought to be as extinct as dodos. Whether looking at the dissolution of the Soviet Union and Yugoslavia, the revitalization of the Orthodox Church in Russia, or the reemergence of tribalism and communalism in Africa, one must be impressed by the durability of old polity forms.

Historical analysis helps explain the relative success and longevity of some polities in comparison with others. The effort of conquerors to eliminate or suppress competing authorities is often a recipe for continued conflict and instability, latent grievances, and claims to irredenta. Preserved in part by ideology, the old forms nest within the new ones and perhaps hibernate, only to resurface at a more propitious moment. By contrast, when dominant polities are flexible, set out to coexist with the old, are tolerant of "foreign" mores, or utilize strategies of cooptation, the resulting crosscutting of authority patterns may work well. Rome prospered by tolerating and availing itself of local religions and nationalisms. Roman citizenship and Latin, as well as other political, psychic, and economic rewards, were available to non-Roman subjects, provided they paid nominal allegiance to Rome and its gods. Conflicts arose mainly when local authorities, the Jews and early Christians for example, refused to reciprocate Roman tolerance; or when subjects like the Samnites in central Italy were denied citizenship and felt the balance between rewards and penalties had shifted against them. Centuries later the British Empire encouraged the study of classics and adapted earlier models, especially the Roman, with remarkable success. Indigenous elites in India, Asia, and Africa were educated in British schools and universities, instilled with the ideology of "civilization," and co-opted to manage imperial institutions. And, when the sun finally set on the empire, Britain's parting of the ways with former colonies was less traumatic than that of other Europeans.

History evolves by simultaneous processes of fragmentation and fusion of polities rather than a progressive movement "toward" any particular type. Some options close—even as others open—when population increases, environmental pressures mount, economies and societies become more complex, communication and transportation improve, and relationships with other groups intensify and present threats or opportunities. Empires may erode, and Westphalian polities may disintegrate at the same time as family-level groups are subsumed into local polities, and these may be swallowed by regional polities. Nevertheless, imperial traditions, ideologies, and memories may remain potent; formerly autonomous local polities may retain some legal rights and constituents' loyalties; and so on. Rosenau (1984, 256–57) captures the contradictory processes of integration and disintegration:

> The two historic processes are familiar features of social systems. They consist of those dynamics that conduce to systemic integration on the one hand and system disintegration on the other, to centripetal forces that today are making groups and nations more and more interdependent even as centrifugal forces are increasingly fragmenting them into subgroups and subnations. It has always been the case that movements toward the coherence of a sociopolitical system normally foster countermovements toward fragmentation on the part of its subsystems and/or the systems of which it is a subsystem. Contrariwise greater coherence within subsystems has always tended to create problems of breakdown for the system of which they are a part.

History does not inevitably produce larger and more inclusive or multifunctional polities. Large polities may simplify the political universe and enjoy economies of scale, yet, as we have observed, they often contain the seeds of their own dissolution. The more inclusive polities incorporate but do not completely overwhelm old loyalties and identities; their very success in creating centralized power may set off a struggle for control. And centralization may result in an ideological revolution, economic take-off, and/or foreign adventures that have an impact upon social groups and loyalties.

Different polities have their own strengths and weaknesses. Small city polities typically develop political parties and cultures that strongly anchor the loyalties of citizens while large imperial polities tend to build centralized bureaucracies and professional armies. "Whereas the former shunned military or political professionals and ran the risks of amateurish performance," argues Liska (1990, 30), "the latter embraced professionalism and courted the danger of seeing their moral or psychological foundation atrophy." He illustrates his claim by contrasting the professional military and bureaucratic castes in Hammurapi's Babylonian Empire and the later Hellenistic kingdoms and empires with the absence of such personnel in the city polities of Sumer and classical Greece (see chapters 3–6).

There is a propensity for polities to become too large to remain efficient and viable, especially as internal conflicts grow and old identities resurface. Bloated entities then fracture into "micro-polities" that are too small to be economically, politically, or militarily viable. Liska (1990, 32) refers to the "ingrained, and subsequently resurfacing, early polarity . . . between narrowly local and parochial and, at least in ambition, universal actors, each caught up in the search for a viable optimum size and scope under existing conditions." The fate of Austria-Hungary is instructive. This polyglot polity whose numerous ethnic and language groups had little in common except their Habsburg ruler, was conquered by Napoleon Bonaparte, challenged by popular uprisings in 1848, and then in the middle of the nineteenth century deprived of its territories in Italy and defeated in war by Prussia. Despite dramatic constitutional revisions (*Ausgleich*) in 1867 that created a dual monarchy, the vitality of the empire was sapped by external and internal foes in the years leading up to World War I. That war was triggered by a desperate gamble on the part of Austro-Hungarian leaders to suppress Slavic separatism. In the words of historian Laurence Lafore (1971, 18): "In tracing almost any of the circumstances that were most critical in 1914, one is led back to the national conflicts of Central and Southeastern Europe."

Although the centrifugal effects of local nationalisms ultimately overwhelmed the centripetal force of dynastic conservatism, the successor states that replaced the empire were less inclusive, more authoritarian, and politically and economically less dynamic. Austria-Hungary, though regarded as an anomalous curiosity by twentieth-century analysts, made sense as an economic entity. It combined thriving industrial (Austria) and fertile agricultural (Hungary) cores, and its rivers (including the Danube) ran north-south and integrated the empire (with the Ottoman port of Salonika, contemporary Thessaloniki, serving as an outlet to the sea for Hungarian grain). By contrast, the polities that replaced the empire made little economic sense, had profound problems of identity, and proved easy prey in the 1930s for Nazi penetration.

Now that the Soviet bloc and Soviet Union have crumbled and Yugoslavia has disintegrated, authority patterns in the region are again in flux. The threat is growing that still smaller national units will emerge. Slovaks and Czechs have already been divorced. Croatians and Bosnians are battling Serbs, and Slovenians wistfully hark back to the Austria-Hungary empire of which they were a part. Indeed, some of the proposals for maintaining the USSR bore an uncanny resemblance to the 1867 Vienna-Budapest *Ausgleich*. Referring to "the small states located between Russia and Germany," Liska (1990, 489) wrote with prescience: "Some of them will again look back nostalgically to the Habsburg formation."

The collision of previously isolated authorities also has important effects on processes of integration/disintegration. Throughout history, divergent polities have coexisted in varying degrees of isolation from and ignorance of one another. The meeting of such authorities symbolizing entire cultures is dramatic. The conquest of Minoan Crete by the Mycenaeans and of the early Indus Valley civilization by the Aryans are examples of such collisions. Between the eleventh and fourteenth centuries, global politics experienced successive shocks owing to the outward expansion of Latin Europe and the movement of warlike nomadic tribes from central Asia. From Europe, crusaders set out to the south and east, intent on forcing the submission of Byzantium and Islam,[25] and the consequences of that collision with an expansive Islam still reverberate. And, from central Asia, waves of Turkish and Mongol warriors overcame the Byzantine Empire and imposed their rule on large areas of Russia, China, and India (Lewis 1988).[26]

In later years, the European voyages of exploration and the ambitions of the conquistadores "encountered" the Indian polities of the New World. Although the Indians either died of disease or were conquered, their culture and institutions influenced Spanish rule, and Indian gold, crops, and diseases had monumental consequences for Europe. Still later, imperial expansion—justified by a mixed ideology created from religious fervor, racial superiority, free enterprise, and a sense of cultural mission—imposed a veneer of European rule and statist bureaucracy on much of Africa, Asia, and the Middle East. Such interpenetration of conflicting cultures mixes both attitudes and resources; emerging polities, whatever they are called, are likely to be different from their antecedents—and also to resemble them—in significant respects.

---

25. The clash between Christian Europe and Islam, the Europeans' continuing sense of siege that lasted until the expulsion of the Moors from Spain (1492), and the defeat of the Ottoman Turks at Lepanto (1571) gave impetus to the European perception that they were members of a Christian Commonwealth. The symbolic importance of Lepanto is reflected in the allusion to the battle in the second volume of *Don Quixote,* by Cervantes, who had lost a leg in that battle.

26. The impacts of these invasions on these areas were quite different.

Currently, much of humanity is still organized into discrete territorial units. In many parts of the world, the symbols of the state—its flag, national anthem, and foundation mythology—elicit a substantial measure of habitual obedience and the voluntary provision of resources from citizens. However, by any standard—size, ethnicity, industrialization, military capability, natural resources, governing capacity, and even function—contemporary states have little in common. To paraphrase Waltz (1979, 97): one *no longer* has to be impressed with the functinal similarity of states. Like members of a biological class, they share some features but are as different as dogs and whales. Asserting that humanity is divided into states is also trivial because it obscures the equally, if not more, important fact that humanity is divided in other ways as well. As in the past, self-definition and political identification both bind and cleave individuals, sometimes issue by issue.

There are few consensual rules of behavior among the inhabitants of a growing number of countries, and there is little loyalty to an abstract state among them. Although paper unity has been reimposed by Syrian troops on Lebanon, that country still breaks down along religious, clan, and charismatic lines. Cyprus and India continue to be ravaged by ancient feuds; in the former, Greeks and Turks refuse to coexist, and in the latter religious and caste identities remain strong. In northern Iraq, as well as Iran, Syria, and Turkey, a large Kurdish minority continues to struggle for political autonomy; the remainder of Iraq pits a dominant minority of Sunni Muslims against the Shi'ite majority. In the Sudan, black Christians and animists in the south war against Arab Muslims in the north—a continuation of the animosity between Arab slave traders and those whom they enslaved. In Rwanda Hutu and Tutsi conduct a tribal war of extermination. In Colombia and Peru, fabulously wealthy drug lords offer income to the underprivileged, control large areas, terrorize government officials, form alliances of convenience with other antigovernment groups, and enjoy links with transnational drug cartels. In the Philippines, a remnant of an old-guard corrupt elite confronts "people power"; radical-left guerrillas battle for what they conceive as social justice for the poor; and a divided military tries to protect illicit profits and institutional prerogatives. The list is endless.

Not only in strife-torn countries are there limits to the applicability of state authority and rules of behavior; everywhere they apply to some issues and some individuals but not to others. In the Irish Republic, it is difficult for any government to challenge the Catholic

Church on reproductive issues; in such matters, many citizens' obedience is to the Church first. In Israel, governments are hopelessly fragmented as voters in two major political parties, which are themselves divided on secular and religious issues, negotiate alliances with tiny religious and single-issue parties.[27]

In many Muslim societies, officials are at risk if they gainsay matters of faith or the dictates of the Qu'ran. The latter speaks to many aspects of human conduct that in secular societies are left as matters of individual conscience or regulated by secular law. In Iran, Saudi Arabia, and the Hausa region of Nigeria, Muslim religious leaders enjoy officially sanctioned political and social power. In other countries, for example, Bangla Desh, Algeria, Egypt, Afghanistan, and even Turkey, the authority of Muslim clerics over secular politicians is subject to often violent controversy.

CONCLUSION

The world is a living museum in which institutional and ideational artifacts from every stage of human evolution can still be found. Just as there remain pockets of Stone Age culture and predominantly agrarian polities, so, too, there continue to be tribes, city polities, viable regional governments and other subdivisions, myriad self-conscious ethnicities, latent and more substantial nations,[28] classes and masses, interest groups, political parties, monarchs, popes and patri-

---

27. The situation in Israel is exacerbated by a system of proportional representation and by unwritten guarantees made to Orthodox Jews at the time the State of Israel was founded. Resulting cleavages are reflected in the Jewish community globally and impede efforts by moderate Israelis to achieve a settlement with the Palestinians.

28. Nationalism is another vague concept. As an ideology, it may foster or even create an identity. Long before the Roman Emperor Augustus commissioned Virgil to write the *Aeneid*, rulers had been inventing foundation myths and other historical fictions to clothe themselves in legitimacy. Even national "languages are . . . almost always semi-artificial constructs and occasionally, like modern Hebrew, virtually invented. They are the opposite of what nationalist mythology supposes them to be, namely the primordial foundations of national culture and the matrices of the national mind" (Hobsbawm 1992, 54). Yet Smith (1991) reminds us that most nations are not built out of entirely new materials. See also Ferguson 1994.

archs, transnational corporations, alliances, and even putative neoim-
perialisms.

Both past and present vary dramatically in terms of authorities,
loyalties, and issues.[29] Some epochs and places are characterized by
many polities cheek-to-jowl, and others by relatively few. Polities
may be tightly linked—sharing the same space, performing similar
functions, and preoccupied by the same issues—or they may be
physically and/or psychologically isolated from one another. Some
polities are relatively homogeneous in some eras and heterogeneous in
others. They may be highly specialized and function only in relation to
few issues, or they may be unspecialized—like holding companies—
and function across a wide range of apparently disparate issues.

Awareness that polities decay from within and are challenged from
without compels us to pay special attention to transitional epochs
when the hegemony of previously dominant authorities is contested,
and loyalties are seduced to new authorities through the critical issues
of the day (Aronoff 1986). Such periods entail shifts in collective value
hierarchies owing to contextual and situational factors that heighten
widespread perceptions of deprivation of some values and reduce
anxieties about others. Value shifts occur slowly as a result of evolutionary environmental changes, or they may be sharp and sudden as a
result of cataclysmic events. The relatively leisurely evolution in the
nature of polities that accompanied the introduction of guns and
gunpowder, the discovery of iron, and the great voyages of exploration
illustrate one pattern; and the dramatic shifts in loyalties and institutions following the Thirty Years' War, World War I—and in all likelihood the end of the Cold War—illustrate the other.

Our description of authorities competing for loyalties across a
multitude of issues may sound suspiciously like our old friend pluralism, and it does bear some resemblance to that concept. Pluralism,
however, carries the limited connotation of power widely distributed
among government and other institutions coexisting under the overarching authority of the democratic polity. Where is the sovereign state?
Its presence is a vague, almost chimerical one; for most purposes, the
state is absent as an active participant or is dimly visible in the
background. Specific agencies of government can, of course, partici-

---

29. Such variation is used by historians as the basis for "naming" different
epochs (e.g., medieval Europe or Renaissance Europe).

pate in a pluralist arena, but there is no unitary sovereign player. Like the metaphor of God the Watchmaker,[30] the pluralist polity seems to have set the rules of the game, started it in motion, and then stepped back from the scene of the action. Paradoxically, the pluralist idea, precisely because it provides a "soft" definition of the state, makes it easier for theorists who recognize the organizational complexities of the political universe to live with the state concept.

Only a very few political scientists, historians, historical sociologists, neo-Marxist world system analysts, political anthropologists, and archaeologists have seriously applied themselves to the study of long-term political change.[31] The revisions in scope and method that we wish to encourage have implications far beyond any traditional conception of international relations as a field, let alone a discipline. In proceeding, we hope to avoid becoming mired in fruitless epistemological debates. Instead, there is an intense need for what Thomas J. Biersteker (1989, 267) calls "concrete, self-reflexive, nuanced, and theoretically-informed research." Recognition that the social sciences are in the midst of theoretical pluralism allows us to begin to integrate the apparently disparate insights of geography (e.g., location, climate, population, natural resources), biology (e.g., disease), technology (e.g., weaponry, communications), economics (e.g., production and markets), sociology (e.g., social strata), anthropology (e.g., social mores), philosophy (e.g., religion, ideology), psychology (e.g., group ethos and identity), and others into a broad understanding of politics.

A focus on any single era—past or present—or geographical part of the world invites the objection that it may not be representative of other periods or areas. Accordingly, we have selected six historical cases to encompass a wide range of time frames, geophysical environ-

---

30. This Enlightenment metaphor is associated with both Voltaire and William Paley, once fellow and tutor at Cambridge University and later archdeacon of Carlisle.

31. See, for example, Bozeman 1960; Buzan, Little, and Jones 1993; Doyle 1986; Eisenstadt 1986; Hall 1985; Johnson and Earle 1987; McNeill 1963, 1986; Mann 1986b; Skocpol 1979; Tilly 1975; Wallerstein 1974, 1979, and 1984; Watson 1992. The boldness with which some of these scholars approach their task is illustrated by Johnson and Earle (1) who declare that: "Our purpose in this book is to describe and explain the evolution of human societies from earliest times to roughly the present."

ments, and cultural settings. These were our sole criteria in picking cases, and no analytical bias that we can perceive is built into the particular choices we made. All the cases are pre-Westphalian; however, we explain in further detail in chapter 15 how the polities perspective also applies to the Westphalian and post-Westphalian eras. The cases include the world's first great civilization in Mesopotamia that arose in the mid-third millennium B.C. and lasted until the Persian conquest in the sixth century B.C.; the Greek world from the Archaic period of eighth century B.C. until its conquest by Macedonia in 338 B.C.; Mesoamerica from the emergence of Olmec culture about 1250–1150 B.C. until after the Spanish conquest; China from the early Chou era of about 1100 B.C. until the end of the Han era in 220 A.D.; the Islamic world from 622 A.D. until the Mongol sack of Baghdad in the thirteenth century; and Italy from the fourth century A.D. until the Golden Age of the Renaissance in the fifteenth century.

We do draw a few important conclusions across cases but have made no attempt at *systematic* comparison. Our main intention is to *illustrate* how world politics has always involved a crazy quilt of polities—foci of authority of varying domain and influence; distinctive in some respects and overlapping, layered, nested, and linked in others; competing and cooperating across space and issues; trying to attract and hold the allegiance and resources of individuals; and seeking to allocate values that have usually been in inadequate supply to meet demands.

At this juncture the reader might wish to recall from chapter 1 the familiar warnings about the risks inherent in using history,[32] as well as what we said about not wanting to get bogged down in epistemological issues. The difficulty of using history does not allow us to ignore it. We have made a determined effort to look at a great many sources as objectively as possible and, indeed, have repeatedly modified some of our initial theoretical assumptions because of what the cases have taught us. However, to be sure, historical research is inevitably *to some extent* theory-dependent and subjective. In addition to our personal limitations as objective analysts, we have been forced to rely mainly on secondary sources—not that many primary sources are any

---

32. For further discussion of some of the pertinent issues, see, for example, Elton 1969, Finley 1986, Hall and Kratochwil 1993, Martin 1989, Novick 1988, and Puchala 1995.

more reliable—and various historians often (certainly not always) advance different interpretations of what happened, when, and why. In every instance, and especially when there are several interpretations, we cannot avoid making our own careful and informed judgment as to what to believe—that is, which interpretation(s) appear to us to be the most plausible.

What makes any "interpretation" "true"? There are, indeed, few givens—only probabilities, likelihoods, and sometimes only possibilities. We have to live with that amount of ambiguity and proceed as best we can. If the results of our own investigations seem to provide a more convincing view of political reality than other constructions, then they will have at least the pragmatic utility that Puchala (1995) suggests is the most we can hope for.

More important, we submit, is that when we look at a number of wide-ranging cases over such long time frames, it really does not matter much to our central theoretical arguments even if some key facts or interpretations that we or our sources advance in specific cases turn out to be dead wrong. We would not be defeated, for example, if it is eventually shown that the classical Mayas simply boarded alien spacecraft and blasted off into outer space. We would have just another example of "encounter" between nonpeer polities! In the end, we can only echo Mann's (1986b, 30) words: "From the specialist historian, I plead for generosity and breadth of spirit. Having covered a large slice of recorded history, I have doubtless committed errors of fact, and probably a few howlers. I ask whether correcting them would invalidate the overall arguments."

Each of the six cases occupies two chapters. Although subheadings and their ordering in the chapters are somewhat different, reflecting unique aspects of the cases, all follow the same basic analytical framework and plan of organization. The first chapter in each case examines the horizontal dimension of politics—relationships among key polities *across space* and other aspects of system structure broadly conceived—including system discreteness, distribution of capabilities, geophysical setting, production, trade, demographics, warfare, diplomacy, and polity types. The second chapter deals mainly with the vertical dimension—relationships of polities *within all or some of the same space*—including identities and ideology as they affect authorities, political centralization and decentralization (fusion and fragmentation), and hierarchy. In the book's final chapter, we draw conclusions from our cases; give further attention to the concept of nested polities and the interaction of authority, identity, and ideology; apply our theoretical perspective to an analysis of the evolution of the Westphalian polity itself; and argue the utility of the polities framework in accounting for political change.

Part II

PRACTICE

3

MESOPOTAMIA
Fission-Fusion of the First City Polities and Empires

Through archaeological finds and other means we are slowly but steadily learning more about the ancient world and not just in the Mediterranean cradle of Western civilization. What we learn frequently forces us to make rather drastic revisions in our chronologies. Be that as it may, currently, ancient Mesopotamia receives credit for an impressive list of probable "firsts." These include the world's first great civilization,[1] the first cities, the first formal law "codes,"[2] the first standing army, the first empire, and the first writing (though not the first kings, who were in Egypt).

Mesopotamia is an intriguing case from other standpoints as well. For Michael Mann (1986b, 92), Mesopotamia was "a singular civilization, fuzzy at the edges" that illustrates how identities "are the product of confined power interactions over a long period between persons" engaged in "the social exploitation of contrasting adjacent ecologies." Various cores and peripheries emerged that reflected to a great extent the shifting limits of irrigation. As we shall see, depen-

---

1. In addition to other works cited herein, for a useful overview, see Roux 1980. Hawkes 1973, written for a popular audience, discusses the three early civilizations of Mesopotamia, the Indus Valley, and Egypt. Lloyd 1984 focuses on archaeology but relates this to evolving politics and culture. Lloyd 1980 is a history of the archaeological "discovery" of Mesopotamia. Kramer 1963 and 1959 and Oppenheim 1964 are classics but have largely been superseded by recent works.

2. These were not codes in the Napoleonic sense, rather promulgation of royal decisions that were presumed to embody significant modifications in existing practices. The most ancient of the known Mesopotamian codes was that produced during the Third Dynasty of Ur by Ur-Nammu (2112–2095 B.C.), some three centuries before the Code of Hammurapi.

dence on irrigation in the midst of a hostile landscape carried with it a strong potential for environmental disaster.

Mesopotamia also hosted one of the earliest interactions among a host of diverse polity types. There were cycles of fusion and fragmentation as well as different manifestations of nesting. Despite a high degree of assimilation, conquering tribes managed to maintain some separate identity. The relationship between imperial and city polities offers a clear example in which one type of polity (city) nested, only to continue competing for the loyalties of subjects. Mesopotamian empires cultivated a form of nesting outside their core domains to compensate for the lack of a genuine administrative network emanating from the center, which only the late Assyrian empire came close to developing. Of the earlier Assyrians, for instance, Adam Watson (1992, 34) declares: "The imperial system which this hard and calculating people established was the first real attempt to organize politically the whole ancient world. They could not govern it all directly, of course. They evolved a system of vassals, native governments with Assyrian garrisons. Cities were normally accorded municipal autonomy under generous charters."

INTRODUCTION

Mesopotamian civilization emerged only a little before those of Egypt and the lesser-known Indus Valley Harrapan civilization. Civilization in Mesopotamia was unusually long-lived, originating in the mid-third millennium B.C.[3] and lasting at least until Mesopotamia's conquest by the Persians in the sixth century B.C. or subsequently, the fourth century, when it was incorporated into the Hellenistic world by Alexander the Great. Even then, Michael Grant (1990, 59) informs us: "Babylonia had preserved, and was still allowed to retain, large parts of its own native, traditional, centralized governmental and social system. In particular, its ancient law—the most sophisticated legal

---

3. There is debate about many Mesopotamian dates. This is particularly serious for the prehistoric era, when it is estimated that dates could be in error as much as 800 years at radiocarbon 4500 B.C. There is a range of 200 years even in dating Hammurapi's reign in Babylon. Most scholars now use the "middle chronology," in which Hammurapi came to power in 1792 B.C. and Babylon was sacked in 1595 B.C. The controversy is summarized in Oates (1986, 23–24). For a recent assessment, see Crawford 1991, 18–20.

system in the world outside Greece, Rome, and China—was still very much alive, and represented a potent unifying factor. Moreover, the Seleucid monarchs took over the antique Babylonian theocracy. Like Alexander before him (who had rebuilt the temple of the god Bel), Seleucus I Nicator publicly ascribed his rule to Bel and Marduk, and he and his dynasty carefully maintained good relations with the local priesthood of the Magi."

A summary of several key periods may be useful to help orient the reader at the outset. Full-fledged city polities formed in southern Mesopotamia about 3500 B.C. and came to be ruled by their own kings. The Akkadian king (c. 2310–2273 B.C.) of Sumeria, Sargon of Agade and his heirs, created the first large regional Mesopotamian polity and expanded it into an empire. When that empire crumbled, it was succeeded by several large regional polities, the most notable of which was ruled by the Third Dynasty of Ur (c. 2112–2095). Other important dynasties were the First Dynasty of Isin (c. 2017–1794); Lagash (c. 2570–2342), which eventually (c. 2230–2111) came under the sway of the Gutians; and the Larsa Dynasty (c. 2025–1763). The next major imperial polity was Babylon (c. 1894–1595) in the south, established by the Amorites, whose dynasty is best remembered for Hammurapi (c. 1792–1750). Later Kassite rulers reestablished Babylonian authority c. 1370 after some two hundred years of turmoil. Meanwhile, after c. 1813 for nearly a thousand years, in the north of Mesopotamia, Assyrian kings gradually consolidated and extended their reach, until they overwhelmed Babylon and established a mighty empire that was even larger than its predecessors. The Assyrian Empire collapsed in the seventh century, and Babylon enjoyed a splendid, albeit relatively brief revival, under a Chaldean dynasty. The Persian Empire conquered Mesopotamia in 539 B.C., and Alexander the Great arrived in 331 B.C.

SYSTEM DISCRETENESS AND STRUCTURE

The Mesopotamian system was highly permeated, had considerable interaction with its neighbors, and ultimately had a noteworthy impact on the external world. Neighboring tribal peoples regularly intervened or in important ways influenced the course of events. Some of these neighboring peoples evolved their own regional polities or empires, and others founded dynasties in Mesopotamia itself, like the Manchus did in China. As a result, it is difficult to identify "native" political elites in subregions like Babylonia or Assyria. After the

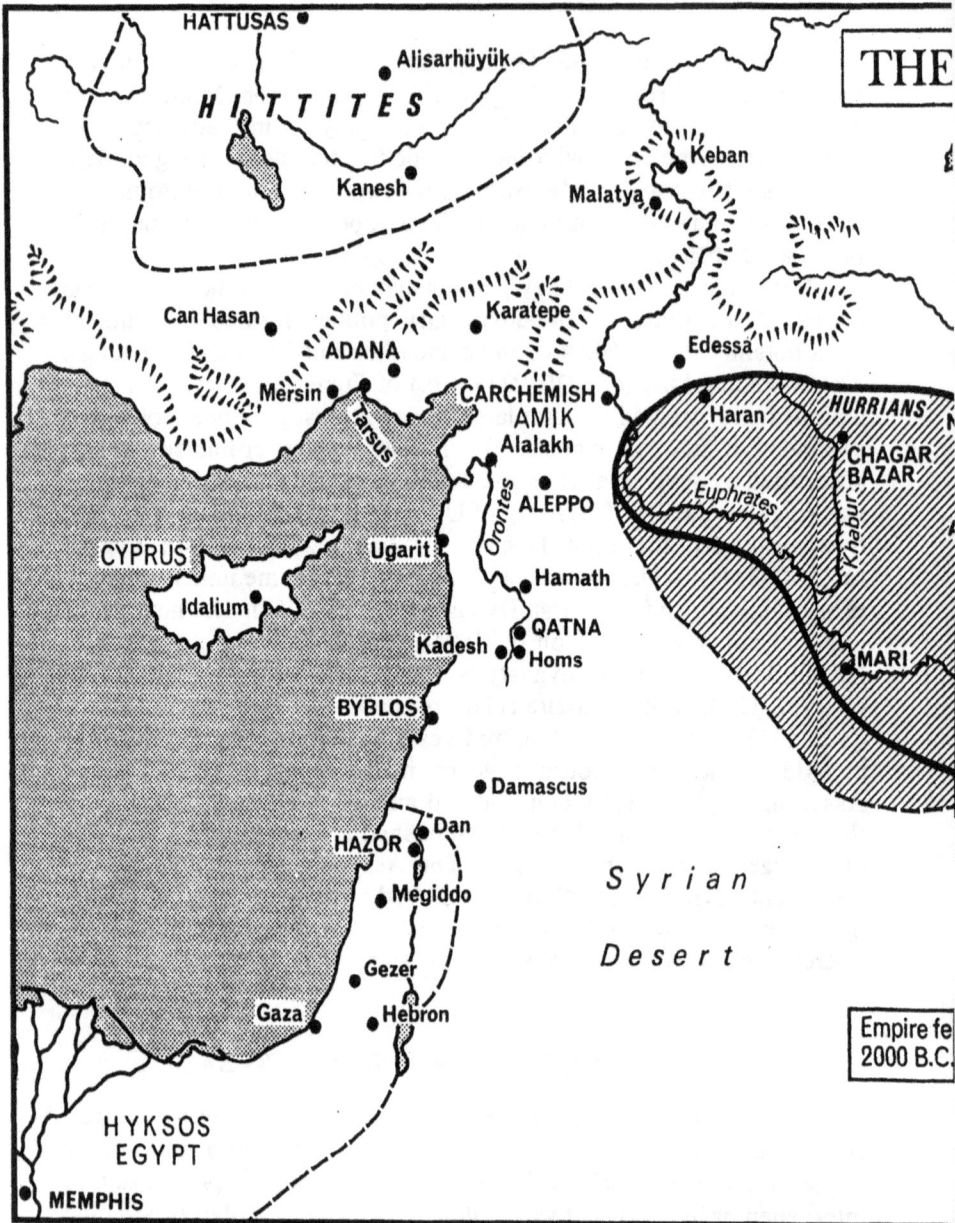

HATTUSAS

Alisarhüyük

H I T T I T E S

Kanesh

Keban

Malatya

Can Hasan

Karatepe

Edessa

ADANA

Mersin

Tarsus

CARCHEMISH

Haran

HURRIANS

AMIK

CHAGAR
BAZAR

Alalakh

ALEPPO

Orontes

Euphrates

Khabur

CYPRUS

Ugarit

Idalium

Hamath

QATNA

Kadesh

Homs

MARI

BYBLOS

Damascus

Dan

HAZOR

Megiddo

S y r i a n

Gezer

D e s e r t

Gaza

Hebron

Empire fe
2000 B.C.

HYKSOS
EGYPT

MEMPHIS

THE

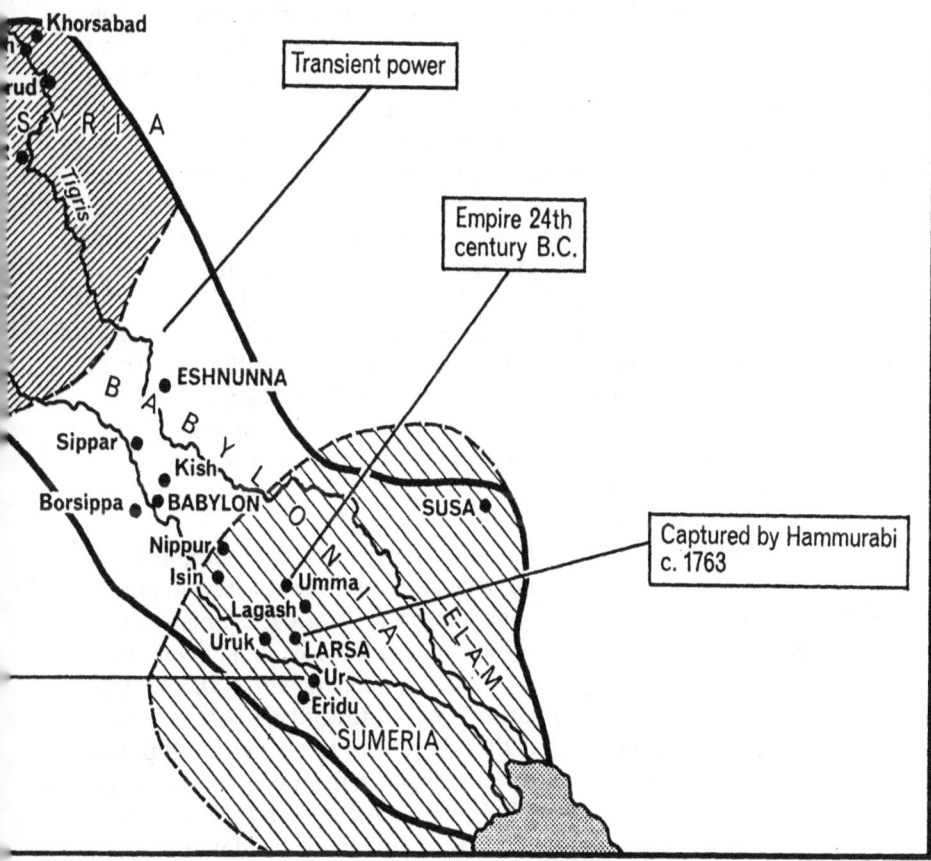

EAR EAST c.1700 B.C.

KINGDOM OF HAMMURABI (early 18th cent.)

KINGDOM OF SHAMSI - ADAD I (died c. 1781)

KINGDOM OF RIMSIN

Some principal cities in CAPITALS

CASPIAN SEA

Khorsabad

rud

SYRIA

Tigris

Transient power

Empire 24th century B.C.

ESHNUNNA

Sippar

Kish

Borsippa

BABYLON

SUSA

Nippur

Isin

Umma

Lagash

Uruk

LARSA

Ur

Eridu

SUMERIA

ELAM

BABYLONIA

Captured by Hammurabi c. 1763

incursions of Indo-European peoples about 1600 B.C., Mesopotamia found itself drawn into a much broader political universe that included Anatolia and Egypt, Iran, and Greece/Macedon (Roux 1980, 208).

The list of peoples who helped to shape political patterns in Mesopotamia is long and somewhat arbitrary, because general ethnic classifications do not do justice to numerous subgroups and also because we do not know the precise identity of certain peoples like the Sumerians and the Sea Peoples. Significant groups include (but are not limited to) the following: Sumerians, Akkadians, Gutians, Amorites, Assyrians, Hurrians/Mitannians, Hittites, Aramaeans, Elamites, the Sea Peoples, Philistines, Kassites, Egyptians, Hebrews, Arabs, Chaldeans, Urartuans, Medes, Persians, Cimmerians, Scythians, and Greeks. Arabs were important in trade, and there were also limited contacts with the Harrapans of the Indus Valley.

Although the intellectual fashion among archaeologists and historians today is to emphasize parallel indigenous developments rather than cultural diffusion, ancient Mesopotamia did have a substantial impact on the world beyond. There is evidence that the Hurrians helped transmit aspects of Babylonian culture to the Hittites, Palestinians, and Phoenicians, and thence to the Greeks (Oates 1986, 87). Raids of the Sea Peoples, which were part of the general turbulence at the time of the collapse of the Hittites, contributed to the demise of the Mycenaean civilization and onset of a Dark Age in Greece. Assyrian imperial campaigns reached deep into Egypt and Persia. Also, the Etruscan predecessors of the Romans seem to have been deeply influenced by the culture of the Near East and may even have originated there (Grant 1979, 13–15).

Because of the permeated nature of the system, the multiplicity of competing polities within it, and change over time, Mesopotamia is difficult to characterize in traditional distribution-of-capabilities terms. To be sure, there were four distinct and successive major centers— Sumer/Akkad, Babylon, Assyria, and Babylon (again)—and to this extent the system might be seen as tending toward unipolarity. One objection to this interpretation is that there was an element of bipolarity involved in the far-from-unilinear transition from one center to the next, particularly the shift from Babylon to Assyria and from Assyria back to Babylon. Seesawing of political and military dominance in response to the leadership abilities and opportunities of successive Babylonian and Assyrian rulers is part of the picture. More basic is what Joan Oates (1986, 95–96) describes as an "Assyrian obsession with, and ambivalence toward, Babylon" that troubled the northern "center" for more than six hundred years. Whenever Assyria got the political and military upper hand, closer contacts with and especially occupation of nested Babylon opened the door further to Babylonian cultural influence. There was always the question whether Babylon should be under the direct rule of Assyria or be allowed to have its own subking under Assyrian overlordship, and vehement pro- and anti-Babylonian factions developed in the royal Assyrian court itself, for example, during the reign of Sargon II's son, Sennacherib (704–681 B.C.) (Saggs 1984, 99–100). Parallel pro-Assyrian sentiments existed in some northern areas of Babylon.

There are other objections to the tendency-towards-unipolarity interpretation. The first is that even when one center was clearly dominant, nearby tribes and adjacent regional polities and empires posed an almost continual threat, often resulting in actual intervention or a more subtle form of infiltration. Any polity that was weakened by war, overextension, or internal political strife became a tempting target for outsiders. Moreover, the political initiative during certain periods came from outside, for instance, from the Hurrians throughout the fifteenth and much of the fourteenth centuries, and from Elam, about the middle of the twelfth century. All of this suggests multipolarity in a wider system or, at best, a highly unstable unipolarity.

Another objection—the most important in light of our assumptions—is that no center ever achieved a secure transfer of the loyalties of its subjects from other competing symbols of identification. The competition was to some extent ethnic, that is, tribal; or more broadly cultural, like the admiration of many Assyrians for Babylonian culture that was distinct from, though associated with, Babylon as a city. However, the principal and most consistently dangerous loyalty competition for would-be empires or large polities was loyalty to city. Despite the continued significance of tribe, as Henri Frankfort (1978, 215) declares, "the original articulation of Mesopotamian society was local rather than tribal," and local identities were strengthened when cities emerged as leading polities at an early stage. Through ideological invention and the provision of concrete benefits that derived from conquering and administering large territories, Mesopotamia's kingdoms and empires periodically seduced their subjects into divided loyalties. But city remained the fundamental attachment,[4] which reas-

---

4. Roux (1980, 20–21) observes that Mesopotamia's ancient inhabitants had no name for their region as a whole. "The terms they used were either too

serted itself whenever empires floundered or the costs of belonging to a larger polity seemed to outweigh the benefits. C. K. Maisels (1990, 132) sees the continued vitality of the "city-state," somewhat paradoxically, as helping to preserve the "millennial continuity" of the Mesopotamian "system" as a whole at times of "external disruption and despoliation." He argues that "because power was dispersed among city-states of differing fortunes and was not centralized, though some could be overrun or disputed, others could continue broadly as normal or even flourish, like Lagash under Gudea despite the Gutians" (2160–2122 B.C.).

A final observation that militates against any unipolar interpretation is that, owing to the combination of factors already mentioned, the region regularly disintegrated into isolated localities or, worse, outright chaos. Small surviving polities were so weak and contact among them so erratic that the term multipolarity, while perhaps technically accurate, seems an overstatement. At times, for example, during the "reign" of the original Sargon's great-grandson Shar-kali-sharri (2217–2193 B.C.), there appears to have been very little political authority at all. The Sumerian King-List describes this period as one of "Who was king? Who was not king?" The formidable challenge facing the famous Babylonian ruler, Hammurapi, upon his succession in 1792 B.C. is evident from a letter written by his contemporary, Zimri-Lim of Mari: "There is no king who of himself is strongest. Ten or fifteen kings follow Rim-Sin of Larsa; the same Ibal-pi-El of Eshunna; the same Amut-pi-El of Qatahum, and twenty kings follow Yarim-Lim of Yamkad" (cited in Hawkes 1973, 78–79). Some of these "kings" were doubtless no more than tribal chiefs. Other periods of chaos followed upon the decline (more than once) of the Assyrians. Georges Roux (1980, 259–60) describes the "dark age" between Tig-lathpileser I (1077 B.C.) and Adad-nirâri II (911 B.C.): "The mounting tide of Aramaean invasion, the desperate efforts made by the Assyrians to dam it up, the irremediable decadence of Babylon, Sumer and Akkad wide open to the Sutû and the Aramaeans, foreign wars, civil wars, floods, famine, such is the pitiful picture offered by Iraq during the tenth and ninth centuries B.C." Over a century later, in 790 B.C., a

---

vague ('the Land') or too precise ('Sumer,' 'Akkad,' 'Assur,' 'Babylon'). So deeply embedded in their minds were cities and other identities that they apparently failed to recognize the existence of a territorial unity."

chronicle could still report of Babylon, that "there was no king in the country" (Roux 1980, 280).

THE GEOPHYSICAL SETTING, PRODUCTION, TRADE, AND DEMOGRAPHICS

Several aspects of the geophysical setting in ancient Mesopotamia, although not deterministic, strongly influenced the political, economic, and demographic patterns that emerged.

Irrigation and the Birth of Cities

The so-called Neolithic Revolution, from hunting and gathering and nomadic pastoralism to settled agriculture, had its origins in the Near East. Barley, emmer-wheat, and einkorn-wheat grew wild, and climatic conditions in certain areas were favorable for agriculture. As H. W. F. Saggs (1984, 7) points out, the timescale involved makes the term *revolution* misleading. The shift to cultivation of previously wild cereals and legumes, and the settled rearing of herd animals, took place over millennia, while hunting remained a crucial means of augmenting the food supply. Paradoxically, these changes encouraged both settlement and migration. Agriculture involved settlement. However, herds could now be fed wherever there was something for them to eat (natural or cultivated), and seed crops could be raised wherever there was adequate water (Saggs 1984, 8).

In the flat alluvial plain created by the Tigris and Euphrates in southern Mesopotamia—unlike the Nile Valley in Egypt—river floods are irregular and violent, and rainfall is sparse. The flood waters often are either excessively high or low; and even when they are normal, they come too late for winter crops and too early for summer crops. The alluvial soil is fertile, but lack of rainfall means that farming away from marshes and lagoons requires intensive irrigation. The earliest hunter-gatherers in Sumer about the late sixth millennium appear to have made their homes in the marshes and lagoons. Initial agriculture seems to have been on the fringes of such areas in southern Mesopotamia and in the northeastern foothills region, where rainfall is more plentiful. However, it is not coincidental that the first cities arose outside the areas of earliest agriculture or that Assyria, in the northeast, remained a land of relatively few cities. Cities were linked to irrigation.

The entire southern plain of Mesopotamia was settled and irrigated with simple dikes and canals during the fifth and fourth millennia, and there was an impressive development of much greater economic, social, and political complexity after about 3500 B.C. It now appears that the city polity as an institution was well-established before the creation of *large-scale* irrigation projects (Oates 1986, 14; Maisels 1990, 213). Nevertheless, there is little doubt that political institutionalization was encouraged by the need to control and mete out scarce water resources, and to redistribute the surpluses that public works projects helped create. Several technological advances about this time also helped increase food surpluses, stimulated markets and trade, and made possible early industrial production: the plough, the sled for dragging grain, the chariot for transport of goods (as well as war), the sail, the potter's wheel, and the casting of copper alloys (Roux 1980, 75–76). Nature, too, boosted surpluses, for barley mutated from its original two-row form into a six-row variety with a far higher yield (Hawkes 1973, 33).

Once cities appeared, many rapidly grew in size, population, and prosperity. Lagash, one of the largest Sumerian city polities, had an area of 1,800 square miles under its control but only 30,000 to 35,000 persons. By comparison, during the sixth-century Neo-Bablylonian period, when Babylon was the center of a polity much larger than Lagash, the city alone covered some 5,000 acres and had a population of 100,000 (Roux 1980, 125, 360). Most population growth appears to have come through migration from surrounding areas. Nature's contribution to surpluses through mutating barley was somewhat undercut by the fact that about 3500 B.C. the climate of the Near East gradually became drier; numerous river tributaries dried up, and marginal agricultural areas received even less rainfall (Roux 1980, 75–76). Migrants came to the cities partly to secure a dependable supply of food in a system of managed agriculture. There were other attractions as well: an expanding economy with an increasingly specialized division of labor, physical security in numbers, the worship of cults in a major center, and the ancient Mesopotamian equivalent of the "bright lights."

Trade and the Development of City Polities

Maisels (1990, 12–13, 254–55, 304) stresses that the Mesopotamian "city-state" resembled the much later "city-state" in Greece, in that an "organic" relationship prevailed between the city and its immediate countryside.[5] The Mesopotamian "city-state" was a genuine economic

---

5. See also Postgate 1982, chapter 4. Part III of Postgatae's book analyzes various dimensions of the early Mesopotamian economy. City-countryside relations in Italy after the Roman Empire are discussed in chapters 13 and 14.

center, not "just" a political and cultic center like the less-integrated "village-state" model prevailing, for example, in China and some parts of Mesoamerica.[6] Moreover, in Maisel's (1990, 135–36) view, the growth of the cities was primarily the result of "political rather than demographic forces," the establishment of new political forms that had broad consequences across the full range of social life in particular areas. He quotes Robert McC. Adams (1981, 81) on the complex and unstable "mix" of relationships between centers and peripheries, which included "intervals of emergent, centralised, military based domination of subordinate centres that had been reduced to the status of clients, alternating with other intervals of fragile multi-centre coalition or local self-reliance." "Coercive extraction of rural resources" alternated with the free exchange of rural subsistence products in return for luxury goods and other items produced in the city. In short, the growth of the cities owed partly to attraction and partly to the subjugation of neighboring areas and polities.[7]

Although the land in ancient Mesopotamia supported nomadic pastoralism and, with irrigation, large-scale agriculture, there was a dearth of other natural resources. Only Assyria had stone and timber for building; the entire region lacked all varieties of metal ores, and many luxury items had to be imported. This situation and the likelihood of occasional crop failures mandated extensive trade. Of course, there were other motives for trade than a need and desire for imported goods, including the fact that a trade monopoly could be extremely

---

6. However, we note in chapter 10 that more careful investigation has revealed that few, if any, of, for example, Maya city polities were strictly political and ceremonial. The problem has been that the perishable nature of building materials has tended to obscure residential areas around the centers, which combined presumably constituted an economic unit. But other polities in Mesoamerica may indeed approximate Maisel's "village-state" model— except that the use of "state" in this context is almost absurd.

7. This brief discussion of the first Mesopotamian cities should not hide the fact that we do not fully understand how they arose. Most scholars agree on the range of factors involved—demographic, economic (including intensified agriculture and trade), ideological, military, administrative, and so on—but not about which factors are the most significant or how they relate to one another. For a summary of the debate and an invaluable bibliography, see Algaze 1989.

profitable. Guaranteeing the safety of caravans[8] and controlling some of the great trade routes of the ancient world were thus powerful incentives for war and empire.

Guillermo Algaze (1989, 591–93, including comments by Philip L. Kohl; see also Crawford 1991, chapter 7) believes that substantial long-distance exchange probably antedated cities, which "crystallized at locations through which long-distance exchange was [already] being funnelled." In any event, he persuasively argues that cross-cultural exchange over a broad area was critical even for the earliest lowland cities. The area involved from the outset extended to Iranian Khuzestan, northern Mesopotamia and Syria, eastern Anatolia, and the Iranian plateau. Early cities actually encouraged some emigration in order to establish enclave settlements at strategic points along the routes of communication.

Records of officials from the Third Dynasty of Ur indicate that merchants were provided with such goods from the temple warehouses as textiles, wool, grain, oil, and leather to trade for copper along the Persian Gulf. Christopher Edens (1992, 127) maintains that by the end of the third millennium, copper from the Gulf to Mesopotamia and grain from Mesopotamia for the Gulf had been "transformed from largely a luxury to a necessity." Trade continued after the fall of Ur under the financial aegis of private entrepreneurs and possibly kings as well. Harriet Crawford (1991, 150) comments: "It is difficult to tell how much of the enterprise was state-controlled and how much private capital played a part. In the Ur III period, for which the records are best, it is clear that much of the trade was financed by the temples; earlier, in the ED period, the palace was a major partner, but by the Old Babylonian period private capital seems to have taken over. . . . at present the evidence shows a real switch from public to private finance." Nevertheless, kings kept trade under close supervision, for merchants could not pass checkpoints along the Euphrates without a "tablet of the king." About the same period, c. 1990 B.C., merchants from Assyria also ran frequent caravans to and from more than twenty trading colonies in Cappadocia (central Anatolia) (Saggs 1989, 140–43).

---

8. Evidence suggests that caravans were in regular operation at least as early as 2750 B.C. (Saggs 1989, 130).

The Hostility of Nature

The cities that raised their ziggurats to the sky were impressive, but they remained vulnerable in a natural setting that could be hostile as well as bountiful. Plagues of locusts periodically destroyed crops, and they were not the only plagues. For instance, the Bible and other sources tell of the virtual destruction of Sennacherib's army as he marched toward Egypt, apparently by a sudden disease or (according to Herodotus) "a legion of rats" (Roux 1980, 295–96).[9] Irrigation was a means of improving agricultural productivity where water resources were inadequate, yet the infrastructure on which managed agriculture depended needed protection and careful maintenance. Wars could damage vital infrastructure and disrupt trade, with grave consequences. A collapse of trade caused a shortage of needed goods and whatever profits and tax revenues derived from trade even in luxuries. A hidden cost of trade was its long-range debilitating effect on agriculture. Since agricultural surpluses provided the bulk of lowland exports, there was a premium on producing as much as possible, which placed an intolerable burden on the land (Algaze 1989, 587).

Overcropping and the inevitable salinization of land under irrigation gradually decreased agricultural productivity,[10] and restoring the land to health was even more difficult than rebuilding war-torn infrastructure. As Maisels (1990, 301–2) observes:

> In the circumstances of declining yields . . . the central authority is likely to intensify what it normally does, seeking a 'fix,' and so making matters worse . . . redoubled efforts, taxes, sacrifices, wars, etc. Or, especially if headed by an autocrat, to be paralyzed by indecision, hoping things will take a turn for the better. Since the underlying causes of the problem(s) may not be known . . . policy could just as well lurch from one line to another, and perhaps back again, thus sowing confusion and so confounding resolution. Or the society as a whole may be so constrained by ecology, technology, ideology, and demography . . . that no

---

9. See Lord Byron's poem "The Destruction of Sennacherib."

10. Powell (1985) suggests that some of the evidence for declining agriculture may have been overrated.

significant policy alternatives are available to keep existing forms
of social complexity in being.

Against this background, then, it is perhaps easier to understand the
rapid collapse of previously flourishing polities, which at times reduced
Mesopotamia to virtual chaos.

Geography and Disunity

The extent to which geography did or did not encourage political
unification is a complex issue. On the one hand, there was some
physical basis for the separation of city polities. On the other hand,
there were few truly "natural" boundaries; extensive trade was essential; and plenty of "space" existed for large kingdoms and empires.
Geography thus played something of a role, but not a controlling one.
Frankfort (1978, 217), for example, remarks that "the character of the
land encouraged separatist and centrifugal tendencies." "The small
settlements of early times appeared lost in the boundless plain. They
remained isolated units, each surrounded by drained or irrigated fields
and separated from the next community by a wilderness of marsh and
desert." Unlike the Nile, the Euphrates had six principal and numerous subsidiary channels, making it difficult for any one center to utilize
river routes as an efficient link with distant points of subjugation. Yet
Oates (1986, 24) observes that the earliest Mesopotamian cities were
literally in sight of one another. If they were "lost," they at least
knew where one another was! The same "boundless plain" that was
punctuated by irrigated field and marsh was also, from a different
perspective, an invitation to closer association.

Much the same might be said about the impact of geography on
larger polities. Assyria offers an example. Saggs (1984, 3–5) writes:
"Comprising . . . four main divisions, Assyria is far from being one
uniform geographical unit; significant differences both of terrain and of
climate exist between one part and another. But on the other hand, the
constituent parts are sufficiently alike to make the whole region
recognizably a single country in its own right, and to set it apart as
distinct from what lies to the south of it" (Saggs 1984, 3–5). As one
moves south, rainfall becomes insufficient for agriculture without
irrigation, and the soil changes from gravelly plains to Tigris alluvium.
"These two features," argues Saggs, "combine to create a geographical boundary between Assyria and the neighbouring land to the
south." Yet: "The political demarcation between Assyria and Babylo-

nia in ancient times did not of course necessarily at all times follow the natural boundary, but shifted back and forth according to the fortunes of the two states." In fact, according to Saggs (1984, 47): "In the south, east of the Tigris, there were three possible natural boundaries between Assyria and Babylonia; from north to south, these were constituted by three tributary rivers, the Lower Zab, the Adhaim, and the Diyala. This border saw innumerable clashes throughout Assyro-Babylonian history, and the line it took at any particular time reflected the current relative status of the two kingdoms." In sum, in this case as in all the others we shall examine, it appears that geography was largely—though not entirely—a function of politics, rather than the other way around.

Roux (1980, 241–42) offers a somewhat different view of Assyrian geography, which is equally inconclusive despite his bold statement that Assyria's "fortune had been written on the map." To the north and east Assyria was "surrounded by high, almost inaccessible mountains haunted by predatory people . . . which could only be kept at bay by frequent and difficult police operations." However, did the mountains not offer some protection as well? On the west was a steppe that stretched hundreds of miles. This "spelled safety for the Assyrians" and allowed them to gain control of important trade routes and even possibly to get a window on the Mediterranean. The steppe, though, was "wide open to hostile armies and to nomadic raiders." To the south lay the Mesopotamian plain and delta, "a constant source of temptation but also of worry, since Akkadians, Sumerians, and Babylonians had always claimed lordship over the northern half of Mesopotamia." If Assyria's fortune was written on the map, it apparently required considerable imagination to read.

One encounters a similar ambivalence in efforts to situate Mesopotamia within the wider world. Frankfort (1978, 217–18) argues: "Mesopotamia is in no sense a geographical entity. Even the powerful Assyrian kings wasted the substance of their people in futile attempts to reach natural limits within which their dominion might remain safe and stable. The plain of the Euphrates and Tigris merges into the limitless deserts of Arabia, and the foothills of its eastern borders rise gradually toward the mountain chains of Persia and Armenia. There are no boundaries from which power may recoil to concentrate at the center." The very absence of natural boundaries might well be seen to have encouraged empire. Watson (1992, 38) suggests, for example, that Assyrian organization of its empire "was much looser . . . than the overtones of our word 'empire' suggest. The ancient empires had no clearly delimited boundaries. Their activities and authority were radial rather than territorial, and spread along lines of penetration." Again, at least in the Mesopotamian case, geography and what it allows and/ or denies appears to have been very much in the eye of the beholder.

War and Modes of Diplomacy

War was endemic in ancient Mesopotamia. Violence provided a means of extending the domain of polities for glory, service to the gods, booty, tribute, and trade. It was also often necessary to defend trade routes or home territories from threats posed by adversaries within and without Mesopotamia.

The style of warfare practiced by Mesopotamians was both pioneering and, from this remove, surprisingly sophisticated. The world's first emperor, the Akkadian king Sargon of Sumeria (2310–2273 B.C.), created the world's first standing army. Its exact size is unknown, but New Kingdom Egyptian pharaohs a few centuries later could put at least 20,000 men into the field (Ferrill 1985, 37), and the mighty Assyrian army in the first millennium numbered well over 100,000 (Saggs 1984, 253). By comparison, as Arther Ferrill reminds us, throughout most of Western history, "well down to modern times, an army of 20,000 was a major striking force."

Mesopotamian armies were well-equipped. The invention of the wheel made the Bronze Age chariot possible, which appeared in the region in the third millenium B.C., a thousand years before it arrived in Egypt. By the second millenium horse-drawn chariots with two or four wheels served as mobile firing platforms. Another important weapon was a composite bow that had a range greater than the European longbow of the Middle Ages. Metal scale armor, helmets, and shields added to defensive capabilities. Sumerians advanced with metal-tipped spears in close-order drill, much as the Greek phalanx did many years later, and used daggers and swords when they fought hand to hand with the enemy. However, Bronze Age Mesopotamians had the advantage over the Greeks of "combining mobility (chariots) and security (pikemen) with short-, intermediate- and long-range firepower (spears, javelins and bows)" (Ferrill 1985, 40–43, 61–62).

The Assyrians raised the science of warfare to new heights, adding to their calculatedly fearsome reputation. A standing central army could be rapidly expanded through conscription and call-up of provincial militias. This was a "complex well-organized force, integrating specialist units of many types" (Saggs 1984, 243), and appears to have been the first effort in history to recruit troops without ethnic discrimination (Keegan 1993, 172). The Assyrians were also the first to use cavalry and benefited greatly from the new technology of the Iron Age. Iron was much stronger than bronze and could be sharpened to a razor's edge. The "iron army" marched, rode, or drove chariots across much of a growing empire on a system of royal roads. Logistical arrangements, including wheeled vehicles, supply depots, transport columns, and bridging-trains, provided a model for later empires. According to John Keegan (1993, 169), the Assyrians had "the first true long-range army, able to campaign as far as 300 miles from base and to move at speeds of advance that would not be exceeded until the coming of the internal combustion engine." Rafts made of skins and large ships with Phoenician crews carried troops and supplies over water. Assyrians, in addition, were early masters of siege warfare. They intimidated target cities by surrounding them with overwhelming force and then, when necessary, stormed the walls with battering rams, mobile towers, scaling ladders, and flaming torches. Prepared earthen ramps or tunnels provided other means of attack. Lastly, an extensive spy network contributed to an efficient system of military intelligence.[11]

We know a great deal about prevailing diplomatic practices from the famous el-Amarna letters, including correspondence between Pharaohs Amenophis III and Akhenaten (c. 1402–1347 B.C.) and Babylonian Kassite kings Kadashman-Enlil (c. 1370) and Burnaburiash II (c. 1350), as well as other documents found in Palestine, Anatolia, Babylonia, and Assyria (see especially Oates 1986, 88–92; and Saggs 1989, chapter 9). During the second half of the second millennium, Babylonian was the lingua franca of diplomacy throughout the entire Near East.

Mesopotamian diplomatic norms foreshadowed features of later "international law," even as gift exchange and the importance of real and artificial kinship ties echoed tribal practices. Rulers regularly exchanged letters and gifts—carefully calculated as to equal or greater value, depending on what was appropriate—as gestures of friendship or respect. Discontinuing such gestures implied hostility tantamount to a break in diplomatic relations. Rulers of equal status addressed one

---

11. This paragraph is based on Ferrill 1985, 70–77; and Saggs 1984, 255–56, 260–61, 267.

another as "brother," and overlord and subordinate were "father" and "son" to one another, respectively. Using the wrong form of address could be asking for trouble. When Assyria was initially growing in prestige, its king, Adad-nerari I (1307–1275 B.C.), had the temerity to address the Hittite king as "brother" and got the reply: "Why should I write to you about brotherhood? Were you and I born of the same mother?" (Saggs 1989, 182–83). (One does not get the impression that the Hittite was really in doubt.) Rulers often concluded formal treaties to establish relationships of alliance and commerce and to fix boundaries. Dynastic marriages sealed formal agreements or symbolized broader understandings. So extensive were diplomatic and matrimonial ties in the early fourteenth century that the entire Near East had "the appearance of a happy family in which Egypt played the part of wealthy relative" (Roux 1980, 237). One king might even give foreign aid to another, as did Assyria's Ashurbanipal when he sent food to Elam during a famine in the seventh century B.C.

Norms governing diplomacy through intermediaries were also clearly established. Kings used one or more regular messengers, who, as Saggs (1989, 183–85) explains, "may be seen as . . . forerunners of today's ambassadors, if we do not press the parallel too closely," to maintain contacts with his foreign counterparts. No local subordinate had the right to dispatch his own ambassador, independent of his superior, and, indeed, this was one test of who was beholden to whom. For example, "when Egypt in the fourteenth century received an embassy from Assyria, the king of Babylon entered a protest, claiming (but contrary to the *de facto* situation) that Assyria was a Babylonian vassal." Although an ambassador was not customarily granted plenipotentiary powers, he might engage in instructed negotiations on behalf of the king who had sent him and normally was not recalled until his king was able to send a suitable parting gift to the host king. An ambassador was entitled to the sort of reception and treatment that befitted the ruler who had sent him, and anything less was insulting. Harm inflicted upon the ambassador's person was such a grave insult to his king that it could be reason enough for war. The property of an ambassador was protected, and he sometimes received exemption from customs duties. On the other hand, if he engaged in objectionable activities or otherwise proved to be offensive, his host might declare him persona non grata and remove him with the permission of his ruler. Finally, not surprisingly, some experienced envoys, when home at their native court, acted as their ruler's "foreign advisers" in residence.

Contrary to the impression that "territoriality" is an invention of the modern Westphalian polity, ancient rulers were keenly aware of the territorial limits of their political jurisdiction. Boundaries (beyond cities) might not usually be marked by walls or guardposts, and authority might be exercised (as Watson suggested about Assyria) in a radial rather than consolidated fashion, but an incursion by a rival people beyond the accepted limits was a challenge that no one on either side of a potential contest could fail to recognize. In such circumstances or for other reasons, a king might agree to a prudent adjustment of boundaries, something that happened regularly between Babylon and Assyria. According to Saggs (1989, 192–93), some foreigners, who had proved their special worth as administrators, commercial agents, or advisers, might be granted land or other special privileges. Sometimes treaties were concluded that guaranteed protection for persons from one polity sojourning in another. Nevertheless, even without such legal protection, "it was accepted that kings had responsibilities for the property and personal safety of foreigners in their land and for the safe and convenient passage of merchant caravans through their territory." Extradition, too, was a well-understood practice. For example, Ashurbanipal went to great lengths to explain why he was justified in refusing the application for extradition from Elam for several members of the Elamite royal family who had fled to him for protection when their immediate kinsman had been deposed by a cousin (Saggs 1984, 112).

POLITY TYPES

As we have indicated, the most significant polities in ancient Mesopotamia were cities, which continued to be important even when they fell under the domination of local hegemons, large regional polities, or still-larger imperial polities. Tribes also continued to be important especially outside, but also to some extent within, Mesopotamia. Temples, large private landowners, and merchants (about whom, unfortunately, we have limited information) were major economic actors. Temples and landowners might be considered as polities for their roles in value-allocation within their respective domains. However, after kingship emerged, there is no indication that they ever seriously questioned the principle of royal authority, and their degree of autonomy varied greatly with time and place. Temples were particularly prominent in the late Babylonian era after the decline of Assyria. Judging by other ancient world societies, it is probable that merchant guilds formed in certain periods to oversee market and trade practices, but we simply do not know.

Of course, any listing of polities ignores significant variety within each polity type, often including institutions, ideas, or patterns of behavior that overlap with those of other types. Political evolution in Mesopotamia, like elsewhere, was not unilinear. Polities interacted with other polity types, and this experience contributed to their evolution.

Tribes and Other Polities

Tribes and other polities in ancient Mesopotamia afford excellent examples of variety, interaction, overlapping, and nesting. Mesopotamian "tribes" include some peoples who were bedouin nomads, whose only interest in civilization was an occasional raid for plunder. Others became (permanently or only occasionally, at times of economic distress) hired agricultural laborers, settled pastoralists, and/or mercenaries, and thereby acquired "civilized" language and culture.[12] Tribal organization included groups under individual shaikhs, some of whom called themselves "king," as well as tribal federations whose names are associated with an entire people or ethnicity, like the Chaldeans, who often fought among themselves and eventually became rulers of Babylon in the eighth and early seventh century B.C.

The Chaldeans and the Kassites,[13] who preceded them in controlling Babylon, merit closer examination. The Chaldean label encompassed at least three distinct tribes: the Bit-Dakuri, the Bit-Amukani, and the Bit-Yakin. As Oates (1986, 112-19) explains, these were "far from impoverished nomads," and "some were even city-dwellers." They "kept large herds of horses and cattle" and apparently controlled the lucrative southern trade routes. With support from the eastern kingdom of Elam, "they became the unwitting champions of Babylonian nationalism" against Assyria, although the residents of some northern Babylonian cities believed that capitulating to the Assyrians offered the best chance for peace and prosperity. (Thus there were

---

12. The situation was similar to that which prevailed in Italy during the period of "barbarian" incursions and Rome's decline (see chapters 13 and 14).

13. The Greek equivalents were broad designations like the Ionians and Dorians (see chapters 5 and 6).

pro-Assyrian factions in Babylon even as there were pro-Babylon factions in Assyria.) The Kassites (Oates 1986, 83, 86–87) were "clearly of non-Mesopotamian origin" but were not exactly "conquering foreigners." They first appear in the seventeenth century as agricultural laborers and were "totally absorbed into the seemingly inexhaustible sponge of Mesopotamian culture and tradition," adopting Babylonian religion, language, and customs. Their dynasty lasted longer than any other in Babylon's history—some four centuries from c. 1570 B.C.—and was also one of the most successful in curbing city separatism.

In these examples, tribal peoples became "civilized" and eventually succeeded to positions of political leadership in different types of polities than their own. But there is more to the story of the interaction of tribes with other polities. The threats and opportunities arising from such interaction provided a powerful incentive for fragmented nomadic peoples like the Amorites to forge a common "tribal" identity. We also have examples of the export of nontribal political identity. Algaze (1989, 572) suggests that this process was at work as early as when the first lowland cities established an asymmetrical pattern of "cross-cultural exchange" with peoples of the surrounding plains and resource-rich highlands. Being plundered, paying tribute, and having able-bodied men conscripted or taken prisoner were net liabilities for peoples on "the periphery," but there were advantages, as well, to be gained from interaction with "the center." The center offered a "powerful stimulus to the evolution of more complex sociopolitical configurations as local elites controlling either the resources being exploited, access to those resources, or the labor involved in their extraction [took] advantage of their natural role as organizers of the means of production and (at times) mediators of the exchange to consolidate and [extend] their power, both in the context of their own socities and vis-à-vis their local rivals." The result, claims Algaze (1989, 601), was that the center soon "had to deal with a variety of more or less powerful polities . . . each centered on a city-state of considerable size." The later Assyrians had a similar experience. Saggs (1984, 90) observes:

In a sense, Urartu—the major rival of Assyria—was the creation of Assyria itself. The constant Assyrian incursions into the Taurus and beyond; the taking of its princes as hostages, its working population for corveé, and its young men for the Assyrian army; and the presence of Assyrian administrators and scribes to control and record deliveries of timber, metals and horses to Assyria; all these must have familiarized the people of Urartu with much of the culture and infrastructure of a major kingdom.

Association not only stimulated neighboring peoples to preserve themselves but also, paradoxically, sometimes offered imperial polities a chance to achieve domination through diplomacy that they would have had a hard time achieving—or at least would have had to pay a higher price for—through war. The fact that the Aramaeans had settled into relatively stable kingdoms in Syria by 1000 B.C. enabled the later kingdom of Israel to engineer control of all of Palestine and Syria. By contrast, at an earlier stage, the Aramaean failure to coalesce into kingdoms made it impossible for the Assyrians to expand east of the Euphrates, since there was no single ruler to accept treaties and none to guarantee the safety of merchants and trade caravans (Saggs 1984, 69).

Having observed the impact of other polities on tribes, the question remains: What of the continuity of tribal elements within cities, large regional polities, and empires? Maisels (1990, 40–41), like many archaeologists, is unconvinced that there was any significant continuity. In his view, at each stage up the evolutionary ladder, "we are dealing with different societies": "Foraging society gave way to sedentary society which was succeeded by fully sedentary cultivating society, and so on. Even if they occupied the same areas and were composed of direct descendants, these are not the same societies in terms of internal structure, dimensions, complexity, cosmology, technology, or politics." In short, what we have, he believes, is step-level change. Kinship is the organizing principle in nonsedentary tribal societies, while the political community itself is the organizing principle in later sedentary societies.

There is some truth to his assertion, but it obscures interesting and significant nested tribalism. For example, a letter from a palace official reminds Zimri-Lim of Mari, that he is only "in the second place, king of the Akkadians," since he is king of the tribal federation of Hanu (Oates 1986, 56). In the Amorite "Old Babylonian" era, the Code of Hammurapi (1792–1750 B.C.), that was in many respects so "progressive," nevertheless changed former Sumerian law by incorporating lex talionis, the rule of "an eye for an eye, and a tooth for a tooth." This was "almost certainly a reflection of Amorite custom" (Oates 1986, 75). The earliest Ur-Nammu code, for instance, had incorporated the more "civilized" concept that the perpetrator of physical injury and some other crimes should pay compensation in silver (Roux 1980, 155). Oates (1986, 103) also observes: "Kassite law governing transfers of land marks a notable departure from Old Babylonian practice, and there is evidence for land tenure by 'households' or territorial districts defined as the property of tribes, that is land owned collectively by tribal communities, a feature characteristic also of Babylonian society later in the 1st millennium." Also, the very names of Aramaean kingdoms usually involved the word bît(u) or "house" and the name of an ancestor, which Roux (1980, 255) characterizes as "a typically tribal way of expressing land ownership: the state, the 'kingdom' is both the territory around the tent (or house) of the chief and all the chief's relatives forming the clan." Finally, as we have seen, rulers of different polities continued to address one another in the language of kinship, tailored to the specific relationship of equality or subordination involved: "father," "son," "brother," and so on. In sum, the persistence of tribe and kinship in Mesopotamian political settings is part of the living museum found elsewhere, for example, in medieval Europe and postcolonial Africa.

Empires, Large Regional Polities, and Other Polities

If city polities and their respective deities were deeply embedded in Mesopotamian tradition, so, too, were large regional polities and empires. Indeed, in the actual Mesopotamian context, it is often difficult to distinguish among these polity types that blur into one another even as they sometimes do with "tribe."

Some early city polities were, in fact, amalgamations of several lesser cities, and various leagues of otherwise independent cities may also have existed. There were fourteen known major cities in Sumer/ Akkad during the Early Dynastic period. According to the Sumerian King-List, after kingship again descended from heaven following the Flood, it was held in succession by a number of cities, each by implication exercising hegemony. Judging by the later popularity of the title King of Kish, Kish was one such city. The ideological source of supreme authority in Sumer was the leading god of the pantheon, Enlil, whose priesthood administered the temple Ekur at Nippur. According to mythological texts, Nippur was where the various city-gods assembled to choose one supreme ruler, presumably reducing the others to the status of provincial governors. Some evidence suggests that, in the early third millennium, an "amphictyonic" league of cities acknowledged Ekur as the paramount shrine and met at Nippur to "elect" a leader (Oates 1986, 27–28; also Jacobsen 1970a).

The reign of the first Akkadian king, Sargon, in Sumer (2310–2273 B.C.) profoundly altered Mesopotamia's political landscape by creating almost simultaneously two new[14] polity types: large regional polity and empire. He not only conquered rival city polities in Sumer, but also, with his grandson Naram-Sin (2246–2190 B.C.), created an empire that encompassed all of Mesopotamia and possibly beyond. Crawford (1991, 147) nonetheless cautions that we are not sure how many of these "so-called conquests were genuine and how many were raiding and foraging expeditions in search of raw materials." Be that as it may, thereafter and certainly with the advent of the Amorites at the start of the second millennium and Hammurapi, large regional polities and/or empires tended to be the prevailing patterns in the overall system. The Assyrian empire at its zenith in the seventh century B.C. extended beyond Mesopotamia to Egypt and Persia. However, as we emphasized earlier, important city identities remained nested and tended to reassert themselves during periods of oppression or declining hegemony. In addition, certain famous cities—Babylon is the best example—served as capitals of far-flung imperial domains. Babylon the empire was associated in the public mind with Babylon the city, and served as the cultural capital of Mesopotamia even when the Assyrians were paramount in every other respect.

CONCLUSION

Ancient Mesopotamia, although the world's first major civilization, nonetheless provides a case study of impressive political and social complexity. The Mesopotamian system was exceptionally open. Neighboring tribes, large regional polities, and empires posed an almost continual threat and were often the source of political change. Consolidation of Mesopotamian polities tended to alternate with periods of severe disintegration.

No single polity ever achieved an exclusive or entirely secure transfer of the loyalties of its subjects from other symbols of identification, most notably loyalty to city but also identities that were tribal or more broadly cultural. Mesopotamian polities overlapped and nested in

---

14. Scholars are still trying to ascertain the accuracy of the boast of Sargon's immediate predecessor, Lugal-zagezi (2335–2310 B.C.), that he ruled from the Arabian Gulf to the Mediterranean (Oates 1986, 28).

complex ways and were forced to "share" authority and its associated symbols and ideologies. Tribal peoples became "civilized" and eventually succeeded to positions of political leadership in more complex polities. Conversely, there were interesting and significant residual tribal elements in some city polities, large regional polities, and empires. Cities themselves were the principal constituents or building blocks of regional polities and empires, but city loyalties persisted and continued to limit the consolidation of larger polities.

4

THE SOURCES AND LIMITS
OF CENTRAL AUTHORITY IN
MESOPOTAMIA

INTRODUCTION

Two key, albeit somewhat overlapping, sets of vertical relationships offer us further insights into the processes of political integration and fragmentation in ancient Mesopotamia. One is the relationship of kings to key groups within their own immediate "government" and society. The second is the relationship of large regional polities and empires to other polities within their wider domain. We focus in particular upon the strengths and weaknesses of empire, which we shall come upon again and again in later cases, and on the critical role that ideologies play in legitimating all forms of authority. Mesopotamian imperial polities borrowed symbols from nested rivals and thereby provided an illusion of continuity in a changing political context.

KINGS AND SOCIETY

The Rise of Kingship

The first kings appeared in an area of southern Mesopotamia between the Tigris and Euphrates, but it is not certain exactly when. Mesopotamian tradition holds that kingship was "lowered from heaven" almost immediately after Creation. According to the Sumerian King-List, this event occurred in the city of Eridu, possibly the oldest Sumerian settlement. Like later Biblical and Greek accounts of a Golden Age of ancestors or heroes, Mesopotamian literature recounts that subsequent kings each ruled for many thousands of years. Then a Flood virtually destroyed the world, and kingship was again lowered from heaven, this time in the city of Kish (Roux 1980, chapter 7). In fact, the first kings on the King-List who can be matched with identifiable persons are those at Kish and Erech about 2700 B.C., more than 700 years after the first Mesopotamian cities emerged and some 300 to 400 years later than the first kings in Egypt (Saggs 1989, 37).

Equally uncertain is who the "Sumerians" were who founded the first royal dynasties. The earliest farmers in the Sumerian subregion were the so-called al-Ubaid people, but the population as a whole was extremely heterogeneous, perhaps explaining why "Sumerian" identity was always more local than tribal.[1] People with both Sumerian and Semitic names may have been mixed as far back as the hunter-gatherer era. All we know is that the Semites were concentrated in northern reaches of the southern plain, near the city of Kish. Moreover, during the third millenium there seems to have been a steady increase in the number of Semitic names and a corresponding decrease in the use of the Sumerian language. We are not sure to what extent this change reflects a growing dominance of the Semitic element of the indigenous population or new Semitic arrivals from the northwest or east. If there was infiltration, it took place gradually, perhaps over a thousand years (Crawford 1991, 20–21).

The first urban communities appeared after 3500 B.C., and by early in the third millennium many were developing into full-fledged city polities. Oates (1986, 24) describes these centers as "a city, occasionally several cities, with its surrounding territory, including dependent towns and villages." Recall also Maisels's observation that what distinguishes "city-state" from "village-state" is the relatively high degree of economic integration, supplementing political and cultic ties. Likewise, Saggs (1989, 33–34) argues that "although the city may have grown out of a group of villages, it was something more than a mere overgrown village; it developed into a new social institution." Most residents continued to work the land, but there was unprecedented room for specialization, including additional roles in the temple, marketplace, and trade. However, Oates (1986, 14) emphasizes, there was

---

1. Mann (1986b, 92) speculates: " 'They' did not exist as a collectivity before the urban revolution but became one as two sets of interdependencies grew: first, lateral dependencies, across the floodplain, of irrigators, wildfowlers, fishers, and some herders; second, vertical dependencies, as each of these cities spread out along the river."

a "definite polarization of society into those who controlled resources such as land, manufacturing or trading enterprises, and those dependent on them." Marxist analysts should note: The same essential mode(s) of production and division of society into "haves" and "have nots" persisted for thousands of years, and yet, as we shall see, there was increasing social differentiation and considerable variety—as well as some important continuity—in patterns of authority.

How did kingship actually emerge? Some scholars, including Thorkild Jacobsen (1970b)—whose argument this was originally (published in 1943)—and Frankfort (1978, 215–28) have maintained that kings most likely evolved out of a form of aristocratic "primitive democracy." The democratic element was a bicameral assembly—that is, an assembly plus a council of elders or senate—made up of leading landowners. According to Frankfort (1978, 228), this form persisted in northern Assyria a thousand years after it had been upstaged by kingship in the south. In the primitive-democracy explanation, the assembly elected a temporary leader—perhaps someone with special charismatic powers or skills like the legendary warrior Gilgamesh—under conditions of emergency, and that office was gradually institutionalized into kingship. It has also been suggested (e.g., Frankfort 1978, 222–23) that the high priest of the temple or a priestly elite may have become too powerful for the landowners, who sought to balance the scales by encouraging the establishment of a more secular centralized authority. Roux (1980, 109) insists, to the contrary, that there is no "clear-cut evidence" Sumerian cities were ever ruled by "collective institutions"; "as far as we can go back into the past" he sees "nothing but rulers or monarchs second only to the gods." He and others think that rulers merely summoned the early assemblies for occasional consultation and that this was hardly "democracy" worthy of the name.

Maisels (1990, 271) approaches this controversy from a different perspective, arguing that the real issue is not who made the actual decisions but who benefited. He writes: "The heads of . . . 'free' or citizen households, whom we may for convenience call patriarchs, constituted the 'ruling class' whether they did the executive ruling or not, for it is they who were the major beneficiaries of the distribution of property and thus wealth secured by the state. They were quintessentially the 'Assembly Men.' " In any event, when strong kings emerged, the assembly continued as an organ of local administration, which could address letters to the king about matters of concern and also render legal decisions regarding a wide range of criminal offenses within its jurisdiction. The landholding nobility do not appear ever to have raised any "constitutional" challenge to royal authority, although there were occasions when they rebelled against corrupt provincial governors or court officials. After a time, of course, many landowners were the king's own family or dependents, who might continue to owe at least occasional service. Other landowners were allowed to operate freely within the private realms of their estates as long as they paid taxes.

Temples

Land in the new cities originally fell into two basic categories, those large plots accumulated and held in common by important extended families, and that belonging to the community as a whole—all or most of which was initially administered by the temple.[2] Saggs (1989, 33) visualizes the process as one in which the earliest settlers took possession of the land that was easiest to irrigate, and irrigation canals were gradually extended to accommodate newcomers, until there was no further room for expansion. At that stage, immigrants had no choice but to work as dependents on large preexisting family, temple, or (later) royal estates. The same fate might befall some of the original landowners if debts forced them to sell or surrender their properties. Most land was worked through tenant farming, with tenants receiving loans at interest for seed, animals, and equipment in return for a specified percentage of the crop (Oates 1986, 70). If there were too few tenants, it was still cheaper for a landowner to employ seasonal labor than to own a slave to do the same agricultural work.[3]

When Mesopotamian cities emerged, the temple was its leading institution, and it continued to play an important role. Each city

---

2. For detailed analysis of landholding patterns, see Diakonoff 1974.

3. Most slaves in Mesopotamia were local persons who were defaulting debtors. Some merchants dealt in foreign slaves. Few private persons held slaves, but those who did used them mainly for domestic service. Most war captives became slaves of the polity and worked on either royal lands or public works projects. Temples acquired slaves from war captives and others through private donations. There was nothing in Mesopotamia comparable to the Roman *latifundia* or mining industries that depended on the labor of enormous numbers of slaves (Oates 1986, 70; also Saggs 1989, 43, and 1984, 134–36; and Maisels 1990, 147–50).

literally "belonged" to its main deity, and worship was a central feature of social life. Mesopotamians had every reason to fear the gods. Unlike the Hebrews, they did not "presume that the gods themselves were bound by any order which man could comprehend." No divine Law had been handed down to guide humankind; the gods need not be just, and the safest course was to try to appease them continually (Frankfort 1978, chapter 20). The most important structure in a city was, therefore, its temple of the city-god. In the larger cities, temples were dedicated to other deities as well.[4] The temple was the home of the god as well as the residence of priests, priestesses, and diviners who presided over religious ceremonies and administered the god's vast estates. Temple officials also helped coordinate some of the early irrigation projects and other public works, collected and distributed agricultural surpluses, and sponsored crafts and industries. In addition, there is evidence that temples initially had some judicial and regulatory functions in matters like weights and measures and interest rates.

Despite the importance of the temple, the Mesopotamian city was never a full-fledged *tempelstadt* (Maisels 1990, 156; see also Postgate 1992, chapters 6 and 14). From the outset, the temple was a community enterprise, and the priesthood as a whole never enjoyed any special status. Almost nothing in ancient Mesopotamia was fully secular, but most political decisions seem to have been made by secular institutions, though to what extent by king or leading landowners in early times remains unclear. Like the landowners, the temple was soon overshadowed by the growing authority of kings. Nevertheless, as we shall see, the king remained a major patron of the temple, and the priesthood continued to help the king interpret the will of the gods and had a role in kingly succession. There was also a revival in the fortunes of the temple in later Babylon.

Kings Versus Temples

Once kingship was established, kings rapidly consolidated their position vis-à-vis actual or potential social groups. Kings took up residence in a palace separate from the temple building. Asserting

---

4. There were an estimated 1,179 temples in sixth-century Babylon (Roux 1980, 360).

divine right, they managed to establish control of temple land, and they and their kinsman also set about acquiring whatever private land became available when leading families wished a quick profit or ready cash (Maisels 1990, 151). Kings grew even stronger when they came to preside, beyond the immediate city, over large regional polities and empires. Expansion brought booty and new taxes into the king's coffers, and he also acquired land by consolidation and conquest, including estates previously owned by local rulers. A distinct royal or "public" Mesopotamian economy and society were well-established in the Early Dynastic period (c. 2700–2334 B.C.), and there was enormous growth in that sector during the Third Dynasty of Ur (2112–2004 B.C.) (Roux 1980, 153, 163). In time, prominent bureaucrats, military officers, and others who had given unusual service to the king—or who were expected to give continued service of one kind or another—received grants of land (rather than rations) as their reward. This practice created a large landholding group that was not necessarily identified with the old families.

Important changes occurred in southern Mesopotamia in the relationships among king, temple, and the private sector during the second millennium with the advent of the Amorites. Frankfort (1978, 252) suggests that the king from time immemorial had the right to appoint at least the high priest. Also, for some 500 years after Sargon, the post of high priestess of the moon-god at Ur was a key royal appointment, which often went to the daughter of the king. Roux (1980, 164) states simply that the kings of Ur "appointed the priests." However, according to Oates (1986, 71), it was under Hammurapi that there was a broad transfer of authority from the temple. The king assumed responsibility for filling temple offices as well as the exercise of judicial functions that previously had belonged to the temple. The changes under the Amorites went further, amounting to the privatization of much of the economy. Argues Roux (1980, 170–71): "Deprived of their privileges, the temples became 'landowners among other landowners, tax-payers among other tax-payers,' " and even the royal domain was purposely circumscribed. "The new monarchs gave or let out for indefinite periods numerous parcels of royal or sacerdotal land, freed the inhabitants of several cities from taxes and forced labour, and seem to have encouraged by all possible means the development of private property. Soon a new society emerged, a society of big farmers, free citizens, and enterprising merchants."

Assyria in the first millennium offers a contrast regarding the roles of the private sector and the temple, and eventually in Babylon itself there was a full-scale revival of the prestige and wealth of the temple. Royal ownership and control of the economy was so extensive in Assyria that the scope for private landholding, apart from the king's own grants, was more limited than it was in the south. Most temples, too, were not wealthy and often did not own even the land immediately surrounding them (Saggs 1984, 171–72, 205). As for Babylon, Roux (1980, 359, 370–73) speculates that Aramaean invaders during the "dark age" chaos after the death of Tiglathpileser I (1077 B.C.) forced farmers and craftsmen to take refuge in the cities, where they became dependent upon the only remaining authority, the temples. The temples' position was reminiscent of the earliest days of Sumer/Akkad and, as Roux points out, also calls to mind the role of monasteries in the European Middle Ages. Later kings of Assyria relied on the temples to keep political order in Babylon and exempted them from taxes, though occasionally borrowing from their treasuries. When the Assyrian empire collapsed, the Chaldean kings of Babylon levied only nominal taxes on the temples, while devoting great attention and vast sums to restoring sanctuaries and celebrating religious festivals. In fact, as Roux suggests, it may have been the effort of the last Neo-Babylonian king, Nabonidus (556–539 B.C.), to rein in the temples and collect more taxes from them that led the priests to favor a Persian takeover. However, the late Babylonian religious revival was definitely not accomplished by diminishing the private sector, for this period involved such a tremendous growth in commerce and banking that some regard it as the true "birth" of capitalism (Roux 1980, 372–73).

Maisels (1990, 140) quotes M. Fortas and E. E. Evans-Pritchard on the profound point—too often underplayed by materialist scholars—that "myths, dogmas, rituals, beliefs and activities . . . endow the social system with mystical values which evoke acceptance of the social order that goes far beyond the obedience exacted by the secular sanction of force." No less than the kings of postmedieval Europe, those of ancient Mesopotamia and their subjects regarded kings as ruling by divine right. It is significant, however, that unlike the pharaoh of Egypt, Mesopotamian kings were usually seen as divinely appointed rather than as gods themselves. This principle was somewhat eroded under Naram-Sin (2246–2190 B.C.), the grandson of Sargon, the first great Akkadian king of Sumeria, who allowed himself to be depicted wearing the "horns of divinity" on his helmet. The subsequent Ur Dynasty kings (2112–2004 B.C.) carried this a step further and unabashedly claimed divine status. Frankfort (1978, 301) believes that their pretension to divinity was an instrument of imperial policy, designed primarily for external rather than internal consumption. In any event, the practice ceased with Hammurapi, and no later king ever assumed the full mantle of a god.

Once again, there were differences in Assyria. Early Assyrian kings were modest with respect to the gods, at least publicly. Until the fourteenth century, only one actually accepted the title of "king," the others preferring instead to regard the god Ashur as king and themselves as "merely" Ashur's earthly representative. When the god Enlil briefly gained ascendancy during a time of Babylonian cultural influence after 1307 B.C., two Assyrian kings dutifully termed themselves "governor of the god Enlil" (Saggs 1984, 44). However, Assyrian temples, as we have noted, were generally much less wealthy than their southern counterparts. Moreover, matters spiritual in Assyria increasingly assumed the character of a polity religion with a spotlight on the king (Saggs 1984, 209), and secular political propaganda began to appear as well. It is significant that later Assyrian monarchs are depicted on bas reliefs not as gods or even in the act of exercising their priestly functions but rather as exceptionally valorous humans (Roux 1980, 325). Saggs (1984, 265) observes that if a god is in the scene at all, "it is the god who is showing awareness of the king," not the other way around.

The king thus stood at the pinnacle of Mesopotamian city polities, with the exception of the gods themselves. Throughout Mesopotamia, the king assumed a dominant position over temple elites and an emerging private sector, but the precise relationships varied with time and place. It only remains to observe that the creation of a large standing army—the first in history—under Sargon, Akkadian king of Sumeria (2310–2273 B.C.), had the effect of strengthening rather than undermining kingly authority. Just as there was no separate priestly class, there was no distinct warrior class, and praetorianism in the Roman sense never became a Mesopotamian pattern.

Constraints on Kingship

The foregoing picture of royal authority, though substantially accurate, nonetheless fails to give a complete picture either of royal accountability or of the challenges and dangers that kings had to face. In part, constraints on kings arose from what Maisels (1990, 149) terms a broad "structure of subordinations" in Mesopotamian society, which was neither classical slavery nor feudalism: "A hierarchy of subordinations, material and ideological, obtained in which [rulers] appear as the slaves of the gods, their high officials are denoted as the slaves of their employers, and so forth right down to the small percentage of true slaves." In the same vein, Frankfort (1978, 251–52) notes that the king's "office combined personal power and servitude in a curious manner." He adds: "This is strikingly documented by letters which certain Assyrian kings addressed to the god Assur and in which they reported to him—as vassal to overlord—the course of their military campaigns."

The gods. The first constraint on a king, then, was imposed by the gods from whom he received the divine mandate, of whom he was to be a faithful slave, and by whom he was continually held accountable.[5] Frankfort (1978, 237–38; also 309–10) expresses it well: "Royalty was something not of human origin but added to society by the gods; the king was a mortal made to carry a superhuman charge which the gods could remove at any time, to bestow it upon another." The king's duties were to interpret the will of the gods, represent his people before the gods, and administer his realm. "This [threefold] division is somewhat artificial, for the king, as representative of the people, interpreted the will of the gods. And his administrative acts were based upon his interpretations" (Frankfort 1978, 252).

The responsibility borne by a king was enormous. Commenting on the "simplicity and sobriety" of the Assyrian coronation ceremony, Frankfort (1978, 247–48, 309–10) observes that "sobriety was the appropriate mood": "The gods, in choosing the king, had given him signal proof of their favor; but the task which he now faced was hazardous in the extreme." Unlike Pharaoh, he was a mere mortal— not a god himself—and, in the Mesopotamian view of these things, there was no clear means of ascertaining the will of the gods. "He could maintain the natural harmony only by watching over the service of the gods and attuning the life of the community to such portents as were vouchsafed him as revelations of the divine will." Accordingly, kings spent (what now seems) an inordinate amount of time and energy presiding over religious rituals (the most prominent of which was the New Year's festival), sacrificing to the gods, building and looking to

---

5. In addition to his city god, a king would often have his personal god, who was held responsible by the chief god for the performance of the king and to whom the king would pray (as though to a patron saint) for intercession with superior deities.

the upkeep of temples, demonstrating piety, consulting diviners, looking for omens, having dreams interpreted, and the like.[6] Priests and diviners who had the royal ear may have exercised considerable influence, but, of course, a determined king might continue to have signs read until he got the interpretation he wished. The stakes were high: If the kingdom prospered, the king still enjoyed the Mesopotamian version of what the Chinese called the Mandate of Heaven. If the kingdom did not prosper, then the king was the principal target for blame.

Norms and mores. In addition to his role as servant of the gods, the king was constrained by a wider set of Mesopotamian customs and beliefs that were more secular in nature. Kings were supposed to be just; to rule within the law; to uphold special privileges extended to particular cities, temples, or officials; and to respect the autonomy of other organs of government that were acting within their limited (but not insignificant) mini-realms of authority. General codes of law like Hammurapi's were proclaimed and supplemented by a variety of decrees and legal decisions. Kings like Ishme-Dagan (1953–1935 B.C.) were proud that they "set justice in the land," which may refer to the promulgation of social or economic reforms (Oates 1986, 53–54). Social tensions were a perennial issue, for law codes often included measures ameliorating debts or curbing administrative abuses. Some kings found it expedient to grant exemptions from taxes, military service, and other obligations. Sargon II of Assyria, for example, did so for the city of Ashur in 722 B.C. and also for all the temples in Assyria. In Babylon, cases were tried by professional judges[7] and the Council of Elders. However, the king was the "ultimate rectifier of wrongs," and there is evidence that individual subjects could at least occasionally appeal directly to him (Tadmor 1986, 216). Beyond the capital-city administration in the larger polities, there were powerful provincial governors and district chiefs (Roux 1980, 318), as well as

---

6. Frankfort (1978, 259) notes that our evidence of Assyrian practices all comes from the first millennium, but these examples are dramatic, e.g., after an earthquake the king had to have all his body hair shaved off, placed in a jar, and deposited at the enemy's frontier.

7. Maisels (1990, 181) argues that there were no professional judges, except perhaps for seven "royal" judges at Nippur.

town mayors or village headmen who presided over a local community council of elders and community law court (Maisels 1990, 181).

How does this all add up with respect to royal accountability? How despotic were Mesopotamian kings? Maisels (1990, 182) describes the situation as "a rather circumscribed autocracy," and he believes the "sphere of despotism" was limited to what I. M. Diakonoff refers to as "super-community and extra-community relations." Tadmor (1986, 216–20) advances a different point of view. He sees a contrast between Mesopotamian and Israelite societies, in that in Mesopotamia there was "no autonomous elite that could criticize the king's equity or question his righteousness." Tadmor asks: "A perverse judge could be punished by the king, but what happened to a perverse king?" The one exception, he allows, were the special privileges won by the citizens of the sacred cities of Babylonia. At least in the Neo-Babylonian period, as part of the New Year's rite, the king had to report to the god on his knees that he had respected those privileges.[8]

Other officials. Tadmor fails to appreciate the full extent of the constraints upon a king arising from the Mesopotamian ideological context. His interpretation also gives inadequate consideration to the threats that individual kings might face from within their own palace and bureaucracies, and to the problems of succession. The answer to his question about what happened to a perverse king—in addition to some who might not fit that description—is that many of them were overthrown or met a violent end.

Administrative abuses increased with the physical distance associated with empires. Some provincial governors and other officials became immensely rich and corrupt, to the point that they became the target of local uprisings. Closer to home, kings had to confront the continual danger of palace intrigues. There are many examples: the

---

8. Interestingly, especially in view of his jaundiced view of the benefits of royal authority, Tadmor (1986, 220) observes: "Privileged elite groups were a hallmark of Babylonian society, and their extensive immunities were one of the causes of its decline and ultimate disappearance. Exempted from military service, the temple cities depended upon external forces for their defense. At first they used Chaldaean mercenaries, who gradually settle in the area, and finally are absorbed by the community. To fight Assyria, the aid of the Elamite army was enlisted, which imposed a heavy financial burden. No wonder the temple cities sided for a while with the kings of Assyria, who reaffirmed their privileged status and undertook to defend them."

first Sargon himself appears to have gained power through a palace revolt (c. 2334). His sons Rimush and Manishtushu were both killed in palace conspiracies, as was Naràm-Sin's successor, Shar-kali-sharri (2193 B.C.). Iahdun-Lim of Mari was killed by his servants, possibly at Assyrian instigation (1810 B.C.). The great Assyrian king, Tiglath-pileser I (1115–1077 B.C.), was murdered, and the Bible tells us that another Assyrian monarch, the notorious Sennacherib (704–681 B.C.), met death at the hands of two of his own sons.

Palace intrigue intensified during the crises that often attended succession. A dynastic system was widely accepted, although it was never certain that the unpredictable gods were pleased either with the past king's performance or his successor's prospects. The system itself was imperiled by the fact that a king was allowed to choose which son (regardless of seniority) was to succeed him. A sitting monarch did not have complete control over the succession. The gods had to signal their approval—giving the priesthood a chance to manipulate oracles—and the royal family and members of the nobility had to swear oaths of allegiance on behalf of the people (Saggs 1984, 104; Roux 1980, 314).

> In the ancient Near East, the main opportunity for public opinion to make itself felt was at the death of a king. In consequence, the end of a reign, particularly a long reign, was often marked by disturbances or even revolt, with rival princes putting themselves at the head of various factions. This happened [in Assyria] at the death of Ashur-dan [1134 B.C.], when two of his sons, one supported by Babylonia, had reigns of no more than a year each, the first being driven out and the second probably murdered. (Saggs 1984, 57)

The first prominent Assyrian king, Shamshi-Adad (c. 1813–1791), was himself "a usurper" (Saggs 1984, 25). In the ninth century B.C., his namesake, Shamshi-Adad V, succeeded to the throne as victor in a power struggle with his brother, but this revolt, involving some twenty-seven cities, was more than a family quarrel. It was an uprising of the rural nobility and free citizens against the corruption of provincial governors and high court officials, and actually in favor of a stronger monarchy and more effective administration (Roux 1980, 278). And, as noted above, when Sargon II became king, after the overthrow of his predecessor, he felt it necessary to grant tax and other concessions to the people of Ashur and to all the temples in the land (Saggs 1984, 92). The internal strife that followed the death of Ashurbanipal (627 B.C.)

for a few months brought to power none other than the chief court eunuch (Tadmor 1986, 208), a humiliating experience indeed for the ruling family of Assyria.

Power struggles over succession, though significant in terms of the tenuous hold of particular dynasties and sometimes administrative reform, apparently never touched off a full-scale popular revolution against the institution of kingship, the nobility as a whole, or social institutions generally.[9] Law codes and kings' testimonies to their "setting justice in the land," as we have noted, do seem to indicate that social tensions existed. Some kings had enough foresight to ease these with progressive measures, and succession crises and palace intrigues themselves acted as safety valves. Discontent appears to have been directed against specific kings, officials, and policies, not at kingly authority or the political system as a whole.[10] The authority of kings—essentially autocratic, however much circumscribed—persisted in Mesopotamia over the millennia, even as particular polities and polity types waxed and waned.

IMPERIAL POLITIES

Motives for Empire

As Saggs (1984, 58) argues with reference to Assyria, no king, however able, could make a polity powerful unless external conditions favored expansion; on the other hand, whenever a polity lacked an able leader, favorable external conditions were of limited consequence. There were several reasons that able Mesopotamian kings might seize whatever opportunities for empire were available. The most obvious

---

9. We have to be cautious about such claims. As Mann (1988, 52) reminds us: "Actually we cannot be really sure whether it is revolts or records that are absent. The literate classes did not seem keen on noticing and chronicling the discontents of their subordinates."

10. Of Assyria, Saggs (1984, 126) observes: "Politically, Assyria was remarkably stable over many centuries. There were occasional intrigues in the top level of society to replace the current king by someone from another branch of the royal family, but there are no known instances of popular rebellion or attempts to change social institutions. The political stability was both a reflection of, and a consequence of, the stability and unfragmented nature of Assyrian society."

and often primary motive was the desire for wealth. Conquering neighboring lands was a means of securing plunder and tribute, easier access to needed commodities and luxuries, control of lucrative trade routes, and an expanded base from which to extract future taxes and military recruits.

Another motive was prestige, looking backward or forward. Past glories were not soon forgotten, perhaps not even for the first Sargon. He may have been inspired to greater ambition by the legendary exploits of his predecessor, Lugal-zagesi, and those of local hegemons like the King of Kish. Sixteen centuries later, an Assyrian monarch (Sargon II, 721–705 B.C.) still found it desirable to proclaim his expectation of glorious accomplishments by choosing the name of Sargon. Oates (1986, 94) also reads a "clear . . . element of *folie de grandeur*" in the later periods of Assyrian expansion. Assyrian incursions into Egypt, though temporarily successful, were terrifically expensive and, realistically, gained them "control" of territory they could never hope to administer.

The Assyrians—not unlike the Romans—expanded their borders to some extent almost inadvertently, in their search for secure frontiers. A perennial concern was the threat posed by various Aramaean tribes. The Assyrians tried to punish them for raids by invading their territory or deter them by staging preemptive strikes. Another threat during the ninth and eighth centuries B.C. was the rise in Armenia of the kingdom of Urartu. Countering Urartu's growing influence seemed to require the Assyrians to secure their position in Mesopotamia and expand into what is today Syria and western Iran. Roux (1980, 282) insists their only choice was "to become an empire or perish." Because neighboring vassal polities like Israel often proved unreliable, Assyria also ended up incorporating them into the empire directly as provinces (Saggs 1984, 86–87). In addition, some neighboring peoples, who themselves felt insecure, actually invited Assyrian control (Saggs 1984, 60). In Roux's (1980, 264) view, "each Assyrian campaign was a measure of self-defence, an act of brigandry, but also a crusade." This points to a fourth and final motive for empire, religious fervor.

Ideology of Empire

Rulers of empires enhanced their legitimacy by drawing upon and sometimes enhancing various symbols of Mesopotamian collective identity beyond the city polity. They not only used such symbols for propaganda but also appear to have been genuinely inspired by them.

Although there was no indigenous word to denote either the territory or the civilization of Mesopotamia as a whole, Peter Machinist (1986, 183–91) identifies various aspects of a "common cultural heritage." First, despite the distinctive role of city-gods—some of whom were elevated to imperial patrons—Mesopotamians had much the same essential pantheon and held sacred some of the same shrines like Ekur at Nippur and that of Nanna the moon-god at Ur.

The second common symbol was the collection of texts that A. L. Oppenheim (1964) calls the "stream of tradition." Writes Machinist: "Assembled, transmitted, and revised over many centuries and from all parts of the south by scribes working under royal patronage, these texts spoke to the basic institutions of the culture—they included legal 'codes,' hymns, omens, rituals, scribal lists, inscriptions of earlier kings, etc.—and represented both the Sumerian and the Akkadian halves of the bilingual tradition, even after Sumerian had died out as a vernacular."

Third, as Machinist explains, the stream of tradition over time developed a distinct Babylonian focus, which drove Assyrian elites almost to distraction. Assyrians adopted or adapted Babylonian gods, used Babylonian literary dialects to compose official texts, and built major libraries of cultural materials. "The climax of such efforts—and of Assyrian expansion generally—came in the military-political conquest of Babylonia by the Assyrian monarchs, and their assumption of the Babylonian royal titles along with their own. Twice, in fact, this entailed even the destruction of the leading city of Babylon and the removal of key cultural treasures to Assyria and its old capital at Ashur."

A fourth element common to Mesopotamians was a sense of superiority as a civilized, urban people, contrasted with neighboring tribal "barbarians," who were regarded with disgust and contempt. Nomads and mountaineers, on the whole, were thought to be "animal-like" and "lawless" (Roux 1980, 166). Nonetheless, Mesopotamians evinced a certain missionary spirit—not unlike the White Man's Burden of modern empires—which held that the poor unfortunates out on the frontier were not absolutely unredeemable. Conquered, they, too, could be taught the benefits of sophisticated urban civilization.

An additional aspect of common culture is the extent to which the idea of political hegemony was itself a part of the Mesopotamian stream of tradition. Successive centers had earlier models to imitate, and they attempted to draw on and adapt the ideological symbols of the past for themselves. The gods got into the act insofar as conflicts between city polities were seen as competitions between their patron divinities. Defeated cities might find some solace in the belief that their divine owners had failed them, at least temporarily, in what was an ongoing contest. Imperial centers sought either to appropriate a god who already had a reputation or to elevate their own city-god to the top of the pantheon (Frankfort 1978, 241–42). J. Hawkes (1973, 160) explains that a larger polity "had a special relationship with the cosmic state of the gods, quite distinct from that of the city-state—which a god simply held for his own livelihood, like a lord of the manor." The "great god" of a larger polity might be the traditional "owner" of the dominant city or one now appropriated because of its greater regional prestige. What is important is that the assembly of gods, the entire pantheon, chose the "great god" and the king of the larger polity, so that both acted as "officials" of the "cosmic state."

Probably the earliest title with hegemonic overtones was the King of Kish. "King of the Land" was coined by Lugal-zagesi, the first Sargon's predecessor. Sargon adopted two titles, one secular and the other vaguely religious—King of Kish and "he who rules the Four Quarters," respectively. Sargon's grandson, Naram-Sin, made it "King of the Four Quarters." The Third Dynasty of Ur kept the earlier titles and added "King of Sumer and Akkad," which rulers preferred to their own "King of Ur" (Frankfort 1978, 226–28). The Amorite Babylonian king, Hammurapi, likewise appropriated "King of Sumer and Akkad" and "King of the Four Quarters of the World" but preceded both of these with "mighty King, King of Babylon, King of the whole country of Amurru" (that is, the Amorites). Most early Assyrian kings eschewed the title of "king" entirely, wanting to be known solely as their god's earthly representative. However, Shamsi-Adad I, in the eighteenth century B.C., was less modest and elevated the Four Quarters of the World to "King of the Universe." Later Assyrian kings continued to use (as well) "King of Sumer and Akkad" and additional titles trailing clouds of glory like "King of Babylon." Even more self-effacing than the early Assyrians, the Neo-Babylonian Chaldean kings preferred to be known simply as "Providers of Esagila and Ezida" (that is, the temples of Marduk and his son Nabu).

As for the gods, it was Enlil who headed the Sumerian pantheon, and his leadership was initially accepted by subsequent Amorite Babylonian kings. Their possession of Enlil's central shrine at Nippur lent them credibility. However, Babylonian kings eventually decided to make their own city god, Marduk, head of the pantheon, and to this end felt obliged to invent the fiction that Sargon had originally taken holy soil from Babylon to found his capital at Agade (Oates 1986, 28,

61). In 1595 B.C. the Hittites sacked Babylon[11] and stole the Marduk statue, which the new Kassite rulers of Babylon retrieved. When the Assyrian/Babylonian rivalry led to direct confrontation during the reign of the Assyrian king Tukulti-Ninurta I (1244–1208 B.C.), the statue of Marduk was again hauled away, this time to Ashur. The obvious message was that Marduk had "theologically abandoned" (Sagg's characterization) Babylon and now favored the upstart Assyria. And, when later Assyrians attempted to establish their distinctive identity apart from Babylon, they gave their own god Ashur pride of place and insisted that it was he who had proclaimed their mission to control all peoples for his glory. According to Saggs (1984, 247), although this "theology of holy war" was adopted only after Assyrian expansion already had begun, it helped to maintain the momentum of the imperial drive by defining it as "an activity decreed on the divine plane." Parallels in our other cases include medieval Crusaders, Islam, the Aztecs, and the Spanish Conquest.

Meanwhile, after a sojourn among the Elamites, who also raided Babylon, Marduk regained his prominence in Babylon in 1157 B.C. under post-Kassite rulers. During a later period of Assyrian ascendancy in Babylon (729 B.C.), it is recorded that the Assyrian king, Tiglathpileser III, "took the hand" of Marduk in the New Year's ceremony as a gesture of reconciliation and offered sacrifices at a number of other important Babylonian shrines (Oates 1986, 114). Forty years later, however, Sennacherib again destroyed Babylon, and Marduk spent another twenty years in captivity before being returned in 669 B.C. by the destroyer's successor, Esarhaddon. When the Persians under Cyrus conquered all of Mesopotamia in 539 B.C., they encouraged the rebuilding of temples and local worship of all the gods of Sumer/Akkad, Babylon, and Assyria as part of a deliberate policy of imperial rule through toleration.

Imperial Governance

An empire's survival required not only building a solid ideological foundation but also an effective administration and policies of gover-

---

11. Saggs (1984, 52) captures the event's significance: "To sack Babylon in the ancient world was like sacking the Vatican or Jerusalem or Mecca in our own time."

nance. The Third Dynasty of Ur were pioneers in these respects. They appear to have been the first to organize their provinces under transferable governors rather than local vassals, entrust military affairs to a separate district general, convert former city polities into simple administrative districts, and provide a network of well-protected roads (Roux 1980, 162; Saggs 1984, 27). The first great Assyrian king, Shamshi-Adad, also gets high marks for unusually effective chancellery and accounting departments, as well as a courier service so rapid that he felt it relevant to date his messages by both day and hour (Oates 1986, 70). Although little is known about their actual policies, the Babylonian Kassites must have been doing something right, for they ruled four centuries after about 1370 B.C., considerably longer than any other dynasty.

Assyrian imperial administrative policies evolved through trial and error.[12] At first, Assyrian kings went on annual campaigns, subduing local chiefs and rulers, and securing from them promises of tribute. Those who failed to make regular payments were subject to punishment in later campaigns. Like the Aztecs, this was rule by fear, depending upon sporadic forays of military terror rather than any effective administration. Kings eventually appointed provincial governors and other officials, but these posts went to certain noble families who came to regard them as virtually hereditary and a source of (often illicit) enrichment. As we have noted, the great revolt of 827 B.C. involved other provincial nobility and subjects who wanted more effective royal rule.

It was Tiglathpileser III (745–727 B.C.), often regarded as the true founder of the Assyrian empire, who undertook needed reforms. The system he created, complete with eunuchs, was rather like an efficient version of later Ottoman administration. A vast bureaucracy of high officials served the king in the capital and assumed all major posts in the provinces. In order to atomize potentially dangerous concentrations of power and tighten centralized control, administrative districts throughout the empire were made smaller, and vassal polities, whenever possible, were turned into provinces. Eunuchs were occasionally appointed to key governorships, since they (like the bishop-barons of the Holy Roman Empire) were unable to sire local dynasties. The

---

12. This analysis draws on Roux 1980, 162, 165, 265–66, 278, 283–84, 318–19.

army, which formerly consisted mainly of peasants and slaves supplied on an ad hoc basis by landlords for annual campaigns, was transformed into a standing force through a system of conscription. As we noted earlier, a network of improved roads and posting stages made for rapid communications.

Another policy of Tiglathpileser III—shifting conquered populations around on a massive scale—had been pioneered by his predecessor, Salmaneser I (1274–1245 B.C.). It was copied, as well, by the later Chaldean rulers of Babylon, most notably in the "Babylonian captivity" of the Jews (see Oded 1979). Why precisely the Assyrians adopted this policy is still a matter of controversy among scholars. One motive, no doubt, was the desire to disorient a potentially disruptive subject people by uprooting them from their home territory and local god. Another explanation is that the policy was part of Assyria's perceived civilizing mission, and there is evidence that Assyrians made a genuine effort to indoctrinate aliens into their culture. The polyglot nature of Assyrian society allowed them to do so with minimal ethnic prejudice; as Saggs (1984, 126) puts it, "the Assyrians were mongrels, and knew it." Since there were fewer cities in Assyria, city snobbism was less pronounced than in the south, and the elevation of Ashur to central god somehow symbolized the coming-to-self-consciousness of a new Assyrian ethnicity. The Assyrian socialization process sometimes worked spectacularly well, as in the case of one troublesome Aramaean tribe, the Itu'a. After reeducation, they became sufficiently reliable to be used as shock troops in the Assyrian army (Saggs 1984, 71, 243–44). In Saggs's view (49), the main motive for the movement of populations was economic: People were shifted wherever more labor and their particular specializations were required.

The Persians, who ruled from 539 to 331 B.C., adopted a posture not unlike that of Alexander and the Seleucids, the Romans, and the modern British Empire. As long as subject peoples did not revolt and were minimally respectful of the laws and customs of their conquerors, they were allowed to retain their own local rulers, religion, and culture.

The Collapse of Empire

It is harder to explain why Mesopotamian empires persisted as long as some of them did, than to explain why they ultimately collapsed. Empires were potentially vulnerable from within as well as from without.[13] Militating against them were almost continual threats to security posed by neighboring tribes, regional polities, and other empires. Moreover, despite the degree of broader identity we have noted, loyalty to city remained primary for most individuals. Assyria in this regard had a modest advantage over the south, in that there were fewer cities in the north and many of those early on were closely associated with the center (Tadmor 1986, 187). A broader common identity might have become securely established in time, except that imperial subjects in the provinces and vassal polities too often saw their wealth being continually transferred to the center, with too little offered in return (Roux 1980, 266–67). Times of military insecurity or economic distress in the provinces increased their sense of exploitation.

There were grave administrative and military burdens associated with ruling vast areas, especially in an age of limited communications and military technology. Local governors, particularly under weak kings, often became independent and corrupt, and might even establish rival dynasties (Saggs 1984, 82–84). Lucrative trade routes fell victim to enemy raids, drying up important sources of funds for the army, public works, and royal largesse, as well as choking the economy generally. Imperial ambitions, like Assyria's adventure in Egypt, sometimes dangerously stretched capabilities. Salinization of the land, too, was a problem. With so little margin, a famine, sudden tax increases, damage to infrastructure from nomad attacks—almost any adverse development of major consequence or a succession of reverses—could bring the entire imperial structure to a quick collapse. It is sobering to recall that the mighty Assyrian empire went from its zenith to utter destruction in less than thirty years.

CONCLUSION

The two main sets of vertical relationships in Mesopotamia were between kings and key groups within their own immediate "govern-

---

13. Roux (1980, 152) comments: "The rise and fall of the Akkadian empire offers a perfect preview of the rise and fall of all subsequent Mesopotamian empires: rapid expansion followed by ceaseless rebellions, palace revolutions, constant wars on the frontiers, and in the end, the *coup de grace* given by the highlanders: Guti now, Elamites, Kassites, Medes or Persians tomorrow."

ment" and society, and between large regional polities and empires and other polities within their wider domain. Authority in each set of relationships rested, in large part, upon ideological foundations that—like the polities themselves—often overlapped and nested.

Despite the continuing importance of religion and notwithstanding a revival of temple influence during the Neo-Babylonian era, "divine-right" kings rapidly consolidated their position over priests and the landed nobility. Nonetheless, there were important constraints on a king, including his accountability to the gods and need to conform to general Mesopotamian norms and beliefs. Kings also had to confront social tensions, palace intrigues, and—in imperial settings—the challenge of corrupt and insubordinate provincial officials.

Cities were deeply embedded in Mesopotamian tradition and remained nested within empires. The establishment of an empire provided elites and masses with additional security, wealth, and prestige. Rulers of empires enhanced their legitimacy by embracing various symbols of Mesopotamian collective identity, including a common pantheon, sacred shrines, and literary texts. Empires also wrung support from the imperial tradition itself, attitudes towards "barbarians," and the elevation of the center's city-god to supreme deity.

Empires needed both a secure ideological foundation and effective administration to survive. Over time rulers replaced local vassals with officials sent from the center and improved communications and military logistics in order to exercise control over greater distance. The Assyrians resettled conquered peoples on a massive scale, but even such a drastic policy was insufficient to overcome loyalty to city and other subversive identities. Eventually, all Mesopotamian empires succumbed, not only to competition from other identities and administrative challenges, but also to a host of related problems like attacks from outside, a collapse of trade, and declining agricultural production from environmental degradation.

The region known as Mesopotamia obviously continues to play an important geopolitical role in contemporary global politics. Centered in modern Iraq, memories and artifacts of this early civilization have largely been effaced by time and by the presence of succeeding civilizations like that of Islam. Nevertheless, Iraq's current rulers seek to remind citizens of their links to this past and have sponsored elaborate restoration projects of ancient monuments and cities.

5

GREECE
Structural Features of a Watershed Civilization

Classical Greek civilization continues to exercise a grip on the imagination of the West. Such Greek ideas as citizenship and democracy, Plato's philosopher king, Sparta's "totalitarian" yet "mixed" constitution, and the power politics of Thucydides' Melian Dialogue[1]— all have had a profound influence on Western political life and thought.

From a polities perspective, a pervasive aspect of the Greek story is the antinomy between relatively small independent city polities and the broader Hellenistic civilization of which they were proudly a part. Unlike the situation in ancient Mesopotamia, ancient China, medieval Islam, and Rome, the appeal of cities in Greece (until the dawn of a new Hellenistic Age) unequivocally triumphed over that of larger polities. And, although Macedonia eventually conquered the Greek cities and incorporated them into an empire—as later did Rome and Byzantium—the cities lived on in more ways than one. They not only nested with some measure of autonomy within their conquerors' bosoms but also transmitted a powerful ideal of independence (along with other ideas) across the centuries. This ideal influenced first the system of city polities that emerged in medieval and Renaissance Italy and thereafter, ironically, the system of exclusive, large territorial polities in Westphalian Europe that brought the Italian experiment to a close (see chapters 13 and 14).

Adam Watson (1992, 315), contrasting the Greek model with the imperial model of the Chinese (see also chapters 7 and 8), makes the point well:

---

1. However, there is a great deal more to Thucydides, as in Machiavelli, than simple-minded *realpolitik*. In fact, recent years have seen a proliferation of writings reinterpreting both theorists. For a sample, see Bagby (1994).

The mythology of Chinese history helped to pull the Chinese system away from the independences half of the spectrum toward the imperial. But the opposite was true of classical city-state Greece, where the mythology of the independent polis as the natural way to organize a community helped to hold the system close to the independences end of the spectrum. The Hellenic assumption was revived in the Italian Renaissance. The seminal Westphalian settlement established a definitive anti-hegemonial legitimacy for the European society of states.

INTRODUCTION

Small, relatively stable city polities first emerged in the vicinity of Greece c. 2000 B.C. in Minoan Crete and, on the mainland, about 1600 B.C. with the appearance of the Mycenaens. After the Mycenaen centers collapsed about 1200 B.C., there was a profound "devolution" in virtually every aspect of Greek life, a so-called Dark Age that lasted several hundred years. Whatever political authority existed during the Dark Age was exercised by local aristocratic family "chiefs" (Ferguson 1991). The development of greater political complexity began anew in the Archaic period, starting around the eighth century B.C. A wide range of city polities—poleis and less-defined ethnos groupings— gradually arose. With the establishment and consolidation of the polis came the single most important shift in identity and ideology, the invention of the key concept of "citizen." Overlapping regional and subregional polities also evolved from peer-polity and center-periphery relationships, and relations with non-Greeks. Philip II of Macedon effectively ended Greek independence in 338 B.C., although his son and successor, the illustrious Alexander the Great, extended the reach of Greek culture (with some noteworthy innovations of his own) to distant lands through his campaigns of conquest.

SYSTEM DISCRETENESS AND STRUCTURE

Ancient Greece was not a closed system, but it was more discrete than many others in ancient times—for example, Mesopotamia. Egypt and successive centers in Mesopotamia were not in a position to pose a significant threat to Greece, nor was any other Near Eastern kingdom, until the Persian Empire loomed on the horizon beginning around the sixth century B.C. However divided the Greeks were among themselves, they were conscious of a shared culture and language that set them apart from non-Greek "barbarians."

MOLOSSIA

EPIRUS

Mt. Olympus
△

Larissa ●

THESSALY

Cynoscephalae

Actium

AEGEAN SEA

Lamia ●

AETOLIA

EUBOEA

Delphi ●   ● Chaeronea

Euripus Strait

BOEOTIA

Thebes

ACHAEA

Leuctra ●   ● Plataea

Tanagra ●

Deceleia ●

Marathon ●

Eleusis ●

Sicyon ●   Megara ●   Colonus ●   Erchia ●

Corinth ●   Athens ●   ● Brauron

Stymphalus ●

Salamis   ATTICA

Laurium

Olympia ●

Mycenae ●

Aegina

● Scillus

Argos ●   ● Epidaurus

IONIAN SEA

PELOPONNESE

MESSENIA

Pylos ●   ● Sparta

LACONIA

0   km   80
0   miles   50

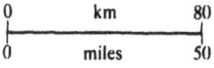

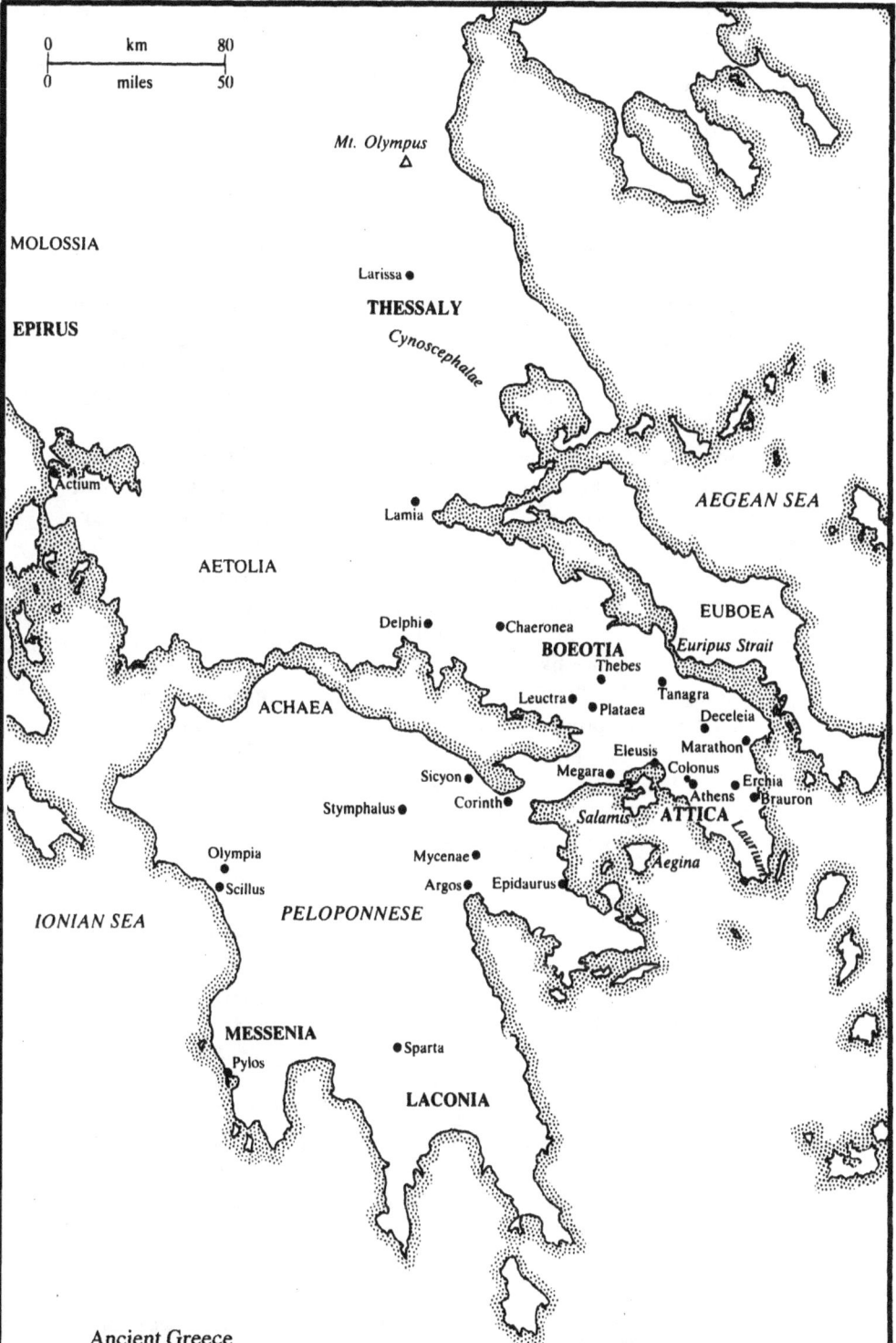

Ancient Greece
Reprinted with the permission of Scribner, an imprint of Simon & Schuster,
Inc. from *A Social History of Greece and Rome* by Michael Grant. Copyright
© 1992 Michael Grant Publications Ltd.

Greeks and Non-Greeks

A debate continues regarding the extent to which Greece was engaged with the rest of the Mediterranean world prior to the late sixth and fifth centuries. Nicholas Purcell (1990) insists that the early Mediterranean milieu was one of great mobility and exchange, that the "small Greece" model is not appropriate until much later when the increasingly xenophobic Greek poleis deliberately tried to cut themselves off from non-Greeks. Most (though not all) scholars agree that the Minoan civilization had at least some cultural links with the Near East and that the Mycenaens were an amalgam of various waves of Indo-European-speaking peoples who came to the mainland over several centuries prior to 1600 B.C. Another traditional view is that Dorian, Aeolian, and Ionian peoples moved into Greece and migrated across the region during the Dark Age.[2] Contacts with the Near East increased from 750 to 650 B.C. (cf. Murray 1993, chapter 6). The Phoenicians were the likely source of the alphabet that made writing possible again after the Dark Age loss of the Mycenaen system. They may also have inspired the trireme warship and the Olympic Games (see Boutroz 1981), and their coastal cities bear an intriguing resemblance to Greek poleis.

As for Greek influence outward, the Mycenaens apparently ranged far and wide. Also, from the Archaic period onward, Greek mercenaries were in demand throughout the Near East, and hundreds of Greek colonies were established along the shores of the Mediterranean from Asia Minor to Italy. After the sixth century, Greece was even less isolated. The threat from Persia initially fostered Greek unity and identity, but eventually Persian influence began to permeate and subvert the Greek system. In due course, the Macedonians arose on the periphery and entered as conquerors. Yet the Greeks substantially "Greekified" the Macedonians before the conquest, and Alexander's campaigns spread Hellenic culture far beyond the areas of Greek colonization. The Romans absorbed and adapted Hellenic culture, including the notion of citizenship, for their own ends (cf. Gruen 1984). Centuries after the Roman Empire had disintegrated, as we have

---

2. An alternative view (cf. Bartonek 1974) is that there was no great influx of outsiders. In this interpretation, migrations during the Dark Age were largely those of previous inhabitants of defunct Mycenaean centers.

observed, a "rediscovery" of the glories of ancient Greece and Rome helped to inspire the Renaissance and to legitimate Westphalian state polities. (On the Greek legacy, cf. Bolgar 1954 and Thomas 1987).

Polarity

The number and variety of polities involved in ancient Greece, and their ebb and flow over time, make it hard to generalize about the distribution of capabilities in the Greek system. The fact that cities were the principal centers of political institutions, resources, and identities in the Mycenaen, Archaic, and Classical periods suggests that the dominant pattern was multipolarity. However, such a conclusion would be misleading in at least three respects. First, Dark Age political disintegration was so complete that the only salient actors were individual households and bands of aristocratic warriors led by local "chiefs." If this was multipolarity, then there are too many "poles" to contemplate. Second, a multipolar characterization gives inadequate weight to the presence of great powers Persia and (later) Macedon on the Greek periphery, which posed not only an external threat but also actively meddled in internal Greek politics.

A third factor undermining multipolarity in Greece was the regular creation of alliances, some of which were transformed into hegemony or empire. The most familiar interpretation of the Peloponnesian War(s) (464–445 and 431–404 B.C.) expounded by Thucydides is that it was essentially a bipolar struggle between the Athenian Empire and the Spartan Alliance, reflecting a mutually reinforcing division of attitudes and resources. Whether this is an adequate reading of the "structure" behind the famous conflict remains a matter for controversy (see especially Lebow and Strauss 1991). Recalling the discussion of outside influence, Sparta finally "won," aided by generous contributions to its defense budget from Persia (Kauppi 1991, 108–9). In addition, the bipolar description neglects the important and relatively independent roles of second-rank city polities like Corinth and Thebes, and two that were not affiliated with either alliance, Corcyra and Argos (Lebow 1991; also Conner 1991 and Kauppi 1991). Moreover, Athen's fortunes were reversed when it engaged in a fruitless campaign against Syracuse. In sum, Mark V. Kauppi (1991, 110) may be correct that, though "bi-multipolarity" is an "inelegant" term, it is probably the most accurate characterization of the Greek system in this critical phase.

The ancient Greek experience as a whole actually offers examples of a great variety of system structures. In several hundred years, the Greek system evolved from the multipolarity of Minoan/Mycenaen city polities; to the almost complete fragmentation of many isolated settlements during the Dark Age and early Archaic period; to more identifiable centers, but still fragmented, as many poleis and ethnos groupings gradually emerged; to loose bipolarity within a general framework of multipolarity, as first Sparta and then Athens slowly grew preeminent and organized their alliance systems; to an alliance of practically the entire Greek world against the advance of the Persian Empire; to tight bipolarity with a smaller but still significant multipolar component (Kauppi's "bi-multipolarity"), as Athens and Sparta converted their unequal bloc alliances into outright empire and hegemony (Doyle 1986, 75), respectively; to two decades of Spartan hegemony after the Peloponnesian War, with support from an outside empire (Persia) and increasing Greek resistence; to growing multipolarity and a highly unstable balance of power, with additional principal actors (including some former ethnos groupings) coming to the fore and the Persians occasionally acting (often unintentionally) as a balancer; to a more definite and competitive multipolarity, with transitory hegemonies, almost continual instability at every level of the system, and Macedonian intervention becoming more frequent; until the Greek system was overwhelmed from outside and became a lesser subsystem of the vast Macedonian empire. Moreover, none of the foregoing discussion of structure adequately captures the important political changes that were going on in individual poleis and ethnos polities.

The Geophysical, Economic, and Demographic Settings

Geophysical, economic, and demographic factors are all additional aspects of structure that afford opportunities for and place constraints on behavior. In the case of Greece, all three were significant.

Although there is disagreement about the extent to which Greece's natural environment changed over the years because of climate shifts and human mismanagement (for example, compare Rackham 1990 with Attenborough 1987), it is still possible to make a few observations. The geophysical setting in some respects encouraged isolation and self-sufficiency, and in others, contact and trade. The most prominent features of the Greek landscape are mountains, sea, and islands. Mountains made distances, with primitive roads and modes of transportation, seem even longer. Yet many distances were short by any measure, and Greeks regularly traversed great distances for purposes of war or commerce. N. G. L. Hammond (1986, 9) comments that the fact that so many islands and mainland territories represented a "cross-section of Greece, comprising highland, lowland, and coast" favored the growth of small polities, because "each possessed the first elements of self-sufficiency." However, one can carry this argument too far. Hammond himself notes that different climatic patterns have made various areas "strongly individual in character and scenary," and, of course, some city polities had special resources (e.g., the silver mines of Laureion in Attica). Not all polities had access to the sea, which provided to those that did an additional avenue to resources and income, a second line of defense as well as vulnerability to attack (dangerous seas made for isolation but could always be crossed in decent weather with a proper ship), and an opportunity for the exercise of influence abroad through seapower.

By contrast to Hammond, Oliver Rackham (1990, 106) contends that nature "intended Greece to be a land of trade rather than self-sufficiency." He notes that, though every city had building materials (stone or mud bricks) and pasturage on land not suitable for cultivation, other resources were unevenly distributed. Olives will not grow in the high frosty inland basins of Acadia. Some cities had broad plains for cultivation, and others could only grow crops, if at all, with extensive terracing. Rackham explains that the degree of reliance on cereals in ancient Greece made self-sufficiency difficult. Crop yield depends on rainfall, which fluctuates each year in different areas of Greece. Chester G. Starr (1986, 71) calculates that no city over 5,000 could have relied solely on local grain and produce, while another study (J.A.C.T. 1984, 230) estimates that the comparable threshhold for Attica's urban population was 10,000.

There was thus reason enough for trade. The Mycenaens (Vermeule 1964, 254–57; also Renfrew 1972, 440ff) sailed with goods as far as Italy in the west, Troy and Syria in the east, and Egypt and Palestine in the south. They carried pottery, olive oil, bronze weapons, and probably wine, textiles, and timber to exchange for bronze, tin, wine, women, silver and gold, possibly horses and textiles, spices, ivory, and other luxuries. Trade reached a peak after the Mycenaens took over Crete and other Minoan outposts. However, Colin Renfrew (1972, 473) stresses that metals were the only essential commodities that were then unavailable in adequate quantities locally and that, partly for this reason, trade was never "commercial in the modern sense," nor did it play a major role in either the Minoan or Mycenaen economies. John Chadwick (1976, 158) suggests that trading at that early stage may have been a state monopoly, with the king himself equipping and dispatching ships.

Following the Dark Age hiatus, long-distance trade resumed and steadily increased from the seventh to the fifth centuries. Greeks emigrating to the northern shore of the Black Sea found themselves near the rich wheatlands of modern-day Ukraine and Crimea, and with ready access to vast quantities of timber. From the Black Sea area, Athens imported grain for its expanding population and timber for its ambitious fleet, and protecting supplies was one aspect of Athenian strategic policy. According to Moses I. Finley (1985, 133–39), the Athenians were self-sufficient only in honey, olive oil, ordinary wine, silver, building stone, potting clay, and fuel; and perhaps almost self-sufficient in wool, fish, and meat. Finley and most other scholars believe that the "bill" for all these imports was not paid for, to any substantial extent, by the export of whatever limited manufactures there were, mainly textiles and some pottery. He sums up (1985, 139): "The ability of ancient cities to pay for their food, metals, slaves and other necessities rested on four variables: the amount of local agricultural production . . . ; the presence or absence of special resources, silver, above all, but also other metals or particularly desirable wines or oil-bearing plants; the invisible exports of trade and tourism; and fourth, the income from land ownership and empire, rents, taxes, tribute, gifts from clients and subjects." Finally, for at least the more powerful city polities like Athens and Sparta, the export of trained soldiers (hoplites) and/or oarsmen was politically and economically significant.[3]

For all that trade was essential and since manufactures contributed only marginally to exports and the standard of living generally, the primary focus of the ancient Greek economy continued to be agriculture. Although some Greek citizens might own a cargo boat, help to finance a particular cargo, or set up a workshop of skilled craftsmen, most preferred to leave trade and manufacturing to metics (resident aliens), visiting foreigners, and slaves (J.A.C.T. 1984, 183). It is significant that coinage was not invented to facilitate trade, was issued by

---

3. From an economic perspective, the export of trained soldiers in ancient Greece helped underwrite military expenditures at home much as contemporary Westphalian polities sell weapons abroad to support their arms production. Such sales also remain politically significant.

fewer than half the city polities, and never came to be of much importance in commerce beyond small-scale local market exchange (J.A.C.T. 1984, 184; Starr 1986, 46–47). Coinage was primarily a political symbol of autonomy, or control in the case of the Athenian Empire, which used a uniform coinage partly to ease payments due from subject cities (Finley 1985, 167–69).

One striking characteristic of the some 1,500 (Starr 1986, 46) city polities from Asia Minor to Italy was their small territorial size, but there were significant variations. Sparta, after it absorbed Laconia and Messenia, was the largest, about 3,200 square miles. Athens, including Attica and Salamis, had 1,060 square miles (Fine 1983, 51). However, John V. A. Fine's (1983, 51) estimate of the average size of most city polities is about 30 to 500 square miles, while Starr's (1986, 46) is an even smaller 50 to 100 square kilometers.

Populations, too, were small, and fluctuated dramatically in some places and, in some key periods, across Greece as a whole. Emily Vermeule (1964, 257) comments that the population of Greece was greater in the thirteenth century B.C. than it would be again until the fifth century. Chadwick (1976, 68) estimates that there was a total of some 50,000 persons in the Mycenaen kingdom at Pylos. Renfrew (1972, 251) calculates that the density per hectare in Aegean settlements throughout the Bronze Age was 300 persons, compared with 400 per hectare in a Sumerian town.

After the collapse of Mycenaen civilization, from the thirteenth to the eleventh centuries B.C., there was a sharp general population decline. Then, beginning about the eighth century B.C., a rapid increase in population accompanied the rise of the polis. Anthony Snodgrass's (1971, 775–76) analysis is controversial (cf. Starr 1986, 38), but he maintains that both the number and size of individual settlements in the Dark Age declined to one-eighth of their previous level and that the later rapid increase was of about the same order of magnitude. He attributes the eighth-century increase partly to a shift to more arable farming from the pastoralism of the Dark Age, which itself had replaced the cultivation that previously took place under the bureaucratic oversight of Mycenaen palaces.

Fine (1983, 51) notes that Greek political theorists thought that 5,000 to 10,000 was an ideal number of adult male citizens, and he believes that most poleis ranged from 2000 to 10,000. Finley (1984, 59) thinks the political theorists had the numbers correct. According to Starr (1986, 46), the *total population* of the "typical" "early" polis was probably just 625 to 1250 persons (Starr 1986, 46). Athens had only about 10,000 persons in the eighth century, but the population was 35,000 to 40,000 by 431 B.C., just before the outbreak of the second stage of the Peloponnesian War (Morris 1987, 99–101). The best estimate of the Joint Association of Classical Teachers' text (hereafter J.A.C.T.) (1984, 157) for the population of Attica as a whole in 431 B.C. is 300,000 to 350,000, including some 50,000 adult male citizens, 25,000 metics, and 100,000 slaves. A year later, with war starting, a virulent plague broke out, seriously demoralizing Athens, reducing its population,[4] and claiming the life of Pericles. By 317 war and disease had reduced the total population of Attica to between 150,000 and 200,000, with only 21,000 male citizens (J.A.C.T. 1984, 157).

Taking territory and population together and following Starr's (1986, 47) "size and strength" classification, Sparta and Athens come out on top. Also impressive were Thebes, Corinth, and Argos on the mainland; Miletus, Samos, and Chios in eastern Greece; and Syracuse and several others in the west. Next, there were some 30 "middling" city polities like Megara, Aegina, Sicyon, and others. The balance of the 1,500 or so poleis were relatively tiny and weak.

"Size," as we are using it, mattered to politics in several respects. First, as happened on a lesser scale in England and elsewhere in Europe after the Black Death during the Middle Ages, the population decline during the Greek Dark Age contributed to the relative independence of the peasantry. The Dark Age economy was predominately rural and pastoral, and most *oikoi* or estates were largely self-sufficient in food and clothing. Oswyn Murray (1993, 46) argues that early Greek society was not "feudal," in that there was no serf class owing obligations to an aristocracy in return for land. The *oikoi* had slave labor, which they probably supplemented with hired labor, and some peasants may have worked modest plots of their own land. Pressures on the land no doubt increased when population again started to rise, which encouraged emigration and agitation over land and debts in many early poleis (see chapter 6). Certainly, Sparta subdued and

---

4. The plague lasted for two years and then recurred after the winter of 427/6 B.C. It appears to have killed at least a third of the population. Thucydides himself had a bout with the disease (Powell 1988, 157; also Kagan 1969, chapter 3).

depended on a class of helots, and something akin to serfdom continued to be part of the way of life in Crete and Thessaly.

A second way that size mattered is suggested by Starr's (1986, 47)
observation that the five top mainland cities also enjoyed a critical
military advantage in later centuries. Apart from other resources,
there was a direct relationship between population and manpower
available for warfare. Sparta and Athens could field hoplite armies of
9,000, while the typical polis could only manage 225 to 625. Whether
they served on the battlefield or on shipboard, if there were going to
be a war, it almost had to involve virtually all able-bodied male
citizens. The style of warfare, too, emphasized the contribution of
every last able man to the community phalanx.

Third, size, coupled with a Mediterranean climate—in which persons circulated outdoors for much of the year—affected the "tone" of
local politics. Although the situation must have differed from large
places like Athens to smaller cities, compared with most modern
polities, Greek polities had a distinct "face-to-face" character (Finley's term, drawn from Peter Laslett). However much tyrants or later
oligarchies curbed popular participation in many poleis, there was a
potential for broad participation and a politically conscious citizenry.
Citizens were educated in politics, not often by formal schooling,
but by "continuing contact from childhood with public life" (Finley
1984, 28).

War and Modes of Diplomacy

Barry S. Strauss (1990, 203) observes: "In the discourse of classical Greek war and diplomacy, the emphasis was on the use of force."
Finley (1984, 60, 67) states that it is hard to overestimate the impact of
war on ancient societies and that "nothing in modern experience is
quite like this." However, even in the ancient-world context, the
sheer routine character of violence and resulting scale of the security
dilemma in ancient Greece stands out. Life for the Greeks, says
Strauss (1990, 202), "appeared to be a choice between dominating and
being dominated." Honorable death in battle was regarded as heroic,
and war, as a natural means of augmenting personal, family, and
community wealth. The rise of the polis created a new community for
which to fight, and changing military tactics involved more social
strata. Kauppi (1990, 104) points to "fear" and its conjunction with
"honor" and interest as the dominant theme in Thucydides' narrative
of the Peloponnesian War. Greeks viewed peace more as merely a

"respite from inevitable war than as the normal state of affairs" (J.A.C.T. 1984, 246). Not only in the experience of Athens and Sparta but also for most Greek cities, there were few years, and still fewer in succession, when there were not military engagements.

Warfare. Although there were some continuities in Greek warfare from "Heroic" to Classical times, innovation and change were more characteristic (see especially Ferrill 1986, chap. 4). Thucydides (I:4) suggests that the Minoans had a maritime empire, or thalassocracy, in the Aegean, and fresco paintings of Minoan warships in action support this assertion. Be that as it may, the Mycenaens came to the fore on the mainland and eventually took over Crete about 1450 B.C., possibly because the Minoans had been weakened by damage to their fleet and other destruction in the monumental eruption of the volcano on Thera (now Santorini) (Chadwick 1976, 11–12). In Arther Ferrill's (1986, 95–97) view, the Mycenaens developed "impressive" and "intricately organized" Bronze Age armies, which resembled those of the ancient Near East in their primary reliance on "massed chariots with infantry support." Some Mycenaen rulers also had warships. After the collapse of the Mycenaens, the Dark Age effectively cut Greece off from Near Eastern military models. "Greece, in a cultural vacuum, reverted to an almost primitive style of war characterized by champions duelling with one another in single combat," against which "almost any kind of formation would have proved effective" (Ferrill 1986, 144–45).

This situation set the stage for what Ferrill, Finley, and other analysts regard as the most important military innovation in Greek history (probably about 650 B.C.), the use in close formation (phalanx) of heavily armed infantrymen called hoplites. Hoplites wore full body armor and marched, armed only with spear and sword, in solid ranks with overlapping shields to engage the enemy head-on. This was heavy-infantry "shock" tactics at its extreme, a form of warfare that required careful drill, iron discipline, and considerable courage (Ferrill 1986, 101–6; also Keegan 1993, 244–54). Hoplites had to provide their own expensive equipment, which gave them a financial investment as well as a new role in the defense of their city. This role, in turn, contributed to what Michael Mann (1986b, 200) terms "an enormous physic intensification of the social relationships of the emerging polis." Commitment to the common good "was not merely a background normative disposition, but an integral part of the battle formation in which the soldier became entrapped."

Not all Greek warfare, of course, took place on land. Except for the battle of Marathon against the Persians, Athens never won a major land engagement or even played a leading role as part of a larger army. The most significant land warriors were the Spartans and Boeotians (J.A.C.T. 1984, 247). Athens was a naval power, and the Athenians and other Greeks who took to the seas "developed naval technology and tactics to a high art." Yet it is the Persians, using mainly Phoenician ships and sailors, who must get credit for pioneering large-scale naval warfare (Ferrill 1986, 106). The Athenians nonetheless perfected the most sophisticated ship of their day, the trireme (Morrison and Coates, 1986), and also innovated by incorporating the lower classes as paid rowers.

The Greek style of warfare was fundamentally indecisive and, however inventive at the outset, became highly conservative. These characteristics help explain both why warfare was almost continuous and also why most poleis managed to remain relatively independent as long as they did. As Ferrill (1986, 105, 143) explains, nearly exclusive reliance on heavy "shock" infantry seems "foolish," especially in a mountainous country like Greece, where seizing and defending strategic positions would appear to offer a better alternative. Hoplite battles tended to be brief, and the outcome usually depended on the first clash, after which the resolve of one side crumbled, and the phalanx disintegrated. This was decisive for the moment, but major battles which nearly annihilated the opposition's forces were rare. Much of Greek "warfare" took the form of skirmishing and ravaging crops in the countryside. Yet "mere" skirmishing could be ruthless. Wounded and disarmed soldiers were often killed, and captured civilians, including women and children, were sometimes enslaved. Actual practices regarding enslavement varied: for example, Sparta did not enslave any captives except the Messenians (presumably Sparta already had enough helots), whereas Argos and Athens did take slaves.

Well-defended positions—especially those with secure sources of supply, like Athens behind its long walls—were especially difficult to seize.[5] Siege techniques were not highly developed. About the only effective method was circumvallation; that is, encircling the city with a wall and trying to starve the enemy out. Pericles apparently used a battering ram and a platform of shields to scale walls in the siege of Samos (440 B.C.), and the Spartans employed siege-engines against

---

5. Josiah Ober (1991) makes the point that the very effectiveness of its defenses twice caused Athens to become fatally overconfident.

Plataia. Nevertheless, it took Pericles nine months to take Samos, and the Spartans two years to defeat Plataia. (J.A.C.T. 1984, 263) At the beginning of the latter siege, Plataia had fewer than 500 defenders and faced the full forces of the Peloponnesian League that must have been twenty times as great (Powell 1988, 160). Hoplites carried only three days' rations, and decent temporary quarters for an army on the move and other logistical support were practically nonexistent (Ferrill 1986, 146–47). Often the core city of an opponent might never be overrun.

Even if there were a clear victory and an enemy city were taken, maintaining control of it was a challenge that most city polities wished to avoid. Few cities had the capacity to incorporate others entirely or administer them at a distance as colonies. Sparta's experience with Messenian helots testified that old identities died hard. By far the easier course was to settle for some slaves and short-term tribute. Anyway, things were so unpredicatable that today's enemy could be tomorrow's necessary ally.

Although there were some changes in Greek warfare techniques between 400 and 350 b.c., they came too late to affect many Greek contests and ultimately worked in favor of the Macedonian conquerors. Greek mercenaries—including such illustrious generals as Xenophon, Iphicrates, and Chabrias—served in campaigns against Persia, elsewhere in the Near East, and in Thrace and wrote about their battle experiences. There was a new professionalism among Greek military officers and an appreciation of the utility of light infantry, skirmishers, cavalry,[6] and proper logistics. Meanwhile, the catapult, possibly invented by the Carthaginians, appeared in the service of Dionysios of Syracuse and revolutionized siege warfare. However, it remained for Philip of Macedon and Alexander to create a fully integrated army and use it to full advantage, with cavalry/infantry "hammer-and-anvil" tactics (Ferrill 1985, chap. 5; and J.A.C.T. 1984, 256–67).

Diplomacy. The ancient Greeks were not without institutions of formal diplomacy, though these were rudimentary by modern standards. The office of herald or *kerux* existed as early as Heroic times and was always considered to be under divine protection. The Heroic herald kept order at meetings and carried messages, and even served

---

6. By contrast, Leslie J. Worley (1993) argues that an emphasis on hoplites has obscured the fact that cavalry continued to play an important role in Greek warfare from the Dark Age through the Classical Period.

wine at the king's meals. In classical Athens, the herald summoned and controlled meetings, and accompanied official deputations—for example, to arrest a prominent citizen. Outside of his city the herald's role—exercised under immunity backed by divine sanction—was to declare war, request a truce, and open peace negotiations (J.A.C.T. 1984, 213–14; also Adcock and Mosley, 1975, 151–54). Although the Spartans and others had a reputation for secrecy and occasional treachery, it was generally considered "impious" to start an "unheralded" war (Nicolson 1954, 10).

Heralds could only deliver messages and never had authority to negotiate, a task which fell to *presbeis* or envoys. The word *presbeis* actually means "elders," and the minumum age for a *presbeutes* in Athens was customarily fifty. It appears that envoys had to have the capacity to engage in very public and sometimes risky diplomacy, for there are accounts of them addressing assemblies in the enemy camp during the Peloponnesian War. During wartime, they would proceed either with a herald or under safe passage previously negotiated. Envoys were not sacrosanct like a herald and received only token public funds, but representing one's city in diplomatic missions surely must have been a prestigious endeavor (J.A.C.T. 1984, 214–16; Adcock and Mosley 1975, 154–58).

From a contemporary perspective, the glaring omission was permanent diplomatic missions, and this had serious implications. Local information in face-to-face city polities, as we have noted, must have been considerable, but the same cannot be said for intelligence as to what was happening even in neighboring cities. Ned Lebow (1991, 144) maintains that during the Peloponnesian War "process variables and patterns of interaction were at least as important as capabilities in influencing the policies of both Athens and Sparta," and "probably the most important . . . was the lack of adequate channels for hegemonic communication."

Active communication on a more private social level did take place and was to some extent useful for public purposes. On the other hand, private ties harked back to societies organized on the basis of kinship and artificial kinship and often were not consistent with loyalty to polis. Starr (1986, 60–61) observes: "Greek upper classes were as linked on an international plane as were those of early modern Europe." Tyrants and their children often married foreigners, and there is evidence, especially in Athens, of noble families having blood relations and other personal ties in many parts of Greece. This was a direct descendant of practices in the Dark Age, when nobles on isolated estates created far-flung networks of ritualized guest-friend-ship or *xenia*, involving gift-giving, reciprocal hospitality, and mutual aid (Herman 1987, 130–42). Preserving and extending such ties abroad provided aristocrats in the later poleis with added stature and re-sources, assistance during difficult political struggles, and a place of refuge or exile in time of disgrace. Solon described a happy man as one who enjoys "dear children, whole-hooved steeds, hunting hounds, and a friend in foreign parts" (quoted in Starr 1986, 61).

The career of the brilliant scoundrel Alcibiades[7] highlights the potentially subversive nature of personal networks, yet there were positive dimensions to them as well, which city polities recognized and partly institutionalized. Desirable private relationships among citizens of different communities were facilitated by the office of *proxenia*, a sort of vice-consulship, whose very name suggests its Dark-Age background. The *proxenos* was a prominent aristocrat in one polis with ties to wealthy households in another polis, whom the latter honored with the title, in the expectation that he would act on behalf of its citizens locally. As Adcock and Mosley (1975, 160) point out, this was as close as the Greeks came to creating some form of permanent diplomatic representation. Another legal institution some-times recognized by the Greeks, isopolity, involved more immediate family, allowing, for example, a man settling in his wife's city to have citizenship rights there in matters such as property.

---

7. Alcibiades was a noble by birth who was raised in the house of Pericles and was a student of Socrates. In 420 B.C. he convinced the Athenians to ally with Argos, which precipitated the renewal of war with Sparta after the Peace of Nicias, and his advice also helped persuade Athenians to embark on the disastrous Sicilian expedition. Accused of having participated in a defacement of sacred statues before he departed with the fleet, Alcibiades was eventually called home to face formal charges. Angered, he took refuge in Sparta and started to advise the Spartans on how to defeat Athens. When difficulties arose in Sparta, he went to the court of Tissphernes, the Persian satrap of southwest Asia Minor. Later he offered to get the Persians to stop assisting Sparta if the Athenians would overthrow their radical democracy and allow him to return. He led the Athenians in a number of successful military engagements and was welcomed back to Athens in 407. The next year, however, Alcibiades was blamed for the defeat of an Athenian fleet, retired to a castle in the Kherronesos, and finally made a last appearance to advise another Athenian fleet prior to the battle of Aigospotamoi (J.A.C.T. 1984, 34–40).

The Greeks enshrined some reciprocal obligations in formal bilateral and multilateral treaties. This practice began in the fifth century B.C. with agreements called *symbolai,* initially between pairs of states, that provided for lawful procedures to be applied in disputes between individuals. The beneficiaries were mainly, but not exclusively, traders (Finley 1984, 161; also Adcock and Mosley 1975, 186–89). In addition to formal alliances and regimes concerning the independence of key shrines and games (discussed in chapter 6), various treaties provided for free trade between or among the parties; proper reception for heralds and envoys; fair treatment for traders, priests, and sojourners; and/or the right of the citizens of each city to marry, hold property, and participate in local religious and sporting events in another city. Adda Bozeman (1960, 79) describes one such treaty that was concluded between Athens and Thessaly in the midst of the chaotic fourth century.

There were also rules and procedures designed to prevent violent confrontations. These included treaties of friendship and nonaggression, like the one in the eighth century B.C. between Sybaris and Serdaioi, which pledged themselves to remain "in faithful, guileless friendship perpetually" (Jeffrey 1976, 45). A feature of many Greek treaties was provision for the use of arbitration, which had long been a "domestic"-arena procedure, to resolve polis-to-polis disputes. The third party might be a single individual like a tyrant, a board drawn from one or more cities, or even the Delphic Oracle. Martin Wight (1977, 52) suggests that what was involved in most such agreements was likely to have been conciliation, allowing the third party only to propose possible terms of settlement. Whatever the practice was exactly, it continued into Hellenic times. Harold Nicolson (1954, 8) reports that some forty-six cases of "arbitration" were recorded between 300 and 100 B.C.[8]

The Greeks also had some rules and agreements whose purpose was to mitigate the effects of war. The dead on the battlefield were not mutilated and were returned to the enemy for burial. Truces were

---

8. Adcock and Mosley (1975, 211) observe: "As in much of Greek diplomacy there was at times an element of gamesmanship in an appeal to arbitration. Such an appeal was used automatically as a first line of defense by the weaker party or it could be seen as a device to present opponents in an unfavourable light."

declared to allow for burial, as well as to facilitate holding certain festivals and games. An exchange of sacred oaths sealed treaties, and hostages might be taken or exchanged as a further guarantee of performance. There were several prefigurations of something like our Geneva Conventions: Megarian villagers took special pains to treat their "spear-guest" captives well. Chalcis and Eretria banned the use of slings and (poisoned?) arrows (Jeffrey 1976, 38). Members of the Delphic Amphictiony might do battle among themselves but pledged not to cut off food, poison wells, or completely devastate one another. (Wight 1977, 50 is skeptical as to whether the pledge was ever really observed.) Finally, some evidence exists that Greeks recognized a status of neutrality (Bauslaugh 1991). Adcock and Mosley (1975, 207) argue that the Greeks "fully accepted" neutrality as a concept and that it "did confer some protection," though it was not usually incorporated into a treaty and was never "clearly and juridically defined."

As Thucydides emphasizes with regret, whatever standards of conduct the Greeks were prepared to accept rapidly eroded during the Peloponnesian War and other times of grave peril. Hammond (1986, 359) lists some cases of surprising behavior: "The Plataeans slew their prisoners, the Spartans killed allied and neutral seamen, and the Athenians executed the Peloponnesian envoys whom Sitacles sent to them. The executions of [thousands of] prisoners from Mitylene and Plataea [by Athens] were more flagrant, in that they were masked by a judicial procedure and were decided in cold blood." Later in the Peloponnesian War the Athenians again shocked their contemporaries by slaughtering all males of military age of neutral Melos and selling their women and children as slaves. Thucydides (V:90) recounts in the Melian Dialogue that the Melians plea to the Athenians not to "destroy a principle that is to the general good of all men—namely, that in the case of all who fall into danger there should be such a thing as fair play and just dealing"—fell on deaf ears.

POLITY TYPES

The city—with "power resources concentrated upon its center rather than under extensive control" (Mann 1986b, 82)—remained the leading type of polity throughout much of the Greek experience. Aristocratic chiefdoms (Dark Age), alliances, hegemonial alliances (Sparta), empires (Athens, Persia, Macedon), large regional polity (Macedon at an earlier stage), federations (Chalcidian League), and functional regimes for shrines and games were also important. Unlike the situation in much of the ancient world, however, tribe in the Greek context had only modest significance.

Tribes

Except insofar as city polities eventually assigned arbitrary tribal names to some of their political subdivisions, the Greek tribe during the time frame we are concerned with (2000–338 B.C.) was more of a vague idea than an organized group. Dorians and Ionians were the most prominent, yet each had traditional internal "tribal" divisions—like Hylleis, Pamphyloi, and Dymanes for the Dorians—whose names tended to be used for political or religious districts by "Dorian" or "Ionian" cities, respectively. Dorian, as well as Ionian, cities also spoke much the same dialect and emphasized many of the same cults and festivals. Dorians (see Andrewes 1967, 85–86) and Ionians were longstanding rivals, but there was no organization grouping all cities in either category nor, for that matter, any suggestion that a Dorian/Ionian tribal subdivision in one city should feel solidarity with its counterpart in another city. Dorians, in particular, were wont to fight among themselves, as the competition between Sparta and Argos testifies.

Although tribes were not polities in our time frame, the Greek tribe does resemble other polity types in that it conceals significant internal variety, overlap with, and nesting within other polity types. Some cities continued to have at least a hazy link with a tribal past, despite the effort of polis politicians to demote the whole idea of tribe to a mere political district (see chapter 6).

Mycenaen City Polities

The Greek city is also an example of internal variety and overlap with other polity types. The Mycenaen city polity is particularly hard to classify, not least because Mycenaen polities were not all that urban, and some had more population and territory than many later city polities (Chadwick 1976, 12). Palaces were constructed at Thebes, Athens, Mycenae, Tiryns, Pylos, and probably Sparta or Elis or in the Corinth area. Finley (1981, 53) suggests that these Mycenaen palaces were the administrative centers of "petty, bureaucratic states." Renfrew (1972, 369) is even less precise in his characterizations of the Mycenaen centers: "something more than chiefdoms, something less than states" or "palace principalities" or "minor states."

Murray (1993, 7) contends that there is, in fact, no close resemblance between the Mycenaen civilization and later Greece. "The world which influenced Mycenae," he believes, "was the [Minoan] world of Knossos, itself on the fringes of an area where the centralized palace economy and the oriental despotisms of Mesopotamia and Egypt had already flourished for some two thousand years." Also, most of Mycenaen civilization vanished by the ninth century (Snodgrass 1980, 15).[9] Nevertheless, not everything vanished. For example, the royal citadel at Athens apparently never fell, and Attica received refugees from many areas (Vermeule 1964, 267; and Sourvinou-Inwood 1974). Chadwick (1976, 191) proposes that the Greek-speaking population of Crete may have broken up into smaller administrative units that kept written records and eventually reemerged as small city polities. And, as we shall see, there was some important ideological continuity between the Mycenaen and post-Dark Age eras.

The Polis and the Ethnos

The later Greeks recognized two basic subtypes of city polity, the polis and the ethnos. Each of these subtypes covered a wide range of forms, and the ethnos in some cases was closer to tribe—a primordial ethnicity with extremely limited organization—than to city. Snodgrass (1980, 42, and 1971, 419) speaks to the difficulty of defining an ethnos. At one extreme, it was "no more than a survival of the tribal system into historical times," a population worshiping a common deity at a single center and assembling periodically for political purposes. Between this and the polis were many intermediate forms. There were "canton-like" entities such as Locris, Doris, or Thessaly; and loose associations of towns and territories such as Arcadia, Achaea, or Boeotia. If a number of urban centers emerged, "they might attain intermittent autonomy as separate states, and pay only occasional homage to the concept of a unified 'nationality.' " Or a single city might forcibly establish itself as the political center of a part of the

---

9. Snodgrass (1980, 15) writes: "That complex and highly-stratified society, with its kings ruling from citadels and palaces, its elaborate system of land-ownership, its laboriously detailed monitoring of production and taxation, its specialization of crafts, its armed forces and its road network, was gone forever. . . . [The Greeks'] own activities now bore so small a resemblance to those of their ancestors that there was little they could have usefully learned from them."

ethnos, making it effectively into a polis. If both processes happened successively, in that order, a large polis with an impressive resource base might result. That is exactly what happened in some cases, and the ethnos "provided the basis for a fresh venture in state formation in the autumn of Greek civilization."[10] The ethnos also offered various models for alliances and hegemony. Hence the ethnos at once reached "back" to something like tribe and "forward," "through" and "beyond" the polis, to polities overarching the city. A contemporary comparison might be with postcolonial territorial polities that combine tribal characteristics with characteristics of the European Westphalian polity.

It is equally difficult to arrive at a satisfactory definition of polis. G. E. M. de Ste Croix (1981, 9; also cf. Starr 1986, 36–37; and Murray 1990) concludes that it is impossible "to give a definition of a *polis* that would hold good for all purposes and all periods, and the best we can do is say that a political entity was a *polis* if it was recognized as such." By the standards of many ancient or modern states, whether judged by territory or population, most poleis were small, but *compared to one another* some were tiny and others enormous. Early poleis (Fine 1983, 56) were little more than "straggling agricultural settlements," with citizens living around the foot of a citadel and scattered throughout the polis in isolated houses or small villages. Most cities were not walled until the sixth or even fifth century, and a real marketplace *(agora)* was slow to develop. Some poleis went on from such humble beginnings to become sophisticated urban centers, while others did not. Some were highly centralized, and others were not. Also, despite some similarities, there were striking differences in the constitutional structures of different poleis. Sparta after it incorporated Laconia and Messenia—with its citizens, "dwellers-round," and subject helots—is particularly hard to classify. It was a polis without a genuine urban center (Runciman 1982, 370–71), which confounds one suggested distinction between polis and ethnos (cf. Ehrenberg 1969, 22). Finally, at the other end of the polis continuum, we have those that at times are almost indistinguishable from hegemon or imperial center. Sparta and Athens spring to mind, but later there

---

10. Quotations in this paragraph are from Snodgrass 1980, 43–44. See also Ehrenberg 1969, 22–25, 120–31; Larsen 1968; and Runciman 1982, 370–73.

were other hegemons, including some like Boeotia that were former *ethnē*.

CONCLUSION

The city polity became and remained the prevailing mode of Greek political organization. The polis was a uniquely successful experiment in civic virtue, and the intense loyalties of its citizens compensated in part for the limited capabilities it afforded political leaders. In fact, the famed polis itself was highly variegated from the outset, as was the ethnos, and each city followed its own distinctive evolutionary path. The Greeks experimented, as well, with a significant range of other more inclusive political forms that we shall examine in greater detail in the next chapter.

6

THE POLIS
Triumph and Challenge of Citizenship

Although the polis remained the dominant political form and Greeks were proud to be called "citizens" of their polis, the city polities themselves evolved and had to confront and cope with other nested identities such as kinship and class. There were also a variety of challenges and opportunities beyond the polis that virtually compelled individual cities to become involved in larger, more encompassing institutional forms.

INTRODUCTION

Political patterns in the Heroic and Dark Ages ultimately disappeared with only a few, albeit significant, vestiges. Once the city had become the dominant polity, the two principal sets of vertical relationships were those within individual poleis; and the relationships of individual cities to a range of overarching polities, including alliances, hegemonical alliances, empire, federations, and functional regimes for shrines and games. Caution to the reader: the overarching polity types should not be regarded as mutually exclusive, and in fact blur into one another even more than is usual in our cases, for the Greeks themselves often used some polity names interchangeably. For example, the Spartan Alliance was also known as the Peloponnesian League and became a hegemonical alliance; the Delian League was the foundation of the Athenian Empire; and the Chalcidian League was a federation. (We shall discuss all of these and other examples later in this chapter.)

Greek city polities thus had to contend with one another and compete, in addition, with other sub-city, trans-city, and supra-city identities and loyalties. For one brief moment, in the midst of the Persian invasion, many independent cities achieved an unprecedented degree of cooperation, and there emerged an almost all-encompassing pan-Hellenic spirit and organization, which could not be sustained.

Ultimately, the Greeks paid dearly for their incessant conflicts, failure to concentrate regional resources, and inability to develop adequate Greece-wide leadership or institutions.

THE EVOLUTION OF GREEK POLITIES

The Heroic Age and Its Antecedents

Archaeology and linguistic scholarship provide what clues we have about prehistoric Greece, and much of this is subject to several interpretations. Finley (1981, 10) writes: "The 'events' in the whole of Aegean prehistory can be counted on one's fingers." Myths and traditions are "highly problematical at best," and archaeology only "reveals cataclysms" without telling us anything about the circumstances or personalities. There is a "remarkable absence of monumental portrayal" and "not a single dated object . . . which is not an import." All dates come from archaeology. One relatively recent breakthrough was the deciphering of Linear B, the script—now accepted to be an early form of Greek—found on clay tablets baked in the fires that apparently attended the destruction of Mycenaen centers at Knossos (c. 1400 B.C.), Pylos and Mycenae (c. 1200 B.C.), Thebes (c. 1320 B.C.), and elsewhere. Unfortunately, these records are fragmentary, inventorial in nature, and cover a period of no more than a single year in each center.

Greece was inhabited from at least the Middle Palaeolithic Age, forty thousand years ago, but not much is known even about much later Neolithic peoples.. The transition from the Stone to the Bronze Age apparently occurred around the beginning of the third millennium B.C. Still in dispute is the extent to which advances in the region derived from diffusion from Near Eastern civilizations and/or central Europe or from indigenous developments in a sort of "multiplier effect" (Renfrew, 1972). In any event, as we have noted, there is some consensus that Indo-European-speaking "proto-Greeks" arrived toward the end of the Bronze Age (c. 2000 B.C.), conquered and blended with the previous inhabitants on the mainland, and may themselves have been conquered by other groups just before 1600 B.C. (cf. Gimbutas 1974; and Marinatos 1974, 108–9).

There is widespread agreement that the distinct Minoan civilization on Crete, Thera, and elsewhere in the Aegean was the first to emerge; that the Minoans were strongly influenced by the Near East (Willetts 1977); and that they, in turn, had some cultural impact on mainland Mycenaens. Perhaps because of volcanic eruptions and earthquakes, the Minoans declined to a point where Mycenaens took control of Crete about 1450 B.C.

We have observed that Mycenaen polities are difficult to classify. They were small kingdoms with centers that were not real cities. Some were larger in territory and population than post–Dark Age poleis, and politically they were closer to Near Eastern models than to later Greek cities. Was there ever a Mycenaen empire? V. R. d'A. Desbourough (1964, 218) insists there was, with Mycenae the capital; however, the balance of opinion is otherwise. Vermeule (1964, 237) sums up some of the pros and cons. On the side of empire are stretches of built roads connecting provincial towns and the legend that Agamemnon could gather all the major cities together to war against Troy. Arguing otherwise are city walls and the poetic record of raids and full-scale conflicts of Greek against Greek. Vermeule concludes: "It is likely that any general organization of Mycenaen power had no more stability than a classical alliance among city-states, that politics were personal and affected by bloodlines and trade convenience, and that it would be quite wrong to think of Greece as a political unity like the Hittite or Canaanite realms."

The ruins of palace centers and especially tombs and tablets offer glimpses of the Mycenaen polity. Finley (1981, 48–49) comments that the tombs testify to the existence of a "power structure . . . different from any Greece had known before," headed by a king and his dynasty. Based on the tablets, Chadwick (1976, 69ff) observes that the ruler of a Mycenaen city polity was called *wanax,* a variation of the Homerian term for "king," and that the title implied large landholdings and may also have had some religious overtones. Several other levels of administration[1] with lesser landholdings are mentioned in the tablets, as well as a class of nobles ("the Followers"), who may have attended the king and constituted an elite military corps. The word

---

1. Chadwick (1970, 70) points out that the other familiar term for king, *basileus,* appears in its ancestral form, *quasileus.* What is surprising is that it had a less exalted meaning for the Mycenaeans than for Homer and "seems to have been used for the 'chief' of any group, even the head of a group of smiths." Reports Chadwick: "Traces of this use can still be found in Homer, for we read of many *basilēes* in Ithaca (Od. 1.394–5), and Alkinoos the Phaeacian king mentions twelve *basilēes,* not counting himself, among his people (Od. 9.390–1)."

damos also appears (foreshadowing *demos*), referring either to "the plot-holders" or to the people of the district collectively.

The palace complex was a center for storage and bureaucratic supervision of a wide range of activities in the larger economy. There seems to have been an "impressive division of labor." Whether there was a merchant class or not is unknown, for there is no mention of such or any indication of a currency. Slaves appear in the tablets, without clear indication of their social rank or political rights. Some were apparently owned by prominent individuals, while others (mainly women and children) received rations from the palace and may have produced textiles (Chadwick 1976, 78–83).

Unlike their Egyptian or Mesopotamian counterparts, religion for the Mycenaens seems to have been more private than public, for no large temples and few shrines or special rooms for ritual purposes have been found. Doctrine probably involved an amalgam of local gods with two separate traditions, Minoan Crete and Mycenaen. Chthonic "earth" gods may have been indigenous, while the proto-Greeks most likely brought the Olympian deities—Zeus, Hera, Hermes, Poseidon, Dionysos, and perhaps Apollo—who first appear in this era (Chadwick 1976, 84ff).

The Mycenaen polities disappeared during a tumultuous century (1250–1150 B.C.) in the eastern Mediterranean that also saw the demise of the Hittite empire in Asia Minor. Why the Myceaneans disappeared is one of the great mysteries of prehistory, rather like the end of the classical Mayan civilization nearly two millennia later (discussed in chapters 9 and 10).[2] The Trojan War of Homer, which perhaps destroyed Troy level VIIa from 1250 to 1200 B.C., may have been the last major success of the Mycenaens. In any event, the Mycenaen palace centers were laid waste, one by one and sometimes (like Mycenae itself) in stages, starting with Knossos about 1400 B.C. Pylos and the last bastions at Mycenae fell c. 1200 B.C., and most of the remnants disappeared by 1150 B.C.

The most likely destroyers were the mysterious Sea Peoples, whom Vermeule (1964, 271)[3] describes as "a phenomenon" rather than a single group, probably coastal tribes who worked as mercenaries and went on freelance rampages between engagements. Some believe that

---

2. As we shall explain, with more information becoming available, the Maya "mystery" is less mysterious than it used to be.

3. See also especially Sandars 1985; McDonald and Thomas 1990, chap. 4; Nibbi 1974; Desborough 1964, 221–25; and Snodgrass 1974.

they devastated Mycenaen centers and soon departed. Nevertheless, if the Sea Peoples are to blame, why did it take them a century to finish off all the centers? More puzzling is that the survivors did not make an effort to rebuild the centers. Was nearly everyone killed, taken away as slaves, or dispersed as refugees? Did the Sea Peoples "decapitate" a complex society that could not function without central direction, or did they just administer the coup de grace to a civilization that was already on the brink of collapse? Did the Mycenaens destroy their own centers? Proposed reasons for the collapse that do not necessarily involve the Sea Peoples include earthquakes, climatic changes, a breakdown in long-distance trade, an invasion from the north, and/or social revolutions.[4] Also in doubt is how complete the immediate collapse was: Jeremy B. Rutter (1992), for example, maintains that much of Mycenaen culture remained intact until after 1100 B.C., when (for reasons no better understood) it rapidly declined.

How relevant is the Mycenaen era to an understanding of later developments? The Mycenaen polities did bear a resemblance to Near Eastern kingships, and, anyway—with the probable exception of the royal citadel at Athens, some possible fragmented groups in Crete, a few dieties, and intriguing ruins—nearly everything disappeared. From an ideological standpoint, however, the Myceanaean era left an important legacy that was transformed into heroic proportions in the collective memory. As Snodgrass (1980, 18, 77–78) observes, the fact that so few details could actually be remembered was, in one sense, beneficial, because myths could "reconstruct" a far more glorious past and were adaptable for any future need. By cultivating their myths, the Greeks were eventually able to revive and advance *on what was essentially a new path* with ideological confidence. Gods and heroes served as patrons for the new city polities that later emerged. Even tyrants could claim that they were merely reviving the proud tradition of palace kings. A strong pan-Hellenic symbol of identification sustained the Olympic Games and shrines like Delphi, and rallied the Greeks, as a people, against the Persian Empire at the time of their greatest peril.

The Dark Age

The demise of the Mycenaen civilization ushered in a period from about 1100 to 800 B.C. that is customarily known as the Dark Age.

---

4. See especially McDonald and Thomas 1990, chap. 10; and Kilian 1988 and 1982.

This name is appropriate, for our information—mainly literary and archaeological—about this period is very limited (Snodgrass 1971, Desborough 1972, and Finley 1981). Homer (Ionia c. 750 B.C.?) draws on an older oral tradition and seems to describe primarily the Heroic (Mycenaen) era, though Fine (1983, 26) and others argue that much of Homer reflects life in the ninth century.[5]

The Dark Age was an era of great migrations, though it is not clear to what extent the Dorian, Aeolian, and Ionian peoples who were involved were newcomers to Greece and/or migrants from former Mycenaen centers. Whatever their background, "Greeks" by the ninth century were living throughout the Peloponnesus, the west coast of Asia Minor, and most of the islands in the Aegean. The decline in overall population after the Heroic Age appears to have been staggering, which suggests that population pressure was not the primary motive for these early migrations. The Ionian migrations across trecherous seas, unlike later migrations, were not government-sponsored; many seem to have embarked from Athens under the leadership of individual aristocrats (Snodgrass 1971, 373–76).

Political development had to begin almost anew in the Dark Age. Powerful kings no longer existed, except perhaps in less-grand circumstances in Athens. The setting for evolving political relationships, as we have noted, was a Greece of extremely small settlements—the more prosperous may have had no more than fifty persons (Starr 1986, 15, citing Snodgrass)—built around the nobility's largely self-sufficient estates (oikoi) and including a relatively independent peasantry. Metals, luxury items, and female slaves came from raids or foreign traders, usually Phoenicians (Fine 1983, 37). In most areas, apparently, there was no "serf" class, and peasants worked their own small plots and occasionally as hired laborers. Nevertheless, Finley (1981, 98) cautions, even much later in fifth-century Athens, we do not know for certain whether labor was "free or half-free" or "whether such concepts are yet applicable in any meaningful way." Although the lower classes had personal and property rights, he proposes, they may have owed some produce or work without pay and may have been tied by law to their land.

---

5. How far to trust Homer continues to be debated. Contrast, for example, Chadwick 1976, 186; and Hammond 1986, 1–91. The Boeotian poet Hesiod (c. 700 B.C.) provides a rare view from the perspective of the nonruling class.

Mycenaen tablets mention a local village official, a *basileus,* and this was the title assumed by those who led residual and new communities. Murray (1993, 38; also Snodgrass 1971, 386–88) describes them as "a group of hereditary nobles" identified as much by their lifestyles as by their "wealth, prerogatives or power." However, Starr (1986, 30–32) stresses that these nobles were not full-fledged aristocrats in that they did not disdain manual labor, nor did they give undue weight to kinship strictly conceived. Greek communities in the Dark Age thus evinced "a fundamental unity" rather than "a rigid stratification." In Starr's view, this is crucial, because "one cannot hope to understand how the *polis* emerged and survived the tensions of the age of expansion after 750 if the social system was divided from the beginning." Mann (1986b, 196–97), too, posits low status rigidity between Dark Age nobles and free people, "a tension between birth and wealth." The duties of any *basileus* who rose above his counterparts to the status of a chief or petty king (presumably the head of an important household) were probably largely military—to lead the people in battle and organize defenses against hostile raids (Fine 1983, 44). The wealthy had a virtual monopoly in warfare; only they could afford weapons, armor, and horses (Finley 1981, 97). Fine (1983, 45) notes that Homer mentions several popular assemblies even in peacetime.

Strict blood-relative kinship may not have been stressed by Dark Age nobility, but there was emphasis placed on artificial kinship, which was eventually to pose a challenge to the emerging polis. Through guest-friendship *(xenia),* including the gift exchange of goods and services, nobles created an extended network of mutual obligations. Bands of *hetairoi* supported one another in cattle raiding or piracy (Murray 1993, 49–53). Ritual friendships, similar to actual kinship, were hereditary in nature, and often spanned great distances (Herman 1987, 16–34). Such artificial kinship ties were linked to the Dark Age social unit known as the phratry *(phratriai)* or "brotherhood," whose name, like "tribe," the polis later appropriated for different purposes. According to Starr (1986, 29, citing Bourriot) another social division long thought to have existed in the Dark Age, the clan or *genos*—a major grouping primarily of upper–class families—appears to have been a "modern fabrication." The "only true clans" were royal ones of Sparta and some priestly clans like those of Eleusis.

The Onset of Social Hierarchy and the Rise of the Polis

The polis emerged at the start of the Archaic Age about the eighth century B.C., probably first on the mainland, and soon became the dominant feature of the Greek political landscape. Many developed in a relatively short time, though there was both significant continuity and variability in political forms.

The key change in the chiefdoms/city polities Dark Age/Archaic Age transition, 800 to 500 B.C., was from group identities based on forms of kinship to those based on locality or territory, the polis. Mann (1986b, 197) notes that Aristotle regarded the polis primarily as "a community of place." Yet this was only a shift in emphasis, in the primary symbol of identification; there were other competing identities both old and new. Family and ritual friendship ties from the chiefdom era posed a challenge to the polis, and kinship groups persisted as social and religious entities even after their political role was diminished. The polis also suffered *stasis* arising from political factionalism as well as a more fundamental division between rich and poor. The *ethnos,* as we explained, was considerably more diffuse than the polis. Other identities continued to be significant in peer-polity and center-periphery relations, and relations with non-Greeks.

Once the polis became prominent, a "demonstration effect" no doubt operated; local communities were both inspired by the example and perhaps fearful of the consequences if they did not imitate it. But how do we account for the initial rise of the polis? Snodgrass (1980, 31–32) thinks the Phoenician coastal cities may have provided a model, but little is known about those cities and there is no hard evidence of influence beyond matters related to trade like the alphabet (Starr 1986, 42).

Changes in Greek social and economic relations were prerequisites for the emergence of city polities, and, once institutionalized, these new entities must have fostered additional changes. Among the major factors involved were apparently an increase in population and agricultural surplus, comparable in magnitude to the post-Mycenaen decline. Snodgrass (1980, 24–40, and 1971, 378–80), as noted earlier, associates these trends with less pastoralism and more arable farming. Mann (1986b, 196) argues that "expansion increased the prosperity and power of the middling-to-large peasant householder as against the aristocracy, who were herders, especially of horses." Be that as it may, as Starr (1986, 39) suggests, increasing population probably led to disputes over land and to territorial disputes among neighboring communities. There was suddenly an urgent need for more formal "government" to help resolve local problems, define vague frontiers, and defend boundaries against encroachments from outside. Starr observes: "By the classical era the boundaries of the poleis seem so firmly set that one may forget how much the wars of the eighth and seventh centuries changed the map of Greece, and in so doing required conscious organization of the body politic and military.''

THE IDEOLOGICAL DIMENSION

Religion and Ideology

Another factor behind the rise of the polis was a desire to regularize the worship of cult deities at a central sanctuary (Snodgrass 1980, 31–34). Certainly the construction of major temples went hand in hand with the development of city polities, and religion (by contrast with the Mycenaen era) was a conspicuous part of daily public as well as private life. The sheer number of Greek deities and their anthropomorphic foibles may seem odd to the modern eye, but it would be an error to underestimate how sincerely the Greeks worshiped their pantheon and sought to discern and follow the will of the gods. As Anton Powell (1988, 383) comments, the lives of Athenians of all social classes ''were profoundly affected by religious prophecy'' and ''divination also influenced decisions on [public] strategy.''[6]

Although the metaphor is inexact, religion provided city polities with the ideological glue that we associate with contemporary ''nationalism.'' A more secularly inclined analyst might wish to stress that impressive temples and religious celebrations glorified the polis and that nowhere in the later Greek context do we find anything like the Near Eastern or medieval European notion of the ''divine right'' of kings. On the other hand, the polis both glorified and depended, to a

---

6. In his reading, the ancient sources occasionally question ''whether divination deserved to be influential, but there seems to have been no dispute that it actually was so.'' Finléy (1984, 95–96) disagrees, insisting that, though everyone ''hoped for divine support in an enterprise, no one argued that the gods were concerned with the substance of a political issue.'' When an augur canceled a meeting, his advice was that ''the *day* was inauspicious for public business, not that the *proposal* to be voted on had received divine disapproval.'' Moreover, Finley can find ''no known case of a genuine deflection of policy because of the protests of private diviners or oracle-mongers.'' Such an interpretation is difficult to square with Thucydides' testimony that divination was influential at virtually every stage of the Sicilian expedition that ultimately wrecked Athens' fortunes (for this and other cases see Powell 1986, chap. 9).

substantial degree, on religion. Skeptical Finley (1984, 132, 95), who flatly states that he is "unaware of a single claim to divine sanction for a particular measure, regime, reform or revolution," nonetheless acknowledges that the "vast body of religious practices was of course an integral part of the traditional *nomos* . . . that upheld the whole structure." One of the leading experts on Sparta, Paul Cartledge (1979, 417), goes so far as to say that religion *was* Sparta's ideology. Christine Sourvinou-Inwood (1990, 304–95) makes a similar generalization: "The Greek *polis* articulated religion and was itself articulated by it; religion became the *polis'* central ideology, structuring and giving meaning to, all the elements that made up the identity of the *polis,* its past, its physical landscape, the relationship between its constituent parts."

Conversely, there was a powerful polis dimension to religion.[7] As Sourvinou-Inwood (1990, 295–97, 301–2) explains, in a religion with no significant texts or clergy, it was the city polity that structured "the universe and the divine world into a religious system"—rather like the Church did for Christianity. "Each polis was a religious system which . . . interact[ed] with the religious systems of other poleis and with the Panhellenic dimension." Each had its own patron diety and other especially sympathetic members of the pantheon, some of whom were associated with specific representative and administrative districts. In addition to regular public worship and religious festivals, there were cults for various mythical and other heroes of the polis (like Theseus in Athens). Many of the same gods and heroes were worshiped differently in different cities, and Greeks knew that they must respect the sanctuaries and cults of others if they were not to offend the gods. One could participate in another city's rites only as a *xenos* and then only with the aid of a citizen, normally one's home city's *proxenos.* On the Panhellenic level, the local city usually oversaw the conditions of access to particular shrines; for example, Delphians offered an initial sacrifice on behalf of non-Delphians before they were allowed to consult the Oracle.

The new city polities fostered nothing less than an "Olympian revolution" among the gods, which helped to legitimize the establish-

---

7. Finley (1984, 94) is extreme and probably incorrect in his position that "government [became] generally secularized in reality though not in appearance."

ment of an ethical order more suited to civilized urban communities than the old code followed by Dark Age nobles. We have noted how, as early as Mycenaen times, the ancient earth gods were joined by some members of an Olympian pantheon. Over time the Olympians gained the upper hand. It was they who supposedly curbed the earth gods' emphasis on family and blood revenge and inspired other city-polity rules—such as accepting gifts under certain conditions is bribery, or consorting with enemies of the polis is treason—to contain the subversive threat inherent in continued ritual friendships.[8] In Richard Kuhns's (1962) analysis, the *Oresteia* illustrates some of the changes in thinking. Orestes is beset by advice from two different quarters, the ancestral Erinyes, and Apollo and other Olympians. An Athenian court, which alone can weigh the pros and cons, ultimately rationalizes Orestes's crime of matricide. The nature of political development is clear in the lesson learned by Orestes: "the right of action is realized through considerations which go far beyond the individual's impulses and desires; the individual and the family, the house and the clan become subordinate to the city" (Kuhns 1962, 56).

Community Versus Hierarchy

Religion was important, but it was not the only ideological factor involved in the rise of the polis. Murray (1990) contends that the celebrated "rationality" of the Greeks was not something that evolved Durkheim-like out of an "undifferentiated religious consciousness." "Political activity," he argues, "had always been the central organizing principle" of "Greek society," and it was that "collective consciousness" which found its expression in the polis. Moreover, Farrar, Finley, and others observe that the polis became, if anything, more secular over time. Farrar (1988, 38) believes that "the conception of order and autonomy shifted from acquiescence in divine determinations to active participation in an order mediated even in its divine aspect by civic institutions" and that an accompanying "transformation" "in the realm of cosmology . . . gradually leached divinity from the cosmos."

Other scholars emphasize the remarkable Greek invention of the polis form itself and the concept of citizenship. From the start, the

---

8. The connection of religion to the development of the law is implicit here.

polis was conceived as a "community" as well as a "place," and for the first time in history what Aristotle described as "political man" became "citizen" rather than mere "subject." Ian Morris (1987, 2, drawing on Runciman 1982) points out that, though it was perhaps predictable during the Dark Age that the Greeks would eventually develop more formal political institutions—by emulating earlier advanced societies or through cluster or peer-polity interaction—there was no predicting that such institutions would assume the specific form of the polis. Each polis was independent of others and unified with a surrounding tract of countryside; inside that area no distinction was normally made between dwellers within and without the city (Snodgrass 1980, 28). As Morris (1987, 3) suggests, the key was citizenship. He says, "the idea of the polis as a *koinonia* emerged quite suddenly, and from that time on we can speak of the existence of the polis."

In Morris's view (1987, 3), the polis "was almost a stateless society, autonomous from all dominant class interests by being isomorphic with the citizen body. The citizens were the state." "The source of all authority was . . . the community." "Force was located in the citizen body as a whole, and standing armies or police forces were almost unknown." One is reminded of the claim associated with the concept of political legitimacy that power that is less despotic is more effective. Internal control, like external defense, became a community task. Morris again (1987, 3, citing M. Godelier): "We might also say that politics functioned as the relations of production." Similarly, Marxist analyst de Ste. Croix (1981, 286–87) emphasizes that Greeks regarded their "state" not mainly as a means of preserving property but rather as the instrument of the body of citizens who had the constitutional right to rule. Hence "class struggle" in this context was an effort by the *demos* to make the city polity sufficiently democratic to curb exploitation by aristocrats.

Ste. Croix's comment about the Greek style of class struggle should caution us not to wax uncritically about "community." Aristotle (*Politics* II i and ii) asserted that the polis was a "natural association," "formed with a view to some good purpose," which had "a natural priority over the household and over any individual." The city was accordingly (in modern parlance) "sovereign," but kings had disappeared altogether or were enfeebled, leaving the "popular sovereignty" of citizens. But, foreshadowing later debates, how was "popular sovereignty" to be exercised in practical terms and what were its full implications? The negative side of citzenship for aristocrats and tyrants was that it seemed to imply an actual role (at least for free males) in political decision making. Whose notion of "good purpose" was to be advanced, and through what political institutions and processes? Aristotle (*Politics* III iii) appears to have recognized the centrality of this issue when he wrote that "the main criterion of the continued identity of a [polis] ought to be its constitution."[9] Finley (1977, 59–60) wisely observes that "the sense of community, strong as it was" could not obscure "gross inequality," which had existed throughout history but not previously in contexts where citizens believed they had the right to seek remedies:

> The citizen felt he had claims on the community, not merely obligations to it, and if the regime did not satisfy him he was not loath to do something about it—to get rid of it if he could. In consequence the dividing line between politics and sedition (*stasis* the Greeks called it) was a thin one in classical Greece, and often enough *stasis* grew into ruthless civil war. . . . [I]n the Greek polis it was not so much policy which caused the most serious divisions, but the question of who should rule, "the few" or "the many." And always the question was complicated by external affairs, by war and imperial ambitions.

In light of socio-economic inequalities in such an intimate political setting as a city, it is perhaps surprising that there was not more sedition than there was. Coercion of any great number of citizens was out of the question, because there was literally no standing professional army[10] and no police force. Also unlike the Oriental regional polities and empires, there was no extensive bureaucracy to "mediate" between the populace and leaders, only a small "unofficial, unpaid entourage" of specialists who acted as advisers (Finley 1984, 77–78).[11]

---

9. In fact, there is no evidence that any Greek polity had a "constitution" in the modern sense of that term. As in the case of "state" or "city-state" for "polis," we are in the hands of translators who ought to find some other line of work.

10. Sparta, Thebes, Athenian rowers, and the mercenaries used by Greek cities in the fourth century are exceptions to this generalization (see Finley 1984, 19).

11. Sinclair (1988, 46) notes that in Athens, even in such a critical area as finance, "it was not until the 350s that we have clear evidence of attempts to

What, then, was the source of the authority enjoyed by the polis polity and its leaders? As we have said repeatedly, coercion aside, authority is an exchange phenomenon, in that individuals trade their loyalty and support for perceived benefits. What were citizens getting out of the polis?

A large part of the explanation, of course, is the psychological satisfaction derived from group identity and ideology. This included the glorification of citizenship in the polis, belief in its links with divine and ancient heroes, and pride in such secular accomplishments as military successes, the exercise of hegemony or empire (in some cases), athletic triumphs, spectacular civic festivals, and brilliant theater. It is crucial that there was an ideological consensus as to who was (and was not) a member of the polis community and their relative standing. Almost no one questioned that only native-born free persons could be citizens and that only free adult males could participate in politics, because women, slaves, and foreign "barbarians" were deemed to be inherently inferior. Thus, a democratic city polity allowed no more than about 14 to 17 percent of its population to participate directly (Sinclair 1988, 200). The population that was entitled to do so had an unprecedented—and expanding—opportunity for participation and no doubt derived satisfaction (or at least reassurance) from their role in marketplace decision making and service in one or another civic office (for Athenian statistics, see especially Finley 1984, chap. 4; and Sinclair 1988, 195–200).

However, even in democracies, the leaders tended to be well-to-do; and democracy, after all, was not typical in Greece, for, as Starr observes (1986, 93), "almost all states by 500 [B.C.] were oligarchic in structure and remained so." Finley (1984, 27) sums it up: "Because no city-state was genuinely egalitarian and many were not democratic either, political stability rested on the acceptance in all classes of the legitimacy of status and status-inequality in some measure, not only of the existence of *boni* but also of their right to greater wealth, greater social standing and political authority." Sinclair (1988, 208) adds: "The willingness of poorer citizens to accept wide disparities in wealth was perhaps encouraged also by their sense of cohesion against the

---

coordinate the various bodies responsible for expenditure of resources in the Athenian state." A Festival Funds Commission was established, which had broader administrative functions than its name might suggest.

slave population, which enjoyed no or few possessions and lacked freedom, and by their tendency to absorb aristocratic values and attitudes.''

Authority in the polis rested on more than satisfaction drawn from group identity and ideology alone; there were also specific practical benefits. As we have seen, population increase pointed up the urgent need for "government" to mediate disputes, demarcate boundaries, and organize community defense. In addition, government proved increasingly useful in sponsoring the foundation of colonies abroad. Emigration was a safety valve for surplus population as well as, in some cases, a tool of hegemony or empire. Moreover, what Finley (1984, 32) terms "conquest-states" secured from abroad substantial resources for their citizens in the form of land, money, and slaves.

Although the fundamental socioeconomic divide in Greek cities was between the rich and the poor, the poor did get material benefits out of the polis community (Finley 1984, 32–36, and 1985, 151–52). In "conquest-states" they received a share of the spoils, despite a distribution system biased in favor of the upper classes. Tribute helped pay for public works and lavish public celebrations that everyone could enjoy. Athens went further than any other polis in providing employment for the poor as rowers in the navy and "state pay"— Finley (1984, 34) calls it "subsistence crisis insurance"—on a per diem basis for jury duty, service in public office, and (beginning in the fourth century) attendance at Assembly meetings.

More important, across Greece as a whole—even in nonconquest states—the costs of government fell almost exclusively on the well-to-do or, to a lesser extent, on foreigners.[12] The urban poor and peasantry paid few taxes. Indeed, there was hardly any direct taxation at all, except extraordinary·levies in wartime or in some tyrannies. Additional taxes were imposed on resident aliens, imports, and use of harbors. Hoplites paid for their own equipment, and other needs of the polis were met through the institution of the liturgy. Wealthy individuals were required, on a rotating basis, to bear both the costs and administrative burden for public services with religious overtones like athletic contests and dramatic festivals. Another type of liturgy was the trierarchy, the personal command and cost of provisioning (crew and stores) of a naval ship for one year. Liturgies were compulsory yet

---

12. On Athenian state finance generally, see J.A.C.T. 1984, 227–30.

were so prestigious that the rich often competed to obtain them and overspent their subscriptions in order to boast of their generosity.

Peasants not only were essentially untaxed, they also rarely paid rent, for the simple reason that most were not tenants. However, with a population that grew beyond the capacity of emigration to alleviate and with the gradual expansion of aristocratic holdings, there was a shortage of land, and peasants acquired an onerous burden of debts. Land hunger and debts, then, were among the major causes of *stasis*.

The City Polity and Deepening Class Cleavages

Not surprisingly, the polis began to evolve internally even after it became the dominant symbol of Greek political identity. Demographic change, economic growth, and changing military tactics affected Greek society, profoundly influencing the constitutions of individual poleis. As social complexity increased, so did pressures to expand the circle of political elites. The fact that Greek society became more complex required a political response. The city symbol of identification had to be strengthened to counter internal diversity. New territorial bases for representation had to be found that would cut across real and imagined ties inherited from the chiefdom era. As we noted with regard to the Olympian revolution, aristocratic behavior that was inconsistent with the polis community had to be outlawed. Government institutions had to be expanded for purposes of representation. Nevertheless, changes in institutions and the degree to which democracy was achieved or remained symbolic differed greatly from city to city.

By the seventh century B.C., several developments—paradoxically, including the emergence of a full-fledged and self-conscious aristocracy—worked together to undermine aristocratic rule.[13] By the seventh century "a fierce competition for public honor and a raw, undisguised drive for riches scarcely ever again equalled in ancient times" (Starr 1986, 63) posed a powerful threat to the "spiritual unity" of the fledgling polis. The formerly rough-and-ready aristocrats made so much money through war, landholdings, and trade that they became gentlemen of leisure, occupying themselves solely with politics and

---

13. Cf. Fine 1983, 94–136; Forrest 1978, 45–97; Snodgrass 1980, 85–159; Starr 1986, chap. 4; Finley 1981, 87–105; Hopper 1976, 52–155; Jeffrey 1976, 39–47; and Ste. Croix 1981.

such amusements as athletic contests and hunting. In most cities, the real political power rested with an aristocratic council *(boule)*. Any remaining hereditary chief-for-life was replaced by an elected functionary known as a *prytanis* or an *archon,* who served a one-year term. Other officials included a war leader (*polemarchus* or *strategus*) and a chief priest. Through their wealth and control of politics, aristocrats steadily expanded their estates and reduced neighboring small farmers to dependence or debt peonage (Starr 1986, 63–65). However, the aristocrats' luxurious lifestyle, flagrant exploitation, and corruption of the administration of justice created resentments that ultimately led to a backlash.

Other changes, too, hastened the end of aristocratic rule. The shift to hoplite warfare meant that a phalanx of equals took pride of place in the defense of the city polity, rather than aristocrats on horseback.[14] Greek colonization stimulated trade and manufacturing, increasing the number of merchants, shippers, and *demiourgoi* artisans. Writing, which was revived about the eighth century, made it possible to keep accounts and establish formal provisions of law that limited the arbitrary personal character of government. The introduction of coinage about the sixth century facilitated exchange and created a new portable form of wealth. A middle range of prosperous *kakoi* farmers appeared—Starr (1986, 94) terms them "semiaristocrats" or "gentry"—and, like aristocrats, they did not hesitate to exploit poorer landholders.

Widespread social conflict or *stasis* led to three major political changes beginning about the middle of the seventh century: the rise of tyrants, the codification of the laws, and the further institutionalization of government to manage demands from a more complex society. Late in the seventh century, tyrants began to appear mainly where urbanization as well as socioeconomic and political development were relatively advanced (Finley 1981, 102–3). Part of the explanation is that hereditary aristocracies could not resolve conflicts in their own

---

14. Whether there was a "hoplite reform" is controversial. Morris (1987, 197–201) finds "not a shred of evidence" for change in Greek warfare tactics. He believes that hoplites were used long before the period in question and sees "absolutely no reason to associate a 'hoplite class' with either the rise of the polis or the rise of the tyrants." (See also Snodgrass 1965, Cartledge 1977, and Salmon 1977.)

ranks. Also, although it would be an exaggeration to say that a full-fledged bourgeoisie had emerged (Starr 1986, 73), there was growing discontent among wealthy commoners, an increasing urban popula-tion, and indebted peasantry.[15] Tyrants arose in Argos, Corinth, Si-cyon, Megara, Epidauros, Pisa, and elsewhere. Solon's constitutional reform in Athens was followed by the Peisistratus tyranny.

In one sense, the so-called age of the tyrants was a backward step toward kingship. Few tyrants, however, were able to establish lasting dynasties, and most became increasingly brutal as their power eroded. In other respects, the tyrants represented a populist step. They bol-stered community spirit through public works and games and festivals. More important, they "broke the habit" of aristocratic rule,[16] which strengthened the *polis* and its institutions, and in some cities (only) led "to government by the *demos,* democracy" (Finley 1981, 104; also van der Vliet, 1987). On the other hand, even where democracy was the outcome, as we have emphasized, participation was limited and the wealthy continued to play prominent roles. Nor was democracy permanently implanted or an unmixed blessing. It is sobering to recall that the next great age of tyrants began with Dionysios I of Syracuse in 405 B.C., when Greek democracy, weakened by the Peloponnesian War, had, in a sense, self-destructed (Davies 1978, 147ff).

Sparta and Athens, in significant respects atypical, nevertheless illustrate two political trends, codification of the laws and further institutionalization of government. Generalizations about Sparta are difficult because of the paucity of evidence and the Spartan myth of equality and democracy.[17] Legend held that Sparta's way of life

---

15. Starr (1986, 80–86) insists that "Marxist and liberal historians" have made too much of the tyrants, particularly their relationship to social and economic tensions in the seventh century. He notes that few city-states experienced tyrannies and that those that did not seem to have "progressed" as much as those that did, so "widespread and irresistible" were the "proc-esses of change." In his view, most tyrants had to depend on mercenaries to remain in power and favored, if anyone other than themselves, the "middling and smaller farmers, though there is no certain evidence that they redistributed the lands of exiled aristocrats."

16. Starr (1986, 86) admits that tyrants "weakened the hereditary position of aristocrats as unquestioned leaders of the state."

17. See Fine 1983, 137–76, from whom we draw heavily; Forrest 1980;

derived from an ancient law-giver, Lycurgas, whose constitution created *eunomia* or "the reign of good law." The Great Rhetra, probably an ancient document (supposedly from the Delphic Oracle) preserved by Plutarch in a confusing form, purports to distribute the powers of state among kings, council of elders, and an assembly of all the equals.[18] Sparta's principal features likely date from the latter half of the sixth century—a century or so after the Spartans forceably extended their control over Laconia and Messenia—and were part of a militarization of the city polity to insure the continued domination of subject helots (serfs). An additional concern were the *perioeci* ("dwellers round"), other Spartan subjects in surrounding villages with limited rights and obligations, and their own local governments. Thus, Murray's (1980, 153) description of Sparta as "the ideal hoplite state of classical Greece" is accurate, although the hoplite "garrison state" was as much for internal control as for defense against external threats. Sparta also had to conduct peer-polity relations with the full knowledge that overextension or military reversals abroad would likely lead to helot revolt at home.

The Spartan polity was more equal in theory than practice (Fine 1983, 147–51, 155–61). All Spartan male citizens were bonded from an early age into a military "brotherhood" to supersede all other loyalties. Whatever equality prevailed in the barracks did not exist outside. Powell (1988, 102) describes fifth-century Sparta as "an oligarchy within an oligarchy": "A few thousand citizens dominated the masses of helot poor, and within the few thousand citizens a few wealthy families had special power." Land was not held in equal portions. Moreover, a nobility of citizens over age sixty elected to life terms on the *gerousia* (senate of thirty, replacing the earlier Council of Elders) controlled the government. Their wealth and influence probably swayed the "popular election" of members of the board of ephors, who were chief administrative officers during their one-year, nonrenewable terms. Sparta retained a dual kingship, but kings were primarily military leaders. After conflict between the two kings in the sixth century, only one was allowed to lead a military campaign and then

---

Cartledge 1979 and 1986; Powell 1988, chaps. 4 and 6; Hamilton 1979; and David 1986.

18. Sparta's "mixed" constitution was of interest to the Founding Fathers of the United States.

only in the company of two ephors. At an elaborate oath exchange ceremony every nine years, the ephors could depose a king. The full assembly of citizens, the *ecclesia,* met about once a month to elect persons to high office and pass on any legislative questions referred to them. However, debate on such occasions may have been limited to the *gerousia,* ephors, and kings; and the *ecclesia* apparently could be overruled in the event that the people decided "incorrectly."

Athens, though different from Sparta, also provides an example of a law-giving stage[19] and the elaboration of governmental institutions to accommodate a changing society.[20] Any unity Attica may have had during the Mycenaen era had to be reestablished. Thucydides credited (re)unification or *synoecism* to the national hero, Theseus, a legendary figure like Lycurgas. Presumably one or more kings succeeded in getting various settlements to accept Athens as a political center, brought nobles from them into the royal council, and extended Athenian citizenship to freeborn native residents of the entire territory. By the early seventh century the king or *basileus* had only religious functions; and the leadership of Athens consisted of a ruler archon, a polemarch or military leader (including jurisdiction over resident aliens), and six other judicial archons. An aristocratic council, eventually known as the Council of the Areopagus, probably held much of the real power, electing archons directly or nominating them for election by a popular assembly. The aristocratic families who controlled Athenian politics called themselves the *Eupatridai* or "wellborn." When tyranny was fashionable, c. 632 B.C., there was an abortive attempt by Cylon to establish one in Athens. About 621, Dracon codified the laws of Athens, partly to meet criticisms that the administration of justice had become corrupt.[21] Little is known about

---

19. Powell (1986, 238) quips that "what Sparta had was not so much law as *order.*"

20. See sections on Athens in general works previously cited, especially Sinclair 1988, Stockton 1990, Powell 1988, J.A.C.T. 1984, Hansen 1991, Starr 1986, Farrar 1988, Forrest 1966, Fornara and Salmon 1991, Ehrenberg 1973, Davies 1993, and Jones 1957, on the fourth century. The leading primary source, traditionally and probably incorrectly attributed to Aristotle, is *The Athenian Constitution.*

21. The penalties imposed for failure to pay debts and others offenses were harsh (hence "draconian").

the terms of the code, except the law on homicide, which partly survived in a late fifth-century copy and is significant as an effort to limit the blood-feuds characteristic of pre-polis society.

In 594 B.C. when Solon became archon, there was a general clamor over debts in Athens. Many small farmers, *hectomoroi* ("sixth-partners"), owed one-sixth of their annual crop to an overlord. Failure to pay this or any debt could result in enslavement of both offender and his family. Some scholars have looked for crisis conditions that might have increased agitation over debts—economic problems from overcropped land, bad harvests, a foreign invasion, or even the introduction of coined money which made it easier to lend and borrow. W. G. Forrest (1978, 150–56) maintains that the economy may actually have been improving owing to a growth in trade, but Dracon's code created resentments. Be that as it may, Solon confronted the problem head-on by abolishing the status of *hectemoros,* canceling existing rural debts, forbidding the use of persons as security in future transactions, and allowing debt exiles to return.

Solon, together with Cleisthenes several generations later, removed the last vestiges of primordial kinship from government. Solon divided the population into four census classes based on wealth rather than birth—*pentakosiomedimnoi* (owners of estates producing 500 measures of grain), *hippeis* (cavalrymen), *zeugitai* (hoplites), and *thetes* (those unable to afford hoplite arms).[22] The archonship was limited to the top two census classes, thereby breaking the Eupatrid monopoly.[23] Solon also created a new Council of 400 (100 from each tribe) to check, how we do not know, the power of the Council of the Areopagos. In addition, he gave the existing popular Assembly an extra title, the *Hiliaea,* to express its new function of acting as a court

---

22. Although the thetes were presumably the most numerous group, Aristotle and/or another ancient commentator (*Constitution* 7 [4]) informs us that "no one" would admit to belonging to that class.

23. Starr (1986, 78) writes: "Essentially the aristocracy as political master was now replaced by a timocracy in which the degree of public participation depended not on ancestry but on the basis of wealth, measured in terms of agricultural produce." Solon himself (Aristotle *Constitution* 12) stated in his poetry that he had "stood in the middle ground . . . like a marker" between "the people" and "those who had power and were admired for their wealth"— and "did not allow either to win an unjust victory."

of appeal even against the magistrates themselves. He rewrote the legal code of the city, abolishing the laws of Dracon. Finally, Solon encouraged the rising commercialism of Athens, welcomed foreign craftsmen, and ordained that fathers should teach all their sons a craft. Not surprisingly, Athens' economic success exacerbated social tensions. In 561 B.C. Peisistratos established a tyranny, which lasted through his son Hippias to 510 B.C.

In 508 B.C. Cleisthenes completely reorganized the administrative and electoral system of Attica.[24] He made about 150 small demes *(demos)* the basic city administrative units, cutting across the old tribes, and superimposed over demes ten new artifical tribes, each to elect one general and fifty members of a Council of 500. Each tribe was further subdivided into three *trittyes,* one from each of the three geographical divisions of Attica—the City, the Coast, and the Inland. Snodgrass (1980, 196) observes that each new tribe was "a microcosm of the Attic state," muddying and undercutting both locality and kinship loyalties. Aristotle (*Politics* 1319b19 and *Constitution* 21.1) flatly declares that Cleisthenes' intention was to "break-up . . . former associations" and "mix" "citizens through ten tribes instead of the old four," so as to create "as much social intercourse as possible" and to give "more men . . . a share in the running of the [polis]." Nor can we overestimate the import of the statement: "[Cleisthenes' reform] is the origin of the saying 'Don't judge by tribes,' addressed to those who inquire into a man's ancestry."[25] The reforms supposedly gave all male citizens equal rights in the election of officials (Hammond 1986, 190), which lends credence to *The Athenian Constitution*'s

---

24. Similar reorganization occurred in other Greek cities. Starr (1986, 79) observes: "Reorganization of voting districts had earlier been carried through at Sicyon, Corinth, Miletus, and elsewhere; at Corinth the eight tribes were even divided into 'thirds' of non-contiguous territory."

25. Sinclair (1988, 3) explains that previously the old aristocratic families "controlled membership of the phratries (or brotherhoods) and thus admission to the tribes," on which rested "the social, religious and political organization" of Attica. Cleisthenes "opposed rigid investigation of family backgrounds and favoured the recognition of those whose claim to being Athenians was in doubt, and in particular his reforms transferred control over these questions from the old aristocratic families to the demes or local communities in which all free Athenians were now to register."

characterization of Cleisthenes as "champion of the masses" and its assessment that "the people put their trust" in him.

The long-range effect was more democracy, with an ostracism procedure for unwanted statesmen after 488 B.C., the selection of archons by lot after 487, and the decline of the Areopagus until it was replaced by a Council of 500 in 462. The Council was chosen by lot from all male citizens who agreed to serve. The term of office was one year; a man could only serve twice in a lifetime; and geographical representation was maintained. Officials of the city polity were held accountable, including being subjected to a financial audit, possible impeachment, and other procedures (Sinclair 1988, 79). The election of officials as well as most other matters of importance came before the Assembly of the city's entire male citizenry, the Ecclesia. Some idea of its size is suggested by the facts that a quorum of 6,000 was required for decisions like ostracism and that in the fourth century a modest sum had to be paid to induce enough persons to participate (Sinclair 1988, 67). David Stockton (1990, 113) comments:

> Looked at from one point of view, the Athenian system was egregiously inefficient, unprofessional, cumbersome, uncoordinated, time-consuming, and plagued by discontinuity. . . . From another point of view, it was remarkably efficient. . . . [The Athenians] achieved great success in creating and maintaining a society in which . . . the citizenry exercised a control over the legislative, executive, and judicial branches of their state to a degree unmatched before or since. Whatever was lost in speed, expertise, and continuity was counterbalanced by the constraints which were erected against the emergence of over-powerful ministries and unrepresentative and irresponsive bureacracies, by the wide pool of practical experience, local knowledge, and common sense that was drawn on, by the provision of a platform for the free expression of every interest, in short by the absence of that "them-and-us" dichotomy between government and governed which has been a feature of so many other societies.

Much of the success Athenian democracy enjoyed is directly attributable to the fact that Athens was a city, but a city had disadvantages too.

BEYOND THE POLIS: GREEK PEER-POLITY, CENTER-PERIPHERY, AND NON-GREEK RELATIONS

Because the polis was small, outside relationships assumed unusual importance, and a variety of informal and somewhat more formal institutionalized arrangements evolved beyond the city polity.[26] These included postcolonial ties, alliances, hegemonial alliances, empire, federations, and functional regimes for shrines and games. Those arrangements at the informal end of the spectrum might be classified as "regimes" in the least restrictive modern sense of that term. However, some arrangements such as the Athenian empire constituted full-fledged polities with significant domains of authority. In Victor Ehrenberg's (1969, 100) words, "We see, in fact, that the conception of autonomy was shrinking: not only did the inter-state relations gain more scope, but actual authorities above the single Polis were recognized." Poleis recognized most such authorities only grudgingly, but the complicated relationships that resulted nonetheless had an important impact on the course of Greek politics.

Alliances, Empires, and Federations

Alliances were essential in a system in which the units were small, numerous, and vulnerable. Some of the major cities perceived that alliances could serve for exploitation as well as for mutual defense. Not for nothing did the Greeks coin the term "hegemon."

At one level were longstanding informal links between colonies and mother cities. Tarentum, founded in southern Italy by Sparta at the close of the eighth century, provides a useful example (Adcock and Mosley 1975, 131). Tarentum became a democracy c. 475 but closed its gates to the Athenians at the time of the Sicilian expedition and gave the Spartan commander Gylippus a haven. A century later Sparta reciprocated by sending forces to help Tarentum resist incursions from Italian tribes. As this example suggests, historical ties could affect the choice of allies, but so could other factors, including considerations of realpolitik. Barry S. Strauss (1991) concludes that Greeks were typically engaged in "balancing," though they might "bandwagon" when resistance to a rising local hegemon seemed futile. Thucydides described the shifting alliances during the Peloponnesian War, a pattern that grew more pronounced in subsequent years after

---

26. Original sources include Thucydides, Xenophon, Herodotus, and Polybius. See also especially Adcock and Mosely 1975,; Lebow and Strauss 1991, Ehrenberg 1969, Wight 1977, Burn 1984, and Fleiss 1966.

more leading actors appeared. It is intriguing that "although a few large states such as Athens, Sparta, Thebes, sometimes Persia, and, later, Macedon could have [had] a decisive influence on affairs they never all stood together" (Adcock and Mosley 1975, 137–38). As it was, their "suspicions and their several strategic requirements led some of them now into alliance or even into professions of friendship, now into conflict," and this "situation always engendered hopes and fears in smaller states."[27]

Ancient tribal identities, especially when reinforced by common combat experiences, may have had some relevance to alliances. Powell (1988, 44) observes that early "warfare between the Spartan alliance, mainly composed of Dorian Greeks, and the Delian League, consisting chiefly of Ionians, must have strengthened the feeling that there was a natural opposition between the two linguistic and cultural groups."

Another influence on alliances was ideology regarding forms of government, but precisely how much influence is difficult to establish. Adcock and Mosley (1975, 139–40) are skeptical about such ideology, arguing that no city "had such a deeply ingrained faith in its own political system as to lead it to attempt to convert with a missionary zeal others to its ways." We find leading poleis like Athens and Sparta not only "prepared to work with régimes of different complexions" but even occasionally coming to their aid, as Athens did Sparta at the time of the helot revolt of 465 B.C. Adcock and Mosley point out that democracy and oligarchical forms were not completely antithetical and were sometimes mixed in particular constitutions, "as can be seen readily from even a brief glance at Aristotle's *Politics*." Moreover, there were often substantial democratic or oligarchical factions competing for dominance in the same city (Sabin 1991).

Nevertheless, the very existence of ideological factions made subversive meddling in neighboring cities a temptation, and ideological cleavages became more evident during the era of the tyrants and the

---

27. Adcock and Mosley (1975, 137) also suggest that the very nature of city governments, "which lacked bureaucracies and depended upon the ascendancy of politicians and régimes of the moment," tended to favor short-term rather than long-term diplomatic aims. They conclude that "it is surprising that many alliances were as durable as they turned out to be," considering "the multiplicity of states and the nature of their government."

later rivalry between Sparta and Athens that fueled the Peloponnesian War.[28] Lebow (1991, 149) argues that what initially worried Sparta most was not Athenian military power but their fostering throughout the Greek world "material, individualist, and democratic values" that were "rightly seen to threaten the survival of the Spartan way of life." There is some evidence that the Athenians may have encouraged the helot revolt they later agreed to assist in putting down (Powell 1988, 109). In all events, reports Thucydides (I, 102), the Spartans, after first asking the Athenians for help, grew fearful and suspicious of their intentions and sent the Athenian contingent home. This offended the Athenians, and they promptly concluded alliances with two cities hostile to Sparta, Argos and Thessaly.

The second century after the rise of the Spartan Alliance, c. 560 B.C., to the era of Macedonian intervention saw an intermittent military contest between Sparta and Athens eventually broaden into system-wide endemic instability. Argos, in the seventh century, was the first dominant power to appear. The Spartan Alliance ("the Lacedaemoni-ans and their Allies" or the Peloponnesian League) began as a sort of Holy Alliance in reverse, ostensibly aimed at Argos and other tyranni-cal regimes. Sparta arranged it so that pro-Spartan oligarchies came to power. Spartan intervention in 510 B.C. freed the Athenians from the Peisistratid tyranny and inadvertently set the stage for Cleisthenes. In sum, the development of the two leading city polities illustrates how important a role alliances played in Greek politics.

The Spartan Alliance was the earliest Greek example of a hege-monial alliance *(symmachia)*. It was based on a series of loose bilateral treaties that were gradually concluded as the conditions of the moment dictated. More significant than their specific terms were general under-standings that Sparta was preeminent both diplomatically and mili-tarily, and that the hegemon would neither interfere in the affairs of its allies nor make unnecessarily burdensome demands (Adcock and Mosley 1975, 232–33). In fact, Sparta was unusually "vulnerable to the special pleadings of its allies" because of its underdeveloped economy and unbalanced force structure relying on land-based hop-lites. Corinth provided critically needed naval forces and financial

---

28. On the Peloponnesian War, aside from Thucydides' central account, see especially Donald Kagan's monumental four-volume study (1969, 1974, 1981, and 1987) and de Ste. Croix (1972).

support, and it could be argued that the demands of Corinth, Megara, and Aegina dragged Sparta into a war it did not want with Athens (Lebow 1991, 148, 129).[29] Although Spartan policy became more domineering late in the fifth century, the Spartan Alliance "proved to be one of the most durable diplomatic associations in history," lasting with the addition of outside members until 366 B.C. (Adcock and Mosley 1975, 231).

The approach of the Persian Empire precipitated the formation of a Hellenic League around the Spartan Alliance in 480 B.C. (see Burn 1962). Some thirty-one city polities eventually joined, and the League finally won a narrow victory. Fine (1983, 329) suggests the Greeks were then "almost thinking in terms of a Greek nation." Wight (1977, 59) observes that thirty-one "must have been a very small proportion" of all Greek cities, and, in any event, unity rapidly dissolved after the victory, partly because some former allies perceived that Athens was attempting to build its own empire through the Delian League.[30]

Although the Delian League was supposed to seek revenge against the Persians, gain compensatory booty, and possibly free some Greek cities still under Persia, Athens's allies soon found themselves exploited. The rules of the League's decision-making council or Synod theoretically gave each member city one vote,[31] but Athens firmly controlled the votes of numerous minor cities. Athens became dependent on cash from allies to maintain its fleet and fund the state pay extended by Pericles and his successors to lower-class Athenians. In 454–453 B.C. the treasury of the League moved from Delos to Athens. Hammond (1986, 304) comments that the treasury "became a department of Athenian finance" and subsidized the city's building program. About this time, no more formal Synods were convened, and Athens began to refer to its "allies" as "the cities over which the Athenians hold sway" (Meiggs 1972, 171). The number of tribute-paying cities increased from 135 to between 155 and 173. Athenian poor were

---

29. "It speaks volumes for the loose ties that bound the allies that Sparta in the Peace of Nicias of 421 B.C. proceeded alone and afterwards tried in vain to induce her allies to accept it" (Ehrenberg 1969, 114).

30. See Rhodes 1985; Hornblower and Greenstock 1984; Meiggs 1972; Kagan 1987; and Doyle 1986, 54–81.

31. For differing views as to voting arrangements, see de Ste. Croix (1972, 303–7).

dispatched to serve as outposts of empire in *cleruchy* semigarrison settlements throughout the Aegean. The use of Athenian coins, weights, and measures was obligatory, and "a surprising amount of legal activity concerning the affairs of the individual states took place in Athenian courts" (Adcock and Mosley 1975, 238). Athenian warships, in an ancient exercise of gunboat diplomacy, collected arrears in payment of tribute. In 440 B.C. Athens brutally forced Samos into line regarding its conflict with Miletus. Then in 428, during the Peloponnesian War, Mitylene's abortive attempt to leave the League precipitated an Athenian massacre of thousands. As events proved, only the defeat of Athens in the second part of the Peloponnesian War (421–404 B.C.) could end the Empire (Kagan 1987).

The Delian League thus evolved beyond a hegemonial alliance into a full-fledged empire *(arkhe),*[32] which Carlo M. Santoro (1991, 76–77) describes in this instance as "a relationship between a metropolis and a periphery linked to the metropolis by a transnational society based in the metropolis"—"a sort of imperial confederation based on the absolute supremacy of the metropolis (Athens) in terms of wealth, military power, structure of the political system (democratic), and alliance structure." Yet, as Forrest (1991, 29, citing de Ste. Croix) reminds us: The Athenian allies "on the whole were rather happier than sadder to be allies," and we should not accept without qualification Thucydides' gloomy picture of them "being ground down dismally and unhappily under a nasty Athenian iron heel."

What Athens got out of empire is clear, but what were the rewards, if any, for Athens's subjects? An important point is that the tribute *(phoros)* they paid was probably not unduly oppressive. In exchange for tribute and loyalty to Athens, they basked in the glory of the Athenian Empire and received protection against the menace of Persia, relief from the responsibility of organizing their own military defense, fewer incursions from pirates, a boost for trade, and lucrative service as mercenaries under imperial command (Powell 1988, 75–76). How-

---

32. Athens was able to sign the 421 B.C. Peace of Nicias on behalf of its allies and maintained the right to negotiate any revision of it directly with Sparta. When Athens subsequently concluded the One-Hundred Year Alliance with Argos, Mantinea, and Elis, Athens ratified for the entire Empire, while each of the other three parties ratified separately. But in the 404 Peace with Sparta Athens could sign only on its own behalf.

ever, there is more to the story in the realm of identities. The bipolar rivalry had a self-reinforcing impact on "internal" political structures, since Athens and Sparta both tended (albeit not unfailingly) to support democratic and oligarchical factions, respectively, within their spheres of influence. As both blocs became increasingly ideological in character, more appeared to be at stake than simple military victory or defeat (see Powell 1988, 76; and Sabin 1991, 240).

Ultimately, both blocs came to grief—as did their successors—in part, because there never developed in the Greek world any enduring ideological justification for either hegemony or empire beyond their weak association with ancient tribes or constitutional types. Greeks continued to believe that the only *legitimate* rule was one that effectively preserved the freedom *(eleutheria)* and independence *(autonomia)* of individual poleis (see Perlman 1991). Entities that seriously threatened the polis might enjoy for a time effective governance within their domains, but they lacked fundamental legitimacy and never succeeded in establishing an enduring identity.

The half-century following the Peloponnesian War (404–354 B.C.), which Hammond (1986) terms "The Period of Transient Hegemonies," was a complex and unusually turbulent era. Bozeman (1960, 69) observes: "During the eighty-five years that divided the Peloponnesian War from the conquest of Greece by Macedon, fifty-five considerable wars were waged by one Greek state against another. . . . [E]very Greek city experienced at least one war, or one internal revolution, every ten years." The first two decades saw the consolidation of the Spartan Empire—no less autocratic (though not as durable) as the Athenian—with Persian support. By 360 B.C., however, Sparta had lost not only its empire but also half of its nuclear territory, when the helots revolted one last time and successfully established their own polis of Messene. Xenophon attributed this sudden fall to a variety of factors (summarized by Cartledge 1987, 400), including Sparta's "arrogance, greed, and fondness for intervening in the internal affairs of her subjects, with her small number of citizens and lack of clear-cut military superiority by land or by sea" and—the least convincing explanation except to Xenophon and therefore perhaps to the Spartans themselves—divine anger because Sparta had occupied the Theban acropolis in peacetime. Cartledge (1987, 409–10) argues, as well, that the Spartans were tainted by the Persian connection and that the Spartan social compact to minimize differences in lifestyle between rich and poor (in the interest of keeping *stasis* at bay and the helots under control) somehow broke down. In any event, thereafter, Spartan influence declined to the vanishing point, and the proliferation of new major and minor actors across Greece was nothing less than astounding: the Boeotian League under Thebes, the Chalcidian League, a second Athenian Alliance, the Arcadian League, the Aetolian League, a League of the Western Locrians, the Thessalian League, and the Achaean League.

The earlier and more "primitive" ethnos polity now served as one model for relations *among* polities. Various federations of autonomous entities developed, each one of which might previously have been polis or ethnos, but which now accepted a central political and military authority (Snodgrass 1980, 43–44).[33] Snodgrass remarks: "The success of this notion is shown by the fact that the Achaean League of the third century B.C. attracted no less than 60 cities into its orbit, including such distinguished former exponents of the polis idea as Argos, Corinth, Sikyon and Megara." Another example, the Chalcidian League, was founded early in the Peloponnesian War and expanded in the fourth century on the initiative of Olynthus. This city was a "simpolity," an ethnos grouping of settlements that formed a single political entity with a common Olynthian citizenship. The city was also an administrative center of a larger group comprising most of the cities in Chalcidice, with a common Chalcidician citizenship and federal government. The latter had "sovereign" powers in its own realm and controlled coinage, while the member cities of the League retained their own local citizenships (in addition to Chalcidician citizenship) and control over local affairs.

The convulsive transient-hegemonies period in Greece ultimately ushered in the rule of Macedon and "relayering" of the system under the conqueror's auspices. In 362 B.C., during a lull in the fighting, all mainland states except Sparta made a final unsuccessful attempt to revive an all-inclusive League of Cities, with an added collective security dimension. All pledged to remain at peace, to settle disputes by negotiation, and defend one another against aggression. Nevertheless, internecine conflict soon resumed.

Greekwide Institutions: Shrines and Games

In another realm of functional integration and institutionalization beyond the polis, regional amphictionies arose in the Archaic period

---

33. Ehrenberg (1969, 121) notes that the "boundary between a federation of states and a federal state was not always very clear."

to secure the sacred and independent character of worship centers at Delphi, Argos, Delos, Triopium, and elsewhere. Temples were places of sanctuary, which were rarely violated, but Delphi and other leading shrines had additional functions. Delphi was more important than all the others combined. The Delphic Oracle (Pythia) was a woman over fifty who nine days a year, when the god consented, chewed laurel leaves and muttered incoherently in the Temple of Apollo. Petitioners made a generous gift, ritually sacrificed and purified themselves, and then were ushered in to the Oracle. Priests "translated" her pronouncements into suitable verse, and any misinterpretation was the recipient's responsibility. The Oracle could be ambiguous or flat wrong, usually (not always) favored the most powerful petitioner, "leaned to conservatism and had aristocratic sympathies" (Wight 1977, 49), and initially displayed an unpatriotic pro-Persian orientation.

Although the Delphic Oracle sometimes failed to deliver value for offering and was not incorruptible, she was a principal source of legitimacy in Greece from as early as the eighth century. Wight (1977, 48) terms the Oracle "the nearest equivalent in Hellas to the papacy in Christendom."[34] Delphi acquired its early reputation and fortune as the patron of colonization embarking from the far west of Greece to Cyrene in Libya and to the Hellespont. Subsequently, many Greek colonies traced their foundation, however tenuously, to the Oracle. Tyrants, too, sought Delphi's blessing, as later did leading city polities at virtually every critical stage of their evolution. The *promanteia,* right of first consultation, was an important honor for the city that received it. Sparta attributed its dual kingship to Delphi, and each king was represented by two Spartans elected as "Pythii," who sought the oracle's advice and preserved responses (including the Great Rhetra). In Athens, Solon consulted the Oracle prior to his reforms, and each archon and councillor vowed to dedicate a gold statue at Delphi were he to violate a decree of Solon's. In 511–510 B.C. Delphi advocated Sparta's attack on the Peisistratids in Athens, and Cleisthenes' new

---

34. The text compiled by the J.A.C.T. (1984, 98–98) notes that there were many methods of divination throughout the Greek world—"clanging pots, rustling leaves, warbling doves, rushing waters, reflecting mirrors." Then it wryly observes: "We turn to experts in politics, economics and social policy with as little or as much chance of success as Greeks turned to their oracle." Who can gainsay, except perhaps *less* chance of success!

system of tribes and electoral representation also received Delphic approval. Athens decided on a naval strategy to defend against the Persians on the advice of the Oracle, and Sparta gained a fateful pledge of support from Delphi when it was on the brink of launching the Peloponnesian War.

The Greeks tried to ensure Delphi's inviolability and impartiality, even as they were tempted to subvert the Oracle and appropriate Delphi's treasures. (Temples at Delphi and Olympia had the resources to offer loans, but loans were not as attractive as owning the bank.) In the seventh century a small amphictiony at Anthela was transferred to the sanctuary of Apollo at Delphi. The amphictiony then placed the sanctuary under its protection and proclaimed Delphi's independence from neighboring Phocis. In principle, the translated Amphictiony consisted of the twelve tribes of Greece rather than representatives of separate poleis. Some adjustment occurred in actual voting; for example, Athens cast a vote for Ionian colonies and Sicyon had a second Doric vote alongside of Doris. No less than four Sacred Wars were fought over the status of Delphi. The First was in 601 B.C. when the Phocians of Kirrha and Krisa were charged with levying unreasonable fees on pilgrims enroute to Delphi; the two towns were laid waste, and their territory was dedicated to Delphi. Delphi became a political football between Sparta and Athens and acted as an arbiter of peace treaties punctuating their wars. Philip of Macedon led the Fourth Sacred War in 339 B.C. and went on to conquer Thebes and Athens. Delphi thus was present at the creation and demise of the independent city polity in Greece.

As with Delphi, the Greeks attempted to preserve their most important games, which had religious and political overtones. Tyrants sponsored games to enhance the stature of their regimes, and Athens similarly held regular Panathenic festivals after Solon's reforms. Moreover, tyrants and aristocrats who had the requisite courage, physical prowess, and wealth (for dedications and expensive equipment like chariots) participated in games for personal prestige.

We know from a list of victors, which is actually our first record of interpolity significance in Greece, that the Olympic Games were founded in 776 B.C. (Finley and Pleket 1976). They remained the most important of four major events, including the Pythian Games at Delphi, games at Nemea honoring Zeus, and others at Corinth for Poseidon. The choice of the Olympus site was partly because it already had a major shrine, the Temple of Zeus, second only to Delphi's Temple of Apollo. The Olympic temple, too, received a steady stream of thank-offerings and served as a repository of treaties. Religious observances were prominent in the games themselves.

Finley and Pleket (1976, 23) point out that the selection of the agrarian backwater district of Elis for the Olympic Games was also for protection. Games held there would not contribute to the prestige of any powerful host city. In addition, during the festival of Olympian Zeus, the entire area was blanketed by a special truce forbidding the carrying of arms, and polities across Greece granted athletes safe-conduct to attend the games. Occasionally the truce or games were disrupted, but the record to Roman times is one of remarkable continuity.

CONCLUSION: THE DECLINE OF THE POLIS

Why did the ancient Greek world of city polities ultimately succumb to their Macedonian conquerors? The most fundamental explanation is simple: Independent poleis were overwhelmed by a large kingdom with greater resources and, as we have noted, a revolutionary conception of military tactics. Also, the Greeks themselves had become profoundly disillusioned and demoralized. Strauss (1991, 200) observes: "What is striking is not so much fear of Philip—as fear of Persia is striking in 480—as a lack of commitment to the prevailing order in Greece. From enlightened opinion . . . to petty politicians . . . to overtaxed Athenians, many people in the Greek poleis preferred risking a new hegemon to perpetuating the endless wars of fourth-century B.C. Greece."

In some respects, it is surprising that the polis world lasted as long as it did. Peter Burke (1986) is largely correct when he concludes that, as a rule, "city-states" can flourish only in the "interstices" between other major polities. (We would only add that nesting *within* a major polity can sometimes provide almost as much autonomy as genuine independence.) Until the Macedonians came on the scene, the only major outside contender was the Persian Empire, which presented a formidable challenge, but one the Greeks narrowly managed to summon enough unity to beat back. After their stunning victory over the Persians, why did the Greeks not evolve some overarching polity of their own that could have provided adequate protection against other external security threats?

W. G. Runciman (1991, 353–54ff.) suggests that the polis was "an evolutionary dead-end" that was "doomed to extinction" when matched against any major polity that did not have its peculiar characteristics. The first of these was an *ideological* insistence on its independent and autonomous status, which ultimately undermined both hegemony and empire—and any other wider association. As we have seen, overarching polities (for example, the Athenian empire) affecting certain issue domains were important and to some extent institutionalized at particular stages of Greek history. But except perhaps for regimes affecting shrines and games (which had their occasional problems too), no adequate ideological framework to support larger polities on a long-term basis ever evolved. Even in the "federations," comments Runciman, there were "no innovations in constitutional theory, no extension of the criteria of citizenship, no mergers of autonomy within a common Hellenism, no binding alliances, and no ideology of subordination beyond recognition of *de facto* sovereignty and the obvious need to preserve the safety of the *koinonia*."[35]

The second characteristic of Greek city polities mentioned by Runciman was also ideological: Greeks in many cities tolerated oligarchic constitutions but did not condone anything like the concentration of power and wealth in a ruler or ruling class that might have allowed an individual city to achieve lasting domination over its peers.[36] Nor was there any great interest in entrepreneurship and foreign trade. Runciman's apt contrast is between Greek poleis and later Venice. In sum, the Greek city was at once both too militantly parochial and, whatever its "constitution," too essentially egalitarian in spirit. Whatever might be said for localism and citizenship, the polis was unable to overcome the limitations of smallness through its own individual "take-off," sustained peer-polity cooperation, or lasting domination or conquest.

Macedon offered kingship, autocracy, a more generous conception of citizenship, new military tactics, imperial ambitions that extended beyond the traditional Greek homeland—but, most of all, an end to

---

35. Sinclair (1988, 27) observes: "There is no evidence to suggest that . . . the Athenians seriously contemplated as a principle the incorporation in the citizen body of peoples over whom they exercised political power. They thereby denied themselves the opportunities of expansion supported by engaging the active involvement of other peoples in the manner of Philip II."

36. Recall, as well, the earlier discussion of the difficulty of achieving a decisive military victory when tactics favored defense over offense, and the burden that administering distant territories presented for a small Greek city.

bitter internecine warfare. After generations of conflict and facing the apparent bankruptcy of their once pioneering political model, the Greeks finally ended their active resistance to Philip and embraced the future with little more than a sigh of relief.

The decline of Greek city polities and the end of their independence did not, however, dampen the admiration of later generations of practitioners and scholars for their achievements. As we commented at the outset of this case, if Greek city polities lost the struggle with larger political forms, their ideal of independence triumphed, at least in the West. Watson (1992, 315) again:

Reinforced by practice, by the interests of princes and by some of the most effective political theory ever written, the classical Greek legitimacy of independence has continued to exercise a powerful effect on the European system and on the contemporary world, little though a modern "nation-state" is like a Greek polis, and though in fact the nominal multiple independence of the Greek cities was tempered in practice by leagues, hegemonical alliances and a succession of hegemonies and bids for domination of the whole society. . . . The same was true of the European *grande république*.[37]

---

37. The reasons that the Greek experience exercised such a hold on Western political thinking is also succinctly summarized by Bozeman (1960, 60, fn. 3) in an illuminating footnote: "The Greeks occupied this preferred place in our thinking about history because 1) they were by all standards a remarkably creative people; 2) they had a 'modern' sense for history equalled perhaps only by the Chinese; 3) they knew how to convey their history in terms meaningful to posterity; 4) their legacy remained accessible while that of other nations did not; 5) their experiences were directly relevant to history-conscious Western peoples; 6) their 'discovery' was psychologically satisfying because the West could in this way come to an identifiable father and establish a continuity of existence."

7

ANCIENT CHINA
Overlapping Polities in an Imperial Framework

Perhaps it is impossible to do justice to a polity that encompasses what "was once the superior civilization of the world, not only the equal of Rome but far ahead of medieval Europe" (Fairbank 1992, 2). By 2 A.D. China had a population of almost sixty million,[1] more than Rome at its peak. Our analysis of polities would hardly be representative if it did not include the emergence in ancient China of centralized government with a complex bureaucracy staffed by officials chosen on the basis of merit who penetrated deeply into, and thereby controlled, many aspects of Chinese society. Fairbank again: "Our repertoire of social science concepts derived from a pluralistic Western experience seems still inadequate to encompass this early Chinese achievement" (1992, 3).

It is not only because Chinese civilization is the oldest uninterrupted civilization in the world or because modern China is becoming an economic giant and major military power that ancient China merits our attention. More important, if the great heritage of Greek experience and political thought are the ideas of individual autonomy and the

---

Note: The Romanization system for Chinese words and names in Chapters 7 and 8 is that of Wade Giles, "generally considered standard in the English-speaking world for historical purposes" (Fairbank and Reischauer 1989, xi).

1. This figure is based on a Han census that is probably more reliable than most Chinese compilations that were for tax purposes and tended to underestimate population. One of the problems in dealing with pre-Han China is the absence of documentary evidence such as the clay tablets of Mesopotamia or the stone inscriptions of Egypt. In its absence, archaeological finds of oracle bone and bronze inscriptions are key sources (Schwartz 1985, 18–19). Recent finds include oracle bones dating back to between 3000 and 2500 B.C. (Mote 1989, 4).

independence of many small city polities, the heritage of Chinese experience and thought are the ideas of achievement through collective action and responsibility to the collectivity. Order, continuity, and central control, as opposed to change and competition—and the certainty that all who lay beyond China's culture were barbarians—pervaded Chinese political thought and conceptions of empire. "The pivot of China's normative order as it had prevailed on all levels of thought and society until the mid-twentieth century," declares Adda Bozeman (1984, 388), "was belief in the unchanging demands of the heavenly order and determination to maintain this harmony by strict control of human behaviour." In Chinese eyes, their polity was unique—"the abode of civilization writ large rather than as a territorially bounded state, China was deemed to constitute a family of nations" (Bozeman 1984, 388).

INTRODUCTION

Our focus is on the formative age of imperial China including the triumph of the Chou over the Shang, the decline of the Chou that began with a barbarian invasion in 771 B.C., the centuries of struggle known as the Spring and Autumn[2] and Warring States[3] eras, unification under Ch'in, and the changing fortunes of Han. During this period, many of the later features of Chinese politics became apparent, especially the persistent tension between powerful centrifugal and centripetal forces.

The Eastern Chou—so named because of the location of its capital—is regarded as the period during which Chinese civilization surpassed its contemporaries in Asia and the Mediterranean (Rodzinski 1979, 24). The Chou have been described as a "peripheral people with martial qualities and a genius for government who burst in upon a nuclear area in some respects Greek-like, appropriated its esthetic and philosophical achievements, and amalgamated it into their own state and society, thus producing a new stage in the growth of the civiliza-

---

2. The name of the Spring and Autumn period derives from one of the Five Classics of Chinese thought, the *Spring and Autumn Annals (Ch'un ch'iu)* which is a record of events in what is sometimes termed the "statelet" of Lu.

3. This name of this era derives from a history entitled *Intrigues of the Warring States (Chan kuo ts'e)*.

tion" (Mote 1989, 6). Following the collapse of Chou hegemony in northern China, there ensued an extended period of anarchic competition among city polities[4] during which war was endemic, but in which philosophy and the arts flourished. Reunification under the Ch'in was brutal and brief, giving way to renewed turmoil and the Earlier Han.

After some two centuries, the Han Empire itself became the victim of turmoil that lasted some two decades until a descendant of the ruling Han family of Liu restored central control. In a real sense, then, the history of China is a story of struggle between centralizing and decentralizing polities and tendencies, "fragmegration" in Rosenau's sense. It is a story told and retold; extending into the twentieth century as in the effort of the Boxers to expel Europeans, the struggles among the warlords of the 1920s, and the clash between Kuomintang and Communists out of which Mao Tse-tung emerged triumphantly as emperor of a "new" socialist China.

Like medieval Europeans, the traditional Chinese were more conscious of a "society of people" rather than a "society of territory." During the period we are covering, the "frontiers" of cultural China were never identical with the "boundaries" of polities that lay within those frontiers. K. C. Chang has argued that the first three Chinese dynasties—Hsia, Shang, and Chou—may have existed for long periods as "overlapping polities" (cited in Schwartz 1985, 16). A further similarity to European conditions makes the emergence of the Chinese imperial system all the more intriguing. While the highly variegated east Asian topography and climate promoted sufficient differentiation of polities to assure contention among them, the eventual cultural accretion—"unification"—of China is a unique outcome. It contrasts with Western historiographic assumptions attributing Europe's economic and technological achievements to conflicts between divergent cultures which had also "resulted" from diverse geography and climate.

Key Dates

Western Chou 1122–770 B.C.[5]
Eastern Chou 770–256 B.C.

---

4. Chinese city polities were urban and commercial centers usually dominated by a single lineage.

5. An alternate date for the Chou conquest of the Shang is 1111 B.C. (Mote 1989, 7).

Spring and Autumn *(Ch'un-ch'iu)* era 722–481 B.C.
Warring States era 403–221 B.C.
Ch'in 221–206 B.C.
Earlier (Western) Han 202 B.C.–8 A.D.
Hsin (New) Dynasty 8–23 A.D.
Later (Eastern) Han 25–220 A.D.

SYSTEM DISCRETENESS AND STRUCTURE

Geographic Effects

In contrast to the great civilizations of Europe and the Near East, traditional China was isolated from other major power centers by distance and natural obstacles, a fact of enormous import in explaining the Chinese view of the world and their place in it. As a result, culture and technology—for example, the Chinese writing system[6]—were largely indigenous, as were modes of governing and underlying ideologies.

Geography has been a key factor in China's political and economic evolution. China's isolation, especially the plain north of the Yellow River that served as the cradle of Chinese civilization, meant that foreign trade was of little importance. That isolation conditioned early Chinese elites to believe that there was little of value that could be imported from abroad. On one side of the relatively dry and cold plains of the north is the impassable Pacific. On the other lay the mountains and deserts of Central Asia—the Himalayan, Altai, and Pamir ranges, and the Tibetan Plateau. To the north stretch the thinly populated deserts and steppes of Central Asia, and to the south the mountains and jungles of southeast Asia and southwest China.

In contrast to the unifying effects of the Mediterranean and the deserts of Arabia, geography divides China. Two parallel mountain ranges run southwest to northeast, and three additional ranges cut China from west to east, breaking up the country "into a sort of checkerboard" (Reischauer and Fairbank 1960, 19). One of these three divides the area around Canton from the Yangtze and Yellow Rivers—the division of north and south China—and another separates North China from Mongolia.

---

6. Evidence of literacy in China dates back to between 2000 and 1500 B.C. (Mote 1989, 3).

While the Mediterranean inspired expansion by serving as a highway for trade, cultural exchange, and conquest during the Greco-Roman eras, the vast trackless "sea" of the inner-Asian deserts and steppe was the domain of marauding nomads possessing few tangible incentives for conquest other than security-related forays. The lure of foreign trade for Chinese elites was only to increase later, during the growth in Chinese power in the Han era, as China's civilization consolidated and gradually expanded its contacts with peoples on the immediate periphery and beyond. Even then, trade was less a means to prosperity (let alone exploration as in the West) than a source of tribute. The two key trade routes skirted the northern and southern edges of the Tarim River Basin and required crossing the Pamir Mountains. The most important Chinese export was silk, for which the Chinese received horses, ivory, glass, linen, and other items.

The political dominance of both Chou (and the location of their capital Ch'eng-chou), and later Ch'in, derived in part from their location in the Wei Valley (Hsu and Linduff 1988, 68–69, 123). This valley was easily defended, as access from elsewhere in China was only possible through a narrow defile astride the Yellow River. By controlling this passage, the armies of the Chou, Ch'in, and Han were able to move eastward to attack rivals whenever they chose while enjoying security from enemies. The Wei Valley also allowed strategic access to the nomadic peoples living to the northwest and aided the exploitation of rich agricultural regions in the Szechwan Basin to the southwest. As a result, the Ch'in were able to stay abreast of technological developments that aided them in wars with competing polities.

The other key feature of China's geography are its two great rivers, the Yellow and Yangtze. Both flow eastward from the mountains of Central Asia, bringing the fertile silt that is crucial to China's agriculture. But there the resemblance ends. The Yellow River runs across the north China plain depositing huge amounts of silt on its own bed, regularly producing devastating floods (and famines), changing course when it breeches the system of dikes that has been built and rebuilt for centuries to cope with it. Its economic value grew dramatically when the emperor Han Wu-ti constructed a system of canals to move tax grain from East China to his capital at Ch'ang-an. By contrast, the Yangtze to the south, though flooding from time to time, has a deeper channel and is navigable along much of its length. Part of the reason the Ch'in outlasted other warring polities was the economic power gained by building a canal for irrigation and transportation in the Wei Valley in the third century B.C.

Horseback riding figured prominently in both the political centralization of China's imperial systems and, later, in the gradual reduction of China's isolation. Cavalry facilitated communication and transportation and permitted central control of potential competitors and rapid response to social unrest. Horses also permitted the movement of ideas and innovations from India and the Middle East to China during the first millennium A.D. Horses were a source of danger and vulnerability too, threatening China's secure isolation. As China became more vulnerable to incursions by nomadic horsemen during the late Chou, the polities of north China began constructing walls for defense. For the nomadic tribes, mounted warfare was an extension of their hunting vocation, transforming them into "the most natural warriors ever produced by ecological circumstances" (Kierman and Fairbank 1974, 13). Toward the end of the first century A.D., horses were conveying the predecessors of Attila's Huns, the seminomadic Hsiung-nu, toward Europe.

The Chinese were unable to subdue the nomadic peoples of inner Asia and north of the mountain ranges rimming the Yellow River basin until the eighteenth century. An extensive system of walled fortifications, culminating in the 1,400-mile-long Great Wall, reflected a defensive mentality imposed by generations of aggressive frontier nomads. The Great Wall was never intended to serve as a Chinese Maginot Line. Instead, it was to be a sufficient obstacle to slow down marauders and permit the dispatch of defenders to points that were in peril. Of greater consequence in China's political history were the interactive effects of both defending against and assimilating those peripheral actors.

Economic Factors

To the south of the Tsinling Mountains, moist summer monsoon winds bless Chinese agriculture, and to the north China's massif has cold dry winters. Grain and pasture thrive in the north; and intensive rice cultivation, able to support larger populations than European or Near Eastern civilizations (aided by relatively easy water transportation), is the basis of economic life in south China. Cultural China ends further north where rainfall is insufficient to support agriculture and forms a boundary between traditional Chinese civilization and the nomadic tribes beyond.

Fortunately, iron is abundant throughout China, and it was exploited before the fifth century in the manufacture of farm tools and weapons. Francesca Bray (quoted in Schirokauer 1991, 61) observed that Chinese iron plows had attained "a perfection and sophistication . . . achieved nowhere else in the world," featuring struts allowing for control of furrow depth and curved metal mold-boards which reduced friction, and hence the number of draft animals required for cultivation. The use of iron implements may have provided the Chou with economic advantages over the Shang whom they conquered (Hsu and Linduff 1988, 70). The expansion of irrigation and flood control projects, fertilization, field rotation, and transport canals, and the introduction of the iron-tipped plow in north China during the mid-Chou era brought about a dramatic increase in agricultural production (Hucker 1975, 64–65). This increase was a prerequisite for urbanization and the mobilization and maintenance of large armies. Growing food production, along with territorial conquest, produced rapid population growth.

Agriculture has remained the basis of China's economy,[7] but only a small proportion of Chinese land is arable. Consequently, land ownership played an important role in Chinese politics. Intensive rice cultivation south of the Tsinlings was essential to support China's enormous population (as many as sixty million were concentrated mainly in north China during the Han era). Rice cultivation permitted the use of every plot of arable land, which was enriched by the extensive application of night soil. Much of the population was tied to the land, and the ready availability of labor made growing rice, which is a labor-intensive endeavor, feasible. It also meant that the fate of polities and dynasties was closely tied to factors such as ownership of land and natural disaster.

Land hunger was a persistent problem that public policy sometimes exacerbated and, at other times, eased, usually by remission of taxes, resettlement on undeveloped land, or public works like irrigation and canal building. In 7 B.C., the Han emperor sought to equalize landholdings by limiting the maximum available to a single family to about 500 acres (30 ch'ing), but the limit was not enforced. Wang Mang (9–23 A.D.) sought to bring all land under imperial control, break up large estates, and redistribute land to the indigent. He also tried to end slavery. Both efforts failed "because the men called on to enforce the reforms were precisely those most disadvantaged by them" (Hucker 1975, 183).

Poor communications and transport conspired to make much of the Chinese economy local. Typically, peasants lived in village communities, within walking distance of market towns. Merchants regularly visited such towns selling manufactures. Reischauer and Fairbank (1960, 27)

---

7. There is evidence that the Chou were also herders (Hsu and Linduff 1988, 76).

capture the essential implication of this economic pattern: "The fragmented and cellular nature of the traditional village economy enabled it to survive with a high degree of inertia, or persistence, in established channels, in spite of wars, invasions, and great social changes in the cities and administrative centers where history was recorded." Thus, since time immemorial, the peasant village, based on the extended family, has been a basic polity in Chinese political life. Nevertheless, a copper-based system of coinage enhanced commercial activity during the Eastern Chou; and, even earlier, Shang civilization used cowry-shell currency to facilitate trade based on silk, jade, and bronze. During the Han era, rag paper and porcelain were invented, adding new dimensions to China's export trade.

During the brief Ch'in era, road systems built for the army by forced labor also served to reduce community isolation. The requirement that farmers provide the equivalent of a month every year to work on imperial projects like roads and canals had a political as well as economic purpose. The Ch'in unification (Bodde 1986, 52–81) was a period of extensive enforced standardization—for weights and measures, coinage, and even the axle-lengths of wagons and carts so that all vehicles could fit the same ruts in the road. These reforms were especially beneficial to the new merchant class that emerged after the death of Confucius to take advantage of a money economy. Of great significance was the introduction of a standardized system of written characters, providing the basis for communication among people with different spoken dialects and making possible a common cultural community that facilitated political cohesion (Schirokauer 1991, 51).

Two opposing currents dominated imperial economic policy during the Ch'in and Han eras. Some officials were inclined toward direct intervention and control of agricultural and material production, while others held that the "will of heaven or the natural rhythms of the cosmos would let the earth develop her own fullness in the interests of man" (Loewe 1986d, 488). The former view prevailed during prosperous times, and the latter "laissez-faire" pattern, during times of imperial weakness.

Practices and Patterns of Warfare[8]

The evolution of military practices, technology, and organization in early China reflects the problem of extending dynastic control across

---

8. This section draws heavily on Kierman and Fairbank 1974.

time and space and serves as an example of institutional adaptation to unique challenges. Military innovation had to overcome tactical and logistical limitations to governing and making an expanding empire secure. Changing military practices thus exemplify Bozeman's (1960, 143) observation that "understanding is not served by the mere recognition of identities or similarities between different civilizations. It is the historical processes . . . which must be studied if understanding and adjustment are to be attained."

As early as the twelfth century B.C., the "fast-moving chariot, pulled by two or four galloping horses" (Hsu and Linduff 1988, 81) was the decisive weapon. Both the Chou and the Shang whom they conquered had similar war chariots, but the typical Chou "tiger warrior" enjoyed important advantages with bronze armor and swords, and an improved striking halberd. The organization of the Chou army, numbering some three thousand soldiers (mainly infantry) and more than three hundred war chariots provided an additional advantage:

> The burials of the royal guards . . . showed that combat formation consisted of a phalanx of infantry in the front and war chariots with attached foot soldiers in the rear. Five chariots made a squad, and each squad formed one of three columns. The infantry was organized into squads of ten, which were lined up into left, right, and central columns. Three hundred soldiers, therefore, constituted a functionally independent combat unit. . . . Since the war chariot was used as a movable command platform, its combination with the foot soldier was rather flexible. (Hsu and Linduff 1988, 85; also, 77–81)

The Chou triumph over the Shang sometime between 1122 and 1027 B.C. owed much to a strategy that used broken terrain in flanking attacks and involved alliances with strategically located polities such as the Shao and the I that enabled the Chou to surround the domains of the Shang. In all, the Chou forged alliances with as many as eight other polities in its conquest of the Shang (Hsu and Linduff 1988, 91–94).

Chinese civilization crossed the threshold between conflict among irregular groups and formally organized armies sometime early in the Shang era. And the later Ch'in era beginning in 221 B.C. is distinguished from the Warring States period by a new level of military control suited to the scale of empire. During this period, the use of cavalry and the crossbow began; large infantry armies replaced the smaller aristocratic armies of the Chou; and professional generals replaced aristocratic amateurs (Lewis 1990, 5). Warfare during this period often pitted clans against one another in vendettas, reflecting the importance of these units as polities. Lewis summarizes the changes in warfare and military organization of this period and their consequences:

> The shift to reliance on infantry armies pioneered by states at the northern and southern frontiers . . . made possible a tremendous increase in the number of men who could be trained and put into the field. In the competition to mobilize ever larger bodies of men, various states began to claim the services of the populations of their rural hinterlands and the lower social classes, which had hitherto played no political role. These reforms involved the allocation of land—gained through the opening of new territories to cultivation or through conquest—in exchange for the payment of taxes and the provision of labor and military service. (1990, 9)

Ch'in—"where the entire adult male population was registered, ranked, and allocated land on the basis of military service" (Lewis 1990, 9)—took advantage of these changes more than any of its competitors. Unification brought the problems of consolidating empire and the requirement to defend against an emerging threat of nomadic tribal confederacies forming in Central Asia, which were to become an enduring preoccupation. "The First [Ch'in] Emperor. . . . sent armies campaigning northward into Inner Mongolia, where the first great confederation of Altaic-speaking nomads, the Hsiung-nu, was just forming. The Ch'in court was too preoccupied with consolidating its control of China proper however, to pursue a vigorously expansionist policy in the north. It was content to keep the Hsiung-nu out of raiding range, beyond the Great Wall that was coming into being" (Hucker 1975, 45).

By the Han era, the size of armies had grown dramatically. Han Wu-ti's expeditions against the Hsiung-nu featured between 50,000 and 100,000 cavalry with additional infantry and supply trains. Like the Chou, the Han also sought allies, and in 139 B.C. Wu-ti sent an officer named Chang Ch'ien in an unsuccessful effort to forge an alliance against the Hsiung-nu with a people called the Yueh-chih. Another unsuccessful effort, this time to conclude an alliance with a tribe known as the Wu-sun, was undertaken by Chang Ch'ien in 115 B.C. (Reischauer and Fairbank 1960, 99).

To meet military needs, every male in the Han realm had to receive military training for one month every year after the harvest and, thereafter, to serve a year in the militia. In practice, the system broke down, and it "became common for 'substitute money' to be levied on draft-eligible men, with which volunteers—or draftees too poor to pay—were paid for a year or more of duty on the frontiers and even in the capital guards. In Later Han local militias were abolished, no doubt to prevent the local and regional warlordism that nevertheless flourished by the end of the second century A.D." (Hucker 1975, 166).

Han Wu-ti also sought to outflank the Hsiung-nu by occupying parts of northern Korea and southern Manchuria and creating a new commandery (an administrative subunit) from them. Three additional commanderies were created in Korea, and the region became a flourishing center of Han culture. In the west, this flanking effort led to an extension of the Great Wall into the heart of Central Asia all the way to the edge of the Tarim Basin, followed by the colonization of the region. Subsequent Chinese military expeditions even crossed the Pamir Mountains and reached modern Turkestan. In 73 A.D., Pan Cha'ao undertook a major campaign to deal with the Hsiung-nu, using local troops and bribery to supplement his armies. His first attempt failed, but his second brought the entire Tarim Basin under Chinese rule. Some years later, Pao Ch'en crossed the Pamirs and reached the Caspian Sea. After his death in 102 A.D., however, Chinese control of Central Asia again began to erode.

Chinese emperors required three types of forces. Permanent garrisons stationed along China's northern and northwestern frontiers defended against marauding nomads. Additional forces concentrated around the imperial capital were available to put down rebellion or move quickly to threatened frontier zones, and military forces were also used for routine police activities. Great distances and networks of mountains and rivers were impediments to the movement of armies and contributed to a defensive mentality, a mentality that was reflected in the proliferation of walled towns. Herbert Franke (1974, 151) points out: "The importance of walled towns to the power structure in traditional China can hardly be overrated. Domination of the empire as a whole was guaranteed by a network of walled strongholds, whereas . . . control of the vast countryside between towns must have been less strict. The possession of towns has. . . . always been a paramount objective of general strategy."

Great distances favored well-provisioned defenders as much as it inhibited Chinese expansion or Hsiung-nu invasion. Invading armies laying siege to fortified towns or lengths of wall could be starved into capitulation. Prolonged logistical support was usually beyond the capability of besieging nomadic armies.[9] The Han practiced a technique called *chien-pi ch'ing-yeh* ("strengthen the walls and clear the fields") by which "everything which could be of potential value to the enemy should be transported behind the walls" (Franke 1974, 152). Crops were hastily harvested or burned; brush and obstacles cleared to facilitate observation and create open "killing zones"; and wells poisoned. These measures, along with the protection offered in built-up areas, imposed heavy costs on besieging forces.

Polarity and the Tributary System

During the period under consideration, the horizontal distribution of capabilities in China ranged from virtual unipolarity at the height of the Ch'in and Han Empires to anarchic multipolarity during the Warring States era (relieved only in part by a formal hegemonic system). Although the numerous independent polities continued to acknowledge Chou suzerainty, the Royal Chou was actually no more than a tiny polity surrounded and dominated by feudal polities. Even at the height of imperial centralization, however, there were usually internal and external military threats with which Chou emperors had to deal.

China was especially vulnerable to the Hsiung-nu during cycles of civil strife and political decentralization. Military prowess was an essential social and cultural norm among the Hsiung-nu, and limited food supplies and fodder provided incentives to prey on wealthy neighbors. The great Han emperor Wu-ti, known as the "Martial Emperor" after conquering the poorly organized peoples of south China as far as Vietnam, Kweichou, and Yunnan, made a serious effort to bring the Hsiung-nu to heel (Loewe 1986b, 163–70). Wu-ti's wars against the nomads of Central Asia gave the Han control of much of these vast wastelands. By 127 B.C., the Hsiung-nu had been pushed out of the Ordos area in Shensi and were gradually pressed further north to the Gobi. Finally, in 52 B.C., the southern half of the Hsiung-nu submitted to Chinese suzerainty and paid tribute to the Han emperor, while others began to migrate westward (Reischauer and Fairbank 1960, 99; also Yu 1986, 381–405).

---

9. See Loewe 1974, 97 for an analysis of the logistical requirements of Han military operations.

The conduct of relations between a unified China and the relatively weak polities along China's periphery posed different problems than those caused by relations among the relatively equal polities within China in the preimperial multipolar system. Succeeding dynasties differentiated between "internal" and "external" peoples, and among the Chinese there evolved a world view based on the premised existence of nine continents divided into nine regions.[10] The meaning of "All under Heaven" gradually came to connote the emperor's authority as "Son of Heaven," rather than China's natural order, and China itself was increasingly described as "within the seas" (Yu 1986, 378). However, "the Han tributary system never achieved the same degree of stability in the realm of foreign relations as it did internally. The balance of the system hung on a host of factors, such as the rise and fall of various foreign powers, which lay largely beyond Chinese control. The Han success in maintaining a desired world order was . . . at best limited" (Yu 1986, 383).

Tribute requirements were based on a hierarchy of "Five Zones," rooted in the concept of five phases through which *yin* and *yang* interact to bring about changes in the natural order (Loewe 1986d, 690). For tributary purposes, the Five Zones included the "Royal Domain" *(tien-fu)* at the political center, controlled directly by the court and directly serving the needs of the emperor. The second was the "Lord's zone" *(hou-fu)* that consisted of polities established by the king and provided monthly tribute to the center. The "Lord's zone" was surrounded by the "Pacified" or "Guest' zone" *(sui-fu)* that included conquered territory added to the empire and that was required to contribute every third month. Beyond these three interior vassalages lay two types of barbarian regions: a "Controlled zone," consisting of the relatively pliant Man and I peoples who were required to provide annual gifts, and an outermost "Wild zone" from where the autonomous Jung and Ti were expected to send tribute only intermittently.

A marriage treaty system, lasting from the third century to the reign of Wu-ti (141–87 B.C.), seems to have originated at the suggestion of a court official named Liu Ching. Liu negotiated terms of reconciliation with the first great Hsiung-nu Confederation under Mao-tun, as a result of Han defeat at the battle of P'ing-ch'eng in 200–199 B.C. A

---

10. This system was conceived by Tsou Yen (305–240 B.C.).

bride for Mao-tun was part of a tribute "package" settlement, and Liu personally escorted the first treaty bride to Mao-tun's harem in 198 B.C. Mounting annual "requests" for material tribute led to the collapse of such relations, along with matrimonial offerings (Yu 1986, 386-89).

POLITY TYPES

Family and Clan Polities

For much of China's history, the extended family has been the focus of the most intense individual loyalties, and early sources depict a society based on patriarchal clan relations. The family or clan rather than the individual, the city, the church, or any other polity was the essential unit in society. China's ethical system was oriented toward the family rather than a supreme being (as in medieval Christian Europe or Islam) or an encompassing polity (as in ancient Greece). Since the patriarchal family was regarded as the model for and analogous to other polities, there was no distinction made in China between private and public spheres as in Greece, and Chinese thinkers accepted hierarchy as a normal organizing principle for polities. "To Confucius, it is precisely in the family that humans learn those virtues which redeem the society, for the family is precisely the domain within which authority comes to be accepted and exercised not through reliance on physical coercion but through the binding power of religious, moral sentiments based on kinship ties" (Schwartz 1985, 70, also 99–102).

The family, rather than any more-encompassing polity, provided the individual with basic economic and personal security and was the source of social and personal values. Religious ideas, military organization, even agricultural labor mobilized from above tended to revolve around the family (Schwartz 1985, 26), and ancestor worship, reinforced by the concept of heaven or nature (t'ien), dates back to the earliest recorded history (Mote 1989, 5, 17–21; Loewe 1986d, 704–8). Thus, larger polities in China have always had to deal with the nested status of the family. When successful, larger polities utilized ideologies and fashioned policies that took advantage of the central importance of the extended family. The Confucian hierarchy, for example, was built on analogies to family relationships, especially father-son, husband-wife, and younger brother-elder brother. The relationship between ruler and subjects in Confucian eschatology was analogous to the father-son relationship. Submission to the parent (hsiao) was a key virtue, followed by loyalty to the polity and its ruler *(chung)* (Mote 1989, 39).

The family or kinship group extended five generations in each direction (e.g., great-great-grandchildren, third cousins, great-great-grandparents). Relations among family members were typically hierarchical, depending on status as determined by birth and marriage. Age and gender were sources of authority, and the omniscient and omnipotent patriarchal father stood at the apex. The analogy of the father-child relationship was repeated in the context of larger Chinese polities, and "this authoritarian pattern was applied to the whole of society, providing a basis for authority and social order in political as well as domestic life" (Reischauer and Fairbank 1960, 30). Filial piety was at the heart of China's ethical system, and ancestor worship was the basis of rituals designed to reinforce authority. Ancestors in this context were "members of a familial community across the barrier of life and death," and their worship "reflects the extraordinary strength of kinship in ancient Chinese social structure" (Schwartz 1985, 22, 23). Arranged marriages were a source of political power and prosperity, and a means by which kinship "boundaries" could be altered.

During the Chou era, "the Chinese polity consisted of a cluster of city-states, in which each capital city was the political base of a lineage" (Lewis 1990, 243). The "sublineage constituted the basic unit of elite society and was itself a political entity and a potential state, so the ruler of an actual state was only *primus inter pares* in the collegial authority of the aristocracy" (Lewis 1990, 13), and the role of this entity was legitimated by ancestor worship. Constant war eroded most of these powerful families, as their lands were conquered and divided and redivided, and led to the territorial expansion of a few city polities. Mark Edward Lewis argues that this process "entailed a transformation of the basic units of society, including a redefinition of the nature of kin ties and the creation of a new 'public' realm outside the networks defined by common descent, shared ancestral cult, and blood covenants" (1990, 9). Loyalties to a variety of crisscrossing authority patterns, sealed by blood covenants, became common. Benjamin I. Schwartz observes: "Over the course of the centuries . . . the covenants also came to play the key role in forming alliances between several lineages, between lineages and alien states, and between the various contestants for supremacy in the state, and the capital populace" (1990, 44).

As Chou authority eroded, "the basic unit of society became the individual household . . . grouped into units of five for purposes of military recruitment, mutual surveillance, and collective responsibility for crimes'' (Lewis 1990, 13, 244). By atomizing society this way, the families that ruled the surviving polities, especially Ch'in, concentrated power in their hands and reduced the likelihood that family loyalties would compete with loyalty to them. These rulers also surrounded themselves with officials drawn from defeated lineages and from all classes who swore loyalty with blood oaths and who were dependent on the rulers alone. And, with the triumph of Ch'in, Heaven became a more powerful source of legitimacy than a ruler's lineage.

"Warring States"

Whatever the pretensions of early Chinese dynasties, they actually governed relatively small territorial entities. The earliest dynasty for which there is historical evidence, the Shang, ruled a small city in north China which probably controlled agrarian settlements on the surrounding plain and found itself in periodic conflict with similar cities. The Chou who conquered the Shang had come from the west and settled near the present city of Sian. The Chou adult male population is estimated at between only sixty and seventy thousand with an army of some three hundred chariots (Hsu and Linduff 1988, 69). Although Chou influence extended across much of north China, technology was insufficient to prevent local autonomy, and small polities—walled cities and their environs—in the eastern territories that acknowledged Chou suzerainty retained independence under vassal lords.

Some of these lords were Shang descendants; others were relatives of the Chou rulers; and still others were Chou military commanders who became "localized." By the eighth century B.C., there may have been as many as two hundred such polities within the boundaries of the Chou domain (Reischauer and Fairbank 1960, 50). In general, there was a self-conscious distinction between the older sinecized polities in the cultural core of the central plain and the "semibarbarian" polities along the peripheries (Schwartz 1985, 18).

Chou hegemony ended in 771 B.C. when an alliance of nomadic tribes and rebel cities destroyed its capital, Hao. The weakened dynastic heirs reestablished themselves in the city of Loyang which was less vulnerable to nomadic incursions. However, the dynasty never again enjoyed widespread political influence and, until its extinction in 256 B.C., controlled fewer subjects and less territory than many of its vassal polities. The dynasty was permitted to survive in order to

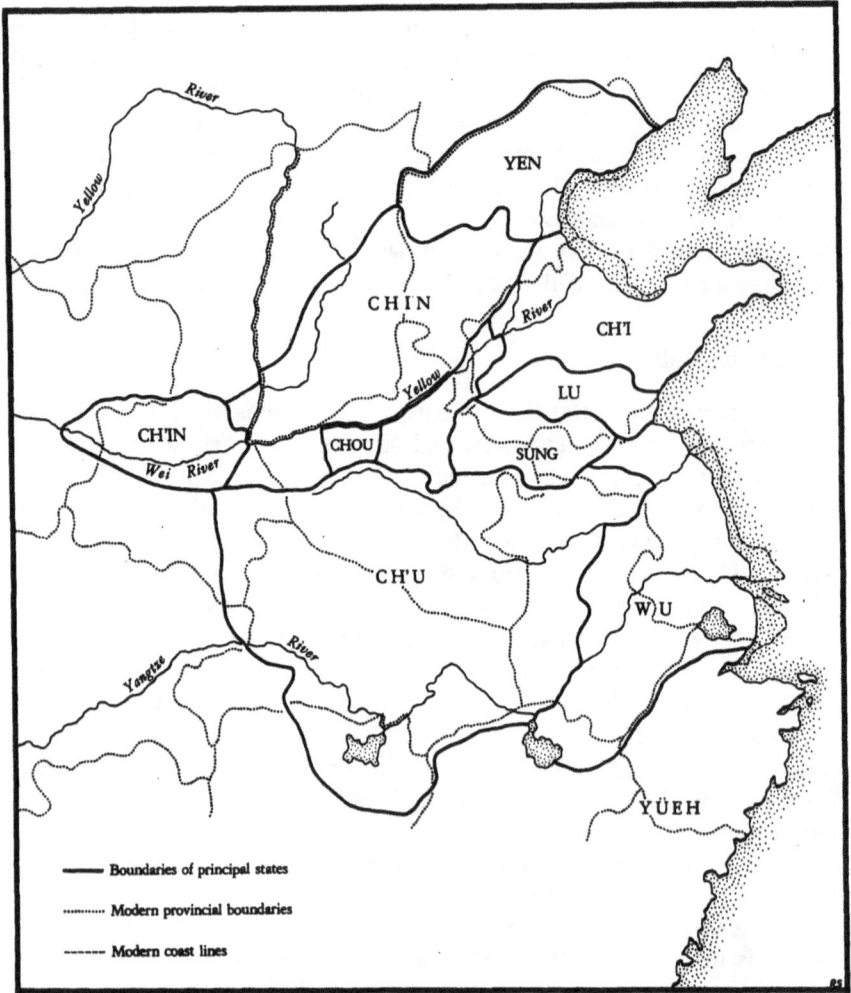

China in the Sixth Century B.C.
John K. Fairbank and Edwin O. Reischauer. *China: Tradition and Transformation,* Revised Edition. Copyright © 1989 by Houghton Mifflin Company. Reprinted with permission.

maintain the myth of Chinese unity and because polities found it convenient to prevent any one of them from achieving dominance. The Eastern Chou is looked upon as an era of political decentralization in China when the situation was mostly one of competitive polities.

The decline of the Eastern Chou left numerous competing polities in control of the north China Plain—some ten to fifteen by the eighth century B.C. Some, like Lu and Sung, dominated the others. These centrally located polities provided the Chinese-language term for "China" *(Chung-kuo)* (Sun-Tzu 1993, 3). Gradually, competitors were brought into the orbit of a few polities located at the periphery of cultural China. It was at the periphery, in polities like Ch'i on the Shantung Peninsula, that economic and technological advances made their greatest impact. It was also at the periphery that assimilated nomadic "barbarians" provided polities with expansive energy. Thus, Ch'i increased its territorial expanse dramatically during the seventh and eighth centuries and augmented its political capacity by instituting a uniform tax system, dividing the territory into geographic and functional units that had to provide troops for the army, regulating weights and measures, and instituting salt and iron monopolies. The government obtained additional resources by taxing agriculture, built political support by permitting private ownership of land, and increased administrative efficiency by relying on professional bureaucrats (Bodde 1986, 34–38). Dennis and Ching Ping Bloodworth (1976, 4) capture what was happening: "The central authority of the [Chou] dynasty was progressively sapped, and the realm split into fifteen rival feudal states fringed and patched with many minor fiefs, so that the map looked like a motley of papal Italy familiar to Machiavelli. Few paid more than lip service to their royal pope, the Chou 'Son of Heaven,' and with his frightened formal consent the buffer states rose in succession to establish their hegemony over the rich Central Plain that was the heart of 'All under Heaven.' "

Along with Ch'i, competitors for power included Chin in present Shansi, Ch'in in the western Wei Valley, Yen in southern Manchuria, Ch'u in the middle Yangtze Valley, Wu in the lower Yangtze, and Yueh still further south along the coast. Chin was itself partitioned among three clans in 453 B.C.—Han, Wei and Chao—and their recognition by the Chou in 403 B.C. marks the onset of the Warring States period. Any pretense that China remained unified under the Chou was dropped in 880 B.C. when the Ch'u rulers, and later the rulers Wu and Yueh, started referring to themselves as "kings" *(wang)*. Several polities, such as Ch'u and Wu, were dominated by peoples who originated outside of China's core cultural area, which expanded as these became more powerful. Whatever their origins, the rulers of the contending polities claimed legitimacy based on (often false) descent from the Chou and emphasized the importance of tradition, ancestor worship, and civilized forms. By the fourth and third centuries B.C., however,

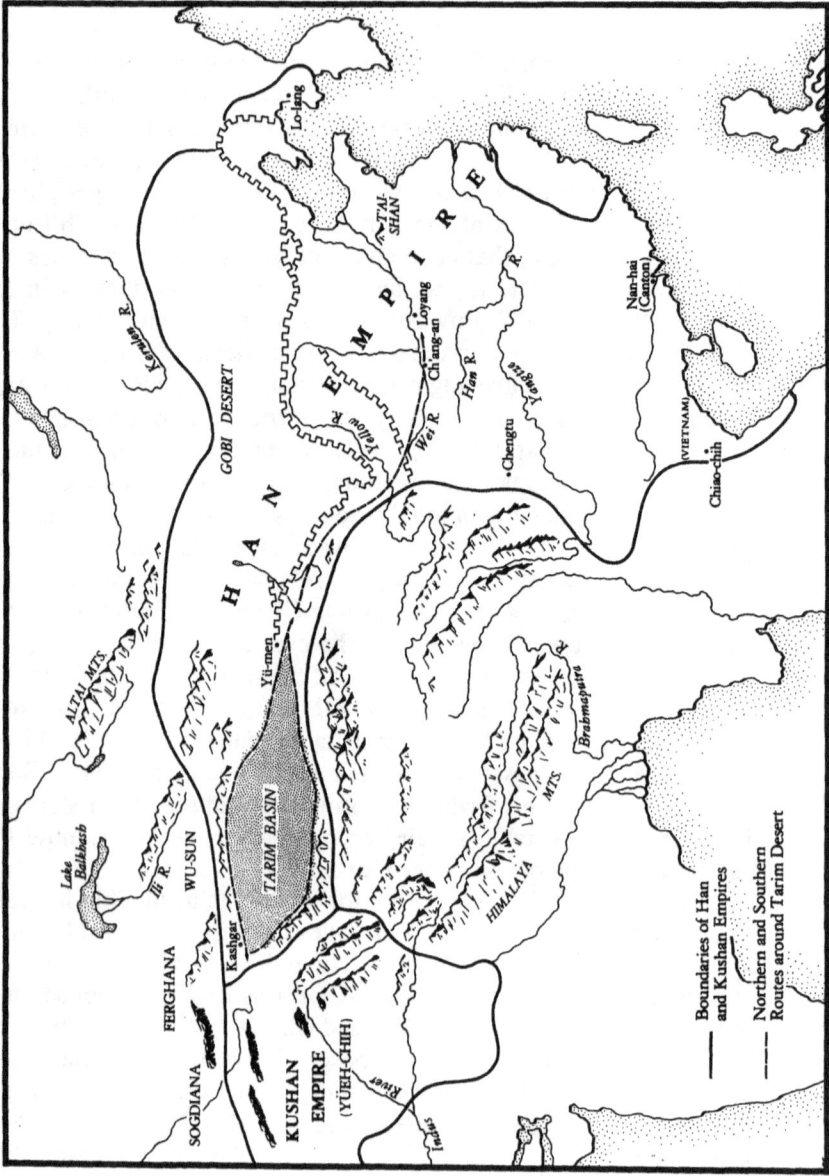

The Han Empire
John K. Fairbank and Edwin O. Reischauer. *China: Tradition and Transformation*, Revised Edition. Copyright © 1989 by Houghton Mifflin Company. Reprinted with permission.

less effort was made to observe the proprieties, and warfare became less restrained. Rulers increasingly referred to themselves as "kings"; conquered polities were extinguished; and pitched battles among peasant armies, assisted by chariots and cavalry, became common. It was during this turbulent period that the most widely studied work on military strategy—Sun Tzu's *The Art of Warfare*—was written.[11]

Relations among the warring parties increasingly resembled the "anarchic" European system of the Thirty Years' War as enshrined in the power-politics tradition.[12] Marriages among clans and the use of hostages to secure alliances, efforts to achieve disarmament, and diplomatic conferences all characterized the Chinese system in this period. Even a rudimentary consciousness of the idea of balance-of-power was apparent. The small polities of the early Eastern Chou period sought to build alliances to protect themselves from the predatory policies of the southern polity of Ch'u. From time to time, during the sixth century B.C., there even existed a formal balancing of power between Chin in the north and Ch'u in the south.

A novel approach to instability was adopted in 651 B.C. at the suggestion of the Ch'i minister Kuan Chung when several small polities, including Chou, met and designated the Ch'i ruler Duke Huan as hegemon or lord protector *(pa)* of their confederation (Hucker 1975, 36; Mote 1989, 104–5; Schwartz 1985, 57). In 632 Duke Wen of Chin became *pa*. "For a time in the seventh century," argues Schirokauer (1991, 29), "the inherent instability of a multistate system was remedied by the formation of a league headed by a strongman *(ba, pa)* and sanctioned by the Zhou court, but unlike the Japanese shogunate of much later times, this arrangement never developed into an institutionalized system." The hegemonic system arose from a belief that the stability of China's multipolar system required a political and military balance that could be reinforced by affirming the myth of the rulership and legitimacy of the powerless Chou kings. In this way, at least the theory of Chinese unity and the continuity of authentic rulership could

---

11. "Sun-tzu," meaning "Master Sun," was the title given to Sun Wu from the state of Wu who was probably a contemporary of Confucius.

12. As in Europe, the competition among autonomous polities was accompanied by a strengthening of "domestic" organization involving officials *(shih)*, probably from the nobility, with clearly differentiated and specialized functions (Schwartz 1985, 57–58).

be maintained. The hegemonic system lost its reason for existence when King Chuang of Ch'u became the third hegemon. It became largely irrelevant when Wu emerged in 482 as China's leading military power, and was in turn defeated and annexed by Yueh nine years later. As described by Reischauer and Fairbank (1960, 62): "With the extermination of the great state of Wu and the assumption of the role of hegemon by Yueh, the southernmost and most 'barbarian' of the Chinese states, the attempt to prevent radical change and halt 'barbarian' domination through the system of hegemony was reduced to its ultimate futility."

Thereafter began a period of ferocious warfare as remaining polities sought to eliminate one another. In 453 B.C., Chin was partitioned, leaving Ch'i, Ch'in, and Ch'u as contenders. In 334, Ch'u destroyed and occupied Yueh. In 286, Ch'i annexed Sung. Owing to military skill and organization, Ch'in (which gave its name to "China") proved the ultimate winner, formally ending the Chou dynasty by occupying that polity in 256 and conquering the remaining independent polities between 230 and 221 B.C. (Bodde 1986, 40–53).

Empire

Notwithstanding the variety of polities that took root in China, a strong sense of cultural unity developed at an early date (Schwartz 1985, 16–39). The Chinese regarded their civilization as superior to others, a continuation of the Shang belief that the central Yellow River Valley was "the center of the Civilized world" (Hsu and Linduff 1988, 99). "The term *t'ien-hsia,* meaning 'all under heaven,' was also applied by the early Chinese to the civilized world known to them, and in time it came to mean 'the empire' "[13] (Reischauer and Fairbank 1960, 37; Hucker 1975, 55), and *t'ien* appears in early Chou oracle inscriptions. King Wu, one of the first in the Chou dynasty, had a "grandiose plan to govern the civilized world of his day . . . from the Central Kingdom in the old Shang domain." His attitude "reflects the assumption that the Chinese world should be drawn together and integrated by the Chou," a mission he undertook "because he received a Mandate from

---

13. The use of the term *empire* to apply to China does not, as in the case of many other applications of the concept, refer to the relations between the polity and those living beyond its boundaries (Mote 1989, 112).

Heaven, bestowed on him because he occupied the Central Kingdom"
(Hsu and Linduff 1988, 96–97).[14]

Just as Arabic fostered the cultural unity of medieval Islam, so the
unity of China—even in the absence of central political control—grew
out of a common written language. Written characters (pictographs
and ideographs) that exist to the present day have been found on
artifacts originating in the semimythical Shang era of the second
millennium B.C. Reischauer and Fairbank (1960, 39–40) capture the
crucial role that this factor played: "It was very much as if the Arabic-
speaking inhabitants of Egypt and Iraq were able to recognize in
hieroglyphics or cuneiform the same language they now use. . . . The
Chinese have always felt a complete cultural and racial identity with
the ancient inhabitants of their land . . . They have good reason to feel
a greater degree of affinity with the people of Shang than we feel for
the ancient Romans and Greeks."

Historically, only a small number of elites had the ability to
write complex Chinese characters. Regional differences among spoken
Chinese dialects have always been so great as to inhibit unity; and, in
the absence of the unifying force of writing, it is hard to imagine that a
common sense of "Chinese" identity would have evolved. Its existence meant that literate Chinese everywhere, however divided politically, always fostered the myth of unity and were prepared to follow
those with an ability to make the myth real. Emphasis on the written
word further reinforced unity because it was translated into respect for
a core of classic texts that educated Chinese esteemed and sought to
master. However, the difficulty in mastering the language and its
calligraphy meant that the skill was a key element in assuring the
perpetuation of a stable social hierarchy. Thus, the written language
unified geographically remote regions while creating barriers between
different social classes.

Indeed, the myth of a single unified kingdom governed by sage-
kings took root early and persisted even through periods of anarchic
localism. It was thought that the creator P'an-ku was succeeded by
three series of brothers—the Three Huang—representing heaven,
earth, and mankind, and these were succeeded by the Five Ti. "These

---

14. The inscription on a vessel unearthed at Pao-chi in 1965 (the "*Ho tsun
vessel*") provides evidence of the evolution of the idea of the Mandate of
Heaven early in the Chou era (Hsu and Linduff 1988, 96–101).

mythical sovereigns, together with some lesser figures, were culture heroes, that is, the magical individuals, who were credited with having provided the basic elements of civilization known to the early Chinese" (Reischauer and Fairbank 1960, 38). In a sense, then, China's history reflects a constant effort to make the political frontiers of the dominant polity identical to China's cultural frontiers, a congruence that rarely existed.

The cultural and political unity of China gradually was expressed in the idea that a ruler enjoyed the Mandate of Heaven, that is, the consent and good will of the governed. After conquering the Shang, the Chou referred to themselves as "Son of Heaven" and claimed they held the Mandate of Heaven *(t'ien-ming)*. "What strikes one first of all is the extreme anxiety of the spokesmen of the new dynasty to identify with the political and religious system of their predecessors" (Schwartz 1985, 46). The Confucian philosopher and teacher Mencius (Meng-tzu) (372–289 B.C.) seized upon and adapted this justification to explain the central role of ethical behavior and benevolence by a ruler toward his subjects. Mencius argued that a true king had to be beloved by his subjects, and that they would do so only if they prospered under his rule. A king's acceptability to his subjects represented the Mandate of Heaven; his overthrow reflected the withdrawal of the mandate. Since Heaven favored no particular dynasty, the doctrine was double-edged, as Hucker (1975, 55) explains:

> The Duke of Chou understood, and emphasized to the young king for whom he acted as regent, the double-edged implications of the new doctrine. Chou could not retain its primacy, he warned, unless the kings conscientiously ruled in such fashion as to remain in Heaven's good graces, and to do that they must rule fairly and benevolently. Thenceforth no Chinese ruler was invulnerable to challenge, and any challenger proved the validity of his claim merely by succeeding. . . . The doctrine of the Mandate of Heaven . . . remained thereafter the cornerstone of all Chinese political theory.

Nomadic Tribes

Nomadic tribes, ethnically similar but linguistically different from the Chinese, represented another form of polity. Called by the Chinese Hsiung-nu, these nomads spoke a Turkish dialect. Horses provided them with mobility and allowed them to adapt to the grasslands of the northern steppe that could not support the sort of intensive agriculture which evolved in China's Yellow River basin. And even as China was being united, a tribal federation of Hsiung-nu in the third-century B.C. was exercising authority over a vast tract across Mongolia from western Manchuria to the edge of the Pamir Mountains in Turkestan. This federation appears to have had an emperor with a title similar to the Chinese "Son of Heaven" (Reischauer and Fairbank 1960, 94–95).

Hsiung-nu mobility posed a permanent threat along the frontiers of cultural China. In response, the Chinese erected walls during the late Chou, and introduced cavalry into Chinese armies, replacing the chariots that had previously been the mainstay of Chinese armies but that mounted nomads easily outmaneuvered. At their peak, the Hsiung-nu could put as many as 300,000 mounted archers in the field. Chinese rebels might get assistance from nomadic raiders and in turn could provide them with intelligence and technical information. In addition to passive defenses, the Han emperors sought to pacify the frontier by combining offensive military operations with incentives like marriage to imperial princesses.

A comparison of Hsiung-nu and Han forces by an adviser to Wen-ti (180–157 B.C.) conveys the dynamic of their encounters. The Hsiung-nu, he argued, enjoyed three advantages: Chinese horses were inferior to Hsiung-nu breeds; Hsiung-nu archery skills were greater as a result of practice in hunting and herding; and the Hsiung-nu were a hardier people, able to tolerate adverse climate and little food longer than the Han. The "mobility of the nomads was an asset not only in attack but also in defense for, traveling lightly with their flocks and tents, they could elude Chinese military expeditions and avoid complete destruction or permanent control, even when the Chinese were able to mobilize their superior resources in manpower and wealth" (Schirokauer 1991, 59). While Hsiung-nu fighting skills were an extension of their daily lives, "military service for a Chinese peasant required that he interrupt the normal pattern of his life, leave his work, and undergo special training" (Schirokauer 1991, 59). However, the Han were said to enjoy five advantages:

> Given flat ground, their light cavalry could throw the Hsiung-nu mass into confusion; their strong crossbows and long halberds could strike at a distance and the Hsiung-nu found them irresistible; equipped with stout armour, sharp swords . . . and crossbows, the Chinese servicemen could advance in formations of five to ten men which the Hsiung-nu could not confront; they

could concentrate volleys of arrows on a target in a way that the leather or wooden protection of the Hsiung-nu could not withstand; and finally, the Hsiung-nu were no match for the Chinese when fighting dismounted at close quarters. (Loewe 1974, 100–101)

CONCLUSION

The relative isolation in which early Chinese polities and civilization developed meant that a "Chinese" identity and loyalty to the ideal of a united China were rarely at issue. Nevertheless, the aspiration toward unity often flew in the face of the reality of disunity and civil strife. As Adam Watson (1992, 85) observes: "The monumental Chinese achievement in the field of statecraft is usually held to be the more or less effective imperial unity that has assured domestic peace and order for most of Chinese history. But for five and a half crucial and creative centuries China consisted of a number of genuinely independent states." System polarity and the changing relationship among major polity types—lineages, village polities, city polities, tribes, and empire—were both consequence and cause of innovations in technology and military tactics, and economic growth; but all contestants agreed in principle that China constituted a single and superior cultural entity. Historical myth, language, and custom all reinforced the ideal of unity and maintained it even in the face of political and military turmoil. In this sense, there was great continuity in ancient China. In a broader sense, however, the power of the center in China waxed and waned dramatically. In the next chapter, we will examine some of the factors that contributed to or undermined political unity, especially the role of religion and philosophy as sources of legitimacy.

8

THE MANDATE OF HEAVEN
Authority in Ancient China

Turning to factors that reinforced or undermined the centralization of authority in ancient China, we must pay special attention to the ideologies that evolved to legitimize different polities. On one hand, the ideas of historical continuity and political unity received lip service and supported the ideal of an imperial polity even during eras of turmoil when there was no real central authority. On the other hand, the influence of other polities remained great even during periods of despotic rule from an imperial center. What Michael Mann calls ideological power (1986b, 46–48) featured importantly in China.

INTRODUCTION

The theme of history as a cycle of order and chaos—despotic central authority and anarchic decentralization—is standard fare in Chinese historiography and philosophy. Each dynasty is described as beginning when a small and dynamic elite seizes power from corrupt rulers. After eliminating rivals, the new dynasty initiates an era of peace and prosperity. For a time, the country seems blessed by fiscal stability, plentiful grain, and a growing population. In time, however, rulers are again corrupted; and their arrogance and poor judgment are revealed in massive expenditures on showy projects, a bloated bureaucracy, a growing imperial court living in luxury, and wasteful foreign military campaigns.

To support their profligate ways, rulers increase taxes on the peasants who are forced into pauperism or flee to the tax-exempt lands of nobles where they become serfs. In time, the tax base shrinks; taxes on remaining peasants are increased; and resentment is fanned in the countryside. Financial crises ensue, sometimes relieved by temporary reforms. Schisms at court widen; factions form within the imperial family; and these seek allies within and outside the palace. Financial crises prevent completion of necessary public works like repairing dikes and canals; and this, combined with the effects of the growing tax burden, produces famine. Banditry and peasant uprisings then spread; pressures grow on overstretched frontier garrisons; and provincial armies and officials cease obeying the center (Reischauer and Fairbank 1960, 116–18). For the Chinese, then, history is a repetitive story in which eras of expansive strength follow periods of debilitating weakness and penetration from without.

FROM EMPIRE TO EMPIRE

The Chou Empire actually embraced little of China, and the primacy of the Chou kings gave way to the decentralization of warring polities. Former Chou domains, especially on the periphery, emerged as key actors, and they amassed greater economic and military power than the Chou king, whose influence was gradually limited to the immediate vicinity of his capital city. However, as we have seen, the intense rivalry of the warring polities was eased, at least for a time, by "the hegemon (pa), which gave to the Spring and Autumn era much of its unique quality." In Hucker's words: "This was a device to offset the ineffectiveness of the Chou kings without challenging their sovereignty. It originated in reaction to the aggressiveness of Ch'u against the small states of the central plain in the 680's. The threatened central states turned for protection to Ch'i in Shantung" (1975, 36).

A new imperial order began to take shape after 318 B.C. with Ch'in's triumph over the combined forces of Chao, Wei, Han, Ch'i and Yen, and its victory in 312 B.C. over Ch'u. In 256 B.C., Ch'in eliminated its predecessor, Chou. China's reunification was accomplished by the king of Ch'in who assumed the throne in 246 B.C. Between 230 and 221 B.C., Ch'in ended the autonomy of its rivals, and the King of Ch'in adopted the title of "First Emperor" (Shih Huang-ti).[1]

The Mandate of Heaven was lost by the Ch'in dynasty after the death of the First Emperor in 210 B.C. By Legalist theory, which, as we shall see, so influenced Ch'in, individual rulers should not have mattered, and the machinery of government should not have missed a beat. The reality was quite different. Initially, the emperor's death was

---

1. Reischauer and Fairbank (1960, 87) point out that this title was formed by combining words that had previously referred to deities and the mythical founding sage-emperors.

concealed, and his heir and leading general, Meng T'ien, were purged by the chief eunuch, Chao Kao, and the emperor's chief lieutenant, Li Ssu. Chao Kao then managed to eliminate Li Ssu and the Second Emperor who was still a juvenile. A military rebellion engulfed China in 209. With no legitimate Ch'in successor, the dynasty disappeared three years later as its armies collapsed before the most powerful of the military rebels, Hsiang Yu. The Ch'in capital fell to Liu Pang, one of Hsiang Yu's generals (Bodde 1986, 81–90).

Ch'in rulers lost the Mandate of Heaven by a combination of bad luck and brutal policies (Bodde 1986, 85–90). Its successor, the Han Empire, survived until 8 A.D., collapsed briefly when a usurper seized the throne, and then was renewed in 23 A.D. under a descendant of the Han emperors. Later Han lasted for two more centuries. Together Earlier Han and the Later Han were contempories of the Roman Empire and represented one of the apogees of Chinese civilization.

Earlier Han "bequeathed to China an ideal and a concept of empire that survived basically intact for two thousand years" (Loewe 1986c, 103). Its power peaked during the reign of the Emperor Han Wu-ti (141–87 B.C.). Ruling through palace advisers, Wu-ti largely ignored established bureaucratic procedures, made extensive use of criminal labor for construction and war, administered the law with vigor, and extended imperial borders. This activity produced a need for additional revenues, which were obtained by purchasing grain in times of plenty and selling it in times of shortage, and by reinstituting imperial monopolies for profitable commodities like salt and iron. Wu-ti's reforms provided stability for several decades until the flight of peasants to the untaxed lands of large landowners forced the government to overtax the remaining peasants who predictably fled or resisted (Loewe 1986b, 152–63, also 198–222).

To halt the deterioration of the empire, Wang Mang (8–23 A.D.) seized power, claiming that he wished to return China to its pre-Ch'in Confucian origins (Bielenstein 1986b, 223–31). Although he made Confucianism the official ideology of the empire, his methods actually reflected a harsher Legalist bent (Bielenstein 1986b, 232-40). To overcome the fiscal crisis, Wang Mang debased the currency, provided peasants with agricultural loans, and used the practice of storing grain in fat times and selling it when supplies dropped. He also tried to expropriate and redistribute the tax-free lands of the large landowners in order to add land to the tax lists and end the flight of peasants to these lands where they became virtual serfs. The government was too enfeebled and resistance of the landowners too great to carry out this reform, and it was rescinded a few years later.

If anything, Wang Mang's efforts hastened the center's collapse. Poor harvests and flooding that caused famine, and the resistance of powerful landed interests led to an epidemic of armed rebellion that included both secret societies and wealthy landowners who claimed to be the rightful heirs to the mantle of Han. Simultaneously, the Hsiung-nu attacked the empire from without. Following the death of Wang Mang in battle with the Hsiung-nu, a wealthy landowner and descendant of the Han rulers named Liu Hsiu (later called Kuang Wu Ti) assumed the throne, thereby inaugurating the Later Han era (Bielenstein 1986b, 240–56).

In more than thirty years on the throne (25–57 A.D.), Liu Hsiu succeeded in getting imperial finances in order and re-creating a powerful center. Northern Vietnam and south China were reconquered, and, under Liu's successor, a major effort was made to deal with the nomads of Central Asia. But fiscal stability was tenuous at best because Han rulers were unwilling to challenge the untaxed status of hereditary landowners. This meant that it was impossible to increase tax revenues except by placing greater burdens on peasants. And, as that burden grew, more and more peasants fled to large estates or became bandits.

The decline of the dynasty was hastened by bloody struggles for power between the imperial bureaucracy and the court eunuchs (Bielenstein 1986b, 287–90) that were followed by rebellions in east China and Szechwan. While these sapped the strength of the dynasty, its collapse was actually precipitated by its own generals who were also members of the landowning class. Widespread rebellion made the generals *de facto* rulers of the districts in which they were stationed. In 189 A.D. one general purged the court eunuchs, and the next year another looted the capital city. Gradually a process began by which the realm was divided among three principal generals, a process that was complete by 220 A.D. (Loewe 1986b, 291–316; Beck 1986, 317–76).

IMPERIAL EXPANSION AND NESTED POLITIES

With their triumph, Chou and, later, Ch'in authorities confronted the dilemmas of all imperial systems. As the empire swallowed up smaller polities, it did not completely digest them. Problems of control and obedience multiplied as one moved away from the center; and, as we have seen (and will again later), there were difficulties enough *within* the center. The Chou sought to co-opt those whom they conquered, using the carrot with the stick. A Shang prince was even employed to govern the old Shang capital region. The Chou simultaneously moved "large numbers of the formerly powerful Shang to new locations" and used them as officials in local governments. In this way, the Chou were able to keep their former foes under surveillance and make use "of their special skills of writing and familiarity with ritual" (Hsu and Linduff 1988, 112, 117).

The Chou also made use of a ready-made corps of skilled workers and professionals like scribes and historians. In constructing their capital at Ch'eng-chou, the Chou used Shang aristocrats to manage the labor force and Shang rituals to bless their new city (Hsu and Linduff 1988, 124). In contrast, the Ch'in employed the severe norms of Legalism to deal with divided loyalties, and, though severity facilitated unification, it also hastened the dynasty's rapid collapse. Ch'in officials imposed tight control over cultural and economic life, mobilized peasants for construction, and instituted the first genuinely centralized administration in China's history. The First Emperor, King Cheng, ruled for thirty-six years. He built countless palaces and took innumerable "inspection tours." His tomb, discovered near Sian in 1974, contained more than seven thousand life-size sculptures of horses and warriors. Mote declares: "The use of the terms 'Chinese empire' and 'Imperial China,' . . . starting with the Ch'in unification in 221 B.C., indicates a new era in the structure and the manner of domestic politics and designates in a general way the political life of China in the two millennia of that era" (1989, 112).

Family identities, as noted earlier, remained potent in imperial China. The shift from ancestor worship to the universalism of Heaven under the Chou was gradual, retaining patriarchal authority and stressing ancestral protection (Hsu and Linduff 1988, 102). Confucian virtues were a direct extension of the ideal of filial piety. The Five Relationships on which the political and social hierarchies were based comprised five pivotal personal relationships. Foremost was the dominance of father over son, which was regarded as higher than loyalty to the ruler. In descending order, the others were that of ruler over minister, husband over wife, elder over younger brother, and relationships among friends. The Ch'in sought to weaken the authority of the extended family and the obstacle that divided loyalties would pose to the throne. Believing that nuclear families would be easier to govern, taxes were doubled on households with more than two adult sons.

The village, too, remained an important polity in imperial China.

The Confucian bureaucracy that Ch'in built and that played a key role in sustaining Han rulers left the economic and political life of China's innumerable agrarian villages largely untouched. Han officialdom cared little about regulating the lives of peasants as long as they paid taxes and did not threaten the stability of the center. This relatively relaxed attitude was reciprocated by the villagers' lack of concern about events at the center.

Pre-Ch'in city polities and ruling lineages also remained objects of elite loyalties. For this reason, after the collapse of Ch'in, Hsiang Yu, assuming the title of Hegemon, gave the imperial title to a member of the royal house of Ch'u and divided imperial domains among the heirs of other royal houses. It proved impossible, however, to turn back the clock because the Ch'in had so thoroughly extirpated the old order, and, in short order, Hsiang Yu and Liu Pang found themselves struggling for the throne. In 202 B.C., Liu Pang defeated his rival, set up his capital in Ch'ang-an, and called his dynasty Han (Loewe 1986c, 110–19).[2] After his death, Liu Pang became known as Kao Tsu ("High Progenitor").

When Wang Mang assumed the throne, he, too, sought to reward his supporters by conferring ancient noble titles and restoring the rights and powers of the old Chou nobility. As part of his effort to reinvent feudal practices, he also reaffirmed the ancient claim that all land belonged to the emperor. In the end, these and other policies alienated all social classes and groups, including the Hsiung-nu who proceeded to renounce their vassalage to the empire (Hucker 1975, 129, and Bielenstein 1986b, 223–90).

SOURCES OF IMPERIAL COHESION

A tradition of authoritarian centralization predated the establishment in China of any large imperial polity. That tradition was compatible with the customs of the patriarchal family and with the military technology of Shang China, which featured bronze metallurgy. Fear of nomadic invasions and, as in Mesopotamia, the need to coordinate irrigation and flood control efforts, along with the power-projecting mobility of horse-mounted cavalry, may also have encouraged authoritarianism.

---

2. Liu Pang had been declared King of Han (named after the Han River) by Hsiang Yu four years earlier

Shang and Chou societies resembled what we think of as feudalism in that a legally omnipotent ruler sat atop a hierarchy in which a class of hereditary aristocratic warriors governed a larger class of peasants (and some slaves). However, Reischauer and Fairbank caution against drawing too close an analogy between ancient China's socioeconomic organization and Western feudalism, arguing that China's system lacked the "complex contractual and legal concepts" associated with Western and Japanese history and might better be regarded as "simply an extension of tribal-type organization in which effective control, both in the Chou realm as a whole and in its component states, depended more on bonds of blood relationship than on feudal legal principles" (1960, 52; also, Schwartz 1985, 42–44).

Chou kings in no way resembled the authoritarian despots of the Ch'in era. Their authority, like those of other members of the aristocratic elite, rested on family lineage; and they were merely regarded as "first among equals" (Lewis 1990, 33). Chou rulers sought to enhance their legitimacy, initially by giving some fifty strategically located fiefs to members of their clan and relatives by marriage and an additional twenty to allies. Beyond these 70 or so vassal polities, there may have been as many as two hundred other local lords who were confirmed in control of their territories. Most of these were so small and unimportant that their names scarcely appear in historical sources, and their number steadily diminished. By the eighth century B.C. the total number of independent polities may have been about 150, of which 25 were relatively important (Mote 1989, 7).

The brief Ch'in era was characterized by rigid centralization and standardization, accomplished and maintained by coercion and ideology. The Chou practice of dividing the territorial fruits of victory among members of the ruling family and their friends ended. Feudal fiefs were replaced by political units called commanderies (chun) that were jointly governed by civil and military governors, who, in turn, were overseen by traveling censors. The initial thirty-six commanderies grew to forty-two and were subdivided into counties (hsien). County magistrates supposedly were direct representatives of the emperor (Hucker 1975, 53). The feudal elite, already weakened by changes in the nature of warfare, was no longer a factor in politics.

While maintaining intact the essential elements of Ch'in administration, Han emperors eased some of the harshness of Ch'in policies and restored some elements of Chou feudalism. They reduced taxes and the demand for forced labor, and resorted to harsh punishment less frequently. Autonomous vassal polities were permitted, especially those in remote regions that could communicate and interact with the center only episodically. In such regions imperial vassals were responsible for governing themselves and collecting taxes. As in Rome, such a system also seemed a way to assure the loyalty of generals and imperial relatives. Newly added territories were laboratories in which to test different administrative practices, as imperial officials wrestled with novel problems involved in extending authority further from the center. Officials in such areas, with populations not yet imbued with Chinese culture, faced challenges in taxing, conscripting, and policing.

Territories were either governed as fully subject commandaries *(chun),* or somewhat more federated kingdoms *(kuo).* The latter initially had considerable autonomy. Local rulers selected their own officials to govern in organizations patterned after imperial institutions. In 145 B.C., however, this discretion was withdrawn, and senior appointments were henceforth made from the center, not only in order to exert greater control over the activities of kings, but also to change the order of succession to local thrones and so tie their loyalty to the imperial court. Although this policy prevented regional challengers from emerging, it ultimately failed because it also left the provinces without "any effective authority." Administrative units were poorly linked, thereby making it difficult to coordinate military forces. In Michael Loewe's (1986c, 111) words: "The imperial regime had forfeited such advantages as might lie in a system of fiefs without acquiring the strength of a fully organized central system."

The Ch'in era was a brief transitional period, and by the time it ended, a number of principles were firmly established. Hucker (1975, 55–56) summarizes these as follows:

1. The Chinese world should be united under a single Son of Heaven, and his control should be effectively centralized.
2. In order to govern well, rulers need and should heed capable, wise ministerial advisers. . . .
3. Government exists to provide peace and order. . . . From the early Chou decades there existed a clear, forcefully stated and reiterated concept that Heaven willed mankind to live together in harmonious cooperation and in harmony with the cosmic universe. It was the responsibility of the Son of Heaven to see that such a condition was achieved.
4. Government should be humane and paternalistic, giving a high priority to fostering the welfare of the people. . . .
5. The scope of government was all-encompassing. . . .

IMPERIAL-MILITARY RELATIONS

Although ideology and religion reinforced and sustained an imperial model in early China, political unification under Chou and Ch'in was fostered and later maintained by force of arms. As in many imperial polities, one crucial dilemma confronting the center was how to delegate the command of military forces stationed in peripheral areas while retaining their allegiance. One answer was absorbing peripheral peoples, including conquerors, into Chinese civilization while utilizing the technological and ideational innovations they brought with them.

Chinese officials actually had less of a problem with the growth of alternate power centers at the periphery than did, for instance, Roman and Islamic officials. Martial virtues were never admired in China to the extent they were in other imperial settings. The Legalist and Confucian ideal of an able ruler was one who, "as the highest product of self-cultivation, should be able to attain his ends without violence"; "resort to violence was an admission that [the emperor] had failed in his own conduct as sage pursuing the art of government" (Fairbank 1974, 7). In dealing with the Hsiung-nu, Chinese officials preferred to co-opt and bribe, especially during times of weakness; and force was used only after other stratagems had failed. Although war was frequent, the military caste did not acquire the sort of prestige and social status that would have threatened imperial rule (Fairbank 1974, 1–26). Instead, the subordination of military institutions to imperial officials in early China reflects belief in an hierarchical ethic as critical to dynastic stability and survival.

Han genius for imperial organization included centralized government's manufacture and distribution of the accoutrement of war. Everything from the breeding of horses to the production of weapons and body armor contributed to the institutionalization of imperial rule. "The same agencies turned out arrowheads of various types, as well as the precision-made trigger mechanisms which formed an essential part of the crossbows with which Han soldiers were armed. Crossbows were made in standard grades which were measured by the pressure required to be exerted on the bow" (Loewe 1974, 98).

RITUAL, RELIGION, AND PHILOSOPHY:
THE IDEOLOGICAL SANCTION

From the earliest times, ritual and religion functioned to provide legitimacy for Chinese polities. What was uniquely Chinese is that no external creator or supreme being was part of that religion or the process of political legitimation.[3] Religion—mainly ancestor worship, and divination and shamanism—sanctified the clan, and larger polities invariably drew sustenance from philosophies that were constructed on clan-based analogies.

Perhaps the most effective use of ritual and religion involved the Mandate of Heaven. The Chou used the idea to legitimize their conquest of the Shang and create a sense of political continuity in a time of instability. The Chou argued that theirs was the Central Kingdom, an extension of the earlier Shang claim that they were at the physical center of the universe (Mote 1989, 5). Heaven was the supreme authority, with a Chamber of Heaven that overlooked the earth.[4] The Chou proclaimed that the Mandate of Heaven passed on from the Shang to them as a result of Shang improprieties—ignoring tradition, employing thieves, and so forth. "Dynasty founders who received the Mandate of Heaven are depicted by the ancient historian as men of extraordinary ability. . . . Those unworthy of the mandate are depicted as libertines" (Bielenstein 1986a, 259). Ancient inscriptions suggest that the first Chou king personally conducted Shang rituals to legitimize his rule. Hsu and Linduff (1988, 100) reconstruct what took place:

> The conquest of Shang was symbolically proclaimed by the Chou not as a hostile act against the Shang, but rather as a pledge to

---

3. An exception was the ideas of Mo-tzu (early fifth century B.C.) who, rejecting the secularism and fatalism of the Confucian *ju*, started from a premise that there existed a supreme being and anthropomorphic gods and spirits who enforced moral behavior through punishments and rewards. The will of Heaven worked through a ruler who has rescued his egoistic subjects from an anarchic and brutal state of nature. Mo-tzu associated morality with material benefit and profit, and denounced war, music, and art because they were wasteful and did not narrowly contribute material benefits. So popular was Mohist philosophy for a time that for "a period of perhaps two centuries, the Mohist organization flourished throughout many parts of China as 'states within the states' of late Chou . . . Within the Mohist organization, the leader's rules prevailed regardless of the laws of the state" (Mote 1989, 81). For an elaboration of Mo-tzu's beliefs and the relationship between Mohism and Legalism, see Schwartz 1985, 135–72 and 329.

4. There may have existed an actual place known as the Chamber of Heaven where Chou ceremonies honoring Heaven were held. However, the evidence on this point is murky (Hsu and Linduff 1988, 98–99).

continue the Shang level of domination over the world of the Chinese. Moreover, their commitment was countenanced by Heaven. . . . The Chou had accomplished the nearly impossible task of allying and uniting the semi-independent and independent powers of north China. The small armed force that they controlled directly was not strong enough to hold the vast territory by force. Part of their solution was to maintain the ties established by the Shang and to legitimate them through moral decree.

The Mandate of Heaven provided the Chou and later dynasties with the "moral decree" they needed. Its effect was to replace pantheism and shamanism with a powerful abstract and universal principle. Both the Shang and the Chou had to "include" guardians of tribes over which they sought to rule. When the Chou defeated the Shang whom they had earlier served and to whom they were linked by marriage, they did not wish to appear to be usurpers. Instead, they sought to depict themselves as having succeeded the Shang because of their own right conduct.[5] In sum, the development of the Mandate of Heaven under the Chou was a critical source of legitimacy (and restraint) on all Chinese dynasties. As the idea took form under the Chou: "God had not committed his will to a single ruling house. God . . . took the Mandate away from the vicious and gave it to the worthy and virtuous. Principles are rewarded before personalities" (Hsu and Linduff 1988, 104). Hsu and Linduff summarize the ideological importance of the concept:

The showdown between the Shang and Chou brought to the fore a profound question: Why had such a drastic change occurred? In the effort to answer that question, a fundamental change in thinking emerged. Justification of their own cause allowed the Chou to moralize—first about the will of God, and then about the new ideology of the Mandate of Heaven reflected in the will of man. . . . The Chou contribution provided the cornerstone for their own political legitimacy, but it also opened the course for the long Chinese tradition of humanism and rationalism. (1988, 111)

---

5. A number of Chou-era poems suggest this preference. See Legge 1970, 428–510.

Reacting to Ch'in excesses, new precepts of imperial authority evolved during four hundred years of Han rule. Gradually, it became necessary to legitimize rulership by reference to the will of Heaven and the phasing of the natural order. During the Han era, a desire to explain and legitimize the devolution of the Mandate of Heaven from the Ch'in led to the growing popularity of correlative cosmology. This took the form of claiming a correlation between five elements—wood, fire, earth, metal, and water—and the cyclical patterns of history. The crucial selection of a patron element, identifying a dynasty's place in the universal order and relation to past rulers, was complicated by the existence of several interpretations of phase sequences. Loewe (1986a, 738) observes: "When Former Han adopted earth in 104 B.C., it was conforming to the theory that one phase of existence came into being by supplanting or conquering its predecessor. . . . However, subsequent decisions . . . were based on the belief that the phases succeeded one another not by means of conquest, but as a result of natural growth."

By this theory, the dominant element under the earliest emperor had been earth; under the Hsia, it had been wood; under the Shang, metal; and under the Chou, fire. A new dynasty, then, would necessarily be dominated by the principle of water, and in conformity with yin/yang it would presumably be the antithesis of what went before. As Schwartz (1985, 379) puts it, "after the excessive overdevelopment of the machinery of culture under the Chou, the dominant principle of the Han dynasty—the true successor of Chou—ought to be that of austere simplicity." Each phase was, it was believed, correlated with other phenomena like particular norms, colors, and types of human behavior. If the human order were out of phase with the natural order, there would be disorder in human affairs until a new cycle began. Rulers liked correlative theory because, unlike the Mandate of Heaven, it afforded prediction and prescribed how they should behave (Schwartz 1985, 362).

As all this suggests, philosophy played a powerful sanctioning role in China. The political instability of the middle and late Chou, an epoch of great change and growing wealth, produced an outpouring of philosophy, much of which was concerned with the place of human beings in society.[6] Many of the principal Chinese philosophers of

---

6. So abundant was the proliferation of philosophies during the late Chou that the period is referred to as The Hundred Schools era.

the time, like Machiavelli in Renaissance Italy, were also political practitioners and professional bureaucrats—for example, Kuan Chung, chief minister of Ch'i and founder of the hegemon system of the seventh century B.C. (Bloodworth and Bloodworth 1976, 5–8). In China, a combination of veneration for the written language (calligraphy) and for the past magnified the influence of philosophers.

As a result of social and political change, "the educated man" (*ju*) was highly prized and esteemed; and, with the decline of Chou feudalism, the *ju* and their talents increasingly replaced the Chou aristocracy in providing public service. Their opportunity was made greater by the instability of the late Chou.

> The old aristocracy was losing its prerogatives, especially those of automatic right to officeholding in the national and local governments. There were new and great opportunities for upward mobility: The competition among the states to succeed in economic development, warfare, and diplomacy offered a broad market for talent, a market that was not stuffy about social background (Mote 1989, 32–33).

The *ju* were heirs to a tradition of shamanism in which holy men advised rulers, and only gradually did their semireligious role acquire secular and ethical functions. In Mote's words: "The wise man's command of written records had replaced the holy man's ability to summon the spirits" (1989, 28). The *ju* oversaw rituals with the spirits of the ancestors of the Chou rulers, observed the seasons and proclaimed the calendar, and made known historical precedents. Mote again: "Thus, they filled the purely bureaucratic functions of recorders, advisors, and technical experts on government. In all of the roles of the *ju* it was their wisdom and their command of specialized book learning that gave them their competence" (1989, 29; also, Kramers 1986, 747-49). Owing partly to *ju* expertise and ability, the Chou were able to retain the prerogatives of rulership five hundred years after they had surrendered real power to neighboring polities. And, as the *ju* came to reflect Confucian principles, rulers eagerly sought them for their talent and loyalty.

During the first century of the Han era, a sustained effort was made to recover the classics of Chinese philosophy, many of which had been destroyed or banned by the Ch'in. Han philosophers and historians were unable to distinguish between original and altered versions of the classics and between historical fact and fiction, and they assumed that China had always been united under the Mandate of Heaven. One consequence was the evolution of highly eclectic ideas drawn from a variety of classical traditions that included cosmology and omen lore.

Confucianism

The most powerful and durable Chinese political philosophy was inherited from Confucius (K'ung-fu-tzu) who lived from 551 to 479 B.C. Confucius was a citizen of Lu in the southwestern part of Shantung, a polity that prided itself on remaining loyal to Chou ideals. Although he never achieved the immediate political influence he sought, his teachings became the basis of the most prominent school *(chia)* of thought in Chinese history. His ideas were almost entirely humanistic and practical (Schwartz 1985, 117–27), and proved a potent formula for imperial unity and stability based on conservatism and continuity, a strong sense of ethics, and an emphasis on problem solving. Confucian ethics contributed not only to personal satisfaction but also to public well-being.

Confucius began by expressing veneration for the past, especially the peace of the early Chou (Schwartz 1985, 63–67), the need for continuity with it, and the importance of social responsibility (Kramers 1986, 747–50). In his view, nature was based on moral order, and political affairs must reflect that order. His ideas took root in part because Chinese politicians were searching for a legitimizing ideology suitable for a period of instability and rapid political, social, and technological changes—many of which Confucius feared and disliked because they seemed the antithesis of the normative order that had previously existed. Confucius succeeded in raising the status of teacher-scholars, reinforcing the tradition of learning (especially history) as a prerequisite for public service and virtue, and breaking down the social rigidity of the decaying feudal system (Mote 1989, 33–35; Schwartz 1985, 85–99).

Later philosophers, most importantly Mencius (Meng-tzu) (390–305 B.C.), kept Confucianism alive and revised some of its tenets (Mote 1989, 46–54; Schwartz 1985, 257–90). Mencius argued that human beings were born with an innate propensity to behave morally and that all had the potential to develop Confucian virtues, but that the way to do so was by education rather than Taoist meditation. Human passions and society were corrupting without the cultivation of Confucian virtues. Recognizing that claims arising from the general interest often degenerate into the pursuit of private interests, Mencius denounced utilitarian logic and argued instead for the pursuit of virtue as an end in itself. Writing at a time of political upheaval and war, Mencius used the doctrine of rectification of names that is described below to challenge rulers to behave in "kingly" fashion. Failure to do so justified rebellion and the loss of the Mandate of Heaven.

The ideas of Mencius were disputed by his fellow Confucian, Hsun-tzu (298–238 B.C.), who along with Mencius helped set the stage for using specialized Confucian education to train scholar-administrators (Mote 1989, 54–58; Schwartz 1985, 290–320). Hsun-tzu, himself an experienced regional administrator, argued that human beings, far from having an innate propensity to do good, were naturally evil. He was confident, however, that formal education in the classics with competent and righteous teachers could overcome the defects in human nature. Unlike Mencius, Hsun-tzu believed in strong government and the use of rewards and punishments, though, like other Confucians, he accepted the premise that government existed to serve the people rather than vice versa. His assumptions about human nature led him to place special emphasis on *li*—the roles, rituals, and ceremonies that reinforce right conduct by force of repetition and habit. Among his students were the politician Li Ssu (Chaliand 1994, 245–284) and the philosopher Han Fei-tzu, who deserted their mentor and became contributors to the Legalist tradition in Ch'in.

The reason for authorities' attraction to Confucianism was its emphasis on the proper roles of individuals in society and the stability of the social and political hierarchy (Hall and Ames 1987, 152–56). Individual behavior should conform to role and rank, and what something was called should conform to reality (Schwartz 1985, 91–94; Hansen 1983, 77). This idea, known as "the rectification of names" *(cheng ming),* is described by Mote (1989, 44): "A discrepancy between name and reality was . . . evidence of breakdown at the top. . . . A name implied content; when it was lacking, it was evidence of a human deficiency. . . . Restore the content, and thereby restore order. . . . That is, the name 'king' implies the content of one who is morally worthy and politically effective because his words and deeds are all kingly."

For Confucius, what justified the social pyramid and the exalted position of those atop it was the virtue of rulers and elites and the contentment of the masses. Order existed when the names *king, minister, father,* and *son* accurately reflected the reality of ethical relationships. All authority—including inherited dynastic authority—could, he believed, only survive on a firm moral foundation, which in turn legitimized the rule of those in power. The trust of those who are ruled is the most important characteristic of good goverment, more important than food or weapons. The ideal ruler was a "superior man" or "person of nobility" *(chun-tzu)*, that is, a cultured and virtuous individual who was a genuine social being. Mencius, even more than Confucius, emphasized the ethical basis of legitimacy; rule by conquest or force, he believed, must be ephemeral. By contrast, good government by virtuous and wise rulers creates a good society and enables commoners to be virtuous.

What were the virtues of a Confucian ruler? They were love (concern for others) or goodness *(jen)*,[7] integrity or intelligence *(chih)*, courage *(yung)*, righteousness *(i)*, loyalty *(chung)*, altruism *(shu)*, culture *(wen)*, and propriety or an understanding of etiquette and ritual *(li)* (Ch'en Ch'i-yun 1986, 788; Fingarette 1972, 7–8). Talent and virtue, not inheritance, were the essence of Confucian legitimacy. Writing of Wang Mang, Hucker declares:

Carried to its logical extreme, Confucianism lends support to the Platonic notion that government properly belongs in the hands of philosopher-kings. Wang Mang's accession is understandable only in the light of this intellectual climate, since he had no military base or following. Originally an obscure provincial member of a powerful family that had repeatedly married its women to Liu-family emperors and princes, Wang gained public attention as a paragon of filial piety, humanitarianism, and other Confucian virtues and as a generous patron of Confucian scholarship. (1975, 128–29; also Ch'en Ch'i-yun 1986, 767–79)

For Confucius, human virtues and relationships were the bases of good government and, by contrast, dependence on laws necessarily implied coercion that was to be avoided (Mote 1989, 42).

The emphasis on ritual, manners, and deportment in Confucian thought reflected a belief that external forms could produce, or at least reinforce, virtue and that observing ritual was a bond with antiquity that could provide added legitimacy. Ritual or *li* governed all relationships between the living and between the living and the deceased (Loewe 1986c, 706–8). Ritual facilitated moderation and compromise and rubbed

---

7. For a discussion of *jen*, see Schwartz 1985, 75–85.

the hard edges off extreme views. Schwartz captures the importance of *li* when he declares: "What makes *li* the cement of the entire normative sociopolitical order is that it largely involves the behavior of persons related to each other in terms of role, status, rank, and position within a structured society. . . . The Chinese commentaries stress again and again the function of *li* in teaching human beings to perform their *separate* roles well in a society whose harmony is maintained by the fact that everyone plays his part as he should within the larger whole" (1985, 67, 68). Thus, *li* is much more than mere ceremony; "it is a sociopolitical order in the full sense of the term, involving hierarchies, authority, and power" (Schwartz 1985, 68).

Those ideas in Confucianism that appealed to the uneducated survived best; and gradually during the Han era a synthetic Confucianism took root in China. The dominant philosophy incorporated ideas from Legalism and Taoism and permeated Chinese life alongside of ancestor worship and animism, and the dualism of yin and yang.

Taoism *(tao-chia)*

Unlike Confucians, Taoists like Chuang Tzu, who also emerged during the late Chou, denounced authority, hierarchy, and the ornaments of civilization and saw little value in Confucian ethics and ritual. In the words of Reischauer and Fairbank: "It was in large part a philosophy of protest—the rebellion of the common man against the growing despotism of his rulers, and the rebellion of the very uncommon man of intellect or sensitivity against the growing rigidity of moralists, who were following in the footsteps of Confucius" (1960, 72). Taoism's emphasis on individual freedom had little appeal for China's rulers, but it nonetheless served the needs of authorities. Although Taoism was a protest philosophy, it was a passive sort of protest, encouraging quietism *(wu-wei)* in its followers and providing an apolitical avenue for those who were not part of the Confucian ruling class.[8] A successful Taoist ruler presumably would be impartial, and would remain aloof from subjects and not intervene in their lives (Schwartz 1985, 212).

Taoism placed the independent individual rather than society at

---

8. The major Taoist texts from the Chou era are the *Lao-tzu* or *Tao te ching*, the *Chuang-tzu*, and the *Lieh-tzu*.

the apex of its value system and sought to teach individuals how to live in conformity with the natural order *(tao)*. Taoism, argues Mote, "has urged egocentric individualism as persuasively for some as Confucianism has stressed the development of the individual through proper performance of his role within the social system for the rest" (1989, 60). The mystic nature of Taoist beliefs suggests they may be linked to pre-Confucian religious traditions. The Tao or Way is best expressed as the natural processes of the universe to which man is subject, and Taoists sought to make their lives compatible with these processes ("doing nothing") rather than resisting them or seeking to change or harness them. In this sense, Taoism was antithetical to Confucian emphases on ethics, law, and ritual.

Taoism was a leveling philosophy that dismissed the gradations in rank, wealth, and privilege endorsed by Confucianism and Confucian law. Knowledge—the object of Confucian respect—was viewed by Taoists as a source of corruption. Instead, Taoists praised the putative tabula rasa of the infant. From these beliefs emerged the Taoist conception of a utopian polity as a "small settlement with few inhabitants" from which the cocks and dogs of nearby settlements could be heard, but whose people were so contented that none had bothered to visit these neighboring settlements (cited in Schwartz 1985, 212).[9] In other words, in apparent contradiction to the Machiavellian element in Taoism,[10] Taoists also seemed to recommend withdrawal from the danger of politics in a dangerous age and emphasized simplicity in order to attain harmony with nature.

Taoist ideas made their way into the ruling elite and became part of the ideology of rulership that came to be known as Imperial Confucianism. Thus, *The Art of Rulership,* which is a chapter in an anthology presented to the court of Han Wu-ti sometime around 140 B.C., "advocates a synthesis between reliance upon universal laws and the ruler's godlike power of transformation. This notion of 'godlike

---

9. This characterization of the Taoist utopia is similar to Jean-Jacques Rousseau's description of an ideal polity.

10. Some observers have interpreted Taoism as "Machiavellian political advice in mystical verbiage." "One empties the people's minds in order to make them docile instruments of the ruler's policies. . . . The large state's policy of winning over small states by kindness and humility is nothing more than a more subtle brand of imperialism" (Schwartz 1985, 213–14).

transformation' *(shen hua)* is decidedly Taoist in tone" (Ames 1983, 62). At the other extreme, there were militant Taoist cults like the Red Eyebrows that rose up against Wang Mang, and the Yellow Turbans and Five Pecks of Rice that fought imperial rule late in the second century A.D.

Legalism *(fa-chia)*[11]

If Confucian ideas saw the nesting of elements from earlier polities as the way to assure continuity and, therefore, political stability, Legalist theory advocated extirpating the nested remnants of earlier polities and the loyalties and identities associated with them. The most authoritarian and ruthless Chinese philosophers and those least concerned with conventional ethics were the Legalists, notably Han Fei-tzu (the great synthesizer of Legalist ideas) and Li Ssu. Like Hsun-tzu, the Legalists believed that human beings were innately selfish and could only be motivated by pleasure and pain. Like Taoists, Legalists believed that nature was amoral. In their view, only negative conditioning provided by harsh punishments and strict but clear laws *(fa)* and administrative methods *(shu)*, buttressed by force *(shih)*, could assure obedience and provide order.

Impersonal rewards and punishments, not virtue and ethics, the goodness of individuals, or charisma, were necessary for a ruler to survive; and subjects, including officials, should be held strictly accountable for fulfilling their obligations. Describing the Legalist statesman-philosopher Shang Yang (Lord Shang), Schirokauer argues: "He emphasized that people should be controlled by the two handles of punishments and rewards. Given the proper legal system, the ruler will not have to do anything and yet will be all powerful" (1991, 47). Confucianists, though also advocates of stability, believed that Legalist reliance on impersonal law was misguided. As Schwartz poses the difference: "In Confucianism we do have a vision in which the agency of living persons (albeit the agency of a vanguard elite) plays a dominant role in shaping society. Individual humans may achieve the highest norms of sociopolitical order or they may effectively outwit it. In Legalism we will have a vision of a society in which 'objective' mechanisms of 'behavioral' control become automatic instruments for achieving well-defined sociopolitical goals" (1985, 328).

---

11. For a discussion of *fa*, see Schwartz 1985, 321–23.

Legalist theory was put into practice by Shang Yang who was influential in Ch'in between 361 and 338 B.C. (Bodde 1986, 34–40). "He is said," according to Reischauer and Fairbank, "to have instituted a strict system of rewards and punishments in Ch'in, forced all persons into 'productive' occupations, set up a system of mutual responsibility and spying among the people, and attempted to replace the old hereditary families by a new, purely honorary aristocracy based on military exploits" (1960, 86). Another of his "reforms" was to centralize and standardize rule in Ch'in territories by replacing existing local subdivisions with prefectures, each governed by a Ch'in-appointed prefect *(ling)*.[12] In this way, Shang Yang eliminated large hereditary territories that might have become sources of opposition to, or competition with, the center. Thereafter, Han Fei-tzu[13] became the leading theorist of Legalism, and Li Ssu its leading practitioner.

The Legalists sought to aid rulers to consolidate personal power and build a strong military establishment. They argued that the word of the ruler should be law and that subjects should have no rights beyond those designated by the ruler (Schirokauer 1991, 56). All policies should aim at increasing the military power of the polity, especially improvement of agriculture and war. Agriculture, Shang Yang argued, was the basis of wealth. Believing that tax revenues would flow directly to the center if individual peasants owned the land, Shang Yang did away with Ch'in's system of communal land ownership (Reischauer and Fairbank 1960, 84; and Schwartz 1985, 332).

Legalism was less a sophisticated philosophical system than an enumeration of principles of rulership. It has few ideological premises and was justified by its advocates on the basis of its accomplishments. Legalists were concerned with stability in a time of turmoil and viewed ethics as a superfluous impediment to the ruler's capacity to maintain

---

12. There is a parallel between prefectural rulership in China and the rationalization and consolidation of European polities in the nineteenth century.

13. Ch'in rulers thought Han Fei-tzu and his doctrines were so dangerous that they forced him to commit suicide rather than let him wander from court to court as did other philosophers (Mote 1989, 107). His synthesis adds to the ideas of penal law and bureaucratic devices the "principle of the mystery of authority" of rulership (rather than of individual rulers) (Schwartz 1985, 339; see 339–43).

stability. The ideal Legalist polity was one in which uneducated masses would routinely obey the draconian laws set down by an omnipotent ruler. Professing a doctrine of power politics, they admired the system of hegemony that had been instituted to mitigate the anarchy of the Warring States era.

The development of Legalism is inextricably bound up with an era in which ethical behavior was insufficient to assure the survival of small polities (Schwartz 1985, 324–27), and the practice of Legalism accompanied the accretion of power by Ch'in rulers and their triumph over competing polities in the struggle to unite and rule China. Although Legalist severity helped unify the empire, its brutality and the drain on resources that accompanied Ch'in expansion created widespread disaffection.

CONFUCIAN OFFICIALDOM

Imperial Confucianism—"a monumental structure of ideas of largely Confucian origin that provided an all-encompassing state philosophy" (Fairbank 1992, 62)—was an ideal ideology for an impersonal and efficient bureaucracy of the sort needed by the polities of the late Chou and the empire that followed. Mann (1986b, 343) extols Confucianism as "a marvellous instrument of imperial/class rule. It appropriated the rationalistic side of salvationist currents. . . . It added universal values and legitimation to a modified particularism of aristocracy and dynasty; it confined egalitarian values to an enlarged ruling class; it provided unified culture to a ruling class otherwise prone to decentralization; and by allowing new entrants into the gentleman category, it could admit educated barbarians into its ruling elite and thus into civilization." As Chou authority vanished in the centuries following the death of Confucius, professional bureaucrats began to replace aristocratic officials in the polities competing for power (Schwartz 1985, 134).

The emphasis of Mencius and Hsun-tzu on formal education and on proper conduct that reflected status were compatible with Legalist ideas of political centralization and hierarchy (Ames 1983, 63)[14]. And,

---

14. The Legalist Shen Pu-hai paid much attention to organizing and controlling bureaucracy by means of impersonal and objective rules in the context of how a ruler acquires and sustains power (Schwartz 1985, 335–39).

despite its emphasis on right conduct, Confucianism, as Fairbank reminds us, was an ideal ideology for a hierarchical officialdom with an omnipotent emperor on top:

> Perhaps we can understand the emperor's capacity to kill his officials only by appreciating his role as the central divinity of the Chinese state and society. The Confucianist had no fear of retribution in an afterlife because he lived in a day-to-day environment in which the imperial power might reward and also extinguish him. Where the West Asian or European, focused upon a faith in an afterlife, might fear going to Hell, the Confucianist, concerned with the here and now, could live in fear of the imperial wrath. God was on his throne within the palace at the capital. (1992, 69)[15]

Given the Confucian emphasis on right conduct, however, it is hardly surprising that an emperor's use of "terroristic violence was usually accompanied by outbursts of moral indignation aimed at achieving normative justification in the minds of the elite" (Fairbank 1992, 70). Nevertheless, the syncratic Confucianism that triumphed was a significant advance over Ch'in Legalism. Indeed, Han Wu-ti actually banned Legalist philosophers from his court.

The hobbling by Ch'in of the old aristocrats and efforts to crush feudal remnants proved a giant step in clearing the way for creating a bureaucracy that could knit the disparate pieces of the empire together. Han ideology and practice fostered the growth of a cohesive and loyal officialdom. By the first century B.C. there existed a bureaucracy staffed by scholars who were indoctrinated in an eclectic Confucianism (Hucker 1975, 128) and "who shared not only a generally similar family background but also an education grounded in classical learning, a common set of historical references, and a fund of basic ideas and widely held values" (Schirokauer 1991, 57; also Schwartz 1985, 377).[16]

---

15. For a different interpretation of the role of an "immanental cosmos" in Confucian thinking, see Hall and Ames 1987, 12–17.

16. As Schirokauer (1991, 57) points out, one should not exaggerate the cohesiveness of Confucian officials. Georgraphic and family ties, for example repeatedly created factions and policy differences among them.

As early as 201 B.C., the Han emperor had a scholar design court rituals.

Han emperors sought talented men who were required to pass written examinations. In 124 B.C., an imperial institution was created to train officials, which "is said to have grown to 3000 students in the second half of the first century B.C. and to 30,000 students under the Later Han dynasty" (Reischauer and Fairbank 1960, 106). After 58 A.D., government schools had to undertake ritual sacrifices to Confucius. Although the Han class of officials was an elite, it was an elite based on wealth (usually derived from land), talent, and education unlike the hereditary aristocratic class of the Chou era.[17] More than any other empire, the Han succeeded in forging an alliance with scholars and in constructing a meritocracy to provide effective government. And the Confucian emphasis on education fostered in officials a serious preoccupation with moral virtue and right conduct.

Part of the process of creating a bureaucratic structure involved elevating and glorifying the emperor. A new palace and a great tomb were built for him, and he made a series of grand tours with an eye toward overawing those who witnessed him. Ch'in officials also sought to reduce the independence of aristocrats by forcing them to reside (in 223, 219 and 213 B.C.) in the capital where they could be kept under surveillance. "In one of these resettlement programs alone," declares Hucker (1975, 44), "some 120,000 families were reportedly transported." In the end: "The outstanding achievement of Ch'in as a national dynasty, which makes the short period of Ch'in supremacy a major watershed in Chinese history, was defeudalization—that is, centralization of Chinese government in a nonfeudal, nonhereditary, bureaucratic administration. All the old feudal states were abolished, and the Ch'in pattern of freehold farmers was extended throughout China" (Hucker 1975, 43).

Although the Han emperors explored restoring some elements from pre-Ch'in China, they retained most Ch'in bureaucratic practices. Officials, graded by salary and rank, were controlled from and concentrated in the Han capital Ch'ang-an (modern Sian). By the first century B.C., the Han bureaucracy had become enormous, numbering perhaps over 130,000 (Reischauer and Fairbank 1960, 96). These officials con-

---

17. Merchants were explicitly excluded from higher bureaucratic positions and forbidden from buying land.

stituted an elite that enjoyed privileges like lower taxes and, in return, saw their first task as serving the emperor and protecting his dynasty.

As in the practice of dividing military command among several generals, the division and overlap of administrative responsibilities during the Ch'in and Han eras was designed to prevent usurpation of power by any single official. At the top were three senior ministers (*san kung,* the "three excellencies") who shared power to develop, critique and implement policy, and "may be described as the imperial cabinet, with collective responsibilities and overlapping duties" (Bielenstein 1986a, 493). One was the Chancellor (*ta ssu-t'u,* "grand minister of finance" or "grand master over the masses") who presided over meetings of high bureaucratic officials.[18] A second was the Director of the Secretariat who (until 68 B.C.) was responsible for deciding which documents would be brought to the emperor. Finally, the Great Commandant was in charge of military forces. Nine other ministers, with specific and overlapping responsibilities, served under these three officials, and they "supervised the business of government and also were charged with palace administration and the conduct of ritual observances" (Schirokauer 1991, 56; also Loewe 1986b, 120–22, and 1986d, 466–70).

EARLY HAN CENTRAL GOVERNMENT ca. 100 B.C.
From the *Han-shu* (Loewe 1986d, 466–470)

Location: Imperial city of *Ch'ang-an* (modern Sian)

Emperor
(huang-ti)

Three Senior Statesmen *(san kung)*

Chancellor
(ch'ing-hsiang)

Imperial Counsellor   **Supreme Commander**
(yu-shih ta-fu)   *(t'ai-wei)*

---

18. As imperial government was divided between the regular bureaucracy and inner court Secretariat *(shan-shu)* of eunuchs serving as administrative aides under the Marshal of State, power shifted to the Marshal of State *(ta ssu-ma)* (Loewe 1986f, 467).

<u>Nine Ministers</u> *(chiu-ch'ing):*

Superintendent of Ceremonial *(t'ai-ch'ang)*
{Astrology, divination, music}

Superintendent of Palace *(kuang-lu-hsün)*
{Supervised counsellors and courtiers awaiting appointment}

Superintendent of Guards *(wei-wei)*
{Palace security}

Superintendent of Transport *(t'ai-p'u)*
{Imperial transport, maintained coaches, horses and their
scarce grazing lands}

Superintendent of Trials *(t'ing-wei)*
{Legal processes, adjudicated cases sent up from provinces}

Superintendent of State Visits *(ta hung-lu)*
{Received foreign dignitaries, provided interpreters. Also
involved in official sacrifices}

Superintendent of Imperial Clan *(tsung-cheng)*
{Tracked imperial family to maintain correct order of
precedence. Only office to be held by a member of the Liu
family}

Superintendent of Agriculture *(ta ssu-nung)*
{Collected land and poll taxes, bureaucratic payroll, supplied
army. From 120 B.C. operated state monopolies on salt and
iron, balanced prices and transport}

Superintendent of the Lesser Treasury *(shao-fu)*
{Received taxes on produce from hills and lakes, maintained
emperor's workshops, agencies for medicine, music, etc.
Secretariat subordinate}

<u>Other Independent Offices</u>: **Senior** and **Junior Tutors** of the heir apparent;
Court Architect; Supervisors of households of empress, heir apparent, and
empress dowager; **Commandants** of independent states; **Superintendent of
Waterways and Parks.**

On the whole, people were left alone provided they paid taxes and
performed services and did not pose a threat to the center. However,
as Loewe (1986c, 106) argues, the "ideal of a perfectly ordered
hierarchical society which is described as Confucian could not with-

stand the grim realities of crime, dissidence, or invasion without some effective measures of Legalist controls." A key role in enforcing imperial obedience was played by "censorial officials." The Censorate consisted of officials with limited judicial powers who were responsible for maintaining surveillance over other government officials and who reported violations of the law or administrative regulations. "Because the censors had the right to submit their impeachment memorials directly to the throne, bypassing routine communication channels, they enjoyed considerable independence of action and high prestige" (Hucker 1975, 162).

CONSTRAINTS ON IMPERIAL AUTHORITY

Classes

During the seventh and sixth centuries B.C., an aristocratic elite stood atop China's society. Chou kings had to share power with and seek resources from the great lineages of the land. These lineages formed a hierarchy with that of the Chou king on top, and each had its own capital city, temple for ancestor worship, and military forces. The great families controlled sacrifice, warfare, and hunting that were, as Lewis (1990, 15) observes, "the central rites of the cults of the ancestors and the state altars, and the performance of these rites set the aristocracy apart from the common people."

Rapid growth in population and wealth during the Eastern Chou era, the emergence of a wealthy commercial class, and changes in military technology eroded the aristocratic feudal order that sought to propagate an ideology based on a hierarchy of four classes with merchants at the bottom. Confucianism sought to rationalize the relationship among different classes and so reduce social and political friction arising from differences in status and wealth. Confucius himself played a key role in institutionalizing the idea that access to public service should be based on merit rather than ascription. "China's society," argues Mote (1989, 35–36), "found in Confucius' teachings the mechanism for regulating and for encouraging social mobility."

Nevertheless, class consciousness was never far below the surface, and Confucianism reinforced the principle of hereditary authority even while it fostered merit criteria. During the Han era, for example, there was an explicit bias against wealth based on commerce and a cleavage between wealthy landowners who were the basis of the Confucian bureaucracy and peasants (some of whom were virtual serfs) who paid the bulk of the taxes and had to provide the government with periodic unpaid labor.

The Ch'in triumph did not alter control by hereditary aristocrats. The First Emperor was a member of that class, and the Ch'in empire had its roots in one of the aristocratic Chou city polities. By contrast, Liu Pang had peasant roots and had engaged in banditry prior to serving under Hsiang Yu. Liu had little sympathy for the ancient aristocratic families, and the civil disorders out of which the Han era arose seriously eroded traditional mores and philosophies. Of the founders of Han, Reischauer and Fairbank assert: "As self-made men, rather than proud aristocrats, they showed themselves more pragmatic and flexible than their predecessors" (1960, 92; also Schwartz 1985, 348–49). As a result, they were less imperious than their predecessors, moved cautiously in reimposing centralized direction on China, and avoided Legalist excesses and rigidity. Nevertheless, the imperial family, and its relatives and friends continued to constitute a small hereditary aristocracy at the apex of the social pyramid.

As we have seen, both Earlier and Later Han were unable to deal effectively with the great hereditary landowners by granting them a substantial measure of autonomy. The great landowners paid only nominal land tax while enriching themselves on rent paid by peasants. The landowners also controlled trade and many of the higher positions at the imperial court. Wang Mang's effort to redistribute the land failed, and Later Han emperors, themselves from the landowning class, made little effort to reduce the autonomy of the landowners, even though their independence threatened imperial prosperity and cohesion (Reischauer and Fairbank 1960, 124–25).

Ideology and Officialdom

The erosion of aristocratic tradition aided the consolidation of the Han imperial system, but continuing class friction set limits on Han policies. Taoism became the ideology of many of those who turned their backs on politics or who rejected the Confucian-based system. However, even Confucianism and those officials who were "heirs to a tradition that, however adulterated, did not teach unthinking compliance to the whims or policies of the ruler . . . restricted the power of the central government and tended to soften the impact of absolutism" (Schirokauer 1991, 57). In addition, Han tradition "called for emperors to heed their advisers; and chief counselors were particularly prestigious and influential as the acknowledged leaders and spokesmen for the officialdom in general" (Hucker 1975, 150). Those who sought to enforce policies opposed by the bureaucracy might find those policies undermined, as did Wang Mang is his effort to redistribute land and end slavery.

Vassals

We have already observed how the Han emperors reversed, at least in part, the centralizing tendencies of their Ch'in predecessors (Loewe 1986c, 123–27). Although this shift served to reduce the discontent that had climaxed in the collapse of Ch'in, it also produced powerful centrifugal forces. It forced Liu Pang to overthrow the kings he had created who were not members of the imperial family. Thereafter, only relatives of the emperor could hold the rank of king. The efforts of seven of these semi-independent kingdoms to maintain their independence by rebellion was crushed in 154 A.D. Liu Pang's successors continued to erode the independence of the remaining kings by dividing and subdividing their territories among their heirs and, in the end, by appointing imperial officials to rule each kingdom. By the end of the Han era, there remained slightly more than 300 semiautonomous polities (including 20 kingdoms and 241 "marquisates"), and most of China was divided into centrally controlled subdivisions (83 commanderies and 1,314 prefectures) (Loewe 1986f, 476–78).

In-Laws and Eunuchs

Once again, concentration and increasing complexity at the center produced some of its own nemesis. A source of dissension and threat to imperial rule during the Han era was the plotting of members of the imperial family (Loewe 1986c, 107–8). As a rule, Chinese emperors took a number of consorts. When an heir to the throne was declared, his mother typically became empress. Following the heir's accession, the former empress, now known as the Empress Dowager, became a major political force at the imperial court. This tradition began following the death of Liu Pang when, with his heir still a minor, the Empress Lu became effective ruler of China. She proceeded to appoint members of her own family to high positions; and, until her death in 180 B.C., it appeared that her family might replace the ruling Han dynasty. However, after her death Liu Pang's followers massacred her clan, and Liu's son assumed the throne. As in the Earlier Han, imperial cohesion in Later Han was challenged by the families of empresses who were well connected at court. In several instances, the emperor sought the aid of court eunuchs to deal with the threat.

Aside from the emperor's immediate family, uncastrated males were prohibited from palace residence areas. Eunuchs thus enjoyed high positions in the imperial household, even coming to command the palace guards. During the Later Han era, eunuchs sometimes fully controlled the court. Once in favor, "eunuchs found it easy to insinuate themselves into influential roles even in government—as confidential adviser to the ruler if nothing more." This placed them in direct competition with imperial officials, who feared and resented the eunuchs' impact upon royal decision making, "especially in dealing with notably strong and notably weak rulers, but [had] to tolerate and even make allies of eunuchs in the interest of orderly administration" (Hucker 1975, 54).

In time, this system weakened the ties between court and bureaucracy, destabilizing the latter. Officials looked down upon eunuchs who were their social and educational inferiors and often their rivals for influence. An absence of direct and uncontested leadership from the center caused officials to form factions around spokesmen— "honest critics"—to compete for imperial approval. Power devolved to residents of the inner court, empresses and eunuchs, who eventually decided issues of succession. Eunuchs, "being entirely dependent on a young emperor as his servants and companions, might be his only reliable supporters against an empress's family" (Fairbank 1992, 59). The clash between officials and eunuchs often led to open conflict. In 166 A.D. and again two years later, the eunuchs imprisoned or executed thousands of their foes in seeking to consolidate power at court.

CONCLUSION: CHINA YESTERDAY AND TODAY

The continuity and longevity of Chinese civilization and politics make it imperative to recognize that change in China, in Schwartz's words, "must be studied within the framework of a civilization in which the modern Western premise of a total qualitative rupture with the 'traditional' past has not occurred" (1985, 2). China's historical experience continues to shape rulers and ruled today. Bozeman (1960, 133) observes: "Just as medieval Europeans thought of themselves as constituting the center of world happenings, so the Chinese regarded China as the sole world state and the center of all humanity." As a result: "Every intellectual effort to understand the place of that 'Middle Kingdom' in contemporary world affairs . . . should issue from a preliminary understanding of these views." Historical continuity and historical self-consciousness, combined with the sinocentric nature of Chinese historical scholarship, mean that Chinese political behavior and ideas reflect China's unique historical conditions and experience. That uniqueness makes it dangerous to draw analogies to Western experience.

Following prolonged weakness and turmoil that featured foreign invasion and occupation and fierce conflict among competing warlords, Mao Tse-tung reunited China. The era after his triumph over the Kuomintang and the flight of Chiang Kai-shek witnessed reunification and resurgence of authority at the center. Communist efforts to weaken potentially competing authorities, including the family, were only partly effective, and recent decades of uneven economic growth have witnessed the reawakening of loyalties to family, regional, city, economic, ethnic and other authority patterns not fully controlled from Beijing.

Events in China that climaxed with the 1989 massacre of prodemocracy demonstrators in Tiananmen Square reawakened fears of an imminent historical turning point. Will chaos again engulf China as the Mandate of Heaven is withdrawn from China's aging communist leaders? Will economic reform in China be accompanied by the triumph of democratic ideas? Whatever happens, Chinese of all ideological persuasions seem to agree that a powerful center able to maintain unity within historic borders is desirable. Communists and noncommunists, for example, argue from tradition that Tibet and Taiwan are parts of China.

China's historical models and myths, in contrast to those in the West, provide little basis for a peaceful transition to democracy. Nor does the economic progress enjoyed by neighbors like Singapore and Taiwan indicate to China's rulers that political democracy is a prereqiuisite to economic prosperity. Instead, China's own history and these examples seem to point to a "new authoritarianism" (Tsai, 1992), perhaps tempered by a Confucian sense of noblesse oblige on the part of rulers, but almost certainly accompanied by a reassertion of China as the Middle Kingdom and dominant force in Asia.

9

MESOAMERICA
A Multitude of Polities

The case of Mesoamerica comes closest to the "clash of civilizations" that Samuel P. Huntington (1993, 22–49) envisions in the post–Cold War world. This case introduces us to the relationship between expansive Europeans and non-European peoples, which obviously still has important echoes today. With no previous contact, the Europe/Mesoamerica relationship began in an exceptionally "pristine" fashion. Moreover, Michael Howard (1984, 35) observes: "Acquisitiveness and fanaticism were to characterize subsequent empire-builders as well, but none fought on quite the same basis of technical equality and quantitative inferiority as did the *conquistadores*."

In the present intellectual climate of political correctness, it is especially important to get the record straight. The Spanish were vastly outnumbered, but, as we shall explain, and contrary to Howard, their technical equipment (though cumbersome) was superior. Acquisitive, fanatical, and "ruthless" (Howard again) are all adjectives that would apply equally well (or more so) to the Aztecs as to their conquerors, although *perhaps* a little less so to the Mayas, Incas, and others. However, Watson's (1992, 219) description of New World peoples as "primitive" and "oppressive Stone Age empires" unfortunately fails to convey how sophisticated and complex their polities and general civilizations were. Mann's (1986b, 120) characterization of Mesoamerican civilizations as "multi-power-actor" appears to be close, until he elaborates: "They were normally composed of two levels of power, a number of small political units, often city-states, and a broader civilizational 'cultural/religious' complex." In fact, the Mesoamerican case involves a *much* greater diversity of polity types—layered, overlapping, and nested within one another. Mann is nonetheless correct that, despite some similarities between the political evolution of Mesoamerica and that of Mesopotamia and China, "the analogy with Eurasian civilizations should not be pressed too far."

INTRODUCTION

When the Spanish conquistadores arrived in Mesoamerica, they were surprised to find peoples who were, in many respects, remarkably civilized. The Europeans were as amazed by the size, beauty, and cleanliness of the Aztec capital of Tenochtitlán, as they were shocked by the Aztec practice of mass human sacrifice. Mesoamericans had developed complex political structures, economic organization, social strata, cosmology and ideology, and architecture and art. Mesoamerica was inhabited as early as 40,000 B.C., and the first settlements appeared about 25,000 B.C. After 5000 B.C., the domestication of maize, beans, and other plants made it possible to develop a genuine agricultural economy. Civilization started evolving—and devolving—at least by the time of the full emergence of Olmec culture about 1250–1150 B.C.—a period roughly parallel with the collapse of the Mycenaen centers in Greece. The Spanish who ventured across the Atlantic in the late fifteenth and early sixteenth centuries were also the product of a long and complicated process of political evolution, most recently the reconquest of southern Spain from the Moors and the union of Castile and Aragon.

SYSTEM DISCRETENESS AND STRUCTURE

Pre-Conquest Mesoamerica was a distinct system, though it was never fully unified politically or integrated economically. The area was isolated from the rest of the world until the Spanish interrupted what had been a long and varied pattern of independent evolution. Within Mesoamerica, numerous local polities developed and interacted in relatively large symbiotic regions. From the time of the Olmecs there were also noteworthy contacts and influences stretching across different regions.

Richard E. W. Adams (1991, 15, 19–20) observes that "interaction among cultures adopted to different ecological areas is a constant and recurring phenomenon in Mesoamerican prehistory." Mesoamerica was one "vast diffusion sphere" with some elements of a common culture. All polities relied on agriculture and Stone Age technology; most were linked in regional market systems; and many engaged in long-distance trade. Major polities were ruled by aristocrats and maintained a distinction between elites who customarily were warriors, a middle tier comprised of merchants and artisans, and the mass of farmer-laborers. All cosmologies involved gods that needed to be appeased and often similar rituals as well.

The pre-Conquest structure of Mesoamerica included a mosaic of different polities, many with urban centers, clustered, as previously noted, within several symbiotic regions. Some regions—like the Basin of Mexico and its vicinity, and the south and east near modern-day Oaxaca—were important for most of Mesoamerican history, while others waxed and waned or were prominent only early or late. The area near modern-day Villahermosa in southeast Gulf Coast Mexico that was a focus of Olmec activity, for example, never regained significance after the Olmec decline, and a similar fate befell the Lowland Petén (current northern Guatemala and extending into neighboring Mexico, northern Belize, and western Honduras), where the Mayas had flourished. The Yucatán was on the periphery of Maya culture until the Itza/Toltecs arrived c. A.D. 800; the Lowland Maya centers collapsed; and a Mexicanized variant of Puuc Maya civilization arose. Likewise, a region well west of the Basin of Mexico became noteworthy only when the Tarascan Empire emerged there about a century and a half before the Spanish arrival.

Polarity

There was no truly unipolar period before the Spanish came, because no single polity ever encompassed or achieved domination over all of Mesoamerica. Until recently, though little was actually known about the Olmecs,[1] the presumption was that, beginning about 1150 B.C., they provided a mother culture for Mesoamerica as a whole (Bernal 1969 and Piña Chan 1989). When most settlements had not yet evolved beyond simple villages, they already had several small urban centers on the Gulf Coast plain, possibly grouped into a single polity or loosely affiliated in some form of league. Their trading and perhaps tribute relationships extended well beyond their Gulf Coast homeland. These contacts directly and indirectly transmitted elements of Olmec culture that persisted in various locations long after the original Olmec centers waned. For example, during a much later period (about A.D. 960–1162), when the Toltecs had their imperial seat to the northwest, an "Olmec tyranny" at Cholula reputedly controlled most of the Basin of Mexico and the Valley of Puebla. Nonetheless, the latest view in Olmec studies is that they

---

1. Only two of their centers, La Venta and San Lorenzo, have been well-excavated.

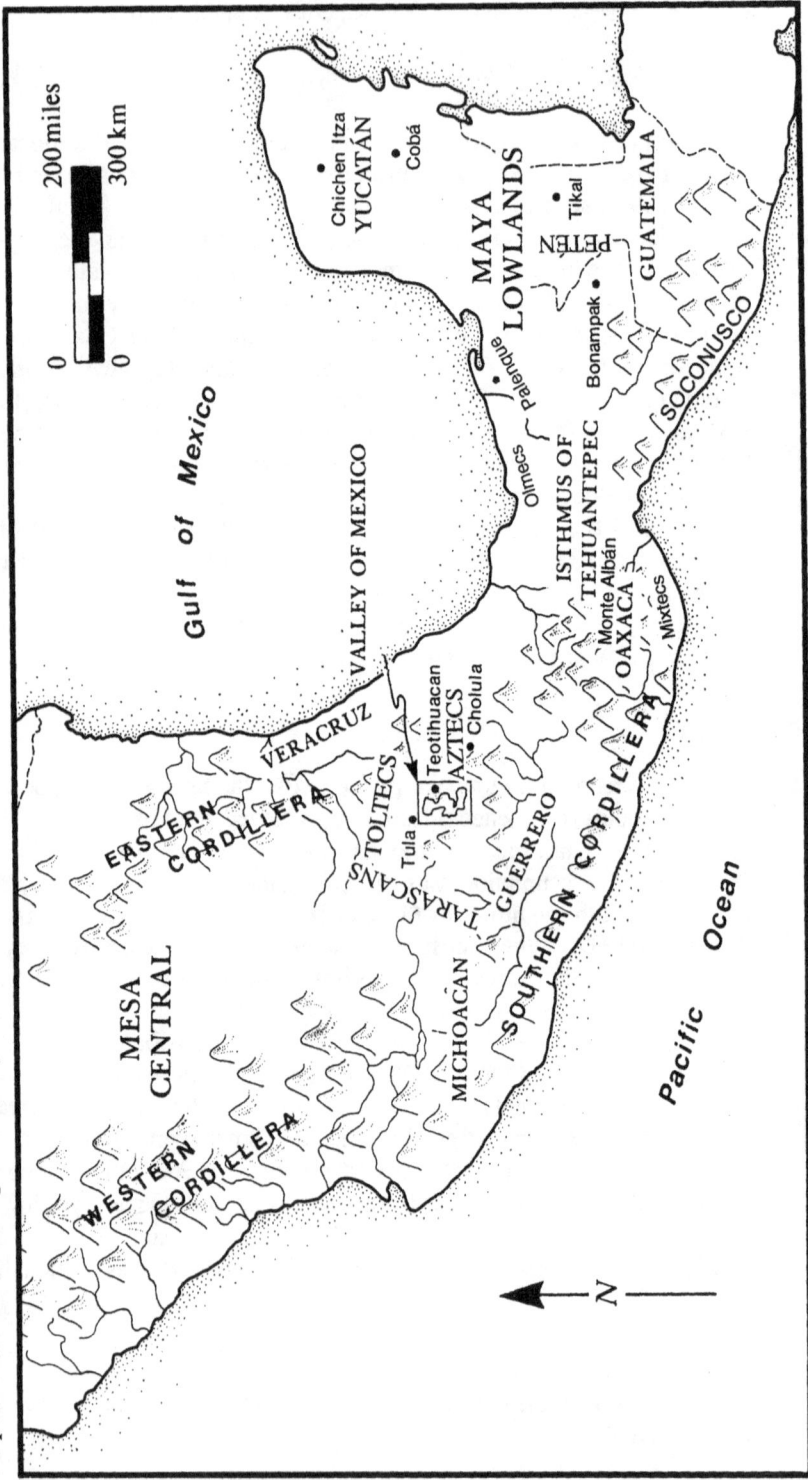

Pre-Conquest Mesoamerica
Geoffrey W. Conrad and Arthur A. Demarest, *Religion and Empire: The Dynamics of Aztec and Inca Expansionism.* Copyright © 1984. Reprinted with the permission of Cambridge University Press.

The Valley of Mexico in Aztec Times
  Geoffrey W. Conrad and Arthur A. Demarest, *Religion and Empire: The Dynamics of Aztec and Inca Expansionism*. Copyright © 1984. Reprinted with the permission of Cambridge University Press.

probably were but one—albeit the most prominent—of several regional civilizations that emerged in Mesoamerica in essentially the same time frame (Sharer and Grove 1989; also Grove 1974 and 1984).[2]

Most periods were multipolar in the sense that several major polities existed in or near the Basin of Mexico or the Central Valley of Oaxaca. Since none had the capacity to incorporate the others, the result was coexistence, albeit threatened by clashes and sweetened by tribute when one or another edged ahead. All leading empires, including the most extensive—those of Teotihuacán (200 B.C.–A.D. 650) and the Aztecs (after A.D. 1350)—had important geographic gaps. For instance, the Aztecs never conquered either the Tarascans or six independent enclaves including the Tlaxcalans and the Mixtec States of Tototepec.

Another variant of system structure was one of general fragmentation precipitated by the collapse of a major polity, which provided an unusual opportunity for new local and regional developments. The leading example was the period of turmoil following A.D. 650–700, after the fall of Teotihuacán and the great Oaxacan regional polity of the Zapotecs, Monte Albán. The result in Oaxaca was "balkanization" (Marcus 1983), but the withdrawal of Teotihuacán's influence from the Lowland Petén provided a stimulus for the rise of the Classic Maya civilization (A.D. 650–900). The Toltec empire eventually filled the power vacuum in central Mexico, probably combining migrants from the north with some peoples loosed from Teotihuacán.

---

2. Adams (1991, 85) argues that "there was an order of magnitude difference . . . heavily in favor of the Olmec." In his view: "They indeed did have cultural priority in Mesoamerica as a whole. They probably did invent and diffuse much of the cultural equipment used and reformulated in later cultures. On the other hand, like any sophisticated culture, the Olmec had no inhibitions about adopting good ideas and new fashions from their neighbors. Therefore, interaction among the regional cultures of Mesoamerica on economic and cultural levels was as important in the Early and Middle Formative as in later times." Grove (1974, 126) writes: "I believe that the archaeological data today strongly suggest that the origin of Olmec culture is southern Mesoamerican and strongly related to early cultures on the Pacific Coast of Chiapas and Guatemala, with many of the basic ideas probably derived ultimately from a tropical forest hearth in South America." Piña Chan (1989) claims that the origins of Olmec culture were in South America, specifically Ecuador-Colombia, c. 4000–3000 B.C. Meggers (1975) goes so far as to posit an initial trans-Pacific contact about 3000 B.C.

Since the most consistent and intensive interaction among polities was at the local and regional level, that structure appears to be at least as significant as system-wide structure, if not more so. Certain local polities established their control over others in their immediate area, and these groupings often (though not always) came under the sway of regional hegemons. When regional hegemons weakened or collapsed, local polities were again preeminent and had more freedom to maneuver. This consolidation/fragmentation process had an impact on system-wide trends and helped produce a broad range of polity types and considerable variety within each type.

Geophysical Setting

Mesoamerica's geophysical environment is unusually diverse, partly owing to great mountain ranges. There is a distinction between highland and lowland, which often lie in close proximity, and vast plains exist at various altitudes in the northern and western deserts, the central Mexico plateau, the lowland Petén, and the Yucatán peninsula. The Valley or Basin of Mexico where Mexico City is today is actually a bowl some 7,500 feet above sea level, surrounded by higher mountains. Nearby, the snow-capped volcanoes of Popocatepetl and Ixtacchihuatel soar to about 18,000 feet. Mountains and dense vegetation at lower levels make communication across substantial distances tedious. Adams (1991, 124) calculates that it would have taken about two weeks to get from the Cobán zone of the northern Guatemala highlands to Tikal in the central Petén. Yucatán Mayas built an elaborate network of elevated roads or causeways *(saches)* that connected many of their urban centers.

Except for the extreme north, all of Mesoamaerica lies in the tropics, with annual wet and dry seasons, and many microclimates influenced by mountain ranges and altitude. Only about half the land receives adequate rainfall for dependable crops, so shortage of water is a perennial problem that can become acute with even a slight variation in climate. In some places (for example, the Petén) reservoirs are essential for survival during the dry season; and in the Basin of Mexico, Oaxaca, and elsewhere large-scale agriculture requires extensive irrigation.[3] The Aztecs solved their water problem initially

---

3. The Palerm-Wolf theory holds that civilization arose first in locations

by weaving a network of floating gardens or *chinampas* into an artificial island in the middle of a lake. Their two main cities on the island, Tenochtitlán and Tlatelolco, were crisscrossed by canals and joined by causeways. From a political standpoint, possession of scarce water resources and the need to increase them through ambitious public works were important reasons for settlements in particular locations and offered a potential means of social control.

Indeed, one of the perennial controversies in Mesoamerican archaeology is the degree to which Karl Wittfogel's (1957) argument that "oriental despotisms" were "hydraulic societies" can be adapted—and combined with other ecological considerations like the balance between natural resources and population—to explain the rise of powerful regional polities like Teotihuacán and Monte Albán (Sanders, Parsons, and Santley 1979; Sanders and Nichols 1988).[4] If there is any consensus, it is that no analysis relying on a single dimension can adequately explain anything as complex as the development of a major civilization and that the balance of factors involved was probably somewhat different for each.[5]

---

where agriculture was easiest with primitive techniques and eventually spread to more challenging areas. The theory works well for the Basin of Mexico and also Oaxaca.

4. For instance, Flannery (1988, 57–58) on Monte Albán: "What we reject is [the] simplistic notion that all civilizations arose in the same way for the same environmental reasons, . . . Political maneuvering and entrepreneurship, warfare and defense, transformation of an egalitarian ideology into one that rationalizes stratification, justification of inequality with state religion and royal ancestor worship, manipulation of tribute—these and countless other factors went into the rise of the Zapotec state." On Teotihucán, see Millon 1974, 357–60, and Kurtz 1987. On ancient irrigation patterns generally, see also Price 1971. Actually, neither Teotihuacán nor Monte Albán were ideally situated for irrigation-assisted agriculture. In the Basin of Mexico a location nearer one of the lakes, like the later capital of the Aztecs, would have been more sensible. Monte Albán's mountaintop was an excellent site as long as control could be maintained over the valley but offered limited means of self-support (Blanton 1983c).

5. For a study of irrigation politics in modern Mexico that illustrates its continuing importance, see Hunt and Hunt 1978: 105, 118–19. They observe (105): "Water control is located in a set of institutions which are territorially localized and hierarchically nested in a vertical ladder of increasing power.

That said, there was an incentive for larger polities in the symbiotic regions because different localities had different resources and specializations. Part of the symbiosis was a response to market conditions that themselves reflected the natural environment. Lakeside bottomland communities tended to have intensive agriculture, supported by rich soil, drainage, and irrigation; while other areas practiced only limited slash-and-burn agriculture and therefore often supplemented their livelihood with craft industries. Controlling a larger region assured access to a greater variety of resources and products, which might be critical when crop failures or other reversals reduced local supplies. However, as Geoffrey W. Conrad and Arthur A. Demarest (1984, 155ff.) point out, we cannot take this line of reasoning too far, because there existed many highland/lowland combinations (for example, the Highland and Pacific Coastal or the Highland/Petén subregions of Guatemala) where little actual economic symbiosis occurred, much less noteworthy political expansion or imperialism.

Features other than access to water, food, or crafts sometimes influenced the siting of political centers. Monte Albán, for instance, is situated on a ridge system that overlooks the entire Valley of Oaxaca. Although the extent to which the Monte Albán polity at one stage involved a "voluntary" confederation with headquarters on symbolic neutral ground (Blanton, 1983a) or was a matter of domination is still debated, the ridge location could have served either purpose. Karl H. Schwerin (1988, 64) points out: "If I wanted to exercise hegemony over the area and knew nothing more than the layout of the three valley arms, I wouldn't stray far from the Oaxaca-Monte Albán area, where the three arms come together. It is the logical spot for an administratrative/religious/symbolic/trade, etc. center. . . . [In addition to defense, Mesoamerican] cosmology regularly represents mountains as inhabited by the gods or at least nearer the gods."

This power ladder is isomorphic with the political and economic power ladder of the region and of the national state, and thus is ultimately centralized in a normative pyramidal arrangement but simultaneously decentralized and semiautonomous at the local level in terms of control of each physical system." Among the present-day local nested polities is the family: "Essentially, a few families which make up the San Juan upper class have unified ultimate decision making at the local level in their own hands by effectively controlling all dimensions of the body politic [including the decision-making roles connected with irrigation]" (118).

Lastly, the environment contributed both indirectly and directly to the vulnerability and even demise of some polities. Indirectly, public works like irrigation networks that were necessary to support large populations were hostage to man-made and natural disasters. There often were not only droughts, storms, and floods but also regular plagues of locusts, outbreaks of disease, earthquakes, and volcanic eruptions. In the Basin of Mexico in 1450–51, there were record snows and frosts, and for three years thereafter, no rain fell. Fifty to eighty percent of the population either starved or emigrated (Brundage 1972, 130–33). About 400 B.C. Cuicuilco built the first significant public architecture after the Olmec era in the Basin of Mexico and, over the next two hundred years, developed a city of some twenty thousand. However, c. 150 B.C. a volcanic eruption destroyed Cuicuilco, eliminating Teotihuacán's strongest competitor and altering the political evolution of the Basin.

Economic Features

Before the Spanish arrived, the peoples of Mesoamerica possessed only Stone Age technology. They did not have the wheel, beasts of burden, many domesticated animals, or the true arch for construction. Metal appeared relatively late and served mainly nonutilitarian purposes. The only forms of transportation were foot or canoe.

The foundation of Mesoamerican economies was agriculture. By about 1500 B.C. the transition from hunting-and-gathering to agricultural-village societies was largely complete. The next big shift, beginning with the Olmec era, was the establishment of urban centers with substantial populations that required intensive agriculture. In general, this transition involved a shift from kin-based production on family plots to a more feudal patron-client style of production, whereby an elite provided protection and owned the water and land that commoner families worked in exchange for tribute (Adams 1991, 140). This pattern was much the same throughout Mesoamerica, though there are still some unanswered questions, as in the Aztec case, about whether extended-family *calpulli* (plural: *calpullin*) units actually held the formal title to lands in common or received merely the right to work the lands from a local ruler or noble. In any case, both supreme and local rulers had lands for the support of themselves, their family, and their court; and as a reward for service, Aztec rulers gave "eagle nobles" a lifetime grant of small landed estates to operate as private preserves (Zantwijk 1985, 273–78; Harvey 1984).

In recent years, the view of many aspects of Maya life, including the Mayan economy, has changed (cf. Clancy and Harrison 1990; Hammond 1982, chapter 5.; Chase and Rice 1985, Introduction). Previously the belief was that Classic Maya cities were mainly administrative and ceremonial centers inhabited by elites and that the rest of the Mayas lived in family pole and thatch huts scattered over a wide territory. However, recent archaeological work has demonstrated that many of the Maya cities had large populations that lived in areas immediately adjacent to the impressive temples and palaces. Only increasingly intensive agriculture could support such numbers, especially when the ambitious building programs of the Late Classic era drafted more and more labor, and attracted more elites and commoners to the city. Remaining wetlands were drained and cultivated, and severe deforestation occurred since wood was in demand for heating and cooking and for the production of the huge amounts of slaked lime needed for construction. An ecological crisis loomed and doubtless played some role in the sudden collapse of Maya civilization.[6] In addition to periodic locust plagues, there is also some evidence from tree rings and other sources that a prolonged drought affecting all of Mesoamerica may have begun about 850 A.D.

As the existence of massive building programs suggest, there was more to Mesoamerican economies than agriculture. Many persons engaged in crafts, which in Maya cities included construction trades, sculptors, and pottery makers. Craftsmen were, if anything, more numerous in other cultures—an estimated 25 percent of the population in Teotihuacán (Millon 1976, 233)—including workers in obsidian, stone masks, tripod vessels, feathered headdresses, leather sandals, as well as quarrymen, masons, plasterers, and mural painters. Similar patterns prevailed in Aztec times (Zantwijk 1985, 172–75).

Adams (1991, 375) observes that the symbiotic region of the Basin of Mexico, was actually "an economic unit before it was politically unified," and, of course, the two aspects were closely related. Support from within the region for the main urban center derived from farmers and craftsmen who lived in family apartment houses and other dwellings, and worked lands or practiced their crafts in the major city and nearby communities; and also from supplies and tribute gleaned from

---

6. Adams (1991, 265) comments that "we must discard any notion of the Maya as the 'noble savage' living in harmony with nature."

more distant satellite cities and farmers across much of the central plateau. Tribute varied according to family unit, social class, and subject polity. Writes Adams: "Commodities and goods were exchanged in a barter relationship, and there was only a skeletal monetary system based on cloaks, cacao beans, and gold dust." Nonetheless, it was "fully as rational a system as our own international monetary arrangements." Also contributing to the unity of the Basin was the fact that both merchants and craft associations included guilds from several cities.

The degree of unity achieved in the Basin should not obscure the localism and kinship involved in economic exchanges. Charles Gibson (1964, 349–50) observes that each town had its own specialty products such as salt, fish, or lime and that the Aztecs encouraged even more specialization: "The organization of Texcoco . . . had entailed a division of the community into thirty parts, each with its own economic function. Silversmiths, lapidaries, painters, feather workers, and others each occupied a barrio. In Aztec practice, sons normally adopted the trades or crafts of their fathers, and genealogy, location, and profession were thus identified in a single composite loyalty. Moreover, because the members of a barrio ordinarily worshipped their own local deity the integrity of the unit was further reinforced by religion."

Extensive as the local support network was, it is still difficult to explain how it managed to sustain the large populations that often crowded into the Basin of Mexico—especially considering drought and other environmental problems. In fact, the situation for the rural poor was probably even worse than it is today. But, until expansion finally reached a point of diminishing returns under the Aztecs, regional hegemons managed to stay ahead of growing internal strains partly through external conquests. Conquered lands increased the supplies of food and tribute, which, in turn, supported the expenditure of the polity on public monuments and ceremonies, and enhanced the appeal of an imperial ideology.

In contrast to cases like that of Mesopotamia, most basic necessities were obtainable locally in Mesoamerica, and long-distance trade therefore developed primarily to provide exotic or luxury goods. The Olmecs obtained obsidian from the Basin of Mexico and the Morelos Valley, cacao from the Guatemalan-Chiapan Pacific plain, iron ore to make mirrors from the Valley of Oaxaca, and kaolin for ceramics from several areas including Chalcatzingo. It was partly through contacts fostered by trade that the Olmecs disseminated aspects of their sophisticated culture, and David C. Grove (1974) argues that what is labeled as "Highland Olmec" is almost entirely a reflection of trade patterns.

Trade was of limited importance for the Lowland Mayas, and except for the important Teotihuacán period,[7] outside influences had little to do with the emergence of their classic civilization. The traditional assumption is that, during the Classic period, what trade there was took place almost exclusively within a closed regional system and consisted mainly of luxury items for elites. Peter D. Harrison (1990) nonetheless maintains that at least some Classic Maya centers further intensified their agriculture in order to export edible produce or items like cotton or cacao at considerable distances within the region. Such "industrialized" agriculture would have made those centers even more vulnerable to variations in water supply and, he believes, might have contributed to the Classic collapse. Anthony P. Andrews (1983, 125–29) and others go further to insist that Tikal and perhaps other centers acted as middlemen for east-west river trade at the base of the Yucatán peninsula, as well as north-south trade, and that growing competition from northern maritime traders was another factor in the collapse.

There is evidence that riverine and maritime trade was significant in Yucatán as early as the Pre-Classic era, and it did assume great importance in the Terminal Classic and Post-Classic periods (Andrews 1990 and 1983; Chase and Rice 1985; Friedel and Sabloff 1984).[8] In fact, Jeremy A. Sabloff et al. (1974) argue that Maya rulers of the post-Toltec era were recruited from a merchant class. Be that as it may, east-coast Maya centers actively traded among themselves and participated in a network of long-distance trade that extended south to Panama and north to central Mexico by the time the Spanish arrived (Hammond 1982, chapter 8). Columbus on his fourth voyage encountered a splendid Maya trading canoe with sails in the Bay of Honduras. In the sixteenth century, the west-coast Yucatán plains of Tabasco were the home of the Chontal Maya, who were renowned as prosperous middlemen for trade between the Maya Yucatán and the rest of Mesoamerica (Adams 1991, 311–12).

---

7. We do not know for certain whether this period involved trade between equals or a colonial relationship under Teotihuacán's hegemony (Hammond 1982, 237–38).

8. Andrews (1983, 135) believes the key items in ancient Maya trade were salt and—to a lesser degree—cotton, obsidian, and jade.

Merchant traders occupied a relatively high status between noble and commoner in central Mexican civilizations. The forerunners of the Aztec *pochteca* were similar persons in Olmec, Teotihuacán, and Toltec societies. Teotihuacán set aside barrios in the capital for the residence of foreign merchants, one enclave (it appears) exclusively for Oaxacans, and the Aztecs, too, reserved certain barrios for merchants. Teotihuacán probably decided to occupy the distant outpost of Kaminaljuyu to protect the security of trade routes to the Maya Lowlands and Tazumal in El Salvador, which supplied cacao and perhaps cotton. During the Toltec period, about 800 A.D., knowledge of metallurgy appears to have entered Mesoamerica from the south through trade contacts.

Demographic Features

In Mesoamerica, as elsewhere, population growth and decline are associated with the rise and collapse of major polities. However, establishing a precise causal relationship between demographic and political patterns is difficult. Often population growth seems to reach explosive proportions and then just as precipitously drop or shift to a different geographic location. In the Lowland Maya case, for example, what had been a region of small agricultural villages inhabited by a few families, suddenly after 550 B.C. had communities of three or four different sizes. Population in the region soared from thousands to tens of thousands in the Early Classic period and then to hundreds of thousands in the Late Classic era. And, when Classic Maya civilization collapsed, a population of some 12 million fell to only about 1.8 million in a 150 years (Adams 1991, 153, 269). Similarly, a population of some 200,000 about A.D. 650 at Teotihuacán dropped to around 30,000 by A.D. 900. Several other centers in the Basin of Mexico like Azcapotzalco and Cholula experienced a spurt of growth soon after this decline (Adams 1991, 257).

What statistics like these do not tell us is whether either the establishment of major political centers or their subsequent expansion/contraction is a result of population trends. On the one hand, urban centers typically develop when small kinship-oriented villages experience levels of population growth sufficient to require more intensive agriculture with attendant public works like drainage, water storage, and irrigation. Social organization on a larger and more complex scale seems to entail the emergence of political elites, differential access to resources, and social stratification. On the other hand, it is often hard to determine whether population growth preceded, went hand in hand with, or was produced by the improvements in agriculture and political consolidation that we are trying to explain. And, of course, other factors like the need for physical protection in times of warfare, an effort to improve the capacity to wage war for booty, or even the attraction of a common religious shrine can help explain the development of urban centers and more complex polities.

Population pressures alone cannot offer a sufficient explanation of why existing polities expand, either through colonization or conquest. Not all large growing populations place serious strains on food supplies, and sometimes even stable or shrinking populations are unable to support themselves because of the collapse of a polity. In the latter circumstance, most remnant populations in Mesoamerica simply dispersed. When successful polities grow beyond local supplies, one alternative is to plant colonies, as did Greek city polities, and we need to explain why some polities chose conquest instead. Conquering more land and sources of supply can help allieviate shortages. But warfare has a price, not just the costs of military equipment and administering subject territories but also damage to infrastructure in the event there are reversals and—directly in terms of food supply—loss of males who are primary food producers. Finally, the Aztec case points up that population increase by expanding polities can be a deliberate aim of public policy, in this instance to increase the numbers of warriors. The Aztec religion deified women who died in childbirth and commemorated them with small shrines all over Tenochtitlán (Conrad and Demarest 1984, 171).

Conrad and Demarest (1984, 167–70) demonstrate that the population-pressure interpretation has been carried to ridiculous lengths by some analysts (Harner 1977a and 1977b; and Harris 1977 and 1979) who seek to explain both the Aztecs' military expansionism and their practices of human sacrifice and cannibalism as a desperate search for protein. First, the only Aztecs who were allowed to eat the victims were those who could easily afford the animals readily available in local markets, not to mention the vegetable proteins that were staples in the Aztec diet. Second, persistent military campaigns burned countless calories and killed many of the young males who were the persons who contributed most to the cultivated food supply.

War and Modes of Diplomacy

The technology of warfare was as unsophisticated as other Mesoamerican technology. Groups of warriors moved on foot or by canoe and wielded stone knives, stone-tipped spears, or rocks with slings. The bow and arrow did not appear among the Yucatán Mayas until the Post-Classic period (Chase and Rice 1985, 7). Mesoamerican warriors were poorly equipped even by the standards of ancient Mesopotamia's wheeled vehicles and siege machines. Although Mesoamericans were hardly defenseless and had far more troops, their weapons were no match for Spanish gunpowder, muskets, artillery, armor, horses, and ships.

Until the Spanish appeared, lack of firepower to some extent favored the defense. Location and architecture were both important in this regard. Some Mayan and central Mexican polities occupied hills, ridges, or ravines. Many had long dry or water-filled moats, walls, or other fortifications. Long causeways protected the Aztec's capital of Tenochtitlán. The height and steepness of most Mesoamerican temples and connections among other buildings in the urban centers made them a formidable last line of defense.

Under these circumstances military victory usually required marshaling large numbers of warriors, effective organization, and high morale. The more serious and sustained the warfare, the higher the stakes. For example, an increase in the scale and frequency of warfare was probably one contributing factor in the demise of Classic Maya civilization, absorbing more and more manpower, ever-scarcer resources, and creating general turbulence that invited external military intervention. Some of the Mayan polities seem to have employed mercenaries, and resort to this expediency was common elsewhere. It seems likely that the Toltecs first entered the Yucatán in the mercenary service of some of the Epi-Classic Puuc Maya polities they later overthrew, and the Aztecs began their careers as mercenaries in the employ of the Tepanecs headquartered at Azcapotzalco. In time the Aztecs were so successful that they became almost equal partners of the Tepanecs and eventually led a coalition of subject cities in revolt.

Teotihuacán may have started the practice of creating a more professionalized military that was a hallmark of later Aztec imperial rule (Millon 1976). The Aztecs relied less on administration than on intimidation. Like the Assyrians, they developed a reputation of having an awesome capacity to deliver overwhelming and fanatically brutal military force quickly to any part of their empire that was so foolish as to delay tribute payments or challenge Aztec rule (see Hassig 1988, chapter 2). The military provided one avenue for social mobility and also had a special role in the religious rites of human sacrifice.

The Aztecs did not have have a standing army as such, but all males received military training and were ready for action at short notice, usually some seven to eight thousand from a pool of about half a million. The extended-family *calpulli* often fought as a unit and hence was a vital part of military organization. Initial military training took place either in a *calmecac* school that was attached to a leading temple and drew most of its students from the nobility, or in a *telpochcalli* school run by a *calpulli*, which mixed nobility and commoners from associated families. Experienced warriors offered some students advanced training. Nobles tended to have more opportunities for training and prestigious service, but they were not always officers. Commoners could also attain officer rank and gain fame and fortune in campaigns. Commoners and nobles of various ranks from enlisted man to officer held membership in military societies, albeit graded by the proportion of nobles to commoners. As Adams (1991, 397) explains: "Kinship, social status, military achievement, and personality determined rank, and these elements seem to have occurred in different mixes, all of which made the Aztec armies unendingly fluid and volatile organizations." (See also Hassig 1988, chapter 3; Fagan 1984, 125–33.)

Mesoamerican polities interacted with one another not only through warfare and trade but also through a variety of formal and informal diplomatic channels, ranging from couriers who carried messages to more official emissaries or ambassadors. In fact, warfare and trade were intimately bound up with diplomacy. Some of the compounds for foreigners at Teotihuacán and Tenochtitlán may have included embassies or trade missions. Merchants from all societies doubled as intelligence-gathering agents in foreign territory. Brian M. Fagan (1984, 126) argues that an Aztec "declaration of war was a highly ritualized, formal business" in which a delegations of diplomats from Tenochtitlán paid visits at set intervals to an intended target polity, "inviting" them in increasingly threatening terms to become part of the empire. The amount of tribute an incorporated polity subsequently paid depended on whether it had joined when invited, or when Aztec military forces actually appeared on the scene, or only after having been defeated in battle.

Great emphasis was placed on keeping open channels for communication and interaction. Ambassadors had certain immunities when they traveled on main roads (Hassig 1988, 50). Recognized reasons for war at least in central Mexico were closing roads to commerce or subjecting merchants to physical harm (Hassig 1985, 120–21). Classic Maya roads "gave rights-of-way through crowded landscapes" (Adams 1991, 160) and served, in addition to commercial and military purposes, as pathways for religious processions. The patron deities of one urban center could pay a ceremonial visit to their counterparts in another polity.

Another instrument of diplomacy—and also a means of avoiding incest among a few high-ranking families—was dynastic marriages. Royal marriages helped to cement alliances among Classic Maya regional capitals and their dependencies (Marcus 1976, 192; also Molloy and Rathje 1974; Hammond 1982, 220). In addition, such marriages were a "crucial and carefully considered activity" among Zapotecs and Mixtecs in the post-Monte Albán "balkanized" period in Oaxaca (Marcus and Flannery 1983, 220) and were no less important in the Basin of Mexico (Carrasco 1984). Millon (1974, 352) speculates that they were part of the special relationship between Teotihuacán and Oaxaca symbolized by the Oaxaca barrio at Teotihuacán.

The foreign policy of Colhuacán, one of the three powerful city polities in the Basin of Mexico at the time the Aztecs were on the rise, consisted mainly of peddling the putative Toltec pedigree of its ruling elite. Aztec ideology was already attaching increasing significance to their supposed Toltec roots, and one account has it that they petitioned Colhuacán for the necessary royal breeding stock.[9] Colhaucán gave them a half-Colhua prince, Acamapichtli, who became ruler of Tenochtitlán about 1370, and subsequently the hand-in-marriage of a full-blooded Colhua princess. Acamapichtli's successor married a daughter of the ruler of Azcapotzalco, and she persuaded her father to reduce the Aztec's tribute payments. Not all marriages were so felicitous, as witness that between Montezuma's sister and the ruler of Texcoco, Nezahualpilli. He had his wife executed for adultery and also to get revenge on Montezuma, who, he believed, had arranged the ambush of the Texcocan army.

POLITY TYPES

The Mesoamerican record reveals a rich variety and range of polities along a continuum of complexity from families to empires, with considerable overlapping and nesting.

---

9. Conrad and Demarest (1984, 25) believe that it is more likely that the Tepanec alliance simply imposed the new rulers. In any event, the alliance more or less simultaneously granted a separate ruler to Tlatelolco, Tenochtitlán's sister city.

Family

The patrilineal extended family or clan was the foundation of early Mesoamerican society, and actual and artificial kinship continued to be important in society and politics. In many polities, including those of the Classic Maya, a hereditary aristocracy emerged from the former heads of various lineages and came to control virtually all productive land. Client commoner families worked the land in an essentially feudal arrangement. However, especially in central Mexican polities, extended-kinship units appear to have retained a higher degree of identity and autonomy. A modern tourist visiting the Pyramids just outside of Mexico City can still see the remnants of about 2,200 one-story apartment compounds in which such groups were almost literally nested in Teotihuacán. One of the main excavators of Teotihuacán, René Millon (1974, 353; also Wilford 1993), suggests that the compounds housed extended-family networks "with a variety of diffuse relationships of dependency," including at its "outermost circle . . . people linked to each other by patron-client ties in a framework of ritual kinship."

These compounds bear a striking resemblance to the "small ward" or *barrio pequeño* that was the urban residence of the *calpullin* of later Aztec times. Each *calpulli* worked a particular plot of land or engaged in the same craft, sent its members together into battle, educated young boys in its own *telpochcalli* school, provided a shrine to honor the *calpulli*'s own patron deity, and shared worship at a local temple complex with certain other *calpullin*. The *calpulli* structure was amazingly resilient and even managed to weather the Spanish Conquest, surviving "virtually intact to the mid-sixteenth century" (Gibson 1964, 182). Nonetheless, the Indian *calpullin*, without disappearing entirely, eventually lost most of their lands and identity. The beneficiaries of this process were a new Spanish extended-family elite, based on *haciendas* and ranchos, and the Catholic Church.

Church

One of the consequences of the Conquest was to add the Church to the list of Mesoamerican polities. As far as we know, no Indian temple priesthood ever matched the degree of autonomy and wealth that the Spanish Church in the New World enjoyed (however humble the deameanor of some friars). When the New World was little more than the island of Hispaniola, the Pope granted to Spain "islands and mainlands . . . towards the West and South," as well as the *Patronato* charge of spreading the Catholic faith in those dominions.[10] In 1512, the King delegated to New-World bishops the right to collect and distribute a tithe on all products of the Indies except precious metals, which gave the Church an enormous permanent income and also insured that the money would be spent by his own appointees. At least until the eighteenth-century Bourbons,[11] Church-Crown relations were mutually supportive. The same relationship prevailed with postindependence Mexican governments, although anticlerical sentiment began to build after the mid-nineteenth century. The Church received some early grants of land directly from the King and steadily extended its holdings. Wealthy Spanish laypersons also made generous gifts of land and, later, money, which the Church often applied to land purchases. In time the Church came to own or control a large proportion of the arable land in Mexico. The Church became too wealthy and powerful for its own good, inviting the extreme anticlerical policies the Mexican government pursued after 1910.

Tribe

Beyond family, clan, and artificial kinship groups is "tribe," a troublesome concept in most contexts, not least in Mesoamerica. There is confusing overlapping between ethnic groups and various polities, which themselves sometimes overlap, and the confusion is compounded by the efforts of successor authorities to label and govern the peoples they inherited. R. Brian Ferguson (1992, 110; also Ferguson and Whitehead 1992b) observes that "there is strong evidence that much of the tribal structure recorded by Europeans was in fact called into being by their presence" because they had "great

---

10. Parry (1966, 154) declares: "The *Patronato* . . . conferred upon the Spanish Crown an immense, a unique, authority. Except in the little kingdom of Granada, nothing like it existed in Europe; not until the eighteenth century did the Spanish kings secure a similar power in the rest of Spain. Neither Ferdinand or Julius, of course, can have had any notion of the magnitude of the concession the Pope had made."

11. The Bourbons relied more on the army and recruited administrators primarily from that quarter. In 1767 the King falsely accused the Jesuits of seeking to convert Paraguay missions into an independent kingdom and expelled them from the New World (Parry 1964, 326).

difficulty dealing with indigenous people as they are often organized—without authoritative leaders or fixed group identities." The "artificial cultural and political boundaries" the Europeans imposed out of administrative necessity rapidly became "integrated into the fabric of native society." Again, the result was fusion, retaining many traditional groupings among the indigenous population. Gibson (1964, 28) notes that Spanish secular and religious authorities "favored programs of Indian resettlement *(congregación)*, and these occasionally resulted in new associations of peoples derivative from separate 'tribes.' " An example is the sixteenth-century ecclesiastical foundation of Tlalnepantla, which combined the Tepaneca of Tenayuca and the Otomi of Teocalhueyacán. Yet Tepaneca and Otomi peoples "remained separate, with distinct internal governments" in the new single community. Some other groups "whose names suggest tribal origins," like Mexicapan and Culhuacan, successfully resisted *congregación* plans, partly by arguing "their long-standing hostility to one another." Meanwhile, large numbers of Otomis, Tarascans, and others moved to Mexico City, where they constituted new political subdivisions.

In fact, there was substantial confusion about tribes in central Mexico long before the Spanish.[12] The Aztecs were confused about the legendary Toltecs from whom they claimed descent, which actually made it easier for them to invent whatever myths served their purposes. But who were the Aztecs? According to their official chronicles, they were originally part of a group of seven Chichimec tribes that migrated over a period of generations from their original home in western Mexico known as Aztlan (whence "Aztec"). One of their prominent leaders was named Meci, from whom they acquired their own tribal name, Mexica (whence "Mexico"). The Mexica arrived in the Basin of Mexico about A.D. 1193, founded the sister cities of

---

12. This confusion was probably part of a broader pattern described by Richard Fraser Townsend (1979, 11): "The complex interactions of migrant tribesmen with the urban heirs of Classic culture constituted a long, continuous process of acculturation. . . . Acculturation was not a simple matter of assimilation of the less sophisticated by established complex societies, nor one of onslaught and overthrow by invading barbarian hordes. It was instead a process of synthesis, compromise, and consolidation, as newcomers settled, developed individual cultural variations from pre-existing patterns, and in time asserted the new identity of their communities."

Tlatelolco and Tenochtitlán, and became the Colhua-Mexica by settling in with the peoples of the already well-established city of Colhuacán.

The name Aztec came to refer, as well, to the empire polity constructed by a Triple Alliance of the Mexica (capital at Tenochtitlán), the Acolhua (capital at Texcoco), and the small city of Tlacopan. In this sense, "the term 'Aztec' referred not to one particular people or nation but rather to a religious and cultural current with a political ideology of its own that had certain social and administrative implications and followers among the different ethnic groups" (Zantwijk 1985, 83). Many post-Conquest accounts used the Aztec label more inclusively yet, to refer to all the diverse peoples that inhabited the Basin of Mexico at the time the Spanish arrived. Gibson (1964, 21–23) reports that the "hierarchy of power and status" in 1519 just prior to the Conquest, was roughly as follows: Mexica, Acolhuaque, Tepaneca, Chalca, Xochimilca, Cuitlahuaca, Mixquica, Culhuaque, and Otomi. Each of these peoples was proud of its distinct identity, discouraged miscegenation, and normally occupied separate wards in the cities and towns where they lived. Aztec imperial authorities also tended to keep them separate in military cadres and labor projects.

Merchant Guilds

Long-distance merchant-traders may have been an occupational-identity category as early as the Olmecs, and it was one that became increasingly important and autonomous as societies became both more complex and connected. The best-documented long-distance merchant-traders are the Aztec *pochtecas,* who practiced their profession on a hereditary basis, lived in separate *barrios* or wards in Tenochtitlán-Tlatelolco and probably elsewhere, usually married within their group, and maintained their own shrines, priests, and sacrificial rituals (Kurtz 1978, 172; Hassig 1985, 117–18). The *pochtecas'* local guild "formed a political enclave in Aztec society," which was internally governed by two principal merchants and had its own courts and laws. Part of the guild's responsibility was regulation of lesser merchants whose trade was limited to selling foodstuffs or crafts in the local market. The *pochtecas* wore special dress and owed neither personal nor military service to the ruler, though they did pay tribute in kind. The local guild was affiliated with a regional merchants association stretching across the twelve towns in the center of the Aztec empire (Hassig 1985, 118; Zantwijk 1985, 132; Berdan 1977, 97).

Villages, Cities, and Large Regional Polities

As a rule, local/subregional identities and loyalties proved more durable than those associated with more inclusive polities. One of four known major Olmec centers, San Lorenzo, probably had a population of about a thousand and may have controlled tens of thousands in surrounding areas (Coe 1981b; and Coe and Diehl 1981). Chalcatzingo, an important highland center on the frontier of Olmec culture between the Basin of Mexico and the Gulf Coast seems to have been just a large village of about 400 persons at its height in 700–500 B.C.

In the Valley of Oaxaca, a pattern of widely spaced independent villages with dependent hamlets gave way to subregional centers, then to a single dominant regional polity—and ultimately to subregional centers again, albeit with a shift both in geographic focus (south from Oaxaca) and in dominant tribal/ethnic mix (from Zapotec to Mixtec) (Flannery and Marcus 1983 and Spores 1967). By 550 B.C. San José Mogoté, with a dependent population of about 1,300, was fifteen times larger than the other local village polities, but a subsequent population explosion and other factors propelled Monte Albán and perhaps six other comparable subregional centers into the lead. By 400 B.C. Monte Albán had about 5,000 persons, and its domain extended at least twenty-five to thirty miles. At its peak, Monte Albán dominated the entire Valley of Oaxaca, with a population of some 30,000, and its public buildings, terraces, and residences alone covered fifteen square miles (Adams 1991, 106; Fiedel 1987, 268–69; Drennen 1991, 270; Blanton 1983d, 1978, 1976; Blanton and Kowalewski 1981).

In the Lowland Petén prior to 250 B.C., Maya culture was one of scattered small villages. Over the next five hundred years some six subregional fortress centers emerged, including Tikal and Becán, which in the fourth century A.D. came under the influence of the extra-regional power, Teotihuacán. After Teotihuacán's decline and sixth-century civil wars, there were, during the Classic period, some twelve to sixteen subregional urban-center or city polities that exercised control over surrounding territory to a radius of about eight to sixteen miles. The largest, Tikal and El Mirador, had populations of perhaps 80,000 (Fiedel 1987, 280–96). Palenque and Copán, in the southwestern and southeastern corner of the lowlands, respectively, were more isolated and, no doubt for that reason, rather different. These two cities had smaller urban centers with temples and housing for elites, while a large population with political, economic, and religious ties to the center lived over a wider area. When Classic Maya civilization collapsed in the Petén circa A.D. 900, the area reverted to small villages for the next thousand years.[13] Mayan evolution continued in the Yucatán, where subregional city polities—some sixteen when the Spaniards arrived—were again the norm.[14]

Similar city polities were also what Adams (1991, 386) calls "the ultimate unit of political stability" in and around the Basin of Mexico, before the rise and after the fall of two regional hegemons—Teotihuacán and the Aztecs—whose ambitions and impact extended far beyond the region. (The Toltecs had their capital to the north and did not control much of the Basin of Mexico in their empire.) There were some six small city polities in the Teotihuacán subregion before Teotihuacán established its dominant position. The Spanish in 1519 counted no fewer than fifty city polities in the Basin of Mexico, most of which had owed allegiance and/or tribute to the Aztecs.

Alliances, Empires, Confederation

Overarching local and subregional polities were alliances, empires, and at least one entity that is customarily labeled a "confederation" (Roys 1962 and 1957, and Freidel 1983). This last arose in the Yucatán after the Toltecs' decline about 1200 A.D. undermined the status of their colonial provincial capital at Chichén and its Mexicanized Itza elite. Traditional Maya local and subregional polities revived, and the head of one Maya family (the Cocom) succeeded in grouping these into a single regional polity under his leadership at Mayapán. Once again, nesting was almost literal, insofar as the rulers of other polities were required to establish residence at Mayapán. There is also some overlapping, in this instance with empire. How much of this confederal arrangement was voluntary, to curb destructive interpolity conflict, or the product of outright coercion by the Cocoms is unclear. The confederation had most of the features usually reserved for empire except ethnic and linguistic diversity, though, of course, not all empires have been diverse in that sense. However, the fact that a high

---

13. Hammond (1974, 331) believes that the collapse of Classic Maya civilization may have "interrupted the emergence of even larger political entities in the Central Area, based on more widely-spaced giant centres such as Tikal and El Mirador."

14. Hammond (1982) offers an excellent overview of Maya civilization.

degree of coercion was not always involved is demonstrated by the circumstances surrounding the demise of the confederation. A later Cocom ruler triggered a general revolt by bringing in Mexican mercenaries to impose his will. Most of the Cocom family were killed, and Mayapán itself was abandoned. Many of the constituent units of the Mayapán confederation are presumed to have been among the sixteen subregional polities the Spanish ultimately encountered.

As in the case of Greece, the overlap between alliances, hegemonial alliances, and empire is even more pronounced. To be sure, alliances were a common feature of relationships among polities whenever a multipolar structure prevailed in a region, and alliances in this regard did not necessarily imply empire. Indeed, individual polities required them to provide security or extend political influence under fluid conditions fraught with both threat and opportunity. But one of the perennial threats was that a single member of the alliance might end up in a dominant position.

Consider the situation that existed after the fall of the Toltecs and the weakening of residual Olmec control in the Basin of Mexico. Three city polities—Azcapotzalco, Culhuacán, and Coatlichan—joined in an alliance which the Tepanecs of Azcapotzalco came to dominate, and the newly arrived Aztec-Mexica, who for a time served as mercenaries for the Tepanecs, eventually formed a Triple Alliance with Texcoco and Tlacopán that successfully overthrew Azcapotzalco.[15] The Tepanec War marked the start of the Aztec Empire, yet the empire from the outset had a novel structure because its foundation was the Triple Alliance. Each of the major city partners had its own cluster of subservient polities and could wage wars separately or jointly with its partners. When the allies waged war jointly, they could either assign the spoils totally to one member or divide them up in a 2:2:1 ratio (Tlacopán receiving the smaller share). A new ruler raised to the throne of one alliance member had to be acceptable to the other two,

15. Calnek (1976, 290) observes: "The city-states that began to emerge during the thirteenth and fourteenth centuries were heterogeneous with respect to ethnic composition and highly unstable insofar as political loyalties were concerned. . . . [T]he ease with which political loyalties could be manipulated and transferred is a background factor of major importance in explaining the rapidity with which individual city-states grew and declined throughout the chaotic era that preceded Tenochtitlan's rise as an imperial power."

and a rival claimant to a throne had a stronger case if his mother had been a princess from one of the other Triple-Alliance cities. Burr Cartwright Brundage (1972, 119–20) tries to explain the arrangement and in doing so he succeeds in demonstrating how inadequate Westphalian terminology is to describe this polity: "When viewed from the outside it appeared to be indeed a single corporate empire. But in terms of its own inner structure it was three mutually supporting empires, interlocked and interspersed, but each quite separate and each sovereign. It was a confederation of three coequal empires, and its executive was a college of three sovereigns. . . . The capital cities were further joined by an exchange of each other's gods and cults, thus forming a kind of amphictyony." As the tribute-division formula suggests, Tlacopán was a minor partner in the Triple Alliance from the beginning, and Texcoco became less important after the death of its illustrious ruler Nezahualcoyotl. Hence, even as the empire steadily expanded through conquest and a patchwork of alliances and tribute relationships, the Aztec-Mexica assumed a leading role.

The Aztec Empire was the last in a series of important pre-Conquest Mesoamerican empires. Teotihuacán, at its height in A.D. 450–650, had at its center an enormous city of up to 200,000, and its influence reached all the way to the Lowland Petén. However, recent evidence suggests that Teotihuacán physically occupied or directly controlled "only the most crucial zones and routes" in Mesoamerica and dealt with the other regional polities by applying strategies of "alliance, intimidation, or isolation" (Adams 1991, 225, 251). Likewise, although the Aztecs ruled five or six million subjects, the system they employed—according to Conrad and Demarest (1984, 53; also Davies 1987, and Hassig 1985 and 1988)—was "conquest without consolidation" and "not really an 'empire' at all." Instead, the so-called empire "was a loose hegemony of city-states pledging obedience and tribute to the Triple Alliance capitals." There was no serious effort to assimilate conquered peoples, and large, almost entirely independent enclaves remained. "Mountainous regions, unyielding opponents, or areas lacking resources desirable as tribute were simply bypassed as the imperial armies swept toward easier and richer prey. As the empire grew in size, these independent enclaves became a substantial problem."

We are left with as much confusion as to the correct or even most useful working definition of "empire" as with "tribe." Is an empire a polity that "merely" exercises control over different ethnic/linguistic groups? Most Mesoamerican empires would qualify, including that of the Tarascans to the west and south of the Basin of Mexico, whose 25,000-square-mile polity was the largest of any at the time of the Spanish Conquest. The Tarascans ruled some 340 settlements, but only four were cities; all were in the Lake Pátzcuaro basin, and the most populous had no more than 35,000 people. Yet a control-over-different-ethnic/linguistic-groups definition for empire would also seem to include modern-day Mexico, and exclude Mayapán. Other issues: How much actual conquest must take place? How should we regard alliances when we are trying to determine an empire's geographical scope? How much genuine consolidation and assimilation of peoples need follow conquest to be a "real" empire?

CONCLUSION

Pre-Conquest Mesoamerica was a distinct system, which was never fully unified even at the height of empires. The Conquest interrupted a long period of independent evolution. Before the Spanish arrived, Mesoamerica had a remarkable range of overlapping and nested polities, including extended-family/artificial kinship groups (for example, *calpullin*), merchant guilds, tribes, villages, cities, subregional urban centers, large regional polities, alliances, hegemonial alliances, at least one confederation, and empires. Mesoamerican polities interacted with one another not only through warfare and trade but also through formal diplomatic channels and royal marriages.

The geophysical environment may have given some advantage to elites who controlled scarce water resources. However, irrigation and other water-related public works made polities more vulnerable to the vicissitudes of nature and warfare. Natural disasters and ecological degradation repeatedly altered the course of political evolution. The fact that different localities had different resources and specializations encouraged the formation of larger polities and extensive trade networks. Trade enhanced the status of whomever controlled it, either rulers or a middle stratum of professionals.

In sum, the sheer variety of polity types and their relationships in Mesoamerica were at least as complex as those in the European system of the *conquistadores*—and became even more complicated when the Conquest added additional layers of authority.

10

MESOAMERICA
AND THE SPANISH CONQUEST
The Collision of Civilizations

The meeting of Old and New Worlds proved a genuine watershed for both civilizations, indeed for world history. (For general background, see Burman 1989 and Wolf 1982.) Some analysts prefer to describe the Spanish Conquest as an "Encounter of Two Civilizations." Both characterizations are to some extent accurate. The Spanish did defeat the Mesoamericans militarily and then ruled them as colonial subjects, yet the conquest forever remained incomplete. The actual result in the New World was mostly fusion, and the Old World experienced profound feedback effects. Those effects included what Boseman (1960, 289) describes as "a revolutionary reappraisal of the Western attitudes toward alien culture areas."

INTRODUCTION

The Spanish superimposed European forms of political, economic, and social organization on Mesoamerica. However, a broader and more reciprocal phenomenon was what Alfred W. Crosby (1972) and others have called "the Columbian Exchange" of Old/New World diseases, animals, and plants. That exchange alone—coupled with the one-way flow to Europe of vast quantities of precious metals—brought about major changes in demographic patterns, modes of production and transportation, food, and lifestyles on both sides of the Atlantic (see also Elliott 1970).

The primary (somewhat overlapping) vertical relationships in the Mesoamerican experience were (1) between pre-Conquest rulers of individual polities and their local subjects; (2) between pre-Conquest expansionist regional and imperial polities, and the other polities within their wider domains; and (3) Spanish imperial rule. Although there are similarities among Mesoamerican polities of the same eras, the differences among those in different regions are sufficient to justify looking at them separately.

RULERS AND RULED IN MESOAMERICA

Olmecs

The Olmecs' region was southeastern to south-central Mexico, but their trade, military operations, and religious and other cultural influences extended over a wide zone. Olmec civilization is only dimly understood, and how much of what followed them is *directly* traceable to their example is still debatable. The Olmecs may have been the first Mesoamericans to produce an elite, possibly those controlling the best land. Elites seem to have succeeded in establishing themselves in ruling dynasties associated with the leading Olmec gods. The jaguar-rain god was especially prominent, and in various guises it reappears—as does human sacrifice, which the Olmecs may have practiced—for the rest of Mesoamerican history. Olmec leaders most likely controlled trade in luxury items and other commodities, and perhaps enjoyed a steady flow of tribute from military conquests. They commanded a large labor force and lavishly funded the work of skilled artisan-craftsmen, who appear to have occupied an intermediate social position between elites and masses. The artists developed a distinctive style that glorified Olmec civilization in magnificent jewelry and sculpture, including the famed colossal stone heads.

Mayas

.   Much about the Mayas, too, remains cloudy, especially the rise of Mayan civilization. However, one of the greatest mysteries of archaeology—why Classic Maya civilization collapsed—is now a long way toward solution. With recent advances in Mayan scholarship, the myth that the Mayas were different than other Mesoamericans—supposedly a peaceful people who were led by philosopher kings—has been disproven. Warfare was endemic, and human sacrifice was common, though not on a scale to compare with the Basin of Mexico. Another misconception was that Maya centers existed mainly for ceremonial and administrative purposes and were not real cities. Finally, most scholars no longer believe that the later period in Yucatán represents a decline in Maya civilization but see instead a transformation that reflected a more egalitarian social structure and an emphasis on commerce.

As far as we know, Maya civilization developed in the Petén Lowlands as a result of the interplay of several factors. We have noted the need for greater social organization arising from population increase and the shift from kin-based production to a tributary feudal-like arrangement in which a hereditary elite controlled most of the land. Early on, assemblies or councils of family leaders may have been the main political structures, but powerful kings who were the heads of distinguished lineages soon emerged. The Maya religion emphasized ancestor reverence,[1] and rulers came to be regarded at least as divinely appointed if not gods themselves.[2] The continuity of some Maya dynasties like those at Tikal and Palenque is impressive. Teotihuacán's involvement especially at Tikal provided a demonstration effect from outside, and the abrupt withdrawal of Teotihuacán's presence—and, indeed, the absence of significant foreign contact for a time—accelerated regional warfare, the decline of some centers, and the consolidation of others that were prominent in the Classic Period. Public works including imposing temple and palace complexes, drainage systems and roads, and the flowering of sculpture and art—as well as the development of mathemathics, writing, and astronomy—all reinforced the faith of Mayans in their civilization.

There were no fewer than five classes in Maya society. Aristocrats were the large landowners and monopolized top roles in government, administration, trade, and the military. Lesser nobility held lower administrative and managerial positions, except perhaps those at the village or district level, which may have been filled by commoners. Next came skilled artisans, then commoner-farmers, and, last, the dispossessed poor. Adams (1991, 192–93) writes: "There were reciprocal obligations between the classes, vertically, so to speak. . . . patron-client relationships between noble households and commoner families.

---

1. Maya temples often housed the tomb of a ruler.

2. See especially Hammond 1982, chaps. 7, 10–11. Freidel (1981, 190) observes about the Lowland Mayas, but with relevance to many ancient civilizations: "Within hierarchical societies the symbols of cosmic and world order that make up a state religion and ideology are often the same as those that signify power relationships. Such central and public symbols do not simply serve to justify extant relationships of power. They also comprise a vital feature of their realization, for the material bases of power, such as labor, land, and wealth, can only be manipulated by means of symbolic denotation."

. . . [W]e can rank them from the highest nonelite, who had intimate and continual contact with the aristocracy, down to those people who rarely interacted with the elite or even saw them. The former would have been those who practiced skills most needed by the rulers, and the latter would have constituted a mass of farmers, many in isolated districts of regional states."

The Classic Maya civilization began to disintegrate rapidly after about A.D. 830, owing to a number of factors that, if anything, were more complex than those that account for its original rise (Adams 1991, 264–70; and Hammond 1982, 138–41). Although the precise mix was somewhat different for each major polity, there do seem to be some common patterns. Increasing populations placed a growing burden on the land, eliminating the potential for agricultural expansion, causing deforestation, and making Maya centers vulnerable to the vicissitudes of weather, insects, and warfare. Weather and warfare took turns for the worse, and elites were unable or unwilling to take corrective action. Indeed, Adams (1991, 266) suggests that "there is a kind of built-in Peter Principle in [aristocratic] leadership: one is born to his level of incompetence," and elites actually aggravated the situation by stepping up building programs. The size and numbers of Late Classic buildings—and presumably the numbers of aristocrats they housed—grew to such an extent that the labor required increased tenfold. There is some evidence of violent revolution from within a few Maya polities and also of growing military pressure from non-Maya groups spreading from the western lowlands. The Lowland Petén was virtually depopulated, and dense jungle spread over ruins that continue to astonish twentieth-century archaeologists and tourists.

Northern Puuc Maya centers in the Yucatán, including Uxmal (which might have been the capital of a regional polity), Chichen Itza, Kabah, Sayil, and Labná, were already absorbing Toltec influences by A.D. 900. The Toltecs may originally have come into the area as mercenaries and then eventually come to dominant their employers. The northern Maya centers seem to have enjoyed something of a renaissance when their southern counterparts collapsed, but they suffered from many of the same problems and, except perhaps for Cobá,[3] lasted no more than a hundred years longer.

---

3. Cobá not only survived but grew, though it appears always to have been "more insular and conservative . . . than the Puuc sphere communities and [had] strong ties to the Southern Classic polities" (Freidel 1985, 287).

The Maya civilization that reemerged in the Yucatán at the end of the Toltec era was different from the earlier pattern, and not all of the difference can be attributed to Mexicanization. For a time the Mayapán "confederation" kept peace among some eighteen scattered urban centers, but the fact that most cities were now walled suggests that warfare remained a possibility. Although there was a supreme Cocom ruler at Mayapán, a ruler or ruling group at each urban center, and an elite class, the social and material gaps in society narrowed. The standard of living of all classes improved, with flourishing markets and unprecedented levels of trade. Public buildings offer the clearest evidence of a shift in social values. There are no more elaborate palaces, no massive temples indicating a centralized religious authority—each family and small social group has its own shrine—and the standard of construction (plaster over crude piles of rubble) is poor. Archaeologists who once regarded all this as evidence of a "decline" now see it as a sign of a more egalitarian ethos (Freidel and Sabloff 1984, 183–85, 192–93).

The relatively good times were not to last. The Mayapán regional polity broke up violently when the leaders of its component entities fell to bickering. The result was a new round of warfare and, by A.D. 1450, political disintegration. Freidel (1985, 309) argues that the principal evolutionary trend in Mesoamerica after Teotihuacán's intervention in the Petén was "toward cultural unification following networks of political and economic alliance" but that Maya elites were never able "to change the worldview of their people from Maya to Mesoamerican." Be that as it may, the Mayas, scattered in a number of small and large towns, were vulnerable when the Spanish arrived. Yet the Conquest of the Yucatán took some twenty years, partly because the region was not rich in resources and was of low priority to the Spanish, and partly because the Maya were skilled in guerrilla warfare.

Nancy M. Farriss (1984, 19) stresses that the conquest of the Yucatán was not really complete until the second half of the twentieth century. The last Maya Great Revolt of the Conquest era was suppressed in 1547, and epidemics greatly reduced the Maya population. Cities withered, but Maya culture survived by retreating into small village polities and families with subsistence plots. The Mayas maintained almost full autonomy from the Spanish administration at least until the Bourbon reforms late in the colonial era. Another revolt flared in 1683 (Jones 1990). Not until the end of the nineteenth century did wealthy Mexicans and foreigners develop large henequen plantations for the world export market.

Meanwhile, the Mayas rose up again in 1847 in the so-called Caste War against what they still saw as foreign domination[4] and came close to defeating the Mexican army. The Mayas only stopped the war to return to their villages for rainy season planting. As it was, they succeeded in pushing the colonial frontier back to where it had been in the mid-seventeenth century and established a rebel Maya *cruzob* polity that gained its name and inspiration from a Maya-Christian cult of a Speaking Cross. The *cruzob* Maya capital fell to Mexican troops in 1901, but the Mayas continued to control most of the Quintana Roo region in eastern Yucatán. Farriss (prematurely) marks the final conquest of the Mayas with the death of the last of the Caste War leaders, the chief of the *cruzob* town of Chumpom, in 1969. His successors decided not to attack the crews who were building a highway that would end Maya isolation. Even today, though some Mayas serve in the Mexican army they once fought, any tourist in rural Yucatán will see that the overlay of Spanish/Mexican culture remains little more than a veneer, and some Mayan descendants, this time in Chiapas, are in open revolt.

Teotihuacán and Monte Albán

Two contemporaneous and indirectly competing civilizations— Teotihuacán in the Basin of Mexico and the Zapotecs at Monte Albán— offer parallels and contrasts. Both began as relatively small centers and steadily expanded, probably through a combination of voluntary association and military coercion, into large regional polities. Monte Albán's leveled mountaintop could have served either as a natural location for the headquarters of a voluntary confederation or a pinnacle from which to dominate most of the Valley of Oaxaca. Teotihuacán controlled most of the Basin of Mexico. Both capitals, judging by their size and monumental architecture, must have been important places of worship and ceremony. Visitors must have been overwhelmed by the beauty and pageantry of the polities they observed. René Million (cited

---

4. Rus (1983) argues that the Indians were initially politicized because they were manipulated by conservative-liberal rivalry among the region's Spanish-Mexican *(ladino)* elite. See also Bricker 1977 and Burns 1977.

in Wilford 1993) attributes much of Teotihuacán's long success to "the instrumental way its leaders used the attraction of its holy places and the prestige of its religion to make it significant to so many for so long a time,"[5] and the same must have been true of Monte Albán on a lesser scale. However, in a matter of decades around A.D. 700, Teotihuacán was destroyed, and Monte Albán was largely abandoned.[6]

This is where the similarities between the two polities end. Teoti-huacán was one of the largest cities in the world of its time—about seven times as large as Monte Albán—and was probably the most important trade hub, center for craft production, and marketplace in Mesoamerica (Millon 1976, 241). Monte Albán dominated a few areas outside the Valley of Oaxaca (Marcus 1988) but nothing to compare with Teotihuacán's empire that reached as far south as the Lowland Petén. One of the apparent gaps in Teotihuacán's empire was the Valley of Oaxaca, though it is not inconceivable that the Oaxaca *barrio* in Teotihuacán housed hostages rather than ambassadors or traders. Also, Monte Albán's leaders were dynastic rulers, like those of the Olmecs and Mayas, whose divine charge must have blurred into divinity itself. Something else appears to have been happening in Teotihuacán. In excavations to date there is no evidence of lavish tombs; and artistic works tend to glorify either deities like a supreme female goddess or the feathered serpent or the accomplishments of the society at large. Specifically, although it is almost certain that Teotihuacán had rulers legitimized by the supernatural, they do not appear to have been raised to the level of a cult of personality (Wilford 1993). Finally, Teotihuacán seems to have set the mold for the later Toltecs and Aztecs, including a precedent for political unification of a

---

5. Coe (1981a, 167) notes: "[Teotihuacán's] odd compass orientation sug-gests a preoccupation with religio-astronomical matters, not practical matters. . . . Why did they put the city exactly there, as there are surely better locations for an urban center in the valley of Mexico? . . . I am convinced that this site was in some important way connected in their minds with the center of the world and the act of creation."

6. Monte Albán experienced large-scale emigration but was not completely deserted (Paddock 1983, 187). According to Blanton (1983b, 281): "During the Late Postclassic, Monte Albán was evidently still a very important place, probably a small commercial center and perhaps also a sacred place where people still deposited offerings and occasionally buried their dead, but it was no longer the center of decision making for a regional polity."

substantial part of the Basin of Mexico, while the aftermath of Monte Albán was political disintegration.[7]

The belief that Teotihuacán's success included the development of a broad-based civic culture fits with other aspects of that polity, but less neatly with its demise. We mentioned earlier the apartment compounds that housed extended family groups and persons of like profession or occupation. Most of these complexes had a small temple or shrine dedicated to a patron deity. In addition, the society was highly militarized, honoring the warrior and practicing human sacrifice associated with warfare. The remains of the ritual sacrifice of two hundred young warriors have been found at the Temple of the Feathered Serpent. Nevertheless, when the collapse came, it was abrupt and total. Some combination of internal discontent—perhaps the effect of a drought, competition among ruling groups abetted by resident foreigners—and the rise of outside rivals must have been involved. In any event, Teotihuacán was burned and systematically looted.

Richard E. Blanton (1983b, 186) suggests that one reason for the demise of Monte Albán at about the same time may have been that Valley of Oaxaca residents believed "such an expensive supraregional authority" was no longer needed to protect against Teotihuacán. Population increases in the Valley may also have led to food shortages during dry years, produced disputes over productive land, and undermined the control of the central polity. Once the mountaintop city could no longer count on large food contributions from the Valley, its doom was sealed.

---

7. Additional legacies of Monte Albán's Classic Period, in Marcus's (1983, 358–59) summary, were a "ruling stratum, including kings who lived in major palaces and nobles . . . ; royal ancestor worship; temples staffed by professional priests, some of them possibly full-time specialists who actually resided in the temple; military conquest, with the possible conversion of captives into slaves for labor or sacrifice." The main political unit of the Postclassic era was the *cacicazgo,* "a small urban center and a whole series of rural communities subject to one hereditary lord." Although some Zapotec polities remained, they were gradually overshadowed by the Mixtecs. The Mixtecs "evolved one of the most highly stratified [social] systems in Mesoamerica, one in which differences were extreme even within . . . royalty and nobility. . . . The direct line of royal descent was so important that rulers sometimes married their full siblings."

Toltecs

The collapse of Teotihuacán, along with Monte Albán, caused turmoil throughout Mesoamerica. The Toltecs emerged as the preeminent polity in the Basin of Mexico, founded their capital at Tula (in the modern Mexican state of Hidalgo) about A.D. 960, and extended their influence as far as the Yucatán. Although they definitely existed, the Toltecs are customarily referred to as "legendary," because little is known about them (Davies 1977, chapter 1). However, it is hard to overestimate their impact on Mesoamerican history, mainly because the later Aztecs were fascinated by them.

The Aztecs created the myth of a Toltec "golden age." They regarded themselves as the heirs of Toltec power—if not the blood relatives of the Toltecs[8]—and went shopping for Toltec or part-Toltec aristocrats from other polities to enhance the pedigree of their own ruling class (Brundage 1972, 10–13, 39–41).[9] Indeed, one of the reasons we know so little about the Toltecs is that the Aztecs deliberately destroyed historical records that might have given the lie to some of their claims of earlier Toltec connections (Brundage 1972, 107–8). Nevertheless, it is not inconceivable that Mexica forebears at some stage in their wanderings might have encountered the Toltecs, served as mercenaries for them, and been a factor in their collapse. Even when the Aztecs faithfully recorded Toltec stories, rather than exaggerating them for propaganda purposes, some of the stories are likely to have been Toltec myths. Like the Aztecs, the Toltecs could have partially invented their own past, drawing on tales of the great civilization of Teotihuacán. To complete the circle, the Aztecs may have confused the Toltecs' "Tollan," referring in part to the historical capital city of Tula, with the vast ruins of Teotihuacán.

---

8. The Mixtecs in the Valley of Oaxaca, too, claimed descent from the Toltec lords of Tula and had some Toltec features in their culture. Whether the Mixtecs were native to Oaxaca and only came to the fore when the Zapotecs declined or whether they were invaders from outside (where they might once have been subject to Toltec influence) is still controversial (Marcus and Flannery 1983, 218–22).

9. This was an expensive policy, as Clendinnen (1991, 24) reports: "When they took the step of choosing as their ruler a prince of Culhuacan of a lineage which could claim Toltec blood, a choice which hinted at their pretensions, the ruler of Azcapotzalco doubled their tribute."

One important legend about the Toltecs is so pervasive it may be partly true. Topiltzin-Quetzalcoatl, Toltec ruler and also high priest of the Quetzalcoatl cult, reputedly attempted to persuade the Toltecs to stop their ruthless military conquests and ritual human sacrifices. One is tempted to draw a parallel with the Egyptian "heretic" pharaoh Akhenaten and to highlight the Topiltzin-Quetzalcoatl episode as the only known Mesoamerican case where "religion" in any form clashed with the dominant political culture. Be that as it may, he apparently lost the contest and had to go into exile. Certainly, the myth of a god named Quetzalcoatl who would someday return became a part of Mesoamerican mythology that the Aztecs accepted, and it was one of the factors adding to their initial uncertainty about how to react to Cortés (Brundage 1972, 252, 266; Gillespie 1989, 226–30).

Nigel Davies (1972, 25, 417, 418, 420) offers a few tentative conclusions about the Toltecs. First, " 'Tollan' and 'Toltec' are not merely the names of one city and its people but are concepts, almost impossible to confine to one place, people, or period." Second, though the Quetzalcoatl story may be true, there is no way to identify the specific ruler-priest involved, not least because "Quetzalcoatl" and "Topiltzin" were titles applied to several persons in Toltec history. The story may even have been based on something that occurred much earlier in Teotihuacán. Third, the Toltecs had an empire, but—owing to limited manpower and resources—it was only a modest one. The Aztecs exaggerated its extent, to add legitimacy to the large empire they were establishing. There was, however, a significant Toltec colony in the Yucatán at Chichén. We have noted that one possibility for the Toltec intrusion into Maya territory was mercenary service, and Davies speculates that it might have involved "some kind of religious proselytism." Finally, though the Toltecs shared the "spirit of militarism" associated with Teotihuacán and the Aztecs, the Toltecs in other respects—including some elements of "theocratic" rule or plural kingship—may have represented more than just a temporal "halfway house" between the other two civilizations.

THE AZTEC HEGEMONY/EMPIRE

We have previously discussed the Aztec economy, including the importance of imperial tribute, and the prominent roles of *pochteca* merchants and *calpulli* farmers and craftsmen. Merchants and *calpullin* were not only crucial to the economy but also were basic units of organization and mobility in Aztec society. They enjoyed a high degree of autonomy within their respective domains, yet in significant respects remained subject to aristocratic rulers. Relative autonomy was its own reward, and there were material benefits, too, as well as some hope for social advancement. However, ideology/cosmology arguably provided the main glue that held Aztec society together. Ideology also generated the fanaticism required for the military campaigns that built a mighty empire. Paradoxically, ideology also guided the empire in directions that made it difficult to consolidate and increasingly vulnerable. Cortés effectively exploited those weaknesses, but whether the empire would have long survived had the Spanish never arrived is doubtful.

The key period in Aztec evolution was the immediate aftermath of the Triple Alliance victory over the Tepanecs.[10] The Aztecs acquired lands that were much more extensive than the lake-bed *chinampas* of Tenochtitlán and carried substantial tribute rights (Conrad and Demarest 1984, 32). Rather than distributing the new lands and tribute to traditional *calpulli* groups, Itzcoatl, the Aztec Great *Tlatoani* (supreme ruler), appropriated most of them for himself, his family, and a warrior elite. Write Conrad and Demarest: "Most of the major chronicles mention the imperial 'reforms' instituted by the principal figures of the new order: Itzcoatl . . . ; Montezuma I, his nephew and successor; and Tlacaelel, a larger-than-life figure said to to have been the *cihuacoatl* (high priest and chief adviser) of the first four imperial rulers." These changes "concentrated wealth, social privilege, and political power in the hands of the ruling tlatoani, his warrior knights, and the noble . . . class."

Then "the new leaders ordered the burning of the existing historical and religious texts" and set about constructing an ideology that would legitimize their rule and continued Aztec expansion.[11] Children of the nobility and commoners alike studied this ideology in temple

---

10. For a summary of Aztec history to this point, see Brundage 1972, chaps. 2–4. Chapters 7, 9–10 chronicle the Aztecs' subsequent imperial expansion.

11. Kurtz (1978, 175) argues that a legend was even manufactured to legitimize the elite's ascendancy after the Tepanec War. "At the time of [the war] the nobles, anxious for a fight, made a pact with the commoners, who were less anxious to fight. If the war was lost the nobles agreed that the commoners could do with them as they wished, even kill them. But if the Aztecs were victorious the commoners would forever serve the nobles."

and *calpulli* schools, artists and architects celebrated it, and rulers and priests reiterated it on every possible public occasion.[12] The Aztecs fused their putative inheritance of the Toltec mantle with a complex and fatalistic cosmology that—like Mesoamerican cosmology from time immemorial—stressed the continual need to appease the gods. To this foundation the Aztecs made two major and related additions that were distinctly their own, though the first paralleled a means of creating identity used in other civilizations and the second drew on previous Mesoamerican practice. First, they elevated their own god, Huitzilopochtli, to the status of one of the four principal deities of the pantheon, interchangeable with Tonatiuh, the sun itself. "In fact, Huitzilopochtli differs from most other ethnic patron deities in the strictly local nature of his following—at least prior to the Mexicas' imperial expansion. . . . It could only have been with the help of the imperial mythographers that the Mexicas' insignificant patron deity was able to elbow his way into the upper pantheon" (Conrad and Demarest 1984, 28).

Huitzilopochtli's calls for imperial adventures and his insatiable desire for sacrifices meshed nicely with the second Aztec "contribution" to ideology, the idea that, without a constant flow of human blood sacrifices, all manner of woe would befall Aztec society—even the end of the universe: "The imperial cosmology held that the Mexica must relentlessly take captives in warfare and sacrifice them; the spiritual strength of the sacrificed enemy warriors would strengthen the sun and stave off its inevitable destruction by the forces of darkness" (Conrad and Demarest 1984, 38; see also Brundage 1972, 92–97). To be sure, earlier Mesoamerican societies—notably those in the Basin of Mexico—engaged in ritual human sacrifice. However, the scale of mass sacrifices—up to a few hundred victims yearly—was "quite small" in comparison to the many thousands whose hearts were ripped out by the obsidian daggers of Aztec priests, whose skin was flayed for wearing or other adornment, and whose flesh went into cookpots for the consumption of Aztec nobility.[13] Is it any wonder that

---

12. On the artistic and ceremonial dimension, see Carrasco 1971; Broda, Carrasco, and Matos Moctezuma 1987; and Matos Moctezuma 1986.

13. The best evocation of Aztec sacrificial rituals is Clendinnen 1991, 2 and chap. 3.

Spanish conquerors and priests regarded the Aztecs as devil worshipers and sought to level their temples as sites for churches?

From the early imperial era onwards, the Aztec social pyramid had a number of different levels (Davies 1987, 120–23). Each major community or equivalent administrative district had one or more *tlatoani(s)* or supreme ruler(s) and various lesser rulers known as *tecuhtli(s)*. Both types of rulers had their own palaces, held court surrounded by their relatives, and owned large plots of the best land. Third in the hierarchy of local nobility came the pillis, descendants of *tlatoanis* and tecuhtlis, most of whom owned plots of land that varied widely in size.[14] *Pillis* grew in numbers because aristocrats (unlike commoners) were allowed to practice polygamy and had numerous wives and concubines. When the office of *tlatoani* or *tecuhtli* became vacant, it was usually filled by a member of the same family, though the Great Tlatoani of Tenochtitlán would also be consulted regarding a *tlatoani*. Further complicating matters is that, at least in Tenochtitlán and perhaps elsewhere, the Great Tlatoani occasionally awarded distinguished non-*pilli* warriors, priests, or traders the equivalent of a life nobility, which carried with it a nonhereditary title to a small landed estate.

Provincial *tlatoanis* owed tribute to the Great Tlatoani, and they taxed the tecuhtlis, who taxed the *pillis* in turn. Aristocratic privileges beyond private ownership of land included wearing special regalia and dress and living in two-story houses. Boys from aristocratic families made up most of the student body of the *calmecac* schools, which trained them for careers in politics, the military, and the priesthood. The few commoners admitted to such schools could only study for the priesthood,[15] though male commoners received instruction in military and other subjects in *telpochcalli* schools, which were attended as well by some aristocrats.

As we have noted, the traditional Aztec *calpulli* was a group—related by extended-family kinship or artificial kinship—that worked a plot of supposedly inalienable common land or engaged in the same

---

14. Those who did not have land could only work as artisans or stonecutters because their social status did not allow them to cultivate the land of others (Davies 1987, 121).

15. Important religious duties in the main temple(s) were probably performed exclusively or primarily by aristocrats.

craft, had their own school and patron deity, and often fought together. However, there is still much we do not fully understand about the *calpullin*.[16] Presumably the element of actual kinship involved in them diminished over time, but some authorities maintain that the Aztec polity had a policy of further diluting *calpulli* identity by deliberately mixing ethnicities where possible (Kurtz 1978, 176). To what extent, then, were *calpullin* transformed from "clan-like" units into units of production and administration? Were aristocratic nobles and priests appointed as "head men" to oversee their political and religious orthodoxy (Kurtz 1978, 173, 176)? What was the *calpullis'* relationship with the nobility? Were the only members of *calpullin* free commoners, or were aristocrats also members? We know that most *calpullin* had "associations" with noble families and were ranked partly by such connections. Many free commoners worked on the lands of the nobility.[17] Were those commoners serfs who had only their own subsistence plots, or were new *calpullin* organized to work whatever new land the nobles acquired? If the latter, how much of the noble's "own" land or production was the *calpulli's* entitlement? For that matter, how much "inalienable" *calpulli* common land was gradually appropriated by the nobility, as did the later Spanish? Finally, when a *calpulli* had either its own common land or an entitlement within an aristocrat's preserve, did it pay tribute directly to the Aztec polity's central bureaucracy or to an associated noble family?

Hierarchical as Aztec society was, there was no strict division between rich and poor. Some commoners were well-off and even had a number of employees, while some *pillis* were relatively impoverished (Davies 1987, 127–28). Everyone could take pride in being Aztec, enjoy the gory pageantry, and hope for a little trickle-down from booty, trade, or tribute. Distinguished service to the polity could bring handsome rewards. A relatively broad middle sector of warriors, *pochtecas,* and artisans profited financially and advanced socially through their professions. Davies (1987, 123) comments that the "no-

---

16. For a range of opinions, see Davies 1987, 121–23; Kurtz 1978, 172–77; Hicks 1987, 94–97; Zantwijk 1985, 81–85; and Adams 1991, 381–86.

17. Since most war captives ended up as sacrifices, there were few slaves. What slaves there were, were usually children sold by destitute parents or persons who wagered their freedom, and these were reserved for personal service or special sacrifice.

bles' real rivals in the quest for power and wealth were less the traditional *calpulli* leaders than the merchants and other intermediate groups." The *pochtecas'* very autonomy in matters of their guild "functionally separated them from Aztec society at large" (Kurtz 1978, 178) and, in a sense, made them less of a threat to central authority. In addition, even as they were allowed to regulate the practices of lesser merchant-craftsmen in the local marketplace, so they themselves were subject to constraints in long-distance trade. Only some *pochtecas* were allowed to trade beyond the boundaries of the empire, and all were at the mercy of local rulers for permission to employ the foot-bearers required to transport merchandise. *Pochtecas* therefore had a stake in imperial expansion, because it opened up opportunities for trade (Hassig 1985, 125).

Nevertheless, all was not well with the Aztec polity. Intermediate levels notwithstanding, Aztec society was highly aristocratic and became more so over time. The Aztec's Great Tlatoani was recruited from the polity's most prominent clan and presumed to speak for whichever god whose counsel might be sought on a particular official occasion.[18] The numbers of aristocrats steadily increased, and supporting them became more of a burden. Conrad and Demarest (1984, 58) observe that the "Mexica social structure had grown top-heavy through some of the very privileges originally granted as incentives to achievement." Montezuma II also adopted a deliberate policy of enhancing his own stature and encouraged greater hierarchy in society at large. The supreme ruler rarely showed himself in public, established separate waiting rooms in his palace for nobles and commoners, insisted that subject rulers serve him in person like menials, organized a corps of the sons of nobles to help around the palace, excluded illegitimate sons of the nobility from temple schools, and created new

---

18. Clendinnen (1991, 81) describes the Mexica's Great Tlatoani's "multiple relationships to the divine": "He went into combat in the customary regalia of the warrior god Huitzilopochtli. His image was set up as a representation of Xiutecutli, the Fire God, on the god's feast of Izcalli, which [acknowledged] the 'naturalness' of human hierarchy. In his priestly performances Moctezoma was associated with Quetzalcoatl, the diety of priestly wisdom. But it was . . . from Tezcatlipoca that he took his power to command, reward or punish. The tlatoani's sacredness was not a state, but a condition, intermittent, yet 'personal' in the most immediate sense, in that his body, properly prepared and adorned, could on occasion become the vehicle of that divine force."

orders of bureaucrats and warriors (Brundage 1972, 232–34). The central royal court was reproduced in miniature in the fifty-odd cities in the Basin of Mexico.

Although the empire served its purposes well at the outset, as the years passed, it became more of a liability than an asset. Island-bound Tenochtitlán needed to acquire productive land and was a poor performer in exports, so tribute—in addition to its other benefits—helped compensate for a trade imbalance. Imperial expansion opened up new areas for trade (Hassig 1985, 103; Davies 1987, 99–100), but, in due course, expansion became counterproductive. As Davies (1987, 100) notes, it was all "a kind of vicious circle"; "new conquests provided the means for lavishness on an ever-increased scale; such rituals in turn, designed to placate the gods of war and to bedazzle the still unconquered guests, exhausted the treasury and thus created the need for further conquests." Conquests at a distance created more difficult administrative and logistical problems and added little to the supply of foodstuffs or the flow of tribute and sacrificial victims. Meanwhile, throughout the empire, wars and sacrifices were destroying some of the empire's productive capacity even as population exploded and the demand for food and victims accelerated. Conrad and Demarest (1984, 58–59) observe: "The wheels of the divine war machine had been set in motion and could not be stopped. The cosmology of solar struggle, the cults of mass sacrifice, and the glorification of war and the warrior were so deeply ingrained into the Mexica way of life that no other ideological perspective could be imagined by either the people or their rulers." When the late empire experienced military reversals and famines, the response—to sacrifice more victims—made matters worse.[19]

Almost all the emphasis was on expansion and not enough on consolidation. The Aztecs relied "on hegemonic rather than territorial control" (Hassig 1988, 26), which up to a point succeeded. They allowed conquered peoples to retain their own dynasties, and Aztec

---

19. Aztec chronicles report that eventually there was such a shortage of preferred victims—warriors captured in battle—that Basin of Mexico polities agreed to engage periodically in "Flowery Wars" to increase the supply for their gods. Some analysts, however, have suggested that Flowery Wars were merely an explanation for the fact that the Aztecs failed to win decisive victories (Conrad and Demarest 1984, 59–60).

nobles often married into local ruling families. The empire was like a large-scale protection racket, yet subjects at least had no one else to fear *but* the Aztecs; and some no doubt enjoyed the prestige of association with a superpower. By Roman or Inca standards, imperial administration was lax. Brundage (1975, 60) argues: "The Incas saw their empire as an administrative responsibility; the Mexica looked upon theirs as loot." There were thirty-eight provinces that represented clusters of subject cities with their own rulers—and some independent kingdoms—but imperial bureaucrats were few and did little more than collect tribute. The only Aztec army garrisons stationed in the field were those along dangerous frontiers and key communications routes.

The Aztecs made no real effort to appeal to or assimilate conquered peoples. "Subjugation did not mean incorporation" (Clendinnen 1991, 25). Quite the contrary. Brundage (1975, 79–80) observes that using the term "Pax Mexicana" would be absurd, for the "last thing in the world the Mexica wanted was peace" because battles would cease and the gods would starve. "Thus the Mexica almost consciously goaded their imperial subjects to a breaking point and were not sorry to have to cope with the insurrections which so inevitably followed." It is not coincidental that most of the pre-Conquest insurrections were at the core of the empire, rather than the periphery, for the core had suffered Aztec domination longer (Hassig 1985, 103).

Montezuma II tried to engage in fewer distant military campaigns and concentrate on strengthening Aztec control of the Basin of Mexico and its environs. But some holdouts like the Tlaxcalans repeatedly defeated the Aztecs, for which the Aztecs expand-or-die ideology simply had no provision. For them, the only possible interpretation was that, despite all the sacrifices, the gods were displeased. Hence, when the Spanish arrived, the Aztecs were already demoralized. Cortés drove a "small wedge . . . into a nonintegrated empire, splitting it along the cleavages inherent in its structure" (Hassig 1985, 150). Many subjects of the empire seized the opportunity to revolt, and not a few gave aid to the Spanish. Conrad and Demarest (1984, 70) regard it as "significant that in the final assault on Tenochtitlán, Cortes's handful of men led an army of tens of thousands of Indian allies, most of them vengeful Tlaxcalans." Nevertheless, many subject city polities fought valiantly for the Aztecs and suffered heavy losses (Davies 1987, 191–92).

THE SPANISH EMPIRE

The *conquistadores* abolished the offices and landholdings of the Aztec nobility and made use of Indian local administrative structures and personnel. As Gibson (1964, 30) explains: "For the tribes, this principle meant that the main groups suffered a loss of identity under Spanish rule whereas subordinate groups survived." *Calpullin* holdings were largely preserved, until epidemics ravaged the Indian population and *calpullin* alienated their land or found it encroached upon by newly established haciendas and ranchos. As time passed, Spanish municipal governments took over most of the functions that had originally been exercised by Indian leaders. In fact, most colonial citizens found themselves effectively ruled by whatever public or private administrative center(s) happened to be nearest at hand, whether viceroy, captaincy-general, audiencia, gobernador, *municipio*—or hacienda. The Mesoamerican economy was reoriented to conform to the requirements of Spanish mercantilism.

The Spanish wrought a revolution in the economic life of Mesoamerica. Silver mining became, after agriculture, the second most important economic activity (MacLachlan and Rodríguez O. 1980, 168–79). There were also important continuities. Fundamental patterns of land and labor in agriculture[20] did not initially change as much as might have been expected, since the Spanish—once they deposed and dispossessed the high-ranking Aztec rulers and nobility—adopted the official position that they would respect the legitimacy of Indian common land titles. Subordinate Indian rulers (caciques) continued to collect tribute from *calpulli* farmers and craftsmen, much as they were accustomed to doing, only now the tribute flowed into the coffers of the King, favored Spanish *encomenderos*, and the Catholic Church. The familiar pattern of community and barrio specialization continued, and forced labor drafts persisted on the Aztec model whenever they were required for public construction projects.

However, some significant changes in land tenure occurred almost immediately, and others over decades and centuries. The only Aztec private landholders had been the rulers and nobility, whose holdings were now technically forfeit because they had rebelled against the

---

20. The discussion below draws heavily on MacLachlan and Rodríguez O. 1980, 79–82, 150–68; and Gibson 1964, chapter 10 and 407–8.

Spanish monarchy. The top echelon of Aztec elites thus lost their properties, had their holdings greatly reduced, or found their rights reassigned. Also, some Indian common land titles were invalidated or consolidated. In 1523 the King authorized Cortés to make outright grants of available land to conquistadores and other important Spaniards. The *encomienda* system, adapted from the reconquest of southern Spain, offered a temporary solution to the problem of how to defend and administer the rest of the territory. *Encomienda* grants were not of land per se but the right to collect tribute from and utilize part of the labor of Indians in a particular area. Labor and materials could help to support a neighboring private estate, possibly one owned by the *encomendero* himself. In return, *encomenderos* were obligated to exercise Spain's authority, protect the Indians from exploitation, and maintain a military force adequate to put down Indian rebellions.

There were several problems with this system. First, a powerful group of feudallike *encomenderos* stood between the King and his subjects, and thus undermined royal authority. The King and his Council never liked the system; indeed, they had already restricted its further use in Spain and agreed to its installation in the colonies only because Cortés had convinced them that there was no other option. Second, the Indian population dropped precipitously because of epidemics, with the consequence that production also fell. A better means of organizing the economy seemed to be required. Third, the preservation of Indian titles and administrative networks limited the advancement of Spaniards. Part of the attempted solution to these problems was to create a multilevel Spanish bureaucracy and elected town councils to take over the functions originally handled through the *encomienda* system and local Indian caciques.

Numerous private haciendas or ranchos also appeared, at first in the interstices between Indian lands or on properties rented from Indian communities. In a sense, the haciendas represented just an extension of the pattern of small estates held by the Aztec nobility, but they steadily increased their domains until the hacienda became the dominant economic unit. "Limitless possibilities for fraud and collusion between caciques and Europeans existed," which resulted in the illegal transfer of some common lands (MacLachlan and Rodríguez O. 1980, 81). Other lands were sold, legally, to satisfy tribute obligations. Municipal councils not only ratified land transfers but also granted Europeans grazing rights *(estancias)* on Indian lands after the crops were harvested. This practice almost guaranteed periodic damage to crops and efforts by ranchers to displace Indian farmers.

Burdened by tribute and the vicissitudes of nature, a declining number of Indians fought a losing battle to retain their properties and autonomy. Gibson (1964, 334) comments: "To an Indian society that had lost its surplus goods and lands and energies the hacienda offered food and agricultural jobs and wages." The contents of Spanish granaries fetched high prices, so "the critical years for Indian agriculture were periods of relative prosperity for the haciendas, which extended their controls from Spanish markets to Indian markets, notably in maize and pulque, displacing Indian supplies and continuously reducing Indian agriculture." The Church, too, coveted Indian land. Colin M. MacLachlan and Jaime E. Rodríguez O. (1980, 1964) report: "Perhaps the largest contributors to the orders were the Indians. It was common for caciques and principales without heirs to bequeath their property to monasteries or other Church institutions. Often the friars persuaded or, if that was not sufficient, pressured the natives into donating land."

The early decline in Indian numbers made the gradual shift to haciendas and ranchos easier (Gibson 1964, 407–8). But in the late seventeenth and eighteenth centuries the Indian population started to grow again, with grave consequences: "Every increase in Indian population in the late colonial period meant an additional number that could not be incorporated in the traditional calpulli tenure. . . . The available land was hacienda land, and the new population could now be incorporated in colonial society only through the mediation of hacienda. . . . An aristocracy had been created through innumerable acts over generations." Actually, the new hacienda aristocracy was a double re-creation, echoing at once the splendid residences of Aztec elites and Spanish castles on the Old World frontier.[21] A new Spanish extended family superimposed itself as an organizing unit for society over the Indian *calpullin* that slowly dwindled in significance.

Some of these changes were long postponed, moderated, or never came at all to the resource-poor, peripheral region of the Yucatán (Farriss 1984 and 1983). There, the Mayas maintained much of their autonomy until the late-eighteenth-century when Bourbon reforms

---

21. We should not think of all *hacienda* estates "as something innately grand." "In actual fact many landowners were marginal, and the struggle to survive took much of the luster out of everyday life" (MacLachlan and Rodríguez O. 1980, 82).

sought to improve local Spanish administration. In fact, the Yucatán skipped most of the hacienda stage until the nineteenth century. At that time, there was a reorganization of much of the entire region into large plantations to produce henequen for the world market.[22]

Finally, as important as the other consequences of the Conquest, were the combined effects of the introduction of European technology and the Spanish accomplishment of what Crosby (1972, 66) calls "the greatest biological revolution in the Americas since the end of the Pleistocene era." The Spanish introduced the horse, donkey, mule, and ox, as well as range cattle, pigs, sheeps, goats, new breeds of dogs and cats, and various domesticated fowls into the Western Hemisphere.[23] The Conquest also doubled or tripled the number of cultivatable food plants in the New World (Crosby 1972, 107), introducing wheat, sugar cane, bananas, grapes, chickpeas, cauliflowers, cabbages, various orchard fruits, salad greens, radishes, onions, and European melons. Many new grasses and wildflowers arrived, too, to the extent that today "an American botanist can easily find whole meadows in which he is hard put to find a single species of plant that grew in America in pre-Columbian times" (Crosby 1972, 72–73). On the negative side, the Spanish ruthlessly exploited New World reserves of gold and silver, and the European plow caused widespread erosion in former grassland areas.

Eventually, long-distance Mesoamerican trade assumed an additional trans-Atlantic dimension. Mesoamerica (New Spain) until the early nineteenth century was the most prosperous part of the sprawling Spanish empire. A mercantilist policy prevailed, by which precious metals and raw materials flowed to the mother country and Spanish producers enjoyed an official monopoly of finished goods sold to the

---

22. Farriss (1984, 393) remarks: "The one aspect of dependency theory that all economists seem to agree on . . . is that time lags between regions both reflect and produce structural differences. If Latin America has been one of the world economy's peripheries since the sixteenth century, Yucatan has been a periphery of a periphery. . . . When the hacienda did finally emerge, it was never tied to a strong local market; the hacienda itself was a relatively brief episode in Yucatan's transition from the semiautarky imposed by the Hapsburg commercial system to the export monoculture of the henequen plantation."

23. The Indians had the turkey, the Muscovy duck, goose, crane, quail, rabbit—and possibly the chicken.

colonies. Smuggling helped alleviate some of the constraints of this system but not enough to placate colonial aristocrats, many of whom regarded the trade monopoly exercised by Spain as one of the reasons to opt for independence when the opportunity presented itself after 1810.

Part of the Mesoamerica story is the reverse impact of New World trade on Spain and the Old World generally. Plants new to Europe included maize, manioc, potato, pumpkin, a variety of table beans, cacao, tobacco, pumpkin, paprika, and American cotton. The addition to European consumption probably played a role in the subsequent population increase in the Old World.[24] Although the outflow of precious metals seemed to provide a bonanza for Spain, the eventual effect was devastating. Prices in Spain rose about 400 percent in the sixteenth century, pushed wages up, made Spanish goods uncompetitive, and ultimately had much to do with Spain's decline as a world power. J. H. Parry (1966, 244) argues that "business profits could be made only by mean of continued technological progress to reduce costs; but the general illusion of prosperity, the feeling of easy money, the accompanying contempt for manual arts, discouraged technological advance when it was most needed." As a result, by the early seventeenth century, "these processes, together with heavy taxation, had raised Spanish costs and prices so far above those of the rest of Europe that all industry was discouraged and export industry in particular." Spain's New World conquered peoples unwittingly had their revenge on the mother country.

Following the Conquest, there was a drop of catastrophic proportions in the numbers of Indians. War, overwork, slavery, malnutrition, and famine all contributed, but it was mostly a matter of microbes. The Indians had no immunities to European diseases. A smallpox epidemic erupted even as the Aztecs initially drove Cortes's forces out of Tenochtitlán and paved the way for the Spaniard's second, successful assault on the Aztec capital (Clendinnen 1991, 270). Especially over the first century after contact with the Europeans, successive outbreaks of smallpox, typhus, typhoid, measles, and other diseases were devastating. Pre-Conquest population estimates vary wildly, for

---

24. Some suggest that the Industrial Revolution would not have happened without the potato, originally from the Andean region, which provided cheap calories for poor laboring families.

example, from 4.5 million to 25 million for Central Mexico. Gibson (1964, 6) tells us that, in the more limited Basin of Mexico, an Indian population of about 1.5 million in 1519 dropped to 70,000 in the seventeenth century. Yucatán had perhaps a million in 1519 and a mere 140,000 by 1580. (Gibson 1964, 6, 136–44; Farriss 1984, 57–67; Crosby 1972, chapter 2; Cook and Borah 1972–1979 and 1960; and Hassig 1985, chapter 9.) Such data, quite apart from other factors, go a long way toward explaining how the Spaniards were able to consolidate their conquest and why a shift in patterns of production and land tenure occurred.

It is hardly surprisingly that the Conquest touched off a debate regarding the validity of Spain's title to the New World; the relationship among King, Pope, and the Church in the Indies; and the respective rights and obligations of the new Spanish rulers and their Indian subjects (Parry 1964, chapters 7–9). The official position of the Crown's lawyers was that the King exercised paramount authority by virtue of "prior discovery," just conquest of tyrannical native rulers, and, not least, the papal bulls of 1493. Some, like the prominent Dominican jurist, Francisco de Vitoria, questioned whether the Pope had any right to determine anything other than the division of missionary activities, but found different reasons to support the Conquest. Vitoria argued that the Indians had committed offenses against natural law, that Spain had a duty to protect those who might prefer to live under Spanish rule, and that the Spaniards properly assisted friendly nations like the Tlaxcalans in a just war.

The debate with the most practical implications was about the rights of the Indians. There were two extremes, represented by the writings of Bartolomé de las Casas and Juan Ginés de Sepúlveda. Las Casas insisted that the conquest obliged the Indians to give their allegiance to the King of Spain, but they, like every Spanish citizen, were entitled to the full protection of the laws of Spain. Specifically, Indian rulers who voluntarily or under duress surrendered to Spanish authority should not have been deposed, and no Indian lands or labor should have been been distributed through the *encomienda* system. The Church was free to evangelize the Indians, but none should be forced to accept the faith. On the other hand, Sepúlveda argued that Spain had been the first to occupy New World lands with no legitimate ruler, that the Pope had ratified the discovery and given the Crown a clear spiritual mission to convert the heathen, that Spaniards were naturally superior to the Indians, and that the inhabitants of the New

World had received many advantages from economic progress under Spanish rule.

These debates had a general influence on the Spanish government's exercise of its authority and the persistence—as well as replacement—of some Indian administrative and landholding structures. However, over the long haul, the pre-Columbian legacy of Mesoamerica reasserted itself in profound ways. Under Spanish rule, a new social division opened up between *peninsulares* (Spanish-born in Spain)—who alone were allowed to occupy the leading political and ecclesiastical offices—and creoles (Spanish-born in the New World). Especially in countries with a large Indian population, indigenous creole elites often came to be mestizos, with a substantial admixture of Indian blood. The Catholic Church found itself substituting Christian saints for some native deities and having to make numerous other concessions to "harmless" pagan aesthetics and practices. Regionalism,[25] localism, extended family, and patron-client relationships continue to characterize Mexican and Guatemalan politics to the present day.

Despite a late nineteenth-century drive for "Europeanization" in Mexico, that country and Guatemala in recent decades have taken renewed pride in their Indian heritage. The fact that modern-day politicians and academics have tended to view the pre-Columbian period through somewhat rose-colored glasses itself more than faintly echoes the Aztecs' own invention of their presumed Toltec past.

CONCLUSION

The Aztecs, in particular, illustrate the importance of fashioning an ideology that is, at once, distinctive and yet incorporates ideas from a wider cultural tradition. Ideology fueled Aztec imperial expansion, but expansion in some respects proved to be counterproductive. Apart from preserving local dynasties, the Aztecs made no effort to assimilate the peoples they conquered. There was only limited consolidation of territory, and imperial administration was also minimal to nonexistent.

---

25. Not until the mid-1930s did Mexican President Lázaro Cárdenas's federal troops defeat the private army of the last regional *caudillo*, in the state of San Luís Potosí.

The Spanish Conquest of Mesoamerica led to the imposition of European forms atop indigenous ones. The primary pre-Conquest vertical relationships between rulers of individual polities and their subjects, and between expansionist regional and imperial polities and the polities they controlled, were severed and replaced by Spanish imperial rule. Nevertheless, the Spanish did make use of some indigenous institutions, and—particularly in the Yucatán—even the military Conquest remained incomplete. As we have noted, regionalism, localism, and other pre-Columbian patterns reasserted themselves. Fusion between conqueror and conquered occurred to such an extent that a new "cosmic race" (MacLachlan and Rodriguez O. 1980) of *mestizos* emerged. The Conquest also inaugurated a transAtlantic "Columbian exchange" of monumental proportions.

The coming of the Europeans did create a revolution in the economic life of much of Mesoamerica, with greater emphasis on mining, but traditional tribute relationships and *calpulli* land tenure persisted for some years. Eventually, however, epidemics and Spanish acquisitiveness elevated a new hacienda aristocracy that was reminiscent both of Aztec nobles and of aristocratic families on Spain's southern frontier.

The Europeans replaced the ideological bases of indigenous polities with new sources of legitimacy, including Christianity. The *Patronato* provided for a wealthy and substantially independent Church polity, which customarily supported the Crown. However, a normative debate erupted over treatment of the Indians. Christian worship, especially in rural areas, assumed a markedly Indian character.

It is somewhat ironic that even as the Indian legacy has finally become a source of cultural pride, it is also a source of continuing tension between Indians and rulers in Mexico and Guatemala (as well as in the more Indian South American countries like Peru and Bolivia). The rising of the Zapatista National Liberation Front in Mexico's southern state of Chiapas owes much to Indian demands for economic and political equality. Robert Wasserstrom's (1983a, 250–51) observation in 1983 now seems a premonition: "Beginning in colonial times, some Indians in central Chiapas have refused adamantly to submit to *ladino*-ization, to the ultimate indignity of transculturation. Instead, they have managed to preserve an independent sense of their own destiny—occasionally by rebelling against their rulers, more often through the less vulnerable mechanism of corporate religious ritual. . . . However much the chapels in Salinas, Nabenchauk, and Sek'emtik may resemble their counterparts in non-Indian communities, they remain Zinacanteco churches, repositories of Zinacanteco history, where Indian men and women may still address their saints in the same language in which their forefathers first prayed to a new and vengeful god nearly five centuries ago.''

11

ISLAM
The Evolution of a Messianic Movement

The following two chapters examine the evolution of political forms in the Islamic world from its inception in 622 A.D. to the early thirteenth century (of the Christian calendar), emphasizing the changing relationships among and within key polities that produced clashes among and revisions in allegiances and loyalties. During the period we are considering, the Islamic world was born, and an Islamic and Arab political and cultural universe spread in all directions and flowered from Spain to the frontiers of India. Muslims throughout the world today recall the epoch with pride, and many brandish it as a model to be emulated and as an alternative to the secular West.

This case involves the emergence of another of the world's great civilizations, in Bernard Lewis's words, "a system of belief and cult" and a "system of state, society, law, thought, and art—a civilization with religion as its unifying, eventually dominating, factor" (1993, 144). Political forms and issues that appeared early on continue to vex the Islamic world. Of special interest was and remains the key role of competing ideologies in the form of religious doctrines and the difficulty they posed for the creation and legitimation of Westphalian states in the Middle East. In addition, the case reflects problems associated with the rapid expansion of polities and the transition from relative ethnic homogeneity to heterogeneity.

Then as now, Arabs and non-Arabs had different perspectives on the conflicts among Islamic polities and provided alternative traditions for governing disparate peoples. At its inception, Islam was an Arab phenomenon, and then, as now, Arabic political identity was amorphous. As Bernard Lewis (1993, 1) observes: "The Arabs may be a nation; they are not a nationality in the legal sense. One who calls himself an Arab may be described in his passport as a national of Saudi Arabia, Yemen, Iraq, Kuwait, Syria, Jordan, Sudan, Libya, Tunisia, Algeria, Morocco, or any other of the group of states that

276

identify themselves as Arab. . . . There are Arab states, and indeed a league of Arab states; but there is no single Arab state of which all Arabs are nationals.''

INTRODUCTION

The Muhammadan movement began as a rebellion against traditional Arab tribal practices (Dabashi 1989, 16), but the death of Muhammad triggered a struggle—the consequences of which remain with us—over modes of political organization and sources of political legitimacy. The elements of the conflict were exceeding complex, involving clashes between tribal and statist practices, struggles among kinship groups, differing class-based perceptions, and strongly held religious positions.

As in our other cases, these chapters touch upon both the horizontal and vertical dimensions of the Islamic system. Owing to the unique wedding and confusion of political and religious elements in Islam, the dimensions repeatedly merge, and the distinction between them is difficult to maintain. As Goldziher (1981, 168) observes: ''In a community based on religion, religious considerations will, however inevitably, pervade political questions and political questions will take on the form of religious issues that give their own coloring to political life.'' Even today, some Islamic societies are characterized by the same condition that W. Montgomery Watt (1973, 7) ascribes to medieval Islam, a condition in which religious doctrine dominated all other aspects of the community, ''including its political life.''

KEY DATES

570 A.D. Muhammad born.
603–628 Byzantine-Sasanian War
622 Muhammad's flight from Mecca to Medina (Hijra)
632 Death of Muhammad. Caliphate founded under Abu Bakr.
634 Beginning of imperial expansion. 'Umar becomes second caliph.
636 Syria conquered.
637 Ctesiphon conquered.
639–642 Conquest of Egypt.
644 Murder of 'Umar. 'Uthman becomes third caliph.
651 Conquest of Iran completed.
656 'Uthman murdered. 'Ali becomes fourth caliph.
656–661 Civil war.

661 Umayyad dynasty established in Damascus.
667 Islam sweeps across the Oxus.
680 Husayn, 'Ali's son, killed at Karbala.
685–705 Caliphate of 'Abd al-Malik.
698 Conquest of Tunisia.
711–714 Conquest of Spain.
713 Arab invasion of Indus Valley.
717–718 Siege of Constantinople fails.
732 Frankish defeat of Arabs at Tours.
750 Umayyads overthrown by 'Abbasids.
755 Umayyad flight to Spain.
763 Founding of Baghdad.
786–809 Caliphate of Harun al-Rashid.
800 Independence of North African caliphate under Aghlabids.
813–833 Caliphate of al-Ma'mun.
827–902 Islamic conquest of Sicily.
861–870 Anarchy in Baghdad created by Turkish mercenaries.
869–883 Zanj revolt in Basra.
875 Beginning of Shi'ite Isma'ili movement.
900–999 Persianized Samanid dynasty in Khurasan.
945 Buyid occupation of Baghdad.
969 Fatimid conquest of Egypt.
1055–1058 Seljuk overthrow of Buyids in Baghdad.
1071 Seljuk victory over Byzantium at Manzikert.
1072–1091 Norman conquest of Sicily.
1095 Pope Urban II launches crusades.
1099 Crusader seizure of Jerusalem.
1069–1093 Reign of Saladin.
1258 Mongol sack of Baghdad and murder of last caliph.

SYSTEM DISCRETENESS AND STRUCTURE

The Arab World before Islam[1]

The Arab world that was thrown into turmoil by the Prophet and his followers was one of tribal traditions, loyalties, and organization.

---

1. Believers referred to the era before Muhammad as *jahiliyyah* or "the time of ignorance" (Dabashi 1989, 149; Hitti 1956, 25).

The Arabs were at the periphery of existing political and economic power in the Mediterranean arena, which, in the early seventh century, was concentrated in two great rival empires to the north. The first, with its center in Constantinople, was the Christian Byzantine empire, since the fourth century the heir to the eastern half of the Roman Empire. Encompassing Syria and Egypt, Byzantium governed through a Greek-speaking elite that would later provide a similar service to the victorious Arabs.

The second great territorial empire, that of the Sasanians, lay to the east of Byzantium, encompassing Iraq and Iran. With its capital in the central Iraqi city of Ctesiphon, the Sasanian realm was a family affair that had originated in southern Iran. The Sasanian empire lacked both the political adhesive of Christianity and the memory of Rome enjoyed by Byzantium. The absence of unifying rivers and the barriers imposed by deserts further impeded unity among the ethnically diverse peoples of the empire. The Sasanians sought to compensate for the absence of unifying factors by formalizing and providing imperial sanction for the ancient Persian religion of Zoroastrianism.[2] Two other important civilizations lay to the south of Arabia, straddling the Red Sea. At the southern edge of the Arabic peninsula was Yemen, with its own language and religion, and, to the west, Ethiopia, a kingdom dominated by Coptic Christians.

Owing to its aridity and the absence of large centers of population, culture, or cultivation, the Arabian peninsula had little to offer to most outsiders. Jewish merchants and Christian monks[3] were sources of external information and ideas, and Jewish tribes resided near Medina. Long-distance commerce was crucial to tribal economies and put Arab merchants in touch with external events and ideas. Camels made it possible for Arabic traders to overcome great distances of inhospitable terrain; and nomads, who depended on camels, and merchants in towns dominated pre-Islamic society. By the middle of the seventh century, large numbers of Arab nomads had immigrated to Iraq and Syria, and some had become tax collectors for the Byzantine and Sasanian authorities. Some Arabic tribal groups (for example, the

---

2. In addition to followers of Zoroaster, the Sasanian Empire was home to Manicheans, Jews, and Nestorian Christians.

3. Christian influences arrived from Ethiopia and Syria.

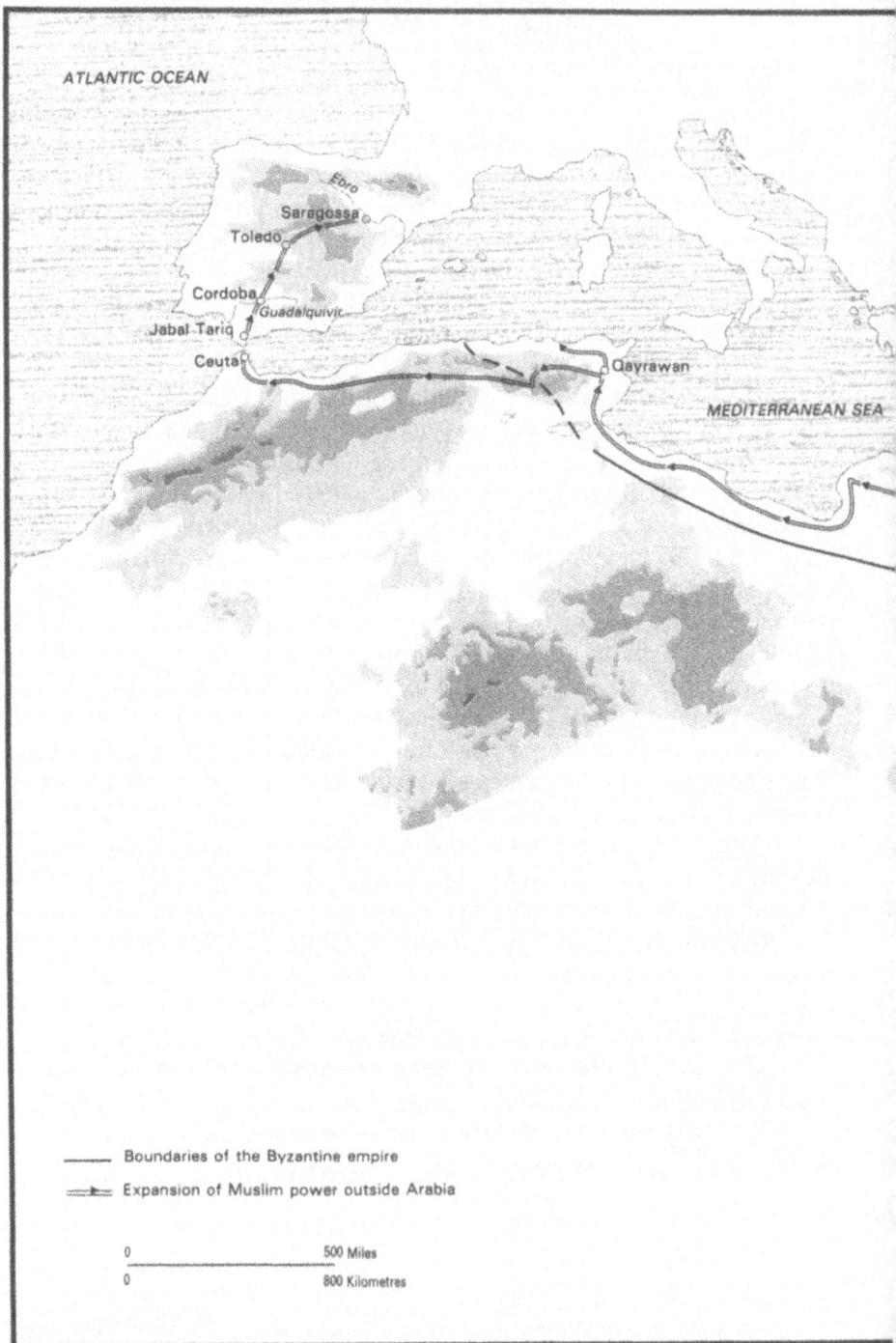

The Expansion of the Islamic Empire
Reprinted by permission of the publishers from *A History of the Arab Peoples* by Albert Hourani, Cambridge, Mass.: Harvard University Press, Copyright © 1991 by Albert Hourani. John Fowler, artist.

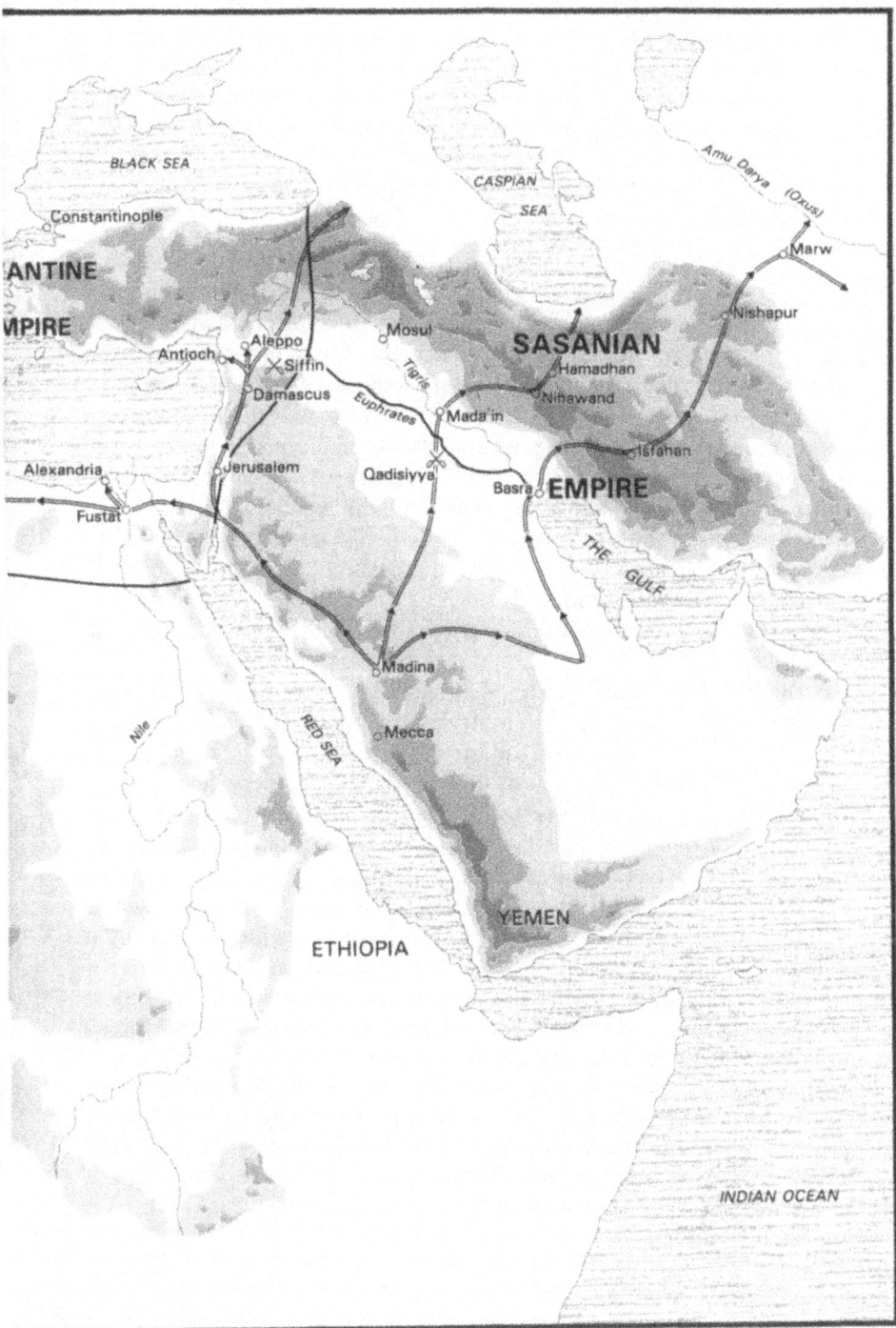

Lakhmids and Ghassanids) enjoyed significant autonomy within the established empires (Hourani 1991, 11–12).

Conquest

The Islamic polity never stabilized within secure boundaries and remained highly permeable throughout its existence. Islamic philosophy, science, and culture were enriched by Hellenistic, Jewish, Christian, and Persian traditions that survived the conquest and even flourished under the caliphate. Islam itself made universalist claims and recognized no territorial limits or frontiers, and the absence of a sense of territoriality also reflected the nomadic roots of the Arab conquerors. As Philip K. Hitti (1956, 60) argues, "the campaigns seem to have started as raids to provide new outlets for the warring spirit of the tribes now forbidden to engage in fratricidal combats, the objective in most cases being booty. . . . But the machine . . . soon got beyond the control of those who built it. . . . [The empire's] creation was therefore due less to early design than to the logic of immediate circumstances."

By the time of his death, Muhammad already enjoyed personal authority over a considerable hinterland beyond Medina and Mecca, and he was determined to spread the Word of Allah to the four corners of the known world. His death, however, triggered desertions among tribal allies and efforts to return to traditional forms of government. "Faced with this challenge," writes Albert Hourani (1991, 23), "the community under Abu Bakr affirmed its authority by military action (the wars of the *ridda*'); in the process an army was created, and the momentum of action carried it into the frontier regions of the great empires and then, as resistance proved weak, into their hearts."

By the middle of the seventh century, all of Arabia, the Byzantine provinces of Egypt and Syria, and additional territory to the north and east had fallen to the young Islamic polity. Indeed, the fact that Byzantium survived at all may owe more to the outbreak of civil war between the Islamic supporters of 'Ali and the Umayyads than to any other factor. Syria fell first, in 636 after the siege of Damascus and the decisive battle of Yarmuk. In a short time, all of the Sasanian holdings in Iraq and Iran were added.[4] In 639, the ancient cities of Egypt,

---

4. Islam and Arabism put down deeper roots in Iran and Iraq than in Syria, a fact that made the Umayyads in Damascus vulnerable.

including the Byzantine naval headquarters at Alexandria fell to an Arab army of some twenty thousand, and, by 643, imperial Islam advanced into the Oxus valley and the frontier lands of India. Thereafter, the Umayyads swept across North Africa, establishing a center in Tunisia. By the end of the seventh century, the empire had incorporated Morocco and shortly thereafter in 710 A.D. crossed the Mediterranean into Spain.

The causes of this rapid success (and later decline) are complex. The charismatic qualities of the Prophet were a key asset, especially at the outset, but do not alone provide a sufficient explanation. The Mediterranean world appears to have been seriously weakened by barbarian invasions, plagues, failure to maintain agricultural projects, and almost continuous war between Byzantines and Sasanians mainly for control of Iraq and Syria. George Ostrogorsky (1969, 110–11) describes the opportunity facing the Arabs:

> The conflict between the Persians and the Byzantines had weakened both empires and so in a sense prepared the way for the Arabs. After Heraclius' victories, Persia had been left in a state of utter chaos; one usurper succeeded another and the backbone of the Sassanid empire was broken. But in spite of her successes, Byzantium too had exhausted her resources in the long exacting struggle. At the same time irreconcilable religious differences had raised up a wall of hatred between Constantinople and her eastern provinces, the separatist tendencies of the Syrians and Copts had been strengthened, and their willingness to defend the Empire finally undermined. Abuses in the military organization of these districts and disruption in administrative circles, due to the overpowerful influence of the big landowners, helped to ease the task of the conquerors, particularly in Egypt.

Many of the Arab soldiers had prior military experience, and camels provided them with unprecedented mobility.[5] Islam sanctioned the search for converts—a "militant polity" Hitti (1956, 36) calls it—and religious conviction assured Arab unity and fervor, but there were actually relatively few conversions during the years of greatest

---

5. Hitti (1956, 64–65) vividly describes how this mobility enabled a smaller Arab army to annihilate the Byzantine defenders of Damascus.

expansion. Hitti (1956, 55) argues that "Islam owes its unparalleled expansion as a worldly power" to the idea of jihad (holy war). The sense of destiny provided by religion was reinforced by early triumphs and rapid forward movement that at once excited the spirit of nomadic warriors and seemed to promise the ultimate victory of Islam. Hourani speculates (1991, 28–29) that, as a faith, Islam spread fairly easily for a variety of instrumental reasons—among Arabs already living in the Byzantine and Sasanian dominions, officials of the former empire who wished continued employment, and immigrants to the new cities who wished to avoid taxes paid by non-Muslims. More important, the simplicity of Islam and its rituals, the absence of structure and hierarchy, its egalitarianism,[6] and its tolerance for ethnic diversity facilitated its spread. Hitti (1956, 59–60; also Watt 1988, 18) claims that, while each of these may have had an impact, the key reason for conquest was economic: "Islam did provide a new battle-cry. . . . It undoubtedly acted as a cohesive agency for masses never before united, and furnished a large part of the driving force. But it is hardly in itself enough to explain the conquests. Not fanaticism but economic necessity drove the Bedouin hordes . . . beyond the confines of their arid abode to the fair lands of the north."

Islam's expansion was also facilitated by the passivity of those who were conquered and their indifference about who ruled them as long as there was peace and reasonable prosperity. The simplicity and egalitarianism of Islam made conversion relatively easy and attractive, especially to those who had fared poorly under previous governments. Finally, Islam's tolerance of other religions and liberal treatment of conquered peoples reduced incentives to resist and rebel. Supervision of the expanding polyglot empire was exercised by Arab soldiers in military settlements, which became centers of Islamic culture and attracted civilians from Arabia and elsewhere. In some cases, these grew into major cities.[7]

Polarity

The idea of polarity cannot do justice to the epoch we are describing because it implies the existence of coherent concentrations of

---

6. The egalitarian bent of Islam probably owes much to the egalitarian nature of the Bedouin society in which it arose.

7. One such settlement, Fustat, later became Cairo.

power across space. Although distinctive centers existed, limits on the exercise of military and economic power imposed by factors like technology and geography meant that localities and regions were beyond their reach much of the time. Consequently, analyses of shifting polarity are only approximations, as would-be predictions of behavior associated with different structural conditions.

In the early seventh century prior to the emergence of Islam, the Mediterranean basin was roughly a tripolar universe. Asia Minor was dominated by the Sasanian empire, and Slavs and Avars were in control of the Balkans from the Adriatic to the Aegean Sea. Squeezed between the two and close to disintegration was Byzantium, heir to the Roman east and guardian of Hellenic traditions. Byzantium reached a crisis in the years immediately before the birth of Islam. The Sasanians conquered Syria, Jerusalem, Cilicia, Armenia, and Egypt (source of much of Byzantium's grain supply) and even reached the Bosphorus. In 626 the Avars reached the gates of Constantinople. Under the Emperor Heraclium (610–641), however, Byzantium experienced a significant revival (Ostrogorsky 1969, 92–109). Through a combination of internal reform, especially reorganization of the armed forces, and adroit diplomacy, Byzantine fortunes were restored. A series of Byzantine military triumphs virtually eliminated the Avar threat and seriously undermined the Sasanians.

By the time the newly mobilized armies of Islam were preparing for their triumphant expansion, the earlier tripolarity had already become an asymmetric bipolarity between Byzantium and Sasanian Persia. Islamic victories eliminated the Sasanians and crippled Byzantium, maintaining an asymmetric bipolarity that bordered on unipolarity. The transformation of this bipolar system into a multipolar one was not the result of the growth of external challenges to the Islamic polity but rather was a consequence of the growth of independent dynastic challengers to the 'Abbasids within the caliphate, especially the Umayyads in Spain and the Fatimids in North Africa and Egypt.

Military Bases of Empire

As noted earlier, mobility was a key factor in Arab military tactics. Hitti (1956, 58–59) describes it as a "military technique adapted to the open steppes of Western Asia and North Africa—the use of cavalry and camelry—which the Romans never mastered."

The army was divided into center, two wings, vanguard and rear guard. The cavalry covered the wings. . . . The infantry used bow and arrow, sling and sometimes shield and sword; the sword was carried in a scabbard flung over the right shoulder. The javelin was introduced later from Abyssinia. The chief weapon of the cavalry was the lance. This, together with the bow and arrow, formed the two national weapons. The defensive armor . . . was the coat of mail and the shield. The order of battle was primitive, in lines or rows and in compact array. . . . The Arabian warrior received higher remuneration than his Persian or Byzantine rival and was sure of a portion of the booty. Soldiering was not only the noblest . . . profession in the sight of Allah but also the most profitable. The strength of the Moslem Arabian army lay neither in the superiority of its arms nor in the excellence of its organization but in its higher morale. . . ; in its power of endurance . . . ; and its remarkable mobility.

Ostrogorsky emphasizes the flexibility of Arab military leaders in the face of new conditions: "For example, although they were desert warriors with no experience with the sea, Muslim military leaders came to appreciate the importance of seapower during their collision with Byzantium. The first Islamic fleet set sail in 649 and seized the Byzantine stronghold of Cyprus. Some years later Rhodes was looted, and its world famous 'Colossus' was carried away" (1969, 116).

In time, it became difficult to oversee and control the armies of Islam from a single center. The sheer size of the realm, the relative isolation and autonomy of the military, the provision of land and other resources to retiring soliders, and the substitution of mercenaries and slaves for Arab soldiers (especially after the early ninth century) all worked to make the military more independent and politically active. As in the late Roman Empire, this was to prove a key factor in imperial decline.

Economic Bases of Empire

The Arab economy in which Islam grew depended importantly on the raising of sheep and camels, which were herded from oasis to oasis. The common practice of tribal raiding, which was regarded as an important and legitimate economic activity, had both cultural and economic roots. In Hitti's colorful language: "The raid . . . is raised by the economic and social conditions of desert life to the rank of a national institution. It lies at the base of the economic structure of Bedouin pastoral society" (1956, 15–16). Conditions in Arabia itself were poor for agriculture, though oases supported date palms, grape vines, almonds, watermelons, and frankincense. The Arab conquerors tended to avoid agriculture, which they regarded as below their dignity and about which they knew little.

The economic heartland of the later Islamic polity lay far from its Arabian roots, and the new rulers wisely husbanded the economic assets of their new provinces. Despite their sense of superiority as regards sedentary cultivators, the nomadic Arab conquerors recognized the economic importance of agriculture and did little to destabilize peasant society. The conquerors quickly realized the importance of agriculture as a source of revenue and took care to restore ancient irrigation systems and protect indigenous peasants. Those whom the conquerors found were treated as *dhimmis*—those outside the faith with whom an arrangement existed permitting cultural and religious freedom. Destabilization of the countryside, when it did occur, was a result of incursions from outside the empire combined with the weakening of the caliphate.

'Abbasid caliphs had access to several sources of revenue. One was a tax on land and produce, which initially was at a different rate for Muslims and non-Muslims, might be paid either in cash or kind, and might be levied either on land or produce. A second source was taxes and duties on urban manufactures and crafts. A final source of revenue, based on wealth, was a poll tax on non-Muslims. From the tenth century, the practice grew up of allowing local officials to collect taxes and retain a proportion of the revenue in lieu of salary and expenses. While this assured a serious effort at collecting taxes, it also provided officials, including provincial governors, with considerable autonomy from the center (Hourani 1991, 134, 139).

The economic system that accompanied Islam's astonishing expansion, like the earlier Arab system, depended heavily on trade but with important differences. The creation of empire meant the existence of a large "domestic" market, which linked the Mediterranean and Indian Oceans as well as enhanced security for caravans. The exigencies of trade were responsible for the growth of thriving urban centers such as Baghdad, Damascus, Cairo, Basra, and Córdoba, usually near rivers or seas. These centers, which were dominated by wealthy merchants, produced the expansion of crafts and industry—for example, glassware, carpets, armaments, paper, and textiles—that might be exported and an accumulation of wealth that fueled the demand for imports such as pepper, silk, camphor, and spices from Asia, slaves and olive oil from Europe, and slaves, ivory, and lumber from Africa.

The urban centers could also provide processed necessities to the countryside in return for the foodstuffs needed to satisfy urban appetites. Workshops were usually small with a master and a few apprentices, and craftsmen constituted a distinctive urban class with its own leaders and representatives.

Trade was largely conducted by Arab, Jewish, and Zoroastrian merchants or merchant families using Arab ships that plied the seas from Spain to Syria and from Constantinople to India and, for a time, even China and Indonesia.[8] Land routes, the most important of which linked Baghdad to Syria and Egypt, Constantinople, and central Asia ("the great silk way"), were traversed by relays of camels.[9]

Urban centers with strong governments and funds to invest provided security for their hinterlands and demand for agricultural products (some of which—rice, cotton, oranges, lemons, and sugarcane—were initially brought from China or India). The Arab conquerors provided Arab immigrants with land on which taxes had to be paid; and, increasingly in the tenth century, bureaucrats and military officers functioned as tax collectors. A new landed class emerged with sufficient wealth to invest in irrigation and new crops. Growing agriculture, commerce, and urban manufacturing provided incentives for and were assisted by the emergence of a monetary system with effective banking facilities that rested on the 'Abbasid gold dinar (Hourani 1991, 43–46; Hitti 1956, 131–36).

Geography and Disunity

The absence of major physical barriers, except for distance itself and the inhospitality of the environment, emphasized the importance of the rapid movement of camel-borne nomads which proved indispensable for creating and sustaining an empire. Unity was reinforced by the relative similarity in climate and geological features throughout the empire. However, the sheer size of the polity and the cultural diversity of those within it made it difficult to govern centrally, especially according to Arab tribal traditions.

---

8. The caliph Harun al-Rashid even considered the possibility of a canal through the Isthmus of Suez.

9. For reasons that are not clear, wheeled transport, even though widely used by the Romans, disappeared from areas conquered by Islam.

At its height, the Islamic polity consisted of five distinctive geographic regions (Hourani 1991, 89–96). The first, the Arabian peninsula—the largest peninsula in the world—was isolated by water on three sides and was subdivided into smaller regions by ranges of mountains running north-south (Hitti 1956, 10; Saunders 1965, 1–3). Hot and dry, much of Arabia, except around oases, was unavailable for intensive settlement and could support only a small population. The land could retain little of the moisture brought by annual monsoons, which, in any event, were limited to southern areas of the peninsula, especially Oman and Yemen.

To the north of Arabia beyond the Syrian desert lay the Fertile Crescent. This region, which included Syria, Palestine, Mesopotamia, and Persia, was the core of the Islamic polity. With few rivers, fixed agriculture and pasturage in Syria were variable. Its prosperity depended on trade. To the west, Syria was linked by sea and land to Egypt and the remainder of the Mediterranean littoral, and, to the east, it was connected to the heart of Iraq by river and land routes. Although much of northern Iraq was either mountainous or poorly irrigated, and so fit mainly for grazing, southern Iraq—the heart of ancient Mesopotamia—was, with the aid of extensive irrigation, among the richest agricultural areas in the empire.

Egypt and the Sudan constituted the third subregion of the Islamic polity. Separated from Arabia by desert and sea, the political and economic life of this region grew up along the Nile River. Two major rivers, one arising in East Africa and the other in Ethiopia, meet to form the Nile, which flowed through Egypt. Although the absence of water limited the productivity of much of this region, a narrow strip along the Nile, for which irrigation could be provided with the aid of devices like the waterwheel, was a major source of grain for the Islamic polity.

The two final regional subdivisions—North Africa (Algeria, Morocco, Tunisia, and Libya) and Spain—were remote from the centers of power in Damascus and Baghdad and found themselves repeatedly depending on each other economically, politically, and militarily. Economic activity in North Africa was largely confined to a narrow strip along the Mediterranean; to the south lay mountains and desert. Caravans, of course, crossed the desert, but the sea trade with Spain, Italy, and Egypt was of far greater importance. The mountains and rivers of Spain created a series of natural subregions with different economic characteristics. The fact that geography tended to isolate these regions from one another also meant that it was difficult to govern them from any single center.

POLITY TYPES

Three major polity types coexisted uneasily within the medieval Islamic system. As we have seen, tribes and tribal/clan loyalties dominated Arabia prior to the revolution begun by Muhammad, and tribal customs and loyalties were never far below the surface. The Prophet sought to replace tribal attachments with loyalty to a Muslim community of believers *(umma)*. However, Muhammad's authority was putatively derived directly from Allah and not from the community he established in Allah's name, and all of his actions were believed to have divine sanction, which was unavailable to others after his death ('Abduh 1966, 123). As Hamid Dabashi (1989, 34) succinctly puts it: "A charismatic leader does not derive his authority from his followers." Instead of legitimizing authority on the basis of past practice and tradition, Muhammad declared that his authority came from Allah alone, and he sought to establish an all-encompassing sociopolitical structure (Pipes 1983, 11–12). Paradoxically, the identification of religious and secular symbols in Islam proved an insurmountable obstacle to institutionalizing imperial forms and practices after the death of the Prophet. The subsequent absence of stable territoriality in turn reinforced earlier tribal mores and affinities.

All later Islamic polities—the caliphate, the Ottomans, and twentieth-century Muslim Westphalian polities—have had to contend with nested memories of, identities with, and loyalties to the Islamic community. These remain latent for long periods and then threaten to erupt, especially during eras of rapid social and political change. Islamic politicians have to appear to be faithful to the forms dictated by Islamic law and the interpretations of that law by Islamic judges, and failure to do so invites political instability and personal disaster.

Tribe

Any understanding of Arabic politics, medieval or contemporary, must begin with an appreciation of its durable tribal and clan basis; that is, "not controlled by a stable power of coercion, . . . led by chiefs belonging to families around which there gathered more or less lasting groups of supporters, expressing their cohesion or loyalty in the idiom of common ancestry" (Hourani 1991, 10–11). As Hitti describes it (1956, 17): "The clan organization is the basis of Bedouin society.

Every tent represents a family; members of one encampment constitute a clan. A number of kindred clans grouped together make a tribe. All members of the same clan consider each other as of one blood, submit to the authority of but one chief—the senior member of the clan—and use one battle-cry. Blood relationship—real or fictitious (clan kinship may be acquired by sucking a few drops of a member's blood)—furnishes the cohesive element in tribal organization."

Within Arab tribal society, the extended family living together produced powerful loyalties. Since such a unit was not self-sufficient, it would be affiliated with a kinship group that could afford protection and, if necessary, seek vengeance on the family's behalf. Kinship groups identified with one another by claiming a common ancestor (who might be no more than symbolic) and thereby constituted a tribe. Such groups might be dominated by a single family that enjoyed prestige because of religious position, wealth, and/or military experience.

The coming of Islam posed a threat to tribal mores and challenged tribal loyalties. Dabashi argues that, far from being a reaction to the feebleness or corruption of traditional tribal society, as argued by others (Hitti 1956, Watt 1961, Hodgson 1974, Mortimer 1982[10]), Muhammad's "charismatic movement" "should be seen as a total expression of a new cultural order that challenged the Arab traditional system" and as an effort to "set up a radical discontinuity with the Arab past" (Dabashi 1989, 17, 22).

That revolution notwithstanding, tribal forms nested within more inclusive Islamic polities, as these retained many of the tribal characteristics of their traditional precursor; and tribal solidarity, though eroded, was not eliminated. The society into which Islam exploded was, as expressed by Dabashi, one in which "tribal solidarity constituted the single most cohesive element," and in which political authority was associated with factors like "age, tribal genealogy, blood relationship, and religious functionaries" (1989, 20, 21; also Hitti 1956, 9–21). All of these factors express the traditional nature of Arab tribalism—especially, the centrality of the past for the present. Age

---

10. Mortimer's description of conditions in Mecca is typical of the "reformist" argument: "The rich behaved with arrogance and selfishness while widows and orphans starved. The revelations which Muhammad began to receive . . . attacked this arrogance and selfishness" (1982, 33).

was a prerequisite for tribal leadership in a patriarchal context, and "pride of descent" (Saunders 1965, 4) was a key source of tribal unity. Kinship—blood relationship—was the basis of family, clan, and tribal loyalties, loyalties that, as we shall see, remained powerful factors in the Islamic polity. Retention of tribal customs was virtually synonymous with maintaining the Arabic character of the movement. Tribalism and Arabism were inextricably woven together (Bozeman 1960, 360–61), and tribal influences continued to play a role in the advocacy of aspirational polities such as the "Arabic nation" as articulated by secular leaders like Egypt's President Gamel Abdul Nasser.

From the birth of Islam until the division and collapse of the Islamic polity, tribal habits and attachments remained strong. Muhammad himself used the same military strategy in seizing oases and raiding caravans against his Meccan adversaries as the Meccans had used against their rivals decades earlier, and he acquired political support by adroitly adopting and manipulating the traditional role of arbitrator among tribes and clans. Muhammad was a member of a secondary branch of the Quraysh tribe, which was, through its control of trade routes and religious sites, the dominant political and economic force in Mecca and, therefore, in Arabia.[11] As his preaching gained converts, Muhammad earned the animosity of leading figures in his tribe, ostensibly because he threatened traditional tribal authority; however, that opposition also reflected long-term rivalry between two branches of the Quraysh. Rivalries of this kind often involved competition for positions of traditional political authority. The same intra-Quraysh rivalry that led to Muhammad's flight from Mecca resurfaced years later in the struggle between 'Ali and Mu'awiya for the title of caliph and was an important element in the split between Shi'ites and Sunnis. Similarly, a "continuity of common symbols was . . . evident in such aspects of traditional Arab culture and the Muhammadan mission as the supremacy of Allah as the highest authority, the centrality of Ka'bah, the Meccan pilgrimage, etc." (Dabashi 1989, 21, 29).

Tribal practices resurfaced almost immediately after Muhammad's

---

11. The Quraysh controlled the Ka'ba or center of pre-Islamic Arabic religion and the chamber of deputies in Mecca. The tribe was also at the center of the web of trade routes and trading alliances that were sources of Arabian prosperity.

death when a tribal council[12] was held to select his successor and in later debates over the selection of caliphs and the sources of their political legitimacy (Watt 1968, 31; Hitti 1956, 62–64; Dabashi 1989, 82–85). The requirement that claimants to the caliphate demonstrate a familial relationship to Muhammad, for example, reflected the importance of genealogy noted earlier, as did the related role of primogeniture in succession to authority. Similarly, the central role afforded the chamber of deputies *(Dar al-Nadwah)* in Mecca and the mixing of religious and secular functions in the chamber reappeared in the form and function of mosques (Dabashi 1989, 24–26). The centrality of the *Dar al-Nadwah* in traditional Arab society was also reflected in the importance accorded by Islamic jurists to the legitimizing function of community opinion.

The organization of the imperial army was along tribal lines; units were tribally based, and conquered lands were divided among tribal groups. Clan and tribe members tended to associate with one another in the towns and cities of the empire and found themselves cheek to jowl with members of other clans and tribes. Indeed, the emergence of a single Islamic polity may have actually exacerbated tribal cleavages by facilitating contacts among geographically disparate members of tribal units. Such cleavages were manipulated by rivals in struggles for power at the center.

Tribal and clan favoritism was widespread in the caliphate. Indeed, nepotism during the reign of the third caliph roused great discontent and was involved in his assassination. G. E. Von Grunebaum (1970, 59) declares: "'Uthman was a member of the family from which had come the last and most obstinate leaders of the Meccan heathens against the Prophet. He has been repeatedly accused of placing family interests before those of the Muslim commonwealth, since he conferred all the key posts of government to his relatives. Many of these men quite cynically and openly exploited these appointments to their own advantage." 'Uthman's "policy was one of appointing members of his own clan as provincial governors, and this aroused opposition . . . ; some of the tribes resented the domination of men from Mecca" (Hourani 1991, 25). 'Uthman had not been selected because of any

---

12. Dabashi (1989, 65–66) sees this meeting as "the first and most significant instance in which the traditional tribal practices were reintroduced into a fundamentally Islamic event."

particular closeness to the Prophet but, rather, as a result of the influence of the Quraysh elite from whom Muhammad had earlier been estranged. As Goldziher (1981, 169) points out, 'Uthman's family "had offered stubborn resistance to nascent Islam, even if in Muhammad's lifetime they had yielded to success and joined the faith."

'Uthman's successor, 'Ali, was also of Quraysh but of a different clan, and he was resisted by his predecessor's kinsmen—most important, the governor of Syria, Mu'awiya. The importance of tribal mores was again reflected in the resistance to 'Ali based on his responsibility for the death of the fathers of some of his opponents in a battle during which they fought against Muhammad. Mu'awiya, who like 'Uthman, was of the clan Banu Umayya, sought to avenge his kinsman, and the triumph of the Umayyads involved a reassertion of tribal prerogatives (Dabashi 1989, 86–88, 121–22). The assassination of 'Ali and the caliphate of Mu'awiya (661–680) mark a shift in imperial power from Arabia to Damascus and the beginning of the Umayyad dynasty.[13]

The status and class differences that characterized imperial Islam also had their roots in pre-Islamic tribal society and politics. The practice of slavery, for example, was taken from pre-Islamic Arabia into the Islamic empire, as was the commercial hierarchy with merchant capitalists *(sayyids)* on top and tribal clients *(mawali)*[14] at the bottom. Indeed, as Dabashi observes, a "close affinity between cultural institutions and the conduct of commerce was a major characteristic of pre-Islamic Arabia that was also present in the Islamic commercial culture" (1989, 28). Institutions included intratribal alliances and contracts to assure the security of trade routes.

The Islamic Community *(umma)*

As the idea of the *umma* evolved, it came to refer to what Barbara Allen Roberson describes as "a communal, though not a territorial society within which and through which people are to develop and enhance their moral behaviour" (1988, 89). The original community consisted only of Muhammad's wife, Khadija; his cousin 'Ali; and Abu

---

13. Umayya was an ancestor of Mu'awiya.

14. This term was applied to non-Arab Muslims who had to become clients of Arab tribes. Such clientelism was typical of pre-Islamic tribal practice and, in contrast to the beliefs of Islam, reflected a claim of Arabic superiority.

Bakr, though it shortly came to include his immediate companions. The death in 619 of his wife, who had provided him with financial as well as emotional support, and of his uncle Abu Talib, who had protected him from tribal foes, made Muhammad increasingly vulnerable to opponents in Mecca. Three years later he was invited to migrate (the *hijra*) to the settlement of Yathrib (later Medina or the city of the Prophet), two hundred miles to the north of Mecca, by members of two tribes who were seeking an arbiter, and it is from this event that the Muslim calendar is dated (Mottahedeh 1980, 22–23; Hitti 1956, 30–35).[15] Islam at this time assumed those characteristics that distinguished it clearly from Judaism and Christianity. Simultaneously, the community of Islam was formally established by the Constitution of Medina that was written by Muhammad on behalf of the believers who had followed him from Mecca and those in Medina: "They are a single community distinct from other people" (cited in Watt 1961, 94; also Watt 1968, 130–34). In other words, communal unity was not to be based on tribal or social affiliation but on common religious belief, and tribal norms such as the blood feud were to be abandoned. Edward Mortimer (1982, 34) mistakenly contends that the *hijra* "marked neither the birth of a founder nor the begining of the revelation, but rather the founding of a state." In fact, Muhammad's idea of a community had little in common with the territorial Westphalian polity. It was, as Dabashi (1989, 76) observes, "the most significant expression of Islamic solidarity against the traditional tribal structure";[16] and, in contrast to pre-Islamic tribal tradition, the community viewed all individuals, whether or not blood kin, as equals.

Between 624 and 632 Muhammad expanded the Islamic community and its power by force of arms until Meccan resistance had been crushed. In 630 Muhammad returned to Mecca in triumph, and the community of Islam found itself supreme across much of the Arabian peninsula. Two years later, the community's political, religious, and military leader was dead, and there was no one who could succeed him in combining these roles. The fact that three of the first four

---

15. Those who accompanied Muhammad from Mecca to Medina were known as the *Muhajirun* and those who invited him as the *Ansar* (Dabashi 1989, 54–55).

16. The concept of *umma,* with its universal implications, was antithetical to that of tribe *(qabilah)* or state.

caliphs died violent deaths suggests how unsettled were the years following the passing of the Prophet. On the one hand, Muhammad's death triggered efforts by successors to elaborate bureaucratic institutions and forms necessary to govern the growing empire; on the other, it brought to the surface old tribal loyalties and identities that Muhammad had sought to suppress. Muhammad's effort to make "religion, rather than blood" (Hitti 1956, 39) the basis of social organization proved only partly successful.

Religion and language enjoyed a symbiotic relationship in which acceptance of one necessitated the other, and both provided the means by which Muslims could identify one another. Together, religion and language marked, for Muslims, the critical demarcation between themselves and others and provided cement for a community united in theory. The Qu'ran and the traditional stories were almost only accessible in Arabic, and the common language of Islam provided an important sense of community among believers[17] just as Arabic poetry had been a source of solidarity (and an important historical record) to Arabs before Muhammad. With the introduction of paper (brought from China to Samarkand and found there by Muslims in the eighth century), Arab religious writings[18] became available throughout the sprawling empire. Lewis (1993, 155–56) eloquently captures the centrality of Arabic in Islamic civilization:

Arabic is one of the great languages of human civilization and history. Like Hebrew, it is a language of revelation, of sacred scriptures revered by hundreds of millions of believers. Like Greek, it was a language of science and philosophy, providing the basic texts and even the conceptual vocabulary of a whole civilization. Like Latin, it was the language of law and government and the source of both ideas and vocabulary in these fields; like French, the standard of taste and elegance for that same civilization. Like French and English, it has been the language of culture and commerce, of science and politics, of love and war. And even today, like English and Spanish, it is the shared

---

17. Iran was an exception to this. Persian literature and culture continued to flourish, alongside of Arabic, after the Islamic conquest.

18. Especially the Qur'an and stories about Muhammad and the military triumphs of Islam.

heritage of many nations and the binding thread of a cultural and intellectual association which transcends national, regional, and ideological barriers.

In addition to religious belief and ritual and language, architecture and art spoke of the unity of the Islamic community. Mosques were built in the center of cities and towns to serve as sites for communal prayer.[19] Whether in Syria or Spain, all were built according to a standard design with an open court fronted by a covered area that allowed the faithful with their *imam* (religious leader) to face Mecca. Each had a pulpit and an attached tower or minaret from which a muezzin called the faithful to prayer. The fact that mosques were also used to conduct public business reflected the merger of governmental and religious functions. Common rituals—the "pillars of Islam"—including a profession of faith *(shahada),* scheduled prayer *(salat),* required almsgiving *(zakat),* periodic fasting, and pilgrimage—intensified the self-conscious similarity and unity of the faithful. It is a matter of dispute whether going to war to extend Islam was another obligation (Hitti 1956, 49–54; Hourani 1991, 65–66, 147–52).

The Sasanian and Byzantine lands that were incorporated into the Islamic polity were already important cultural centers. However, the caliphs' (especially the 'Abbasids') encouragement of learning—provided it did not threaten political stablility—and the evolution of distinctive Islamic artistic, architectural, and literary forms (Graber, 1973) produced a cultural flowering equal to anything experienced later by Europe during the Renaissance. As Hitti observes (1956, 5): "Arab scholars were studying Aristotle when Charlemagne and his lords were reportedly learning to write their names. Scientists in Cordova, with their seventeen great libraries, . . . enjoyed luxurious baths at a time when washing the body was considered a dangerous custom at the University of Oxford." With a common language and religion to provide the framework, there was an outpouring of scholarship, especially between the ninth and twelfth centuries, in areas as diverse as

---

19. Early mosques showed the influence of Judaism and Christianity; the first genuinely Islamic structure was the Dome of the Rock in Jerusalem. It was built on the site of the ancient Jewish Temple where Abraham was said to have sacrificed Isaac, presumably in order to symbolize the legitimacy of Islam as heir to its two great predecessors.

theology, astronomy, medicine, history, and geography. However, beyond language and religion, the civilization that flourished was not indigenously Arabic but reflected the integration of the Hellenized Aramaic and Persian traditions that the Arab conquerors found when they arrived.

The idea of a community of believers retains much of its potency even in contemporary world politics. The powerful sense of "we" versus "they" that it propagated was and continues to be reflected in the Islamic contrast between "the sphere of Islam" (regions governed by Muslims according to Muslim law) and "the sphere of war" (regions not ruled by Muslims) (Watt 1988, 16).

The Islamic Empire

Michael W. Doyle (1986, 105) argues that, unlike most empires, the medieval Islamic polity did not begin "with a centralized state directing a differentiated society," and he notes that it lacked "substantial transnational economic extensions of domestic society" typical of most empires. Indeed, many of the attributes of a bureaucratized territoral polity were added *after* imperial conquest. Like the Mongols and Ottomans, the Arab entity was what Doyle calls "the puzzle of tribal empire" (Doyle 1986, 105–8). An empire constructed on a tribal foundation, in Doyle's view, will not be durable, and the anomalous and transitory nature of the Islamic polity is perhaps best captured in Bozeman's metaphor of an "empire-in-motion" (1960, 366). She expresses what Doyle means by "tribal empire" with the additional metaphor, "greatest of all caravans," in which dynamism was provided by "the quest of the end rather than the end itself, the moving rather than the arriving."

The rapid spread of Islam and the movement of the center from Medina to Damascus were accompanied by the proliferation of "government attributes." Tribal customs alone were inadequate to govern a polity of enormous size and cultural diversity, and in time the caliphs adopted Iranian, Turkish, and Byzantine practices. Hourani (1991, 26) summarizes this trend: "Gradually, from being Arab chieftains, they [the caliphs] formed a way of life patterned on that traditional among rulers of the Near East, receiving their guests or subjects in accordance with the ceremonial usages of Byzantine emperor or Iranian king." And as power shifted from the Arabian periphery to the Syrian and, later, Iraqi heartland, the ruling elite grew urbanized and hostile to tribal mores; for their part, the 'Abbasid rulers found themselves increasingly dependent on Iranian and Persianized Turkish administrators. Nevertheless, the establishment of an Islamic polity continued to feature many tribal attributes, even as it adopted the attributes of other cultures.

The style of government administration was adapted from Islam's imperial predecessors. Although Arabic became the common language of administration, many of the same groups that had provided personnel to the Byzantines and Sasanians continued to do so for their new rulers. Along with the Arabic language, a new coinage was introduced without the human images forbidden by Islam, and a postal service was established. "More important still," argues Hourani (1991, 27), "was the creation of great monumental buildings, themselves a public statement that the revelation given through Muhammad to mankind was the final and most complete one, and that its kingdom would last forever." This tendency was most evident under the 'Abbasids.

It was under the 'Abbasids, too, that an imperial administration under a *wazir* was centralized in the caliph's palace in Baghdad and subdivided into *diwans* (offices). The *wazir* was responsible for overall civil administration. Hourani (1991, 34–5; also, 131–33) offers a sense of how complex and sophisticated this new structure was: "There was a *diwan* for the affairs of the army, a chancery which drew up letters and documents . . . , and a treasury which supervised and kept records of revenue and expenditure." There was also an intelligence service to keep track of the increasing numbers of bureaucrats as well as a professional army and a proliferation of taxes to underwrite the whole grand edifice. Many officials were recruited from the military, but others emerged from the educated non-Arab urban elites, including Persians, Turks, Egyptians, Syrians, Jews, and Copts.

Over time, recognizable interests emerged within the caliphate. Two of the most powerful were a military class surrounding the caliph and the merchants upon which the prosperity of the caliphate depended. Between the two there grew up an uneasy interdependence; the military required the wealth of the merchants, and the merchants needed the protection of trade routes, the maintenance of urban order, and the collection of taxes. The different religious and ethnic communities of the urban centers acquired representatives as did the different crafts.

If the European concept of the Westphalian polity implies control from the center, then the caliphate would not meet that criterion. Hourani (1991, 138) captures this difference: "Before the modern age, frontiers were not clearly and precisely delimited, and it would be best to think of the power of a dynasty not as operating uniformly within a fixed and generally recognized area, but rather as radiating from a number of urban centres with a force which tended to grow weaker with distance and with the existence of natural or human obstacles.'' The caliph's control was greatest in "his" city and the immediate countryside. A permanent military presence was limited to key cities and a few highly fertile and productive agricultural centers. In other areas, the imperial presence was sporadic and indirect—military expeditions to keep trade routes open and manipulation of local tribal chiefs. Soldiers were recruited from these regions and occasionally might come to challenge the caliph himself.

CONCLUSION

The evolution of the medieval Islamic polity cannot be understood except by reference to a variety of polity forms that accompanied its birth, growth, and fragmentation. During the five hundred years or so that imperial Islam prospered, three major types of polities competed for the loyalties and identities of Muslims—tribe, *umma*, and empire. Competition also went on among entities within each type of polity (among tribes and clans, branches of Islam, claimants to the caliphate and rival caliphates).

Tribal identities that had dominated pre-Islamic Arabia remained important factors within the empire. Tribal perspectives, practices, and mores persist even in contemporary Arab societies, lending Arabic states a peculiarly tribal and clan coloration. The Muslim community only took root outside the Arabian peninsula years after the expansion of the empire itself. However, the community survived the empire, ultimately spread far beyond the empire's limits, and remains a potent aspiration for Muslims in contemporary global politics. The caliphate, though it grew rapidly, proved an ephemeral political form, and the Islamic state never assumed the features of a Westphalian polity.

12

THE CALIPHATE
The Limits of Dynastic Power

Unity based on Arabism and Islam proved elusive, and schisms based on tribe, clan, and even ethnicity were replicated and legitimized by religious divisions that made it difficult for the Islamic polity to survive. Some of those divisions remain potent in the contemporary Arab world. Indeed, the Arabs' common heritage—their religion—actually reduces their sense of national identity. As Anthony Smith (1991, 63) declares: "There is no reason why a common religious culture might not in principle act as the social cement of an Arab nation, were it not for the fact that the Islamic community of the faithful, the *umma*, by virtue of its very different inspiration and geographic extent, constitutes a rival. It creates a unity and a destiny that is, from a purely Arab standpoint, ambiguous, reinforcing yet subtly negating efforts to rediscover an Arab past that is not universalistic and global."

INTRODUCTION

The case of Islam is of interest precisely because of its failure to create a stable and territorial political structure like that enjoyed by Westphalian polities. The Muhammadan revolution began in the early seventh century as a religious movement and cultural aspiration at the edge of the then-dominant Byzantine and the Sasanian Persian empires. Armed with the revelations of the Prophet, Islam expanded with dramatic speed across North Africa and into Spain (or Andalus as its conquerors called it), with raids as far as the heart of France, and into the heartlands of its imperial foes in Syria, Persia, Turkey, all the way to the frontiers of the Indian subcontinent (as far as the Punjab). Assuming the trappings of a despotic multinational empire, the center of Islamic power shifted from the Arabian periphery first to Damascus under the Umayyad caliphs (A.D. 661–750) and then to Baghdad under the 'Abbasids (A.D. 750–1258). However, the collision of polity types—secular empire, religious community, and Arab tribalism—impeded and remains a challenge to the stability of any secular political form in the Islamic world.

THE EROSION OF THE CENTER

The death of Muhammad threw the burgeoning community of Islam into turmoil. All Muslims agreed about the supremacy of God and His word as conveyed in the Qu'ran. Less clear, however, was how to govern the community of believers in the absence of the Prophet, and it was over this question that the community became irremediably divided (Crone and Hinds 1986, 24–42, 97–110). A successor to Muhammad had to be selected from the Islamic elite consisting of his early followers, the influential citizens of Medina with whom he had been allied, and the leading families of Mecca. Among factors that were considered in identifying this successor were kinship to the Prophet, membership in his tribe, date of conversion to Islam, and acceptability to other tribal groups.

The Theory of the Caliphate

One of Muhammad's early followers, Abu Bakr, was selected as his successor or caliph (*khalifa:* the Prophet's successor), and political authority came to be centered around that position (Watt 1973, 276–77). The caliph, however, did not enjoy the authority of a prophet; he received no revelations and, though the guardian of the community and its traditions and defender of the faith, he could not easily claim the legitimacy provided one who was a messenger of Allah (Mottahedeh 1980, 3–39; Hourani 1991, 22, 60–61; Hitti 1956, 75–76). Although the caliph became de facto leader of the Islamic community, he could claim no authentic religious sanction (Watt 1968, 32–33; Goldziher 1981, 182–83).[1] God was the source of Muhammad's authority, and, for Muslims, secular authority without religious sanction was inconceivable. One consequence is that Islamic beliefs could never be

---

1. For a dissenting view, see Crone and Hinds (1986, 19) who argue that "if khalifa meant 'deputy of God' from the start, then the Shi'ites can hardly be altogether wrong in their claim that the legitimate head of state . . . inherited both the religious and the political power of the Prophet."

fully co-opted by a government; this still remains the case (Roberson 1988, 94).

Critical issues remained unresolved: Did a caliph possess religious authority, and, if so, what was its source? If a caliph lacked religious authority, what could be the source of his temporal authority? Were the tribal customs according to which caliphs were selected sufficient? Were caliphs infallible, and if not, could they be overthrown? Did law issue from the caliphs or the jurists, or was the Qu'ran its only legitimate source? Neither the Qur'an (which appeared about 651) nor the stories of Muhammad's actions and prescriptions *(hadiths)* provided clear answers to these vexatious questions.[2]

Muslim jurists sought to legitimize the caliphate by arguing that the caliph had been sent by Allah in order to maintain Islamic law and custom, a theory that, because it was an "expedient that lacked the sanction of the fundamental sacred law" (Bozeman 1960, 368; also Crone and Hinds 1986), became a source of continuing controversy. One of the most influential of the jurists, al-Mawardi, proclaimed in the eleventh century that the caliph enjoyed divine sanction through Muhammad to protect Islam and its community of believers, and must come from Muhammad's tribe. Al-Mawardi also argued that, although a caliph could delegate his authority to others, there could be only one legitimate caliphate at any time. This theory incorporated the traditional secular power enjoyed by Arab tribal chiefs and reflected, as well, Byzantine and Sasanian political influences. In fact, theory and practice regarding the caliphate diverged from the outset. As for practice, Gibb (1962, 8) notes, "the establishment of the Umayyad Caliphate . . . was . . . the outcome of a coalition or compromise between those who represented the Islamic ideal of a religious community, united by common allegiance to the heritage of the Prophet, and the Meccan secular interpretation of unity, against the threat of anarchy implicit in tribalism."

Competing Dynasties

Far more important to the fate of the Islamic polity than conflicts with external competitors like Byzantium or the later Christian crusad-

---

2. For a different view, see Rahman (1982, 2) who argues that "the Qur'an had from the time of its revelation a practical and political application."

ers were conflicts *within* the realm. The first imperial dynasty, the Umayyads, assumed power after a period of civil war and moved the imperial center to Damascus. With the Umayyads, the caliphate came to be regarded as a hereditary or dynastic position, and caliphs increasingly relied on Sasanian and Byzantine bureaucratic procedures to augment the more informal modes of rule associated with their Arabic tribal origins. The Medina-Meccan elite was gradually superseded by an elite dominated by military leaders who abandoned the nomadic mores of tribal ancestors in favor of a more settled urban way of life.

Umayyad preeminence lasted only eight decades and collapsed in civil war. The Ummayad caliphs had sought to institutionalize traditional Arab tribal practices and, in so doing, had alienated those who wanted the precepts of Islam to govern political life. In representing Arab superiority over non-Arab inhabitants of the empire, the Umayyads produced discontent on the part of "the large numbers of non-Arabs who had become Muslims, especially in Iraq and the eastern provinces" (Watt 1974, 27). These proved important sources of 'Abbasid and Shi'ite support. The last Umayyad caliph, who after being defeated in battle was killed in Egypt, was succeeded by Abu'l-'Abbas (749–54), a descendent of Muhammad's uncle, thereby inaugurating the 'Abbasid period.

Unlike the Umayyad, whose influence had been greatest in Syria and Arabia, the source of 'Abbasid power lay to the east, in Iran and southern Iraq. Like their predecessors, the 'Abbasids assumed power as part of an uneasy alliance and quickly turned upon their former allies. The family itself was torn by disagreements, so the caliphs relied upon others to administer the empire (Hourani 1991, 33). It was under the successors to Abu'l-'Abbas, especially al-Mansur (754–775) and Harun al-Rashid (786–809), that the medieval Islamic polity reached its political and cultural zenith. The shift in power away from Damascus was reflected in the construction of the city of Baghdad at a site which enjoyed a rich agricultural hinterland and controlled both the main north-south and east-west routes that linked the disparate provinces of the empire. In splendor and ritual nothing of the time could rival the new planned city, the city recalled by the *Arabian Nights*.

There are several events from which one might date the beginning of the collapse of the Islamic empire. One candidate is the establishment of a powerful rival caliphate in Egypt. The Isma'ilis, described later, carved independent territories for themselves first in eastern

Arabia and in 910 in Tunisia, where 'Ubaydullah, claiming descent from 'Ali and Fatima, established the Fatimid dynasty. In 969, the Fatimids occupied Egypt and clashed with the 'Abbasids in Syria and Arabia. The Fatimid caliphs sought to combine the roles of imam and caliph in themselves and emulated 'Abbasid pomp and ceremony; the dynasty marked the first time since the Pharaohs that Egypt had enjoyed political autonomy. Fatimid power rested on the fertility of the Nile delta, an easy tolerance of Sunnis and nonbelievers, and a mercenary army of Berbers and Turks. The dynasty survived until 1171 when a Kurdish general, Saladin, seized power, established his own dynasty (the Ayyubids), and then ousted the Christian Crusaders from Palestine and Syria.

Rival caliphates to both the 'Abbasids and Fatimids were established in Morocco (the Idrisids) and, more important, in Spain. Both areas were geographically remote from Cairo and Baghdad, and local officials acquired local interests and autonomy. A branch of the Umayyads that had been cast out of Damascus gained ascendancy in Spain and ruled informally for many years before adopting the title of caliph in the tenth century. Like the Fatimids, the Spanish Umayyads tolerated religious and ethnic diversity, centralized power in a capital city (Córdoba), enjoyed a high level of regional economic self-sufficiency, and utilized a mercenary army. Also, like the Fatimids, the Spanish Umayyads mimicked the court in Baghdad, even in moving the caliphate and isolating it from the capital city. The Umayyad polity split apart early in the eleventh century, and its successors found themselves under virtually continuous pressure from the Christian kingdoms to the north. Islam was isolated in a pocket around Granada and then, in 1492, finally swept from Spain.

Thus, by the tenth century there was no longer a single centralized imperial entity nor even a secular center to which all Muslims could look. One caliph (Baghdad) governed Iran, much of Iraq, and regions to the east. A second (Córdoba) governed North Africa and Spain, and a third (Cairo) ruled Syria, Egypt, and much of the Arabian peninsula. Actual collapse may be dated from 1055 when the Seljuks, representing Turkish military mercenaries, seized power in Baghdad and governed through figurehead 'Abbasid caliphs. An alternative date would be 1258 when the 'Abbasids were formally deposed by non-Muslim Mongols.

Hourani (1991, 130) argues that a successful dynasty "needed to strike roots in the city: it needed the wealth to be derived from trade and industry, and the legitimacy which only the 'ulama could confer.

The process of formation of dynasties consisted in the conquest of cities. A conqueror would move up a chain of cities lying on a trade-route. The creation and growth of cities in their turn depended upon the power of dynasties." Thus, the 'Abbasids were associated with Baghdad, the Umayyads with Damascus and Córdoba, the Fatimids with Cairo, and the Idrisids with Fez. Once in control of a core city, dynasties would try to appoint as provincial governors individuals who were beholden to them. Even if they were successful in placing their supporters, time usually eroded the ability of dynastic rulers to exercise authority at a distance, and provincial governors would increasingly come to exercise autonomy.

Imperial Decline

If the great expansion of Islam owed much to the military prowess of its armies, the employment of Turks in the imperial army and the failure to assure their loyalty were key factors in the decline of the empire. As the Iranian recruits upon whom the 'Abbasids had relied were integrated into Baghdad, they became less effective. In the early ninth century, the manpower needs of the caliphate were met increasingly by the recruitment of soldiers from Turkish-speaking tribes in central Asia and the purchase of slaves. These "slaves on horses" (Crone 1980) were aliens with no stake in the polity they pacified, and they were dependent on the caliphs whom they served. They neither enjoyed the political and social status of a formal elite nor did they acquire the stake in society of a landed elite. Patricia Crone (1980, 84) sees the practice of employing such mercenary slaves as decisive: "Because *mamluk* armies are essentially bodyguards writ large, they have all the virtues of elite troops at their best, but all the vices of private servants and foreign mercenaries at their worst: the facility with which palace officials can manipulate the state apparatus without ever considering the wider interests of politics, and that with which a hired soldiery can mutiny, ravage, loot and enter rebel service without ever going home, came together in the persons of the military slaves. A well-controlled *mamluk* army might have kept the unitary state intact, but an uncontrolled one could not fail to bring about its total disintegration."

Like the French kings at Versailles, the caliphs sought to distance themselves from popular urban forces and the pressures such forces might exert; they sought also to keep the army isolated from those popular forces. To this end, the caliph al-Mu'tasim (833–842) moved his capital north from Baghdad to the new city of Samarra. There, the political life of the empire was increasingly shaped by the leaders of the Turkish forces who also created virtual anarchy in Baghdad; simultaneously, the caliphate was threatened by the independence of strong provincial governors and by slave rebellions in southern Iraq. As early as 868, a Turkish soldier, Ahmad ibn-Tulun, seized power in Baghdad.[3] In Hitti's words (1956, 213): "Ahmad served as an example of what could be done in the matter of achieving military and political power at the expense of a bulky and unwieldy caliphate through the strong-handed and confident ambition of a subject soldier and his slave satellites."

On the surface, geographic impediments to unity and the shock of the Mongol invasions are sufficient to explain the imperial collapse. However, the former was not a determining factor, and the latter took place long after the empire had already been parceled into hostile parts. In reality, the Islamic polity, having grown so quickly, never managed to stabilize itself or get beyond its tribal and clan-based origins. Hourani (1991, 38) captures the process of decline:

> Even when the 'Abbasid caliph's power was at its height, his effective rule was limited. It existed mainly in the cities and the productive areas around them; there were distant regions of mountain and steppe which were virtually unsubdued. As time went on, his authority was caught in the contradictions of central-ized, bureaucratic systems of government. In order to rule his far-flung provinces, the caliph had to give his governors the power to collect taxes and use part of the proceeds to maintain local forces. He tried to keep control of them by a system of intelligence, but could not prevent some of the governors building up their own positions to the point where they were able to hand power on to their own families. . . . In this way local dynasties grew up. . . . As this happened, less revenue flowed to Baghdad, at a time when there was a certain decline in the system of irrigation and agricultural production in lower Iraq itself. In order to strengthen his position in the central provinces, the caliph had to rely more upon his professional army, whose leaders in their turn acquired greater power over him.

---

3. The Tulinid dynasty was short-lived and came to an end in 905 A.D.

Heavy taxation of conquered lands precluded deep loyalties, especially among non-Arabs and nonbelievers, and stimulated class differences.[4] Floods, plagues, and other natural disasters sapped the
imperial economy and produced political discontent. Islam provided a
veneer of unity among Arabs, Berbers, Turks, and Persians, but it was
not sufficient to wipe away deep cultural and ethnic self-consciousness
that was reinforced by geographic distance and differences in wealth.
Sectarian differences in Islam weakened the bonds afforded by religion
and, in some cases (for example, the Fatimids), provided justification
for political independence. Finally, in 945 A.D. one Turkish military
clan, the Buyids, seized power in Baghdad. One hundred years later
the Seljuk Turks replaced the Buyids and embarked on additional
conquests in western Asia. The 'Abbasids remained nominal and
shadowy caliphs until the middle of the thirteenth century. In 1258,
Hulagu, the grandson of Genghis Khan, occupied and pillaged Baghdad and the remaining 'Abbasids were annihilated.

Islamic Continuity and Imperial Collapse

As Hitti (1956, 193) expresses it: "If anything parallels the
astounding rapidity with which the sons of the Arabian desert conquered most of the civilized world in the first Islamic century, it is the
swift decadence of Arab domination between the middle of the third
and the middle of the fourth centuries after the death of Muhammad."
The collapse of the unitary imperial structure did not mean the disappearance of Islam. Instead, the weakening of loyalties to dynasties and
territorial frontiers intensified identification with religious symbols and
thereby reinforced the bonds uniting individuals in the community of
Islam. Although the medieval empire proved transitory, the community of Islam prospered after its demise. It was after the collapse of the
Arab polity that Islam expanded into Turkey, India, Africa, and
southeast Asia.

Many of the ideas and practices that evolved during the spread of
Islam retain relevance for contemporary Muslims. Watt (1988, 1)
argues that "the thinking of the fundamentalist Islamic intellectuals
and of the great masses of ordinary Muslims is still dominated by the

---

4. This process was intensified by the ostentatious display of wealth by
urban upper-class Arabs.

standard traditional Islamic world-view and the corresponding self-image of Islam." According to him (1988, 3–23), key elements of this worldview are: (1) the world is unchanging; (2) the Islamic religion is a final answer to all moral and religious questions; (3) Islam is intellectually self-sufficent and neither rests upon nor requires insights from Judaism or Christianity; (4) Islam is destined to become universal; and (5) all guidelines for society can be found in the Qur'an and in the "perfect" life followed by Muhammad. The "Islamic world" was destined to outlive the demise of the "statist" caliphate. Hourani summarizes this achievement:

> A traveller around the world would have been able to tell, by what he saw and heard, whether a land was ruled and peopled by Muslims. These external forms had been carried by movements of peoples: by dynasties and their armies, merchants movings through the worlds of the Indian Ocean and the Mediterranean Sea, and craftsmen attracted from one city to another by the patronage of the rulers or the rich. They were carried also by imported and exported objects expressing a certain style. . . . The great buildings above all were the external symbols of this 'world of Islam'. . . . By the tenth century, then, men and women in the Near East and the Maghrib lived in a universe which was defined in terms of Islam. The world was divided into the Abode of Islam and the Abode of War, and places holy to Muslims or connected with their early history gave the Abode of Islam its distinctive feature. . . . [Muslims] were aware of belonging to something broader: the community of believers (the *umma*). The ritual acts which they performed in common, the acceptance of a shared view of man's destiny in this world and the next, linked them with each other and separated them from those of other faiths. (1991, 54-55, 57)

The Contentious Religious Community: Schisms and Schismatics

In practice, most inhabitants of the Islamic empire had no way to participate in public affairs or desire to do so except in battling infidels or applying Qur'anic law (Pipes 1983, 144). If common religious beliefs initially fostered unity, differences in doctrine served to legitimize competitors for power. Factionalism characterized the ruling elite from the outset. In the years immediately following the death of Muhammad, early converts and personal friends of the Prophet found themselves at odds with "careerists" from Medina and Mecca. Tribal loyalties also clashed repeatedly, and the elites in Medina and Mecca resisted the efforts of governors of the wealthy provinces of Syria and Iraq to carve out greater autonomy. In fact, the powers of the caliph were limited from the outset, and the role, according to Watt (1968, 40), was "conceived in terms appropriate to the chief of a nomadic tribe"; that is, as first among equals.

On one hand, the bureaucracy that grew up around the caliphate was necessary for day-to-day administration of newly urbanized centers and a far-flung empire. On the other hand, it also produced alternate centers of power that the caliph sought to control and with which he had to contend. Among the new sources of official power in the caliphate were the positions of *wazir, amir* (general), and *ulama* (religious scholars). Increasingly the secular power of caliphs and later Islamic leaders was circumscribed by the "holy law developed by jurists from the Qur'an and the traditions of the Prophet" (Lewis 1993, 145). Since caliphs had no authority to interpret Islamic law, the role of religious judge *(qadi)*, established during the Umayyad period but with some similarity to tribal arbiters, became important, especially since *qadis* enjoyed an exclusive right to interpret Muslim law *(shari'a)*. In this way, caliphs were deprived of authority to legislate or, at best, had to share that prerogative with those who represented the Islamic community. Like the caliphs, subsequent secular Islamic leaders have had to compete with one another to make it appear that their policies and actions were compatible with the *shari'a,* described by Lewis as "not only a normative code of law but also, an ideal towards which people and society must strive," regulating "every aspect of life, not only belief and cult, but also public law, constitutional and international, and private law, criminal and civil" (1993, 145).

Judges were trained in special schools *(madrasas)* that instructed them in how to interpret and apply the *shari'a* or make inferences from it to matters to which it did not explicitly refer. To this end, the judges and the theologians who constituted the *ulama* used the Qur'an and the deeds and words of the Prophet as confirmed by a chain of authority, putatively going back to witnesses of Muhammad. In fact, judicial interpretation was more significant than this suggests because the record of Muhammad's deeds and words was not brought together until several generations after his death. Thereafter, as Lewis (1993, 33) observes, "new social, political, legal, and religious problems and concepts came into Islam from the conquered peoples, and many of the ideas and solutions that resulted were projected backwards into the mouth of the Prophet.'' All in all, interpreting the law remained a source of considerable authority in Islamic lands, especially when applied to phenomena unknown during the Prophet's liftetime. In Dabashi's words (1989, 92): ''Occupying a distinct position of authority, the *qadis* were designated as deputies *(na'ibs)* of the Prophet. They gradually developed into a powerful class that could use their office for the legitimation, or illegitimation, of a ruler.''

All Muslims agreed that Muhammad was the last in a line of prophets that included Moses and Christ; that, in the words of Ahmad al-Badawi, ''the Qur'an contains the words of Allah directly and verbatim revealed to . . . Muhammad . . . through the Angel Gabriel''; and that ''the Qur'an is the last revealed Holy Book, which supersedes previous scriptures and the only one still available in the exact words and language uttered by Prophet Muhammad'' (cited in Hick and Meltzer 1989, 191–92; also Mortimer 1982, 31). In time, however, there arose divergent interpretations of the Qur'an, focusing on issues such as free will, the attributes of Allah, the relationship between belief and action, and the relative importance of reason and revelation. Various schools of thought arose around these issues: Mu'tazelism (rationalism), Ash'arism (scholasticism), Sufism (mysticism), and Hikmat (science) (Muzaffar-Ud-Din Nadvi 1965; also Mortimer 1982, 51–55; Watt 1973, 180–250). For the most part, these differences, though manipulated for political ends, were theological and remained academic (Zubaida 1989, 5).

By contrast, Islamic society was violently divided by disputes over the bases of political and religious authority. Although clothed as doctrinal questions, the real issues involved power and rulership and were rooted in tribal and class rivalries. According to Dabashi (1989, 3), ''the charismatic authority of Muhammad,'' his struggle ''against the traditional patrimonial mode of Arab tribal authority,'' and process of disintegration of authority after Muhammad's death—''three simultaneous, forceful, and interacting processes, which may be visualized as three horizontal lines moving along early Islamic history, are then cut across by three vertical lines, known historically as the different branches of Islam. Each of these branches (vertical lines) will have a particular position vis-à-vis those forceful trends (horizontal lines), which were already independently and yet interconnectedly in process.''

The sometimes ferocious schism among the three branches of Islam—Shi'a, Sunni, and Kharijite—was never bridged, and it was partly responsible for the failure of Islam to produce a stable territorial polity. Although Sunnism triumphed, it would be wrong to regard it as religious orthodoxy because, in Watt's words (1973, 6), "Islam has no machinery comparable to the Ecumenical Councils of the Christian Church which could say authoritatively what constitutes 'right doctrine'." In time, followers of the different branches came to be identified with different regions of the empire.

As noted earlier, Muhammad's successors could not claim a direct link to Allah; their authority could only be legitimized indirectly.[5] Nevertheless, an empire existed; it had to be ruled, and disputes had to be settled. Abu Bakr, an early follower of Muhammad and the Prophet's father-in-law, was selected as first caliph. He and his three successors—'Umar ibn 'Abd al-Khattab (634–44), 'Uthman ibn 'Affan (644–56), and 'Ali ibn Abi Talib (656–61)—are known collectively as the *Rashidun* ("Rightly Guided") (Watt 1988, 18). The cracks in Islam only became visible with the fifth caliph, Mu'awiya ibn Abi Sufyan (661–80), who assumed power after a civil war, which climaxed with the murder of 'Ali. 'Ali was a cousin of Muhammad, a close personal friend, the husband of Muhammad's daughter Fatima, and father of Muhammad's favorite grandchildren; he could, therefore, claim kinship, even a blood tie, to the Prophet. Mu'awiya, the governor of Syria, could assert no such claim. 'Ali's authority could neither be surrendered to others nor legitimately seized by them. As a result, with 'Ali's death, authority had to pass to his sons, Hasan and Husayn. Hourani summarizes the civil war and its resolution:

> The two forces met at Siffin on the upper Euphrates, but after fighting for a time they agreed on arbitration by delegates chosen from the two sides. When 'Ali agreed to this, some of his supporters abandoned him, for they were not willing to accept compromise and submit the Will of God, as they saw it, to human judgement; the honour due to early conversion to Islam was at stake. In the months of discussion between the arbiters, 'Ali's

---

5. The first caliph, Abu Bakr, is supposed to have proclaimed to the community: "O men, if you worship Muhammad, Muhammad is dead; if you worship God, God is alive." Cited in Hourani 1991, 22. In other words, there was no longer on earth a direct messenger from God whose dicta carried the authority of God.

alliance grew weaker, and finally he was assassinated in his own city of Kufa. Mu'awiya proclaimed himself caliph and 'Ali's elder son, Hasan, acquiesced in it. (1991, 25; also Mortimer 1982, 41–42, and Watt 1973, 12–18)

Shi'a

The *shi'at Ali* ("followers of 'Ali") refused to accept as legitimate rulers anyone except the male heirs of Muhammad, insisting that the caliphate required a familiy, not merely a tribal, link to the Prophet. Only if the line of succession went through the sons of 'Ali would a portion of Muhammad's charismatic authority be preserved (Dabashi 1989, 95–120; Watt 1968, 119).[6] From the moment of the Prophet's passing, some of his companions were unhappy with the succession and would have preferred 'Ali. (Goldziher 1981, 169). Their view reflected resistance to the resurgence of tribal traditions that followed the death of the Prophet.

According to one branch of Shi'a (the Imamis), there were twelve descendents of 'Ali—known collectively as the Twelve *imams* (spiritual leaders). Most of the twelve were believed to have been murdered, but the twelfth and last *imam*, also called *mahdi* (leader guided directly by God), was believed to have disappeared in 878 A.D. and not to have died at all.[7] Imami belief held that the *mahdi* would remain invisible until the day he chose to return and rule all Islam. In Mortimer's view: "The Imam is not equal to the Prophet: the divine revelation of the Koran remains final and complete. But the interpretation of the Koran is not simply a matter of learning. Divine guidance is necessary and this is imparted through the Imam. Thus Shi'ism accepts the notion of spiritual authority in a sense that Sunni Islam does not, and it makes a distinction between spiritual and temporal authority" (1982, 44; also 45–49, 54; and Watt 1973, 38–40, 275–77). In other words, *imams*, unlike caliphs, were believed to be infallible and to enjoy a divine right to leadership of the Islamic community (Goldziher 1981, 170).

---

6. Dabashi (1989, 107–8) notes the possibility that Shi'ite belief in hereditary succession was influenced by pre-Islamic contact with the Sasanids in Iran.

7. The second son of 'Ali, Husayn, who was killed in 680 at Karbala in Iraq, was regarded as a *mahdi* by his followers.

Initially, the Shi'a were only a loose group of opponents of Mu'awiya, but, in time, they became bitter foes first of the Umayyads and later the 'Abbasids. Spiritual and temporal power were, in their view, distinct; but, since the latter depended on the former, which could be held only by the male descendants of 'Ali, Sh'ites regarded all caliphs after 'Ali as usurpers. Since Muhammad was believed to have designated 'Ali as his successor, Sunni caliphs must be usurpers with no moral, legal, or religious legitimacy. Shi'ite beliefs, described by Mortimer as a "doctrine of opposition," were fundamentally incompatible with secular rule and bureaucratic institutions. Although the *shi'at Ali* itself broke apart in time, Shi'ite sects, especially in the eastern provinces of the empire, continued to oppose the Sunni caliphs in Damascus and later Baghdad.

Although most Iraqi Shi'ites co-existed with their Sunni rulers, one sect, the Zaydis, refused to recognize as *imam* anyone who would not fight the usurpers, and they carved out an independent *imamate* in Yemen in the ninth century. More notable was another sect, the Isma'ilis, who regarded Isma'il, son of the sixth Shi'ite *imam*, as his father's successor and believed that Isma'il's son in turn would return as the *mahdi*. The origins of this movement are obscure, though J. J. Saunders (1962, 128) suggests that we "get the impression of a vast network of 'cells' extending to the remotest corners of the Muslim world, of an 'underground' constantly striving to evade the police, of spies and traitors and internal feuds and schisms." Ultimately, one of the Isma'ilis established the Fatimid dynasty in Egypt. In Saunders's view (1962, 132), "The emergence of the Fatimid Caliphate is a major event in Islamic history. For the first time a large part of Dar al-Islam had passed under the control of a sect which not only rejected the spiritual claims of the Abbasids, but declared its resolve to replace them by a new universalist Imamate. The progeny of Ali were to govern the whole Muslim world, not as civil magistrates but as the sinless and infallible spokesmen of God." Shi'ites of different stripes remained a threat to the caliphate, and some may even have assisted the Mongol conquest of Baghdad in the thirteenth century.

Sunni

Those who supported the Umayyads and accepted the legitimacy of the caliphs after 'Ali were known as Sunni (from *sunna*, which means "standard practice" or "normal and normative custom") (Watt 1973, 256). Caliphs, they insisted, should be selected from Muhammad's tribe according to the consensus of the community or its surrogates. The Sunni tradition was ostensibly based on the general principles of the Qur'an or on Muhammad's practice. In reality, Sunnism entailed a rejection of charisma and an acceptance of much of pre-Islamic Arab tribal tradition as the source of political authority and practice (Dabashi 1989, 71–93). Muhammad was viewed by Sunnis as a tribal, as well as religious, leader, and early caliphs had to be Quraysh.

More important (and anathema to their adversaries), when issues arose for which neither the Qur'an nor "standard practice" offered a clear answer, Sunnis permitted leaders to decide or render an opinion based upon their interpretation of original religious sources (Mortimer 1982, 41–42; Watt 1973, 180–81). The Sunni tradition, then, was a pragmatic concession to necessity and changing circumstances. And even though all practices had to conform to the principles of the Qur'an, Sunni rulers permitted significant regional variation in customs and behavior (Watt 1973, 256). The absence of any mechanism for making official doctrinal changes led to divergent practices and the proliferation of various Sunni schools of belief, but also encouraged tolerance of such divergences (Mortimer 1982, 41–42; and Watt 1973, 266–68, 317).

In time, the Sunni tradition became the ideology of the ruling elite, especially the 'Abbasids. 'Abbasid caliphs freely adopted religious symbols and used Islam to legitimize their rule.[8] They claimed divine sanction by kinship with the Prophet and made decisions that putatively were based on the Qur'an and the Prophet's behavior. The triumph of Sunnism probably permitted an imperial Islamic polity to survive as long as it did. In Watt's words (1973, 75), its "basic positive feature . . . may be said to have been the attitude to community and state." The Sunnis' "common attitude was one of attachment to the state and to the underlying Islamic principles; and this attachment led to devout loyalty or even to a practical zeal for the maintenance and advancement of the community."

Kharijite

In the midst of the battle of Siffin (657 A.D.) between the supporters of 'Ali and Mu'awiya, 'Ali was persuaded to permit arbitration

---

8. *Qadis* who were supposed to arbitrate disagreements according to Islamic law were important in this regard.

between him and his enemies in accordance with tribal tradition. The third and least known of the branches of Islam, the Kharijis ("those who seceded"), originated among those of 'Ali's supporters who turned against him when he agreed to this concession (Watt 1973, 15–19; Dabashi 1989, 121–45). The Kharijis argued that the struggle (which 'Ali was winning) should be decided by Allah alone, not by human arbitration. Violence then ensued between 'Ali and the Kharajites, and in 661 'Ali was assassinated by a Kharijite.

Centered around Basra, Kharijites had much in common with the Shi'a. Like the Shi'a, they were unwilling to accept the idea of inherited rule or the possibility that secular politics could be severed from religion. Authority, in their view, came solely from the community and was not reinforced by any external source of legitimacy; tribal sources of authority were explicitly rejected. In addition, the Kharijites claimed that only the most virtuous—pious and strong—could govern and that a ruler could be overthrown at any time if he showed himself to be sinful or unworthy.[9] Kharijites believed that Sunni Muslims were sinners who were no longer Muslims, and that violence should be used against them.[10] By this logic, waging holy war (jihad) was a religious duty of all Muslims (Mortimer 1982, 41–43; Hitti 1956, 54–55). Ultimately, Kharijite fanaticism alienated them from other Muslims, and they had little long-term impact.

From time to time, Kharijite ideas found favor among tribes that sought leaders or arbitrators who would not undermine the existing tribal power structure and who could be used to justify separatist movements. Where Kharijites governed themselves, as did the Najdites in southern Arabia during the late seventh century, they had to limit their extremism (Watt 1973, 18–19). Perhaps the most important of these was the Ibadi imamate that lasted in Oman for over a hundred years until crushed by the 'Abbasids at the end of the ninth century. For the most part, however, Kharijite dogma made them anarchists

---

9. The most extreme puritans among the Kharijites, known as the Azraqites, believed that there could be no excuse for sin, that all sinners were automatically infidels, and that sinners should be executed.

10. Watt (1962, 12) suggests that Kharijite readiness to use violence in their cause was related to "old Arab usage" that "there was no wrong in killing someone not a member of one's tribe or an allied tribe."

and revolutionaries, unable to construct or cooperate with any stable governing structure (Von Grunebaum 1970, 69).

Classes

Doctrinal cleavages were linked to the emergence of socioeconomic classes and hostility among them. To some extent, class and economic differences reinforced ethnic divisions (notwithstanding Islam's tolerance of ethnic diversity). Not surprisingly the Arab conquerors became a privileged elite, enjoying social and economic advantages. For the most part, they lived apart from those whom they conquered and retained a sense of distinctiveness and superiority.

Non-Arabs who converted to Islam enjoyed theoretical, but not practical, equality with the Arab elite. For instance, Muslims were not supposed to pay "tribute," yet, as Hitti (1956, 96) points out: "Here Arabian chauvinism, pitted against theoretical claims, proved too strong for those claims to be realized. There is no doubt that throughout practically all the period of the Umayyads, holders of land, whether believers or unbelievers, were made to pay land tax. . . . Reduced to the position of 'clients,' these neophyte Moslems formed the lowest stratum of Moslem society, a status which they bitterly resented." Among converts to Islam—and in particular among Iranians who enjoyed an ancient culture—there was resentment against the tax and other privileges given to those of Arab origin. This resentment intensified as memory of the first Arab conquests began to fade. Even when they became clients *(mawali)* of Arabs, local converts could not easily enter the new elite (Von Grunebaum 1970, 73).

Christians, Jews, and others who were nonbelievers but were tolerated constituted the class of *dhimmis*. They and their property were under Muslim protection and allowed to practice their religion provided they paid tribute or tax *(jizya)* (Saunders 1965, 33). In theory, such groups were protected because they were esteemed by Allah as the precursors of Islam just as Moses and Jesus were regarded as prophets before Muhammad. Although *dhimmis* could not participate in judicial proceedings involving Muslims or bear arms, were forbidden to wear certain colors associated with Islam, and could build houses of worship only with permission, the tolerated communities enjoyed considerable autonomy.

At the bottom of the social hierarchy were the large number of slaves who were captured in war or were purchased by Arab merchants. Although the enslavement of Muslims was outlawed, the practice was common, especially by Arabs as applied to non-Arabs. However, the freeing of slaves was regarded as the charitable act of a pious Muslim. One special category of slaves—those purchased for military service—were destined to play a key role in the decline of the caliphate.

As a "doctrine of opposition" to statist institutions and to the elites who managed those institutions, Shi'ism had a natural appeal to the poor and non-Arabic elements in Islamic society, especially in southern Iran. Mortimer (1982, 43–44) declares that Shi'ism's "primary appeal is to the defeated and the oppressed," "the underdogs in the Muslim world." He adds: "Central to Shi'ism's appeal, especially for the poor and dispossessed, is the theme of suffering and martyrdom." While the merchants of Mecca became Sunnis, many *mawalis*, especially those who chafed under the Arab Umayyads, took refuge in Shi'ism.

In some ways, Kharijism was an even more powerful magnet for the non-Arab poor, the *dhimmis*, Muslim slaves, and the *mawalis* because of its antiestablishment and radically democratic character. In its fierce egalitarianism, the Kharijites wished to carry out the promise of the Qur'an. As Dabashi (1991, 123, 124) observes:

> The Kharijite movement was essentially an embodiment of the aspirations of a multitude of disillusioned and disinherited Muslims who, while in the acceptance of their new faith, were released from the stabilizing bonds of their traditional order, and yet did not come totally under the cohesive command of a new political culture, stemming from the predicates of Islam as the new moral demand system. Most of the Kharijites, whether tribal Arab or mawali, were primarily from the lower social and economic strata of their respective societies. . . . Brought into the new collectivity—the Islamic community *(ummah)*—the Kharijites believed their aspirations had been betrayed by both the Umayyad aristocracy of the Quraysh tribe and the Shi'ite oligarchy of the Prophet's household. Disillusioned with both, the Kharijites vowed to establish a form of Muslim "democracy" in which anyone, "even a black slave," could become the leader of *ummah* through popular "election" and consent.

Conversions

In its early years Islam attracted relatively few converts outside of Arabia, and many of them were probably officials in conquered areas, captured soliders, or Arabs already residing in the new imperial provinces. In time, the number of conversions outside Arabia increased owing to immigration to the new imperial cities, the hope of avoiding taxes or tribute, the relative ease of the conversion process itself, and the prospect of employment with their new rulers. Nevertheless, by the end of the Umayyad period,[11] perhaps only 10 percent of the empire's inhabitants were Muslim; by the end of the tenth century, however, relatively few non-Muslims remained (Bulliet 1979). Little pressure was exerted on nonbelievers to convert. Non-Islamic religious communities, though required to pay tribute, were permitted to live in peace and worship as they wished. Non-Arabs could find acceptance by mastering Arabic and converting to Islam. In large measure, Islamic society was tolerant of regional and ethnic differences; many Iranians, for example, were attracted to the new religion (though, unlike others in the empire, not to the Arabic tongue) (Hourani 1991, 28–30, 47–48).

Islamic Law and the Jurists

There can be no stable and independent political structure in the absence of a legal framework to legitimize it and provide the guidelines for it to adapt to changing conditions. Since Islam regarded law and religion as identical, the purpose of which was to assure right conduct in this world in preparation for the next, it was almost impossible to establish a durable foundation for a secular Islamic polity.[12] Government was regarded as an epiphenomenon, subordinate to religious dogma. The principles and practices of politics and government could evolve only with difficulty and had to find justification within the narrow confines of religious doctrine. As Mortimer (1982, 56) argues, the "political disintegration of the Islamic state corresponded to a gradual ossification of Islamic thought."

The Qur'an united Islam by providing a clear and simple code of

---

11. The fall of the Umayyads was probably hastened by the fact that the Islamic population of Iraq and Iran grew more quickly than that of Syria, their power base, whose cities had thriving pre-Islamic communities and cultures.

12. Bozeman (1960, 363) suggests that in both Byzantium and in Western Europe "the influence of Roman jurisprudence proved to be stronger than that of the religious norms," thereby abetting the establishment of stable territorial political units.

ethics, fundamental values, and behavior for individuals, enabling Muslims to differentiate themselves from nonbelievers but providing little that might serve the practical day-to-day needs of government. Although it may be argued that the limitations inherent in religiously derived law contributed to the demise of the Islamic empire, it should also be noted that such law was vitally important in maintaining Islamic unity—the Islamic community—after the empire collapsed. As Bozeman (1960, 364) comments: "Later developments seemed to justify the emphasis placed upon the ideological and cultural, rather than political, aspects of the idea of unity; for even when the military and political foundations of the commonwealth crumbled during the tenth and eleventh centuries, the unifying social fabric that theology and the law had produced did not give way. In fact, Islamic history shows, on the contrary, that the widest possible measure of religious, social, and cultural unity was attained only after the political unity of Islam had been disrupted, partly recreated, and then disrupted again."

In time, the gap between theory and practice and between Islamic values like equality and the reality of despotism widened. Especially after the 'Abbasids had assumed power, the caliphs, their governors, administrators, and judges effectively legislated and adjudicated and, in doing so, took account of tribal customs and regional differences. Necessarily, they also sought justification for their acts and decisions in the beliefs of Islam. As caliphs came to resemble oriental despots, Islamic law and society were transformed. Sami Zubaida (1989, 4–5) describes this process:

The theologians and jurists of those dynamic periods for the most part accepted the state of their time as an Islamic state representing the unity and power of the Islamic community. . . . The elements of political activism of the community present in the early charismatic Islam . . . had by the medieval period developed into mere formalities: *Shura* (consultation) . . . was only practiced . . . as a show . . . ; *Ijma'*, originally consensus of the community . . . seldom pronounces in matters of state . . . ; and the injunction to command the good and forbid evil, binding on every Muslim and extending to watchfulness over the actions of princes and leaders, soon became confined to the private and ceremonial sphere, its extension to matters of state lapsed. . . . It would seem that the ulama took a realistic view of the state, that is, that they and their followers were powerless to change it.

Islamic specialists in jurisprudence *(fiqh)*, really a body of religious scholars *('ulama)*—who combined the attributes of theologians, constitutional scholars, and political philosophers—tried to overcome the gap between theory and practice (Mortimer 1982, 35–38). The leading members of *'ulama*, which included leading *qadis*, teachers, and religious preachers, constituted a political and social elite. Religious scholars of all stripes agreed that law and government had to reflect the Qur'an, Muhammad's habitual behavior *(sunna)* as recorded in traditional biographies and stories *(hadiths)*,[13] and the wisdom of the Islamic community *(sunna* of the community) about what was just. However, caliphs and jurists differed about the meaning and relative importance of these sources of law and about how they related to one another. They argued especially about the role of contemporary community consensus *(ijma')*, which reflected local traditions (including those handed down in a tribal context), preferences, and interests. They also differed over the accuracy of the traditional stories about Muhammad and his companions.

Some scholars sought to apply reasoning to reach interpretations of the law. Others emphasized the customs of Muhammad and his companions in Medina, and still others gave greater weight to community consensus and interests. The jurist who had perhaps the greatest impact was al-Shafi'i (767–820 A.D.), who argued that the Qur'an had to be viewed as the literal Word of God on all matters referred to in it whether large or small. Of equal importance, especially in matters to which the Qur'an did not refer, were the customs of Muhammad as traditionally handed down. *Ijma'*, he argued, was of lesser importance. But what was to be done in the event that the Qur'an or other traditional sources did not refer to an issue or was obscure about it, or in the event that conditions had changed? The dominant response, given by al-Shafi'i among others, was that they themselves, as the most competent religious scholars, should reach decisions by analogous reasoning from traditional sources; that is, that the *'ulama* could determine the community consensus.[14] Not all agreed, however, and,

---

13. *Hadiths* could be falisified relatively easily to accomplish some legislative or administrative purpose.

14. There remained significant differences about whether such a consensus was permanent or could be questioned by later generations living in changed conditions.

by the eleventh century, different schools had been ceded de facto dominance in different regions of the empire.

The decisions and interpretations that jurists provided collectively constituted the sacred law or *shari'a*. The sacred law not only concerned public conduct but also private issues of ethics, indeed, all aspects of life. Although such law was supposed to arise solely from Islamic sources, it actually mirrored local custom and tradition as well. On the one hand, the *'ulama* and its legal interpretations *(fatwas)* provided the caliphate with a critical source of legitimacy. Even though the jurists were divided, they were all within the Sunni tradition. On the other hand, jurists were a source of power independent of the caliphate; caliphs might be deterred from certain actions by fear of disagreement with jurists, or jurists might actually denounce a particular decision or policy. Indeed, within a century, the 'Abbasid caliphs had no input into determining the law even though they were expected to obey it (Crone and Hinds 1986, 108–9). Thus, the imperial Islamic polity lacked the principal attribute of sovereignty as it evolved in Europe—the power to legislate and interpret the law (Crone and Hinds 1986, 80–96). Consequently, as Roberson argues (1988, 94), Islam "was not the captive of any government, nor dependent for survival upon the state, nor could it be predictably manipulated by centralized authority."

CONCLUSION

The issues raised by medieval Islam remain relevant for the contemporary Muslim world. The effort of secular governments to harness the *umma* and deepen secular loyalties—or, as Roberson puts it, "nationalize" Islam (that is, encourage those elements in Islam which support or rationalize the needs of a modernizing society)—have failed or are likely to fail. Arab national loyalties and frontiers have proved tenuous, and the barrier between internal and external politics almost nonexistent.

The Islamic community and the religion of Islam continue to exert a stronger attraction for many Arabs than do Arab "states" or the "Arab nation" (a phrase that has roots in the original caliphate). Some of the region's sharpest and most dangerous conflicts, like those in Lebanon and Syria, can be traced to sectarian conflicts within the original Islamic community. The territorial polities of the Middle East were created by European rulers, and postcolonial nationalists and their political parties tried but largely failed to instil enduring national loyalties among citizens.

Instead, these polities reflect the nested consequences of their tribal origins. King Hussein and his Bedouin followers in Jordan (originally Transjordan) preside over a territory that was given to the son of Hussein, the sharif of Mecca, and his Hashemite heirs for services rendered during the 1916 Arab Revolt against Ottomon rule.[15] Modern Saudi Arabia traces its origins to the Wahhabi movement of the eighteenth century, which, like modern Islamic fundamentalism, preached a return to strict obedience to the Qur'an and the teachings of Muhammad, and the rule of the Sa'udis began in 1921 at the expense of their tribal foes, the followers of sharif Hussein. The policies of Hafiz al-Assad of Syria show strong clan loyalties to the minority Alawite religious community in Syria, and Saddam Hussein has surrounded himself with followers from his Tikriti family clan in Iraq. In a word, contemporary Arab states are weak in the sense that they are not the principal targets of loyalties of many of their own inhabitants. Whether one looks at Shi'ites, Alawites, Druzes, Hashemites, Maronites, or others that determine cleavages in the region, the potency of religious and tribal symbols inherited from the early years of Islam and before are evident (Merad 1981, 37–48).

Efforts to make loyalties to the medieval Islamic empire identical or even compatible with loyalties to the Islamic community (or sects within it) succeeded only temporarily, if at all. The awkward relationship between *umma* and government that arose in the seventh century persisted and produced "a religious outlook . . . that was and is suspicious of the state" (Roberson 1988, 99). The triumph of the idea of an Islamic community (and the simultaneous demise of a united polity) separated from and superior to the non-Islamic world became frozen in time. As a result, "Islamic reform is always governed by and drawn inexorably to the past: . . . nothing in the present and future could possibly ever be as good as that exquisite society erected by Muhammad and transfixed forever by his death" (Naff 1981, 28). Islamic societies thus have found it difficult to accept change and adapt to modernity. In the words of Watt (1988, 142), "One of the important points at which this . . . unhistorical self-image of Islam affects contemporary events is in the idealization of early Islam, when it is regarded as a perfect society to which a return is possible and desirable; no such return can solve our contemporary problems."

---

15. King Hussein's willingness to accept a special role in protecting Islamic holy sites in Jerusalem despite the opposition of the Palestine Liberation Organization is based on a claim of familial and tribal links to the Prophet.

13

ITALY AFTER ROME
Complexity at the Nexus of the Ancient
and Modern Worlds

The rather lengthy period of Italian history that is our final case encompasses the end of the Age of Antiquity in the West, the Medieval era, and the dawn of the Westphalian system in Europe. No case involves more varied and significant transformations among polities. We are dealing here with the gradual demise of the western branch of the Roman Empire, the intrusion of barbarian tribes, and the evolution of several major, interrelated rivalries during the Middle Ages among Western Catholicism, Orthodox-Byzantine Catholicism, and Islam, as well as among different forms of empire and city polities.[1] Contests among Pope, Holy Roman Emperor, and cities (some of whom eventually acquired empires) persisted through the Renaissance and Early Modern era, when politics became more secular, the Holy Roman Empire faded, and cities—themselves internally transformed—were overshadowed by emerging Westphalian polities to the north.

INTRODUCTION

Of all the systems we treat in our cases, Italy was perhaps the most penetrated from the outside. J. K. Hyde (1973, 2) observes of Italy that no "medieval country lived less exclusively unto itself," and the same was true during the historical periods that bracketed the Middle Ages. Rome built its initial empire in Italy on the foundations laid by Etruscans, Greeks, and others and, as the empire expanded,

---

1. Italian city polities had far more in common with the Greek polis and the early Roman republic than with the later Roman empire, illustrating again that there is no inevitability about the direction in which political history moves.

became a clearing house for peoples, goods, and gods from the entire Mediterranean world and as far north as Britain. At its peak, Rome provided relative security and prosperity for millions of citizens.

After the third century A.D., incursions of German tribes—Huns, Visigoths, Ostrogoths, Vandals, and others—themselves pushed by other peoples and perhaps deteriorating climate conditions further to the east, threatened the Italian base of the empire. The Roman strategy for dealing with the threat, apart from straightforward military defense, was multifold: Rome joined in shifting alliances with some tribes and tried to play them off against each other. Successive emperors also incorporated into the imperial army Franks and Alamanni, Visigoths, Ostrogoths, Vandals, and Burgundians and allowed German immigrants to settle peacefully on lands within imperial frontiers.[2] Nevertheless, in Edward N. Luttwak's (1976, 5) words, "the provision of security became an increasingly heavy charge on society. . . . Even then the empire retained the loyalties of many, for the alternative was chaos. When this ceased to be so, . . . then the last system of imperial security lost its last support, men's fear of the unknown."

Thereafter, Italy was host to a bewildering array of competing polities. Tribal entities like the Huns, dynasties like the Merovingians, the imperial polity that emerged in northern Europe, groups of freebooters, the Church, and numerous city polities competed vigorously in Italy. Waves of invaders ebbed and flowed up and down the peninsula as Italians repeatedly served as pawns in the conflicts among powerful rulers.

SYSTEM DISCRETENESS AND STRUCTURE

The character of the Roman Empire, not only in its far-flung extensions but also at its center, became increasingly "barbarianized" as Germanic tribes settled within its frontiers. In 476, after twenty years of political instability that included the elevation and deposition of no fewer than eight emperors, Odoacar, the general of an imperial army that consisted mainly of Germans, simply dismissed the last western emperor, Romulus Augustus. Odoacar pledged his loyalty to the Emperor Zeno at Constantinople, which event marked the end of

---

2. Useful sources for this period include Goffart 1980, Musset 1975, Heather 1991, and Wallace-Hadrill 1985.

the Roman empire in the West. For a time, barbarian rulers went on ruling Italy much as their imperial predecessors, but it brought Italy little long-range stability. Zeno successfully encouraged the Visigoth leader, Theodoric, to overthrow Odoacer.

The Persistence of Disunity

In 535 the Byzantine emperor Justinian sent his armies to liberate the western empire from barbarian rulers whom he viewed as Arian heretics. Although Justinian's forces were ultimately victorious, two decades of warfare left Italy devastated. Next, in 568, came the Lombard invasion and occupation, which for a generation plunged much of Italy into a genuine Dark Age. As J. K. Hyde (1973, 14) describes it, "the elaborate drainage and irrigation works created by the Romans fell into disrepair, and great tracts of country even in the most favoured areas like the Po valley, reverted to marsh, forest and waste." At the same time, cities lost their role as administrative centers and withered or simply disappeared. Hyde points out that "significantly, no historian has succeeded in proving the continuance of civic institutions from late Roman to medieval times for any city north of Rome."

Italy gradually recovered, mainly because the Lombards did not capture all of it. Once again, the Byzantine connection was crucial. Byzantium, through control of the sea, held on to the northwest Ligurian coast until the 1640s and administered the eastern part of the Lombard plain from Ravenna until 751. Settlements of Roman peoples in the Venetian lagoon remained relatively undisturbed, and in the ninth and tenth centuries it was a rising Venice that linked to Byzantium. Meanwhile, the city of Rome maintained its independence under a succession of Christian popes. The popes regarded themselves as subjects of the emperor at Constantinople until the Byzantines withdrew from northern Italy after 751 and forbade the use of religious images in worship. This iconoclast controversy was so bitter that the pope could no longer rely on Constantinople's protection against the Lombards, and the only choice seemed to be to appeal to the Franks. The Byzantines had remained in Italy long enough to "civilize" the Lombards, a process facilitated by trade as well as by the Lombards' abandonment of the Arian heresy and fusion with local Catholics. Hence, when Charlemagne's Franks conquered Lombardy in 774, "they found not only scholars superior to those of Francia but also a state at least as sophisticated as their own, and, in some respects, more so."

In subsequent centuries, external actors continued to influence Italy's political evolution. The Frankish conquest tied north and central Italy to a large, albeit loose and unstable continental empire, and the Franks allowed the pope to claim territories beyond Rome in central Italy. Islam presented another threat, which Charles Martel, King of the Franks, turned back from France at the battle of Poitiers in 732. Nevertheless, Saracens captured Sicily in the mid-ninth century and moved onto the mainland, from which the Byzantines ejected them several decades later. Those areas in the north and south within the Byzantine sphere tended to prosper, while the Franks' Carolingian Empire—divided among Charlemagne's heirs—proved unable to cope with Saracen raids and the advances of Magyars and Vikings. At a critical juncture, however, Otto the Great gave the Holy Roman Empire a new lease on life by rallying German forces to defeat the Magyars decisively at Lechfeld in 955.

The First Crusade (1095) and its successors (the last in 1270) inaugurated a new phase in which influences emanated from and then fed back to Italy. The Crusades failed to do lasting damage to Islam, but they fatally weakened Byzantium, creating a vacuum in the eastern Mediterranean that the Turks and others eventually filled. Byzantium's weakness also invited predators into southern Italy. The Normans arrived as mercenaries in the mid-eleventh century, soon established their own large mainland kingdom, and conquered almost all of Sicily. However, the primary beneficiaries of the Crusades, in addition to the pope and the peace of Europe generally—with quarrelsome knights away besieging the Holy Land—were the Venetians, Genoese, Pisan, and other Italian seafarers, who transported and supplied the crusaders, and wrung trade concessions from Constantinople. Even the Holy Roman Empire gained indirectly, insofar as its last great emperor, Frederick II, received his youthful education in the wealthy Norman kingdom of Sicily.

The Holy Roman Empire fell into disarray in the fourteenth century, and the new arbiters of politics in northern Italy were, first, armies sent by various German princes and rulers of the nascent polity of France and, then, between 1340 and 1380, companies of mercenaries from Germany, France, and England. A combined army of Hungarians and Germans temporarily seized the Norman kingdom of Naples from Joanna I. When Joanna supported the Avignonese pope in the Great Schism of 1378, the Hungarians returned and had her murdered. The next year Italian mercenaries defeated mercenaries fighting for the Avignon pope, which inaugurated a century of relative freedom from outside interference for Italy. This was the Golden Age of the Italian Renaissance (Holmes 1975, 101–4). Holmes (1975, 282) attributes the "emergence of Italy from the domination of northern European armies" not to "the brilliance of Italian commanders and troops but to the relative decline of the northern powers."

Golden Age it was, but not an era of peace, especially in the first half-century, owing to the ambitions of Milan's Visconti family. By 1453 Italian polities had reached a modus vivendi of sorts. Yet wars among some of them continued, intense rivalries persisted, and factions within individual polities engaged in frenzied competition. Perhaps the absence of a foreign threat had lulled Italians into a false sense of security that discouraged them from achieving the sort of political cohesion that was slowly emerging to the north. M. V. Clarke (1926, 154) argues: "The renewal of foreign dangers at the end of the fifteenth century came too late: by that time local variations and jealousies had become so stereotyped that the cities and principalities of Italy found submission to a foreign enemy easier than confederation with each other."

Lack of unity, as Machiavelli later lamented, cost Italy dearly. The Golden Age gave way to thirty-six years of warfare that changed everything. In J. R. Hale's words (1985, 15):

> From an invasion by Louis XI's successor Charles VIII in that year which led to his conquest of Naples, a series of campaigns waged in Italy by his successors, Louis XII and Francis I, by Ferdinand and his successor as king of Aragon and Castile Charles V, by Maximilian and by the Swiss, left Milan and Naples by 1530 subject to Spain and no other state except Venice unaltered in its form of government, unscarred by battle losses or unshaken from its tradition of independence. Even Venice had been for a while stripped of its mainland possessions by a coalition comprising France, Spain, Maximilian, the Pope and the neighbouring rulers of Mantua and Ferrara. Florence had been transformed, through one military crisis after another, from a free republic into a duchy under Imperial tutelage. Rome itself had been brutally sacked.

Polarity

Italy from Roman times to the early modern period ran the gamut from unipolarity to fragmentation, although because of overlapping polities and external intervention, it is often difficult to identify a dominant overall structure in traditional distribution-of-capabilities terms.

The Roman era resembled unipolarity, and Rome's power made it an ideal vehicle for preserving and transmitting the wisdom of the ancients. Roman laws and other aspects of its culture had an enormous impact on the Middle Ages and western civilization generally. In some respects, however, regarding the Roman era as unipolar is misleading. Rome overextended itself to a point where a second capital at Constantinople was necessary, not only to provide a fall-back in the event of further barbarian attacks in the west but also for the task of day-to-day administration of its sprawling territories. Rome's imperial system involved the active presence of Roman administrators and garrisons but gave scope to local rulers and cultures. Even as Rome's high culture was attractive to many of its non-Roman subjects, local cultures and barbarian incursions had an important impact on what it meant to be "a Roman." Who were the Romans by the sixth century, asks R. H. C. Davis (1988, 60–61)? "Were they the people of Rome, battered and besieged now under Gothic, now under imperialist rule? Or were they the members of the imperial court—Justinian who was an Illyrian, Belisarius who was a Thracian, the eunuch Solomon who came from Mesopotamia, and the eunuch Narses whose origin was unknown?" In any event, the late Roman Empire was beset by internal conflicts that contributed to its demise.

After the Roman Empire, the dominant structure in Italy was multipolarity, but there were dramatic variations on that theme. For example, after the Lombard invasion, Italy was shared by the Lombards, Byzantium, the pope—and soon the Franks' Holy Roman Empire, Venice, Saracens, and Normans. These "poles" were very diverse. The Lombards were a nomadic people who only slowly settled in cities. Popes were also secular princes with feudal estates and broad territorial claims, and they ultimately laid spiritual claim—exercised through local priests and churches—to all of Christendom. The Holy Roman Empire much of the time was merely an aspiration of German princes and, even under Otto or Frederick II, had difficulty establishing effective administration over its domain, which overlapped that of the pope. Venice expanded from a group of island communities to a seaborne commercial empire, competing with Genoa, Pisa, and others. The Saracens were an advance contingent of a universalist religion spread by the sword, and the Norman kingdoms in southern Italy and Sicily were good-sized regional polities.

Rivalry between emperor and pope discouraged the formation of large kingdoms in northern and central Italy and helped create conditions that were favorable for the emergence of strong cities. According to the fradulent Donation of Constantine, the Emperor Constantine had ceded vast territories to the pope in the fourth century, and in the late eighth century Pepin and Charlemagne recognized the pope's title to much of central Italy and the former Exarchate of Ravenna. Yet successive emperors continued to assert their authority over the same territory. The clash of jurisdictions made it virtually impossible for any new kingship to establish itself over a large territory (Hyde 1973, 39–40). After the brief Dark Age, cities again flourished and during the Middle Ages became even more prominent in Italian politics than elsewhere in Europe.

Independent cities arose all over Italy, and some, like Venice, Verona, Florence, Siena, Pisa, and Genoa, soon were more important than others. In time, conflict among and within Italian polities grew, coupled with more threats from outside, especially during the catastrophic fourteenth century when fragmentation was more in evidence than anytime since the Lombard invasion. Hyde (1973, 178) recounts that *signori* treated their cities "as if they were private property, eroding the distinction between public and private law in a manner scarcely equalled in the Dark Ages": "Cities were bequeathed at will and even bought and sold. An extreme example is Lucca, once one of the great free communes of Tuscany, which in 1329 was sold to Gherardo Spinola of Genoa by Lewis of Bavaria's German troops. During the next thirteen years the city changed hands five times—once by cession, twice by purchase and twice by conquest." The result of this turbulence, not surprisingly, was the expansion and consolidation of the leading polities at the expense of others. After about 1378 there were only six major Italian polities—Milan, Venice, Genoa, and Florence in the north—plus the pope and the kingdom of Naples.[3] At intervals, Milan or Naples (under Ladislas, 1402–14) appeared poised to swallow up the others, and Genoa dropped out of the top tier. However, consolidation was insufficient to provide a basis for effective resistance to renewed foreign interventions after 1494. The political evolution of key Italian polities continued, but under conditions that foreshadowed the Europe of Westphalia.

---

3. For a discussion of politics in Renaissance Naples, see Bentley 1987.

Geophysical Setting

"Within the two extremes," writes J. P. V. D. Balsdon (1979, 1) citing the elder Pliny, "the frozen North and the torrid South, was the temperate zone; and in this Italy had the finest position in the world, 'for the land juts out in the direction which is most advantageous, between the East and the West.' " E. L. Jones (1981, 90) points out that "opportunities of the environment" provided an incentive for European trade: "Climate, geography, and soils varied greatly from place to place. The portfolio of resources was extensive, but not everything was found in the same place. . . . Transport costs were low relative to those obtaining in the great continental land masses." The climate gradually improved all over Europe until it reached what historians speak of as the "little optimum" during the eleventh and twelfth centuries. Warmer weather extended the growing season in fringe areas and contributed to a revival of European economic activity generally. Then, for a century and a half after about 1200, average temperatures fell to such an extent that this cycle has been called the "little ice age."

Italy's geography and Mediterranean climate provided the foundation for a variety of polities and economic pursuits. High mountains, hills, and rivers break up most of the Italian landscape and make for numerous microclimates. Hyde (1973, 10–11) observes that "the close juxtaposition of mountain and plain in almost every region, by creating areas of contrasting challenges and potentialities has at all periods impeded the emergence of uniform social and political structures even within the restricted territory dominated by a single city." For much of Italian history, peoples who learned to exploit the plains and valleys have been dominant, but the mountain regions, too, have been important.

One important geographic distinction was between polities that enjoyed easy access to the sea, good harbors, and timber and those that were landlocked. Italy had a long coastline and was the main peninsula of peninsular Europe. The sea provided a highway for long-distance trade, defense against attack by all but naval forces, and an opportunity to exercise influence through seapower. Lagoons and reedy marshes also played a crucial role in physically isolating and protecting Venice.

Climate combined with marshes and mountains affected land-based military operations in Italy. The countryside was poorly suited for cavalry. Especially in winter, military activities almost ground to a standstill, and in summer, troops and supplies were confined to roads and a limited amount of open country. Opposing armies were constantly having to maneuver for position, marching and countermarching with no conclusive outcome.

Although there were few good maps, boundaries were reasonably clear and sometimes even geographically logical. Davis (1988, 152) remarks that "feudal geography was not as haphazard as is sometimes imagined," that "feudal domains, since they had grown up from small beginnings, were likely to be defensible units, and therefore to conform with the natural geographical divisions of the land." Such "feudal geography" was, for instance, in evidence in the final division of Charlemagne's empire. One hundred and twenty "emmisaries" labored for more than a year to determine the boundaries of the parcels distributed to Charlemagne's heirs. Some boundaries remained unclear or were disputed, but others followed earlier Roman administrative divisions or markers like "stones, rivers, trees, and sometimes man-made trenches" (Sahlins 1989, 5).

Economic and Demographic Factors

The Roman economy in late antiquity was agrarian. Because unsettled conditions of the third century made it possible to acquire ever-larger estates and because of patronage from the Emperor Constantine and his successors, the fourth and early fifth centuries saw the rise of an immensely wealthy and powerful class of senatorial landlords. Much of their land was worked by slaves or tenants with varying degrees of freedom, which may have prefigured medieval feudalism, but this is uncertain. First, "there was no simple chronological transition from late Roman *coloni* to medieval serfs." Second, most landlords in Italy felt it desirable to maintain at least one luxurious town house, a tradition that tempted later aristocrats into upper-middle-class family alliances and commercial pursuits (Cameron 1993, chapter 4). Hyde (1973, 13) points out that, during the disturbances of the fourth and fifth century, landlords in Italy were more likely to stay in town rather than withdraw to their country estates, the reverse of the pattern in Gaul.

The traditional view of the period after the third-century Diocletian "reforms" is that Roman government expenditures and oppression increased. Contemporary sources complain of tax collectors and laws forbidding tenants from moving from one property to another. By contrast, recent scholarship holds that the constant reiteration of harsh laws bespeaks a weak government in the western empire, trying to cope with the growing burden of imperial defense. Leading Senate landlords—apart from those directly affected by barbarian settlement—were largely exempt from taxes or found it possible to have their arrears canceled; restrictions on tenant mobility reflected a failing attempt by government to create a stable tax base; patron-client relations permeated society at large, and many government offices were sold to the highest bidder (Cameron 1993, chapter 4).

Successive Germanic incursions and Justinian's campaign of reconquest gravely harmed the Roman economy. Many aristocratic families that had been prominent in the Senate fled to the east, where some formed a Latin-speaking colony in Constantinople (Cameron 1993, chapter 5). Much of the infrastructure that had supported agriculture and urban life was destroyed or abandoned. Population declined—devastating outbreaks of plague occurred between 541 and 543—and many towns, if they did not disappear entirely, "shrivelled up into a corner of their ancient walls" (Le Goff 1988, 70). Thereafter, as Averil Cameron (1993, 79) puts it, "the fragmentation of the western empire, combined with the conversion of all the invading tribes (something which was not at all a foregone conclusion), allowed the church to assume a leading role." In addition to its growing political clout, the Church acquired a preeminent economic position. Local bishops became the primary urban and rural patrons, and the Church and its monastic orders received gifts of money and land from wealthy and poor alike.

The rich and civilized Byzantines remained in Italy just long enough to mitigate some of the economic and cultural shocks of the Lombard invasion. Hyde (1983, 13) writes that wherever the Lombards "established their control, written records cease for a time; when they resume they reveal that the Roman world has died and a new culture, much poorer and more primitive but strongly influenced by Byzantium, has arisen in its place." From the seventh to the tenth centuries, interior sections of Italy were economic backwaters, while a few key ports like Venice, Naples, Amalfi, and Salerno profited handsomely from trade in eastern luxuries. Venice came to prominence in the ninth and tenth centuries after unification of its lagoon communities and successful campaigns against local rivals. The Golden Bull of Basil II (A.D. 992) allowed the Venetians (alone) concessionary tolls in the Dardenelles. However, there are some signs of gradually increasing trade in Lombard areas from about 690, including the establishment of a royal mint at Pavia that issued Byzantine-style gold *solidi* (Hyde

1983, 16–22). As for agriculture, the feudal manorial pattern appeared over much of north and central Italy beginning in the ninth century—and later in the Norman south—but it was never as extensive as elsewhere in Europe and declined earlier.[4] Most of the estates owned by noble families and monasteries seem to have been "grossly under-exploited" and began to be divided into smaller, more intensively cultivated units during the general economic revival of the eleventh century (Hyde 1983, 5, 25).

The passing of A.D. 1000 not only relieved fears that the world might end that year but also ushered in better economic times. (For an overview of the medieval economy, see Pounds 1974 and Lopez 1976.) Viking, Saracen, and Hungarian raids had ceased; the weather improved; and agriculture expanded into new lands aided by the availability of iron tools (including the iron ploughshare), new techniques for shoeing and harnassing animals, watermills, and windmills (in flat country). A food surplus fed a rapidly growing population and encouraged nonfarm occupations. Towns and regions began to develop specialities: those in England focused on wool, Germany on silver, Spain and central Germany on iron, and Flanders and northern Italy on high-quality cloth manufacture. By the twelfth century Flanders and northern Italy were "economically the most advanced parts of Europe," to such an extent that "trade between them became a kind of commercial axis along which much the economic life of Europe was to evolve" (Koenigsberger 1987, 144; also 136–43). This was a highly organized trade protected by new commercial laws and treaties, and carried on by merchants who attended international trade fairs and conversed in "an international language" (mainly Latin but German in the Baltic and Norman French about the English Channel). However, next to war, the most important economic activity, which began early

---

4. Henri Pirenne, in his well-known thesis, argues that Islamic conquests were the major factor in the emergence of feudalism, because they cut the west off from trade with the east and left a western "economy with no outlets" during the ninth and tenth centuries. Partly because of the links with Byzantium enjoyed by Venice and a few other port cities, Italy had more of an outlet. In fact, trade in this period was at a low ebb, but only partly because Islam made the Mediterranean more dangerous. Justianian's reconquest and the Lombard invasion were so devastating that there was limited wealth to support trade. Elsewhere in Europe, the Baltic provided an alternative outlet, and Viking and Hungarian raids were more disruptive than distant Islam.

and peaked in the High Middle Ages (1200–1340) was a building boom—parish churches, pilgrimage churches, cathedrals, monasteries, and castles—sponsored by the Church, monastic orders, and secular lords.

By the thirteenth century, towns were growing wealthy and independent, reflecting in many cases the fact that commerce, trade, and finance were becoming more lucrative and institutionalized.[5] Hansa merchants dominated trade in the north, including Flanders cloth through Bruges; and in the south, Genoa, Pisa, Milan, Florence, and Siena began to compete with Venice. The Venetian government-owned Arsenal and private firms in Genoa emerged as centers for building ships powered by sails instead of oars and steered by a hinged rudder.[6] Venice, Genoa,[7] and Pisa gained immense business and booty, as well as profitable trading stations in the eastern Mediterranean, from the Crusades. As early as 1072, Venetian merchants had the idea of forming companies to buy shares in several trading ships, to spread risk and profits beyond a single voyage. Later *compagnias* included both active and passive members—often a single family group formed the core—and were even able to arrange dependable insurance for cargoes.

Institutionalized and international banking in Europe[8] originated in Florence and Genoa. Italian bankers safely ignored the Church's prohibition against usury not least because popes were regular borrowers (Gilbert 1980). During their heyday in the early fourteenth century,

---

5. Hyde (1973, 12) cautions that unlike the situation in northern Europe, in Italy "the great majority of cities have lived as centres of consumption and distribution of the surplus produce of the rural areas around them; apart from a few exceptions, they have been dominated not by merchants and manufacturers but by landowners. . . . The apparent self-sufficiency of the ancient or medieval city, cut off from the fields by its walls and gates, is, in fact, an illusion."

6. Ships were now built more cheaply by constructing skelton rather than hull first. The compass came into widespread use by the late thirteenth century and made it easier to sail in all seasons (Jones 1981, 58).

7. On the Genoan connection with Byzantium and its impact on Genoa's "internal" politics, see Day (1988).

8. As early as the ninth century, Baghdad banks had branches with genuine checking accounts in key cities throughout the Islamic Empire (Davis 1988, 143).

the Florentine houses of the Bardi and Peruzzi were "the biggest business organisations the medieval world was to see." However, the legendary banking wealth of Florence derived from an "almost unique" level of industrial development, primarily in textiles. Florentine companies beat out rivals from Siena, Pistoia, Lucca, and Piacenza; and Florence's very success spilled over into Tuscany as a whole. San Gimignano, for instance, made its fortune from locally grown saffron dyestuff, sold to Florence and then worldwide (Hyde 1973, 157–58).

Until the end of the thirteenth century, what Davis (1988, 377–79) calls "the central clearing-house of European trade and finance" were the Fairs of Champagne. There were six fairs a year, and each lasted six weeks and was genuinely transnational. "Italian bankers sent agents who issued letters of credit which could be cashed in almost any stated currency and in any part of Europe." One may even begin to speak of "the essential unity of the European economy": "Before 1250 there were no national customs-systems, no 'tariff walls,' and no restriction on the movement of merchants, ecclesiastics, scholars, or labourers from one country to another. The Pope 'presented' Italians to English benefices; English scholars studied in Paris where the great master was Thomas Acquinas, the son of a German baron from the *Regno* of Naples and Sicily; Catalan merchants were employed in the Byzantine Empire; and Italian merchants resided at Lübeck and Bruges." This "transnationalism" was primarily among the educated and highly skilled,[9] and the prosperity that fostered it gave rise to further development, variety, and competition.

The major economic changes of the later Middle Ages had more immediate social and political consequences, including the decline of the feudal manorial system.[10] Required to equip himself and his retain-

---

9. Hale (1971, 32) comments that "we should probably not be far wrong if we took the average longest journey made by most people in their lifetimes as fifteen miles."

10. Jones (1981, 88) proposes that "a tightly organized feudalism" had actually been a "suitable setting" for the initial "rise of commerce," strong enough to protect the market without posing a serious threat—until the market developed its own momentum. He observes: "for landless men to become traders instead of bandits may require a society strong enough to protect itself and to offer good legitimate profits."

ers with arms, armor, and sound horses, all costly, the crusader—if he survived—usually came home poorer than he went, or left his estate poorer, especially since none of the crusades after the first was victorious or lucrative. The only recourse, since it was unthinkable to sell land, was to sell communal privileges or commute labor services and bonds of serfs for a money rent. In the expanding economy of the twelfth and thiteenth centuries, the profits of commerce and agricultural surplus brought burghers and peasants the cash to pay for rights and liberties (Tuchman 1978, 10).

Population growth provided a growing supply of free laborers, who were more efficient than serfs; and, as farming became more profitable, there was an incentive to hire them. At the same time, landowners were steadily lured into nonagricultural pursuits, a trend especially apparent in northern Italy where the feudal pattern had been weak from the outset. Many of the remaining large estates were more intensely exploited through concessionary agreements with tenants that evolved into a sharecropping system.

Manufacturing in towns and cities gave rise to guilds, which gradually evolved, as H. G. Koenigsberger (1987, 222–25) observes, from social/religious fraternities into a vertically integrated capitalist mode of production. Many guilds gained rights to regulate apprenticeship, working hours, product quality, and sometimes even prices. Although most production still took place in the home and master craftsman continued to employ journeymen and apprentices, in time a "proletariat" emerged that owned only their labor. Laborers suffered from fluctuations of an international market and found their guild employers determined to keep them from organizing. The result was a widening gap between patricians and *popolo minuto* that added another source of factionalism in Italian cities to family feuds, party rivalry, and Guelph-Ghibelline quarrels. Occasional strikes and urban disturbances in Italy were echoed in places with similar conditions, like Flanders, but Italy was at least spared the peasant revolts that attended the demise of the manorial system elsewhere in Europe.

The progress of the previous centuries continued until a series of calamities in the mid-fourteenth century. In fact, progress and calamities were related, insofar as a burgeoning population made Italy vulnerable to the perennial scourges of famine, plague, and warfare. The population of cities like Palermo and Pisa surged to over 50,000; Florence had about 90,000; and Venice, Genoa, and Milan probably had more than 100,000 (Koenigsberger 1987, 215; also Hyde 1973, 153). Barbara W. Tuchman (1978, 96) writes: "Following the Florentine bankruptcies, the crop failures and workers' riots of 1346–47, the revolt of Cola di Rienzi that plunged Rome into anarchy, the plague came as the peak of successive calamities'' and ''coincided with a massive earthquake that carved a path of wreakage from Naples to Venice.'' With the largest population in Europe, Italy suffered the worst. The Black Death killed from one-third to two-thirds of Italians.[11] The death rate in Pisa was 500 a day, and Siena never fully recovered from the loss of half of its citizens. Venice lost about three-fifths of its population (Lane 1972, 19). The Black Death also ''was eventually to have profound effects on the position of the papacy by undermining the high population level on which its income ultimately depended'' (Holmes 1975, 92). Warfare, too, took an increasing toll partly as a result of city polities' greater wealth and administrative efficiency. Armies grew larger and were ''cripplingly expensive.'' The heavy tax burden fanned popular discontent and fostered unrest in another respect, by purchasing the services of unreliable mercenaries (Hyde 1973, 182-83).

As the Middle Ages gave way to the Renaissance in the fifteenth and early sixteenth centuries, not a great deal changed in Europe from an economic standpoint. Ahead lay the next wave of government bankruptcies and the dislocations caused by the influx of wealth from the Spanish colonies in the New World. The Veneto-Tuscany area lost ground to southwest Germany, especially in banking, as the Fuggers surpassed the Medicis partly because of the difficulty of getting raw wool for the Italian clothing industry. Nevertheless, ''Europe was still almost entirely a self-contained unit, full of areas servicing one another on more or less equal terms.'' The largest single industrial plant in Europe continued to be Venice's Arsenal, employing up to four thousand workers (Hale 1971, 155). Portents of the next stage of development were the issue of the first patent by Florence in 1421, Venice's first formal patent law in 1471, and the Gutenberg printing press (c. 1456). The latter created an information revolution that was dangerous

---

11. Jones (1981, 56) provocatively suggests that the ''fall in population as a result of the bubonic plague'' was ''a kind of Marshall Plan.'' He cites Herlihy on the point that ''Europeans were psychologically prepared for the better diet that a reduced population could afford, and 'perhaps' by the greater energy that came from being better fed, to enter a renewed age of expansion.''

to the established ecclesiastical and secular authorities (Jones 1981, 60).

Since Roman times, Italy had been more urban than elsewhere in Europe, and this pattern persisted after the Black Death. By 1550, Naples' population swelled to 210,000 and Venice to 160,000. More than forty Italian towns had populations of 10,000 or more, and twenty had 25,000 or more. Peter Burke (1986, 220–21) observes: "In the rest of Europe, from Lisbon to Moscow, there were probably no more than another 20 towns of this size. About a quarter of the population of Tuscany and the Veneto was urban; in all the regions of Europe, only Flanders is likely to have had a higher proportion of townsmen." Nevertheless, traditional links with the countryside remained and were strengthened in some cases. A number of wealthy merchants in Venice and Florence shifted their investments from trade to land, and the result was a phenomenon that some historians describe as limited "refeudalization."[12]

War and Modes of Diplomacy

Warfare. The existence of so many autonomous polities complicated security calculations in medieval Italy. Nevertheless, war in the Middle Ages (Contamine 1984 and Verbruggen 1977) was as much influenced by ideas as by geography or technology. Medieval society had an "overwhelmingly military ethos." The "upbringing of princes and nobles in the arts of combat and the values of chivalry" instilled this ethos "into young men in the highly idealized form of romances, chronicles and tournaments" (Koenigsberger 1987, 299). Tuchman (1978, 14–15) notes: "The status of nobility derived from birth and ancestry, but had to be confirmed by 'living nobly'—that is, by the sword. . . . The clergy was to pray for all men, the knight to fight for them, and the commoner to work that all might eat." The noble was not, in theory, to engage in "fighting for fighting's sake," but in "defense of the two other estates and the maintenance of order and justice." For this virtuous calling, he was exempt from many taxes on the assumption that "taxpaying was ignoble" and that "the knight's sword arm" was his contribution to society.

---

12. As a result, the splendid Palladio villas were built by leading Venetian families on the mainland (Burke 1986, 240).

War could also satisfy greed for land or territory. "Political Europe," Hale (1985, 22–23, 31–32) remarks, "was like an estate map, and war was a socially acceptable form of property acquisition." The ownership of territory, usually "expressed in the idiom of inheritance," offered attached jurisdictional rights, opportunities for patronage, and "a weaker motive almost always . . . profits obtainable from rents, fees and the acres farmed directly." "Land, and the 'glory' it brought with it, was a far more potent motive than any anticipated profit."

Hale (1985, 37–38, 31–32, 21) notes that the significance of chivalry "long outlasted the withering away of the relevance of its international code of behavior and training to the actual practice of war." Knights of the old aristocracy were gradually replaced by soldiers of fortune, and tournaments no longer offered training for the new age of infantry and firearms. But Renaissance princes were still reading "a particularly heady brew compounded of . . . chronicles [of wars], of chivalrous and crusading romances, and of humanistic potboilers which stressed the exploits of Alexander, Hannibal, and Caesar." Likewise, although aristocrats were less inclined to personal military service and more reluctant to pay for it, they continued to idealize violence, the hunt, and tournaments to such an extent that "rulers could broadly rely on this essential echelon in the mobilization process to support a call to war."

Military history over our period begins with barbarian invasions, continues through an era of feudal knighthood and sea battles, and ends with the large mercenary armies hired by Italian cities being overwhelmed by the even larger armies and resources available to emerging Westphalian polities. Though nomads caused Roman legions and settlements no end of grief, the invaders needed up to ten horses per armed rider and thus could not sustain warfare beyond the vast grazing grounds of the steppe (Koenigsberger 1987, 21). Nonetheless, the inability of other authorities adequately to protect against the raids of Magyars and others was a factor in the reorganization of early medieval society into a manorial hierarchy of lords and vassals, bound by oaths of fealty, and resting on the defensive unit of a castle defended by armored knights on horseback. The Franks were successful warriors because of their superior swords and coats of mail. Armored regalia for rider and horse soon became so elaborate that only wealthy lords could afford it. Riders bearing lances sat on a saddle with a high pommel and canticle, their armored feet firmly secured in stirrups, and horses' hooves had metal shoes. Meanwhile, ships for war (as well as commerce) added sails, hinged rudders, and a compass for improved navigation.

For much of the Middle Ages, difficult topography, armored fighters, castle fortresses, and walled towns favored defense over offense. There were few major battles, many minor skirmishes and long sieges, and continual pillaging and devastation. The aim of armies beyond booty and rape was to live off the land, deny resources to enemies, and starve them out of strongholds. It was a slow business that often ended indecisively, with besiegers exhausted, defeated by bad weather and disease. Death tolls from minor wounds or illness were regularly more than half of the total deaths (Hale 1985, 119–20). However, almost imperceptively at first, the balance in military technology began to shift to the offense. Swiss halberdiers and pike men started to counter the mounted knight. By the mid-fifteenth century, cannons using shells propelled by gunpowder and capable of leveling castle and city walls began to replace catapults. Charles VIII used the new guns with startling success in his 1494–95 campaign for the Kingdom of Naples (Keegan 1993, 321–22).

Cities were willing to use their newfound wealth to buy the necessary forces for protection and expansion. During the Renaissance, armies steadily grew larger and more professional, with good and bad consequences. Knights were less inspired by crusades, local obligations, or errands of mercy, and more willing to accept pay—and lesser folk were too. Bands of mercenaries served the highest bidder. Hale (1985, 70, quoting Sanuto; also 44) describes these as "Noah's ark" armies, men of various "nationalities" fighting against one another in non-civil wars, which made possible a Renaissance society "adequately organized to produce wars on demand, in spite . . . of a sluggish resistance to paying for or serving in them." On the other hand, this development mitigated the intensity of warfare because mercenaries were reluctant to fight to the death. Mercenaries were expensive and posed a threat to their own employers. Despite the obvious problems with mercenaries and the pleas of the likes of Machiavelli to return to citizen militias, only Venice built a standing army. Venice in 1560 had an army reserve of 20,000 and a naval reserve of 10,000, which involved about one in seven of an estimated rural peasant population of 200,000 (Mallett and Hale, 1984). By contrast, the Medicis in Florence opposed militias because militias tended to be republican in sentiment (Hale 1985, 200–1).

Historical sociologists like Michael Mann argue that war had much to do with the growth of powerful central governments in Europe, and it is worth examining the extent to which this relationship prevailed in Italy. The situation was mixed, as Hale (1985, chapter 9; 1971, 100) explains. On the one hand, war threatened governments with defeat, unruly mercenaries, and/or financial ruin. Local militias (when they could be formed at all) were unpredictable when it came to putting down riots or revolts of citizens. Cannons threatened castles, and governments tried to establish a monopoly over the manufacture of artillery. Some lords secured their own cannon, and in any event "the complex shifts towards more effectively centralized forms of government began before cannon were effective or readily transportable." Newly constructed "citadels projected little more than a whiff of naked force over the vast landscapes covered by authority in general." Florence was the only major city with a citadel poised like a "knife . . . at its throat."

On the other hand, rulers' urgent need to take or defend against military action "was the chief factor that underlay constitutional and institutional developments before the Reformation." Ever-larger bureaucracies collected taxes, planned for defense, and conducted diplomacy. Government coffers, swelled by tax revenues and voluntary or forced loans, rose to levels that, in a few important cities, even exceeded the resources of leading banking houses. Meanwhile, the creation of a public debt increased the interdependence of private lenders and government.

Diplomacy. Medieval diplomacy took place on the premise that all polities were, in some sense, part of a broader Christendom (the devil was in the details). Byzantium established a special government department to deal with external affairs, train professional negotiators to serve as ambassadors, and provide them with a commercial incentive in the form of rich goods to exchange for local currencies on arrival. The Duke of Milan established the first resident embassy in Florence. Other Italian cities followed suit, though the hardships and expenses incurred by ambassadors were so severe that it was difficult to recruit them. Venice in 1271 had to impose a stiff fine on individuals who refused to serve. Many ambassadors were, therefore, men of modest social stature. The code of behavior governing their missions often included secret instructions and an occasional assassination, so it is no wonder that host authorities regarded them with suspicion. Permanent missions had an impact on substance as well as form, facilitating the shifting alliances that were a hallmark of Renaissance diplomacy. (Nicholson 1954, chapter 2; Hale 1985, 58–59; also Queller 1967, and Mattingly 1955)

One view is that permanent missions were an important step on the road to modern diplomacy among sovereign equals. This is correct in the sense that, in the century before Westphalia and earlier, monarchs of fledgling European territorial polities gradually established a near monopoly over the *formal* mechanisms of diplomacy that were enshrined in newly codified "public international law." Harold Nicholson (1954, 33) reports that the title of "ambassador" "became current not earlier than the middle of the sixteenth century, when the Emperor Charles V decreed that it should be accorded only to the representatives of crowned heads and the Republic of Venice, and should not be used to designate the representatives of other republics or free cities." This example captures transitional ambiguities: Charles V himself was an "Emperor." Venice got special treatment, and Charles was trying to assert his own supremacy over city polities that were subversively independent and still in a few cases "republican." City polities in that period were increasingly an endangered species, and most were moving toward authoritarian rule, yet the "republican" ideology that many intellectuals continued to espouse[13] prefigured later political struggles.

Any suggestion that permanent missions, like patterns of warfare, enhanced the centralization of polities neglects the additional fact that diplomacy in the High Middle Ages and Renaissance embodied complex relationships among a wide variety of polities. Aristocratic families established their own alliances, cemented by marriages, that created once and future claims to territory and jurisdiction. Feudal ties often hampered the conclusion of treaties, when an overlord might complain that a vassal had no right to enter into an agreement without consent. The Peace and Truce of God,[14] practices that gained widespread acceptance from the late tenth century, can best be understood,

---

13. Skinner (1978, 139) declares: "The history of political theory in the later Renaissance offers a striking exemplification of Hegel's dictum to the effect that the owl of Minerva spreads its wings only with the falling of the dusk. . . . [It was during the twilight of the city republics] that incomparably the most original and important contributions were made to republican political thought."

14. The Peace of God was aimed at protecting the clergy and other noncombatants from harm. The Truce of God forbade fighting from Thursday to Monday morning (the span of Christ's Passion), on any special feast day, and during the seasons of Advent and Lent.

Susan Reynolds (1984, 34) suggests, "against a background in which collective oath-taking and some collective responsibility for law and order were already taken for granted." The Peace and Truce of God ameliorated feudal conflicts, but they were promoted by the clergy and were linked to yet another polity, the emerging firm. Jones (1981, 88) points out that even a slight reduction in violence contributed to the commercial revolution of the Middle Ages: "Truces of God were called to permit mingling in the marketplace. Abbeys took fairs under their wing." Soon companies created the "transnational" institution of the medieval fair and a network of resident missions rivaling those of governments. The "great banking and trading firms . . . established their 'factors' in foreign cities in order both to obtain a constant flow of information and to have agents at hand to carry out commercial instructions from headquarters" (Koenigsberger 1987, 348–49). Commercial treaties provided that foreign merchants could appoint and pay their own *baglio* or consul (the origin of "consulate"), who represented their interests abroad and with the local ruler formed a "mixed tribunal" to adjudicate disputes with citizens in the host community (Nicholson 1954, 41).[15]

The diplomatic role of the Church was broader than its sponsorship of the Peace and Truce of God. From earliest times, papal emissaries and other Church officials traveled far and wide, trying to maintain a unified Church and defend its positions on a host of issues vis-à-vis secular authorities. Popes regularly intervened in secular politics, reiterating the principle that it was a papal responsibility to maintain peace among Christian princes (Nicholson 1954, 39).

POLITY TYPES

Italy's experience after the decline of the Roman empire involved a wide variety of polities, with considerable overlapping and nesting. Reynolds (1984, 138) writes of the Middle Ages: "There was no one sort of group which acted collectively. . . . Many people must have thought of themselves (if they thought consciously about the subject at

---

15. As late as the sixteenth century, a merchant with an unsatisfied claim against a foreign merchant could obtain a "letter of reprisal" allowing him to seize the property of *any* merchant from the same foreign jurisdiction (Nicholson 1954, 41–42).

all) as belonging to overlapping groups within their immediate locality and also to layers of collective activity beyond it.''

Tribes

Tribes presented a continuing threat to the late Roman empire, though (as we have seen in other cases) what constituted a "tribe" is unclear. Most were foederati, like the Huns, whom Koenigsberger characterizes as "a federation of clans and tribes under one king" (1987, 28). The Lombards, for some years after their invasion, imposed tribal rule over a large part of Italy. The situation in early Lombard Italy doubtless resembled that of the early Frankish kingdom (Merovingian Gaul), described by Davis (1988, 106, 109) as having existed "simultaneously on two different planes": "the world of high politics" in which most of the participants were Frankish and "thoroughly brutal and barbarian" and the civilized world of merchants, artisans, and townspeople who "continued to provide a civilized environment for their barbarian masters, supplying them with luxuries and paying their taxes." The Merovingian Franks "were living in, and ruling over, Roman Gaul, but did not 'belong' to it." "Government was not really their business, but as there nobody to stop them interfering with it, they took it over as a valuable source of additional revenue."

In time, however, the Lombards—like the Goths who proceeded them, and the Carolingian Franks and Magyars and others who came to Italy later—found their ways of life transformed by Rome's cultural legacy. In fact, in Italy, tribe ceased to be a significant identity, while identities based on kinship found more than adequate expression in family and clan. The situation was somewhat different to the north among the Germans, where tribal identities persisted even when lifestyles became more civilized (see McKitterick 1983). When, in the tenth century, Otto the Great spoke of the German parts of his kingdom, he talked of Francia, but he referred to its four duchies (ruled by members of his family)—each of which claimed a tribal origin—as Saxons, Franks, Bavarians, and Swabians (Alemanni). Davis (1988, 204) writes: "The distinct identity of each of these four peoples is indeed an undoubted historical fact. The Bavarians are not mentioned by name before the sixth century, but the Saxons, Franks, and Swabians . . . were well known to the writers of imperial Rome. Each people had its own laws which, in spite of their general resemblance, often differed from each other on important points of detail, and each people had its own historic traditions." Tribe, family, kingdom, and Holy Roman Empire identities thus overlapped.

Family

The basic unit of Italian society and those of Italy's neighbors was family or clan. Whatever the tribal nature of the Frankish kingdom, the Merovingian kings thought of the whole of Gaul as a family property and their "palace" as a mobile family household. Davis (1988, 108, 155) remarks: "When the sons or grandsons of Clovis divided Gaul amongst themselves, they divided it as if it were an 'open field,' giving to each a portion of the land in the south and a portion in the north. It did not matter to them if the shares were disjointed and had no territorial unity, or if their frontiers cut across districts that had the appearance of geographical units." Likewise, the Carolingian Empire ended "by becoming family history." It was critical for medieval kings to have sons, but not too many of them. "Lothar I had had too many, but Lothar II, alas! had none." Charles the Bald and Louis the German divided the empire between them, into the kingdoms of the West and East Franks.

Centuries later, in 1152, when Emperor Frederick I Barbarossa ascended the throne, Germany was still suffering from a dispute between those who had supported Henry IV (Ghibellines) and those who had rejected him (Guelphs). Rather than a principled quarrel between papalists and imperialists, the conflict was really between Guelph supporters of the dynasty of Welf who opposed Henry's descendants "as if by hereditary instinct" and Ghibelline supporters of the hereditary dynasty of Hohenstaufen. When the Guelphs eventually lost, their lands were forfeit and all of the medieval duchies of Germany were redrawn. Thus began a process of disintegration of what little unity Germany had, until in the seventeenth century the "empire" consisted of more than three hundred separate jurisdictions ruled by princes from noble families. These were a closed corporation whose number could not be increased except by their consent, interposing themselves as the *Reichfürstenstand* between the emperor and his subjects, including less favored noble families (Davis 1988, 303, 321–22).

In northern and central Italy, kings early on became as obsolete as the Holy Roman Emperor was after Frederick II, and the effective rulers of Italian city polities were groups of families dubbed the patriciates. One such group was the Book of Gold families of the Venetian Republic, but less exclusive patriciates, including well-heeled families of commoner origin, were the norm in many Italian cities. Most of the great commercial and trading companies and banking houses were identified with particular families. Family and clan—*gente* in Florence, *albergo* in Genoa—were often, quite deliberately, blurred through extended family linkages resulting from marriage or artificial kinship, what Bernard Guenée (1985, 157) describes as "the simple custom of long propinquity." Hyde (1973, 104–5) explains that such *consorterie* predated the communes and continued to spread and evolve in the twelfth century. Most *consorterie* were either interfamily alliances or an important family with its clients. In every instance, the purpose was "the conservation of the persons, property and interests of the members."

Sometimes conserving the interests of an extended family militated against external authority and even civil peace. Typically, the *consorterie* regulated marriages and the inheritance of property and arbitrated disputes. Some enacted statutes or ordinances that were enforced by their own officials. Hyde points out: "Where the members [of the *consorterie*] were the leading landowners in a particular area, the *consorterie* could easily acquire something like territorial jurisdiction. . . . In such cases the distinction between a powerful *consorterie* and a small commune might be a fine one." Many extended families symbolized their independent status by constructing family towers, which can still be seen clustered in a few places like San Gimignano. The towers were defensive bastions as well as symbols of family autonomy and pride.

Vendetta was the accepted social code for repaying "insults" in city polities, and Capulets and Montagues set to regularly all over Italy. Family rivalries complicated other divisions—Guelph/Ghibelline, other parties, *popolo grasso/popolo minuto*, and so on—and resulting conflicts threatened public order in any number of cities. Machiavelli (1988, 11) grumbled: "And it has been given from above, so that there be nothing perpetual or quiet in human beings, that in all republics there be fatal families that are born for their ruin." That was the immediate origin of the single *podestas* and *signori* whose appearance signaled the end of the republican tradition of the communes. In effect, many cities eventually installed family dynasties—of which the later Medicis of Florence were an example—local kings in all but name. Nevertheless, families outside of the ruling circle still preserved some of their traditional autonomy. "Even Milan, a duchy brought forward in evidence by Jacob Burckhardt for his thesis that in Italy the state became a 'work of art,' was so little a work of art that Lodovico Sforza, strongest of the rulers in his period, had to allow some of the leading families in the Milanese to issue their own statutes and to allow

them to accept oaths of fealty from men in their neighbourhoods"
(Hale 1971, 63).

Towns and Cities

Italian society in the Middle Ages and later was unique both in its
degree of urbanization—encompassing one in three persons by the late
thirteenth century in parts of Lombardy and Tuscany—and in the
character of its towns and cities. What distinguished other European
cities from those of Italy was that their inhabitants were engaged in
trade, industry, or other commercial activity setting them apart from
the rest of society and that leading burghers managed to establish their
independence from kings, the landed noblity, and the Church. In Italy,
towns and cities managed, to a great extent, to incorporate the landed
nobility from an early stage and faced less resistance from external
authorities (except the Church) because feudal structures were weak
from the outset. Most Italian aristocratic families had a town house in
which they spent at least a part of the year, and they were attracted to
marriage and business alliances with wealthy merchants and traders.
Cities regarded their right to rule the surrounding countryside as a
given, and a number of cities came to be ruled by merchant aristocracies (Hyde 1973, 6–7).

There was a growth of towns and cities in much of Italy between
900 and about 1150. Many were on previous Roman foundations, while
others developed around a local church or shrine, at the intersections
of travel routes, or from clusters of small villages or farms. Many
towns were new walled *castelli* settlements, some built by local lords
and others by groups of neighbors acting on their own (Reynolds 1984,
105, 159, 127). "How far the change in each area was a defensive
measure, a sign of the troubles endured by those who lived in dispersed
settlements, and how far it was a sign of growing population and
prosperity, and of the desire of lords to profit from it, is debated"
(Reynolds 1984, 105). Most of the people involved came initially from
nearby. The very construction and maintenance of the walls may have
been a factor in creating the communal spirit that developed in the
twelfth and thirteenth centuries. Local identity was also enhanced by
the association of cathedrals or *pievi* (mother churches) and patron
saints with specific towns and cities. In the case of former Roman
sites, some traditions of civic solidarity may have survived, preserved
in part by a core of lawyers and notaries known as *civitates* (Reynolds
1984, 105, 149, 160). By 900 "the society and institutions of former

Roman towns, like Roman law itself, had become so much adapted to current conditions that Roman inheritances were matters of antiquarian interest and pride rather than real determinants of civic practice" (Reynolds 1984, 158).

Towns and cities, along with local bishops and priests, helped fill the authority vacuum created by the absence of kings and the weakness of the Holy Roman Empire. Only in southern Italy did duchies and marquisates become firmly entrenched. In northern and central Italy, the Carolingian counties *(contadi)*, though still largely intact in the tenth century, rapidly disintegrated thereafter. Counts who headquartered in cities "found their rights disputed by bishops and citizens, while their control outside was steadily lost to the lords who dominated smaller districts." Then in the twelfth and thirteenth centuries, towns and cities established a new system of *contadi* by extending their control into the surrounding countryside, circumscribing the collective government of lesser towns and villages and drawing *castelli* lords and other notables "into the community of the whole city" (Reynolds 1984, 240, 242). The process in Venice was somewhat different, owing to its Byzantine roots and unique geography. There a central city polity was formed, c. 1200, by literally bridging some sixty neighborhood parishes, "each with its own saint, festivals, bell tower, market center, local customs, and first citizens" (Lane 1973, 12).

Conceptions of town and city polities began to change in the mid-twelfth century when the term "commune" came into fashion. The word had no real legal significance and was used to refer to everything from government to the people of a community, or both (Reynolds 1984, 170, 181–82). Yet a new sense of community identity did evolve, rooted in the practical achievement of greater independence. For many towns and cities there was a transitional stage in which local church authorities played a key role. Some bishops "during the troubled years of the tenth and eleventh centuries [shifted] from being the natural leaders and protectors of their cities to being their most effective if not sole governors." Elsewhere, in humble market towns, mother churches also "served simultaneously as places for judicial, religious, and commercial assemblies—assemblies in which townspeople must have been present if not predominant." Residents of towns and cities did not initially seem to be "motivated by any new political ideology." They "took over powers from their bishops, and from viscounts and other lay lords, by slow stages which often allowed them to remain on good terms throughout." The process often was so gradual that it was "very difficult to say when independence was really achieved."

Sometimes landmark charters were granted, but these were not always faithfully observed. (Reynolds 1984, 162, 169)

In this manner, Italian towns and cities reemerged both as living-museum remnants of Rome and in the interstices within the domains of Church and Holy Roman Empire. Towns and cities did not suddenly appear as a result of some communal "revolution," though the increasing independence of some may have inspired others. Degrees of autonomy varied for a long time, and it was not even clear who were citizens of these new communities. Length of residence seems to have been one criterion for citizenship, though wealth or marriage helped, and some noncitizens also had to pay taxes or serve in the military (Reynolds 1984, 186). From the outset the consolidation of towns and cities also implied some loss of autonomy, or at least switch of allegiances, for neighboring settlements. This process of consolidating continued until, in the late fifteenth century, most urban centers were overshadowed by Milan, Florence, or Venice. Like Greek polities, a number of Italian cities planted colonies, whose leading residents continued to enjoy citizenship in the parent city. For instance, Treviso established Castelfranco; and Padua, Cittadella. Such new towns absorbed surplus population and served "as a bastion of communal power" (Hyde 1973, 77) in subduing neighboring peoples.

The consolidation of a polity, as we have repeatedly stressed, is never complete, because the process involves establishing dominance over other groups and loyalties that tend to persist and because a new polity generates new institutions and groups. Consolidation breeds complexity, and so it was with Italian cities. "The powers deriving from independence reinforced the stimulus given both to solidarities and to conflicts by economic and social change, so that towns became at once the focus of intense patriotism and the scene of fierce civic dissension" (Reynolds 1984, 155). Hyde (1973, 8) observes: "The commune was a particular form of association for which the legal term was societates. . . . Trade and professional guilds, the universities and political parties based on class or other interests were also societates. The clash of these associations within the commune and their struggles to control it produced extreme political instability which was cured eventually only by the establishment of despotisms."

Economic and Social Polities

Important fraternities, guilds, companies, and banks often overlapped with family groupings. By the late twelfth century, many Italian towns and cities were "positively riddled" by fraternities and guilds. We are inclined to accept Reynold's (1984, 73–74) interpretation that their primary function was social—providing a sense of belonging in an unfamiliar town setting—though they also advanced economic interests, upheld standards, and regulated membership in crafts or trades. "The action that people took because they were guildsmen was first and foremost drinking, with some performance of religious ceremonies (especially burials) and charitable works thrown in for good measure." Most of the fraternities and guilds we know about are documented because they owned property, were involved in town government, or were downright subversive. Secular lords might fine or license guilds, and church authorities might use them to promote piety, but both religious and secular officials were deeply suspicious of sworn associations, viewing them as potential sources of heresy and political faction.

By the later thirteenth century, trading companies and banks had become powerful actors. Single-venture enterprises or family businesses developed into permanent firms drawing capital from a variety of sources. Some Italian traders settled in foreign trading centers, where they formed local associations or "nations" for mutual advancement and protection. Large banks established such a symbiotic relationship with local and foreign governments, as well as various popes, that it was often difficult to determine who was beholden to whom. Edward III of England so drained the houses of the Bardi and Peruzzi that they went bankrupt in 1346 and ruined other leading families, which in turn made it difficult for Florence to raise money for its defense. In some cities—notably Pisa, Florence, and Venice— governments fell into the habit of borrowing locally at interest rather than levying a new tax, thereby amassing a substantial public debt. The public debt grew larger and larger until there was no hope of repayment, a problem officials dealt with by borrowing at enforced bargain rates—an ingenious form of direct taxation of patricians who had previously paid no direct tax (Guenée 1985, 106–8).

A wild card among Italian polities were independent "companies" of mercenary soldiers (condottieri), who became the virtual arbiters of Italian politics from about 1340 to 1380. Conditions both inside and outside Italy help account for the rise of the condottieri. George Holmes (1975, 104) explains it as a side effect of the Hundred Years' War. Following the defeat of France at the Battle of Poitiers and the devastation caused by the Black Death, it was hard for soldiers to find employment elsewhere in Europe. In Italy, by contrast, the progress

of commerce and industry undermined civic militias, as did the reluctance of popular communes to elevate aristocrats to military leadership
positions (Clarke 1926, 156). Greater wealth also made it possible to
pay the prices foreigners demanded for their services. At this stage,
most mercenary soldiers came from Germany, France, and England.
The Essex knight Sir John Hawkwood was the most famous mercenary
general, waging war in the 1370s for the pope, Milan, and Florence.

By the fifteenth century, the *condottieri* had become largely Italian. During the many wars of this period, only Venice had sufficient
wealth and foresight to maintain anything like a standing army. It
retained *condottieri* at half-strength in peacetime, thereby keeping
them fairly loyal in contrast to mercenaries elsewhere. In general, the
condottieri of this century plundered less than those of the previous
century because rulers and cities were consolidating their own defenses. Ever inventive, *condottieri* leaders like Francesco Sforza coun-
tered such adversity by striving to capture themselves a city or group
of cities that would serve as their permanent base (Clarke 1926, 159).
Sforza—the son of a *condotierre*'s mistress—ruled part of the papal
territorial preserve given him by the pope, fought for Florence, and
defected to Milan when promised the hand of Filippo Maria Visconti's
heiress daughter.

Polities with Universal Pretensions

The two polities that occupied center stage in the drama of the
Middle Ages were an empire centered in Germany and a church in
Rome. Both wanted to inherit the mantle of Rome and exercise
temporal authority over Christianity. Both the Holy Roman Empire
and the Papacy were territorial empires that sought to extend their
territory, and their struggle waxed and waned for centuries. In the
end, both had to cede primacy to the territorial princes whose allegiance they sought. Since both attempted to centralize authority and
create a "universal" and unified polity, we will treat their conflict in
the next chapter.

During the period under consideration, however, there were other
empires than the original Roman Empire, its Byzantine counterpart,
the Holy Roman Empire, and the papacy. In fact, Italy in the Middle
Ages offers several examples of empires that were almost exclusively
commercial and largely seaborne—notably Venice, Genoa, and Pisa.
Each city had some land possessions—and Venice, at one stage,
quite a large land area—and exercised authority partly through the

application of force and use of local administrators stationed abroad. The primary goal of such empires was to acquire as many trading enclaves in the Mediterranean area as possible, usually captured or won as concessions from the Byzantines or others in connection with a crusade. Competition was fierce, often leading to armed conflicts. Venice and Genoa fought spectacular naval battles with one another on and off from 1350 to 1355. The so-called War of Chioggia erupted in 1376 and continued through 1381 with Genoa encamped across the lagoon from Venice. Holmes (1975, 101) terms that war "perhaps the most remarkable clash of two rival commercial empires in the Middle Ages," and it left both sides exhausted.

CONCLUSION

"The word 'frontier,' " argues Peter Sahlins (1989, 6), "dates precisely from the moment when a new insistence on royal territory gave to the boundary a political, fiscal, and military significance different from its internal limits. The 'frontier' was that which 'stood face to' an enemy." However, "frontiers" in much the same sense were characteristic of many polities before and after early-modern kings. Certainly the Roman Empire had such a frontier, and the fact that it was inadequately defended—that the barbarians managed to breach it by forceful incursion and peaceful settlement—outraged Roman citizens in the countryside. Every polity has a territory, although its frontiers may not be clearly demarcated, contiguous, or exclusive.

The complexity of Italian political organization in the period under discussion resists any statist interpretation. This complexity was made to appear even greater by the presence in the Middle Ages of what Benedict Anderson (1983) calls "imagined communities" that reflected the aspirations of rulers and philosophers.[16] For example, "the French monarchy," as Sahlins (1989, 6) observes, "continued to envision its sovereignty in terms of its jurisdiction over subjects, not over a delimited territory, relying on the inherited notions of 'jurisdiction' and 'dependency' instead of basing its administration on firmly delineated

---

16. Anderson is referring to "nations" in this context. Since the end of the Cold War there has been a veritable explosion of imagined or remembered "nations." See, for example, Gottlieb 1993 and Pfaff 1993.

territorial circumscriptions." Likewise, in the Middle Ages, lords had presumed vassals, both a pope and emperor claimed jurisdiction over all of Christendom, and kings laid claim to often distant lands based on family ties of blood or marriage. In the end, what counted most was the extent to which polities actually controlled persons and resources, by whatever combination of ideology and coercion they could muster.

MEDIEVAL ITALY
Competing Visions of Unity and Authority

Only once in its tumultuous history did Europe enjoy the sort of unity and central rule that characterized China for many centuries. This was the great achievement of Rome at its height. Although there were later pretenders to the authority of Rome, none would prove a worthy heir to the empire created by Augustus and mythologized for centuries after its demise. Italy avoided much of the feudalism that characterized other areas of medieval Europe. Instead, despite the pretensions of pope and Holy Roman Emperor, a multitude of independent city and regional polities emerged in Italy that began to compete intensively with one another. Under these circumstances, overlapping and divided political loyalties and identities became common, and the nesting of local polities within more extensive polities was widespread.

INTRODUCTION: FROM ROMAN EMPIRE TO CHRISTIAN COMMONWEALTH

Among the many internal conflicts that contributed to the demise of the Roman Empire were those between army generals and civilian authorities, rich senatorial landlords and other Roman citizens, and Romans and tribal barbarians. Ironically, the glorification of the Roman Emperor not only elevated him far above his subjects but also, after the first century, tempted generals with the support of the praetorian guard to ursurp his position. Even as the military raised and deposed emperors, a senatorial aristocracy steadily increased their wealth until most of them were much richer in the fourth century than they were in the first. Meanwhile, barbarian tribes posed a growing threat, whether raiding across imperial borders or settling peacefully as farmers and Roman military recruits—and thus becoming nested tribal polities—within frontiers. How barbarian settlers were accommodated peacefully on lands that were already occupied is still a matter for scholarly debate (see Musset 1975, 215ff; Goffart 1980; Thompson 1982). A fundamental norm was that of *hospitalitas,* whereby landowners were required to bear the expense of quartering troops. However, it is not clear whether this principle, as extended to barbarians especially after they actually came to constitute Roman government, involved the outright transfer of one-third to two-thirds of large landholdings (including produce and revenues from that land) or simply a government formula for grants derived from general tax revenues.

The tumultuous two centuries between A.D. 400 and 600 saw the steady decline of Roman civilization in the West and the onset of a process that Robert Markus (1990; also Grant 1970; Fox 1986; Brown 1982; and Chadwick 1967) describes as a relentless "drainage of secularity"—to the benefit of a Church that was itself divided. In previous centuries there had been a steady growth in major cities at the expense of lesser towns (Brown 1971, 34), but now urban life either collapsed entirely or suffered major reversals. When "older traditions of civil authority and secular administration became weakened, clerical power naturally assumed growing dominance, and in doing so, contributed to the eclipse of secular traditions." "Christian discourse shrank to scriptural," and a "biblical culture emerged." "The secular became marginalized, merged in or absorbed by the sacred, both in discourse and in the social structure and institutions." "Ascetic ideals" found wide acceptance "in Christian circles beyond monastic communities;" "secular Roman time was transformed into Christian liturgical time;" pagan entertainments and customs were curbed or modified; and "the geography of the Roman Empire received a thick overlay of sacred topography" (Markus 1990, 226–27).

As time passed, the Church faced growing competition from several quarters and a gradual trend toward resecularization began, culminating in the Renaissance. The Holy Roman Emperor demanded his role in the governance of Christendom, and the notion of Christendom itself began to wane. In fact, for all the poet Dante and others sang its praises, Christendom was always honored more in the breach than the observance and never had much substance beyond the chivalric romantic ideal of the crusades—in contrast to the disorganized rivalries that were the reality. There was precious little Christian unity or any sense of a sacred obligation to achieve it even vis-à-vis the infidel.[1] Venice, for example, concluded a secret treaty in 1222 with

---

1. For a comparison of the relationship between monotheism and imperial ambitions in the west, east, and Islam, see Fowden 1993.

the Mongol empire, by the terms of which the Venetians were to spy and propagandize for the Mongols in exchange for the Mongols' closure of rival trading stations. In the early 1500s the Papacy joined the League of Cambrai in a determined assault against Venice, despite the Venetians' valiant record as a bulwark for Christendom against the Turks (Jones 1981, 111).

EMPIRE VERSUS PAPACY

The Papacy and the Holy Roman Empire were major polities during the entire period. From the outset, their domains and fortunes so overlapped that it is necessary to consider them together. The seeds of the relationship were sown with the spread of Christianity in the first centuries A.D. and especially with the conversion of the Roman Emperor Constantine early in the fourth century. By summoning the Council of Nicaea, Constantine helped to codify and impose mainline Christian doctrine (the Nicene Creed) against the Arian heresy, which regarded Christ (the Son) as lesser than God and not wholly God. Yet Constantine's own prominence raised the issue of the balance between sacred and secular authority that—in one form or another and involving various religions, as well as numerous polities—continues to the present.

From Empire to Empire

With Rome's declining capacity to defend its western possessions, the pope inherited some of the glamour and burdens of Rome in the West. Leo I was instrumental in convincing Attila to leave Italy in 452 and thereafter helped preserve parts of the city of Rome from an attack by the Vandals. "To the barbarians," Davis (1988, 68) declares, "the Papacy represented the magic and power of the Roman name. And this was important, for the Roman Catholic Church grew to its greatness as the Church not only of Rome, but of the barbarians." Also contributing to the preservation and spiritual renewal of the Church during the disastrous time of Justinian's attempted reconquest—while beginning a tradition of separate institutions that would later be a source of tension as well as renewed inspiration—was the development of Benedictine monasticism. Gregory the Great, pope from 590 to 604 during the aftermath of the Lombard invasion, had himself been a Benedictine monk. Fortunately for its future, the patrimony of St. Peter was large, including many estates in Sicily, and grew steadily when tax-poor landowners gave their properties to the Church. Rome had been spared from the Lombards, and from that base Gregory set about converting the English and establishing a system of church government that relied on bishops being supervised by archbishops, and archbishops by the pope. In the eighth century missionaries from the English Church brought the concept of papal authority to the Continent, and eventually convinced the Frankish Church to accept it.

The pope's link with the Franks was a fateful one and came about primarily because of the continued threat from the Lombards. The pope waived return of church property previously seized by Charles Martel and agreed to consecrate Pepin III as king. In exchange, the Franks agreed to protect the pope from the Lombards, and Pepin led his forces into Italy in 755. More important in the long run was that Pepin confirmed the Donation of Constantine, which recognized the pope as Christ's vicar on earth, made all bishops subject to him, and granted the pope full government powers over Rome and all Italy. The Frankish Church, as well, agreed to recognize papal authority and reform itself in accordance with his instructions.

The relationship between the Franks and the pope intensified, not without frictions, during Charlemagne's reign (768–814). Bishops actively participated in the government of Charlemagne's kingdom, symbolized by their gathering with counts in an annual *conventus generalis*. Charlemagne conquered the Lombards and became their king in 774, thus eliminating any possibility of the pope's playing the Lombards off against the Franks. In a revised Donation, king and pope divided Italy between them, though Charlemagne later sought to limit his recognition to territory the Lombards had previously taken from the Papacy. On Christmas Day 800, the pope crowned Charlemagne in Rome, where he was proclaimed Caesar Augustus, the Christian Emperor of all Christendom. It was a portend of future disputes that Charlemagne later resented the pope's insistence that the coronation had ratified the Papacy's superior authority. When an elderly Charlemagne in 813 wished to make his son Louis the Pious coemperor, Charlemagne pointedly crowned himself and did so at Aachen rather than Rome. Louis was a pious man and envisaged a perfect unity between empire and church over all of Christendom, but the Carolingian Empire disintegrated in the face of raids from Saracens, Vikings, and Hungarians.

The Holy Roman Empire Ascendant

Saxon rulers revived the empire after a series of civil wars, and the ceremony elevating Otto I suggests the compromises required by the complexities of political theory in those times, complexities that owe much to a system based on "a nonexclusive form of territoriality, in which authority was both personalized and parcelized within and across territorial formations and for which inclusive bases of legitimation prevailed" (Ruggie 1993, 150). The ceremony in Charlemagne's palace-chapel at Aachen was a double one, a secular "election" involving the nobility, followed by a religious investiture conducted by the local archbishop. Otto gradually consolidated his authority, gaining support from the fact that the Germans urgently needed to unite in defense against Hungarian incursions. When the kingdom of Italy fell heir to Adelaide, Otto invaded Italy and married her. Having won his empire, Otto then sought to devise a means of governing it. His initial impulse had been a familiar ploy of replacing existing dukes with members of his own family and other trusted supporters. However, "no king could trust even his own family implicitly—not, at any rate, in the tenth century, when the revolts of brothers and sons were amongst the more common dangers to which kings were exposed" (Davis 1988, 211). Hence Otto invented an ingenious new system: he would govern his kingdom through clergy (who, being celibate, could not found rival dynasties) and appoint them himself. Henry's appointees received vast lands and "immunity" from direct royal authority.

One snag in Otto's plan to rely on bishop-barons was that the system depended on the continued cooperation of the pope. An opportunity seemed to present itself when Pope John XII appealed for military assistance against a rival. Otto sent help, and John dutifully crowned him emperor. Otto then formally recognized the independence of the Papal State, which he immediately regretted. An ensuing quarrel led to Pope John's deposition, the installation of the more compliant Leo VIII, and the new pope's acceptance of the proposition that no future pope could be consecrated until he had taken an oath of allegiance to the emperor. During the first half of the eleventh century, the Papacy was at a low ebb. The emperor was far away, and Roman noble families appointed popes of their choice. So it continued until they disagreed to such an extent that, in the mid-eleventh century, there were no fewer than three popes. That was too much for the pious Emperor Henry II, who marched on Rome and elevated Pope Clement II.

When Henry III died and was succeeded by a woman, subsequent popes tried again to establish their independence. Nicholas II went so far as to enlist the aid of the Normans in an effort to balance the empire. Then, under popes Hildebrand and Gregory VII, the so-called Investiture Controversy reached crisis proportions. Popes forbade clerics to accept secular commissions; Henry IV demanded his rights as emperor; the popes excommunicated Henry; Henry made war on Gregory VII; the pope escaped with the aid of the Normans (who paused to loot Rome); Gregory died in exile; the emperor tried to impose a compliant successor; and reforming cardinals instead succeeded in electing Urban II. Urban II boosted the authority of the Papacy by urging support for the First Crusade. Pope Calixtus II also came to an agreement of sorts with Henry IV and his son Henry V, by the terms of which elections to bishoprics and abbeys within the German kingdom would be a joint responsibility. The conflict between pope and emperor thus remained fundamentally unresolved, with implications for the continued disunity of Italy. Meanwhile, the Church itself accommodated the foundation of thousands of new semi-independent monasteries, including those of the Cluniac and Cistercian Orders.

The contest between Holy Roman Empire and Papacy erupted again during the reign of the Emperor Frederick I Barbarossa (1152–1190). This was an era when interest in the "rediscovered" ancients reached almost fever proportions, and Frederick I saw himself as grand Roman emperor destined to reestablish imperial rule over Italy and the Mediterranean world generally. To his mind, Roman law was sufficient ground for his authority, requiring no sacerdotal blessing. Not surprisingly, the pope was alarmed by Frederick, as were the Normans and the prospering cities of northern and central Italy. Relations between the Papacy and the Normans had never been good, not least when Innocent II had excommunicated Roger for supporting an antipope and Roger had replied by humiliating Innocent on the battlefield. However, Frederick practically forced the pope and the Normans into alliance against him.

Frederick might still have succeeded with his design, except that he overestimated his capacity to subdue the communes. He and the cities could not have been further apart ideologically. As Frederick saw it, not only was everyone subject to him as Holy Roman Emperor, but also any proper town belonged to a feudal lord whose wealth rested on land. In his view, it was irregular for cities to have republican governments, not monarchies, and for upper-class citizens to draw their livelihood from trade and mix with plebians in business and politics. No wonder most cities were at war with their neighbors, and charges of corruption among magistrates regularly made. Frederick believed he was obliged to reorder matters. For their part, cities were guilty of all the ideas and actions that Frederick attributed to them—and, worse, a parallel hubris about their own putative ancient Roman birthright.

Frederick's armies swept south over many of Italy's cities, even capturing Rome. He obliterated Milan physically and legally, and tried to raise a compliant antipope. No sooner had the emperor returned to Germany than his success provoked an unprecedented reaction. The antipope failed to gain widespread recognition, and sixteen Italian cities buried the hatchet long enough to form the Lombard League. The League rebuilt Milan, and its forces succeeded in defeating those of the empire, which suffered from the defection of Frederick's powerful cousin, Henry the Lion, head of the house of Guelph. In a dramatic encounter, on July 24, 1177, Frederick submitted himself to Pope Alexander III. As Davis (1988, 318) describes it: "The meeting took place outside St. Mark's church. Frederick approached the Pope, threw off his imperial garment and prostrated himself at his feet. The Pope, with tears in his eyes, raised him, embraced him, and led him into the church, where he gave him his blessing. Afterwards Frederick held the Pope's stirrup as he mounted his palfrey and showed himself willing, if the Pope had not excused him, to lead him to his barge." Frederick then took his revenge on Henry the Lion, who was tried for disputing with a bishop and driven into exile. Guelph lands were divided, which worked to the advantage of local princes and helped to splinter Germany.

The empire defeated, Pope Innocent III extended his discipline to rebellious kings and tried to reform a Church that seemed to be losing ground among believers generally. When Alfonso IX of León married a close relative and Philip Augustus of France divorced, the pope brought them to heel by interdicting their entire kingdoms, so that no services except infant baptisms and deathbed penances could take place. King John of England faced an even harsher penalty when he refused to accept the pope's nominee for Archbishop of Canterbury: the pope excommunicated John and threatened to encourage the French to invade, until the king surrendered his kingdom, which the Pope then returned to him as a fief for one thousand marks a year. Hungary, Portugal, and Aragon were also vassal kingdoms of the pope.

However, the looting of Constantinople by Christian forces engaged in the Fourth Crusade deeply embarrassed the Church, as did the relentless progress of the Manichaean Albigensian heresy. That heresy preached a dualist doctrine of the separation of spiritual and material worlds, denied the divinity of Christ, opposed procreation, and therefore was charged with advocating prostitution over motherhood. At length, however, the Church received a tremendous assist from the popularity of the Franciscan movement, founded by St. Francis of Assisi.

The final round in the two-hundred-year contest between empire and church began with the crowning of Frederick II in 1215 first at Aachen and then by Pope Honorius III at Rome in 1220. Frederick recognized that, after over two decades of civil war in Germany, the empire needed a new base of power. He found that base in the *Regno* or rich Norman kingdom of Sicily where he had spent his youth and reputedly had acquired his religious skepticism. Pope Gregory IX, fearing that Frederick planned to conquer all of Italy eventually and, resenting the emperor's initial reluctance to obey his instructions to embark on crusade, excommunicated Frederick in 1227. Although Frederick did set out and capture much of the Holy Land through skillful diplomacy, Gregory not only refused to lift the excommunication but also invaded the *Regno* and released Frederick's subjects from their oaths of allegiance.

War between emperor and pope was inevitable. Religious fervor in Italy reached a peak in 1233, the year of the great Allelulia, when many cities gave popular preachers authority to remake the laws. Church authorities sought to direct such fervor against the "anti-Christ" Frederick, and Gregory did his best to revive the Lombard League. The next few years were chaotic, as papal and imperial forces clashed all over Italy; Guelph/Ghibelline quarrels added still more fault lines within, between, and among city polities; and the cities failed to forge a united front against the threats to their independence. Pope Gregory died (aged over a hundred) even as Frederick marched on Rome to depose him, and the emperor obtained a Ghibelline successor, Innocent IV—only to have Innocent turn against him. A General Council of the Church summoned by Innocent formally deposed Frederick, and papal forces defeated those of the emperor in 1248. Frederick's heirs, legitimate and illegimate, continued to seek restoration of their family's authority until 1268, when Frederick's grandson Conradin was captured and beheaded in Naples.

Thus ended for the near future any serious threat from the empire and the possibility of European unity under its aegis. German electors went on electing kings, usually from weak families chosen for the honor for that reason. Some kings marched briefly into Italy and crowned themselves emperor, but without lasting success. However, the title of Holy Roman Emperor retained enough prestige for ambitious Hapsburgs to covet it. Charles V of Spain, a Hapsburg, played a key role in the final consolidation of Medici rule in Florence. In the early nineteenth century, Napoleon Bonaparte obtained the title by marriage from the Hapsburgs.

The Imperial Papacy

The Papacy's authority, rejuvenated at great cost, almost proved its undoing. The pope claimed the right to make all appointments to bishoprics and other high church offices, entertain appeals from local ecclesiastical courts, tax the clergy, and maintain control of the important Dominican and Franciscan orders—as well as use the weapons of interdiction and excommunication against secular rulers whenever circumstances seemed to warrant. In 1296, when England and France were at war and their kings sought to tax their respective churches in that connection, Boniface VIII commanded the clergy to resist. The dispute escalated until Philip IV of France captured and held Boniface until he died, and then installed a French Pope, Clement V, at Avignon.

In some respects, the Avignon "Babylonian captivity" was the high point of the medieval Papacy. The Avignon popes—despite their sometime debauchery—established themselves in the midst of a powerful kingdom and a cultural center for Europe as a whole, and achieved for the Church the administrative status of a genuine international organization:

> They pronounced on matters of faith and doctrine with complete authority. They extended papal taxation of the clergy and perfected their financial control. They appointed bishops and abbots all over Christendom. They called up cases from ecclesiastical courts to the curia. By exercising the papal "plenitude of power," the right to bind and loose, which included release from oaths, the popes could and did set aside electoral promises which they had made in conclave before being chosen. Personal absolutism could not go further. (Koenigsberger 1987, 324)

In all this, the popes were dependent on the resources of Italian bankers who alone "had the network of representatives necessary for financial dealings on a European scale" and "the reserves of cash at Avignon and in Italy to finance papal operations" (Holmes 1975, 90).

Despite the successes of the Avignon popes, the essential bases for papal authority were eroding. Kings were starting to demand a cut from clerical taxes and were trying to influence papal appointments. The Papacy was also losing control of the education of both clergy and laity. Fredrick II had established the first university in Europe, in Sicily, and later kings and their rich subjects created their own secular systems of education. Moreover, in 1376, Gregory XI's decision to return to Rome precipitated the Great Schism and further undermined papal authority. Within a few years there were no fewer than three Popes—one Roman, one at Avignon, and another appointed by a general church council in 1409. The Council of Constance ended the dispute by electing Martin V. Martin and his successors, supported by the emperor, defeated the Hussites and temporarily reunited the Greek Orthodox Church and other Christian churches in the East with Rome. But the papal revival was more apparent than real. Educated clergy and laity looked less and less to Rome, and kings insisted on taking control over clerical appointments. The earlier Investiture Controversy was soon to be reenacted with kings replacing the emperor, and the Reformation was just over the horizon.

For all its strength and coherence in some periods, the Catholic Church was never a genuinely unified polity, and its identity tended to overlap with others. At the very pinnacle of Church authority, the pope and his ecclesiastical entourage resembled a secular feudal king who, with his court, ruled over the Papal State, collected vassals and tribute, made war and, all too often, wined, dined, and fornicated as well. Even popes who were reformist in spirit were far removed from what was happening in local communities. Bishops were literally rulers at a formative stage in some cities, and a "cathedral, towering over its city, was a potent focus of civic loyalty, and its symbolic function was shared not only by its campanile, which summoned the citizens to prayer, counsel, or defence, but also by its baptistry, where all continued to be baptized in the same font" (Reynolds 1984, 83). Outside of the major cities, the "untidy overlaps of secular and ecclesiastical units, combined with the apparent indifference of medieval people about the particular unit in which to act at any moment, often make it difficult to separate parish activity from the activity of villages or units of lordship." "Everywhere churchyards were liable to serve as marketplaces, church bells summoned people to secular as well as religious duties, and churches themselves doubled as warehouses or fortresses." (Reynolds 1984, 90–91) In the countryside, mother churches had dependent churches (tituli, *capelle*), sometimes built by lesser lords, and there was a gradual decentralization of parish rights. During the twelfth and thirteenth centuries, it was "an Italian custom"—apparently accepted by canon lawyers—for town councils or parishoners to elect parish clergy. Also, monasteries of various orders grew rich and independent, and managed village churches that they received as gifts. Monks at those monasteries preserved texts of the ancients that contained subversive ideas about the authority of the emperor and the proud heritage of Roman cities.

OVERLAPPING AND DIVIDED LOYALTIES IN MEDIEVAL EUROPE

Pope and emperor occupied center stage after about the year 1000, and it may be going too far to dismiss their contest, with Jacques Le Goff (1988, 96), as "a mere shadow play behind which the serious events took place." Nonetheless, much of what was vital in terms of political authority and identity lay elsewhere. During the Middle Ages, "the reality for the west . . . was not only the fact that government was split up into small particles but also the fact that vertical and horizontal powers were entangled. People in the Middle Ages did not always know to which of the many lords, the Church and individual churches, the towns, princes, and kings, they were subordinate." As Hale (1971, 112, 119, 124–25) suggests: "Meaning lay in the familiar and near." Any sense of loyalty to or involvement with larger polities "was all the weaker because of the vigor of local associations and their ability to cater satisfactorily to the desire for mutual aid, spiritual fraternity, recreation and simple gregariousness." The family, not least because it was often the center of production, continued to be *the* most important focus of identity and loyalty for the individual.

Communal Polities and Politics

The communes in Italy emerged with the waning of the Carolingian system, at a time when Christian ideology had triumphed and Church institutions were well-established but the Papacy had not yet established practical control beyond part of central Italy.[2] In time, the communes became powerful symbols of identity, though they set in

---

2. General sources include Hyde 1973, Clarke 1926, Waley 1988, and Wickham 1981.

motion institutional, economic, and social changes that simultaneously made government less manageable and society at large more difficult to govern. Like other successful polities, they ultimately helped create their own nemesis.

The feudal offices of marchio, count, and viscount came to mean little more than entitlement to lands and property enjoyed by certain families, who in fact weakened their control by subdividing estates among their heirs. During this confusing era, Hyde (1973, 44–45) explains, "it was the bishops with their stronger sense of office, their deep roots in the history of the city and their access to the virtues of its saints and martyrs, who were often able to rally the frightened and impoverished citizens." Emperors in a sense only made matters worse for the imperial cause when they tried to discourage the foundation of local aristocratic dynasties by giving celibate bishops secular authority. The bishops, then, were those who at least temporarily prevailed in the nascent-commune *civitates*,[3] though the extent of their role varied from place to place. Citizens were supposed to have a say in the administration of church property and sometimes elected the bishop's lay officials at a traditional general assembly meeting in front of the cathedral. In time, many bishops and other churchmen lost some of their legitimacy by aligning themselves too closely with the feudal aristocracy.

Town rule became *somewhat* more secular when the concept of a "commune" developed and gained acceptance over synonyms like *compagna* and *popolo*. A "consulate"[4] of citizens typically drawn from prominent families assumed control of local affairs from the bishop or other local church officials. The consulate was responsible—in principle more than practice—to a broader citizen council (parlementum, concio, or *aregna*) with membership of a hundred or more. This institutional framework evolved in a relatively spontaneous and haphazard fashion; it was essentially a successful experiment by some urban centers in difficult times that seemed to be worth imitating. The new system was hardly democratic, "only the resettlement of

---

3. The *civitas* was the Roman city and its countryside, ruled in the heyday of the empire by an oligarchy of local landowners who formed a council or *curia*, sometimes grandly called a local senate. Rome substituted its own officials for the *curiae* in the last two centuries of the Empire (Hyde 1973, 42).

4. Another Roman echo.

power within the existing ruling classes on a new basis'' (Hyde 1973, 48).

There were only three precedents for communal rule—and these were only tangentially relevant—in the old regime. One was the "world of less formal associations which had at best been little more than tolerated at the lower levels," although such associations were to become a prominent characteristic of the Middle Ages. A second was the feudal oath, which evolved into a consular oath enshrining "the principle that authority was granted by the community" (Hyde 1973, 54–55). Soon medieval rhetoricians (dictatores) were writing ecstatically about the joys of republican liberty and the responsibilities of citizens of a commune.[5] A third precedent was the ancient Greeks and Romans, who were "rediscovered."[6] Centers for the study of Roman law were established as early as the eleventh century, the most important in Ravenna and Pavia (Hyde 1973, 63). In the thirteenth century, in Arezzo and Padua, a humanist movement began a systematic search of monastic libraries for "undiscovered" texts by favorite writers like Cicero. As Quentin Skinner (1978, chapter 4) recounts, Petrarch and other Italian humanists focused on the Ciceronian concept of virtus—the perfectability of man through proper education in rhetoric and philosophy—the precious legacy of Roman law, and their own era's links to the Roman Republic. From the fourteenth to mid-fifteenth centuries, in early Renaissance Florence, there was a flowering of writings on "civic humanism"[7] inspired, in part, by that city's lengthy struggle to preserve its republic against assaults from the Visconti of Milan (Baron 1966 and 1988; Black 1992, 58–71, chapter 4).

Readings from the past were highly selective, downplaying, for example, the fact that the legal code of Justinian was at its root imperial law. Hyde (1973, 64) surmises that to "the academic Roman lawyer the commune could only appear as a highly irregular and probably illicit institution, unknown to classical Roman law." There were additional legal legacies from feudal and Lombard traditions,

---

5. For the Scholastic context, see Baldwin 1971.

6. The Roman heritage was most influential in Italy, but it was Aristotle's praise of the polis that had the greatest impact on Marsilio of Padua.

7. Associated especially with Coluccio Salutati (1331–1406) and Leonardo Bruni of Arezzo (1369–1444).

which had to be "tamed and domesticated by the prevailing Roman spirit . . . codified and glossed as if they were part of Justinian" (Hyde 1973, 85). Moreover, the "pagan and Christian heritages were not reconciled . . . but were simply aggregated together" (Hyde 1973, 63). The early humanists did not carefully explore the potential conflict of *virtus* with the Church's Augustinian view of the sinfulness of man. Indeed, the humanists often employed Biblical examples, language, and imagery (Skinner 1978, 92–93; Hyde 1973, 62). The "idea of 'community' as an ethical value" merged with "the full might of the Christian value of love," and the "very word *commune* could be associated with the *communio* of Christians in the Eucharist" (Black 1992, 120). No better symbol could be found of the living-museum effect and overlapping polities—blending ancient and medieval, sacred and secular—than the magnificent Romanesque cathedrals built with a hefty contribution of city funds, to the combined glory of God and the commune. In church and civil processions alike marched many of the same grand families, heirs to feudal titles and oft-subdivided properties that once had been granted by the Holy Roman Empire.

Christian love and civic virtue were tested to the full as the communal experiment evolved. Even at the outset, although threats from emperor and pope temporarily subsided, intercity rivalries and aristocratic tower societies and their vendettas threatened the peace. Between 1150 and 1250 more serious problems accompanied rapid economic growth, increased migration to the cities, the rise of the guilds, and the conquest of the *contado*. As Hyde (1973, 106–7) explains, leading communes struck "individual bargains with the families or consorterie, minor communes or religious communities" in the surrounding countryside. Cities expanded their territory and number of citizens, thereby adding to "the complexity of the society which they sought to govern." The communes "did not build up a citizen body with uniform rights" but "divided into numerous legal and social categories," because there was rarely an attempt made "to modify the structure of the groups brought under control." They simply nested, along with old and new polities, in communal niches. "Each section with its resources of men and money and its own particular interests constituted a potential pressure group or faction." No wonder communal history was tumultuous, "for the communes were trying to practise government on conciliar principles in a society which remained intensely hierarchical." Tower societies proliferated, while a wealthy *popolo* class of guild masters and other successful newcomers arose between the nobles[8] or magnates on one hand and ordinary laborers and the urban poor on the other.

The result of these developments was almost continual faction and party strife, occasionally growing so bitter that there were "prolonged periods of civil war" and "virtual anarchy" (Hyde 1973, 105). A small group of dedicated communal administrators continued to draft laws and invent an administrative infrastructure, but the situation was beyond their control or that of the governing aristocracy. At this juncture Emperor Frederick I advanced into Italy, established his rule over many of the communes, and sent an imperial vicar or *podesta* to each of the captured cities to oversee its affairs. When the Lombard League finally defeated Frederick, the office of *podesta* lingered on in modified form. Many cities chose to elevate a single executive from outside their city to the post of *podesta* for a limited term, usually one year, to increase administrative efficiency and mediate among factions. There was a link here with intercity relations, which were at a delicate stage with the dissolution of the Lombard League. Cities exchanged *podestas* almost like royal marriages to pledge fidelity to a new alliance (Hyde 1973, 101–3).

By the mid-thirteenth century, most cities had accomplished nothing less than a "democratic revolution" in which the *popolo* gradually supplanted the older elite. This revolution typically took place in three stages: the *popolo*'s appearance as a powerful faction,[9] the creation of a separate public body identified with the *popolo* that shared authority with the old council, and the *popolo*'s final success in dominating elected offices and administrative positions (Hyde 1973, 114–15). However, the new arrangement hardly ameliorated civil conflict because some of the nobility refused to accept defeat and because of the divisiveness introduced by another contest among Frederick II, the papacy, and the communes. Rivals exploited long-standing animosties between and within cities, and even managed to construct fleeting political alignments that cut across city loyalties. One *popolo* might

---

8. Reynolds (1984, 205) cautions not to read too much into the term "noble." By the time the communes got underway there was no clear distinction between the aristocrats of ancient lineage and the nouveaux riches.

9. A separate office, *capitano del popolo,* was sometimes created parallel to the *podesta,* with the responsibility of defending the *popolo* from violence and injustice perpetrated by the elite.

call on their counterparts in a neighboring city for assistance against aristocrats, and aristocrats from one city might even appeal to the *popolo* in another. Once again an emperor's strategy appeared to have a lasting impact, though civil conflict may have reached a level where the future was inevitable. Frederick II appointed despotic rulers over the communes he managed to subdue, and when he was finally defeated, the stage was set for a new age of the *signoria* (Hyde 1973, 119–23).

The transfer of power to a single individual or family in most communes was the most important political development in Italy in the century from 1250 to 1350. Hyde (1973, 141–42) attributes the trend to conflicts within and among individual cities, rather than interference by emperor or pope. This interpretation, though correct, is somewhat misleading. Although the new *signoria* model spread most rapidly after Frederick II when the empire was in eclipse and popes were preoccupied with problems other than northern Italy politics, the complicated Guelph/ Ghibelline alignments of the thirteenth century increased the complexity and bitterness of factional strife in the cities. Machiavelli looked back on those times in Florence: "Everyone believed that when the Ghibellines were destroyed, the Guelphs would then live for a long time happily and respected; nonetheless, in a little while they divided into the Whites and the Blacks. After the Whites were conquered, the city was never again without parties." Meanwhile, the larger cities were extending their territory beyond the bounds of their previous contado, and warfare with bigger armies was becoming more expensive. In these conditions, there was a temptation to abandon republican squabbles for a single authoritarian leader. Siena somehow managed to remain republican throughout the Renaissance, and Bologna was sometimes republican. But of the major cities only Venice (with qualifications), Florence (with some lapses), and Genoa (intermittently)[10] maintained republican institutions for long stretches of time (Holmes 1975, 79).

---

10. Genoa's republicanism was unstable, consisting of feuds among the great trading families, until the tyrant Simone Boccanegra (of the Verdi opera) created the institution of the doge (occupying it from 1339 to 1344). From the mid-fourteenth century on, Genoa repeatedly fell under the sway of Milan and had to accept members of the Visconti family as *signore* (Holmes 1975, 80).

The Florentine Experience

The example of Florence illustrates the perils of late medieval/ Renaissance republicanism.[11] One problem was the complicated and cumbersome government institutions necessary to give factions the representation they demanded and provide for sufficient rotation in office to make it difficult for any one to consolidate power. At the top were six *priori* and an additional standardbearer of justice who served for only two months and could not soon be reelected. These officials initiated legislation and conducted diplomatic relations. Below them were a *podesta* (executive) and *capitano* (judicial), who were always foreigners serving short terms, and various councils involving hundreds of citizens who did the actual legislating. However, this elaborate system was not enough to preserve republicanism during three periods of external threat, when even Florence felt obliged to submit to rule by a *signore:* King Robert of Naples (1313–1322); King Robert's son, Duke Charles of Calabria (1325–1328); and the Frenchman, Walter of Brienne, known as the Duke of Athens (1342–1343).

After the Duke of Athens, Florence remained republican, with one serious interruption, for about a century—until the Medicis gradually transformed it into a virtual monarchy. Politics initially became somewhat more inclusive, allowing "lesser guilds" of shopkeepers and artisans more access to office. "During the period 1343–82 the constitution on the whole favoured the smaller men. . . . Great merchants and proprietors still had a disproportionate share of power. It was impossible for a city state to be more than a narrow oligarchy tempered by a wider oligarchy" (Holmes 1975, 83). The system suffered a rude shock in 1378, when artisans and laborers *(popolo minuto)* who were not organized in recognized guilds rose in rebellion and terrorized the commune for several weeks. This episode was labeled the revolt of the *Ciompi,* or wool carders, because they were among its leaders, protesting their treatment by the Wool Guild. Its long-term effect was to strengthen the seven major guilds in the overall republican-oligarchical regime (Holmes 1975, 129–30, 83).

Although there had been a gradual trend toward single executives in Italy, the "Age of the Princes" and political theorists whose writings

---

11. See especially Brucker 1962 and 1969, Becker 1967 and 1968, Hale 1977, Rubinstein 1966 and 1968, and Kent 1978.

served as a "mirror-for-princes" began with the invasion of the French Charles VIII in 1494 and continued through—and decades beyond—Charles V's decision in the early 1520's to challenge French control of Milan. It was an era of endemic warfare and political instability that further undermined what remained of republican rule. The Florentine Medicis and Machiavelli's *The Prince* are the symbols of the Age. "Of kingship," Pope Pius II said, "[Cosimo de Medici] lacked only the name and the pomp" (Holmes 1975, 295). Cosimo's descendant, Grand-Duke Cosimo I still lacked the title, but effective kingship and pomp he had aplenty. Hale (1977, 144) describes his funeral: "The body was embalmed and an effigy prepared for the lying-in-state in the Palace of the Signoria, dressed in robes of state, crowned and sceptred, its waxen hands and face modelled by Giambologna. The notion of the lifelike effigy and its message, 'the king never dies,' was borrowed from the funeral ceremonies of the king of France."

The Medici's rise to near absolute power, beginning with Cosimo's return from exile in 1434, took many years and suffered two serious reversals. Cosimo and his grandson, Lorenzo Il Magnifico, shifted most advisory and legislative authority away from the traditional large councils to a Council of a Hundred and then to a Council of Seventy (respectively), which they controlled by electoral manipulation and appointment (Rubinstein 1966 and 1968). The first reversal came in 1494, when Piero de Medici was driven from the city after ingloriously capitulating to the French. A revived republic, directed until his execution by the charismatic friar Girolamo Savonarola,[12] tried to create a Great Council so open that its membership might have reached three thousand. The Medici returned in 1512, supported by Spanish troops, only to face another republican revolt in 1527. However, in 1529 the Medici pope, Clement VII, reached an agreement with Charles V to reinstall his relations, whom Clement made Grand Dukes of Tuscany. In all, the Medici Dukes governed Florence for two hundred years.

The Venetian Experience

The political evolution of Venice[13] offers contrasts to, as well as parallels with, tumultuous Florence and other Italian cities. What

---

12. See Weinstein 1970. The Pope whose morals Savonarola denounced conspired to have him overthrown and burned at the stake.

13. See Lane 1973 and Norwich 1982, also Hodgson 1901, Chambers 1970, Finlay 1980, and Rowden 1970.

made Venice different were two factors present from the outset—its secure lagoon location distant from mainland conflicts and its ties with Byzantium. Venice was founded in the late sixth century when wealthy Roman refugees from the Lombard invasion joined the local population, which had eked out a living from the lagoons. Later Venetians would boast that their city had always been independent, that it was the residence of the last real western Romans, and that it enjoyed a special relationship with the eastern Romans in Byzantium. In fact, "paradoxically, it was through her very submission to the Empire of the East that her independence was achieved and her future greatness assured" (Norwich 1972, 25).

Byzantium's treaty of 811 with the Franks granted the latter imperial status in exchange for Charlemagne's recognition of Byzantine claims to the province of Venetia. Venice "was to enjoy all the advantages, partly political but above all cultural and commercial of being a Byzantine province, without any real diminution of her independence" (Norwich 1982, 24). Nevertheless, the relationship was strained by the time of the crusades, when Venice won trading enclaves in the eastern Mediterranean, and had to steer "a difficult course between the shoals of the empires of east and west and the Norman kingdom in the south." Venice sought the protection of the Emperor Manuel against Frederick I and then supported the beleaguered Hungarians to keep the Byzantines from closing in on the northern Adriatic (Nicol 1988, 94–96).

Venice (under a *dux* or doge) started as a Byzantine dukedom, that is, with the sort of one-person secular autocratic rule that other Italian cities were to arrive at only later, by which time the Venetian doge had gotten weaker. The Venetians were also unique because they alone claimed to possess the body of the Apostle St. Mark, stolen from Egypt by two merchants c. 828. It is significant that, on its arrival, the body was conveyed directly to the doge and not to the bishop or other church authorities (Lane 1973, 88). Other cities might have patron saints, but St. Mark was an Evangelist, a fact that "would endow Venice with Apostolic patronage and place her on a spiritual level second only to Rome itself, with a claim to ecclesiastical autonomy— further strengthened by the patriarchal status of her bishop— unparalleled in Latin Christendom" (Norwich 1982, 29).

Venice thus forged much of its special identity as a polity early on, but that identity continued to evolve and was never exclusive. The first five or six centuries of Venetian history were very violent, not unlike civil strife elsewhere in Italy, reflecting primarily the feuds and ambitions of powerful families. While doges slowly unified the small lagoon communities around the Rialto and spread Venetian control over the northern Adriatic, a central aim of most of the rulers was to make the dukedom hereditary. Many early doges were assassinated or deposed, and mob violence in 976 got so out of hand that fire destroyed both the ducal palace and the church of San Marco. Accordingly, the subsequent task of Venetian political reformers was to ensure that the doge received his position by election rather than birthright and that, while in office, his power was curbed by aristocratic councils. When authority gradually shifted to leading families, eventually enshrined as the Book of Gold nobility, politics became stable enough to add to Venetian identity the coveted appellation of *La Serenissima*[14] (Lane 1973, 88–89).

From the ninth through the eleventh centuries, the doge enjoyed virtually absolute control. In later years, though his authority diminished, he continued to be "the symbol of the unity and authority of government" and "at the center of the practical problems of commanding the armed forces, conducting foreign affairs, and supervising administrative officers." By the mid-twelfth century, however, Venice like other Italian cities was calling itself a commune, and in 1172 a nominating committee was created to name a new doge. Each new doge had to speak an oath, which grew more elaborate over time, detailing the restrictions he accepted on assuming power. There were soon several layers of councils, starting at the bottom with a General Assembly of three or four hundred, then a Council of the Forty, a sixty-person Senate (which became more influential), and a Ducal Council of Six. The Ducal Councillors, the doge, and the three heads of the Forty constituted the *Signoria,* which acted as the government on a day-to-day basis. A genuine bureaucracy was almost nonexistent, since elected committees of the various councils ran almost everything except the church of San Marco, which had its own Procurators. State Attorneys watched over the actions both of the several councils and individual officials. Venice at the local level consisted of some sixty to seventy parishes, each of which had a priest elected by the parish and installed by the bishop, and a parish chief named from one of the great families and supervised by the doge and Council (Lane 1973, 90–99).[15]

---

14. Venice's reputation for being free of factions was no less a myth than the later impression that the city was controlled by a tyrannical oligarchy (Lane 1973, 88–89).

15. Settlements in the lagoons outside of Venice, such as Murano and

Lane (1973, 100–101) describes the overall system as "aristocratic" but not narrow "oligarchy." A hundred or more families, including twenty to fifty leading families, were involved in communal rule one way or another. The doge served for life, but other terms were short and nonrenewable, so persons tended to rotate through important posts. Moreover, in Venice as elsewhere, the rise both of new monied interests, including major guilds *(popolo grasso)* and artisans and craftsmen *(popolo minuto)*, forced changes. Two reforms aimed to accommodate more of the newly rich and discourage factions. One was a complicated system of nominating for high office through nominating committees that were themselves chosen by other nominating committees *and* by lot. In 1297 the Great Council was expanded to 1000 and made hereditary. Even as the ruling class was thus enlarged and secured, the *popolo minuto* found a place in local parish and professional groupings, which, in turn, played a prominent role in the festivals that regularly celebrated the life and constitution of the polity as a whole.

Venice maintained its republican constitution, to the envy of other Italian cities, but the Venetian system became more oligarchical and corrupt as the years passed. In 1310, a Council of Ten was created to act swiftly in the event of security threats. In the mid-fifteenth century, the General Assembly was abolished, and the Great Council abandoned all pretense of seeking broader approval for changes in legislation. The Senate named several chief ministers to sit together with the *Signoria,* framing agendas and overseeing the execution of resolutions. In matters of foreign policy and finance, the *Signoria* could bypass the Senate by consulting the Council of Ten. Government also became more bureaucratized with the growth of secretarial staffs under aristocratic officeholders. Meanwhile, after 1381, the Book of Gold nobility who were eligible for service on the Great Council closed ranks, admitting no new families. Doges no longer were vigorous leaders, because most were elderly. Elections were often rigged; public service in elected or appointed office was increasingly sought for private gain or avoided; and more disputes between individuals and factions

---

Chioggia, had their own laws and councils but a *podesta* chosen by the doge or the Venetian commune. Beyond the Adriatic, those colonies established by merchants were eventually placed under consuls elected in Venice, and colonies acquired outright from Byzantium immediately received Venetian governors (Lane 1973, 98–99).

resulted in violence and bloodshed (Lane 1973, 250–73; Logan 1972; Finlay 1980; and Queller 1986).

CONCLUSION

Some analysts argue that the authoritarianism of Medici family rule in Florence—like the Venetian, Milanese, and papal polities—foreshadowed the bureaucratized European governments of later eras. To be sure, there was a gradual increase in the number of bureaucrats, and some effort was made to encourage appointments by merit. However, as Burke (1986b, 215–18) emphasizes, there are several reasons one cannot carry the "Renaissance state" idea too far. First, apart from later Venice, "public administration was not separated from the private household of the ruler; loyalty was focused on a man, not an institution; and the ruler by-passed the system whenever he wished to grant a favour to a suitor." As for appointments and promotions, the prime necessity was the prince's favour. "A second consideration is the sottogoverno, the fact that some offices were sold outright, not to mention the continued importance of family connections and what was known euphemistically as 'friendship' *(amicizia)* . . . the links between powerful patrons and their dependents or 'clients.' "

Third, "impersonal administration was impossible in what was still essentially a face-to-face society . . . citizens might know officials in their private roles" (Burke 1986b, 217–18). Hale (1971, 106) observes that "even Machiavelli, writing as an ex-career civil servant, frequently used the word 'state' in the sense of 'those individuals in power for the time being.' " It took only twenty minutes on foot to cross all of Florence. "The leading figures in Florence were constantly to be seen as they walked from their palaces to the cathedral, to their place of business or to the centre of government, the Palace of the Signoria." Most citizens were not directly involved in councils, but "the sense of involvement in public affairs, through gossip, through sheer physical proximity, penetrated into all sectors of society" (Hale, 1977, 15).

Finally, although a nascent bureaucracy's primary loyalty might, of necessity, be to the prince, he—and even the less personalized Venetian polity—continued to face many competing identities and loyalties within the city at large. Distinct from but often overlapping the loyalties attached to the polities we have discussed were still others. Burke (1986b, 217) again:

Loyalty to one's quarter of town, or ward, or *rione* (as in Rome), or *sestiere* (as in Venice) was strong, a loyalty which has survived

. . . among the *contrade* of Siena today, and is symbolized on the famous *palio*. Within the quarter, the neighbourhood *(vicinanza)* was a meaningful unit, a stage for local social dramas of solidarity and enmity. In Florence, the neighbourhood, or more exactly the *gonfalone* (a quarter within a quarter, or a sixteenth of the city) was a focus for political activity. . . . The parish was often a community, and so was the street, which was frequently dominated by a particular trade.

Such identities and loyalties came to the fore when issues were perceived to affect them directly, and just as frequently subsided, fragmented, or blended into other identities and loyalties when other issues arose.

So it was at other levels. Cities fought cities with patriotic passion, yet "local patriotisms could merge into regional loyalties, and both at times could become aware of a larger shared identity . . . a shared space . . . which nature had appointed as a home; a sense that somehow 'they' had contributed something to the world that set them apart. It was this that, on occasion, led armies comprising mutually competitive peninsular units to battle against crude northerners with the cry of 'Italy!' " (Hale 1985, 43). Machiavelli of *The Discourses* fervently appealed for Italian unity even as he sang the virtues of city-polity republicanism. At times Italy did come close to achieving a significant measure of unity, although the moment always passed. The Lombard League of 1167 against Frederick I included many cities[16] and succeeded both in defeating the emperor and rebuilding Milan. Later, in 1347, the megalomaniac Cola di Rienzi (the subject of Wagner's early opera) proposed a grand Italian Federation centered on Rome. A number of cities expressed interest and sent envoys but withdrew their support when Rienzi made clear that what he had in mind was nothing less than a revival of the Roman Empire with himself as emperor (Clarke 1926, 155–56).

Italy finally joined the Westphalian club late in the nineteenth

---

16. Its principal members were Milan, Cremona, Brescia, Mantua, Ferrara, Venice, Verona, Vicenza, Padua, and Treviso. These cities elected a group of Rectors to whom citizens swore obedience, to work for the common good and not make war or sue for peace without the League's consent (Clarke 1926, 152).

century, but a century later regional and city identities persist; there is still a pope in Vatican City with a global diplomatic network, whose bankers are occasionally in the news. Factionalism and ideological extremes remain the norm in politics, despite the existence of major parties; fascist Mussolini, like Rienzi, sought to recreate the glories of Rome; post–World War II Italy has relied mainly on NATO for its defense and has been an enthusiastic advocate of European Union integration; much of Italy's "private" economy is autonomous, un-taxed, and unaccounted-for in "national" statistics like GDP; and weak and divided politicians have had to wage "war" against first the Red Brigades and then the Mafia. And, with the disintegration of postwar political parties like the Socialists and church-affiliated Chris-tian Democrats amidst charges of corruption, regionalism and fascism have again raised their heads with the Northern (Lombard) League and National Alliance respectively.

We are told (Hale 1971, 111–12) that Machiavelli, for all his passionate desire for Italian unity, once responded to a friend's en-quiry about the prospects for an Italian alliance with the comment, "Don't make me laugh." Let us reclaim the estimable Niccolò from contemporary realists and neorealists and turn our attention from a static world consisting exclusively of Westphalian state polities to a richer universe of varied and constantly evolving polities.

Part III

CONCLUSION

15

THE PAST AS PRELUDE

How do human beings organize and reorganize themselves for political ends (value satisfaction)? How do they identify themselves and distribute their loyalties? What authorities control or influence what persons, resources, space, and issue outcomes? How do these patterns arise and change? These are the central questions of politics.[1] We have tried to address these questions in our six cases. Our primary aim—rather than to compare the cases in systematic fashion—has been to show how our conception of a world of polities is appropriate to understanding political patterns in different time frames, geophysical environments, and cultural settings. In this chapter we draw some general conclusions from the cases and continue the discussion of theory begun in chapters 1 and 2, with further attention to the concept of nested polities and the relationships among authority, identity, and ideology. We contend that the polities framework not only helps us explain the fortunes of the Westphalian polity but also is essential to understand political change in any era.

Recall that polities, as we defined them, have a distinct identity, the capacity to mobilize persons for value satisfaction, and a degree of institutionalization and hierarchy. All of our cases revealed the interaction of a wide variety of layered and overlapping polities, some so embedded in others that we described them as nested polities (more on this shortly). Depending on the issue and prevailing circumstances, polities coexisted, cooperated, and/or contended. Each exercised authority within a domain of persons, resources, space, and issues. Nevertheless, authority often was not exclusive, and no single polity or type of polity was dominant to the point of omnipotence in any of the cases.

---

1. We thus return to some of the classic issues raised by Lasswell and Kaplan (1950).

Polities attract loyalties and exercise authority that is as effective as the conventional notion of rule by governments. It is, as Rosenau (1990, 40) observes, critical to "recognize that what makes actors effective in world politics derives not from the sovereignty they possess or the legal privileges thereby accorded them, but rather lies in relational phenomena, in the authority they can command and the compliance they can thereby elicit." The effectiveness of governance ultimately rests on the loyalties of those who are governed and on their willingness to obey commands and provide resources to the polities with which they identify. Identities can be imposed, but most are not; rather, they are willingly accepted or even enthusiastically embraced because they promise value satisfaction. Individuals obey mainly because they are getting something worthwhile in exchange, the psychological satisfaction inherent in group identity as well as material benefits.

THE HORIZONTAL DIMENSION OF POLITICS

The capacity of polities to provide value satisfaction is only partly determined by the choices leaders make. For example, although we shall soon be discussing the need for an ideology that helps to shape identity and legitimate authority, no smoke and mirrors or pomp and ceremony will long suffice to preserve rulers and their polities if they are routed in war or if the crops repeatedly fail. Hence we cannot ignore horizontal-dimension attributes and variables—aspects of system structure broadly conceived—that we examined in the first chapter of each case.

System discreteness. Polities emerging in a particular territorial space have sometimes remained relatively isolated from outsiders for long periods of time—most notably in our cases, China and Mesoamerica[2]—but every system ultimately was profoundly influenced by external forces. The other side of the coin is that polities within each system also expanded into or otherwise significantly influenced their own external universe. In this sense there was a significant outside-in and inside-out aspect to every case, supplementing inside-inside vertical interaction among polities.

---

2. Although, recalling the debate about the origins of the Olmecs, perhaps not entirely from South America or even Polynesia.

In every instance, outsiders who penetrated or conquered found themselves to some extent transformed in the process. Even the Spaniards, whose arrival was a watershed in Mesoamerican politics, had to adapt to local patterns of rule; and New-World gold, crops, and diseases had a major reciprocal impact on mother Spain. Much of Mesopotamia's history is infiltration and/or conquest by one alien tribe after another and their absorption into mainstream culture. Greek culture probably began with incoming tribes influenced by the Minoan civilization, and city polities were overwhelmed in the end by Macedonia's regional polity. But the Macedonian conquerors were "Hellenized" long before their arrival and subsequently spread Greek culture over much of Alexander's empire. China nurtured its unique identity in relative isolation, yet nomads posed a regular threat on the periphery. Islam had to contend with two empires, Byzantine and Sasanian, as well as European crusaders. Italy after the Roman Empire faded was a busy political crossroads.

Distribution of capabilities. There was wide variation in the distribution of capabilities category not only across cases but within them as well. The usual structural power models—bipolar, multipolar, and so on—are hopelessly inadequate to describe the range of political complexity we encountered *within* historical systems. To be sure, a more or less multipolar pattern prevailed at certain times in Mesoamerica, but major polities were isolated from one another by modern standards, and at all times a host of local polities were physically closer to inhabitants and played a vital day-to-day role. Much the same might be said for villages in China and medieval Italy. Can one begin to characterize in traditional realist/neorealist terms a system like Italy's, where so many polities *of different types* overlapped and contended? Or Mesopotamia and Greece, where nested city loyalties remained paramount even when cities were under the sway of a hegemonical alliance or empire? Or the fragmentation in Dark Age Greece, Italy following the Lombard invasion, or Mesoamerica after the collapse of Teotihuacán?

Everywhere recognition of processes of integration and fragmentation is more useful than any static assessment of polarity. Large polities tend either to draw others into their orbit or cause them to consolidate in some fashion for protection. Conversely, the breakup of large polities sets up a condition of general turbulence that allows local polities greater freedom to maneuver and regroup.

Geophysical setting. The geophysical setting, not surprisingly, had influence in every case. No one can deny the significance of Venetian

access to timber for ships, Athenian control of Laureion silver, Mesopotamia's lack of metal, or the peripheral location of successful Chinese contenders for power. Equally important were the vicissitudes of
the natural environment with which ancient polities were ill-equipped
to deal. Mesoamerican chronicles are filled with accounts of volcanic
eruptions, droughts, insect plagues, and bitter winters. Attempts to
tame nature were fraught with risks. Land-clearing and irrigation might
encourage a greater population and production for trade than the
environment could support. Irrigation and other infrastructure were
hostages to war. There are indications that environmental degradation
and infrastructure damage were significant factors in the collapse of
major Mesopotamian polities and the classical Maya civilization.

However, the claims about "natural frontiers" that geographers
are so wont to advance were rarely supported by the evidence.
Boundaries and frontiers are more a function of political will and
capabilities—and one's conception of political space—than of geography. Mountains, rivers, deserts, and jungles do offer some protection
and deter expansion, but the likes of Alexander the Great and the
Aztecs were able to establish their empires across them. Moreover, as
we continue to stress, numerous polities of many types typically
shared at least part of the same territorial space.

Economic production and trade. The variable of economic production and trade had an impact on political evolution in all cases, but the
relationship is much less clear than a Marxist analyst might suppose.
The same or similar modes of production often persisted for long
periods of time (even millennia) while political forms changed dramatically. A prosperous economy—like a growing population—was often
associated with political consolidation or expansion and helped support a larger military. However, as with population growth, it is not
clear whether economic consolidation and prosperity preceded, went
hand in hand with, or was a consequence of political change. Moreover, the demand for additional resources, booty, or trade could lead
to disastrous foreign adventures and imperial overstretch.

Expanding commerce and trade usually made society more complex, increasing social strata between landed aristocrats and peasant
masses. Middle-sector hoplites were (literally) central to the political
culture of the Greek polis. Merchants enjoyed prestige and autonomy
in Mesoamerica, Islam, Italy, and Mesopotamia; and their associations
and guilds in Mesoamerica and Italy are clear examples of polities.
Islamic banking enterprises and Italian firms, banks, and medieval
fairs were forerunners of contemporary globalized business and fi-

nance. One can even find stirrings of proletarian organization in the Italian lesser guilds.

War. Wars played a role in all cases and were a major source of political change. Although good strategy and tactics could make a difference, as in Islam's dramatic expansion (Chaliand 1994, 387–426), success on the battlefield often went to the side with more men and resources and/or superior military technology. Apart from other considerations, Greek cities were outmatched by Macedonia's large polity; rather like individual Italian cities were later, by emerging Westphalian polities to the north. Phalanx warfare revolutionized fighting and affected political participation in Greece but could not cope with the Macedonians' more numerous, varied, and flexible but integrated forces. The introduction of gunpowder weapons in Europe, especially heavy artillery, made offensive warfare more feasible and accelerated the demise of feudal knight-and-castle enclaves and the medieval siege mentality.

Mesopotamian and Chinese empires created large professional armies. Assyrian, Aztec, and Islamic warriors get high marks for mobility. Citizen militias worked well in Greece, but often proved an abysmal alternative in Italy, not least because Italians who might otherwise have served preferred to seek their fortunes in commerce. This problem did not afflict Italian navies, which—like those of the Greeks—acquitted themselves well. Incorporation of the lower classes as rowers on Greek triremes gave even the lowest social sector a significant role in the polity. Hiring mecenaries, as in Mesoamerica, Islam, and Italy, was often an accepted but dangerous expedient. The Aztecs and Turks turned on their employers; and Italian *condottieri* often terrorized the countryside or, like the Aztecs and Turks, captured the city polities that had hired them for protection.

Diplomacy. Diplomatic norms reflect relationships among dominant types of polities, and as Watson (1992) suggests, formal norms tend to follow practice rather than the other way around. In any historical epoch, including our own, some diplomatic norms reflect political change and others lag behind. Ancient rulers customarily viewed their relationships in terms of extended family or artificial kinship, father/brother/son as the actual hierarchical situation might require. Dynastic marriages often gave substance to professed kinship connections. Formal agreements, official emissaries, and guaranteeing foreigners privileges upon local marriage or for purpose of commerce were common practices in the earliest civilizations. The Greeks pioneered in creating the consul-like institution of *proxenia* and established regimes to protect shrines and games. Italian cities, notably Venice, get credit for setting up the first permanent diplomatic missions. Less often recognized is the fact that Italian firms were simultaneously establishing their own private outposts abroad.

A RANGE OF IDEAL TYPES

As we stressed in chapter 2, polity types are ideal constructs, which fail adequately to capture the range of actual forms, the continuous process of political evolution, and the extent to which different types and the identities associated with them—for example, family, tribe, city, and empire—consequently blur into one another.

Family played a key role in all cases,[3] but the concept has an enormous range and overlaps with other polity types. Frequently family was "extended" to include distant kin and artificial kin as well. Examples include Dark Age Greek aristocratic raiding brotherhoods, Chinese lineages, Aztec *calpulli,* and Italian tower societies. At some point the extended family extends even further into clan and tribe, as it did in Arab and Aztec society. However, family blurs into other types of polities as well. In Italy, for instance, it was also associated with the Roman Senate, aristocratic feudal fiefdoms, the Holy Roman Empire's bishop-barons, merchant guilds, companies and banks, and cities under princely dynasties. In China, family was the basis of most other polities. Warring State cities were ruled by distinct lineages or sublineages. Imperial Confucianism preached obedience to father-emperor. Religion and military organization, too, revolved around the family. China's ethical system rested on filial piety, and ancestor worship was a key ingredient in rituals designed to reinforce authority.

Tribe, albeit ill-defined, also appeared in all cases, usually though not always as a major identity or polity. Ancient Greek tribes became little more than a vague memory, and the tribal concept evolved mainly into an electoral district. Among nomadic invaders of China, the tribal idea was fundamental. When the Italians succeeded in civilizing the last of the barbarians, tribal identity faded away, though it retained some relevance for the Germans. At the other extreme is the Islam

---

3. Perhaps least so in Mesopotamia, where we encounter family mainly as kings and their relatives, but this is probably because we have little information about the role of aristocratic families.

case, which continually reflected Arab tribal traditions, loyalties, and organization.

What exactly constituted a "tribe" is often not easy to determine, and in some cases conquerors or later analysts assigned names rather arbitrarily. "Tribes" like the Mesopotamian Kassites or Chaldeans, Mesoamerican Aztecs, or even the German Franks were made up of identifiable subgroups that were more than mere clans. Tribal peoples in our cases ranged from nomads, to settled farming communities, to virtually entire civilizations. Today, of course, tribal loyalties merge with the ideas of "ethnicity" and "nationality."

Cities, too, were key polities in all cases and—in Greece and Italy, and probably in Mesopotamia and Mesoamerica—were more important than larger units. Some of the early Greek poleis were little more than hamlets or villages and did not even have a full-fledged marketplace, while others were large urban centers. Some cities like Venice were created from the union of smaller communities in vicinity, which nested as wards or neighborhoods within the larger whole. Other cities reached out into the surrounding countryside, as elsewhere in Italy, to incorporate (nest) whatever polities (smaller towns/cities, castles, churches, and monasteries) were found there—often at the price of granting them continued autonomy. Cities sometimes evolved into large regional polities—Milan, Florence, and Venice—or Monte Albán; or even empires—Babylon, Athens, Rome, Venice, Teotihuacán, and the Aztecs' Tenochtitlán.

Empire also blurs into other polity types and is itself a murky concept. One general distinction among empires formed by conquest is between those that were administratively consolidated (for example, the Chinese in certain periods and the Roman) and those that depended more upon their capacity to visit occasional raids and terror on subjects (for example, early Assyrian, Aztec). The Assyrians went at least one step further than the Aztecs in physically moving around subject peoples, partly for the purpose of assimilating them. The Athenian empire and that of the Aztecs, initially, were built from alliances. Venice, Genoa, and Pisa were essentially seaborne trading empires. Medieval Islam was "the greatest of all caravans," and imperial China evolved without the conquest of non-Chinese peoples. Lastly, there were empires like the medieval Papacy, the Holy Roman Empire, and the Chinese in other eras that were largely aspirational.

AUTHORITY AND IDEOLOGY

All of our cases have emphasized the role of ideology or what Hobsbawm (1992, 101) describes as "exercises in programmatic mythology." Normally communicated and reinforced through an active process of political socialization, ideology helps to legitimate authority and reinforce or weaken identities. When the Babylonians eclipsed the Sumerians, they elevated their own god to the top of the pantheon, and the Assyrians later did the same for their chief god. Athens and Sparta each cultivated a special ideological image: liberal democratic Athens versus disciplined oligarchic Sparta. The Venetian empire—formed by literally bridging sixty neighborhood parishes—rested on several reinforcing identities: Venice the Christian city with the patron saint of the Apostle St. Mark (versus cities with less favored patron saints and heathen Mediterranean Muslims), Venice the residence of the last real Western Romans who maintained a special relationship with the Eastern Romans in Byzantium, and Venice the city dominated by a distinguished group of families (the Book of Gold nobility) whose stable rule guaranteed that the coveted appellation *La Serenissima* was not misplaced.

Even as Venice built bridges, in building a polity, it is best to fashion not only a distinctive ideology but also one that is not so distinctive that it fails to incorporate useful ideological strands already within the expanded domain. Broad cultural norms can provide an ideological foundation for larger polities. For example, rulers of the Mesopotamian and Chinese empires made much of the common and unbroken cultural heritage of their peoples, which contrasted with the supposed inferiority of outsiders; and this common culture gave serious competition to equally long-standing city and regional identities. Successive Mesoamerican empires also incorporated important ideological strands from the distant past.

The closest parallel in ancient Greece was an overarching sense of Greekness, which sustained the alliance against Persia, supported the role of the Oracle at Delphi and other shrines, and helped make possible the Olympic Games. However, Greece was different from Mesopotamia and China in that the Greeks never developed a persuasive ideological justification for empire. Greece and Mesopotamia were similar in one very key respect (and thereby different from China): the primary identity in both regions continued to be cities and always seemed to reassert itself in the end.

Today the aspirational ideologies that realists and neorealists contrast with *Realpolitik* and dismiss as "idealism" and "utopianism" (Carr 1962, 22–40) are, like *Realpolitik* itself, efforts to legitimize selected authorities and their policies. This has been the case with virtually all officially sponsored religions—whether the temple gods of ancient Mesopotamia or the Calvinism of theocratic Geneva. It is also the case with normative systems like Roman Stoicism, Wilsonian national self-determination, the Rights of Man of revolutionary France, Marxism-Leninism in the Soviet Union after 1917, and even the free market philosophy of contemporary America.

Although an appealing ideology is a necessary resource for durable polities, no ideology, however persuasive, can forever mask a failure to satisfy values (or overcome serious value deprivation). For many reasons, the demands of the "faithful" may mount, sometimes rapidly, and so exceed a polity's capacity to satisfy them. As we emphasized earlier, the capacity of polities to provide value satisfaction is only partly a function of the choices leaders make. Nevertheless, authorities must be able to mobilize whatever resources they do possess effectively. Effective mobilization, as Stalin discovered in 1941, entails appropriate ideological nuancing, but, as the dissolution of the Soviet Union reminds us, it also requires management skills and perhaps charisma as well. Bureaucratization at some "center" and the establishment of specialized administrative roles appear to be virtually unavoidable. Sometimes pressure from within is affected by pressure from competing polities without. Often, as in the USSR, the one can be abated by playing up the threat of the other, but, if this fails, the survival of the polity may be jeopardized. As dominant political affiliations and loyalty hierarchies erode, and as other political forms challenge dominant polities, new "theory" emerges (or is revitalized) to legitimize the challengers.

The emergence of large territorial monarchies in Europe during the Early Modern era, for example, was accompanied by a proliferation of statist theory using concepts like divine-right monarchy, sovereignty, and the balance of power. Bishop Bossuet's defense of divine right, Emmerich de Vattel's praise for balance of power, and Hugo Grotius's analysis of the law of nations all contributed to legitimizing the Westphalian polity and the state system of Europe. Both Hobbes's *Leviathan* and Bodin's *Six Books* were aspirational, expressing partisan preferences for an expansion of monarchical power and prerogatives during periods of political and religious turmoil. More recently, the realist and neorealist traditions have served to legitimize and deflect criticism of the Westphalian polity.[4]

---

4. The debate between "realists" and "utopians" that was a staple of international relations theory after World War II can be understood, in part, as a clash between "statists" and "antistatists."

The symbiotic relationship between theory and practice appears to be universal. The rise of the polis in ancient Greece went hand in hand with the glorification of the city polity (Aristotle's "man is a polis being") and the idea of citizenship, and even Thucydides—not least through the speeches of Pericles—is hardly a dispassionate narrator of political forms. Imperial Rome harnessed historians like Tacitus to glorify the empire, just as Augustus commissioned Virgil to provide a new foundation myth in the *Aeneid*. The triumph of an imperial institution in China coincided with the spread of Confucian doctrine that made use of early sage-kings, and the existence of administrators schooled in Confucian principles fostered imperial unity. Without a belief in the divinity of pharaoh, no Egyptian ruler could long have overcome divisive forces in that civilization. And sixteenth-century England reinforced the dynastic claims of the Tudors and their nation-alization of the English Church with the cultural and national identity provided by a common language (Helgerson 1992).

The power and omnipresence of the Catholic Church in medieval Europe rested not least on its control and self-serving interpretation of Holy Scripture. Church doctrines—with their synthesis of political, legal, and theological themes—provided some measure of stability for a turbu-lent age. Predictably, the reinterpretation of doctrine and the Protestant denial of papal authority contributed to the independence of territorial princes. The Church and its Germanic archcompetitor, the Holy Roman Empire,[5] had already been the targets of theorists like Marsilio of Padua and Niccolò Machiavelli, both representative of a shift in loyalties to smaller secular polities. Although contemporary theorists are sometimes less overtly normative than earlier philosophers, the ideological content of their scholarship is no less central. For example, Marxists and neo-Marxists urge us to recognize the class basis of behavior; feminists declare gender to be a basic authority category; and liberal regime theorists promote structures whose authority is legitimized by presump-tions about the implications of interdependence.

In sum, what appear to be scholastic debates over abstract ideas may be the tips of ideational icebergs of conflicts among competing polities and their surrogates. Debates over the interpretation of scrip-

---

5. The poet Dante Alighieri was a prominent defender of that empire in its conflict with the Church and shows his scorn for the popes of his era by placing them in the eighth circle of hell in his *Divine Comedy*.

ture, for instance, however dry and scholastic in appearance, had real consequences for human loyalties and authority patterns generally. If secular rationalism might inform the reader of Holy Scripture as well as the doctrine handed down by church hierarchy, what might be next? The answer was the Reformation, with its subversive implications both for the Church of Rome and for secular authorities. Martin Luther recognized this subversive potential and urged his followers to obey their princes, but this was not the message that followers of Oliver Cromwell wanted to hear as they extolled parliament and decried the rights of kings.

Our cases—all of them pre-Westphalian—suggest a number of distinct sources upon which a polity may draw to build a legitimating ideology. The first is *blood relationship* (whether real or fictive), which extends outward from family to clan and tribal polities like those in medieval Arabia, Chinese Warring States, and Italian cities. A second is *artificial kinship,* which is the source of "fraternal" loyalties like those that bind Mafia "families" or patrons and clients in Latin America. Artificial kinship was the basis of the fraternities and guilds (in their nonprofessional dimension) that served as urban substitutes for traditional family and village ties in medieval Italian cities. A similar relationship characterized the informal raiding-party brotherhoods formed by neighboring nobles in Dark Age Greece.

Shared history and/or culture (whether real or mythic) makes legitimate many national and ethnic polities. The role of historical myths is perhaps greatest in the cases of ancient China and the Aztecs, but it is present in some form in all our cases. Sometimes, this justification shades into blood relationship, especially when a foundation myth posits common ancestry as in Rome or Mesoamerica.

Religion is also an important source of legitimacy. Every empire had its principal god or pantheon, and every significant city polity its sponsoring deity or saint. One variant is *charisma* or *revelation,* illustrated by the Islamic community, especially during Muhammad's lifetime, and also by the Christian pope. Mesopotamian kings and Mesoamerican rulers, too, played the role of special intermediary between their peoples and the gods. Patron deities, saints—or in the instance of Venice, the Apostle Saint Mark—were sacred conduits for city dwellers who had secular local rulers. Another variant of religion is the idea of *divine right* as a source of dynastic legitimacy. Unlike revelation, divine right does not require direct communication with gods but does entail their sanction. The Chinese equivalent of the divine right claimed by European kings was the Mandate of Heaven.

Dynastic legitimacy is also conferred by *property rights,* especially in feudal settings, such as Chou China and medieval Europe.

With the demise of feudal relationships in Europe and the spread of Enlightenment ideas, the notion of a *general will* came to the fore. One variant, resting on popular sovereignty and democratic symbols, gained impetus from the American and initial French Revolutions. However, a similar ideology legitimated the classical Athenian polity. According to Confucian ethics and China's Mandate of Heaven, a dynasty could be ended if rulers failed to serve the welfare of subjects. Another variant, as debates over Rousseau and France's revolutionary Terror reveal, is an authoritarian conception of the general will. Sparta, Stalinist regimes, and Hitler's Germany are extreme examples of this.

Finally, *functional ties* provide some legitimacy for all polities. They are especially important for polities based on professional or economic advantage, such as the Italian *condottieri,* merchant associations in Mesoamerica, Italy's guilds, Europe's medieval Hanseatic League, and trading firms like the Dutch East India and British East India Companies. Modern examples are transnational corporations and financial firms, as well as functional intergovernmental and nongovernmental regimes.

The content and meaning of these legitimizing devices vary by time and place; they may assume different forms and sometimes resemble one another. The process assumes a form similar to what Liah Greenfeld (1992, 5) calls "the zigzag pattern of semantic change":

> The meaning of the word, which comes with a certain semantic baggage, evolves out of usage in a particular situation. The available conventional concept is applied within new circumstances, to certain aspects of which it corresponds. However, aspects of the new situation, which were absent in the situation in which the conventional concept evolved, become cognitively associated with it, resulting in a duality of meaning. The meaning of the original concept is gradually obscured, and the new one emerges as conventional. When the word is used again in a new situation, it is likely to be used in this new meaning, and so on and so forth.[6]

---

6. Greenfeld (1992, 4–5) illustrates the "zigzag pattern" by tracing the evolution of "nationalism" from its early derogatory usage to denote foreign-

The Westphalian transformation added a new source of legitimacy, the legal conception of *sovereign statehood;* however, older sources of legitimacy continued to be used. The assumption that the Westphalian state is universal makes it difficult to theorize about sources of legitimacy. If polities are functionally homogenous—all legitimized by being sovereign—why are they so different? Surely one reason is that they are heirs to the ideologies on which they were built. For example, the idea of a general will—so important in European polities that are heirs to an Enlightenment tradition—is absent in Arab states in the Middle East. There, the heirs to the traditional blood relationships of tribal polities (for example, Saudi, Jordanian, and Kuwaiti rulers) compete with those who claim a principal role for charisma/revelation (for example, Iranian mullahs and Islamic fundamentalists). And, even as shared history and culture reinforce the unity of some European polities, cultural and linguistic dissimilarity undermine the fragile unity of countries like Canada. The concept of nested polities helps explain, among other things, how old ideologies remain potent and are handed down from generation to generation.

NESTED POLITIES: TOWARD A NEW CONCEPTION OF POLITICAL SPACE

Different conceptions of political space permeate all of our cases. Just as many analysts exaggerate the significance of "territoriality" and boundaries with reference to Westphalian polities, there is a propensity to ignore the extent to which pre-Westphalian polities were territorial and sometimes demarcated as well.[7] Each polity had a territory in the sense of a space occupied by persons who identified with it, but that space was neither always contiguous nor often exclusive. Sometimes, as in many Greek city polities, there were actual boundary markers, and even when there were not, rulers of particular polities usually knew at least generally where the limits of their domain were. The territorial limits of aspirational domains like that of medieval "Christendom" or the "Islamic community" were less clear. Polities

---

ers ("heathens") in Greek *(ta ethne)* and Roman Latin *(natio)* to "those who did not belong to the chosen monotheistic people" in Hebrew *(amamim)* to its favorable usage by Montesquieu.

7. Barkin and Cronin (1994, 107) declare: "International relations scholars rarely examine how definitions of populations and territories change throughout history and how this change alters the notion of legitimate authority."

did not always have a center, though it was a disadvantage not to have one—or to have more than one—like the medieval papacy at one stage, or the later Islamic caliphate.

All cases reflect the value of Peter Sahlin's (1989, 4) distinction between "boundaries" and "frontiers." A boundary, such as that of a Westphalian polity, is a "precise linear division within a restrictive, political context"; whereas a frontier "connotes more zonal qualities, and a broader, social context." The linear boundary of the Westphalian polity built upon Greco-Roman theory and practice and was reinforced by the European principle of contract and Euclidean conceptions of space. By contrast, the zonal frontier is more like the Chinese conception of overlapping "civilizations," with continuity regardless of changing linear boundaries.

Just as important as the fact that the polities in our cases had different notions of territorial space is that many of them shared the *same* space. All cases revealed layered and overlapping polities, sometimes lacking a clearly established hierarchy— certainly any that was applicable to all issues. In most cases—not least in Italy—local polities had their own patterns of authority and also effectively managed relationships with more inclusive polities. The larger the polity, the more polities it is likely to encompass, thereby presenting a greater challenge for top-down management.

Conflict among different polity types is usually avoided because there exists an understanding (sometimes but not always embodied in law) about the role that each is expected to play. The family has its customary domain; likewise, the local school board (in the United States), the Iowa legislature, the transnational firm, the U.S. Department of Agriculture, the Ayatollah, the Church of England, the Bundesbank, the Fisheries Directorate-General of the European Commission, and so on. Few of these domains are exclusive, but each polity has its own identity, resources, and raison d'être. Thus, overlap gives rise to simultaneous and sometimes crosscutting patterns of coexistence, cooperation, and conflict among polities. Individual polities occupy particular niches in the lives of adherents, and the loyalties they evoke are usually activated only in the context of specific issues.

Tensions arise, however, when authorities perceive incompatible interests in the same issues and compete with one another to become the objects of affection for the same constituents. Bloody clashes like those that pitted communists against the family during China's cultural revolution or the church against the communist regime in Poland and

Hungary in the 1950s reflect such conflicts. Contests for loyalties and the changes in affiliation that they produce are the stuff of changing global history.

Layering and overlapping also produce the nesting or embedding of polities in one another.[8] It is as though one political form were superimposed on another. The latter may lose some of its separate identity, but in the process, the dominant polity may assume some of the trappings and features of the nested polity. The impact of nested polities will be felt in the unique attributes of the successor polity and show up in significant variations among institutions, ideologies, and behavior in each type of polity. Even in this century, some Westphalian polities have been hard to distinguish from empires (for example, the Soviet Union), tribal conglomerates (for example, Rwanda and Kenya), religious movements (for example, post-Shah Iran), cities (for example, Singapore), or even coteries of families (for example, El Salvador). In other words, each polity reflects the impact of its origins and the nesting of other polity types that are the bases of its history. Inheritance from embedded polities helps explain why some states are "strong" and others "weak," and why imperial or tribal forms vary dramatically.

In some cases, the impact of nested polities on a dominant polity is so great that the latter is transformed into something genuinely new. We may continue to use the old term, but, at best, the new entity is a mutant or "bastard" version of its earlier form. The process can be one of imposition and emulation, as was the case of Europe's impact on many of its colonies, or it may involve outright subversion of some polity types by others. Occasionally, it is less a matter of direct confrontation than gradual transformation. In any event, the process by which some polities assume the features of others with which they interact is a major source of change.

Rome had to deal with the Huns head on but succeeded in accommodating Goths and Visigoths to such an extent that the western Empire was "barbarized." That is one reason that Rome never "fell," as Gibbon claimed, but was transformed gradually, and why many Roman practices and ideas lived on. Neither Rome nor the barbarian tribes were as they had been before. The result was a

---

8. Krasner's (1982a, 499–500) metaphor of "tectonic plates" to replace the model of "billiard balls" in global politics implies the nesting phenomenon.

temporary amalgam that received an even greater push in the direction of tribalism when the Lombards swept through Italy after Justinian's disastrous attempt at reconquest. Ultimately, the Lombards themselves were Romanized, and the story continued with the emergence of new polity types in the run-up to the Renaissance and beyond— Venice, the pope's Church, the Holy Roman Empire, city polities, families like those that built San Gimignano's towers, and so on.

A nested polity is either the remnant of an earlier form or the incubus of one yet to come, depending on the direction of political evolution. Polities are always changing or "becoming," sometimes coming from or moving toward another polity type. Authorities recognize this and may seek, with varying degrees of success, to manage the direction of political evolution by means of familiar institutional arrangements like confederations, federations, and international organizations.

Political evolution, as we have stressed, is not unilinear. In some eras, like our own, change is tumultuous, and in others it is so slow as to be almost imperceptible. In Greece, the polis gradually emerged and established itself as dominant over kinship and artificial kinship. However, kinship ties retained importance among aristocratic families in different poleis and in the diplomatic institution of *proxenia*. Meanwhile, each polis became more internally complex and linked to various external associations—alliances, functional regimes, and virtual empires. Similarly, kinship and village authority patterns remain potent in contemporary China despite communist efforts to eliminate them.

Today's European polities are in the midst of an awkward transition. Europeans are experimenting with alternative ways of organizing political space, and tensions exist as Westphalian polities compete with other polities for the loyalties and resources of citizens. No Westphalian polity in Europe is fully responsible for its own defense; some vital economic functions have been "EU-ized," and others effectively surrendered to multinational firms and worldwide financial markets—not to mention the challenges of coping with a more organized and demanding citizenry. There has been such to-ing and fro-ing that there probably is no historical model that can do justice to the political arrangements taking shape in Europe.

Simultaneously, Central Europe and, to a lesser extent, Western Europe are in the midst of an upsurge of passionate nationalism and national separatism that are regarded by many as attempts to turn back the historical clock. After World War II, national identities became dormant, awaiting the end of Soviet and communist dominance or the appearance of an issue like European political integration against which they could rally. Though he does not say so explicitly, the nesting phenomenon is central in Yael Tamir's description: "National movements are regaining popularity, and *nations that had once assimilated and 'vanished' have now reappeared.* Estonians, Latvians, Corsicans, and Lombards awake from the long slumber" (1993, 3, emphasis added).

We ignore the impact of nested polities at our own peril. Just as the imperial form assumed by the ninth-century Islamic caliphate was at odds with its Byzantine and Persian predecessors because of its tribal and clan patrimony, so contemporary Muslim polities of the Middle East (or for that matter Israel with its Zionist roots) have little in common with Westphalian polities of different parentage. And the facile assumption that all states are fundamentally the same—with similar motivations or institutions—plays no small role in the errors of Western policymakers when they meddle in states with nested tribal or clan polities like Rwanda, Iraq, or Somalia.

Samuel P. Huntington's argument (1993, 26) that loyalties to religious "movements" are filling the "gap" left by the weakening of nation-state identities ignores nesting and so misses the mark. Certain polities, like those in the Islamic world, have *for centuries* reflected a tension between secular and religious values. Religious polities have from time to time dominated secular polities (as in seventeenth-century Salem and Calvin's and Zwingli's Geneva) and in other eras have quietly nested in secular polities.

Polities do not evolve in a vacuum. The path that political evolution takes—toward centralization and larger polities or toward decentralization and fragmentation—depends on structural attributes and variables, and other factors that have a different impact in specific contexts. Different issues mobilize different interests, identities, affiliations, and coalitions. In some countries governments believe they can survive only by accepting the issue position of a potential competitor. For example, in the 1970s and 1980s the position of Jordanian authorities on regional issues was subject to the virtual veto of the Palestine Liberation Organization.[9]

---

9. Jordanian authorities met the PLO challenge with force in "Black September" in 1970. Since then, the autonomy and capability of the Jordanian

Depending upon the context, any polity can display *status-quo, expansive,* or *contractive* tendencies. Polities that are the dominant authoritative foci of loyalties for an issue generally wish to maintain their status. For example, education policy and the taxes to pay for schools in the United States are set mainly by local community school boards and town/city governments, and those local polities want to maintain that status quo. However, there are others who seek a greater role for families or a state government (for example, the State of New Jersey), seeing them as alternative and preferred sources of authority. Some families insist, for instance, that sex education belongs entirely in the home. The family is a contractive polity in this regard, in that authority for this issue would be exercised by a smaller, nested entity. Some persons argue that state governments should assume more responsibility for taxing and financing education so as to eliminate the inequities that stem from reliance upon local property taxes. The state government here represents an expansive polity.

The collision of status-quo, expansive, and contractive preferences is apparent in a range of issues. When the German Bundesbank failed to lower interest rates during Europe's 1992 exchange-rate crisis, pressures on other European currencies drove them down against the Deutschmark and encouraged wide swings in the frenetic international financial markets. In no case was the limited capacity of Westphalian polities more clearly revealed than in their inability to insulate themselves from hot-money speculation; not even the Bank of England had sufficient currency to defend the pound. The collapse of the Mexican peso in late 1994 and the dramatic decline of the U.S. dollar against the yen and mark suggested that even the concerted action of the "Group of Seven" was insufficient to cope with the financial power of currency traders. These crises reflected the power of polities like transnational banks and corporations that have substantially broken free from the straitjackets imposed by national borders. Governments and central banks lack the means even to track much of what is happening in the private sector, let alone to design effective policies to

---

Westphalian state have diminished owing to demographic and other factors. Consequently, Jordan, along with the PLO, were among the few supporters of Iraq's Saddam Hussein during the Persian Gulf War. Partly because of the threat from Islamic fundamentalists, both have now made formal peace with Israel.

control unwanted practices. As Susan Strange (1991, 33–49), who popularized the term *casino capitalism* points out, we need to give more scrutiny to two new forms of diplomacy: government-to-firm and firm-to-firm.

The resistance of status-quo polities is reflected more broadly in efforts to sabotage the Maastricht Treaty, although it was ultimately adopted in modified form. Recessionary conditions, long-standing resentments over regulatory decisions of the Brussels bureaucracy, fears of diluting national culture in a wider Europe, and the Yugoslav debacle eroded support among some publics for further integration. The exchange rate and Maastricht crises also coincided with a clash between EU and U.S. officials in the last stages of the GATT Uruguay Round negotiations.

Along with a troubled United States–Japan trade relationship, the threat of one expansive polity—"Fortress Europe"—provided incentives for the negotiation of another—the North American Free Trade Agreement. Mexico's decision to join NAFTA was part of a shift by that country's ruling political elite to a more free-market and less nationalist stance than at any time since 1910. Facilitating the shift was a similar trend in much of the developing world, hastened by the debt-crisis adjustments of the 1980s and the loss of bargaining leverage for a New International Economic Order (NIEO).

The United States' other NAFTA partner, Canada, has political difficulties of another kind, as it confronts the challenge of contractive nationalisms. Unlike Yugoslavia, the outcome of the struggle between status-quo and contractive goals remains in doubt. Polls suggest that only a relatively small proportion of the total voting public actually wants an end to Canada, weak as its collective identity is. Were the country to divide, it is unclear along what lines—far West, agricultural heartland, French speakers, and maritime provinces?—because Quebec is not the only distinct identity. Also uncertain is the long-range effect of NAFTA. If NAFTA increases general prosperity, it may enhance the rewards of being Canadian. On the other hand, separatists argue that larger associations like NAFTA have made membership in a Canadian national economy superfluous. Canada is a victim of Rosenau's "fragmegration."

In the United States, the conflict between status-quo and expansive positions regarding NAFTA assumed a different form, focusing mainly on the Mexican connection. NAFTA received strong support from transnational corporations like Navistar International, Allied Signal, Pepsi, and General Instruments (some grouped into an Emergency Committee for American Trade), which are eager to expand sales and production facilities in a wider market. Also supportive were some environmental groups like the World Wildlife Fund and Conservation International that believed a more prosperous Mexico bodes well for conservation efforts. Opposed—in addition to the populist demogogue Ross Perot—were industries like textiles and winter fruit and some small business associations; major organized labor groups like the AFL/CIO, UAW, and Teamsters; environmental groups like the Sierra Club, Friends of the Earth, Environmental Action, and Greenpeace, which feared that companies would move across the border to escape U.S. environmental standards; some consumer groups like Ralph Nader's Public Citizen; and certain religious and human rights organizations that were dissatisfied with Mexico's progress toward a more open political system.

The NAFTA debate reflected trade-offs across issues between advocates of status-quo and expansive policies, and bargaining was not limited to the foreign ministries of the United States and Mexico. Robert A. Pastor (1992, 194–95) explained: "Not only are the issues debated openly in both countries, but groups within each country have built transnational coalitions with counterparts in the other two North American countries to stimulate government attention and substantive progress on issues of mutual concern." Trade-offs involving trade, environment, drugs, and immigration were all important in negotiations at more than one level.

As such issues suggest, centrifugal and centripetal forces continue to tug polities in different directions. Even when a few become dominant, the processes of integration and fragmentation continue. During Europe's Middle Ages, there were Western and Byzantine variants of Christianity, religious heresies (Albigensian, Arian, Manichaean), rival popes in Rome and Avignon, and ascetic monastic orders decrying the worldliness of the Church hierarchy. The Holy Roman Empire waxed and waned; kings bickered about rights of investiture; and powerful towns, merchant guilds, trading associations, and local nobles were loath to recognize any higher authority. Today, as in that epoch, the elaboration of larger networks of interaction and interdependence exist alongside the fragmentation of other collectivities into tiny units of self-identification. Some polities are nesting even as other formerly nested polities reassert their autonomy or independence.

CHANGE, STASIS, AND THE STATE CONCEPT

Richard Hooker is credited with observing that change "is not made without inconvenience, even from worse to better." What was true for Hooker in the sixteenth century is no less true for today, both for our hopeful, yet turbulent post–Cold War world and for the theories we use to make sense of that world. Contemporary events present a strikingly different and more complex picture than traditional models of global politics allow, including less of a distinction between inside and outside the Westphalian state/polity and a proliferation of crosscutting polities—the European Union, other formal and informal regimes, transnational corporations, interest groups, and organized crime, to name a few. Westphalian polities struggle with these as well as their own bureaucracies, free-wheeling legislatures, "people power," and resurgent ethnicities for the privileges of sovereignty. The results are civil wars; tribal, ethnic, anti-*Ausländer,* and anomic violence; the melting of some long-established boundaries; and floods of migrants and refugees.

The state concept provides an illusion of stability and continuity that contrasts with a restless reality. The question is not whether the state exists, is observable, and matters, but to what extent it explains the things we need to understand. Although the state has many definitions (Ferguson and Mansbach 1989), international-relations theory usually equates it with the Westphalian model, supposedly enjoying a monopoly of authority within and legal equality without. As we have stressed, this model is an ideal type that few actors approach.[10] The European experience of a particular era is generalized to all times and places. As Huntington (1993, 24) reminds us: "Westerners tend to think of nation states as the principal actors in global affairs. They have been that, however, for only a few centuries." The Westphalian state is only one polity type, distinguished less by criteria focusing on loyalties or resources than by a legal claim to legitimacy and the formal recognition of other members of the "sovereign club" that it is what it claims to be. Unfortunately, there is no official certification board comparable to the community of Westphalian states to provide formal recognition for other polities.

Generalizing from the Westphalian model fails to acknowledge the

---

10. A second usage, favored by historical sociologists, anthropologists, and archaeologists equates the state with any institutionalized authority. It could be a democratically elected government, a dictator and his cronies, a city like ancient Corinth, a medieval monarchy, an Inca hierarchy, or the Ottoman Empire.

diversity of authorities present in all societies since ancient Sumer, and history gainsays the claim of any single polity to universality, exclusivity, or permanence. The ways in which people organize themselves for political ends change along with nearly everything else, and a map that limits its boundary lines to some two hundred "states" captures only a small slice of reality. Today, as in the past, individuals identify themselves in a variety of politically relevant ways, have loyalties to a variety of authorities, and distribute their resources (including their energies) among them. Every polity has a potential to mobilize adherents to act in the context of issues that touch their interests or excite their passions. Each polity has a hierarchy and institutions (however minimal), resources, ideology, and frontiers. Patterns of loyalties and resulting polities overlap and cross each other's frontiers.

Change is continuous as loyalties, like cards, are shuffled and reshuffled and as people are seduced to follow new authorities on new adventures (or misadventures). Contests are rarely sufficiently decisive to eliminate polities permanently; and new polity types often synthesize features of old ones. Thus, Napoleon's effort to replace the Westphalian polity by an empire of nations was rebuffed by the older states at the gates of Moscow, and efforts to build a new entity—the nation-state—succeeded, but only for a time. The murder of an Austrian archduke in 1914 highlighted the tension between the Westphalian polity, and nationalist and cultural passions, and the Wilsonian doctrine of national self-determination revealed the incompatibility of "nation" and "state" as organizing devices.

History bites those who ignore it. Such is the case with the end of the Cold War, which has pointed up the ill fit between "state" and "nation" in many parts of the world. In the words of U.S. Secretary of State Warren Christopher, if the fires of contemporary nationalism continue to burn unchecked "we'll have 5,000 countries rather than the hundred plus we now have" (*New York Times*, February 7, 1993, 1). One might even be tempted to contemplate the prospects of a final divorce of "nation" from "state,"[11] thereby severing the link established in 1789: "From Haiti in the Western Hemisphere to the remnants of Yugoslavia in Europe, from Somalia, Sudan, and Liberia

---

11. Tamir (1993, 3) pronounces the end of the "era of homogeneous and viable nation-states."

in Africa, to Cambodia in Southeast Asia, a disturbing new phenomenon is emerging: the failed nation-state, utterly incapable of sustaining itself as a member of the international community" (Helman and Ratner 1992–93, 3).

Although the Westphalian polity triumphed in its collision with the tribal polities of Africa and the Americas between the fifteenth and twentieth centuries, no polity type remains unchallenged or unchanged forever. Old loyalties remain, sometimes dormant, sometimes on the march, and they may be triggered by tumultuous events like the fall of communism in Eastern Europe. The challenge for any polity is to cope with old memories, identities, and loyalties within its domain. While it is easy to make martyrs, it is almost impossible to eradicate an old identity. The simile used earlier of the world as a living museum is again useful. In this museum, some exhibits are currently on show; some are being refurbished; and still others are in storage. Polities are successful to the extent they co-opt or incorporate the old memories, identities, and loyalties—that once supported other polities—into their own ideological framework.[12] Otherwise, these old identities—like those of the Mayas in Mexico[13]—may be reactivated even in later centuries and become the bases of rival political associations and faiths.

The genius of Rome, as it spread beyond its republican origins, was its willingness to coexist and even share authority with potential rivals and to fashion integrative symbols that allowed Roman officials to govern with the assistance of local elites. In the case of religion, for example, Roman conquest did not entail the replacement of the local religion. "Rather, a new element," as John Kautsky (1982, 258) notes, "that is, a new god, was merely added to it." He continues: "Indeed, both Romans and Incas not only imposed new gods on their subjects but also managed to integrate the religions of the people they conquered into their own."

The manner in which the Westphalian polity evolved and was

---

12. The manner in which early Christianity embraced symbols from precursors ranging from the cult of Isis to Germanic paganism illustrates the value of co-optation.

13. Now joined with memories of Emiliano Zapata's peasant forces during the Mexican Revolution, as well as secular Marxism and Catholic priests' Liberation theology.

modified illustrates the fate of all polities. Its ideology grew in a particular historical soil. It never stood as a singular identity but from the outset drew much of its substance from other identities. The model prospered—both as an idea and as a fact—to the extent it incorporated other identities, some of which have remained actual and potential challengers to the authority and legitimacy of the state to the present.

THE WESTPHALIAN POLITY AND THE CHALLENGE OF NATIONALISM

Medieval monarchs who sought to extend their authority beyond their family holdings looked to the universal Church and/or Holy Roman Emperor to establish a divine right to rule over a particular territory. Medieval conceptions of legitimacy rested on an assumption of the unity of Christendom. Legitimate rule proceeded only from God, though God's earthly intermediaries had to ratify the grant. The problem was that some saw the pope and others the emperor as God's certifying agent. Fortunately, one or the other could usually be found to give the blessing, normally in exchange for a supplicant king's pledge of support in the Church-Empire rivalry.

The emergence of the Westphalian polity took place gradually, as dynastic property rights and divine-right monarchy in the early modern period merged with the concept of sovereignty. A monarch continued to claim authority to rule over a territory that included and extended beyond his own lands, but in other respects the situation was changing. The authority of Church and Holy Roman Empire waned with the consolidation of local polities. The stirrings of secular humanism in the Renaissance also undermined the influence of the Church. Henry VIII and Cardinals Mazarin and Richelieu sought to capture what remained of Church authority and link it to the monarchy, thus providing ideological glue for a new polity. The king's divine right to rule was presumed to derive directly from God, with no intermediary.

Although even the most absolute of divine-right monarchs was never fully autonomous, kings did consolidate their position enough to give their pretensions some substance. They extended their territory and acquired standing military forces, significant police capabilities, extensive bureaucracies, and growing tax revenues. Historical sociologists (for example, Mann 1986b and 1993) stress the role of continual warfare in consolidating the power of early modern kings. As historian McNeill (1986, 39) observes, the Hundred Years' War (1337–1453) "disentangled the French and English kingdoms from one another geographically [and] endowed the French king with a standing army and a tax system capable of supporting an armed force that was clearly superior to any and all domestic rivals in peacetime." McNeill notes that "challenges to royal absolutism did not disappear until after a final flare-up in the seventeenth century." Nevertheless, "armed rebellion was decisively defeated in France with the suppression of the Fronde (1633); whereas in England, where absolutism had never taken firm root, a remarkably flexible parliamentary sovereignty emerged from the Civil Wars and Glorious Revolution of 1688."

Nascent national consciousness thus enhanced the authority of early kings, and their consolidating activities in turn gave greater credence to the doctrine of sovereignty. Moreover, for all the significance of the establishment of national churches, the theoretical justification for sovereignty became increasingly secular, for example, Hobbes's claim that the only alternative to a single source of absolute power was unacceptable chaos. Early writers of international law like Grotius and de Vattel provided an external dimension to sovereignty, by positing the existence of a European system of independent states and accepting that states were not obliged to recognize any higher authority. This was the external face of sovereignty.

After Cromwell's revolution in 1640 and especially in the second half of the eighteenth and the nineteenth centuries, national consciousness began to take on a broader yet more intense form. It became less focused on rulers presiding over their literal and figurative domains and more on a fictive partnership between rulers and peoples. The extent of change here can be overstated. Medieval rulers, too, were presumed to have obligations to the community to rule justly (Reynolds 1984). The community had rights, derived from custom and extended by law, and English nobles believed they were reminding King John of those historic rights when they forced him to sign Magna Carta in 1215.

As McNeill (1986, 38) sees it, "what mattered for the later rise of nationalism was the pattern of town and rural life in France and England, where sufficient homogeneity between urban populations and the surrounding countryside was sustained between the eleventh and seventeenth centuries to make an extension of the ancient civic ideal of citizenship to the kingdom as a whole seem conceivable by the mid-eighteenth century." Not that anything like homogeneity was achieved. In France, for example, he writes: "Apart from German-speakers in Alsace-Lorraine, and Celtic speakers in Brittany, the gap between Langue d'oc and Langue d'oïl divided peasant France into significantly different communities. Indeed, one may argue that the incandescent quality of revolutionary propaganda in the crisis of 1793–4 was partly a deliberate effort to override such local divergences by insisting on the sacredness of the republic, one and indivisible.''

The legacies of American and French revolutionaries in this regard were distinct, however, and not entirely compatible. The new America was a republic but had to weave a separate ethnos out of almost whole political cloth. Except for being colonials, most white Americans had cultural roots in the former metropole. In later years, of course, the United States attracted immigrants of so many ethnicities that the only possible "American" ethnos was one based on myths of individual liberty and citizenship in a democracy. The American experience points up the fact that democracy is a brilliant ideological invention, not least because it does not demand that citizens give up their ethnic, religious, and other loyalties, unless those threaten the democratic process itself. It is significant, for example, that African-Americans in the United States demand not a separate state but a share of the pie promised by their status *as* Americans.

The model advanced by the French Revolution was similarly republican at the start. French nationalism was supposedly based on the universal rights of man, although the Revolution did help to forge a French ethnos. Training in citizenship, including the *levée en masse,* were for *la patrie.* Mixed with fraternity were the ideals of liberty and equality, but not all who extolled *la patrie* were democrats or social levelers. Quite the contrary, there were dark currents of political authoritarianism and imperial ambition, which the very notion of a *universal* rights of man seemed to legitimate.[14] Napoleon convinced the French that they should support him not because he was a divine-right aristocrat but because he was their leader, and emperor and people together could do glorious things. Having no need of a papal blessing, Napoleon had Jacques David mythologize him crowning himself.

Nation as ethnos was more directly a German and East European concept. As Bismarck was to demonstrate, when a Westphalian state/polity becomes entangled with ethnos, it may be only a short step to Hegel's view of the state as a moral idea, the highest realization of self; to a side connection with Social Darwinism's survival of the

---

14. Napoleon planned to create a French citizenship in his Empire following the Roman precedent of civis Romanus.

fittest; and to Treitschke's ecstatic hymns of praise for the race. In this fashion, national identity—expressed through democratic or authoritarian institutions—provided ideological glue for a polity that could no longer rely on aristocratic bloodlines and divine right. Ironically, as McNeill (1986, 52) observes, it was Napoleon's spectacular effort "to build a transnational empire on the strength of an aroused and mobilized French nation" that "assured the idea and practice of the ethnically unitary nation-state of rather more than a century of florescence." European rivalries fueled by that idea only ran out of steam after two world wars.

Meanwhile, Woodrow Wilson had given the nation-state idea new currency by advancing the principle of "national self-determination." The twist was dangerous because it forced global politics to confront what J. Samuel Barkin and Bruce Cronin (1994, 108) describe as the "historical tension between state sovereignty, which stresses the link between sovereign authority and a defined territory, and national sovereignty, which emphasizes a link between sovereign authority and a defined population."[15] In fact, as Magda Adám (1993, 35) explains: "Wilson was decisively against the disintegration of the [Austro-Hungarian] Monarchy. He did not think the creation of a large number of small states was politically or economically rational. He was afraid of Balkanization. . . . His well-known principles of self-determination did not envision national independence. He wanted to federalize rather than disintegrate." Wilson only had in mind granting minorities autonomy in some federal arrangement or certain guaranteed rights.

Unfortunately, no one, including Wilson, could offer a coherent definition of "nation," which invited dissident groups to claim nationhood and demand independence. National self-determination was subversive to Westphalian polities without providing incontestable rights to any group demanding legal independence. The Versailles conferees tried to limit the principle to the Hapsburg and Ottoman empires,

---

15. Barkin and Cronin (1994, 108) argue that "sovereignty should be used as a variable rather than as a constant and therefore that the state as a basic analytical unit should be scrutinized in international relations theory." However, treating sovereignty as a variable muddies matters because state and nation are only two of many critical identities in global politics, and sovereignty acts to legitimize a particular type of polity. Other ideologies in turn provide legitimacy for other types of polities.

which because of their polyglot character were the worst places to start. The unsatisfactory result set the stage for World War II and is echoed in current Balkan conflicts. The self-determination principle was also enshrined in the UN Charter, where it was invoked after 1945 by colonial entities in support of independence movements. Decolonization proceeded despite the fact that in some cases the only unity in evidence was that imposed by colonial boundaries. Now the self-determination principle lies like a ticking bomb, waiting for the next round of ethnic claimants. Referring to that bomb, Daniel Patrick Moynihan (1993, 174), recalls Milton's "Pandaemonium" that "was inhabited by creatures quite convinced that the great Satan had their best interests at heart."

Wilson's "nation" was not the only challenger to the Westphalian polity. Another was the idea of "class," as proclaimed by Marx and Lenin. In their eyes, the state apparatus was an instrument of bourgeois coercion, and when the proletariat seized the levers of power, the Westphalian polity would wither away. Although the Soviet Union only recently withered away (for reasons unforeseen by Marxists), the 1917 Revolution saved the Russian Empire from the fate of the Hapsburgs by substituting the dictatorship of the proletariat for a Westphalian-polity Tsar.

The popularity and durability of the ideology of the Westphalian polity owes much to European imperialism. There is a parallel here to McNeill's observation, noted earlier, about Napoleon's campaigns and the growing popularity in the early nineteenth century of the ethnos model of identity. Later in that century, statist ideology followed the conquering flags of the Europeans. When the sun finally set on those empires in mid-twentieth century, a host of new polities appeared in the former colonial boundaries. They were sovereign entities like the European metropoles but different from them in every other respect.

THE PRESSURES OF CHANGE: PRESENT AND FUTURE

The contradiction between the expanding functions of the European Union and the centrifugal pressures of separatists as diverse as Basques and Scots reflect the continuous and simultaneous pressure on polities to grow and fracture. It is to this pattern that Benjamin Barber (1992, 53) alludes when he declares that the "planet is falling precipitantly apart and coming reluctantly together at the very same moment." One solution is to create polities that can "specialize" in meeting specific human needs and encourage citizens to divide their loyalties for particular purposes. It may make sense, for example, to look to large specialized polities to achieve economic efficiency while nourishing local loyalties to provide psychological satisfaction. Unfortunately, it is difficult to maintain those boundaries, so the different polities tend to collide. Resulting trade-offs may be excruciating—for example, welfare for security.

The Westphalian polity has been much admired because it seemed a successful multifunctional experiment—large enough to satisfy values requiring economies of scale but small enough to satisfy values demanding intimacy. In reality, the Westphalian model, as noted earlier, was an ideal type that is linked with the success of only a few polities in creating a viable "national" identity and institutions that allowed them to exercise authority within stable boundaries. Nearly everyone thinks of England and France, though France fleshed out its present boundaries only late in the nineteenth century and the United Kingdom still has problems with its Celtic fringe. But why should England and France be considered "typical" when, in fact, most of Europe's Westphalian polities have always had to find ways to cope with dangerous identity fault lines?

Late bloomers like Germany and Italy also have a claim to being considered typical. Germany, like Italy, was forged in the late nineteenth century. Prussian power and Bismarck's *Zollverein* provided the core for Germany. Nevertheless, the Holy Roman Empire model and spread of the German language and culture seriously complicated the problem of identifying "natural" German boundaries. Italy, on the other hand, only appeared to create a viable state. Local and regional loyalties remained primary; the most dynamic sectors of the economy have never been integrated—or documented and taxed—and the Mafia established itself as the most effective authority in southern Italy and Sicily. Even as the divided Italian central government wages a desperate battle against organized crime, the separatist Lombard League has emerged as a political force in the prosperous north.

Overall, the Westphalian polity prospered in Europe but not in isolation. Since 1949, European security—the hallmark of sovereignty—has been almost entirely bound up in NATO, and there is little doubt that the Cold War standoff kept the lid on change. Events in the former Yugoslavia and in Brussels, nevertheless, suggest that the fission and fusion of polities has not ceased even in the cradle of state-centric mythology. The European Union has gradually extended its authority over matters historically regarded as the exclusive preserve of Westphalian polities. Protecting "national security" in traditional fashion is inconceivable without cooperation and institution building, within the region and across the Atlantic. Although each step along the integration path has preserved the legal nicety of countries' "voluntarily" surrendering sovereign rights, this does not alter the fact that, as a result of these steps, decisions are made in an EU context that used to be made only by decision makers in their respective capitals. Borders have gradually dwindled in significance, including the establishment of common European citizenship and a Single Market; and all members have ratified Maastricht, albeit in truncated form.

None of this means that the Westphalian polity is disappearing. Instead, it is evolving into something different alongside new polities. As B. Guy Peters (1992, 106–7 and 107n) explains, there are "at least three large games being played" in Europe today. One is a "coping with interdependence" game in which governments seek "to extract as much as possible from the EC, while relinquishing as little . . . as possible." Another involves competition among European institutions themselves. The third is a bureaucratic game "that is apparently becoming an important subtext for everything else happening within the EC." Twenty-three directorates-general develop "their own organizational cultures and approaches to policy," compete for "policy space" and attempt to establish "their own working relationships . . . with relevant elements of national governments." Writes Peters, "there may also be still other games being played simultaneously, including those involving interest groups." "Firms, for example, may believe that they would find a less restrictive regulatory environment if the Community had greater control of environmental policy."

The future of "Europe," like that of all polities, rests on establishing authority in a particular domain, supported by an appropriate ideology. Whether or not Westphalian polities will become fully nested in the future remains to be seen. What do we mean by "Europe"? What is the scope of Europe geographically and functionally—how "wide" and how "deep"—and how shall the inevitable compromises regarding these matters be legitimated ideologically? "Federalism" has uncomfortable Anglo-Saxon nuances and seems to suggest a "United States of Europe." "Confederation" implies little more than a loose association. "Subsidiarity"—the idea that control should be exercised at the lowest possible level—has a Catholic and Continental ring to it. On the other hand, subsidiarity is attractive in theory to the British and others who seek a decentralized Europe, but it is not clear how the principle might apply in practice. How are members to decide what the appropriate level for control actually is? Finally, "consociationalism" draws on the experience of democratic polities like those of Switzerland and Holland, which preserve the segmental autonomy of internal minorities by demanding consensus if major changes in common tasks and decision making are to be made (Taylor 1991). Like subsidiarity, consociationalism might reassure those who have been dubious about aspects of the common European enterprise from the start. But the formula is close to the long-standing EU arrangement whereby each member has an effective veto, and it is not encouraged by Switzerland's rejection of further involvement in a European union.

The degree to which the Westphalian polity remains a powerful symbol of collective identity varies from place to place. Imagine the answer that would be given on the streets of Moscow, in a hotel lobby in Sarajevo, on a Venetian *vaporetto,* on a Belfast bus, at a crossroads in Somalia, in a Teheran mosque, or a Sikh temple in India. Around the world, we should emphasize again, loyalties to self and extensions of self like family, clan, village, tribe, city, nation, religion, or profession limit support for government policies.

It also bears reiterating that the very "growth of the autonomous power of the state" in the early modern period that so impresses historical sociologists created its own nemesis. Various processes were involved, which we also saw at work in the other cases we examined: First, the growth of bureaucracy and institutions at the center and a far-flung administrative network makes decisive action more difficult to accomplish. Freewheeling bureaucratic infighting, conflict among ministries, factionalization in legislatures, aggressive interest-group politics, official corruption, and restive military establishments threaten sovereign polities from the inside. Second, the consolidation of almost any polity sets in motion changes that may undermine whatever unity and concentration of resources have been achieved. Political fusion tends to generate greater complexity in the relations among authorities. Over time the result is greater social complexity, new loci of power and wealth, new identities, more political factions, and rising popular demands. Fusion may also invite foreign adventures or lead outside polities to consolidate, with uncertain consequences for military security and economic competition.

In the end, no Westphalian polity exercises the degree of autonomy and control that sovereignty implies, and only a few even put on an impressive show. Far from possessing a Weberian monopoly on the legitimate use of violence, sovereign polities, especially in areas of the developing world, often are unable to preserve a modicum of domestic tranquillity. They are routinely challenged by malaise and insubordination as well as street demonstrations, corporate power, guerrillas in the countryside, terrorism, ethnic conflicts, religious fanatics, party strife, drug cartels, and warlord gangs. All feature the collision of loyalties based on interest and sentiment. "The smallness or weakness of many States," declares Robert Jackson (1993, 358), "draws them into external relationships of quasi-trusteeships with international organizations and important States."

The relevance of sovereign boundaries should not be dismissed too lightly. The response to Saddam Hussein's invasion of Kuwait attests that boundaries still count when someone gathers an army and assaults them from outside. As Jackson (1986, 246–64; and 1990) reminds us, sovereignty continues to provide some freedom from external interference. Throughout Africa and elsewhere in the developing world, "negative sovereignty" has for years helped to preserve illogical borders and corrupt governments. Yet assertions of sovereignty in this instance are those of the weak, with elites appreciating that boundary adjustments would lead to chaos and their own political demise. These are sovereign polities but certainly not Westphalian polities in any real sense. From Liberia to Rwanda, governments represent little more than a veneer of political ineptitude and opportunism plastered over long-standing tribal divisions.

In sum, challenges to the Westphalian polity are intensifying with an increase in "turbulence" in global politics (Rosenau 1990). The rising capabilities of individual citizens and a tendency to subgroupism are interacting in unpredictable ways with trends like interdependence and regional integration. More and more persons and groups are traveling, negotiating business deals, transporting goods, offering services, moving money, listening to mass media, telephoning, sending faxes, and sharing electronic data—and ideas. Sovereign boundaries in these respects are not so much being altered as ignored or transcended. The developments that *overarch* sovereign polities also have an impact *within* them. They promote democracy and capitalism, and a resurgence of ethnic identity. Ironically, largeness has helped foster smallness; sovereignty-eroding economic and political integration has encouraged fragmentation. Self-determination seems more important to many people, partly because others are demanding it, but also because of economic unions, the revitalization of international organizations, and an increasingly globalized economic system. French Canadian separatists, Baltic republics, Croatians, and others do not necessarily have to go it alone; they have other potential relationships to replace those they choose to end.

CONTEMPORARY CHALLENGERS TO THE WESTPHALIAN STATE

Scholars have begun to move away from viewing the Westphalian polity as a universal, dominant, and unchanging unit of analysis. That polity, like other organizations, is a jurisdiction with authorities who act in its name. Whether or not those authorities can actually do so is an empirical issue. Their claims to govern may or may not be honored by individuals and groups in society, and other authorities—both within and without the state's boundaries—compete for citizens' loyalties and resources.

Governments today are besieged by challengers that involve both traditional and novel claims to loyalty. The seriousness of these challenges varies by issue and polity. For example, the Catholic Church exercises traditional influence over Catholics in countries like Ireland and Poland. Even at the acme of Soviet/communist dominance in Poland and Hungary, the Church remained a force with which to be reckoned; and the collapse of communism has again allowed the Church to play an even more influential role in those societies.[16]

Other longtime challengers include tribal and ethnic groupings that threaten the territorial and political integrity of Westphalian imitations. Somali and Lebanese clans, Liberian and Rwandan tribes, Russian nationalities and provincial authorities, and Indian castes and language groups are among those that are engaged in conflicts with government authorities. Loyalty to a "state" is irrelevant to many participants in these conflicts, and traditional "interstate" issues are relevant only as they affect communal relations within a society. By contrast, transnational corporations, subnational and transnational environmental groups, and regional organizations typify the emergence of modern rivals (although there are some interesting historical precedents) for the loyalties and affections of citizens.

Sometimes government authorities are able to ward off challenges

---

16. Although the Church's pressure on the Polish government to outlaw abortion was successfully resisted, the presence of a Polish Pope in Rome enhances the authority of the Church in Poland.

from competitors and extract resources from citizens by combining what Mann (1986b, 171) refers to as "infrastructural power"—"the capacity to actually penetrate society and to implement logistically political decisions" with the systematic application of coercion (for example, Stalinist Soviet Union). Others may be even more successful by substituting for coercion an effective capacity to satisfy the demands of citizens along with an ability to balance disparate constituencies that are potential challengers. However, some governments are vulnerable to challenge and unsuccessful in warding off competing authorities because they are unable to avail themselves of either strategy.

Challengers may arise within or without sovereign boundaries or from both. In traditional international-relations theory, the focus has been on the challenge posed to one polity by external polities. That challenge may be physical as in war or provision of aid to a regime's domestic opponents, or it may entail efforts by governments to seduce the citizens of other polities to shift loyalties. External challengers have often sought to recruit allies from within a polity. Since the sixteenth century, for example, adversaries of Great Britain sought to make common cause with Scottish and Irish separatists. In the chaos of sixteenth-century France, the British sought to return the favor by making common cause with French Huguenots in their conflict with Catholic extremists who were also aided by the Spanish monarchy.[17] In the nineteenth century, Serbia and Piedmont sought to erode the loyalties respectively of Slavs and Italians living in Austria-Hungary. And, in the more recent past, the Soviet Union tried to mobilize and manipulate the loyalties of communists throughout the world to provide the USSR with a reliable cadre of supporters. External competitors for the loyalties of citizens have included imperial, religious, transcendental ideological, class, national, and even tribal appeals.

Winners write history so that the species of polity that dominates an epoch has a profound influence on the norms for that epoch. Norms are expressed in legal forms (for example, sovereignty) and rules of conduct (for example, diplomatic immunity), and the flouting of such laws and rules are omens of change. Although traditional international relations tries to be sensitive to shifts in power among Westphalian

---

17. The Valois monarchy—the repository of French sovereignty—was caught between the two factions and was largely impotent.

polities, the field has largely ignored more far-reaching loyalty shifts. That shortcoming certainly characterized scholarship on the Cold War. The Cold War not only pitted governments and their allies against each other but also entailed fierce competition with other polity types (labor unions, political parties, and revolutionary groups).[18] The end of the Cold War was less the result of a stalemate between two powerful governments than of competition between two rather different empires and sustained vertical pressures on governments by competing nongovernmental authorities. Nongovernmental authorities were responsive to and helped to mobilize a participation explosion among citizens not tranquilized by the nostrum of a collective national interest. This explosion constrained the autonomy of governments as much as, if not more than, the more celebrated global interdependence (to which it is related).

The susceptibility of governments to social and political mobilization became apparent in the endemic instability of postcolonial polities. The wave of nationalism that accompanied decolonization proved transitory because the loyalties of inhabitants remained anchored in a variety of authority patterns that antedated colonial boundaries and institutions. However, Third World instability did not, as might have been expected, render developing countries susceptible to external control. Social mobilization meant that foreign efforts to impose control would be met by popular resistance, in contrast to the European conquests of earlier centuries. The French experience in Vietnam and Algeria in the 1950s and 1960s were harbingers of American and Soviet experiences in Vietnam and Afghanistan. The sophisticated mechanisms that permitted the exercise of influence in developing societies without direct military intervention were never as pervasive or successful as *dependencia* theorists claimed. Such phenomena as external investment and mountains of debt proved two-edged swords, providing leverage to both the weak and the strong.

The 1960s witnessed an erosion of government autonomy in foreign affairs even in the West. Elite control over foreign affairs was diminishing, and the barriers between processes of foreign and domestic politics were breaking down. The anti–Vietnam War movement in

---

18. The replication of the system-wide conflict at all levels of social organization during the Cold War was analogous to events in Europe during the medieval struggle between secular and religious authorities.

the United States was a watershed and affected Europeans, as well, especially the young. That movement had a major impact on the way in which the U.S. government waged war and forced authorities to defend policies publicly that previously would have been carried out with minimal debate. Simultaneously, the Congress and many private groups became much more active in the foreign-policy arena that the Executive had previously dominated. The Vietnam War forced Washington to fight a two-front war—at home and abroad—in which victories on one usually exacerbated problems on the other. Domestic resistance to the war reinforced Hanoi's conviction of ultimate victory, and Hanoi waged war with at least one eye on events in the United States.

It did not take long for the virus to cross the Atlantic. Like Americans, Europeans had long been used to pressure from below in the form of lobbying for policies by orthodox interest groups. However, the virtual overthrow of President Charles de Gaulle by student and worker riots in Paris in 1968 signaled a new relationship between government and society in the protected area of foreign policy (Mansbach and Waterman 1988, 277–99). The growth of European peace and environmental movements—many with religious and university roots—reflected a genuine struggle for the political loyalties of the young. The 1960s also spawned extremists like the Red Army Faction in Germany and the Red Brigades in Italy. In the late 1970s, counter-culture movements—increasingly allied with environmental groups[19]—played a key role in preventing the deployment of enhanced radiation weapons and, in the early 1980s, almost halted the deployment of intermediate-range nuclear weapons.

The Soviet bloc was the last to be infected. In East Germany as well as elsewhere, environmental, peace, and human rights activists began to form rudimentary links with each other and with activists in the West in order to articulate social discontent and press for social, economic, and political reform. In the absence of economic collapse

---

19. The ambiguous status of nontraditional social movements is reflected in the behavior of the various Green parties that arose in Europe. Although initially environmental movements, these groups began to take issue with governments over a broad spectrum of issues. They also began to split over the question of whether or not to share responsibility for governing in the tradition of political parties or continue to resist the government.

and technological stagnation, nonparty groups in the East might have remained peripheral. However, the concatenation of a fruitless adventure in Afghanistan, a critical need for infusions of capital and knowledge from the West, and a need to reduce military spending forced Soviet leaders to try a different approach. They attempted unsuccessfully to co-opt a variety of ethnic, reformist, and religious elements in Soviet society that previously had been pariahs. In the end, the USSR was torn apart by the revival of national memories such as the division of Ukraine in 1667 by Poland and Russia. Nested polities in the Soviet empire reasserted their cultural identity and political independence.

Events in the East should not be viewed in isolation, but rather as part of a broader contemporary trend that we may characterize as *a revolt against the prerogatives of the Westphalian state*. We may be approaching one of those historical sea changes (such as the conquest of tribal forms in the New World by Westphalian polities) in which one polity form is forced, at a minimum, to share its dominion with others and perhaps even to yield pride of place. Political groups of many stripes are seducing the loyalties of citizens away from the "center" and make governments everywhere increasingly responsive to demagogues, narrowly defined interests, public opinion polls, and public demonstrations. As the world grows less and less to resemble the Westphalian system of classical theory, it acquires features of what William Kornhauser (1959, 227) described as "the politics of mass society." He explained: "Mass politics occurs when large numbers of people engage in political activity outside of the procedures and rules instituted by a society to govern political action." The general atmosphere of malaise has grown even more pronounced with the end of the Cold War. David Deudney and G. John Ikenberry (1994, 21) observe: "The end of the East-West conflict holds deeper implications for the American polity than is generally recognized. Despite the widespread expectation that relations *among* the Western democracies would be disrupted by the end of the Cold War, the reality is that relations *within* those democracies has been more profoundly disturbed."

CONCLUSION: FUSION AND FRAGMENTATION IN A POST–COLD WAR WORLD

As at other moments of rapid change, the end of the Cold War has made it easier for advocates of expansive and contractive polities to make their cases persuasively and reawaken old identities. Whatever the taboo regarding the alteration of sovereign boundaries, the fact remains that they have lately been radically rearranged *from the inside* in the former Yugoslavia and Soviet Union. With ethnic conflict simmering in Central Europe, one wonders what claims for self-determination will be advanced next.[20] Will there be external intervention, especially by neighboring groups with claims of kinship? At the very least, there will have to be new forms of autonomy invented for pockets of ethnicity. Then, no doubt, when the smoke has settled on the battlefields, there will be need of newer formulas to knit the pieces back together into larger polities for functional ends.

This brings us again to the units to be ordered, and here the going gets difficult. Certainly, the growing importance of economic issues opens up a broad field of polities that, until recently, political scientists were pleased to leave to analysts in management schools. But what are we to make of a world in which, in the words of a U.S. assistant secretary of state, much of the African continent appears to be reverting to a precolonial order characterized by tribal enclaves? How shall we regard the bloody remnants of Yugoslavia? Georgia? Afghanistan? Rwanda? Somalia? Cambodia? The list goes on and will grow longer.

Like the cases we reviewed, this list of disintegrating states defies the implicit realist premise that history somehow culminated in the European polity. In this ethnocentric and ahistorical interpretation, that polity is the crowning achievement and possible end-all of political evolution. Westphalia supposedly ratified a Platonic form rather than, simply, a statist ideology and a few European legal boundaries. In fact, as we have seen, statist ideology was altered by its post-Napoleon linkage with nationalism, and the Westphalian ideal has never been *fully* realized in practice *anywhere* and hardly at all in most polities. The cases we have examined provide a richer and more dynamic picture of the way polities evolve. All are rather normal eras in the small "r" real world of polities. It was the "Westphalian Moment" that was exceptional.

---

20. Etzioni (1992–93, 21) regards self-determination and democracy as competitors: "While they long served to destroy empires and force governments to be more responsive to the governed, with rare exceptions self-determination movements now undermine the potential for democratic development in nondemocratic countries and threaten the foundations of democracy in the democratic ones."

The real world has always been one of numerous layered, overlapping, and nested polities. Our task as theorists is to explain that most defining characteristic of politics—the manner in which people come together (or are brought together) to behave collectively. We need to understand the sources and consequences of change—the processes through which polities emerge, evolve, expire, and are sometimes resurrected. The Westphalian ideal seems remote from the solutions that must be found, both to accommodate contemporary mini-nationalisms or issues of global scope. It seems destined to remain as a reassuring symbol, rather like the British monarchy before the latest scandals, while most of what is really important politically takes place among other polities in a variety of arenas. We are in an era in which there will be many experiments with new polity forms. This sort of thing has happened repeatedly in human history, and it will not cease because Hegel, Fukuyama, or someone else declares history to have ended.

Sources

'Abduh, Muhammad. 1966. *The Theology of Unity*. London: George Allen and Unwin.

Adám, Magda. 1993. In *Ethnicity and Nationalism: Case Studies in Their Intrinsic Tension and Political Dynamics*, edited by Peter Krüger. Marburg, Germany: Hitzeroth.

Adams, Richard E. W. 1991. *Prehistoric Mesoamerica*, rev. ed. Norman: University of Oklahoma Press.

Adams, Robert McC. 1972. *The Urban Revolution in Lowland Mesopotamia. In Population Growth: Anthropological Implications*, edited by B. Spooner. Cambridge, Mass.: MIT Press.

———. 1981. *Heartland of Cities*. Chicago: University of Chicago Press.

Adams, Robert McC., and H.-J. Nissen. 1972. *The Uruk Countryside*. Chicago: University of Chicago Press.

Adcock, Sir Frank, and D. J. Mosley. 1975. *Diplomacy in Ancient Greece*. London: Thames and Hudson.

Agger, Ben. 1994. *Gender, Culture, and Power*. Westport, Conn.: Praeger.

al Faruqi, Isma'il R., and al Faruqi, Lois Lamya'. 1986. *The Cultural Atlas of Islam*. New York: MacMillan.

Algaze, Guillermo. 1989. "The Uruk Expansion: Cross-Cultural Exchange in Early Mesopotamian Civilization." *Current Anthropology* 30.

Allan, Pierre. 1992. "The End of the Cold War: The End of International Relations Theory?" In *The End of the Cold War: Evaluating Theories of International Relations*, edited by Pierre Allan and Kjell Goldman. Dordrecht, Netherlands: Martinus Nijhoff.

Allison, Graham T. 1971. *Essence of Decision: Explaining the Cuban Missile Crisis*. Boston: Little, Brown.

Allison, Graham T., and Morton H. Halperin. 1972. "Bureaucratic Politics: A Paradigm and Some Policy Implications." In *Theory and Practice in International Relations*, edited by Raymond Tanter and Richard H. Ullman. Princeton: Princeton University Press.

Ames, Roger T. 1983. *The Art of Rulership: A Study in Ancient Chinese Political Thought*. Honolulu: University of Hawaii Press.

Anderson, Benedict. 1983. *Imagined Communities: Reflections on the Origin and Spread of Nationalism*. London: Verso.

421

Andrewes, Antony. 1967. *Greek Society*. Harmondsworth, Middlesex, England: Penguin.

Andrews, Anthony P. 1983. *Maya Salt Production and Trade*. Tucson: University of Arizona Press.

———. 1990. "The Role of Trading Ports in Maya Civilization." In *Vision and Revision in Maya Studies,* edited by Flora S. Clancy and Peter D. Harrison. Albuquerque: University of New Mexico Press.

Aristotle. 1981. *The Athenian Constitution*. Translated by T. A. Sinclair, revised by Trevor J. Saunders. London: Penguin.

———. 1984. *The Athenian Constitution*. Translated by P. J. Rhodes. London: Penguin.

Aronoff, Michael J. 1986. *The Frailty of Authority*. New Brunswick, N.J.: Transaction.

Ashley, Richard K., and R. B. J. Walker. 1990. "Speaking the Language of Exile: Dissident Thought in International Studies." *International Studies Quarterly* 34:3.

Attenborough, David. 1987. *The First Eden: The Mediterranean and Man*. London: William Collins Sons.

Bagby, Laurie M. 1994. "The Use and Abuse of Thucydides." *International Organization* 48:1.

Baldwin, David A., ed. 1993. *Neorealism and Neoliberalism: The Contemporary Debate*. New York: Columbia.

Baldwin, John W. 1971. *The Scholastic Culture of the Middle Ages, 1000–1300*. Lexington, Mass.: Heath.

Balsdon, J. P. V. D. 1979. *Romans and Aliens*. Chapel Hill: University of North Carolina Press.

Barber, Benjamin. 1992. "Jihad vs. McWorld," *Atlantic Monthly* 269 (March).

Barkin, J. Samuel, and Bruce Cronin. 1994. "The State and the Nation: Changing Norms and the Rules of Sovereignty in International Relations." *International Organization* 48: 1.

Barnet, Richard J., and Ronald E. Muller. 1974. *Global Reach: The Power of the Multinational Corporations*. New York: Simon and Schuster.

Baron, Hans. 1966. *The Crisis of the Early Renaissance*. Princeton: Princeton University Press.

———. 1988. *In Search of Florentine Civic Humanism: Essays on the Transition from Medieval to Modern Thought,* vol. 1. Princeton: Princeton University Press.

Bartonek, Antonín. 1974. "The Place of the Dorians in the Late Helladic World." In *Bronze Age Migrations in the Aegean,* edited by J. A. Crossland and Ann Birchall. Park Ridge, N.J.: Noyes.

Bashkar, Roy. 1979. *The Possibility of Naturalism: A Philosophical Critique of the Human Sciences*. Atlantic Highlands, N.J.: Humanities Press.

Bauslaugh, Robert A. 1991. *The Concept of Neutrality in Classical Greece*. Berkeley: University of California Press.

Beck, B. J. Mansvelt. 1986. "The Fall of Han." In *History of China*, edited by Denis Twitchett and Michael Loewe. Vol. 1, *The Ch'in and Han Empires, 221 BC–AD 220*. Cambridge: Cambridge University Press.

Becker, Marvin B. 1967. *Florence in Transition*. Vol. 1, *The Decline of the Commune*. Baltimore: Johns Hopkins Press.

———. 1968. *Florence in Transition*. Vol. 2, *Studies in the Rise of the Territorial State*. Baltimore: Johns Hopkins Press.

Bentley, Jerry H. 1987. *Politics and Culture in Renaissance Naples*. Princeton: Princeton University Press.

Berdan, Frances F. 1977. "Distributive Mechanisms in the Aztec Economy." In *Peasant Livelihood: Studies in Economic Anthropology and Cultural Ecology*, edited by Rhoda Halperin and James Dow. New York: St. Martin's.

Bernal, Ignacio. 1969. *The Olmec World*. Berkeley: University of California Press.

Bielenstein, Hans. 1986a. "The Institutions of Later Han." In *History of China*, edited by Denis Twitchett and Michael Loewe. Vol. 1, *The Ch'in and Han Empires, 221 BC–AD 220*. Cambridge: Cambridge University Press.

———. 1986b. "Wang Mang, the Restoration of the Han dynasty, and Later Han." In *History of China*, edited by Denis Twitchett and Michael Loewe. Vol. 1, *The Ch'in and Han Empires, 221 BC–AD 220*. Cambridge: Cambridge University Press.

Biersteker, Thomas J. 1989. "Critical Reflections on Post-Positivism in International Relations." *International Studies Quarterly* 33:3.

Black, Anthony. 1992. *Political Thought in Europe, 1250–1450*. Cambridge: Cambridge University Press.

Blanton, Richard E. 1976. "The Origins of Monte Albán." *In Cultural Change and Continuity: Essays in Honor of James Bennett Griffin*, edited by Charles E. Cleland. New York: Academic.

———. 1978. *Monte Albán: Settlement Patterns at the Ancient Zapotec Capital*. New York: Academic.

———. 1983a. "The Founding of Monte Albán." In *The Cloud People: Divergent Evolution of the Zapotec and Mixtec Civilizations*, edited by Kent V. Flannery and Joyce Marcus. New York: Academic.

———. 1983b. "Monte Albán in Period V." In *The Cloud People: Divergent Evolution of the Zapotec and Mixtec Civilizations*, edited by Kent V. Flannery and Joyce Marcus. New York: Academic.

———. 1983c. "The Urban Decline of Monte Albán." In *The Cloud People: Divergent Evolution of the Zapotec and Mixtec Civilizations*, edited by Kent V. Flannery and Joyce Marcus. New York: Academic.

———. 1983d. "Urban Monte Albán During Period III." In *The Cloud People: Divergent Evolution of the Zapotec and Mixtec Civilizations*, edited by Kent V. Flannery and Joyce Marcus. New York: Academic.

Blanton, Richard E., and Stephen A. Kowalewski. 1981. "Monte Albán and

After in the Valley of Oaxaca." In *Supplement to the Handbook of Middle American Indians,* vol. 1, edited by V. R. Bricker and J. A. Sabloff. Austin: University of Texas Press.

Bloodworth, Dennis, and Ching Ping Bloodworth. 1976. *The Chinese Machiavelli: 3,000 Years of Chinese Statecraft.* New York: Farrar, Straus and Giroux.

Bodde, Derek. 1986. "The State and Empire of Ch'in." In *History of China,* edited by Denis Twitchett and Michael Loewe. Vol. 1, *The Ch'in and Han Empires, 221 BC–AD 220.* Cambridge: Cambridge University Press.

Bolgar, R. R. 1954. *The Classical Heritage and Its Beneficiaries.* Cambridge: Cambridge University Press.

Boulding, Kenneth E. 1962. *Conflict and Defense: A General Theory.* New York: Harper and Row.

———. 1978. *Ecodynamics.* Beverly Hills, Calif.: Sage.

Boutroz, Labib. 1981. *Phoenician Sport: Its Influence on the Origin of the Olympic Games.* Amsterdam: J. C. Gieben.

Bozeman, Adda B. 1960. *Politics and Culture in International History.* Princeton: Princeton University Press.

———. 1984. "The International Order in a Multicultural World." In *The Expansion of International Society,* edited by Hedley Bull and Adam Watson. Oxford: Clarendon Press.

Bricker, Victoria Reifler. 1977. "The Caste War of Yucatán: The History of a Myth and the Myth of History." In *Anthropology and History in Yucatán,* edited by Grant D. Jones. Austin: University of Texas Press.

Broda, Johanna, Davíd Carrasco, and Eduardo Matos Moctezuma. 1987. *The Great Temple of Tenochtitlan: Center and Periphery in the Aztec World.* Berkeley: University of California Press.

Brotherston, Gordon. 1974. "Huitzilopochtli and What Was Made of Him." In *Mesoamerican Archaeology: New Approaches,* edited by Norman Hammond. Austin: University of Texas Press.

Brown, Peter. 1971. *The World of Late Antiquity, AD 150–750.* London: Thames and Hudson.

———. 1982. *Society and the Holy in Late Antiquity.* Berkeley: University of California Press.

Brucker, Gene. 1962. *Florentine Politics and Society, 1343–1378.* Princeton: Princeton University Press.

———. 1969. *Renaissance Florence.* New York: John Wiley and Sons.

Brundage, Burr Cartwright. 1972. *A Rain of Darts: The Mexica Aztecs.* Austin: University of Texas Press.

———. 1975. *Two Earths, Two Heavens: An Essay Contrasting the Aztecs and the Incas.* Albuquerque: University of New Mexico Press.

Bull, Hedley. 1977. *The Anarchical Society: A Study of Order in World Politics.* New York: Columbia University Press.

Bulliet, R.W. 1979. *Conversion to Islam in the Medieval Period.* Cambridge, Mass.: Harvard University Press.

Burke, Peter. 1986a. "City-States." In *States in History*, edited by John A. Hall. Oxford: Basil Blackwell.

———. 1986b. *The Italian Renaissance: Culture and Society in Italy.* Princeton: Princeton University Press.

Burman, Edward. 1989. *The World Before Columbus, 1100–1492.* London: W. H. Allen.

Burn, A. R. 1984. *Persia and the Greeks*, 2nd ed. London: Duckworth.

Burns, Allan F. 1977. "The Caste War in the 1970's: Present-Day Accounts from Village Quintana Roo." In *Anthropology and History in Yucatán*, edited by Grant D. Jones. Austin: University of Texas Press.

Burton, John W. 1972. *World Society.* Cambridge: Cambridge University Press.

Butters, H. C. 1985. *Governors and Government in Early Sixteenth-Century Florence, 1502–1519.* Oxford: Clarendon Press.

Buzan, Barry. 1993. "From International System to International Society: Structural Realism and Regime Theory Meet the English School." *International Organization* 47:3.

Buzan, Barry, Richard Little, and Charles Jones. 1993. *The Logic of Anarchy.* New York: Columbia University Press.

Calnek, Edward E. 1976. "The Internal Structure of Tenochtitlan." In *The Valley of Mexico: Studies in Pre-Hispanic Ecology and Society*, edited by Eric R. Wolf. Albuquerque: University of New Mexico Press.

Cameron, Averil. 1993. *The Mediterranean World in Late Antiquity, AD 395–600.* London: Routledge.

Carlsnaes, Walter. 1992. "The Agency-Structure Problem in Foreign Policy Analysis. *International Studies Quarterly* 36:3.

Carr, E. H. 1962. *The Twenty Years' Crisis, 1919–1939: An Introduction to the Study of International Relations.* New York: St. Martin's.

Carrasco, Pedro. 1971. *To Change Place: Aztec Ceremonial Landscapes.* Np: University Press of Colorado.

———. 1984. "Royal Marriages in Ancient Mexico." In *Explorations in Ethnohistory: Indians of Central Mexico in the Sixteenth Century*, edited by H. R. Harvey and Hanns J. Prem. Albuquerque: University of New Mexico Press.

Cartledge, Paul. 1977. "Hoplites and Heroes: Sparta's Contribution to the Techniques of Ancient Warfare." *Journal of Hellenic Studies* 47.

———. 1979. *Sparta and Laconia: A Regional History, 1300–362 B.C.* London: Routledge and Kegan Paul.

———. 1987. *Agesilaos and the Crisis of Sparta.* Baltimore: Johns Hopkins University Press.

Chadwick, Henry. 1967. *The Early Church: The Story of Emergent Christianity from the Apostolic Age to the Foundation of the Church of Rome.* London: Penguin.

Chadwick, John. 1976. *The Mycenaen World.* Cambridge: Cambridge University Press.

Chaliand, Gérard. 1994. *The Art of War in World History: From Antiquity to the Nuclear Age*. Berkeley: University of California Press.

Chambers, D. S. 1970. *The Imperial Age of Venice, 1350–1580*. London: Thames and Hudson.

Chang, Kwang-chih. 1983. *Art, Myth, and Ritual: The Path to Political Authority in Ancient China*. Cambridge, Mass.: Harvard University Press.

Chase, Arlen F., and Prudence M. Rice. 1985. *The Lowland Maya Postclassic*. Austin: University of Texas Press.

Cheetham, Nicholas. 1982. *Keepers of the Keys: A History of the Popes from St. Peter to John Paul II*. New York: Charles Scribner's Sons.

Ch'en Ch'i-yun. 1986. "Confucian, Legalist, and Taoist Thought in Later Han," In *History of China*, edited by Denis Twitchett and Michael Loewe. Vol. 1, *The Ch'in and Han Empires, 221 BC–AD 220*. Cambridge: Cambridge University Press.

Clancy, Flora S., and Peter D. Harrison. 1990. *Vision and Revision in Maya Studies*. Albuquerque: University of New Mexico Press.

Clarke, M. V. 1926. *The Medieval City State*. Cambridge: Speculum Historiale.

Clendinnen, Inga. 1991. *The Aztecs: An Interpretation*. Cambridge: Cambridge University Press.

Coe, Michael D. 1981a. "Religion and the Rise of Mesoamerican States." In *The Transition to Statehood in the New World*, edited by Grant D. Jones and Robert R. Kautz. Cambridge: Cambridge University Press.

———. 1981b. "San Lorenzo Tenochtitlan." In *Supplement to the Handbook of Middle American Indians*, vol. 1, edited by V. R. Bricker and J. A. Sabloff. Austin: University of Texas Press.

Coe, Michael D., and Richard Diehl. 1980. *In the Land of the Olmecs*. 2 vols. Austin: University of Texas Press.

Cohen, Ira. 1989. *Structuration Theory: Anthony Giddens and the Constitution of Social Life*. London: Macmillan.

Coleman, Daniel Harvey. 1993. *The Medieval Christian Commonwealth: A Theoretical Approach*. M.A. thesis, Iowa State University.

Conner, W. Robert. 1984. *Thucydides*. Princeton: Princeton University Press.

Conrad, Geoffrey W., and Arthur A. Demarest. 1984. *Religion and Empire: The Dynamics of Aztec and Inca Expansionism*. Cambridge: Cambridge University Press.

Contamine, Philippe. 1984. *War in the Middle Ages*. Translated by Michael Jones. Oxford: Blackwell.

Cook, Michael. 1981. *Early Muslim Dogma*. Cambridge: Cambridge University Press.

Cook, Sherburne F., and Woodrow Borah. 1960. *The Indian Population of Central Mexico, 1531–1610*. Berkeley: University of California Press.

———. 1972–79. *Essays in Population History: Mexico and the Caribbean*. 3 vols. Berkeley: University of California Press.

Crawford, Harriet. 1991. *Sumer and the Sumerians*. Cambridge: Cambridge University Press.

Creel, Herrlee. 1949. *Confucius, the Man and the Myth.* New York: J. Day.

Crone, Patricia. 1980. *Slaves on Horses: The Evolution of the Islamic Polity.* Cambridge: Cambridge University Press.

Crone, Patricia, and Martin Hinds. 1986. *God's Caliph: Religious Authority in the First Centuries of Islam.* Cambridge: Cambridge University Press.

Crosby, Alfred W., Jr. 1972. *The Columbian Exchange: Biological and Cultural Consequences of 1492.* Westport, Conn.: Greenwood.

Culbert, T. Patrick. 1973. *The Classic Maya Collapse.* Albuquerque: University of New Mexico Press.

Dabashi, Hamid. 1989. *Authority in Islam: From the Rise of Muhammad to the Establishment of the Umayyads.* New Brunswick, N.J.: Transaction.

Dahl, Robert A. 1967. *Pluralist Democracy in the United States: Conflict and Consent.* Chicago: Rand McNally.

Dante Alighieri. 1969. "De Monarchia." In *Great Political Thinkers,* 4th ed., edited by William Ebenstein. New York: Holt, Rinehart and Winston.

David, Ephraim. [1981] 1986. *Sparta Between Empire and Revolution, 404–243 B.C.: Internal Problems and Their Impact on Contemporary Greek Consciousness.* Reprint, Salem, N.H.: Ayer.

Davies, J. K. 1993. *Democracy and Classical Greece,* 2nd ed. Cambridge, Mass.: Harvard University Press.

Davies, Nigel. 1977. *The Toltecs: Until the Fall of Tula.* Norman: University of Oklahoma Press.

———. 1987. *The Aztec Empire: The Toltec Resurgence.* Norman: University of Oklahoma Press.

Davis, R. H. C. 1988. *A History of Medieval Europe: From Constantine to Saint Louis,* 2nd ed. New York: Longman.

Day, Gerald W. 1988. *Genoa's Response to Byzantium, 1155–1204: Commercial Expansion and Factionalism in a Medieval City.* Urbana: University of Illinois Press.

Demieville, Paul. 1986. "Philosophy and Religion from Han to Sui." In *History of China,* edited by Denis Twitchett and Michael Loewe. Vol. 1, *The Ch'in and Han Empires, 221 BC–AD 220.* Cambridge: Cambridge University Press.

Der Derian, James, and Michael J. Shapiro, eds. 1989. *International/Intertextual Relations: Postmodern Readings of World Politics.* Lexington, Mass.: Lexington Books.

Desborough, V. R. d'A. 1964. *The Last Myceneans and Their Successors: An Archaeological Survey c.1200–c.1000 B.C.* Oxford: Clarendon.

———. 1972. *The Greek Dark Ages.* London: Ernest Benn.

Deudney, Daniel, and G. John Ikenberry. 1994. "After the Long War." *Foreign Policy* 94.

Deutsch, Karl W. 1978. *The Analysis of International Relations,* 2nd ed. Englewood Cliffs, N.J.: Prentice-Hall.

———. 1989. "A Path among the Social Sciences." In *Journeys through World*

Politics: Autobiographical Reflections of Thirty-four Academic Travelers, edited by Joseph Kruzel and James N. Rosenau. Lexington, Mass.: Lexington Books.

Diakonoff, I. M. 1974. *Structure of Society and State in Early Dynastic Sumer.* Berkeley: University of California Press.

Diehl, Paul F., and Frank W. Wayman. 1994. "Realpolitik: Dead End, Detour, or Road Map?" In *Reconstruting Realpolitik,* edited by Frank W. Wayman and Paul F. Diehl. Ann Arbor: University of Michigan Press.

Doyle, Michael. 1986. *Empires.* Ithaca, N.Y.: Cornell University Press.

Drennan, Robert D. 1991. "Pre-Hispanic Chiefdom Trajectories in Mesoamerica, Central America, and Northern South America." In *Chiefdoms: Power, Economy, and Ideology,* edited by Timothy Earle. Cambridge: Cambridge University Press.

Dreyer, Edward L. 1974. "The Poyang Campaign: Inland Naval Warfare in the Founding of the Ming Dynasty." In *Chinese Ways in Warfare,* edited by Frank A. Kierman and John K. Fairbank. Cambridge, Mass.: Harvard University Press.

Easton, David. 1965. *A Framework for Political Analysis.* Englewood Cliffs, N.J.: Prentice-Hall.

Ebrey, Patricia. 1986. "The Economic and Social History of Later Han." In *History of China,* edited by Denis Twitchett and Michael Loewe. Vol. 1, *The Ch'in and Han Empires, 221 BC–AD 220.* Cambridge: Cambridge University Press.

Eckstein, Harry, and Ted Robert Gurr. 1975. *Patterns of Authority: A Structural Basis for Political Inquiry.* New York: Wiley.

Edens, Christopher. 1992. "Dynamics of Trade in the Ancient Mesopotamian 'World System'." *American Anthropologist* 94.

Ehrenberg, Victor. 1969. *The Greek State,* 2nd ed. London: Methuen.

———. 1973. *From Solon to Socrates: Greek Civilization During the 6th and 5th Centuries* B.C., 2nd ed. London: Routledge.

Eisenstadt, S. N., ed. 1986. *The Origins and Diversity of Axial Age Civilizations.* Albany: State University of New York Press.

Elliott, J. H. 1970. *The Old World and the New, 1492–1650.* Cambridge: Cambridge University Press.

Elton, G. R. 1969. *The Practice of History.* London: Fontana.

Etzioni, Amitai. 1992–93. "The Evils of Self-Determination." *Foreign Policy* 89.

Fagan, Brian M. 1984. *The Aztecs.* New York: W. H. Freeman.

Fairbank, John K. 1974. "Introduction: Varieties of the Chinese Military Experience." In *Chinese Ways in Warfare,* edited by Frank A. Kierman and John K. Fairbank. Cambridge, Mass.: Harvard University Press.

———. 1992. *China: A New History.* Cambridge, Mass.: Harvard University Press.

Fairbank, John K., and Edwin O. Reischauer. 1989. *China: Tradition and Transformation,* rev. ed. Boston: Houghton Mifflin.

Farrar, Cynthia. 1988. *The Origins of Democratic Thinking: The Invention of Politics*. Cambridge: Cambridge University Press.

Farriss, Nancy M. 1983. "Indians in Colonial Yucatan: Three Perspectives." In *Spaniards and Indians in Southeastern Mesoamerica: Essays on the History of Ethnic Relations*, edited by Murdo J. MacLeod and Robert Wasserstrom. Lincoln: University of Nebraska Press.

———. 1984. *Maya Society Under Colonial Rule: The Collective Enterprise of Survival*. Princeton: Princeton University Press.

Ferguson, R. Brian. 1992. "Tribal Warfare." *Scientific American*, January 1992.

Ferguson, R. Brian, and Neil L. Whitehead. 1992a. Introduction. In *Expanding States and Indigenous Warfare*. Santa Fe, N.M.: School of American Research Press.

———. 1992b. *War in the Tribal Zone: Expanding States and Indigenous Warfare*. Santa Fe, N.M.: School of American Research Press.

Ferguson, Yale H. 1991. "Chiefdoms to City States: The Greek Experience. " In *Chiefdoms: Economy, Power, and Ideology*, edited by Timothy Earle. Cambridge: Cambridge University Press.

———. 1994. "Ethnicity, Nationalism, and Polities Great and Small." *Mershon International Studies Review* 39: Supplement 2.

Ferguson, Yale H., and Richard W. Mansbach. 1988. *The Elusive Quest: Theory and International Politics*. Columbia: University of South Carolina Press.

———. 1989. *The State, Conceptual Chaos, and the Future of International Relations Theory*. Boulder, Colo.: Lynne Reinner.

———. 1991. "Between Celebration and Despair: Constructive Suggestions for Future International Theory." *International Studies Quarterly* 35:4.

———. 1995. "The Decline of Inside/Outside: Reintegrating Interstate and Intrastate Politics." Paper at the annual meeting of the International Studies Association.

Ferrill, Arther. 1985. *The Origins of War: From the Stone Age to Alexander the Great*. London: Thames and Hudson.

Fiedel, Stuart J. 1987. *Prehistory of the Americas*. Cambridge: Cambridge University Press.

Fine, John V. A. 1983. *The Ancient Greeks: A Critical History*. Cambridge, Mass.: Harvard University Press.

Fingarette, Herbert. 1972. *Confucius: The Secular as Sacred*. New York: Harper and Row.

Finlay, Robert. 1980. *Politics in Renaissance Venice*. New Brunswick, N.J.: Rutgers University Press.

Finley, Moses I. 1981. *Early Greece: The Bronze and Archaic Ages*, rev. ed. New York: Norton.

———. 1984. *Politics in the Ancient World*. Cambridge: Cambridge University Press.

———. 1985. *The Ancient Economy*, 2nd ed. London: Hogarth.

———. 1986. *The Use and Abuse of History*. London: Hogarth.

Finley, Moses I., and H. W. Pleket. 1976. *The Olympic Games: The First Thousand Years*. London: Chatto and Windus.

Fischer, Marcus. 1992. "Feudal Europe, 800–1300: Communal Discourse and Conflicted Practices." *International Organization* 46:2.

———. 1993. "On Context, Facts, and Norms: Response to Hall and Kratochwil." *International Organization* 47:3.

Flannery, Kent V. 1988. "Comment." In *Ecological Theory and Cultural Evolution in the Valley of Oaxaca*, by William T. Sanders, Deborah L. Nichols, et al. *Current Anthropology* 29.

Flannery, Kent V., and Joyce Marcus. 1983. *The Cloud People: Divergent Evolution of the Zapotec and Mixtec Civilizations*. New York: Academic Press.

Fleiss, Peter J. 1966. *Thucydides and the Politics of Bipolarity*. Baton Rouge: Louisiana State University Press.

Fornara, Charles W. and Loren J. Salmons II. 1991. *Athens from Cleisthenes to Pericles*. Berkeley: University of California Press.

Forrest, W. G. 1978. *The Emergence of Greek Democracy: The Character of Greek Politics, 800–400 BC*. London: Weidenfeld and Nicolson.

———. 1980. *A History of Sparta*, 2nd ed. London: Duckworth.

Fowden, Garth. 1993. *Empire to Commonwealth: Consequences of Monotheism in Late Antiquity*. Cambridge: Cambridge University Press.

Fox, Robin Lane. 1986. *Pagans and Christians: In the Mediterranean World from the Second Century AD to the Conversion of Constantine*. New York: Knopf.

Franke, Herbert. 1974. "Siege and Defense of Towns in Medieval China. In *Chinese Ways of Warfare*, edited by Frank A. Kiernan and John K. Fairbank. Cambridge, Mass.: Harvard University Press.

Frankfort, Henri. 1978. *Kingship and the Gods: A Study of Ancient Near Eastern Religion and the Integration of Society and Nature*. Chicago: University of Chicago Press.

Freidel, David A. 1981. "Civilization as a State of Mind: The Cultural Evolution of the Lowland Maya." In *The Transition to Statehood in the New World*, edited by Grant D. Jones and Robert R. Kautz. Cambridge: Cambridge University Press.

———. 1983. "Lowland Maya Political Economy: Historical and Archaeological Perspectives in Light of Intensive Agriculture." In *Spaniards and Indians in Southeastern Mesoamerica: Essays on the History of Ethnic Relations*, edited by Murdo J. MacLeod and Robert Wasserstrom. Lincoln: University of Nebraska Press.

———. 1985. "New Light on the Dark Age: A Summary of Major Themes." In *The Lowland Maya Postclassic*, edited by Arlen F. Chase and Prudence M. Rice. Austin: University of Texas Press.

Freidel, David A., and Jeremy A. Sabloff. 1984. *Cozumel: Late Maya Settlement Patterns*. Orlando, Fla.: Academic Press.

Gamble, Clive. 1987. "Hunter-Gatherers and the Origin of States." In *States in History*, edited by John A. Hall. New York: Basil Blackwell.

George, Alexander, and Juliette George. 1964. *Woodrow Wilson and Colonel House*. New York: Dover.

Gibb, H. A. R. 1962. *Studies on the Civilization of Islam*. Princeton: Princeton University Press.

Gibson, Charles. 1964. *The Aztecs Under Spanish Rule: A History of the Indians of the Valley of Mexico, 1519–1810*. Stanford, Calif.: Stanford University Press.

Gibson, Mc G. 1973. "Population Shift and the Rise of Mesopotamian Civilization." In *The Explanation of Culture Change: Models in Prehistory*, edited by C. Renfrew. London: Duckworth.

———. 1976. "By Cycle and Stage to Sumer." In *The Legacy of Summer*, edited by D. Schmandt-Besserat. Malibu, Calif.: Undena.

Giddens, Anthony. 1984. *The Constitution of Society: Outline of the Theory of Structuration*. Berkeley: University of California Press.

Gilbert, Felix. 1980. *The Pope, His Banker, and Venice*. Cambridge, Mass.: Harvard University Press.

Gillespie, Susan D. 1989. *The Aztec Kings: The Construction of Rulership in Mexica History*. Tucson: University of Arizona Press.

Gilpin, Robert. 1981. *War and Change in World Politics*. New York: Cambridge University Press.

Gimbutas, Marija. 1974. "The Destruction of Aegean and East Mediterranean Urban Civilization around 2300 B.C." In *Bronze Age Migrations in the Aegean*, edited by R. A. Crossland and Ann Birchall. Park Ridge, N.J.: Noyes Press.

Goffart, Walter. 1980. *Barbarians and Romans, A.D. 418–584: The Techniques of Accommodation*. Princeton: Princeton University Press.

Goldstein, Judith. 1993. *Ideas, Interests, and American Trade Policy*. Ithaca, N.Y.: Cornell University Press.

Goldziher, Ignaz. 1981. *Introduction to Islamic Theology and Law*. Princeton: Princeton University Press.

Gottlieb, Gidon. 1993. *Nation Against State: A New Approach to Ethnic Conflicts and the Decline of Sovereignty*. New York: Council of Foreign Relations Press.

Gourevitch, Peter. 1978. "The Second Image Reversed: The International Sources of Domestic Politics." *International Organization* 32:4.

Graber, O. 1973. *The Formation of Islamic Art*. New Haven: Yale University Press.

Grant, Michael. 1979. *History of Rome*. London: Faber and Faber.

———. 1990. *The Fall of the Roman Empire*. London: Weidenfeld and Nicolson.

———. 1992. *The Hellenistic Greeks: From Alexander to Cleopatra,* 2nd ed. London: Weidenfeld and Nicolson.

Grant, Robert M. 1970. *Augustus to Constantine: The Rise and Triumph of Christianity in the World.* New York: Harper and Row.

Greenfeld, Liah. 1992. *Nationalism: Five Roads to Modernity.* Cambridge, Mass.: Harvard University Press.

Grieco, Joseph M. 1988. "Anarchy and the Limits of Cooperation: A Realist Critique of the Newest Liberal Institutionalism."*International Organization* 42:1.

———. 1993. "Understanding the Problem of International Cooperation: The Limits of Neoliberal Institutionalism and the Future of Realist Theory." In *Neorealism and Neoliberalism,* edited by David A. Baldwin. New York: Columbia University Press.

Grove, David C. 1974. "The Highland Olmex Manifestation: A Consideration of What Is and Isn't." In *Mesoamerican Archaeology: New Approaches,* edited by Norman Hammond. Austin: University of Texas Press.

———. 1984. *Chalcatzingo: Excavations on the Maya Frontier.* London: Thames and Hudson.

Gruen, Erich S. 1984. *The Hellenistic World and the Coming of Rome.* Berkeley: University of California Press.

Grunberg, Isabelle, and Thomas Risse-Kappen. 1992. "A Time of Reckoning? Theories of International Relations and the End of the Cold War." In *The End of the Cold War: Evaluating Theories of International Relations,* edited by Pierre Allan and Kjell Goldman. Dordrecht, Netherlands: Martinus Nijhoff.

Guenée, Bernard. 1985. *States and Rulers in Later Medieval Europe,* translated by Juliet Vale. Oxford: Blackwell.

Gulick, Edward Vose. 1955. *Europe's Classical Balance of Power.* New York: Norton.

Haas, Ernst B. 1964. *Beyond the Nation-State: Functionalism and International Organization.* Stanford, Calif.: Stanford University Press.

———. 1986. "What Is Nationalism and Why Should We Study It?" *International Organization* 40:3.

———. 1993. "Nationalism: An Instrumental Construction." *Millennium* 22:3.

Haggard, Stephan, and Beth A. Simmons. 1987. "Theories of International Regimes." *International Organization* 41:3.

Hale, J. R. 1971. *Renaissance Europe 1480–1520.* London: Fontana.

———. 1977. *Florence and the Medici: The Pattern of Control.* London: Thames and Hudson.

———. 1985. *War and Society in Renaissance Europe 1450–1620.* London: Fontana.

Hall, David L., and Roger T. Ames. 1987. *Thinking Through Confucius.* Albany: State University of New York Press.

Hall, John A. 1985. *Powers and Liberties: The Causes and Consequences of the Rise of the West.* New York: Basil Blackwell.

————. 1987. Introduction. In *States in History*. New York: Basil Blackwell.

Hall, Rodney Bruce, and Friedrich V. Kratochwil. 1993. "Medieval Tales: Neorealist 'Science' and the Abuse of History." *International Organization* 47:3.

Hamilton, Charles D. 1979. *Sparta's Bitter Victories: Politics and Diplomacy in the Corinthian War*. Ithaca, N.Y.: Cornell University Press.

Hammond, N. G. L. 1986. *A History of Greece to 322 B.C.*, 3rd ed. Oxford: Clarendon.

Hammond, Norman. 1974. "Distribution of Late Classic Maya Ceremonial Centres in the Central Area." In *Mesoamerican Archaeology: New Approaches,* edited by Norman Hammond. Austin: University of Texas Press.

————. 1982. *Ancient Maya Civilization*. New Brunswick, N.J.: Rutgers University Press.

Hansen, Chad. 1983. *Language and Logic in Ancient China*. Ann Arbor: University of Michigan Press.

Hansen, Mogens Herman. 1991. *The Athenian Democracy in the Age of Demosthenes*. Oxford: Blackwell.

Harner, Michael. 1977a. "The Ecological Basis for Aztec Sacrifice." *American Ethnologist* 4.

————. 1977b. "The Enigma of Aztec Sacrifice." *Natural History* 86.

Harris, Marvin. 1977. *Cannibals and Kings: The Origins of Cultures*. New York: Random House.

————. 1979. *Cultural Materialism: The Struggle for a Science of Culture*. New York: Random House.

Harrison, Peter D. 1990. "The Revolution in Ancient Maya Subsistence." In *Vision and Revision in Maya Studies,* edited by Flora S. Clancy and Peter D. Harrison. Albuquerque: University of New Mexico Press.

Hart, Jeffrey A. 1991. "Theories of Hegemonial Stability: Opening the Black Box." Paper at the annual meeting of the Midwest Political Science Association.

Harvey, H. R. 1984. "Aspects of Land Tenure in Ancient Mexico." In *Explorations in Ethnohistory: Indians of Central Mexico in the Sixteenth Century,* edited by H. R. Harvey and Hanns J. Prem. Albuquerque: University of New Mexico Press.

Hassig, Ross. 1985. *Trade, Tribute, and Transportation: The Sixteenth-Century Political Economy of the Valley of Mexico*. Norman: University of Oklahoma Press.

————. 1988. *Aztec Warfare: Imperial Expansion and Political Control*. Norman: University of Oklahoma Press.

Hawkes, J. 1973. *The First Great Civilizations: Life in Mesopotamia, the Indus Valley, and Egypt*. New York: Knopf.

Heather, P. J. 1991. *Goths and Romans 332–489*. Oxford: Clarendon.

Helgerson, Richard. 1992. *Forms of Nationhood: The Elizabethan Writing of England*. Chicago: University of Chicago Press.

Helman, Gerald B., and Steven R. Ratner. 1992–93. "Saving Failed States." *Foreign Policy* 89.

Herbert, P. A. 1978. *Under the Brilliant Emperor: Imperial Authority in T'ang China as Seen in the Writings of Chang Chiu-ling*. Canberra: Australia National University Press.

Herman, Gabriel. 1987. *Ritualized Friendship and the Greek City*. Cambridge: Cambridge University Press.

Herz, John H. 1959. *International Politics in the Atomic Age*. New York: Columbia University Press.

Hick, John, and Edmund S. Meltzer, eds. 1989. *Three Faiths—One God*. London: MacMillan.

Hicks, Frederic. 1987. "First Steps Toward a Market-Integrated Economy in Aztec Mexico." In *Early State Dynamics*, edited by Henri J. M. Claessen and Pieter van de Velde. Leiden, The Netherlands: E. J. Brill.

Hitti, Philip K. 1956. *The Arabs: A Short History*. Chicago: Henry Regnery.

Ho, P. T. 1975. *The Cradle of the East*. Chicago: Chicago University Press.

Hobsbawm, E. J. 1992. *Nations and Nationalism Since 1780: Programme, Myth, Reality*, 2nd ed. Cambridge: Cambridge University Press.

Hodgson, F. C. 1901. *The Early History of Venice: From the Foundation to the Conquest of Constantinople*, A.D. 1204. London: George Allen.

Hodgson, M. 1974. *The Adventure of Islam*. Chicago: University of Chicago Press.

Holmes, George, 1975. *Europe: Hierarchy and Revolt, 1320–1450*. London: Fontana.

Holsti, K. J. 1985. *The Dividing Discipline: Hegemony and Diversity in International Theory*. Boston: Allen and Unwin.

Hopf, Ted. 1993. "Getting the End of the Cold War Wrong." *International Security* 18:2.

Hopkins, Raymond F. 1976. "The International Role of 'Domestic' Bureaucracy." *International Organization* 30:3.

———. 1987. "Interests and Regimes: The Subjective Dimension of International Politics." Paper presented at the annual meeting of the American Political Science Association.

Hopper, R. J. 1976. *The Early Greeks*. New York: Barnes and Noble.

Hornblower, S., and M. C. Greenstock. 1984. *The Athenian Empire*, 3rd ed. London: London Association of Classical Teachers.

Hourani, Albert. 1991. *A History of the Arab Peoples*. Cambridge, Mass.: Belknap.

Howard, Michael. 1984. "The Military Factor in European Expansionism." In *The Expansion of European Society*, edited by Hedley Bull and Adam Watson. Oxford: Clarendon.

Hsu, Cho-yun, and Katheryn M. Linduff. 1988. *Western Chou Civilization*. New Haven: Yale University Press.

Hucker, Charles O. 1975. *China's Imperial Past: An Introduction to Chinese History and Culture*. Stanford, Calif.: Stanford University Press.

Hulsewe, A. F. P. 1986. "Ch'in and Han law." In *History of China,* edited by Denis Twitchett and Michael Loewe. Vol. 1, *The Ch'in and Han Empires, 221 BC–AD 220.* Cambridge: Cambridge University Press.

Hunt, Eva, and Robert C. Hunt. 1978. "Irrigation, Conflict, and Politics: A Mexican Case." In *Origins of the State: The Anthropology of Political Evolution,* edited by Ronald Cohen and Elman R. Service. Philadelphia: Institute for the Study of Human Issues.

Huntington, Samuel P. 1971. "The Change to Change: Modernization, Development and Politics." *Comparative Politics* 3.

———. 1993. "The Clash of Civilizations?" *Foreign Affairs* 72:3.

Hyde, J. K. 1973. *Society and Politics in Medieval Italy: The Evolution of the Civil Life, 1000–1350.* London: Macmillan.

Jackson, Robert H. 1986. "Negative Sovereignty in Sub-Saharan Africa," *Review of International Studies* 12.

———. 1990. *Quasi-States: Sovereignty, International Relations and the Third World.* Cambridge: Cambridge University Press.

———. 1993. "Continuity and Change in the States System." In *States in a Changing World: A Contemporary Analysis,* edited by Robert H. Jackson and Alan James. New York: Oxford University Press.

Jackson, Robert H., and Alan James. 1993. "The Character of Independent Statehood." In *States in a Changing World,* edited by Robert H. Jackson and Alan James. New York: Oxford University Press.

Jacobsen, Thorkild. 1970a. "Early Political Development in Mesopotamia." In *Toward the Image of Tammus (and Other Essays),* edited by W. L. Moran. Cambridge, Mass.: Harvard University Press.

———. 1970b. "Primitive Democracy in Ancient Mesopotamia." In *Toward the Image of Tammus (and Other Essays),* edited by W. L. Moran. Cambridge, Mass.: Harvard University Press.

Janis, Irving L., and Leon Mann. 1977. *Decision Making: A Psychological Analysis of Conflict, Choice, and Commitment.* New York: Free Press.

Jeffrey, L. H. 1976. *Archaic Greece: The City-States, c. 700–500 B.C.* London: Earnest Benn.

Jervis, Robert. 1976. *Perception and Misperception in International Politics.* Princeton: Princeton University Press.

———. 1989. "Change, Surprise, and the Hiding Hand." In *Journeys through World Politics: Autobiographical Reflections of Thirty-four Academic Travelers,* edited by Joseph Kruzel and James N. Rosenau. Lexington, Mass.: Lexington Books.

Johnson, Allen W., and Timothy Earle. 1987. *The Evolution of Human Societies: From Foraging Group to Agrarian State.* Stanford, Calif.: Stanford University Press.

Johnson, G. A. 1973. *Local Exchange and Early State Development in Southwestern Iran.* Ann Arbor: University of Michigan Museum of Anthropology.

Joint Association of Classical Teachers. 1984. *The World of Athens: An Introduction to Classical Athenian Culture*. Cambridge: Cambridge University Press.

Jones, A. H. M. 1957. *Anthenian Democracy*. Oxford: Basil Blackwell.

Jones, E. L. 1981. *The European Miracle: Environments, Economics and Geopolitics in the History of Europe and Asia*. Cambridge: Cambridge University Press.

Jones, Grant D. 1983. "The Last Maya Frontiers of Colonial Yucatan." In *Spaniards and Indians in Southeastern Mesoamerica: Essays on the History of Ethnic Relations*, edited by Murdo J. MacLeod and Robert Wasserstrom. Lincoln: University of Nebraska Press.

———. 1990. "Prophets and Idol Speculators: Forces of History in the Lowland Maya Rebellion of 1683." In *Vision and Revision in Maya Studies*, edited by Flora S. Clancy and Peter D. Harrison. Albuquerque: University of New Mexico Press.

Kagan, Donald. 1969. *The Outbreak of the Peloponnesian War*. Ithaca, N.Y.: Cornell University Press.

———. 1974. *The Archidamian War*. Ithaca, N.Y.: Cornell University Press.

———. 1981. *The Peace of Nicias and the Sicilian Expedition*. Ithaca, N.Y.: Cornell University Press.

———. 1987. *The Fall of the Athenian Empire*. Ithaca, N.Y.: Cornell University Press.

Katzenstein, Peter J., ed. 1978. *Between Power and Plenty: Foreign Economic Policies of Advanced Industrial States*. Madison: University of Wisconsin Press.

———. 1989. "International Relations Theory and the Analysis of Change." In *Global Changes and Theoretical Challenges: Approaches to World Politics for the 1990s*, edited by Ernst-Otto Czempiel and James N. Rosenau. Lexington, Mass.: Lexington Books.

Kauppi, Mark V. 1991. "Contemporary International Relations Theory and the Peloponnesian War." In *Hegemonic Rivalry: From Thucydides to the Nuclear Age*, edited by Richard Ned Lebow and Barry S. Strauss. Boulder, Colo.: Westview Press.

Kautsky, John H. 1982. *The Politics of Aristocratic Empires*. Chapel Hill: University of North Carolina Press.

Keegan, John. 1993. *A History of Warfare*. New York: Knopf.

Kegley, Charles W., ed. 1995. *Controversies in International Relations Theory: Realism and the Neoliberal Challenge*. New York: St. Martin's.

Kent, Dale. 1978. *The Rise of the Medici: Faction in Florence, 1426–1434*. Oxford: Oxford University Press.

Keohane, Robert O. 1984. *After Hegemony: Cooperation and Discord in the World Political Economy*. Princeton: Princeton University Press.

———. 1986. "Theory of World Politics: Structural Realism and Beyond." In *Neorealism and Its Critics*, edited by Robert O. Keohane. New York: Columbia University Press.

———. 1988. "International Institutions: Two Approaches." *International Studies Quarterly* 32:4.

Keohane, Robert O., and Joseph S. Nye, Jr. 1987. *"Power and Interdependence* Revisited." *International Organization* 41:4.

———. 1989. *Power and Interdependence,* 2nd ed. Glenview, Ill.: Scott, Foresman.

Kierman, Frank A., Jr. 1974. "Phases and Modes of Combat in Early China." In *Chinese Ways in Warfare,* edited by Frank A. Kierman and John K. Fairbank. Cambridge: Harvard University Press.

Kierman, Frank A., Jr., and John K. Fairbank, eds. 1974. *Chinese Ways in Warfare.* Cambridge.: Harvard University Press.

Kilian, Klaus. 1982. "Zum Ende der Mykenischen Epoche in der Argolis." *Journal of the Mainz Museum* 27.

———. 1988. "Mycenaens Up to Date: Trends and Changes in Recent Research." In *Problems in Greek Prehistory,* edited by E. B. French and K. A. Wardle. Bristol, England: Bristol Classical Press.

Knightly, David, ed. 1983. *The Origins of Chinese Civilization.* Berkeley: University of California Press.

Knorr, Klaus, and James N. Rosenau, eds. 1969. *Contending Approaches to International Politics.* Princeton: Princeton University Press.

Koenigsberger, H. G. 1987. *Medieval Europe, 400–1500.* London: Longman.

Kornhauser, William. 1959. *The Politics of Mass Society.* Glencoe, Ill.: Free Press.

Kramer, S. N. 1959. *History Begins at Sumer.* Garden City, N.Y.: Doubleday.

———. 1963. *The Sumerians: Their History, Culture and Character.* Chicago: University of Chicago Press.

Kramers, Robert P. 1986. "The Development of the Confucian Schools." In *History of China,* edited by Denis Twitchett and Michael Loewe. Vol. 1, *The Ch'in and Han Empires, 221 BC–AD 220.* Cambridge: Cambridge University Press.

Krasner, Stephen D. 1978. *Defending the National Interest: Raw Materials Investments and U.S. Foreign Policy.* Princeton: Princeton University Press.

———. 1982a. "Regimes and the Limits of Realism: Regimes as Autonomous Variables." *International Organization* 36:2.

———. 1982b. "Structural Causes and Regime Consequences: Regimes as Intervening Variables." *International Organization* 36:2.

———. 1993. "Westphalia and All That." In *Ideas and Foreign Policy, Beliefs, Institutions, and Political Change,* edited by Judith Goldstein and Robert O. Keohane. Ithaca, N.Y.: Cornell University Press.

Kratochwil, Friedrich V. 1986. "Of Systems, Boundaries, and Territoriality: An Inquiry into the Formation of the State System." *World Politics* 39:1.

———. 1989. *Rules, Norms, and Decisions: On the Conditions of Practical and Legal Reasoning in International Relations and Domestic Affairs.* New York: Cambridge University Press.

——. n.d. "Sovereignty as Dominium: Is There a Right of Humanitarian Intervention?" Unpublished.

Kratochwil, Friedrich V., and John Gerard Ruggie. 1986. "International Organization: A State of the Art on an Art of the State." *International Organization* 40:4.

Kreml, William P., and Charles W. Kegley, Jr. 1990. "Must the Quest Be Elusive? Restoring Ethics to Theory Building in International Relations." *Alternatives* 15.

Krüger, Peter, ed. 1993. *Ethnicity and Nationalism: Case Studies in Their Intrinsic Tension and Political Dynamics*. Marburg, Germany: Hitzeroth.

Kuhns, Richard. 1962. *The House, the City, and the Judge: The Growth of Moral Awareness in the Orestia*. Indianapolis: Bobbs-Merrill.

Kurtz, Donald V. 1978. "The Legitimation of Early Inchoate States." In *The Early State*, edited by Henri J. M. Claessen and Peter Skalník. The Hague, The Netherlands: Mouton Publishers.

——. 1987. "The Economics of Urbanization and State Formation at Teotihuacan." *Current Anthropology* 28.

Lafore, Laurence. 1971. *The Long Fuse: An Interpretation of the Origins of World War I*. Philadelphia: Lippincott.

Lakatos, Imre. 1970. "Falsification and the Methodology of Scientific Research Programmes." In *Criticism and the Growth of Knowledge*, edited by I. Lakatos and A. Musgrove. Cambridge: Cambridge University Press.

——. 1978. *The Methodology of Scientific Research Programmes: Philosophical Papers I*. Cambridge: Cambridge University Press, 1978.

Lane, Frederic C. 1973. *Venice: A Maritime Republic*. Baltimore: Johns Hopkins University Press.

Lapid, Yosef. 1989a. "Quo Vadis International Relations? Further Reflections on the 'Next Stage' of International Theory." *Millennium* 18:1.

——. 1989b. "The Third Debate: On the Prospects of International Theory in a Post-Positivist Era." *International Studies Quarterly* 33:3.

——. 1989c. "Without Any Guarantees: The 'Third Way' (in the 'Third Debate') to International Theory." Paper at the annual meeting of the Northeastern Political Science Association.

Lapid, Yosef, and Friedrich Kratochwil. 1994. "The Taming of the Shrew? Neorealist Approprations and Theorizations of Nationalism." Paper at the Western Political Science Association annual meeting.

Larsen, J. A. O. 1968. *Greek Federal States*. Oxford: Oxford University Press.

Larsen, M. T. 1976. *The Old Assyrian City-State and Its Colonies*. Copenhagen: Akademisk Forlag.

——. 1979. "The Tradition of Empire in Mesopotamia." In *Power and Propaganda*, edited by M. T. Larsen. Copenhagen: Akademisk Forlag.

Lasswell, Harold D., and Abraham Kaplan. 1950. *Power and Society: A Framework for Political Inquiry*. New Haven: Yale University Press.

Lebow, Richard Ned. 1991. "Thucydides, Power Transition Theory and the

Peloponnesian War." In *Hegemonic Rivalry: From Thucydides to the Nuclear Age,* edited by Richard Ned Lebow and Barry S. Strauss. Boulder, Colo.: Westview Press.

Legge, J. 1970. *The Chinese Classics.* Vol. 4, *The She King.* Hong Kong: Hong Kong University Press.

Le Goff, Jacques. 1988. *Medieval Civilization.* Translated by Julia Barrow. Oxford: Blackwell.

Lewis, Archibald R. 1988. *Nomads and Crusaders, 1000–1368.* Bloomington: University of Indiana Press.

Lewis, Bernard. 1993. *The Arabs in History.* New York: Oxford University Press.

Lewis, Mark Edward. 1990. *Sanctioned Violence in Early China.* Buffalo: State University of New York Press.

Liska, George. 1990. *The Ways of Power: Pattern and Meaning in World Politics.* Cambridge, Mass.: Basil Blackwell.

Litchfield, R. Burr. 1986. *Emergence of a Bureaucracy: The Florentine Patricians, 1530–1790.* Princeton: Princeton University Press.

Lloyd, S. 1980. *Foundations in the Dust: The Story of Mesopotamian Exploration,* rev. ed. London: Thames and Hudson.

———. 1984. *The Archaeology of Mesopotamia,* rev. ed. London: Thames and Hudson.

Loewe, Michael. 1974. "The Campaigns of Han Wu-ti." In *Chinese Ways in Warfare,* edited by Frank A. Kierman and John K. Fairbank. Cambridge: Harvard University Press.

———. 1986a. "The Concept of Sovereignty." In *History of China,* edited by Denis Twitchett and Michael Loewe. Vol. 1, *The Ch'in and Han Empires, 221 BC–AD 220.* Cambridge: Cambridge University Press.

———. 1986b. "The Conduct of Government and the Issues at Stake." In *History of China,* edited by Denis Twitchett and Michael Loewe. Vol. 1, *The Ch'in and Han Empires, 221 BC–AD 220.* Cambridge: Cambridge University Press.

———. 1986c. "The Former Han Dynasty." In *History of China,* edited by Denis Twitchett and Michael Loewe. Vol. 1, *The Ch'in and Han Empires, 221 BC–AD 220.* Cambridge: Cambridge University Press.

———. 1986d. "Introduction," In *History of China,* edited by Denis Twitchett and Michael Loewe. Vol. 1, *The Ch'in and Han Empires, 221 BC–AD 220.* Cambridge: Cambridge University Press.

———. 1986e. "The Religious and Intellectual Background." In *History of China,* edited by Denis Twitchett and Michael Loewe. Vol. 1, *The Ch'in and Han Empires, 221 BC–AD 220.* Cambridge: Cambridge University Press.

———. 1986f. "The Structure and Practice of Government." In *History of China,* edited by Denis Twitchett and Michael Loewe. Vol. 1, *The Ch'in and Han Empires, 221 BC–AD 220.* Cambridge: Cambridge University Press.

Lopez, Robert S. 1976. *The Commercial Revolution of the Middle Ages, 950–1350.* Cambridge: Cambridge University Press.

Luttwak, Edward N. 1976. *The Grand Strategy of the Roman Empire: From the First Century A.D. to the Third.* Baltimore: Johns Hopkins University Press.

Machiavelli, Niccolò. 1988. *Florentine Histories,* translated by Laura F. Banfield and Harvey C. Mansfield, Jr. Princeton: Princeton University Press.

Machinist, P. 1986. "On Self-Consciousness in Mesopotamia." In *The Origins and Diversity of Axial Age Civilizations,* edited by S. N. Eisenstadt. Albany: State University of New York Press.

MacLachlan, Colin M. 1988. *Spain's Empire in the New World: The Role of Ideas in Institutional and Social Change.* Berkeley: University of California Press.

MacLachlan, Colin M., and Jaime E. Rodríguez O. 1980. *The Forging of the Cosmic Race: A Reinterpretation of Colonial Mexico.* Berkeley: University of California Press.

Maisels, Charles Keith. 1990. *The Emergence of Civilization: From Hunting and Gathering to Agriculture, Cities, and the State in the Near East.* London: Routledge.

Mallett, M. E., and J. R. Hale. 1984. *The Military Organization of a Renaissance State: Venice c.1400 to 1617.* Cambridge: Cambridge University Press.

Mann, Michael. 1986a. "The Autonomous Power of the State: Its Origins, Mechanisms and Results." In *States in History,* edited by John A. Hall. Oxford: Basil Blackwood.

———. 1986b. *The Sources of Social Power: A History of Power from the Beginning to A.D. 1760,* vol. 1. New York: Cambridge University Press.

———. 1988. *States, War and Capitalism: Studies in Political Sociology.* Oxford: Basil Blackwell.

———. 1993. *The Sources of State Power: The Rise of Classes and Nation-States, 1760–1914,* vol. 2. New York: Cambridge University Press.

Mansbach, Richard W., Yale H. Ferguson, and Donald E. Lampert. 1976. *The Web of World Politics: Nonstate Actors in the Global System.* Englewood Cliffs, N.J.: Prentice-Hall.

Mansbach, Richard W., and John A. Vasquez. 1981. *In Search of Theory: A New Paradigm for Global Politics.* New York: Columbia University Press.

Mansbach, Richard W., and Harvey Waterman. 1988. "Political Change and the Atlantic Alliance." *Polity* 21:2.

Marcus, Joyce. 1976. *Emblem and State in the Classic Maya Lowlands.* Washington, D.C.: Dumbarton Oaks.

———. 1983. "A Synthesis of the Cultural Evolution of the Zapotec and Mixtec." In *The Cloud People: Divergent Evolution of the Zapotec and Mixtec Civilizations,* edited by Kent V. Flannery and Joyce Marcus. New York: Academic Press.

———. 1988. "Comment." In *Ecological Theory and Cultural Evolution in the Valley of Oaxaca,* by William T. Sanders and Deborah L. Nichols, *Current Anthropology* 29.

Marcus, Joyce, and Kent V. Flannery. 1983. "An Introduction to the Late Postclassic." In *The Cloud People: Divergent Evolution of the Zapotec and Mixtec Civilizations,* edited by Kent V. Flannery and Joyce Marcus. New York: Academic.

Marinatos, Sp. 1974. "The First 'Mycenaeans' in Greece." In *Bronze Age Migrations in the Aegean,* edited by R. A. Crossland and Ann Birchall. Park Ridge. N.J.: Noyes.

Markus, Robert. 1990. *The End of Ancient Christianity.* Cambridge: Cambridge University Press.

Martin, Raymond. 1989. *The Past Within Us: An Empirical Approach to Philosophy of History.* Princeton: Princeton University Press.

Matos Moctezuma, Eduardo. 1986. *Vida y muerte en el Templo Mayór.* México, D. F., Mexico: Ediciones Océano.

Mattingly, Garrett. 1955. *Renaissance Diplomacy.* Boston: Houghton Mifflin.

McDonald, William A., and Carol G. Thomas. 1990. *Progress into the Past: The Rediscovery of Mycenaen Civilization,* 2nd ed. Bloomington: Indiana University Press.

McKitterick, Rosamund. 1983. *The Frankish Kingdoms under the Carolingians.* New York: Longman.

McNeill, William H. 1963. *The Rise of the West.* Chicago: University of Chicago Press.

———. 1974. *Venice: The Hinge of Europe, 1081–1797.* Chicago: University of Chicago Press.

———. 1982. *The Pursuit of Power: Technology, Armed Force, and Society since A.D. 1000.* Chicago: University of Chicago Press.

———. 1986. *Polyethnicity and National Unity in World History.* Toronto: University of Toronto Press.

Meggers, Betty J. 1975. "The Transpacific Origins of Mesoamerican Civilization: A Preliminary View of the Evidence and Its Theoretical Implications." *American Anthropologist* 77.

Meiggs, R. 1972. *The Athenian Empire.* Oxford: Oxford University Press.

Merad, Ali. 1981. "The Ideologisation of Islam in the Contemporary Muslim World." In *Islam and Power,* edited by Alexander S. Cudsi and Ali E. Hillal Dessouki. London: Cromm Helm.

Millon, René. 1974. "The Study of Urbanism at Teotihuacán, Mexico." In *MesoAmerican Archaeology: New Approaches,* edited by Norman Hammond. Austin: University of Texas Press.

———. 1976. "Social Relations in Ancient Teotihuacán." In *The Valley of Mexico: Studies in Pre-Hispanic Ecology and Society,* edited by Eric R. Wolf. Albuquerque: University of New Mexico Press.

Molloy, John P., and William L. Rathje. 1974. "Sexploitation among the Late Classic Maya." In *The Valley of Mexico: Studies in Pre-Hispanic Ecology and Society,* edited by Eric R. Wolf. Albuquerque: University of New Mexico Press.

Morris, Ian. 1987. *Burial and Ancient Society: The Rise of the Greek City-State*. Cambridge: Cambridge University Press.

Mortimer, Edward. 1982. *Faith and Power: The Politics of Islam*. New York: Random House.

Mote, Frederick W. 1989. *Intellectual Foundations of China*, 2nd ed. New York: McGraw-Hill.

Mottahedeh, R. P. 1980. *Loyalty and Leadership in an Early Islamic Society*. Princeton: Princeton University Press.

Moynihan, Daniel Patrick. 1993. *Pandaemonium: Ethnicity in International Politics*. New York: Oxford University Press.

Murray, Oswyn. 1990. "Cities of Reason." In *The Greek City from Homer to Alexander*, edited by Oswyn Murray and Simon Price. Oxford: Clarendon Press.

———. 1993. *Early Greece*, 2nd ed. Cambridge, Mass.: Harvard University Press.

Musset, Lucien. 1975. *The Germanic Invasions: The Making of Europe, AD 400–600*, translated by Edward and Columba James. University Park: Pennsylvania University Press.

Muzaffar-Ud-Din Nadvi, Syed. 1965. *Muslim Thought and Its Source*, 5th ed. Lahore, Pakistan: Sh. Muhammad Ashraf.

Naff, Thomas. 1981. "Towards a Muslim Theory of History." In *Islam and Power*, edited by Alexander S. Cudsi and Ali E. Hillal Dessouki. London: Croom Helm.

Nettl, J. P. 1968. "The State as a Conceptual Variable." *World Politics* 20:4.

Nibbi, Alessandra. 1974. "The Identification of the 'Sea Peoples.' " In *Bronze Age Migrations in the Aegean*, edited by R. A. Crossland and Ann Birchall. Park Ridge, N.J.: Noyes Press.

Nicol, Donald M. 1988. *Byzantium and Venice: A Study in Diplomatic and Cultural Relations*. Cambridge: Cambridge University Press.

Nicolson, Harold. 1954. *The Evolution of Diplomatic Method*. London: Cassell.

North, Douglass C. 1981. *Structure and Change in Economic History*. New York: Norton.

———. 1990. *Institutions, Institutional Change and Economic Performance*. New York: Cambridge University Press.

Norwich, John Julius. 1982. *A History of Venice*. New York: Knopf.

Novick, Peter. 1988. *That Noble Dream: The "Objectivity Question" and the American Historical Profession*. Cambridge: Cambridge University Press.

Nye, Joseph S., Jr., and Robert O. Keohane. 1971. "Transnational Relations and World Politics: An Introduction." In *Transnational Relations and World Politics*, edited by Robert O. Keohane and Joseph S. Nye, Jr. Cambridge, Mass.: Harvard University Press.

Oates, Joan. 1986. *Babylon*, rev. ed. London: Thames and Hudson.

Ober, Josiah. 1991. "National Ideology and Strategic Defense of the Population, from Athens to Star Wars." In *Hegemonic Rivalry: From Thucydides to the Nuclear Age,* edited by Richard Ned Lebow and Barry S. Strauss. Boulder, Colo.: Westview Press.

Oded, B. 1979. *Mass Deportations and Deportees in the Neo-Assyrian Empire.* Wiesbaden: Ludwig Reichert.

Onuf, Nicholas G. 1989. *A World of Our Making: Rules and Rule in Social Theory and International Relations.* Columbia: University of South Carolina Press.

Oppenheim, A. L. 1964. *Ancient Mesopotamia.* Chicago: University of Chicago Press.

Osborne, Robin. 1990. "The *Demos* and Its Divisions in Classical Athens." In *The Greek City from Homer to Alexander,* edited by Oswyn Murray and Simon Price. Oxford: Clarendon.

Ostrogorsky, George. 1969. *History of the Byzantine State,* rev. ed. Translated by Joan Hussey. New Brunswick, N.J.: Rutgers University Press.

Paddock, John. 1983. "Some Thoughts on the Decline of Monte Albán." In *The Cloud People: Divergent Evolution of the Zapotec and Mixtec Civilizations,* edited by Kent V. Flannery and Joyce Marcus. New York: Academic Press.

Parry, Clive. 1968. "The Function of Law in the International Community." In *Manual of Public International Law,* edited by Max Sorensen. New York: St. Martin's.

Parry, J. H. 1966. *The Spanish Seaborne Empire.* Berkeley: University of California Press.

Pastor, Robert A. 1992. "NAFTA as the Center of an Integration Process: The Nontrade Issues." In *North American Free Trade Agreement: Assessing the Impact,* edited by Nora Lustig, Barry P. Bosworth, and Robert Z. Lawrence. Washington, D.C.: Brookings.

Perlman, Shalom. 1991. "Hegemony and *Arkhe* in Greece: Fourth-Century Views." In *Hegemonic Rivalry: From Thucydides to the Nuclear Age,* edited by Richard Ned Lebow and Barry S. Strauss. Boulder, Colo.: Westview Press.

Peters, B. Guy. 1992. "Bureaucratic Politics and the Institutions of the European Community." In *Euro-politics: Institutions and Policymaking in the "New" European Community,* edited by Alberta M. Sbragia. Washington, D.C.: Brookings.

Pfaff, William. 1993. *The Wrath of Nations: Civilization and the Furies of Nationalism.* New York: Simon and Schuster.

Piña Chan, Román. 1989. *The Olmec: Mother Culture of Mesoamerica.* New York: Rizzoli.

Pipes, Daniel. 1983. *In the Path of God: Islam and Political Power.* New York: Basic Books.

———. 1989. *The Long Shadow.* New Brunswick, N.J.: Transaction Publishers.

Posen, Barry R. 1993. "Nationalism, the Mass Army, and Military Power." *International Security* 18:2.

Postgate, J. N. 1992. *Early Mesopotamia: Society and Economy at the Dawn of History*. London: Routledge.

Pounds, Norman J. G. 1974. *An Economic History of Medieval Europe*. London: Longman.

Powell, Anton. 1988. *Athens and Sparta: Constructing Greek Political and Social History from 478 B.C.* London: Routledge.

Powell, Marvin. 1985. "Salt, Seed, and Yields in Sumerian Agriculture." *Zeitscrift für Assyriologie* 75.

Price, Barbara J. 1971. "Prehispanic Irrigation Agriculture in Nuclear America." *Latin American Research Review* 6.

Puchala, Donald J. 1995. "The Pragmatics of International History." *Mershon International Studies Review* 39: Supplement 1.

Putnam, Robert D. 1988. "Diplomacy and Domestic Games: The Logic of Two-Level Games." *International Organization* 42:3.

Queller, Donald E. 1967. *The Office of the Ambassador in the Middle Ages*. Princeton: Princeton University Press.

———. 1986. *The Venetian Patriciate: Reality Versus Myth*. Urbana: University of Illinois Press.

Rackham, Oliver. 1990. "Ancient Landscapes." In *The Greek City from Homer to Alexander*, edited by Oswyn Murray and Simon Price. Oxford: Clarendon.

Rahman, Fazlur. 1982. *Islam and Modernity*. Chicago: University of Chicago Press.

Reischauer, Edwin O., and John K. Fairbank. 1960. *East Asia: The Great Tradition*, vol. 1. Cambridge, Mass.: Harvard University Press.

Renfrew, Colin. 1972. *The Emergence of Civilization: The Cyclades and the Aegean in the Third Milleneum B.C.* London: Metheun.

Rengger, N. J. 1990. "The Fearful Sphere of International Relations." *Review of International Studies* 16.

Reynolds, Susan. 1984. *Kingdoms and Communities in Western Europe, 900–1300*. Oxford: Oxford University Press.

Rhodes, P. J. 1985. *The Athenian Empire*. Oxford: Clarendon.

Riasanovsky, Nicholas V. 1993. *A History of Russia*, 5th ed. Oxford: Oxford University Press.

Roberson, Barbara Allen. 1988. "The Islamic Belief System." In *Belief Systems and International Relations*, edited by Richard Little and Steve Smith. Oxford: Basil Blackwell.

Rodzinski, Witold. 1979. *A History of China*, vol. 1. New York: Pergamon.

Rosenau, James N. 1966. "Pre-Theories and Theories of Foreign Policy." In *Approaches to Comparative and International Politics*, edited by R. Barry Farrell. Evanston, Ill.: Northwestern University Press.

———. 1967. "Foreign Policy as an Issue-Area." In *Domestic Sources of Foreign Policy*, edited by James N. Rosenau. New York: Free Press.

————. 1969. *Linkage Politics: Essays on Convergence of National and International Systems*. New York: Free Press.

————. 1984. "A Pre-Theory Revisited: World Politics in an Era of Cascading Interdependence." *International Studies Quarterly* 28:3.

————. 1986. "Before Cooperation: Hegemons, Regimes, and Habit-Driven Actors in World Politics." *International Organization* 40:4.

————. 1990. *Turbulence in World Politics: A Theory of Change and Continuity*. Princeton: Princeton University Press.

Rosenau, James N., and Ernst-Otto Czempiel, eds. 1992. *Governance Without Government: Order and Change in World Politics*. Cambridge: Cambridge University Press.

Rosenthal, Erwin I. J. 1965. *Islam in the Modern National State*. Cambridge: Cambridge University Press.

Roux, G. 1980. *Ancient Iraq*, 2nd ed. Harmondsworth, England: Penguin.

Rowden, Maurice. 1970. *The Fall of Venice*. London: Weidenfeld and Nicolson.

Roys, Ralph L. 1957. *The Political Geography of the Yucatan Maya*. Washington, D.C.: Carnegie Institution of Washington.

————. 1962. "Literary Sources for the History of Mayapan." In *Mayapan, Yucatan, Mexico*. Washington, D.C.: Carnegie Institution of Washington.

Rubinstein, Nicolai. 1966. *The Government of Florence under the Medici (1434 to 1494)*. Oxford: Clarendon.

————. 1968. *Florentine Studies: Politics and Society in Renaissance Florence*. Evanston, Ill.: Northwestern University Press.

Ruggie, John Gerard. 1983. "Continuity and Transformation in the World Polity: Toward a Neorealist Synthesis." *World Politics* 35:2.

————. 1993a. *Multilateralism Matters: The Theory and Praxis of an Institutional Form*. New York: Columbia University Press.

————. 1993b. "Territoriality and Beyond: Problematizing Modernity in International Relations." *International Organization* 47:1.

Runciman, W. G. 1982. "Origins of States: The Case of Archaic Greece." *Comparative Studies in Society and History* 24.

————. 1990. "Doomed to Extinction: The *Polis* as an Evolutionary Dead-End." In *The Greek City from Homer to Alexander*, edited by Oswyn Murray and Simon Price. Oxford: Clarendon.

Rus, Jan. 1983. "Whose Caste War? Indians, Ladinos, and the 'Caste War.' " In *Spaniards and Indians in Southeastern Mesoamerica: Essays on the History of Ethnic Relations*, edited by Murdo J. MacLeod and Robert Wasserstrom. Lincoln: University of Nebraska Press.

Rutter, Jeremy B. 1992. "Cultural Novelties in the Post-Palatial Aegean World: Indices of Vitality or Decline?" In *The Crisis Years: The Twelfth Century B.C.*, edited by M. S. Joukowsky and W. B. Ward. *Berytus* Supplement.

Sabin, Philip A. G. 1991. "Athens, the United States, and Democratic 'Characteristics' in Foreign Policy." In *Hegemonic Rivalry: From Thucydides to the Nuclear Age,* edited by Richard Ned Lebow and Barry S. Strauss. Boulder, Colo.: Westview Press.

Sabloff, Jeremy A., et al. 1974. "Trade and Power in Postclassic Yucatan: Initial Observations." In *MesoAmerican Archaeology: New Approaches,* edited by Norman Hammond. Austin: University of Texas Press.

Sadao, Nishijima. 1986. "The Economic and Social History of Former Han." In *History of China,* edited by Denis Twitchett and Michael Loewe. Vol. 1, *The Ch'in and Han Empires, 221 BC–AD 220.* Cambridge: Cambridge University Press.

Saggs, H. W. F. 1984. *The Might That Was Assyria.* London: Sidgwick and Jackson.

———. 1989. *Civilization Before Greece and Rome.* London: B.T. Batsford.

———. 1990. *The Greatness That Was Babylon,* rev. ed. London: Sidgwick and Jackson.

Sahlins, Peter. 1989. *Boundaries: The Making of France and Spain in the Pyrenees.* Berkeley: University of California Press.

Salmon, J. 1977. "Political Hoplites?" *Journal of Hellenic Studies* 97.

Sandars, N. K. 1985. *The Sea Peoples: Warriors of the Ancient Mediterranean.* London: Thames and Hudson.

Sanders, William T., and Deborah L. Nichols. 1988. "Ecological Theory and Cultural Evolution in the Valley of Oaxaca." *Current Anthropology* 29.

Sanders, William T., Jeffrey R. Parsons, and Robert S. Santley. 1979. *The Basin of Mexico: Ecological Processes in the Evolution of a Civilization.* New York: Academic.

Santoro, Carlo M. 1991. "Bipolarity and War: What Makes the Difference?" In *Hegemonic Rivalry: From Thucydides to the Nuclear Age,* edited by Richard Ned Lebow and Barry S. Strauss. Boulder, Colo.: Westview.

Saunders, J. J. 1965. *A History of Medieval Islam.* London: Routledge and Kegan Paul.

Schirokauer, Conrad. 1991. *A Brief History of Chinese Civilization.* New York: Harcourt, Brace, Jovanovich.

Schwartz, Benjamin I. 1985. *The World of Thought in Ancient China.* Cambridge, Mass.: Belknap.

Schwerin, Karl H. 1988. "Comment." In *Ecological Theory and Cultural Evolution in the Valley of Oaxaca,* by William T. Sanders and Deborah L. Nichols, *Current Anthropology* 29.

Scullard, H. H. 1959. *From the Gracchi to Nero: A History of Rome from 133 B.C. to 68 A.D.* New York: Praeger.

Shapiro, Michael J. 1989. "Textualizing Global Politics." In *International/ Intertextual Relations: Postmodern Readings of World Politics,* edited by James Der Derian and Michael J. Shapiro. Lexington, Mass.: Lexington Books.

Sharer, Robert J., and David C. Grove. 1989. *Regional Perspectives on the Olmec.* Cambridge: Cambridge University Press.

Sinclair, R. K. 1988. *Democracy and Participation in Athens*. Cambridge: Cambridge University Press.

Singer, J. David. 1961. "The Level-of-Analysis Problem in International Relations." In *The International System: Theoretical Essays*, edited by Klaus Knorr and Sidney Verba. Princeton: Princeton University Press.

Skinner, Quentin. 1978. *The Foundations of Modern Political Thought*. Vol. 1, *The Renaissance*. Cambridge: Cambridge University Press.

Skocpol, Theda. 1979. *States and Social Revolutions*. New York: Cambridge University Press.

Smith, Anthony D. 1991. *National Identity*. Reno: University of Nevada Press.

Snodgrass, Anthony. 1965. "The Hoplite Reform and History." *Journal of Hellenic Studies* 85.

———. 1971. *The Dark Age of Greece*. Edinburgh: Edinburgh University Press.

———. 1974. "Metal-work as Evidence for Immigration in the Late Bronze Age." *Bronze Age Migrations in the Aegean*, edited by R. A. Crossland and Ann Birchall. Park Ridge, N.J.: Noyes.

———. 1980. *Archaic Greece*. London: J. M. Dent and Sons.

Snyder, Jack. 1993. "The New Nationalism: Realist Interpretations and Beyond." In *The Domestic Bases of Grand Strategy*, edited by Richard N. Rosecrance and Arthur A. Stein. Ithaca, N.Y.: Cornell University Press.

Sourvinou-Inwood, Christiane. 1974. "Movements of Populations in Attica at the End of the Mycenaen Period." In *Bronze Age Migrations in the Aegean*, edited by J. A. Crossland and Ann Birchall. Park Ridge, N.J.: Noyes.

———. 1990. "What is *Polis* Religion?" In *The Greek City from Homer to Alexander*, edited by Oswyn Murray and Simon Price. Oxford: Clarendon.

Spores, Ronald. 1967. *The Mixtec Kings and Their People*. Norman: University of Oklahoma Press.

Sprout, Harold, and Margaret Sprout. 1965. *The Ecological Perspective on Human Affairs*. Princeton: Princeton University Press.

———. 1969. "Environmental Factors in the Study of International Politics." In *International Politics and Foreign Policy*, rev. ed. Edited by James N. Rosenau. New York: Free Press.

Spruyt, Hendrik. 1994. *The Sovereign State and Its Competitors*. Princeton: Princeton University Press.

Starr, Chester G. 1986. *Individual and Community: The Rise of the Polis 800–500 B.C.* Oxford: Oxford University Press.

Ste. Croix, G. E. M. de. 1972. *Origins of the Peloponnesian War*. London: Duckworth.

———. 1981. *The Class Struggle in the Ancient Greek World from the Archaic Age to the Arab Conquests*. London: Duckworth.

Stephens, J. N. 1983. *The Fall of the Florentine Republic, 1512–1530*. Oxford: Clarendon.

Stockton, David. 1990. *The Classical Athenian Democracy*. Oxford: Oxford University Press.

Stopford, John, and Susan Strange, with John S. Henley. 1991. *Rival States, Rival Firms: Competition for World Market Shares*. Cambridge: Cambridge University Press.

Strange, Susan. 1991. "An Eclectic Approach." In *The New International Political Economy*, edited by Craig N. Murphy and Roger Tooze. Boulder, Colo.: Lynne Rienner.

Strauss, Barry S. 1991. "Of Balances, Bandwagons, and Ancient Greeks." In *Hegemonic Rivalry: From Thucydides to the Nuclear Age*, edited by Richard Ned Lebow and Barry S. Strauss. Boulder, Colo.: Westview Press.

Sun Tzu. 1993. *The Art of Warfare*. Translated by Roger Ames. New York: Ballantine.

Sylvester, Christine. 1994. *Feminist Theory and International Relations in a Postmodern Era*. Cambridge: Cambridge University Press.

Tadmor, H. 1986. "Monarchy and the Elite in Assyria and Babylonia: The Question of Royal Accountabilty." In *The Origins and Diversity of Axial Age Civilizations*, edited by S. N. Eisenstadt. Albany: State University of New York Press.

Tamir, Y. 1993. *Liberal Nationalism*. Princeton: Princeton University Press.

Taylor, Paul. 1991."The European Community and the State: Assumptions, Theories and Propositions." *Review of International Studies* 17.

Thomas, Carol J. 1987. *Paths from Ancient Greece*. Leiden: E. J. Brill.

Thomson, Janice E. 1994. *Mercenaries, Pirates, and Sovereigns: State-Building and Extraterritorial Violence in Early Modern Europe*. Princeton: Princeton University Press.

Thomson, Janice E., and Stephen D. Krasner. 1989. "Global Transactions and the Consolidation of Sovereignty." In *Global Changes and Theoretical Challenges: Approaches to World Politics for the 1990s*, edited by Ernst-Otto Czempiel and James N. Rosenau. Lexington, Mass.: Lexington Books.

Thorburn, H. G., and Jordi Sole Tura, eds. 1989. "Pluralism, Regionalism, Nationalism." *International Political Science Review* 10:3.

Thucydides. 1972. *History of the Peloponnesian War*, rev. ed. Translated by Rex Warner. London: Penguin.

Tickner, J. Ann. 1992. *Gender in International Relations: Feminist Perspectives on Achieving Global Security*. New York: Columbia University Press.

Tilly, Charles. 1975. *The Formation of National States in Western Europe*. Princeton: Princeton University Press.

Tolchin, Susan, and Martin Tolchin. 1988. *Buying into America: How Foreign Money Is Changing the Face of Our Nation*. New York: Times Books.

Tong, James W. 1991. *Disorder Under Heaven: Collective Violence in the Ming Dynasty*. Stanford, Calif.: Stanford University Press.

Townsend, Richard Fraser. 1979. *State and Cosmos in the Art of Tenochtitlan*. Washington, D.C.: Dumbarton Oaks.

Tsai, Wen-hui. 1992. "New Authoritarianism, Neo-Conservatism, and Anti-Peaceful Evolution: Mainland China's Resistance to Political Modernization." Paper at the Sino-American-European Conference on Contemporary China. Institute of International Relations, National Chengchi University: Taipei, Taiwan.

Tuchman, Barbara W. 1978. *A Distant Mirror: The Calamitous Fourteenth Century*. New York: Knopf.

Twitchett, Denis, and Michael Loewe, eds. 1986. *History of China*. Vol. 1, *The Ch'in and Han Empires, 221 BC–AD 220*. Cambridge: Cambridge University Press.

van der Vliet, Edward. 1987. "Tyranny and Democracy: The Evolution of Politics in Ancient Greece." In *Early State Dynamics*, edited by Henri J. M. Claessen and Pieter van de Velde. Leiden, The Netherlands: E. J. Brill.

Vasquez, John A. 1983. *The Power of Power Politics: A Critique*. New Brunswick, N.J.: Rutgers University Press.

——. 1993. *The War Puzzle*. Cambridge: Cambridge University Press.

Verbruggen, J. F. 1977. *The Art of War in Western Europe During the Middle Ages: From the Eighth Century to 1340*, translated by Sumner Willard and S. C. M. Southern. New York: North-Holland.

Vermeule, Emily. 1964. *Greece in the Bronze Age*. Chicago: University of Chicago Press.

Vernon, Raymond. 1971. *Sovereignty at Bay: The Multinational Spread of U.S. Enterprises*. New York: Basic Books.

——. 1977. *Storm Over the Multinationals: The Real Issues*. Cambridge, Mass.: Harvard University Press.

Von Grunebaum, G. E. 1970. *Classical Islam: A History, 600 A.D.–1258 A.D.* Chicago: Aldine.

Waley, Daniel. 1988. *The Italian City-Republics*, 3rd ed. New York: Longman.

Walker, R. B. J. 1987. "Realism, Change, and International Political Theory." *International Studies Quarterly* 31:1.

——. 1989. "History and Structure in the Theory of International Studies." *Millenium* 18:2.

——. 1993. *Inside/Outside: International Relations as Political Theory*. New York: Cambridge University Press.

Walker, R. B. J., and Saul H. Mendlovitz. 1993. *Contending Sovereignties: Redefining Political Community*. Boulder, Colo.: Lynne Rienner.

Wallace-Hadrill, J. M. 1985. *The Barbarian West, 400–1000*. Oxford: Blackwell.

Wallerstein, Immanuel. 1974. *The Modern World System: Capitalist Agriculture and the Origins of the European World-Economy in the Sixteenth Century*. New York: Academic.

——. 1979. *The Capitalist World-Economy*. Cambridge: Cambridge University Press.

——. 1984. *The Politics of the World-Economy: The States, the Movements, and Civilization*. Cambridge: Cambridge University Press.

Waltz, Kenneth N. 1959. *Man, the State, and War: A Theoretical Analysis*. New York: Columbia University Press.

———. 1979. *Theory of International Politics*. Reading, Mass.: Addison-Wesley.

———. 1990 "Realist Thought and Neorealist Theory." *Journal of International Affairs* 44:1.

———. 1993. "The Emerging Structure of International Structure." *International Security* 18:2.

Wasserstrom, Robert. 1983a. *Class and Society in Central Chiapas*. Berkeley: University of California Press.

———. 1983b. "Spaniards and Indians in Colonial Chiapas, 1528–1790." In *Spaniards and Indians in Southeastern Mesoamerica: Essays on the History of Ethnic Relations*, edited by Murdo J. MacLeod and Robert Wasserstrom. Lincoln: University of Nebraska Press.

Watson, Adam. 1992. *The Evolution of International Society: A Comparative Historical Analysis*. New York: Routledge.

Watt, W. Montgomery. 1961. *Muhammad: Prophet and Statesman*. Oxford: Oxford University Press.

———. 1962. *Islamic Philosophy and Theology*. Edinburgh: Edinburgh University Press.

———. 1968. *Islamic Political Thought*. Edinburgh: Edinburgh University Press.

———. 1973. *The Formative Period of Islamic Thought*. Chicago: Aldine Atherton.

———. 1974. *The Majesty That Was Islam*. London: Sidgwick and Jackson.

———. 1988. *Islamic Fundamentalism and Modernity*. New York: Routledge.

———. 1991. *Muslim-Christian Encounters: Perceptions and Misperceptions*. New York: Routledge.

Weinstein, D. 1970. *Savonarola and Florence*. Princeton: Princeton University Press.

Wendt, Alexander E. 1987. "The Agent-Structure Problem in International Relations Theory." *International Organization* 41:3.

———. 1990. "Sovereignty and the Social Construction of Power Politics." Paper at the annual meeting of the International Studies Association.

———. 1992. "Anarchy Is What States Make of It." *International Organization* 46:2.

Wendt, Alexander E., and Raymond Duvall. 1989. "Institutions and International Order." In *Global Changes and Theoretical Challenges: Approaches to World Politics for the 1990s*, edited by Ernst-Otto Czempiel and James N. Rosenau. Lexington, Mass.: Lexington Books.

Wickham, Chris. 1981. *Early Medieval Italy*. London: Macmillan.

Wight, Martin. 1968. "Why Is There No International Theory?" In *Diplomatic Investigations: Essays in the Theory of International Politics*, edited by Herbert Butterfield and Martin Wight. Cambridge, Mass.: Harvard University Press.

————. 1977. *Systems of States,* edited by Hedley Bull. Leicester, England: Leicester University Press in association with the London School of Economics and Political Science.

Wilford, John Noble. 1993. "Mysterious Mexican Culture Yields Its Secrets." *New York Times,* June 29.

Willetts, R. F. 1977. *The Civilization of Ancient Crete.* Berkeley: University of California Press.

Wittfogel, Karl. 1957. *Oriental Despotism: A Comparative Study of Total Power.* New Haven, Conn.: Yale University Press.

Wolf, Eric R. 1982. *Europe and the People Without History.* Berkeley: University of California Press.

Worley, Leslie J. 1993. *Hippeis: The Cavalry of Ancient Greece.* Boulder, Colo.: Westview Press.

Wright, H. T. 1972. "A Consideration of Interregional Exchange in Greater Mesopotamia: 4000–3000 B.C." In *Social Exchange and Interaction,* edited by E. Wilmson. Ann Arbor: University of Michigan Museum of Anthropology.

————. 1977. "Recent Research on the Origin of the State." *Annual Review of Anthropology* 6.

Wright, H. T., and G. A. Johnson. 1975. "Population, Exchange, and Early State Formation in Southwestern Iran." *American Anthropologist* 77.

Wright, H. T., et al. 1975. *Early Fourth-Millennium Developments in Southwestern Iran. Iran* 13.

Young, Oran R. 1989. "Odysseus Twenty-five Years On: Reflections on the Study of International Relations." In *Global Changes and Theoretical Challenges: Approaches to World Politics for the 1990s,* edited by Ernst-Otto Czempiel and James N. Rosenau. Lexington, Mass.: Lexington Books.

Yu Ying-shih. 1986. "Han Foreign Relations." In *History of China,* edited by Denis Twitchett and Michael Loewe. Vol. 1, *The Ch'in and Han Empires, 221 BC–AD 220.* Cambridge: Cambridge University Press.

Zantwijk, Rudolph van. 1985. *The Aztec Arrangement: The Social History of Pre-Spanish Mexico.* Norman: University of Oklahoma Press.

Zinnes, Dina A. 1980. "Prerequisites for the Study of System Transformation." In *Change in the International System,* edited by Ole R. Holsti, Randolph P. Siverson, and Alexander L. George. Boulder, Colo.: Westview.

Zubaida, Sami. 1989. *Islam, the People and the State.* New York: Routledge.

Index of Names

'Abd al-Malik (ninth caliph), 277
'Abduh, Muhammad, 290
Abraham, 297n
Abu Bakr (first caliph), 276, 282, 294–95, 302, 312, 312n
Abu'l-'Abbas al Saffah (nineteenth caliph), 304
Abu Talib (uncle of Muhammad), 295
Acamapichtli of Tenochtitlán, 240
Adad-nerari I of Assyria, 82
Adad-nirâri II of Assyria, 72
Adám, Magda: on Woodrow Wilson, 407
Adams, Richard E. W.: on Mesoamerica as "vast diffusion sphere," 224; on Olmec importance, 228n; on "symbiotic" Basin of Mexico, 233–34; on Maya as "noble savage," 233n; on rank in Aztec military, 239; city as "ultimate unit of stability" in Basin of Mexico, 246; on Maya patron-client relationships, 252–53
Adcock, Sir Frank: on Greek diplomacy 126–28, 156n, 157, 157n
Adelaide (queen of Italy), 359
Agger, Ben, 36n
Ahmad ibn-Tulun, 307
Akhenaten (pharaoh of Egypt), 81, 259
Alcibiades, 126
Alexander the Great, 66, 108, 112, 124, 340, 384
Alexander III (pope), 361

Alfonso IX (king of León), 361
Algaze, Guillermo, 75n. 7: on long-distance trade in Mesopotamia, 76; center-periphery in Mesopotamia, 85
'Ali ibn Abi Talib (fourth caliph), 276, 277, 294, 312, 313: and struggle with Mu'awiya, 292, 294, 315–16; assassination of, 294, 312–13; and Kharijtes, 316
Allah, 286, 311: as a source of authority, 282, 290, 302
Allan, Pierre, 1
Allison, Graham T., 17: on Rational Actor Model, 18
Amenophis III of Egypt, 81
Ames, Roger T., 207, 211, 213, 214n. 15
Amut-pi-El of Qatahum, 72
Anderson, Benedict: on "imagined communities," 353–54
Anderson, Perry, 43n
Andrews, Anthony P.: Tikal as trade center, 235, 235n
Apollo (Greek god), 136
Aristotle, 145, 152n. 20, 154, 157, 297, 367n. 6, 388
Aronoff, Michael J., 58
Ashley, Richard K., 5
Ashur, Assyrian diety, 97, 106
Ashurbanipal of Assyria, 82–83, 101
Al-Assad, Hafiz: and Alawites, 323
Attila (king of the Huns), 173, 357
Augustus Caesar (Gaius Julius Caesar Octavianus), 57n. 28, 355, 388

453

INDEX OF SUBJECTS

www.ingramcontent.com/pod-product-compliance
Lightning Source LLC
Chambersburg PA
CBHW020448270326
41926CB00008B/532